M000221838

William E. Kovacic
An Antitrust Tribute

Liber Amicorum - Volume I

Editors
Nicolas Charbit
Elisa Ramundo
Anna Chehtova
Abigail Slater

Copyright © 2012 by Institute of Competition Law
60 Broad Street, Suite 3502, NY 10004
www.concurrences.com
contact@concurrences.com

Publisher's Cataloging-in-Publication
(Provided by Quality Books, Inc.)
William E. Kovacic, an antitrust tribute. Liber amicorum.
  Volume I / editors, Nicolas Charbit ... [et al.].
  p. cm.
  LCCN 2012953616
  ISBN 978-1-939007-40-7
  ISBN 978-1-939007-41-4

  1. Antitrust law--United States. 2. Antitrust law--
    Europe. 3. Kovacic, William E.   I. Charbit, Nicolas.

  K3850.W55 2012   343.07'21
                              QBI12-600224

Cover and book design by Yves Buliard, www.ybgraphic.fr

Editors' Note

Nicolas Charbit
Elisa Ramundo

Anna Chehtova
Abigail Slater

This Liber Amicorum was launched on the occasion of Professor William E. Kovacic's retirement from the U.S. Federal Trade Commission where he served as Commissioner from January 2006 to October 2011, as the Chairman from March 2008 to March 2009, and as a General Counsel from 2001 through 2004.

This Volume I pays tribute to William Kovacic's work as a professor, public official and "international entrepreneur," which has tremendously contributed to the development of the U.S. and international antitrust law. This first volume includes 31 contributions by his colleagues and friends mainly from the United States, and it is divided into two sections. Part I, entitled "An Antitrust Career," contains 10 articles that offer an original as well as enthralling picture of Kovacic as professor, lawyer, unconventional thinker and innovator of antitrust law. Part II, entitled "New Frontiers of Antitrust," consists of 21 articles covering different aspects of competition law, ranging from cartels to mergers analysis, private rights of action, antitrust settlements, etc. The overall result is a collective work that offers the opportunity to look over the antitrust world not only as a "cold" field of law, but also as a lively discipline to whose growth Professor Kovacic has contributed so much.

Volume II will focus on the international career of William E. Kovacic and on international and bilateral antitrust issues.

The editors would like to give their sincere thanks to all the 43 authors for their hours of labor in dedication to this Liber Amicorum.

Contributors

Alden F. Abbott
Research in Motion - Formerly
U.S. Federal Trade Commission

Theodore L. Banks
Scharf Banks Marmor

Thomas Barnett
Covington & Burling

Jean-François Bellis
Van Bael & Bellis

William Blumenthal
Clifford Chance

Rachel Brandenburger
U.S. Department of Justice,
Antitrust Division

John M. Connor
Purdue University

Adrian Emch
Hogan Lovells - IP School
Peking University

Joseph Farrell
University of California,
Berkeley

John Fedele
Baker & McKenzie

Andre Fiebig
Baker & McKenzie

Harry First
New York University
School of Law

Albert A. Foer
The American Antitrust Institute

Andrew I. Gavil
Howard University
School of Law

David J. Gerber
Chicago-Kent College of Law

Douglas H. Ginsburg
New York University School of
Law

John D. Harkrider
Axinn, Veltrop & Harkrider

Stephen Harris
Baker & McKenzie

Ronan P. Harty
Davis Polk & Wardwell

Roxann E. Henry
Morrison & Foerster

Hugh M. Hollman
Jones Day

Clifford A. Jones
University of Florida Levin
College of Law

James A. Keyte
Skadden, Arps, Slate,
Meagher & Flom

Joseph Krauss
Hogan Lovells

Abbott B. Lipsky
Latham & Watkins

Joseph S. Nord
Kirkland & Ellis

George L. Priest
Yale Law School

James F. Rill
Baker Botts

J. Thomas Rosch
U.S. Federal Trade Commission

Christian M. Rowan
Hogan Lovells

Seth Sacher
U.S. Federal Trade Commission

Fiona A. Schaeffer
Jones Day

Kristin Shaffer
Covington & Burling

Howard A. Shelanski
U.S. Federal Trade Commission
- Georgetown University

Joe Sims
Jones Day

D. Daniel Sokol
University of Florida Levin
College of Law

Jesse Solomon
Davis Polk & Wardwell

John M. Taladay
Baker Botts

Theodore Voorhees
Covington & Burling

Xiaoye Wang
Hunan University

Spencer Weber Waller
Loyola University Chicago
School of Law

Christine Wilson
Kirkland & Ellis

Joshua D. Wright
George Mason University School
of Law and Department of
Economics

Table of Contents

Part II - New Frontiers of Antitrust

Professor William E. Kovacic Biography

Career

William E. Kovacic is currently a professor of Global Competition Law and Policy at George Washington University, where he is also the director of the Competition Law Center. Since January 2009, Prof. Kovacic has also served as Vice Chairman for Outreach of the International Competition Network.

Before joining the GW Law School in 1999, he was an FTC Commissioner from January 2006 to October 2011, and served as Chairman of the agency from March 2008 to March 2009. Previously Prof. Kovacic was the FTC's General Counsel from 2001 through 2004, and also worked for the agency from 1979 until 1983, initially as a staff attorney in the Bureau of Competition's Planning Office and later as an attorney advisor to former Commissioner George W. Douglas.

In his early career he was the George Mason University Foundation Professor at the George Mason University School of Law. Bill Kovacic also practiced law as an associate with the Washington, DC, office of Bryan Cave, where he was a member of the firm's antitrust and government contracts departments. He also spent one year on the majority staff of the Subcommittee on Antitrust and Monopoly of the U.S. Senate Committee on the Judiciary, which was chaired by Senator Philip A. Hart.

Kovacic has served, since 1992, as an advisor on antitrust and consumer protection issues to the governments of Armenia, Benin, Egypt, El Salvador, Georgia, Guyana, Indonesia, Kazakhstan, Mongolia, Morocco, Nepal, Panama, Peru, Russia, Ukraine, Vietnam, and Zimbabwe. Since January 2009, he has also served as Vice Chairman for Outreach of the International Competition Network.

Education

Kovacic attended the University of Detroit Jesuit High School, and then graduated with a bachelor's degree from Princeton University in 1974. He received a J.D. from Columbia Law School in 1978 where he was a Harlan Fiske Stone Scholar.

Publications

Books

Evolution of U.S. Antitrust Enforcement. Northhampton, ME: Edward Elgar, 2011.

(With Gavil, Andrew I., and Jonathan B. Baker.) *Antitrust Law in Perspective: Cases, Concepts and Problems in Competition Policy.* 2nd edition. St. Paul: Thomson West, 2008. First edition published in 2002.

(With Gellhorn, Ernest and Stephen Calkins.) *Antitrust Law and Economics in a Nutshell.* 5th ed. St. Paul: West Publishing Co., 2004. Fourth edition published in 1994.

Evaluating the Competitive Effects of Defense Industry Mergers on Research and Development. Washington, DC: Federal Legal Publications, 1996.

The Choice of Forum in Bid Protest Disputes. Washington, DC: Administrative Conference of the United States, 1995.

(with Feinstein, Richard and Patrick Sheller.) *Antitrust Analysis and Defense Industry Consolidation.* Chicago, IL: American Bar Association, Section of Public Contract Law, 1994.

(with Sullivan, E. Thomas, et al.). *Nonprice Predation under Section 2 of the Sherman Act.* Monograph No. 18. Chicago, IL: American Bar Association, Section of Antitrust Law, 1991.

The Antitrust Government Contracts Handbook. Chicago, IL: American Bar Association, Section of Antitrust Law, 1990.

A Basic Antitrust Compliance Manual for the Moving and Storage Industry. 1987.

(with Heckmeyer, Steven, et al.). *Coping with a Mature Product in a Changing Industry: White Paper of the National Task Force on the Yellow Pages Industry.* 1987.

(with Blumenthal, William, et al.). *Horizontal Mergers: Law and Policy.* Monograph No. 12 Chicago, IL: American Bar Association, Section of Antitrust Law, 1986.

Law Review Articles & Chapters in Books

(With Anderson, Robert D., and Anna Caroline Muller.) "Ensuring Integrity and Competition in Public Procurement Markets: A Dual Challenge for Good Governance," in *National Seminar on the Revised WTO Agreement on Government Procurement: Basic Documentation*, Chap. III:2. [Geneva]: World Trade Organization, 2011.

"Intellectual Property Policy and Competition Policy," 66 *New York University Annual Survey of American law* 421-434 (2011).

(With Marshall, Robert C., Leslie M. Marx and Halbert L. White.) "Plus Factors and Agreement in Antitrust Law," 110 *Michigan Law Review* 393-436 (2011).

"Redesigning a Criminal Cartel Regime: The Canadian Conversion," in *Criminalising Cartels: Critical Studies of an International Regulatory Movement*, p. 45-73. Edited by Caron Beaton-Wells and Ariel Ezrachi. Oxford; Portland, OR: Hart, 2011.

(With Hollman, Hugh M.) "The International Competition Network: Its Past, Current and Future Role," 20 *Minnesota Journal of International Law* 274-323 (2011).

"The Role of Economic Analysis in Competition Law," in *Intellectual Property, Competition Law and Economics in Asia*, p. 23-33. Edited by R. Ian McEwin. Oxford; Portland, OR: Hart Pub., 2011.

(With Winerman, Marc.) "The William Humphrey and Abram Myers Years: The FTC from 1925 to 1929," 77 *Antitrust Law Journal* 701-747 (2011).

(With Winerman, Marc.) "Competition Policy and the Application of Section 5 of the Federal Trade Commission Act," (Symposium: Issues at the Forefront of Monopolization and Abuse of Dominance) 76 *Antitrust Law Journal* 929-950 (2010).

(With Winerman, Marc.) "Outpost Years for a Start-Up Agency: The FTC from 1921-1925," 77 *Antitrust Law Journal* 145-203 (2010).

"Panel III: Antitrust and the Obama Administration: U.S. Convergence with International Competiton Norms: Antitrust Law and Public Restraints on Competition," (Antitrust Conference in Honor of Joseph Brodley.) 90 *Boston University Law Review* 1555-1610 (2010).

"The Digital Broadband Migration and the Federal Trade Commission: Building the Competition and Consumer Protection Agency of the Future," 8 *Journal of Telecommunications & High Technology Law* 1-24 (2010).

"Rating the Competition Agencies: What Constitutes Good Performance," (Symposium: Antitrust Policy in the New Administration) 16 *George Mason Law Review* 903-926 (2009).

"Competition Policy, Consumer Protection, and Economic Disadvantage," (Access to Justice: The Social Responsibility of Lawyers). 25 *Washington University Journal of Law & Policy* 101-118 (2007).

(With Reindl, Andreas P.) "An Interdisciplinary Approach to Improving Competition Policy and Intellectual Property Policy." 28 *Fordham International Law Journal* 1062-1090 (2005).

"Evaluating Antitrust Experiments: Using ex post Assessments of Government Enforcement Decisions to Inform Competition Policy." 9 *George Mason Law Review* 843-861 (2001).

"Institutional Foundations for Economic Legal Reform in Transition Economies: The Case of Competition Policy and Antitrust Enforcement." 77 *Chicago-Kent Law Review* 265-315 (2001).

"Private Monitoring and Antitrust Enforcement: Paying Informants to Reveal Cartels." 69 *George Washington Law Review* 766-797 (2001).

"The Significance of the Microsoft Litigation for Postal Service Operators." in *Future Directions in Postal Reform*, edited by Michael A. Crew and Paul R. Kleindorfer. Boston, MA: Kluwer, 2001.

"Transatlantic Turbulence: The Boeing-McDonnell Douglas Merger and International Competition Policy." 68 *Antitrust Law Journal* 805-873 (2001).

"Holding Legislators Accountable for their Regulatory Promises." 2000 *Law Review of Michigan State University - Detroit College of Law* 9-15 (2000).

"Lessons of Competition Policy Reform in Transition Economies for U.S. Antitrust Policy." 74 *St. John's Law Review* 361-405 (2000).

"Competition Policy in the Postconsolidation Defense Industry." 44 *Antitrust Bulletin* 421 (1999).

"Designing Antitrust Remedies for Dominant Firm Misconduct." 31 *Connecticut Law Review* 1285-1319 (1999).

"The Crusade against Monopolists: Federal Antitrust Authorities are Jousing with Giant Corporations in a Sudden Reversal of the Government's Noninterventionist Policy." 6 *Corporate Counsel* no. 5, p. 44 (June 1999).

"Evaluating the Effects of Procurement Reform." 33 *The Procurement Lawyer* no. 2, p.1 (Winter 1998).

"Law, Economics, and the Reinvention of Public Administration: Using Relational Agreements to Reduce the Cost of Procurement Regulation and other Forms of Government Intervention in the Economy." 50 *Administrative Law Review* 141-156 (1998).

"Merger Enforcement in Transition: Antitrust Controls on Acquisitions in Emerging Economies." 66 *University of Cincinnati Law Review* 1071-1112 (1998).

"Perilous Beginnings: The Establishment of Antimonopoly and Consumer Protection Programs in the Republic of Georgia." 43 *Antitrust Bulletin* 15-43 (1998).

"Administrative Adjudication and the Use of New Economic Analysis Approaches in Antitrust Analysis." 5 *George Mason Law Review* 313-346 (1997).

"Antitrust Decisionmaking and the Supreme Court: Perspectives from Thurgood Marshall Papers." 42 *Antitrust Bulletin* 93-114 (1997).

"Antitrust Policy and Horizontal Collusion in the 21st Century." 9 *Loyola Consumer Reporter* 97 (1997).

(with Boner, Roger A.). "Antitrust Policy in Ukraine." 31 *George Washington Journal of International Law & Economics* 1-48 (1997).

"Comments on a Paper by Robert Cooter." in *Economic Dimensions in International Law* 317, edited by Jagdeep S. Bhandari & Alan O. Sykes. Cambridge: Cambridge University Press, 1997.

"Competition Policy Analysis of Joint Ventures and Teaming Arrangements by Government Agencies and the Courts." in *Subcontracting, Teaming and Partnering in the Age of Consolidation and Cooperation.* Chicago, IL: American Bar Association, Section of Public Contract Law, 1997.

"Creating Competition Policy: Betty Bock and the Development of Antitrust Institutions." 66 *Antitrust Law Journal* 231-245 (1997).

"Getting Started: Creating New Competition Policy Institutions in Transition Economics." 23 *Brooklyn Journal of International Law* 403-453 (1997).

"Predatory Pricing Standards and Competition in Postal Areas." in *Diffusion of New Regulatory Approaches to Postal Services* 67, edited by Ulrich Stumpf and Monica Plum. Bad Honnif: Wissenschaftliches Institut feur Kommunikationsdienste, 1997.

"The Quality of Appointments and the Capability of the Federal Trade Commission." 49 *Administrative Law Review* 915 (1997).

(with Thorpe, Robert S.). "Antitrust and the Evolution of a Market Economy in Mongolia." in *De-Monopolization and Competition Policy in Post-Communist Economies* 89, edited by Ben Slay. Boulder, CO: Westview Press, 1996.

"Commissions, Courts and the Access Pricing Problem." in *Pricing and Regulatory Innovations under Increasing Competition* 53, edited by Michael A. Crew. Boston: Kluwer, 1996.

"Downsizing Antitrust: Is it Time to End Dual Federal Enforcement?" 41 *Antitrust Bulletin* 505-540 (1996).

"The Competition Policy Entrepreneur and Law Reform in Formerly Communist and Socialist Countries." 11 *American University Journal of International Law & Policy* 437-474 (1996).

"Whistleblower Bounty Lawsuits as Monitoring Devices in Government Contracting." 29 *Loyola of Los Angeles Law Review* 1799-1857 (1996).

"Accounting for Regulation in Determining the Application of Antitrust Rules to Firms Subject to Public Utility Oversight." 40 *Antitrust Bulletin* 483-499 (1995).

"Designing and Implementing Competition and Consumer Protection Reforms in Transitional Economies: Perspectives from Mongolia, Nepal, Ukraine, and Zimbabwe." 44 *DePaul Law Review* 1197-1224 (1995).

(with Graham, Neil E.). "Determining Constraints on Pricing." in *The Strategy and Tactics of Pricing* 360, edited by Thomas T. Nagle and Reed K. Holden. Englewood Cliffs, NJ: Prentice Hall, 1995.

"Expanded Antitrust Scrutiny Requires Greater Caution." 30 *The Procurement Lawyer* no. 3, p. 23 (Spring, 1995).

"Post-Appointment Preference Shaping and its Influence on Judicial Analysis of Economic Regulation Issues." in *Commercialization of Postal and Delivery Services: National and International Perspectives* 93, edited by Michael A. Crew and Paul R. Kleindorfer. Boston, MA: Kluwer, 1995.

"Procurement Reform and the Choice of Forum in Bid Protest Disputes." 9 *Administrative Law Journal of the American University* 461-513 (1995).

"Public Choice and the Origins of Antitrust Policy." in *The Causes and Consequences of Antitrust: The Public Choice Perspective* 243, edited by Fred S. McChesney and William F. Shughart III. Chicago: University of Chicago Press, 1995.

"The Application of Legal Safeguards against Predation to the Postal Service Industry." in *Commercialization of Postal and Delivery Services: National and International Perspectives* 45, edited by Michael A. Crew and Paul R. Kleindorfer. Boston, MA: Kluwer, 1995.

"Competition Policy, Rivalries, and Defense Industry Consolidation." 8 *Journal of Economic Perspectives* 91 (1994).

(with Larson, Alex and Douglas Mudd). "Competitive Access Issues and Telecommunications Regulatory Policy." 20 *Journal of Contemporary Law* 419-477 (1994).

"The Changing Equilibrium of Antitrust Policy." in II *The Antitrust Impulse: An Economic, Historical and Legal Analysis* 575, edited by Theodore P. Kovaleff. Armonk, NY: M.E. Sharpe, 1994.

"The Law and Economics of Privacy: Applications to Regulated Industries." in *Incentive Regulation for Public Utilities* 113, edited by Michael A. Crew. Boston: Kluwer, 1994.

"Comment: Perennial Gales and the International Mail." in *Regulation and the Nature of Postal and Delivery Services* 217, edited by Michael A. Crew and Paul R. Kleindorfer. Boston: Kluwer, 1993.

"Judicial Appointments and the Future of Antitrust Policy." 7 *Antitrust* 8 (Spring 1993).

"The Identification and Proof of Horizontal Agreements under the Antitrust Laws." 38 *Antitrust Bulletin* 5-81 (1993).

"Competition Policy, Economic Development, and Transition to Free Markets in the Third World: The Case of Zimbabwe." 61 *Antitrust Law Journal* 253-265 (1992).

"The Antitrust Law and Economics of Essential Facilities in Public Utility Regulation." in *Economic Innovations in Public Utility Regulation* 1, edited by Michael A. Crew. Boston: Kluwer, 1992.

"The Effect of Government Involvement." in *Antitrust Law Developments (Third)* 963-1016. Chicago, IL: American Bar Association, 1992.

"The Influence of Economics on Antitrust Law." 30 *Economic Inquiry* 294 (1992).

(with DeSanti, Susan S.). "*Matsushita*: Its Construction and Application by the Lower Courts." 59 *Antitrust Law Journal* 609-653 (1991).

"Blue Ribbon Defense Commissions: The Acquisition of Major Weapons Systems." in *Arms, Policy, and the Economy: Historical and Contemporary Perspectives* 61, edited by Robert Higgs. New York: Holmes & Meier, 1990.

"Commitment in Regulation: Defense Contracting and Extensions to Price Caps." 3 *Journal of Regulatory Economics* 219-240 (1991).

"Merger Policy in a Declining Defense Industry." 36 *Antitrust Bulletin* 543-592 (1991).

"Reagan's Judicial Appointees and Antitrust in the 1990's." 60 *Fordham Law Review* 49-124 (1991).

"Regulatory Controls as Barriers to Entry in Government Procurement." 25 *Policy Sciences* 29 (1991).

"The Reagan Judiciary and Environmental Policy: The Impact of Appointments to the Federal Courts of Appeals." 18 *Boston College Environmental Law Review* 669-713 (1991).

"Antitrust Analysis of Joint Ventures and Teaming Arrangements involving Government Contractors." 58 *Antitrust Law Journal* 1059-1115 (1990).

"Antitrust and Competitiveness: Is Legislation to Exempt Production Joint Ventures Necessary?" in *Proceedings of the New York State Bar Association Antitrust Law Symposium* 66 (Jan. 16, 1990).

"Comments and Observations on the Sherman Act: The First Century." 59 *Antitrust Law Journal* 119-130 (1990).

"Government Support for Research and Development." in *The Shrinking Industrial Base: Restructuring the Defense Industry and Ensuring American Competitiveness for the 1990's.* (Annual Meeting Program, American Bar Association, Section of Public Contract Law, August 1990).

(with Larson, Alex). "Predatory Pricing Safeguards in Telecommunications Regulation: Removing Impediments to Competition." 35 *St. Louis University Law Journal* 1-38 (1990).

"The Antitrust Paradox Revisited: Robert Bork and the Transformation of Modern Antitrust Policy." 36 *Wayne Law Review* 1413-1471 (1990).

"The Sorcerer's Apprentice: Public Regulation of the Weapons Acquisition Process." in *Arms, Policy, and the Economy: Historical and Contemporary Perspectives* 104, edited by Robert Higgs. New York: Holmes & Meier, 1990.

"Congress and the Federal Trade Commission." 57 *Antitrust Law Journal* 869-905 (1989).

"Failed Expectations: The Troubled Past and Uncertain Future of the Sherman Act as a Tool for Deconcentration." 74 *Iowa Law Review* 1105-1130 (1989).

"Federal Antitrust Enforcement in the Reagan Administration: Two Cheers for the Disappearance of the Large Firm Defendant in Nonmerger Cases." 12 *Research in Law & Economics* 173-206 (1989).

(with Burnett, William B.). "Reform of United States Weapons Acquisition Policy: Competition, Teaming Arrangements, and Dual-Sourcing." 6 *Yale Journal on Regulation* 249-317 (1989).

"Built to Last? The Antitrust Legacy of the Reagan Administration." 35 *Federal Bar News* 244-250 (June 1988).

"Federal Regulation of Business: Antitrust and Environmental Law." in *Significant Business Decisions of the Supreme Court, 1986-1987 Term* 57, edited by Henry M. Butler, William Fischel & William E. Kovacic. Washington, DC: Washington Legal Foundation, 1988.

"Illegal Agreements with Competitors." in *Tales from Toronto.* (Annual Meeting Program, American Bar Association, Section of Public Contract Law, August 1988).

"Illegal Agreements with Competitors." 57 *Antitrust Law Journal* 517-541 (1988).

"Public Choice and the Public Interest: Federal Trade Commission Antitrust Enforcement during the Reagan Administration." 33 *Antitrust Bulletin* 467-504 (1988).

(with Burnett, William B.). "Teaming Arrangements and the Acquisition Process." *Defense News* 24 (November 27, 1987).

"The Analysis of Mergers in Industries Subject to Rapid Technological Change." in *Manual on the Economics of Antitrust Law* 7-1. Chicago, IL: American Bar Association, Section on Antitrust Law, Economics Committee, 1987.

"The Emerging Role of Competition in the Weapons Acquisition Process." 1 *Antitrust and Trade Regulation Section Report* no. 2. (Federal Bar Association, Summer 1987).

(with Miller, James C. III, Thomas F. Walton, and Jeremy A. Rabkin). "Industrial Policy: Reindustrialization through Competition or Coordinated Action?" 2 *Yale Journal on Regulation* 1-51 (1984).

"Antitrust." in 1 *TMGT 340: The Business Government Relationship Reader* 173, edited by William M. Wolff, Jr. Lexington, MA: Ginn Custom Publ., 1983.

(with Hurwitz, James). "Judicial Analysis of Predation: The Emerging Trends." 35 *Vanderbilt Law Review* 63-157 (1982).

"The Federal Trade Commission and Congressional Oversight of Antitrust Enforcement." 17 *Tulsa Law Journal* 587-671 (1982). Reprinted in *Public Choice and Regulation: A View from Inside the Federal Trade Commission* 63, edited by Robert Mackay, James C. Miller III, and Bruce Yandle. Stanford: Hoover Institution Press, 1987.

"An Analysis of the Commission's Response to Congressional Oversight of FTC Antitrust Enforcement." in *Federal Trade Commission Competition Programs 1969-1980*. Washington, DC: U.S. Federal Trade Commission, 1981.

(with Hurwitz, James D., Thomas Sheehan, and Robert H. Lande). "Current Legal Scholarship of Predation." in *Strategy, Predation, and Antitrust Analysis* 101, edited by Steven C. Salop. Washington, DC: Federal Trade Commission, Bureau of Economics, Bureau of Competition, 1981.

Book Reviews

"The Institutions of Antitrust Law: How Structure Shapes Substance." Review of *The Institutional Structure of Antitrust Enforcement*, by Daniel A. Crane. 110 *Michigan Law Review* 1019-1044 (2012).

Other

"Prepared Statement of the Federal Trade Commission on the FTC's Regulatory Reform Program: Twenty Years of Systematic Retrospective Rule Reviews & New Prospective Initiatives to Increase Public Participation and Reduce Burdens on Business," U.S. Trade Commission before the Subcommittee on Oversight and Investigations of the House Committee on Energy and Commerce, 112th Cong. (2nd Sess., July 7, 2011).

Editor, *Research in Law and Economics*, v.17 (1995) to date. Greenwich, CT: JAI Press.

"The Competition Conundrum (Antitrust Policies of Presidential Candidates George W. Bush and Al Gore)." 23 *American Lawyer* 77 (2001).

"Is Uncle Sam too Easy a Mark? Bid Rigging on Government Contracts." 21 *Legal Times* no. 24, p. S42 (Nov. 2, 1998).

Recommended Action Plan for Implementing Georgia's Antimonopoly and Consumer Protection Laws. Center for Economic Policy and Reform, Analytical Report No. 9, May 1997.

(with Dunn, Karen Turner and Robert S. Thorpe). *Analysis of Competition in Mongolia & Three Case Studies*. University of Maryland, IRIS Center Country Report No. 14, 1994.

Antitrust and the Evolution of a Market Economy in Mongolia. Working Paper No. 97. College Park, MD: Center for Institutional Reform and the Informal Sector, 1994.

"A Knack for Business: Breyer Would Fill a Void on the High Court." 107 *Los Angeles Daily Journal* no. 11, p. 41 (Aug. 2, 1993).

"Anti-Competitive Forces may Stir Anew." 15 *National Law Journal* no. 38, p. 19 (May 24, 1993).

The Reagan Judiciary Examined: A Comparison of Environmental Law Voting Records of Carter and Reagan Appointees to the Federal Courts of Appeals. Working Paper Series No. 36. Washington, DC: Washington Legal Foundation, 1989.

The Antitrust Paradox Revisited: Robert Bork and the Transformation of Modern Antitrust Policy. Working Paper Series No. 32. Washington, DC: Washington Legal Foundation, 1989.

The Reagan Judiciary Examined: A Comparison of Antitrust Voting Records of Carter and Reagan Appointees to the Federal Courts of Appeals. Working Paper Series No. 34. Washington, DC: Washington Legal Foundation, 1989.

(with Fullerton, Lawrence, et al.). *Reliance on FTC Consumer Protection Law Precedents in other Legal Forums*. Working Paper No. 1. Chicago, IL: American Bar Association, Section of Antitrust Law, 1988.

Permanence and Regulatory Change: The Longevity of Reagan Antitrust and Consumer Protection Policy at the Federal Trade Commission. Working Paper Series No. 29. Washington, DC: Washington Legal Foundation, 1988.

"Armed Services Using Competition Strategy to Reduce Expenses." 10 *Legal Times* p. 14 (July 13, 1987).

"The Rules of Reason: D.C. Circuit Adopts Judge Bork's Analysis." 9 *Legal Times* p. 20 (Oct. 6, 1986).

Part I
An Antitrust Career

The Toastmaster

WILLIAM BLUMENTHAL

william.blumenthal@cliffordchance.com
Partner, Clifford Chance, LLP

Abstract

This article discusses Bill Kovacic's skills in delivering ceremonial remarks at events honoring the accomplishments of others. His remarks are successful and well received largely because of the allusions with which they are interlaced—allusions to literature, history, film, music, and sports.

When members of the academic community think of the many accomplishments of William Evan Kovacic, they are prone to focus on his contributions to the scholarly literature in such fields as institutional design of regulatory agencies, policy development for emerging competition regimes, and government contracting. Other communities, though, are at least as likely to focus on other accomplishments, skills, attributes, and contributions. To a generation of funding officers at the U.S. Agency for International Development and similar institutions, Bill is probably best known for his delivery of technical assistance to new competition agencies around the globe. To a generation of competition practitioners in the U.S. and Europe, Bill represents the most gripping, enthusiastic speeches and presentations at any program or conference at which he appears. To a generation of students at law schools in and around Washington, DC, Bill is the award-winning professor who not only delivers the most gripping, enthusiastic classroom performances, but also is particularly decent and approachable, offering a friendly and supportive ear and a willingness to provide recommendations to employers and other onward opportunities. To a legion of law students elsewhere, Bill is the co-author of West's antitrust Nutshell and of a widely-adopted antitrust casebook.

For those who worked with him during his decade-plus of service at the Federal Trade Commission, Bill has been all of those things, and more. Particularly during the later period at the agency when he served as General Counsel, Commissioner, and Chairman, Bill offered thought and insight that drew on his years in academia teaching courses outside the competition and consumer protection missions at the agency's core. Contracts? Torts? Property? For most lawyers those are ancient relics of first-year law school; but for a professor who had to master the subjects and impart them to students, they contained doctrinal gems that might inform a competition or consumer protection decision or provide a critical analogy. (Might the tort principle of least-cost avoider bear on one's analysis of a dominance investigation? Bill saw the link in at least one internal debate.) And in his dealings with staff, he went about the work with a gentility, grace, humanity, and kindness that one sometimes doesn't observe in officials of his rank.

For me, though, the most memorable feature of our shared time at the agency, Bill's most singular quality and the one to which this *festschrift* contribution is chiefly devoted, were his remarks at internal tributes and celebrations.

Most people never receive the honor of being celebrated in a *festschrift*. But they do receive other honors over the course of a career—awards ceremonies, birthday celebrations, tributes as they depart one organization to join another, retirement parties. Sometimes those are open events, but more often they are internal events and sometimes intimate gatherings. And when Bill was tapped to deliver two- or five-minute remarks to applaud someone he knew, the treat was very special. Take the gripping, enthusiastic speaking style known to practitioners and students from more extended presentations, and distill it into brief, concentrated remarks. Stir in a dose of personal knowledge, personal closeness. And because the setting was among friends, allow for an air of informality, less guarded than one customarily finds in public statements. Yes, the two- or five-minute treat was very special.

The remarks were always customized, of course, with a particular focus on the honoree, and they were delivered with the unique pacing and modulation that one always observes when Bill speaks. But individual honorees and their life stories are often lacking in entertainment value. Bill would provide the entertainment through other means, interweaving the remarks with allusions to mass culture and sometimes-bizarre foreign culture and various other apt phenomena.

There were the allusions to sports. Baseball was the most common, but football, hockey, basketball, track, luge, auto racing all made appearances. Spring training was sometimes mentioned, as was the postseason. Reflecting Bill's formative years, Detroit teams were viewed with great favor. Sometimes circumstances called for a reference to the New York Yankees, but if feasible, the preferred reference would point to the Detroit Tigers. Bill often quoted the great managers and coaches, the likes of John Wooden and Morgan Wootten. "Don't confuse activity with accomplishment." And Bill sometimes quoted highlights from players, such as the one who responded to the hackneyed scolding "there's no I in team" by noting "ain't no we, either."

There were the allusions to music, with a particular focus on the genre now known as classic rock. Beatles, Rolling Stones, CSNY, Joni Mitchell, the Eagles, many groups that sold millions fewer albums. It was clear that Bill, unlike many of his contemporaries, had actually listened to the lyrics, since the lyrics would often find their way into his remarks. They were often offered without attribution. "That's familiar," the audience member would think, "I know that line from somewhere," but since the member probably hadn't listened to the lyrics and certainly hadn't memorized them, the words would simply ring like a fitting grace note. Picture the retirement event for a forty-year career staffer: We are stardust. Billion year old carbon. We are golden. Caught in the devil's bargain. And we've got to get ourselves back to the garden.

There were the allusions to historical events, most often of the catastrophic variety. The Hindenburg: "Oh, the humanity." The Titanic: the failure to alert the bridge by shouting "Iceberg right ahead." Pearl Harbor: Wohlstetter and decision makers' difficulties in detecting and sorting the signals among the noise, even if the cables had been decoded. Miscellaneous events from the Civil War and World War II.

There were occasional allusions to literature, though sometimes in disguise or with a twist. "The horror, the horror." (That was Joseph Conrad in *Heart of Darkness*, not the radio commentator at the Hindenburg.) Remarks opening with Kafka's *Metamorphosis*: "As Gregor Samsa awoke one morning from uneasy dreams, he found himself transformed in his bed into a gigantic insect . . . Oops, sorry. Wrong text . . . ."

And there were allusions to movies and quotations from movies. Many, many, many movies. Some were black-and-white films from the golden age of Hollywood. *All About Eve. Sunset Boulevard.* Some were classic films from England's Ealing studios. *The Lavender Hill Mob.* Many were action-adventure films. The *Dirty Harry* series was a particularly fertile source of quotations—"A man's got to know his limitations"—but the *Indiana Jones* and *Die Hard* and James Bond series had their place, too. Some others were classic war movies. *The Bridge on the River Kwai* and its last line, "Madness. Madness." Many were mysteries, detective films, and modern films noir. *L.A. Confidential* and Rollo Tomasi, the fictional-within-fiction villain who always got away with it. *Chinatown* and the line "The future, Mr. Gittes. The *future*." Some were Westerns. Some were modern horror films. *Saw. Hostel.* Some were gangster films. Occasionally a romantic comedy crept in.

Many of the movies had been viewed during Bill's travels while airborne, most often on United Airlines. One of the great ironies was the opportunity to view *Up In The Air* from an airplane seat. A related irony was that the movie's lead character Ryan, played by George Clooney, was described as having flown 350,000 miles in a year,[1] a level roughly comparable to Bill's travels during that particular period. Of course, Ryan's flights were mainly domestic short-hops in the Midwest, whereas Bill's were more often international long-hauls, on which any given volume of mileage is much more easily accumulated. Still, Ryan's flights would have been too brief to allow the viewing of a feature movie, whereas Bill's had time for one or two, even more for transpacific travel. *The Flintstones* on codeshare partner Lufthansa, on connection via Frankfurt to Central Asia? *Der Feuersteins.*

Those travels yielded many anecdotes, which also found their way into Bill's remarks. Some of the anecdotes were entirely domestic. A favorite is Bill's tale of a visit to an air facility crew lounge, where he observed as 777 and 747 pilots, engaging in braggadocio and one-upsmanship based on length of haul and size and sophistication of craft, were humbled upon their realization that a soft-spoken, mild-mannered shuttle pilot had been referring not to the PSA DC9 shuttle or the Eastern 727 shuttle, but to the NASA space shuttle. Recalling the encounter, Bill sometimes said in reference to the quietly self-assured among his honorees, "if you can really do it, you don't need to brag about it."

Most of the travel anecdotes came from overseas, collected during the course of technical assistance activities for the benefit of new competition regimes that resided in cultures that differed materially from our own. From the director of the Hermitage, asked whether his collection was the finest, the response: "it may not be the finest, but there is none finer." From landlocked Ulan Bator, the substitution of "safe harbor" with "pleasant pasture." From a Tanzanian urged to adopt analytical methodologies relying on technology that was nonexistent in his country, the characterization of his instructor as "motu noclu—Master of the Universe. No Clue."

While virtually all of Bill's remarks at tributes and celebrations were offered with bonhomie and good spirits, and while most included at least some twinkle in the eye, the remarks sometimes broached gently against serious substantive issues. A memorable example was Bill's tribute to Tim Muris on the occasion of Tim's receiving the FTC's Miles Kirkpatrick Award. The agency's highest award, the Kirkpatrick is designed to honor "individuals who throughout their public and private careers have made lasting and significant contributions" to the FTC. After some references to baseball (a shared interest of Bill and Tim) and to movies, Bill offered a vignette from the first senior staff meeting with Tim as agency Chairman and Bill attending as General Counsel. Bill recalled that Tim made the point of speaking well of the prior Chairman, Bob Pitofsky, and of noting that the legitimacy of antitrust policy required that it not be perceived as susceptible to political gusts and to sharp changes with shifts of agency leadership. Bill observed that the credibility of the U.S. in conducting advocacy abroad required policy consistency across Administrations. And Bill recounted that Tim told senior staff at that first meeting: "If I ever learn that you have been publicly criticizing our predecessors, you'll be out the next day."

Bill then moved on to the next point in his tribute to Tim. He didn't return to the point of policy consistency, nor did he ever indicate why he elected to include the anecdote in his remarks. He didn't need to, for most of those in attendance understood the unstated message. Bill's successor as Chairman had continued the practice of viewing antitrust enforcement as bipartisan, as a shared undertaking across the political spectrum. Two blocks away, though, on the other side of the National Archives, the new head of the Justice Department's Antitrust Division had been seeding the press with barbed remarks critical of the prior Administration, in a manner that some viewed as an unbecoming and undeserved breach of tradition. Bill was merely recounting Tim's gesture in praising Bob, but in context the unstated contrast was deafening.

No one knew it at the time, but Bill was to receive the Kirkpatrick the following year. He offered brief remarks, a testimonial to the agency and its staff, but he did so as the honoree. Three other speakers served the role that had so often fallen to Bill, as persons delivering the tribute. Their remarks were not shared in advance, even among themselves, for two of them invoked the story that Bill had so often used from his visit to the Hermitage: we wouldn't presume to say the finest, but there's certainly none finer.

NOTES

1   Jason Reitman & Sheldon Turner, UP IN THE AIR, Film Script *available at* http://www.imsdb.com/scripts/Up-in-the-Air.html, ("Last year, I flew three hundred fifty thousand miles. The moon is only two fifty.").

From Here to There: The Life and Works (So Far) of Bill Kovacic

Fiona A. Schaeffer

fschaeffer@jonesday.com
Partner, Jones Day

Hugh M. Hollman

hmhollman@jonesday.com
Associate, Jones Day

Abstract

Bill Kovacic is a great leader and scholar who has made an enormous contribution to the development of U.S. and international antitrust law, enforcement and institution building. Other authors have recognized Bill for these contributions; we wanted to complete this picture by recognizing his other great gifts and contributions—Bill's incredible generosity of spirit, his humility, his ability to raise the game of everyone around him and the indelible impression he leaves on everyone that has been fortunate to work or study with him. Believing that Bill Kovacic's liber amicorum would not be complete without a biographical account, we spoke to a number of Bill's friends and colleagues in the hope of gathering the necessary material to give you a more complete picture of Bill—the man, professor, public official and "International Entrepreneur." We begin with a description of Bill's formative years and early influences and then discuss aspects of his academic career. Continuing this chronological progression, we describe Bill's role as public official, interspersed with his contribution to the worldwide growth of competition law through foreign assistance projects. We entitled this section of the essay: "Bill, the International Entrepreneur," which is how former FTC Chairman Timothy Muris describes Bill. Finally, we provide an account of what Bill is dedicating himself to today. Above all and throughout, we try to capture what we believe are Bill's quintessential qualities—especially his dedication to sharing success and passing it on - Bill the person that has achieved such great heights but has never become too important to help those who need it the most.

I. Introduction—Getting Started[1]

Bill jokes that he wouldn't want anyone to write anything biographical about him as that would be a testament to a life complete and he still has much to do. We could not agree more. This essay is to be read as an appreciation of Bill, the man, and his work for others to share.

A timeless philosophical debate is whether we, as human beings, truly have free will. Few human beings sitting down to breakfast a little earlier than they expected would do anything but grumble before their first cup of coffee. Few would see the opportunity in an early start and resolve to make it a better day. Bill, however, is one of those people. Certainly, he would greet the morning (and afternoon) with customary coffee in hand. But, he would turn it into a brighter day—especially for those around him. Should the day take on a darker hue than he had hoped, Bill would remind everyone that the legal profession is a lot better than many others. After all, he would remark, we could be coal miners toiling underground for hours on end at a coal face. Bill's grandfather was a coal miner in Pennsylvania.

His grandfather mined a lot of coal but he also made time for his son. Bill's father went on to become a nuclear power plant engineer and perhaps an early inspiration for Bill's chilling cold war anecdotes. One can imagine that at the height of the cold war, being the son of a nuclear power engineer must have made the nuclear threat feel much closer to home. But instead of retreating behind protectionist barriers, Bill wanted to better understand people and cultures different to his own.

Bill explains that his love of people, cultures and foreign travel began at the age of thirteen when his father took him on a three-week business trip around Europe. That trip made a huge impression on Bill and inspired a lifelong passion to learn and understand more about the world we live in. He went on to study at the Woodrow Wilson School for Public and International Affairs, followed by law school at Columbia. With this background, Bill seemed destined to find a way to weave law, government and international studies together. Becoming a trailblazer, however, was an evolutionary process that would take time.

Bill attributes his interest in law to his mother's side of the family. Bill's mother, Francis Crow, grew up in the Texas panhandle. Her father and grandfather were both lawyers. With much fondness, Bill describes how he spent summer vacations with his mother's family and a lot of time at the law offices. Unusual for the time, Ms. Crow graduated from the Texas College for Women where she studied biology. But Bill's mother was not the first in his family to go to college, that honor belongs to Bill's grandmother, Carmen Dickinson, who graduated with a degree in pharmacology from the University of Kansas in 1909. When describing the maternal side of his family, Bill often jests that they were probably the only family in the town of Canadian, Texas (population: 2,281) with a subscription to the New Yorker.

Was Bill always destined to become an antitrust scholar? His early scholarship suggested so. Bill took an antitrust course in law school and immediately felt its gravitational pull. He describes antitrust as a "natural home for someone keen on economics, history, and political science." One day, Bill wondered aloud in class about melding his interest in international affairs with competition law.

His antitrust professor responded sharply that there was "no such thing" as "international antitrust." In 1978 only the United States and Germany showed much appreciation for competition law enforcement. But Bill was also beginning his career at a watershed time for antitrust law in the United States and found himself right in the middle of the action.

During law school, Bill took a leave of absence to spend a year as a research assistant for the U.S. Senate Judiciary Committee's Antitrust and Monopoly Subcommittee, chaired by Philip Hart. Among other assignments, Bill worked on legislation adopted in 1976 that became the Hart-Scott-Rodino Antitrust Improvements Act. This legislation led to numerous changes in the antitrust law, not least of which were pre-merger approval notifications, the HSR review process, and a clock ticking for merger review by the U.S. federal antitrust agencies.

After law school, Bill went on to do a clerkship with Hon. Roszel C. Thomsen, Senior U.S. District Judge, District of Maryland. Instead of heading to private practice after his clerkship like many others, Bill decided to enter the FTC's Bureau of Competition as an attorney in what was then known as the "Planning Office." If asked why the FTC, Bill likely will explain that his work on the Hart committee and studies at Princeton and Columbia had inspired a strong interest in antitrust law and the evolution of institutions. Bill had contributed to the drafting of the HSR Act, and working at the FTC would allow him to see it put into practice. This was a real life experiment in institution building that Bill was on the scene to observe first hand.

Bill's next role at the FTC was to become an attorney advisor to Commissioner George W. Douglas. Before starting as an advisor, Bill's boss at the Planning Office, Jack Kirkwood, invited Bill to a dinner that literally changed his life. Bill often encourages younger attorneys who fear they have too much work or looming deadlines to go to social occasions, that "often it is best to simply show up." Had Bill not heeded such advice himself, the world might never have known one of its greatest antitrust duos. Jack and his wife, Heather Kirkwood, had invited another young FTC attorney to dinner that evening. Kathy Fenton was working with Heather on a media concentration project at the time. The rest, as they say, is history.

Kathy and Bill did not announce their engagement until after they left the FTC. Kathy joined Jones Day, and Bill went on to Bryan Cave and then took up a post as an Assistant Professor at George Mason University Law School. In the summer of 1985, when Kathy was an associate at Jones Day and Bill was at Bryan Cave, Kathy and Bill were married. While Bill later took up a career dedicated to academia and public service, Kathy went on to make partner at Jones Day, where she is a preeminent antitrust lawyer in her own right. Kathy is also one of the few people that can match Bill's wit and Bill is fond of quoting Kathy's phrases. "Don't let the perfect be the enemy of the good" is one of Kathy's more popular sayings. Like Bill, Kathy is blessed with the ability to instill courage and a sense of perspective in those around her. No wonder Kathy excels at successfully navigating the most challenging of merger cases.

II. Bill, the Professor

At this point, it perhaps makes sense to pause the chronological account of Bill's life and his work. A straight chronology might not reveal the impact and significance of Bill's earlier years on his future work. To fully appreciate how the seeds Bill planted in his early days in the FTC's Planning Office took root and blossomed, we need to fast forward to a report he published when he was Chairman of the FTC: The Federal Trade Commission at 100: Into Our 2nd Century.

The FTC at 100 Report is a tour de force of scholarship on institution building. The Report examines agency structure, mission building, leadership, and how to utilize agency resources. A key chapter is how to objectively measure agency effectiveness. Bill writes:

> The orientation of this study also is long-term in nature, at least by the customs of national policymaking in the United States. The measures suggested here generally do not lend themselves to instant accomplishment but instead require sustained, incremental effort . . . The public policy environment in the United States does not tend to nurture this perspective. In the eyes of many observers, the reputations of individual agency officials are set by observable events that transpire during the individual's tenure. This point of view discourages investments in activities with long-term, capital qualities that generate benefits to the agency well beyond a single manager's time in office.[2]

This quote captures the essence of Bill's philosophy. The subtitle of the report is "The Continuing Pursuit of Better Practice." That is precisely the point. Sustained incremental improvements, no matter who gets the credit in the end. This has been Bill's approach throughout his career, and is, of course, why Bill makes such a wonderful professor as many very fortunate students have discovered. Maureen Ohlhausen who was recently appointed to succeed Bill as Commissioner at the FTC was one such student.

Bill joined George Mason in 1986 as an Associate Professor. When Maureen began classes in 1988, she was fortunate to have Bill as her property law professor. Maureen still remembers how her first class began. Bill started by quoting from Jonathan Edwards' "Sinners in the Hands of an Angry God." We're not sure exactly which verse Bill chose, but here is a flavor of fire and brimstone language in Edwards's sermon:

> This that you have heard is the case of everyone of you that are out of Christ. That world of misery, that lake of burning brimstone is extended abroad under you. There is the dreadful pit of the glowing flames of the wrath of God; there is hell's wide gaping mouth open; and you have nothing to stand upon, nor anything to take hold of: there is nothing between you and hell but the air; 'tis only the power and mere pleasure of God that holds you up.[3]

Bill told Maureen and her fellow students that he was taught law in this manner: to fear the law and your professors and everything in-between. He, however, would strive to do the opposite. Maureen explains that no-one ever had a stupid question in Bill's classes. Questions that would have attracted scorn and condescension from another professor, Bill regarded as an opportunity to uncover the hidden (sometimes, very well hidden) brilliance buried deep within the question. Having Bill believe in you, said Maureen, expanded the universe of the possible and your belief in your own capabilities.

Maureen attended Bill's night classes as she was a full time mother during the day. Maureen's second child was born (considerately) just two weeks after her property exam. Maureen felt that she gave the appearance of being a less than a dedicated law student. Of course, appearances are often deceiving but they didn't fool Bill. Maureen later took a government contracts class with Bill, which was her inspiration to pursue a clerkship at the U.S. Court of Federal Claims, where she would have the opportunity to put into practice what she had learned from Bill.

Bill was Maureen's referee when she was applying for clerkships. One day Maureen was walking down the corridor past Bill's office pushing a double stroller with her children who were two and three years old at the time. Bill jumped up and told Maureen that a judge at the U.S. Court of Federal Claims was trying to get hold of her and encouraged her to return the judge's call immediately from his office. Maureen protested, gesturing to her children in the stroller, but of course, Bill was not to be deterred. Maureen squeezed the double stroller into Bill's office, and called the judge. She remembers looking down at Bill who was on his hands and knees doing everything he could to keep her children entertained. Bill was offering her kids anything from his desk that might distract them, even his glasses. Those same children are now in law and medical school respectively, and Maureen has just been sworn in as Commissioner and Bill's successor at the FTC.

Bill is quick on his feet. When you speak to him, do not be surprised at his quick wit. With a few ironic twists, Bill will turn a question or comment into a hilarious moment in time you will not soon forget. As quick as his wit, so too is Bill's brilliance as a speaker. Inevitably, any speaker following Bill will apologize to the audience for coming between them and hearing more from Bill. The toughest of all audiences—law students—selected Bill to be their Faculty Speaker at the George Mason School of Law commencement each year from 1989 to 1993, and in 1995, 1996 and 1998. In 1994, Bill was not in the running as he was a visiting professor at American University: Washington College of Law. While there as a visiting professor, Bill won American University's First-Year Class Teaching Award. Of course, Bill won numerous teaching awards at George Mason too.

Although Bill enjoyed teaching, he also quietly hoped he might have the opportunity to return to the FTC in some capacity. At the time, his hope seemed unlikely to be fulfilled. Bill reconciled himself to life as an academic and enjoyed writing and working with students. Then, in 1989, Bill interviewed for a faculty position at George Washington University law school. GW needed a government contracts lecturer and Bill really wanted the job. Surprisingly, he did not get it. Even more surprising was that the job was offered to a construction law professor from Kentucky who then turned it down. This odd turn of events could only have been providence at work. As Bill reflects, if he had been offered the job and become a government contracts professor, antitrust would have become a minor hobby. Nevertheless, at the time, Bill felt quite dejected. An exciting opportunity was just around the corner, though he did not appreciate it at the time.

Characteristically, Bill told himself that he could not spend too long looking at the top of his shoes, as he might miss an opportunity coming up to greet him. Still at George Mason, Bill had the opportunity to work closely with Tim Muris, who would later follow Robert Pitofsky as FTC Chairman. Tim would get to know Bill well enough to know that he wanted him to be his General Counsel at the FTC. Bill also taught a student at George Mason who later would recommend him for the position of foreign advisor to Zimbabwe, which was developing a competition law. If Bill had left George Mason, his return to the FTC, and his international antitrust missionary work could have remained a dream. Divine providence, for sure.

We describe Bill's international work and time in public office in subsequent sections, but regarding Bill's professorial pursuits at this time, suffice to say that George Washington University Law School did call again. In 1999, Bill moved from his faculty position at George Mason University School of Law across the bridge to the George Washington Law School and has been on its faculty ever since. One of Bill's first students at GW was Andrea Agathoklis, now of counsel at Wilson Sonsini Goodrich & Rosati. Andrea described herself as a "typical nervous first year law student" for which Bill was the "perfect antidote" as he ensured everyone was able to master the material while managing to have fun at the same time. Andrea would later take up antitrust law as a career, and served as Bill's attorney advisor when he was a Commissioner and Chairman at the FTC. As she told us, she has been fortunate to have Bill as her mentor and trusted advisor whom she has consulted on every step of her career from the beginning.

III. Public Office

On October 25, 2011, Federal Trade Commission Chairman Jon Leibowitz presented Bill with the Miles W. Kirkpatrick Award for Lifetime FTC Achievement. Chairman Leibowitz described how Bill had made the "FTC stronger, more nimble, and more effective."[4] For the past decade from the turn of the century to the end of 2011, Bill was part of the institutional fabric of the FTC. He was the FTC's General Counsel from 2001 through 2004. From 2006 through October 2011, Bill served as an FTC Commissioner and from 2008 to 2009 he was Chairman of the FTC.

Bill rejoined the FTC as General Counsel when Tim Muris was appointed Chairman. We were fortunate to speak to Tim about his work with Bill. They first met in 1979 when they were both working at the FTC and later worked together at George Mason. When Tim learned that he was being nominated to be Chairman in 2001, his first telephone call was to Bill to ask him to serve as General Counsel. Tim describes Bill as a General Counsel who played an integral role in the FTC's most significant policy initiatives while being extremely effective in ensuring that the General Counsel's office supported the day-to-day activities of other FTC offices.

One of Bill's most valuable talents according to Tim is his role as a remarkable consensus builder. Tim would step out of a contentious meeting leaving others engaged in highly charged debates and return to find that Bill had calmed everyone down and found an appropriate middle ground. Bill's talent for consensus building helped to keep everyone on course in pursuing policy initiatives during Muris's Chairmanship, such as the state action immunity study, and ground-breaking cases, such as Three Tenors. But, Tim noted, Bill never claimed credit for his contribution—he was self-effacing at all times while acknowledging everyone else's contribution. Whether you were a security guard, student intern or staff attorney, you could be assured that Bill would remember your name. He would also pick up where you had left off in previous conversations—even if they had happened months before. Bill has a genuine interest in everyone he interacts with, which makes everyone feel special around Bill.

Tim also described how Bill had a keen appreciation for institutional dynamics and devoted much thought and time to making the FTC a more effective institution. Bill was always careful to consider the institutional perspective on any policy question and how it would reflect on the agency. Bill developed this sensitivity when he was first at the FTC in the 1970s and early 1980s when the agency was known as the "nation's nanny." There was a perception at the time that the FTC was out of control, which led to a series of moves in Congress that threatened its very existence. Accordingly, while Bill had many ideas and plans for the agency, he was always sensitive to how they would be received by the American public. Bill would often comment that you had to be careful not to pursue too many innovative projects at one time—and, as he would write in his FTC at 100 Report, building an agency could only be achieved by a series of incremental changes and long-term, sustained effort.

Bill continued to pursue his policy work and intellectual interests during his time as General Counsel. He worked closely with Susan DeSanti and David Hyman in the FTC's policy office, especially on reforms to the patent system and healthcare. But above all, Tim noted, Bill was an "international entrepreneur" and "ahead of his time," especially in the formation of the International Competition Network and its early years of operation.

IV. Bill, the International Entrepreneur[5]

Perhaps more than any other individual, Bill has been one of the driving forces behind the globalization of competition law. It may sound strange to say today, but as Tim Muris explained, during the 1990s the U.S. antitrust agencies generally gave little thought to international competition law. But Bill could see that competition law was beginning its dramatic international expansion and he was active on the international scene from the beginning, influencing its development and convergence, as he continues to do today. To put in context the impact of Bill's work on the international stage, it seems appropriate to set the scene and explain how and why competition law took off around the world in the 1990s.

Shortly after the Second World War, Winston Churchill gave his Sinews of Peace address at Westminster. Not the English parliament, but Westminster College in Fulton, Missouri. It was a speech to the American people looking to the opportunities of the future after the dark years and sacrifices of war. Churchill's words, of course, are far more eloquent than our own. Here is what he said:

> The United States stands at this time at the pinnacle of world power. It is a solemn moment for the American Democracy. For with primacy in power is also joined an awe-inspiring accountability to the future. If you look around you, you must feel not only the sense of duty done but also you must feel anxiety lest you fall below the level of achievement. Opportunity is here now, clear and shining for both our countries. To reject it or ignore it or fritter it away will bring upon us all the long reproaches of the after-time.[6]

In the same speech Churchill went on to describe how an "iron curtain" had descended across Europe. It was the first time that term had been used. Many at the time refused to believe that their "allies in the east" had now suddenly become an enemy of western-styled democracies and market-based systems. But they had. The figurative expression of an iron curtain became a very real physical wall dividing Europe. To cross from one side to the other could result in shots being fired and instant death. The opportunity that Churchill identified was lost.

As physically divided as Europe was, so too the rest of the world was divided on a free market economy. It took about forty years for those circumstances to change. But when they did, the end seemed to come quickly. A popular depiction of the end of the iron curtain is the television images of the Berlin Wall being dismantled by a wall of people. Young men standing on the top of the wall with sledge hammers. Churchill's words spoken four decades earlier, seemed as applicable to the 1990s as they did after the Second World War. This was another solemn moment for American Democracy. An opportunity had presented itself once again.

The ramifications of what had happened in Europe were felt throughout the world. This is not surprising. Korea and Vietnam were battlegrounds of the "cold war." Countries in the African subcontinent were struggling for independence but it was also a cold war battleground. Communist China and the Soviet Union provided military assistance to those struggling for independence across the African subcontinent. AK-47s and MiGs were present, and so were concepts of a centrally-planned economy. But with the fall of the Wall, there was a crisis of confidence in the centrally-planned model. Nations across the world began to embrace the market system.

Zimbabwe is a prime example of a country that felt the impact of that change in the early 1990s. It was also the site of Bill's first technical assistance project in 1992. While Bill was at George Mason, one of his students recommended him to USAID for a project aimed at developing Zimbabwe's competition law. At the time, the leader of the government was Robert Mugabe, who remains in power to this day. China and the Soviet Union had supported Mugabe's party, the Zimbabwe African National Union ("ZANU") in its war for independence and ZANU was very sympathetic to communist principles. But Zimbabwe was not unaffected by all that was happening abroad at that time. Just the year before the Soviet Union had dissolved and during 1992 the Socialist Federal Republic of Yugoslavia began to break up, with Slovenia and Croatia gaining independence. On Zimbabwe's southern borders, white South Africans voted to end the apartheid government and began reforms to establish a power-sharing multi-racial government. Change seemed inevitable and Zimbabweans briefly looked to the West for solutions.

Zimbabwe was a short trip for Bill—two weeks—and no return. While Bill would never say it, it likely was a tough place to start his international antitrust missionary work. Bill would later report on the lessons he had learned from the tea pot-shaped African country that would serve him well on future technical assistance initiatives. In future articles he wrote about two main faults that beset technical assistance initiatives: an ignorance of local conditions by donors and technical advisors alike and an impatient, short term orientation. Bill was frustrated that his trip to Zimbabwe had been just two weeks with no follow-up, especially since he knew there was no such thing as a quick fix. Lasting change in Zimbabwe would require a sustained effort—not one short trip, which the donors did not seem to appreciate. This first technical assistance mission reinforced Bill's view that lasting change requires considerable and sustained work over a long period of time. After all, the Iron Curtain had shown its first cracks in the 1980s when Mikhail Gorbachev introduced his policy of glasnost and took a decade to finally give way.

Bill learned more about the need to appreciate local conditions during his second technical assistance initiative in Mongolia, towards the end of 1992. When asked about that trip, Bill will tell you the story of how a group of corporate lawyers drafted pages and pages of model legislation for Mongolia. While Bill was waiting to continue his conversation with his Mongolian host, the corporate lawyers stopped by to check if there was anything further that they could do to assist the Mongolian government. Their Mongolian host apparently pointed to the immense binders that the corporate lawyers had dropped off and asked if he could receive more, but to please ensure that it was presented in exactly the same way, that is, in binders and printed on one side. The corporate lawyers were delighted to hear this and took this as evidence of how well their suggested legislative amendments had been received. Once they had left the room, Bill's Mongolian host turned to Bill and explained that his country was short of paper and what is more, American lawyers used very high quality of paper that could be printed on both sides.

After similar experiences elsewhere in the world of foreign advisors thinking that only their law would do for their host countries, Bill later wrote: "Laws and regulatory processes must be adapted to the host country's environment. It is insufficient for reformers to adopt an American law, or even the 'best' law on the subject."[7] In fact, instead of pointing out how antitrust law as applied in the U.S. was "the best," Bill would point out the practical realities of antitrust law practice. To a group of Ukrainian scientists and engineers, Bill explained that "limited data and conceptual uncertainties often required the use of rough approximations and estimates," and that "antitrust analysis was more art than science."[8] Bill describes how this view was a little disconcerting to the workshop participants, but Bill had learnt through his many international advisor experiences that one size does not fit all. He was providing the workshop participants the tools they needed to solve their own local problems. To use an old adage from the international development community, "give a man a fish; you have fed him for today. Teach a man to fish; and you have fed him for a lifetime." But not all cultures wanted sushi so Bill went further and taught how to cook.

Bill's ideas and approach to foreign assistance were crystallized in a paper he wrote on convergence in international competition policy.[9] While serving as the FTC General Counsel during the 2001-2004 time period with Tim Muris, both Bill and Tim outlined principles of convergence for competition policy around the world. The first element they identified was to learn from individual agencies and non-governmental actors; the second was to develop of consensus around best practices and techniques; and the third and final element was to promote the adoption of consensus-based practices. This approach is mirrored in the International Competition Network's ("ICN") structure and is central to the ICN's approach. These should be carefully distinguished from the harmonization or homogenization of competition law, as Bill describes in a recent book chapter:

> . . . uniformity of antitrust enforcement practices is not necessarily favorable, as it reduces the opportunity for experimentation. Competition law is in the process of evolution and constant revision; as such, pursuing convergence

of global competition law (as opposed to homogenization) requires flexibility and adaptation—as economies and markets change, political priorities shift, and new technologies develop, competition laws will need to adapt.[10]

This openness to change and diversity of competition law could only be developed through experiences with many difference cultures and laws. Bill was the right person for the job.

Bill's colleagues agree. Here is what Professor Richard Whish at King's College London had to say about Bill's role in the development of competition law internationally:

> The geographical growth of competition law in the last twenty-five years has been remarkable. It would hardly have been believable in the late 1980s to have been told that in 2012 there would be 120 systems of competition law in the world, with more in the pipeline. Many very eminent people have worked tirelessly at building an international system of competition law and policy, but none has made a greater contribution than Bill Kovacic. I have been fortunate enough to visit many countries where new competition laws have been adopted, but I have never visited one where Bill had not already been. In fact I sometimes think that there must be two of him, since I never see a conference programme—whether in India, Hong Kong, South Africa or South America—which does not include him. What I admire most about Bill's work is that he excels in so many ways - a mastery of the law and economics; a convincing vision of the way in which competition and consumer law reinforce one another; terrific insights into the building of successful competition law institutions; and generous commitment to young academics embarking upon their careers. The 'world' of competition law is a much better place as a result of Bill's work.

And Margaret Bloom, former Director of Enforcement at the OFT and now of counsel at Freshfields,

> I cannot think of anyone else in the world who would have the breadth of knowledge and experience that Bill has on agency effectiveness spanning both competition and consumer powers. On top of that he is always positive and good fun.

Bill would later write about a trip to three southern Russian cities, Chelyabinsk, Novosibirsk, and Irkutsk to give antitrust workshops that were funded by the World Bank. It was arranged to have Ernest Gellhorn's and Bill's Antitrust Law and Economics in a Nutshell[11] translated into Russian and distributed to every workshop participant. Autographing the Nutshell became a standard part of the each workshop. Bill commented that "I could not have imagined that I would sit in the former dacha of a Communist Party official, located near one of Russia's most secret nuclear weapons research centers, and sign copies of an American antitrust text."[12] Times had changed.

To sum up Bill's international assistance work to date, it seems fitting to quote Eduardo Perez Motta, head of Mexico's competition agency and current chairman of the International Competition Network, who recently expressed his appreciation for Bill's international work in this poignant statement:

> Bill Kovacic, undoubtedly, is one of the most inspirational figures in the competition policy landscape. To a certain extent, this is no surprise to me. Bill is not only an expert in the field, but also his commitment to his work (whether in academia or in government) has been really impressive. Even more importantly, I am convinced that what makes Bill unique is that, in addition to being a fervent believer in the merits of competition, he has done

everything in his power to persuade others that competition is good for the economy, the markets and consumers. If we take a look at the state of the art of competition policy around the world (and Mexico is certainly not the exception) we could be positive that Bill´s efforts have not been in vain.

V. Chairmanship—Short Time but Long Legacy

If you were to strike up a conversation with a member of the FTC, and the subject were to turn to Bill Kovacic, inevitably what you would hear is how unfortunate it was that Bill was not Chairman for longer. Bill was appointed FTC Chairman in March 2008, a position he occupied until the following March. Much happened in that year, but instead of trying to amass as many short-term successes as possible, which pundits could later use to define his time as Chairman, Bill did the opposite. He focused on what would happen to the Commission after his tenure. Bill and his team developed a long-term strategic plan to map out best practices that would increase the Commission's overall effectiveness. This was, of course, the FTC at 100 Report. In many ways this Report was the culmination of everything Bill had learned in his early years at the FTC, during his time as a professor, and especially on his technical assistance trips abroad, which is why we drew your attention to it from the outset. Bill invested much of his time as Chairman in a long-term human capital building project that would mostly benefit his successors at a time well past his tenure. As Bill describes it, he wanted to make long-term capital investments, which didn't necessarily generate immediate returns. His question to himself and to others was always: "What am I doing today to ensure that my successors can be more effective five years from now."

With the change of administration in 2009, Bill stepped down as Chairman and continued as a Commissioner until his term ended in October 2011. He resumed his post at the George Washington Law School, where he is today. He is also the head of the George Washington University Competition Law Center. Apart from again dedicating himself to developing subsequent generations of lawyers, Bill also has formed a joint venture with the Oxford Competition Law Center to launch a journal entitled, the "Journal of Antitrust Enforcement." The journal will provide a forum for cutting-edge scholarship on the continual improvement of competition agencies from within, no matter where they are, or in what circumstances they find themselves. The objective of this journal encapsulates what Bill has done professionally, and as many will attest, personally, throughout his life.

In 1986, when Bill had just accepted a position at George Mason, he met Ernest Gellhorn at a reception. Bill would later collaborate with Ernie to write Antitrust Law and Economics in a Nutshell. Speaking loudly over the cocktail party din, Ernie shared his thoughts on how to approach the new job, which Bill realized were not just suggestions for a new member of a law faculty but words of wisdom for living life. Bill later wrote:[13]

> From the notes I scribbled at the reception on that evening in 1986, here are Ernie's suggestions:
>
> First, treat every day as an opportunity to do something special—to give a great class, to help a colleague, to inspire a student, to write an excellent paper. Try each day to paint a masterpiece.
>
> Second, don't show anyone up. Be lavish and open with encouragement and praise for students and colleagues. Be cautious and private with criticism.

Third, don't make a habit of proclaiming your greatness. Others have covered that field exhaustively. Try something different. Take satisfaction in quietly raising the game of everyone around you.

Fourth, brush aside the inevitable slights of academic life. You will find that many academics have a high estimation of their abilities. Some can be acutely tiresome, and you may be tempted to dwell upon their missteps. Each minute you spend to nurse old hurts is time lost, time stolen from pursuits that improve your own life and those around you. You cannot build a good reputation by keeping grudges.

Finally, when success comes your way and you are established as one of the usual suspects in your field, pass the favor along. May you never become too important to help those who need it the most.

Bill needs not have written these suggestions down. These are quintessential Bill qualities. He exemplifies them in everything he does and in so doing has ensured a brighter day for everyone he interacts with, and an assured bright future for international competition law.

NOTES

1   We had the opportunity to speak to a number of Bill's friends and colleagues in the course of writing this essay. We are particularly grateful to former FTC Chairman Timothy Muris, Maureen Ohlhausen, Andrea Agathoklis, Richard Whish, Margaret Bloom and Eduardo Perez Motta for offering up their invaluable time. We had hoped to speak to more of Bill's colleagues and friends but unfortunately publishing deadlines did not make this feasible. We also would like to thank Kathryn Fenton for her insightful comments and thoughts.

2   THE FEDERAL TRADE COMMISSION AT 100: INTO OUR 2ND CENTURY, THE CONTINUING PURSUIT OF BETTER PRACTICES (Jan. 2009).

3   JONATHAN EDWARDS, SINNER IN THE HANDS OF AN ANGRY GOD (1741).

4   FTC Press Release, Former FTC Commissioner William E. Kovacic Named Recipient of 2011 Kirkpatrick Award (Oct. 25, 2011), *available at* http://www.ftc.gov/opa/2011/10/kirkpatrick.shtm.

5   This is the term that Timothy Muris affectionately uses to refer to Bill.

6   Winston Churchill, The Sinews of Peace, Westminster College, Fulton, Missouri (Mar. 5, 1946), *available at* http://www.nato.int/docu/speech/1946/s460305a_e.htm.

7   William E. Kovacic & Robert S. Thorpe, *Antitrust and the Evolution of a Market Economy in Mongolia, in* DE-MONOPOLIZATION AND COMPETITION POLICY IN POST-COMMUNIST ECONOMIES 89 (Ben Slay ed., 1996).

8   William E. Kovacic, *The Competition Policy Entrepreneur and Law Reform in Formerly Communist and Socialist Countries,* AM. U. J. INTL' L. & POL'Y 11:3, 454 (1996).

9   William E. Kovacic, *Extraterritoriality, Institutions, and Convergence in International Competition Policy* (a paper based upon a presentation given at the annual meeting of the American Society of International law, Washington, April 2003), http://www.ftc.gov/speeches/other/03121Okavacic.pdf; Timothy J. Muris, *Competition Agencies in a Market-Based Global Economy* (prepared remarks at the Annual Lecture of the European Foreign Affairs Review) (July 2002).

10 William E. Kovacic, et al., *Building global antitrust standards: The ICN's practicable approach, in* RESEARCH HANDBOOK ON INTERNATIONAL COMPETITION LAW, 89 (Ariel Ezrachi ed., 2013).

11 ERNEST GELLHORN & WILLIAM E. KOVACIC, ANTITRUST LAW AND ECONOMICS IN A NUTSHELL (4TH ED. 1994).

12 William E. Kovacic, *The Competition Policy Entrepreneur and Law Reform in Formerly Communist and Socialist Countries,* AM. U. J. INTL' L. & POL'Y 11:3, 442 (1996).

13 William E. Kovacic, *Ernest Gellhorn: An Appreciation,* GEO. MASON L. REV. 13:6, 1189 (2006).

On the Road with Bill Kovacic

Abbott B. Lipsky, Jr.

tad.lipsky@lw.com
Partner, Latham & Watkins, LLP

Abstract

Bill Kovacic has contributed to antitrust in many different roles, combining keen analytical skills with wanderlust and effective pedagogy. Based on core themes of Bill's extensive and thoughtful work on the subject of unilateral conduct, the author examines a major and persistent problem in U.S. antitrust law: While substantive antitrust standards have been rationalized since structuralism and formalism were rejected by the Supreme Court in the 1970's, the area of unilateral conduct standards has proven more resistant to similar improvements. The author reflects on the slow progress and the wide variety of suggestions on the subject from litigants, lower federal courts and the enforcement agencies. The main thesis is that the complex and diverse challenges of assessing unilateral conduct can only be confronted effectively by the Supreme Court (as distinct from lower courts and agencies). Continued waffling threatens to distract the world's most innovative and productive firms and degrade their competitive performance. The author warns against accepting this risk given the persistent, widespread and intensifying threats to global economic well-being.

I. Introduction

Antitrust has come a long way, and it still has a long way to go. Bill Kovacic has been a chief chronicler and facilitator of that journey. With originality, careful and searching scholarship, objective analysis, clear writing and (last but not least) a flair for succinct and entertaining speaking, Bill has become the Paul Erdös of antitrust. Much as Erdös stimulated, advanced and clarified thinking and analysis on a wide range of topics in mathematics by traveling broadly and incessantly to collaborate with others, Bill has done the same for antitrust. In fact, not to minimize Erdös' extraordinary achievements, we must note that Bill has gone Erdös one better: whereas Erdös traveled a world in which mathematics had long been a subject of universal interest, Bill actually helped to make interest in antitrust universal, transforming the subject from an almost unique obsession of the U.S.[1]

This brief essay tips the hat to Bill's past and continuing contributions by offering a perspective on the current state-of-play of one very important antitrust issue that Bill has focused on with characteristic diligence and impact—U.S. standards governing unilateral conduct. Single-firm conduct is subject to scrutiny (*inter alia*) under U.S. monopolization law (Section 2 of the Sherman Act)[2] and the prohibition on "unfair methods of competition" ("UMC") in Section 5(a)(1) of the FTC Act.[3] Several of Bill's many contributions on the subject are cited in the note,[4] and general familiarity with Bill's views on the subject will be assumed. My objective is not to rehash or provide a critique of those views, but to extend the dialogue to a broader and more fundamental point: the need for further depth and improvement in the quality of the competitive analysis applied to unilateral conduct by the Supreme Court, and for the provision of more focused and effective assistance by our federal agencies (and other *amici curiae*) in helping and encouraging the Court to make these refinements. This will help the Court to provide improved guidance for the other federal courts, the federal antitrust agencies, and the broader antitrust enforcement community as well as the business community. Unless such additional refinement is provided, there is a danger that the continued application of vague antitrust standards (like the test for monopolization stated in *United States v. Grinnell Corp.*,[5] or the UMC standard) to single-firm conduct will prolong unnecessary legal incoherence, leading to reduced innovation and productivity growth, thereby limiting our economy's capacity to create wealth.

Specifying the appropriate antitrust standards for assessment of unilateral conduct has proven to be a very durable and difficult subject. Numerous monopolization cases have generated significant interest and commentary over many years, but with limited narrowing of many important areas of controversy. From 2006-08 the FTC and Department of Justice soldiered through a series of hearings and internal debates regarding unilateral conduct standards, and ultimately the Department of Justice produced a comprehensive report on the subject in September 2008.[6] The FTC took no specific official action on the matter, but three Commissioners jointly issued a blistering and accusatory critique of the Report, representing an historic low in FTC-Antitrust Division relations.[7] When the Obama Administration swept into office shortly thereafter, its newly confirmed Assistant Attorney General for Antitrust quickly orchestrated a somewhat theatrical repudiation of the Report.[8] Over the years the FTC has been exploring ways to expand the legal theories available for challenging unilateral conduct using its UMC authority, and this tendency experienced a notable emphasis following the last change in Administration. Bill has contributed substantially to the debates surrounding these topics, as a scholar, as a sitting Commissioner and as Chairman of the FTC.

The persistence of acute controversy over unilateral conduct standards indicates that neither the Supreme Court nor the Federal Trade Commission has done enough to develop practical criteria to assess specific forms of unilateral conduct that tend to attract antitrust challenge. The Court has done some very helpful work in providing more explicit standards for conduct such as predatory pricing, tying and sham litigation, but the Court's work is incomplete. It has not provided equally helpful guidance for other forms of conduct such as refusal to deal and bundled pricing (in part because it can only decide cases presented by litigants). This has bred opportunistic behavior at the Commission. Great uncertainty remains about the specific standards applicable to unilateral conduct and the relationship between Section 2 and UMC—an unsatisfactory state of affairs that could ripen into an outright institutional failure. The Court should recognize and grapple with the hard questions of competitive analysis that must be confronted in order to provide useful standards in Section 2 and UMC cases. If the Court leads, the federal agencies and lower courts will follow; if the Court does not lead, the agencies and courts will continue to gyrate unnecessarily and aimlessly, with potentially serious adverse effects.

II. Growing Impact of U.S. Unilateral Conduct Standards

Particular care in articulating unilateral-conduct standards is especially important because authoritative pronouncements on antitrust not only carry weight in the U.S., but receive very careful study and often emulation by the 100+ jurisdictions around the world that now have their own single-firm conduct standards to enforce (frequently against large U.S. firms that represent the vanguard of new technologies critical to future economic growth). From hopeful but uncertain beginnings in the U.S.,[9] antitrust has grown into an overpowering international force—a pervasive and influential system of control that governs all major transactions and virtually any other form of business conduct across the entire spectrum of industry and commerce worldwide. Specifically, antitrust and competition rules are brought to bear upon unilateral conduct throughout commerce and trade, and continue to be an increasingly important consideration for our most innovative firms in our largest, most economically critical and most technically advanced industries—the vanguard firms whom we rely upon to generate new employment and wealth sufficient to sustain modern society. Antitrust can compel these firms to pay billion-dollar judgments and fines, and on rare occasions our unilateral conduct rules can pulverize even titanic firms like Standard Oil[10] or the Bell System.[11] Microsoft Corp. came close to suffering the same fate,[12] and other technology giants (Apple, Facebook, Google, IBM, etc.) are being led under the antitrust microscope (again, in IBM's case) as this is written.

The threat of government enforcement is constant and essentially ubiquitous. The imposition of enormous antitrust fines under monopolization/abuse of dominance standards is now a reality in most of the developed world, and is a possibility virtually everywhere. Moreover, the chase for billions in civil damages and fees through private litigation, including class actions (still primarily but no longer exclusively an American enterprise) is also spreading around the world. All these endeavors provide occupation for thousands of lawyers, economists and their various auxiliary professionals worldwide. They can reshape industries and patterns of everyday life. The full potential impact of the ever-expanding global network of antitrust enforcement is probably not yet fully appreciated, even by the business community that feels the consequences most heavily, and still less by the broader public.

Until the 1960's antitrust was almost exclusively an American domain. The competition rules of the six-member European Economic Community (main forerunner of today's twenty-seven member European Union), adopted in the 1957 Treaty of Rome and implemented in 1962, did not begin to bite until much later—notably when Europe inaugurated a compulsory merger review discipline. (There were other, more successful European innovations in the name of competition, most notably the extensive Treaty provisions aiming to provide direct guarantees of various market "freedoms" against Member State encroachment, as well as the rules against Member State causes of "market distortion," including state aid and anticompetitive action by state or state-favored enterprises—public or state-franchised utilities, for example.) In the area of control of private trade restraints, however, the EU enforcement network came on in fits and starts and suffered from some consequential early missteps (mostly with regard to the definition and legal consequences of restrictive agreements). However, the EU competition-rule system now equals and some would say even surpasses the American model in its significance to the conduct of business globally— notably in the area of abuse of dominance. Even before Brussels began its struggle to launch, stabilize and expand its antitrust system, nations like Japan, Mexico, former West Germany and the Philippines, as well as the UK, Canada and other British-heritage jurisdictions, had laws and/or constitutional provisions safeguarding competition, but their enforcement was at best sporadic and largely inconsequential.

Operating in virtual global isolation, by the end of the 1960's American antitrust rules had become rigid, legalistic and highly confining. Judicial hostility to the entire spectrum of modern business arrangements emerged, encouraged by the federal antitrust agencies. For a brief time in the late 1960's and early 1970's, all horizontal restraints,[13] vertical restraints,[14] horizontal mergers[15] and numerous common patent licensing limitations[16] were deemed *per se* illegal (although only in the *de facto* sense where mergers were concerned— "the Government always wins"[17]). It seemed that common-law evolution of U.S. antitrust principles had subverted the Supreme Court's effort to fashion a rule of reason in *Standard Oil*. The result was that a great range of business arrangements could be struck down under the Sherman and Clayton Acts without any consideration of their procompetitive justifications. Most relevant to discussions of unilateral conduct, monopolists were presumed guilty of monopolization unless their power had been both attained and maintained *involuntarily*.[18]

The availability of trail-blazing U.S. civil procedures and other litigation-friendly mechanisms for the pursuit of antitrust claims led to aggressive impositions on business conduct, including single-firm conduct. Antitrust had not only acquired a powerful arsenal of strict substantive rules, they were being enforced with ever-increasing ferocity through the potent American legal system. The adoption of notice pleading, opt-out class-action procedures and liberal pre-trial discovery by U.S. federal courts, when applied to civil claims involving joint and several liability, mandatory treble damages and one-way fee-shifting in favor of successful plaintiffs, gave rise to a system where *per se* rules developed by agencies and courts were applied vigorously to all types of competitive conduct without any serious regard for long-run impact on competition and productivity. Antitrust litigation became one of the most prolific forms of civil litigation in the federal courts.

Added to a consistent program of aggressive enforcement by the federal antitrust agencies, these phenomena undoubtedly contributed to the U.S. economic crisis of the late 1970's. American competitiveness came under serious challenge in a variety of import-competitive economic sectors, and inflation, unemployment and interest rates soared well into double-digits. Of course numerous other fundamental U.S. policies contributed as well—deficit spending, accommodative monetary policy and the enervation of intellectual property protection, to name just a few.

Then, beginning in the 1970's, aided by serious and influential legal and economic scholarship based on empirical research, more sophisticated and persuasive modes of antitrust analysis fashioned by the law and economics movement swept the federal antitrust agencies and the federal courts, led by the Supreme Court. The movement rode the tide that brought the Reagan Administration to office, pervading the enforcement agencies and the federal judiciary with its adherents, its fundamental methods and its beliefs. Vertical arrangements,[19] horizontal arrangements[20] (other than hard-core cartel conduct), and most common patent licensing practices[21] were removed from *per se* or presumptively unlawful categories (although extracting price-related vertical arrangements from the *per se* category took decades, and neither minimum vertical price agreements nor tie-ins are not yet totally out of the *per se* woods). The Supreme Court signaled an end to the strictest form of structural merger analysis. *United States v. General Dynamics Corp.*, 415 U.S. 486 (1974) (government's structural data—and therefore its predictions of anticompetitive effect—rejected because undermined by market developments). The Justice Department's 1982 Merger Guidelines established a consensus methodology for defining markets, measuring concentration, and assessing the likelihood of anticompetitive effects from mergers, acquisitions and other structural transactions, based on economic analysis tested by empirical research. Across the U.S. antitrust spectrum a more sophisticated model for competitive analysis of business conduct based on economic effect had been established, and use of conclusive or strong presumptions based on formal characteristics of business conduct, mere contractual "restraint," or rigid structural criteria had been abandoned or fatally undermined. Other federal policies thought to inhibit productivity were also revised. Specifically, a wide variety of reforms were instituted to strengthen intellectual property protection, including by eliminating the *per se* approach to antitrust analysis of IP licensing provisions.[22]

As U.S. antitrust was being transferred onto its new foundations, the collapse of Communism and the drive for more extensive and intensive unification of Europe released forces destined to spread antitrust throughout the world. As the European Communities expanded and evolved to form the EU, the gaps in the European competition-law system began to be filled in. Each of the Member States (except Luxembourg) was armed with its own competition agency enforcing a replica of the EU rules and welcomed into the European Competition Network; the Merger Regulation brought the EU onto the Broadway stage to co-star with HSR. As of 1990, antitrust had two main acts playing in the developed world.

In the period of the Washington Consensus that formed the background to European integration and the concurrent renovation of European antitrust, the U.S., EU and other OECD jurisdictions, as well as the IMF and World Bank, encouraged the rest of the world to adopt or strengthen market institutions and implement or tune up antitrust-law enforcement regimes. In one unusually visible example, the U.S. urged Japan to enhance its antitrust enforcement as part of a major long-term bilateral trade arrangement known as the "Structural Impediments Initiative."[23] The result of these and similar initiatives was that in less than two decades (1985-2000), antitrust went from being an almost uniquely American phenomenon to its present position as a near-global phenomenon. Although some young antitrust regimes are still struggling to achieve real impact, most are vigorous and seem capable of sustaining a significant role in economic management. And several of the major jurisdictions—notably China—are viewed by business as co-equal with the U.S. and EU in broad impact, at least as to structural transactions. Moreover, the strongest and most important features of U.S. antitrust—starting with mandatory premerger review, but extending more recently to criminal cartel remedies, leniency systems, private damage remedies and even class actions (or other similar collective procedures)—are being replicated in an increasing number of jurisdictions.

American antitrust standards are reflected, absorbed and ultimately magnified in scores of other jurisdictions around the world. Antitrust itself is to some extent an American export to start with—importers will want the most current model. It has become typical for antitrust cases involving unilateral conduct to internationalize quickly—witness the multiple jurisdictions investigating firms like Google, Intel and Microsoft. As important as our unilateral-conduct enforcement standards are from a strictly domestic perspective, it is especially important that American pronouncements on unilateral conduct be fashioned only after careful consideration of how those pronouncements will be understood and applied in the antitrust and competition systems that now exist across the world.

III. The Evolution of U.S. Unilateral Conduct Standards

Antitrust standards for unilateral conduct continue to present a variety of dilemmas for antitrust enforcement. Popular concepts of the "monopolist" and the evil that she does were prominent in driving the public clamor for action that led to passage of the Sherman Act. Concepts of the "dominant firm" and its "abuses" were no less vital to the global proliferation of unilateral conduct standards. One of the first high-impact applications of U.S. antitrust was the break-up of the Standard Oil Company.[24] Based on accusations of predatory pricing and other exclusionary tactics aimed at defending and expanding an alleged monopoly of oil refining and related sectors, the dissolution of Standard Oil was one of the first major divestitures under U.S. antitrust law and it remains a signal event in global antitrust history, still important in any debate about the fundamental purposes, substantive rules and remedial mechanisms of antitrust. Aside from the legal significance of the Supreme Court opinion defining and adopting the now-pervasive "rule of reason" as the dominant mode of judicial analysis of business conduct, the case indelibly stamped antitrust as a tool of great consequence to society. The case made antitrust enforcement a salient issue in the U.S. Presidential election of 1912 and led not only to the passage of the Clayton Act and the creation of the FTC, but it also confirmed antitrust as an important subject in public thought about economic policy.

Fast-forward to 1953 and the first district court judgment in *United States v. United Shoe Machinery Corp.*[25] By that time judicial hostility toward monopoly had reached the point where Judge Wyzanski could condemn one of the largest and most innovative American companies—a mainstay of economic life in a significant part of coastal New England—by employing a presumption that a monopolist was guilty of violating Section 2 of the Sherman Act. Failing to overcome the burden to prove that its conduct—although "honestly industrial" and not otherwise reprehensible—was not *thrust upon it* by historic accident, government fiat or the like, the company was ultimately condemned to dissolution at the direction of the Supreme Court.[26] In this endeavor Judge Wyzanski was building on the reasoning of Judge Learned Hand in *Alcoa*[27] as well as other Supreme Court precedent of the era.

Whether by dint of persuasive scholarship, effective advocacy, or the observable economic benefits flowing from the innovations of leading U.S. firms of the early post-World War II era, such as AT&T, IBM, Kodak and Xerox, the judiciary's paradigm vision of the monopolist as a presumptive abuser seems to have shifted by the 1970's, in parallel with similar developments outlined above. In 1966 the Supreme Court—providing a distant echo of its plea for "reason" in *Standard Oil*—had defined monopolizing conduct in terms of a distinction between "willful maintenance" of monopoly power as distinct from "growth or development as a consequence of a superior product [or] business acumen . . ."—monopoly conduct with a far more benign visage.[28] Favorable judgments for IBM in a series of private antitrust treble-damage suits[29] beginning in the 1970's seemed to confirm that it was possible to defend a monopolist's voluntary competitive conduct successfully based on *Grinnell*.

Like the rule of reason in *Standard Oil*, the instincts toward moderation that may have been present in *Grinnell* did not easily attain broad acceptance. Suggestions for a "no-fault monopolization" law that would allow dissolution of monopoly without proof of specific exclusionary conduct were heard as late as 1979 in the Report of President Carter's National Commission for the Review of Antitrust Laws and Procedures. Moreover, a broad series of even more ambitious "deconcentration" efforts also emerged at about this same time. S.

1167, the "Industrial Reorganization Act", (a favorite of Bill's early employer, Senator Philip Hart), would have formed a federal Commission to identify and restructure concentrated industries. Massive structural cases brought by the FTC and Antitrust Division challenged the integrated petroleum industry (*In re Exxon*), the ready-to-eat breakfast cereal industry (*In re Kellogg*), the Bell System, and IBM Corp.

All (save one) of these massive deconcentration efforts were eventually abandoned. S. 1167 never emerged from committee, "no-fault monopolization" proposals went nowhere, and the structural cases of the late 60's and 70's were all dropped, save the Bell System item. Their legal, economic and policy rationales were almost entirely discredited and the cases themselves were begging for quick and inconsequential termination by the end of Jimmy Carter's term as President. Bill was among the first to survey and summarize this evolution, characterizing some of the deconcentration cases in a 1989 article as "notorious symbols of prosecutorial ineptitude."[30] Only *United States v. AT&T*, filed in the late hours of the foundering Nixon Administration, survived, to be pursued by AAG William Baxter to a consent decree that broke up the former Bell System after a decade of litigation surrounded by intense political maneuvering. Bill's 1989 Iowa Law Review article noted some negative reaction to the settlement at the time,[31] but in light of the explosive growth in a variety of innovative information technologies (mobile and wireless communications, the internet, a wild proliferation of miniaturized information and communication devices), doubts about the Bell System divestiture have receded as time and technology moved on. The Bell System divestiture was a key maneuver that unleashed some of the most powerful creative forces in world economic history. Conversely, antitrust loyalists looking for a nostalgia dose should read the 1969 complaint in *United States v. IBM Corp.*, which tried to evoke apprehension about IBM's power by describing the "thousands" of computers it had sold. Any small business and indeed many households in the present day likely have more information processing capability—in their PCs and Macs, smart phones and automobiles—than IBM had produced in its entire history up until 1969. Antitrust had been drawing and then shooting at static images of moving targets, and was starting to learn the high cost of wasted ammunition and collateral damage that went along with that approach.

Despite all the clear progress made in replacing legal formalism and substantively restrictive rules with more analytically sound and practical approaches in virtually every other area of antitrust—vertical and horizontal arrangements, IP licensing—the standards for assessment of unilateral conduct have made only limited progress since 1966, when *Grinnell* enshrined the "willful maintenance" versus "superior product, business acumen" duality. It bears note that this was all we had to show after more than a half-century (1911-1966) of inconclusive waffling regarding monopoly conduct standards. Indeed, we have seen only limited refinements in nearly another half-century (1966-2012). Lower courts have struggled to find within this confusing and inconclusive record some useable framework for analysis of unilateral conduct, largely without success. The federal appellate courts have offered several glosses on *Grinnell*—most prominently the assessment of refusals to deal using the "intent test" and the "essential facilities doctrine." But the Supreme Court has never adopted either—indeed, has barely deigned to comment on these lower-court efforts to provide some form of objective guidance to trial courts and the enforcement community, to say nothing of the businesses who must comply with antitrust rules or face enormous legal consequences. The Court's continuing negative comments on the essential facilities doctrine suggest it would be rejected in a case presenting the opportunity. (As explained more fully below, the Court's lack of interest in these lower-court approaches is justified; I have previously suggested a different line of attack on the unilateral conduct conundrum, which I repeat and explain below.)

Other tests for the analysis of monopoly conduct have been proposed to the Court by the Solicitor General and other litigants and *amici*: the "profit sacrifice" test; the "welfare balancing" test; the "no procompetitive rationale" test, the "disproportionality test" and the "equally efficient competitor" test. None has won acceptance or even favorable comment in the Supreme Court. (Again, I applaud the Court's skepticism.) The Court has fashioned rules for some specific categories of monopolizing conduct, including predatory pricing,[32] unjustified refusal to sell to customers that patronize other suppliers,[33] and bad-faith litigation.[34] But for the broad run of cases—which often involve some complex mixture of pricing practices, contractual "restraints" and other conduct that may have both benign and potentially anticompetitive aspects—there is no approach more specific than *Grinnell*. Thus when confronting a facially justified refusal to deal, exclusive dealing, "bundled pricing" and the like, lower courts, litigants and business advisors are left to speculate as to which among a broad range of possible legal outcomes—including massive treble-damage liability—might result from their conduct.

In recent cases—encouraged by parties and *amici*, including the Antitrust Division speaking through the Solicitor General—the Supreme Court has articulated a variety of important limiting policy principles (as distinct from operational rules) to guide application of Section 2.[35] Among them: that cartelization is the "supreme evil" of antitrust, and must not be encouraged unnecessarily by mandatory sharing or access remedies imposed through monopolization law; that courts should hesitate to adopt remedies that require them to "act as central planners," setting prices and other terms of trade for mandated access to monopolized products and services (and then adjusting them as economic conditions—demand, cost, technology—change over time); that courts should hesitate to crank up the vast machinery of antitrust litigation to question monopoly conduct absent some solid indication of likely harm, lest the enormous, delays, burdens and error risks common to such litigation lead to a "chilling effect" on legitimate competitive conduct; that low prices and unilateral decisions on such matters as establishing or terminating a course of dealing, product design (including features and product combinations), capacity decisions and other terms of trade should not lightly be questioned lest the independent competitive spirit of even a dominant firm be snuffed out by the heavy impositions of antitrust litigation.[36]

Ken Glazer and I have previously described why it is highly unlikely that any "one-size-fits-all" test for monopolizing conduct will fulfill the important objectives of monopolization law.[37] What is called for is a more discriminating economic analysis of specific cases, and a repudiation of formalistic or formulaic approaches. Antitrust must confront the need to improve the quality of competitive analysis in unilateral conduct cases (and in other types of antitrust cases as well).

The lack of more detailed guidance from the Supreme Court is having another curious effect as well: given the consistent rejection of lower-court offerings of "gloss" on monopolization standards, we have witnessed a repeated series of attempts by the Federal Trade Commission to fill in the gaps in monopolization doctrine by use of the UMC prong of Section 5 of the Federal Trade Commission Act. Notably in the 1970's and early 1980's the Commission seemed determined to extend the UMC definition to a variety of novel areas, including certain forms of unilateral conduct not previously thought to be reachable under Sherman Act Section 2—monopoly conduct at one level of commerce that "distorts" competition at an adjacent functional level.[38] The FTC also attacked unilateral but parallel "facilitating practices,"[39] and other interdependent but unilateral parallel pricing conduct.[40]

Perhaps somewhat chastened by its 0-3 record in the appellate courts in that earlier era, the FTC did not attempt a similar round of expansionary interpretation of UMC until more than a quarter century had passed. In a series of new Section 5 UMC challenges relying on monopolization theory, the Commission undertook to condemn alleged deception in the context of IP rights deemed essential to the practice of an industry product standard. This effort was forcefully rejected by yet another appellate court decision in *Rambus Inc. v. FTC*, 522 F.3d 456 (2008). Despite the continuing record of losses, there is no shortage of additional suggestions for stretching UMC to cover unilateral conduct not reachable under Section 2 of the Sherman Act.

Without sound and specific Supreme Court guidance as to accepted methodology for presentation and resolution of difficult cases, perhaps it shouldn't be surprising to see the FTC attempting to fill the void. There is nothing inherently defective in the idea of an agency looking for new demands for application of its mandate—even this late in the antitrust "day," when one might have expected that most of the major competitive conduct problems and a good many minor ones would have been identified and dealt with—but the Commission has displayed a number of disadvantages in this role. First, significant disagreement is evident among Commissioners regarding the governing legal and economic principles. Public statements and opinions (dissenting and otherwise) issued in conjunction with FTC complaints, decisions and settlements[41] demonstrate a wide variation in the standards considered appropriate for UMC cases challenging unilateral conduct. In a workshop held a few years ago on the subject of UMC standards, a broad variety of opinions from private practitioners (including several former enforcement officials from both the FTC and Antitrust Division) were also on display. There were proposals to use UMC jurisdiction to "converge" with European Commission standards under Article 102, and suggestions that UMC jurisdiction be used to rectify perceived (by others) gaps in coverage in the Robinson-Patman Act. As I said at the time, it seemed like a strange dream to be listening to such proposals at this advanced stage in antitrust history.[42]

Even if an accurate reading of the law might permit a Commission challenge to some novel forms of unilateral conduct that could not be reached under the Sherman or Clayton Acts, that does not necessarily establish the wisdom of any particular challenge. The courts have shown a tendency to strike down Commission initiatives under Section 5 that are not persuasively supported and/or that fall upon ground unprepared by the provision of a well-considered policy framework. I place the *Rambus* reversal firmly in this category: no one supports or encourages deceptive conduct (if that's what was involved in *Rambus*—the Court of Appeals thought the Commission inconclusive on this aspect). But the Commission's discussion of standard setting was so cursory that no reader looking for a sound competition policy basis for the Commission's effort could have been satisfied that the appropriate homework had been done—at least within the four corners of its decision. (Although the Commission's decision was exclusively grounded on a straight reading of Sherman Act Section 2 as encompassed within its UMC authority, the FTC Chairman's *dicta* clearly invited the Court to consider the potential for broader coverage under UMC. Such *dicta* attracted sharp criticism from Commission Rosch and a comment *dubitante* from the Court.)

Bill Kovacic has published a number of searching discussions of these issues: the first (that I'm aware of) in his 1989 Iowa Law Review article[43] in which he traced the history of the ill-fated deconcentration efforts of past eras and persuasively itemized their defects, and later in his more recent deconstructions of the problem faced by the Commission in melding its UMC authority with the framework for unilateral conduct analysis provided by Section 2 of the Sherman Act.[44] He urges the Commission to develop and articulate a coherent policy framework for an approach to UMC coverage, analogous to that represented by the FTC Statement on Unfairness with respect to the deception prong of Section 5.[45] While the analysis is characteristically thoughtful, thorough, scholarly and persuasive—vintage Kovacic, one might say—and his salient conclusion must be regarded as sound, a review of the substantive and institutional difficulties facing the Commission—in the historic and broader context of the century-long tribulations of unilateral conduct analysis—leads me to conclude that the issue requires resolution not at the Commission but "at the top". If our Supreme Court, after 122 years of common-law evolution, cannot fashion appropriate standards for unilateral conduct cases, we may doubt that the FTC could do better. If both should fail, antitrust would be facing a serious and unfortunate breakdown.

In a 1995 article in Antitrust Law Journal, Ken Glazer and I first developed the argument for more refined competitive analysis of unilateral conduct, and I later broadened the argument to cover other conduct subject to rule-of-reason scrutiny, where presumptions no longer provide quick rules of decision.[46] *Sylvania* itself, along with a number of other post-*Sylvania* decisions of the Supreme Court, including *Spectrum Sports, Inc. v. McQuillan*, 506 U.S. 447 (1993), *State Oil v. Khan*, 522 U.S. 3 (1997), *Brooke Group*, *supra*, *Leegin Creative Leather Products v. PSKS, Inc.*, 551 U.S. 877 (2007), and others, demonstrate that the for the last few decades Court seems comfortable—and almost always successful—venturing into the key details of competitive analysis that must be addressed in antitrust cases where it is called for. By extending this form of analysis into the remaining areas of unilateral conduct, further progress seems likely. Without it, further progress may be impossible. The agencies can assist the Court by recognizing the futility of simplistic and procrustean approaches, by trying to maneuver their own cases into position for Court review, and by *amicus* intervention to encourage grant of *certiorari* in appropriate private cases that pose these issues.

IV. Conclusion

Owing to Bill Kovacic's many contributions, the quality of our present debates about numerous aspects of antitrust law and enforcement policy is undoubtedly higher than it would otherwise be. He would be the first to acknowledge that he stands on the shoulders of other strong contributors—Areeda, Baxter, Bork, Bowman, Klein and many others—but he could rightfully claim a variety of original and substantial contributions to our understandings of competition and the proliferating systems for controlling anticompetitive business conduct. I've chosen to focus on unilateral conduct because (1) it's an area to which Bill has made many significant contributions, (2) it perhaps best symbolizes the ever-present need to assure that our global network of competition-law enforcement does not become an albatross around the neck of our most innovative and successful firms.

Especially in our present circumstances, where maintaining even basic equilibrium of our global economic system has become a nerve-wracking high-wire act, the antitrust community must take great care to assure that impositions on aggressive competitors—especially our most successful and innovative competitors—are gauged carefully to what will best maintain the long-run health of the competitive process. History proves again and again that the forces of innovation and dynamic competition unleashed within the private sector (admittedly within essential government-created frameworks) are by far the most powerful engines of productivity growth. While government has a unique role in constructing and maintaining a stable legal and economic environment in which that competition can take place, and in performing and/or stimulating basic research in areas where private market outcomes have proven demonstrably suboptimal, care must be taken to ensure that any intervention—notably the antitrust treatment of unilateral conduct—does not in fact impair the competitive process, rather than assist it.

NOTES

1   One mustn't go overboard with this comparison to Erdös. Those who are aware of Erdös' extraordinary life and career as a mathematician will understand what I mean. Others are encouraged to see one of the many on-line or book-format biographies of Erdös (*e.g.*, PAUL HOFFMAN, THE MAN WHO LOVED ONLY NUMBERS (1998)). Bill may regard this comparison with restrained enthusiasm, but I hasten to observe that Erdös far outdid Bill in the eccentricity department. Bill may also consider that the comparison is offered with ill grace or at least impaired fidelity to the Golden Rule, inasmuch as he once called me—on a for-attribution basis–the "Brendan Sullivan of antitrust lawyers." Mark A. Kellner, *Microsoft and the FTC*, INFOWORLD, June 24, 1991, at 54.

2   15 U.S.C. §2.

3   15 U.S.C. §45(a)(1).

4   William E. Kovacic & Marc Winerman, *Competition Policy and the Application of Section 5 of the Federal Trade Commission Act*, 76 ANTITRUST L.J. 929 (2010); William E. Kovacic, *The Intellectual DNA of Modern U.S. Competition Law for Dominant Firm Conduct: The Chicago/Harvard Double Helix*, 2007 COLUM. BUS. L. REV. 1 (2007); William E. Kovacic, *Failed Expectations: The Troubled Past and Uncertain Future of the Sherman Act as a Tool for Deconcentration*, 74 IOWA L. REV. 1105 (1989).

5   United States v. Grinnell Corp., 384 U.S. 563, 570-71 (1966).

6   U.S. Department of Justice, *Competition and Monopoly: Single-Firm Conduct Under Section 2 of the Sherman Act* (2008).

7   Statement of Commissioners Harbour, Leibowitz and Rosch on the Issuance of the Section 2 Report by the Department Of Justice (Sept. 8, 2008). *Available at* http://www.ftc.gov/os/2008/09/080908section2stmt.pdf. Bill Kovacic, then Chairman of the Commission, issued his own statement on that occasion, characteristically hewing to an objective and moderate tone. *Modern U.S. Competition Law and the Treatment of Dominant Firms: Comments on the Department of Justice and Federal Trade Commission Proceedings Relating to Section 2 of the Sherman Act* (September 8, 2008). *Available at* http://www.ftc.gov/os/2008/09/080908section2stmtkovacic.pdf.

8   Assistant Attorney General Christine A. Varney, Vigorous Antitrust Enforcement in this Challenging Era, Remarks as Prepared for the Center for American Progress (May 11, 2009) ("... I hereby withdraw the Section 2 Report [Competition and Monopoly: Single-Firm Conduct Under Section 2 of the Sherman Act, United States Department of Justice (2008)]... Thus, effective today, May 11, 2009, the Section 2 Report no longer represents the policy of the Department of Justice with regard to antitrust enforcement under Section 2 of the Sherman Act. The Report and its conclusions should not be used as guidance by courts, antitrust practitioners, and the business community."). Although AAG Varney based her announcement on "the need for a clear Department policy regarding enforcement under Section 2 of the Sherman Act," the speech was more notable for retracting very specific views expressed in the Report, rather than advocating any new refinements on Section 2 conduct standards. She adopted no standards for doubtful cases beyond reference to a "need to look closely at both the perceived procompetitive and anticompetitive aspects of a dominant firm's conduct, weigh these factors, and determine whether on balance the net effect of this conduct harms competition and consumers." Although the speech cited three judicial decisions to illustrate the new approach, such decisions (whether considered individually or in combination) provide little clarity. To illustrate, one of the key decisions cited was Aspen Skiing v. Aspen Highlands Skiing Corp., 472 U.S. 585 (1985)—an enigmatic decision based on unusual facts and a questionable stipulation regarding relevant market, and subject to a wide range of interpretations, even though it could have been resolved by a quick citation to Lorain Journal Co. v. United States, 342 U.S. 143 (1951), an uncontroversial precedent also cited favorably by AAG Varney in the speech.

9   Of course U.S. antitrust, like all modern antitrust law, had antecedents—in Periclean Athens, in medieval Europe and in Canadian legislation of 1889, to name just a few. But the scope and intensity of the American enforcement record that began with passage of the Sherman Act far surpassed any other prior system of competition law. As explained further *infra*, other antitrust systems began to attain significant and continuing impact only within the present generation.

10   United States v. Standard Oil Co., 221 U.S. 1 (1911).

11   United States v. Am. Tel. & Tel. Co., 552 F. Supp. 131 (D.D.C. 1982) (consent decree approval), *aff'd mem. sub nom.* Maryland v. United States, 460 U.S. 1001 (1983), *vacated sub nom.* United States v. Western Elec. Co., No. 82-5192 (HHG), 1996 WL 255904 (D.D.C. Apr. 11, 1996) (*vacatur* pursuant to 1996 legislation).

12   Microsoft Corp. v. United States, 253 F.3d 54 (D.C. Cir. 2001) (reversing decree of divestiture entered by district court).

13   United States v. Topco Assocs., 405 U.S. 596 (1972) (*per se* rule applied to horizontal restrictions among joint venturers).

14   United States v. Arnold, Schwinn & Co., 388 U.S. 365 (1967) (*per se* rule applied to all vertical restraints).

15   United States v. Von's Grocery, 384 U.S. 270 (1966) (prohibiting merger between grocery store chains with limited market shares).

16   Remarks of Bruce Wilson, Deputy Assistant Attorney General, Department of Justice Luncheon Speech Law on Licensing Practices: Myth or Reality? (Jan. 21, 1975).

17   United States v. Von's Grocery, 384 U.S. 270, 301 (1966) (Stewart, J., dissenting).

18   United States v. United Shoe Machinery Corp., 110 F. Supp. 295, 343-47 (D. Mass. 1953), *aff'd mem.*, 347 U.S. 521 (1954).

19   Continental T.V., Inc. v. GTE Sylvania, Inc., 433 U.S. 36 (1977) (overruling *Schwinn* as to non-price vertical arrangements), State Oil Co. v. Khan, 522 U.S. 3 (1997) (overruling *Schwinn* as to maximum vertical price limits), Leegin Creative Leather Products, Inc. v. PSKS, Inc., 551 U.S. 877 (2007) (overruling *Schwinn* as to minimum vertical price limits).

20   *See* Polygram Holding, Inc. v. Federal Trade Commission, 416 F.3d 29 (D.C. Cir. 2005).

21   Abbott B. Lipsky, Jr., *Current Antitrust Division Views on Patent Licensing Practices*, 50 ANTITRUST L.J. 515 (1981) (reversing prior Antitrust Division policy of attacking patent license restrictions using *per se* rule).

22   Abbott B. Lipsky, Jr., *To the Edge: Maintaining Incentives for Innovation after the Global Antitrust Explosions*, 35 GEORGETOWN J. INT'L L. 521, 529-30 (2004) (itemizing thematically similar changes and additions to U.S. IP law, federal patent-law jurisdiction, federal acquisition policy, misuse doctrine and antitrust enforcement policy toward IP).

23 Abbott B. Lipsky, Jr., *Current Developments in Japanese Competition Law: Antimonopoly Act Enforcement Guidelines Resulting from the Structural Impediments Initiative*, 60 ANTITRUST L.J. 279 (1991).

24 Standard Oil Co. v. United States, 221 U.S. 1 (1911).

25 *Supra*, note 7.

26 Judge Wyzanski refused to order divestiture both at the time of the initial judgment and years later when the government demanded it, but he was overruled by the Supreme Court. 391 U.S. 244 (1968).

27 United States v. Alcoa, 148 F.2d 416 (2d Cir. 1945).

28 United States v. Grinnell Corp., 384 U.S. 563 (1966). *Grinnell* also listed "historic accident" as a permissible cause of monopoly, but this was very much in line with the type of "involuntary" causes specified as acceptable in *United Shoe Machinery Corp.* and other cases of the "presumptive liability" ilk. It should be noted that the Court did not seem to regard the definition of monopolization as a key issue in *Grinnell*. The case involved a firm with a very substantial market share that had grown by acquisition and other "voluntary" acts. The critical question involved geographic market definition and the Court seemed to assume that if the geographic market definition were resolved in the Government's favor, liability would follow. It was, and it did. One could have read the *Grinnell* definition of monopolization and thought that the phrasing was casual or inadvertent—there was nothing explicit in the opinion to indicate that a shift in attitude toward competitive conduct by monopolists had taken place on the Court.

29 Memorex Corp. v. International Business Machines Corp., 636 F.2d 1188 (9th Cir. 1980) (affirming directed verdict in favor of defendant in private treble-damage action and citing other cases leading to similar results), *cert. denied*, 452 U.S. 972 (1981).

30 William E. Kovacic, *Failed Expectations: The Troubled Past and Uncertain Future of the Sherman Act as a Tool for Deconcentration*, 74 IOWA L. REV. 1105, 1109 (1989) (footnote omitted).

31 *Id.* at 1106 note 7.

32 Brooke Group v. Brown & Williamson Tobacco Corp., 509 U.S. 209 (1993).

33 Lorain Journal Co. v. United States, 342 U.S. 143 (1951).

34 Professional Real Estate Investors v. Columbia Pictures Industries, 508 U.S. 49 (1993).

35 Verizon Comm's v. Law Offices of Curtis V. Trinko, 540 U.S. 398 (2004).

36 "Any device which is workable only because it utilizes the threat of unmanageable and expensive litigation to compel settlement is not a rule of procedure—it is a form of legalized blackmail. If defendants who maintain their innocence have no practical alternative but to settle, they have been de facto deprived of their constitutional right to a trial on the merits. The distinctions between innocent and guilty defendants and between those whose violations have worked great injury and those who have done little if any harm become blurred, if not invisible. The only significant issue becomes the size of the ransom to be paid for total peace." MILTON HANDLER, 25 YEARS OF ANTITRUST 864-65 (1973). Handler may have been speaking primarily with regard to class action litigation, but the sentiment has resonance in the Section 2 field as well.

37 Abbott B. Lipsky, Jr., *Improving Competitive Analysis*, 16 GEO. MASON L. REV. 805 (2009); Kenneth L. Glazer & Abbott B. Lipsky, Jr., *Unilateral Refusals to Deal Under Section 2 of the Sherman Act*, 63 ANTITRUST L.J. 749 (1995).

38 Official Airline Guides v. FTC, 630 F.2d 920 (2d Cir. 1980).

39 E.I. du Pont de Nemours & Co. v. FTC, 729 F.2d 128 (2d Cir. 1984).

40 Boise Cascade Corp. v. FTC, 637 F.2d 573 (9th Cir. 1980).

41 Dissenting Statement of Commissioner William E. Kovacic, *In the Matter of Negotiated Data Solutions, LLC*, File No. 051-0094 (*available at* http://www.ftc.gov/os/caselist/0510094/080122kovacic.pdf, visited March 8, 2012); Concurring and Dissenting Statement of Commissioner J. Thomas Rosch, *In the Matter of Intel Corp.*, Docket No. 9341) (*available at* http://www.ftc.gov/os/adjpro/d9341/091216intelstatement.pdf visited March 8, 2012); Concurring Opinion of Commissioner Jon Leibowitz, *In the Matter of Rambus, Inc.*, Docket No. 9302 (*available at* http://www.ftc.gov/os/adjpro/d9302/060802rambusconcurringopinionofcommissionerleibowitz.pdf (visited March 8, 2012).

42 Internet links to the agenda, webcast, transcript, and papers presented at the workshop (*inter alia*), Section 5 of the FTC Act as a Competition Statute, held October 17, 2008, are accessible at http://www.ftc.gov/bc/workshops/section5/index.shtml (visited March 8, 2012).

43 *Supra*, note 4.

44 *See citations supra*, note 4.

45 *See*, J. Howard Beales, III, *The FTC's Use of Unfairness Authority: Its Rise, Fall, and Resurrection* (tracing history of unfairness jurisdiction, including development of policy framework later codified) (*available at* http://www.ftc.gov/speeches/beales/unfair0603.shtm visited March 8, 2012).

46 Abbott B. Lipsky, Jr., *Improving Competitive Analysis*, 16 GEO. MASON L. REV. 805 (2009); Kenneth L. Glazer & Abbott B. Lipsky, Jr., *Unilateral Refusals to Deal Under Section 2 of the Sherman Act*, 63 ANTITRUST L.J. 749 (1995).

Implementing the Artistry of Bill Kovacic

ALBERT A. FOER[*]

bfoer@antitrustinstitute.org

President, The American Antitrust Institute

Abstract

Bill Kovacic regularly emphasizes the need for excellence in implementation of antitrust policy. In this profile of "the best public speaker on the antitrust circuit," a long-time colleague explores Bill's methods of implementing his own strategies via a uniquely forceful speaking style that makes use of encyclopedic knowledge of antitrust and its history, humor, metaphor, and the ability to encapsulate a thought in a colorful and eminently quotable manner. The sketch explains how Bill became the "go to" guy for reporters during the Microsoft trial, comments on his emphasis on long-term strategy as an underutilized key to successful implementation of antitrust both at the FTC and in his remarkably effective advocacy abroad. His obvious passion for antitrust stands out in a community that has grown too coolly intellectual, too enamored with jargon and mathematical pseudo-science.

One of the important themes that Bill Kovacic returns to time and again is the need for a competition authority to execute well. In his farewell address,[1] the title is "U.S. Antitrust Policy: The underperforming federal joint venture" and one of his words that appears repeatedly here and in many of the speeches I have heard him deliver, is "implementation." Indeed, Bill writes about his farewell address, "This essay focuses squarely on implementation." In *this* essay, therefore, I feel justified in focusing on how Bill has not only articulated but made articulation part of the implementation of his own vision of antitrust. This is therefore not so much about what he has said as how he has said it.

While Bill is an extraordinarily fertile writer, he also chalks up more speaking appearances, both in the U.S. and particularly abroad, than anyone else in the profession.[2] He is rightly considered the very best public speaker on the antitrust circuit. Part of Bill's influence, I cannot help thinking, is his physical presence as he speaks before an audience. He is a larger than the average man, mop-haired (I report with a trace of jealousy), tall and sturdy with widely separated but piercing eyes behind wire-rimmed glasses, a cropped graying goatee and light beard, and what seems to be a scowl even though he has a great sense of humor.[3] This impressive appearance is accompanied by a booming voice that he modulates from loud to very loud when emphasis is needed (he is often told he has no need for a microphone). His remarkably passionate presentation style, in addition, establishes the speaker as a kind of Old Testament prophet focused on the virtues of antitrust institution-building. Agreeing with him or not on particulars, one typically comes away from a Kovacic speech with a clear sense of where Bill stands and why he stands there.

In the interim between Bill's departure from his first tour of duty at the FTC in 1983 and his return to be General Counsel in 2001,[4] he became the favorite source of antitrust quotes for the news media. This peaked during the lively days of the Microsoft investigation and trial, when newspapers and television stations temporarily considered antitrust if not inherently interesting, then at least too important to ignore. In those days, many reporters with backgrounds on business, technology or legal desks, who had little notion of what antitrust was about, were suddenly thrust into an antitrust beat and were eager to identify experts they could quote. How did Bill Kovacic become their number one "go to" guy?

By 1994, the press was becoming aware of a Microsoft antitrust story. That was the year of a settlement between the Department of Justice and Microsoft. It was also the year that Bill co-authored with Ernie Gellhorn the fourth edition of a compendium called Antitrust Law and Economics in a Nutshell. I speculated that this may have been one of his writings that would have brought him to the timely attention of reporters, but David Lawsky, who covered the Microsoft trial for Reuters, has informed me of the following:

> Sadly, no reporter I know of had ever even heard of the document you mention. Instead, Bill was at the trial virtually every single day and highly available. I know; I was the only other one there all the time who wasn't part of the trial. He identified himself as a professor and he was a great schmoozer—he became friends with all the reporters. And as you say he was a good quote.[5]

Three points account for Bill's appeal to the Microsoft reporters. First, his knowledge of the antitrust scene was then—and is even more so today—nothing less than encyclopedic. He can comment confidently off the top of his head on virtually any antitrust topic, domestic or foreign. Second, Bill has an unusual ability to encapsulate a thought in a colorful sound bite, making him a rare as well as eminently quotable expert. And third, at least with regard to the Microsoft case, he could present himself as an academic observer, above the fray.

This third point seems to contradict my description of his forceful speaking style, but my recollection of the Kovacic quotes I used to read in articles about the Microsoft case is that they often left me frustrated as to which side he thought should win. (He was at that time one of the first members of the Advisory Board of the American Antitrust Institute, which I had started in 1995. He recently rejoined, after leaving government.) I don't know whether the contradiction can be explained by the difference between a full-blown speech and an unrehearsed telephone interview with the media, by the difference between an academician and a political appointee in the government, or simply by Bill's particular attitude toward the Microsoft case as it unfolded. But he attracted the press like no other available antitrust commentator at the time or since.

Despite the scowl, Bill is genuinely and frequently funny. He has mastered the knack for turning a memorable phrase that brings a smile. For example, near the opening of his farewell address, he observes:

> Big transactions provide the rare and diminishing occasions when clients say the magic words, "Spend what it takes."[6]

I recall a story he tells about teaching a seminar in the landlocked country of Mongolia. He was trying to explain the concept of a "safe harbor" as it appears in our merger guidelines, but was met with blank faces. After some negotiating, he reported, they agreed to continue the discussion using a substitute term: "peaceful meadows." For Bill, this story could help make the point that the antitrust community has to take into account institutional context, including national political, economic, and cultural differences.[7] Having provided antitrust and consumer protection advice to the governments of such countries as Armenia, Benin, Egypt, El Salvador, Georgia, Guyana, Indonesia, Kazakhstan, Mongolia, Morocco, Nepal, Panama, Russia, Ukraine, Vietnam, and Zimbabwe, he is eminently well-positioned to talk about international comparative law and institutions.[8]

As with "peaceful meadows," Bill often colors his message with metaphor or analogy. For example, in the farewell address he says,

> Merger guidelines are a policy product whose successful application demands intensive post-sale services. There is little point in creating the complex antitrust software of new merger guidelines without careful attention to customer service and to their compatibility with the operating system on which the software runs.[9]

This neatly utilizes two different metaphors. The more obvious, perhaps, is the comparison of merger guidelines to an application for computer software. He then links the software to an operating system, and speaks of post-sale services. The operating system is recognized to be the system that produces public policy products, and the reference to post-sale services is a metaphor for implementing a merger control policy. Yes, one nods in agreement: I see that it is not enough to announce guidelines; there must be an equally important program for follow-up implementation.

Similarly, "[w]e can depict the collection of all competition agency guidelines as the equivalent of the inventory of a policy store. A potential customer will study the age of the products on the shelf. A product last revised in 1992 will suffer by comparison to a product issued more recently. . . ."[10] Another speaker might simply have said that old guidelines need to be updated. Bill makes the point by forcing the listener to use his imagination and convert the words into a visual image, which cognitive science teaches, makes them more memorable.[11]

Later in the farewell address, Bill uses an extended analogy and call to imagination when he talks about the need for deeper policy integration between the two U.S. antitrust agencies. "Imagine that there were two commonly owned hospitals with cardiology units in the same community," he begins.[12] After developing the scenario a bit more, he concludes,

"The DOJ and FTC antitrust hospitals have common ownership but no culture or habit of routine consultation that joins up the work and knowledge of their merger teams, or of any other enforcement units."[13] In fact, this is just one of the ways in which Bill emphasizes the theme of his presentation, which is, of course, that the FTC and DOJ policy collaboration "is an underperforming joint venture with considerable room for further work."[14] Throwing in the concept of "joint venture," of course, is another metaphor for a framework that the agencies have rarely explicitly accepted, and that is Bill's point: they need to perceive of themselves as similar to a joint venture in the production and sale of the antitrust product.

This is a theme he has previously attacked by metaphor. In an interview with Dow Jones in 2007, Bill complained about lack of cooperation between the FTC, DOJ, industry-specific regulators, and state attorneys general. "We have an archipelago of policy makers with very inadequate ferry service between the islands," he said. "In too many instances when you go to visit those islands the inhabitants come out with sticks and torches and try to chase you away."[15]

In addition to encyclopedic knowledge, humor, and the tools of metaphor and analogy, Bill's typical mode of presentation also includes frequent reliance on history.[16] Footnote 5 of the farewell address is to an article on the origins of the FTC by Marc Winerman. It is indicative of Bill's engagement with history that he selected Winerman, like Kovacic a graduate of Princeton, as one of his attorney advisors. Marc has a master's degree in history and authored a number of papers on the history of the FTC, some of which were co-authored with Bill. The farewell address itself looks to history for context (e.g., "For nearly a century, this joint venture, whose members are rivals for policy making preeminence, has displayed a sustained tension that usually arises when two public bodies are assigned the same or similar duties")[17] and a certain flavor of resigned realism (e.g., Bill recalls that when in 2002 the DOJ and FTC were stymied in their effort to change the existing allocation of sectoral oversight, "[t]he agencies had underestimated the value the legislative oversight committees derive from the number and type of companies subject to the jurisdiction of the agencies within their purview").[18]

Respect for history may help one see potential in a more realistic light and lead to a kind of conservatism that values institutions and idiosyncratic differences and empirical analysis more than overarching theories. With Bill Kovacic, history has also taught him the importance of long-term strategy, a topic that was one of his major themes during his relatively brief chairmanship of the FTC, from March 30, 2008 to March 2, 2009. In his considerable work on behalf of the International Competition Network, he has continued to emphasize strategic planning for national competition authorities, urging them, as he has the DOJ and FTC, to pay expanded attention to the details of successful, long-term implementation of policy.

The rapidly growing global antitrust community has benefitted from Bill's various communications skills, from his emphasis on history, comparative institutions, strategy, the multiple goals of policy, and the mundane crafts of implementation.[19] But there is another element in his presentation that bears emphasis, and that is his obvious passion for antitrust. At times this can be extreme, but much of the antitrust community has grown too coolly intellectual, too enamored with jargon and mathematical pseudo-science. Bill's unlimited energy, vigorous advocacy, and patent caring have enlivened the global marketplace.

NOTES

* I appreciate the comments on an early draft offered by Jonathan Baker, Andrew Gavil, Robert Lande, and David Lawsky.

1 By "farewell address," I refer to the keynote address delivered by William E. Kovacic at dinners organized on September 6 and 12, 2011, by Concurrences in New York and Washington, DC. Surely there were other occasions around that time that could also be deemed farewell addresses.

2 Note to doctoral candidates: this can in theory be confirmed by actual research. I rely here on non-systematic personal observation and hearsay. It is possible that France's Frederic Jenny's record is competitive.

3 For a current photograph, *see* http://www.law.gwu..edu/faculty/profile.aspx?id=1731. Compare to his senior photograph at the University of Detroit Jesuit High School and Academy, http://www.uofdjesuit.org/image/9869.

4 Bill's first law job, from 1975 to 1976, was on the majority staff of the U.S. Senate Judiciary Committee's Antitrust and Monopoly Subcommittee. He began his FTC career in 1979 as an attorney in the Bureau of Competition Planning Office and then as Attorney Advisor to Commissioner George Douglas. From 1983 to 1986, he practiced antitrust and government contracts law with Bryan Cave. From 1986 to 1999 he taught at George Mason University School of Law, moving to George Washington University Law School in 1999.

5 Email from David Lawsky to author, November 27, 2011, on file with author. Lawsky also suggested that I should stress Bill's politician-like "ability to make everyone feel that he is their special friend," an important part of the networking he does across the world. *Id.*

6 Farewell Address, at para. 2.

7 *See* William E. Kovacic, *"The Competition Policy Entrepreneur and Law Reform in Formerly Communist and Socialist Countries,"* Am. U.J. Int'l L. & Pol'y 437 (1996), a paper full of anecdotes from his travels, in which he makes the point that "The success of a new legal regime, however well-conceived in theory, depends vitally on 'the human dimension'." *Id.,* at 438.

8 The magazine Mother Jones once went after the FTC commissioners, and especially Commissioner Kovacic, for spending too much time travelling. Since President George W. Bush appointed Kovacic to a Republican slot on the Commission in 2006, Mother Jones reported he had averaged nearly 100 days of foreign travel per year. I was one of those who defended his travel, saying "He gets an enormous amount of work done. He's not a guy to take junkets or enjoy himself on these trips. I don't think the taxpayers are getting shortchanged." Some consumer advocates argued that the commissioners should have stayed home to bring more cases. Kovacic replied that much of what he does overseas "is [to] create the infrastructure for pursuing global investigations and enforcement actions." Stephanie Mencimer, *Where in the World Are the Federal Trade Commissioners?* http://motherjones.com/politics/2009/07/federal-trade-commissioners-world-travel+ posted July 7, 2009, article published July 9, 2009.

9 Farewell Address, at para. 13.

10 Farewell Address, at para. 6.

11 *See* Joshua Foer, Moonwalking With Einstein (The Penguin Press 2011).

12 Farewell Address, at para. 19.

13 *Id.*

14 *Id.* at para. 7.

15 *FTC Commissioner Claims DOJ Attorneys Chase Him Away with Torches*, posted by David Fischer on Feb. 1, 2007, http://www.antitrustreview.com/archives/831. It is not clear that the blogger was thinking metaphorically.

16 A frequently cited example of Bill's influential work on the history of antitrust is *The Intellectual DNA of Modern U.S. Competition Law for Dominant Firm Behavior: The Chicago/Harvard Double Helix*, 2007 Colum. Bus. L. Rev. 1, minimizing the differences between the so-called Chicago and Harvard schools of antitrust.

17 Farewell Address, at para. 7.

18 *Id,* at para. 27.

19 Bill's impact on the International Competition Network and as a technical assistance instructor has been substantial, but many individual foreign officials also speak of the influence of his informal advice and counseling.

The Elephant in the Room

Joe Sims[*]

jsims@jonesday.com
Partner, Jones Day

Abstract

Bill Kovacic understands the American antitrust process from the inside. He has also consulted with countries all over the globe about how to best establish competition law structures and processes. So when he says the U.S. system needs to be improved, people should pay attention. In fact, however, he is either overly optimistic or just too nice to make the real point: American antitrust is in a state that requires outside intervention, since it is (like people who require intervention) unable to fix its problems by itself. The only possible solutions are all hard and require structural change, up to the abolition or complete refocusing of one of the two federal antitrust agencies. Of course, these may be the only solutions, but that does not make them likely. So in the end, this discussion may be purely conceptual. But at least we should be talking about solutions that would solve the problem if implemented. This article suggests four options that could work.

I. Introduction

I have been around a long time—even longer than Bill Kovacic. I started at the Antitrust Division of the U.S. Department of Justice ("DOJ") in 1970, right out of law school. I left for Jones Day in 1978, and the next year Bill began his career at the US Federal Trade Commission ("FTC"). I first met him a few years later, when he was an associate at Bryan Cave.

Eventually he became Kathy Fenton's husband, one of his most impressive accomplishments. I was smart enough to lure Kathy away from the FTC in 1984, and she has become one of Jones Day's most important partners over the years—making me look a lot smarter on a regular basis, becoming recognized as one of the leading antitrust lawyers in the world, and recently serving as the Chair of the ABA's Antitrust Law Section. Bill and Kathy are clearly one of the power couples of antitrust.[1]

In addition to being Kathy Fenton's husband, Bill is one of those relatively rare lawyers with a constantly curious mind. He is definitely not just a mechanic, like many lawyers, merely fixing broken toys; he is more of a designer, as exemplified by his work helping emerging economies create competition regimes, often from the ground up. I remember asking him, when he told me he was going someplace remote and very definitely still developing to help write the local competition laws, whether that country should not focus on getting an economy before they tried to figure out how to regulate it? His answer: better they start with at least some rational competition concepts, even if there is not much to apply them to in the beginning. Pretty good answer.

In addition to his global Johnny Appleseed work, trying to plant rational competition law principles in what was frequently quite infertile ground, Bill has been a very productive antitrust historian, producing analyses of antitrust historical performance that are always interesting and sometimes quite revealing. And he has, ever since his first tenure at the FTC as a young lawyer and throughout his most recent service as a Commissioner and Chairman, always been a big advocate for and fan of the FTC. So it is interesting that in his paper in Concurrences late last year, as he was leaving the FTC for probably the last time, he raises serious issues about the interaction of the two American antitrust agencies, including the possibility of rethinking the whole notion of dual antitrust enforcement.[2]

II. American Antitrust— A Great Ship with Lots of Barnacles

Modern antitrust/competition law is an American invention, albeit with a significant debt to English common law. Like so many American inventions, it has been widely used and misused, in this country and around the world. It has spawned many global imitators, some of which improved on aspects of the original and many of which have not. Even in America, the combination of antitrust enforcement by the various states, private parties, and at the federal level, by not one but two primary agencies and other niche applications (the Federal Communications Commission ("FCC") in telecommunications, the Federal Energy Regulatory Commission ("FERC") in energy, the Department of Transportation ("DOT") with respect to airlines and railroads, etc.) has produced a historical smorgasbord of decisions and approaches—some quite appealing and many unappetizing. The pros and cons of this multiplicity of American sources of antitrust oversight are well known, and will not be recited here. But Bill's recent article at least implicitly recognizes the largest elephant in the room: is it time to reconsider the very existence of two federal antitrust enforcement agencies in America?

There are not many other places in the world that still have multiple national enforcement bodies. The UK, Brazil and France, among others, have either recently combined or are in the process of combining multiple national competition agencies; soon the United States will be alone in this category among the advanced economies of the world. This is not a distinction to be valued. For all the logical reasons, the notion that it is a good idea to have competition between federal enforcement agencies is so hard to justify as to be nonsensical. Bill obviously gets this point, but he also recognizes that the bureaucratic and political forces that have grown up like kudzu around the status quo make it difficult to imagine that changing for the better in the real world. So instead, Bill advocates for better cooperation between the two agencies. Here, he reveals that he is a true academic at heart, since this makes a lot of sense but is never going to happen in the real world.

III. Antitrust Enforcement Competition Is an Oxymoron

While the two agencies do cooperate from time to time (Horizontal Merger Guidelines is the best example) they are never going to fully coordinate their activities or policies, because the people at the two agencies, and the people that are connected to or support each agency, do not really want it to happen. The people at the agencies want their agency to be the pre-eminent national enforcer, and being first is not a goal conducive to cooperation. They want to do the most interesting stuff; they want to be the most influential U.S. enforcer, here and abroad, and they want to attract the best lawyers to their agency.

On the other side, the people that depend on or are closely connected to each agency, which includes the alumni that practice before the agencies and the politicians that oversee each agency, do not want the world to change because that could adversely affect them. For the alumni, the confusion and uncertainty that is endemic under the *status quo* is just one more reason they can give for why you need to hire them. The politicians like the fact that people who want to gain their influence over the agency make contributions to them, hoping that will gain them an audience when and if necessary, and that the audience will result in some positive (from their perspective) effect on the agency. In other words, like most human enterprises, the antitrust agencies and the people that surround them reflect common human instincts of winning over cooperating, being first rather than helping the overall community be better, and putting their interests before those of the commons. They are much more Donald Trump than Mother Teresa, or for that matter, even your typical NGO. This approach will actually serve the greater good in many circumstances in life, but not in government regulation.

This may be a cynical view of the world, but it is also demonstrably true. There are any number of ways to prove this point, but let me fall back to one in which I was personally involved—the effort a decade ago to redo the clearance system between the two agencies that determines which agency investigates a particular merger or other matter. For background, even these two competitive agencies long ago figured out that it would be a bad idea if both of them simultaneously investigated a particular merger or some other conduct. It is easy to imagine the adverse reaction to having two different federal agencies seeking (probably) different sets of information, and then seeking to impose (probably) different conditions on the parties. Even in America this would resonate as stupid, and probably produce some negative impact on one or both agencies. To avoid this reaction, the agencies decades ago created what they call the clearance system—a process by which the two agencies allocate between themselves every individual investigation.

The clearance process has frequently worked reasonably well, but since it is a voluntary accommodation of and between the two agencies, it depends entirely for its success on the approach and attitude of the people at both agencies at any given moment. As a result, there have been regular spurts of working less well, and occasional moments of not working at all.[3] Even when it works reasonably well, it is not consistently predictable which agency will review a particular matter or set of circumstances, as recent history shows, especially in technology related matters or transactions. The current accommodation with respect to Google, where certain of its conduct is being investigated by one agency and its acquisitions by another, is indefensible on any grounds other than bureaucratic parochialism. It should be embarrassing to both agencies, but they have each long since progressed beyond embarrassment in this context, to the point that they actually can assert, as they have, that this completely inappropriate arrangement proves the process works.

Bill Kovacic, in his Concurrences article, argues that the current system is perverse and needs to be replaced, but then notes that any new system will probably require congressional approval.[4] You might wonder why this is so, since the existing system was not authorized or approved by Congress, but Bill explains why: "When an agency ceases to exercise jurisdiction over a company (for example, by allocating oversight to another federal agency), the incentive to provide contributions to the agency's congressional oversight committee diminishes. For the affected oversight committee, this is the equivalent of losing an income stream."[5] And we know that Bill is right because that is exactly what happened in 2002.[6]

IV. A Case Study

The then-heads of the FTC and the DOJ Antitrust Division ("ATD"), Tim Muris and Charles James, had arrived in office with one real advantage over most of their predecessors—they had been there before, either actually running the agency (James was Acting Assistant Attorney General ("AAG") for about a year) or in very senior positions (Muris had run both the Bureau of Consumer Protection and the Bureau of Competition at the FTC). So neither had much of a learning curve, and importantly they also had a good personal relationship. Both knew from their experience at the agencies and in private practice that the clearance process had become a bad joke—eating up time and resources, and generating inter-agency jealousies and animosities that were impairing effective antitrust enforcement.[7]

They also found on their arrival one pending matter, involving a proposed joint venture, that had been pending in the clearance process for more than a year.[8] In the old clearance process, if all else failed, the FTC Chair and the AAG would decide it. Apparently, the previous heads of the two agencies could not reach agreement on this matter, and left it pending for their successors. James and Muris unsuccessfully tried to resolve the dispute themselves. Unfortunately, the arguments for both agencies had some merit, and both were under considerable pressure from their staffs to not give in—in large part because under the existing clearance system, which was largely based on recent experience, once an agency gave up a matter it largely gave up all future matters that were in the same industry area. In desperation, they came up with the idea of going to a neutral arbiter, selected a local law professor, had each agency present their arguments, and let him decide. He decided that the DOJ had the better claim, and on that basis it was cleared to the DOJ.

Although this solved this particular problem, Muris and James had absolutely no desire to go through this again, and certainly not on a regular basis. In addition, both of them were committed to fixing what they saw as a variety of procedural problems for the agencies that, in their view, had gotten in the way of effective enforcement and reduced the bar and business support for the agencies that is critical to long-term enforcement success. This commitment had already resulted in a reorganization of the ATD, a new approach to Hart-Scott-Rodino investigations and second requests at both agencies, and now it produced a new attempt to fix the clearance process.

Given the historical inability to get the agencies themselves to agree on a fix to the clearance mess (agency staffs had become more competitive than cooperative, caused in large part by constant disputes over clearances), Muris and James decided it would be useful to seek help from a small group of respected former agency officials—from Republican and Democratic administrations and both agencies—to come up with a workable plan. The theory was that such a group would have useful experience and knowledge, and (hopefully) because they had long histories of practice before both agencies, less parochialism. In other words, they could be experienced and honest brokers—willing and able to suggest the right thing from the perspective of federal antitrust enforcement in the aggregate.

I was one of that group, having served as a Deputy Assistant Attorney General ("DAAG") in the ATD in the early part of my career. The other three were all experienced and respected antitrust lawyers—Steve Sunshine, also a former DAAG in the ATD, and Bill Baer and Kevin Arquit, each of who had served as heads of the Bureau of Competition at the FTC. Sunshine and Baer had served in Democratic administrations (and Baer is now the Obama Administration's nominee to head the ATD), and Arquit and I in Republican administrations, so the group was both professionally and politically balanced.

This outside expert group spent four months working the problem. They talked with both agency heads, and with the people who actually do the clearance processing. They got statistics and information relating to the historical clearance process. And most importantly, they approached the problem with the starting assumption that it was generally irrelevant which agency did which matter—since both are fully capable of doing any antitrust matter (taking into account certain limited statutory and constitutional exceptions, of which the most important is all criminal matters must be done by the DOJ). We believed that having matters done in a timely and effective way was much more important than which agency did them. This group produced an initial report and recommendations that suggested a revamping of the entire process—from original input to internal agency handling to communicating between agencies.[9] As part of this report, it also suggested updating the existing historical commodity allocation list to (1) make it more effective—broader categories of like matters grouped together, and old exceptions rationalized, and (2) create an essentially even distribution of matters between the two agencies, emphasizing wherever possible historical patterns.[10]

V. Good Government Meets the Real World

The report was considered by both agencies, and after a careful review largely adopted, despite the fact that staffers at both agencies were not at all enthusiastic, and agency alumni from both agencies almost universally did not like the proposed solution—not because it was not workable, not because it did not do a good job of creating a process that would reasonably equally divide the federal antitrust workload, but because looking at the solution from the prism of *their* agency, they believed that *their* agency had gotten the short end of the stick. In my view, this reaction—both sides thinking the other side got the better deal— was a strong affirmation that we had gotten it about right. When all sides to a solution are unhappy, that is strong evidence that no one was unduly favored. And to their credit, that is where Muris and James came out. Despite some significant opposition from their respective staffs, they signed off on it, a majority of FTC Commissioners endorsed it, and with very small modifications it was put into place.

While it is true that, as a public matter, most knowledgeable observers saw the new system as quite positive, the reality is that the public support was fairly tepid. For example, the American Bar Association Antitrust Law Section concluded that "a publicly announced agreement allocating responsibility by industry will lead to a more expeditious, efficient and transparent review process at least with respect to the allocated industries . . . ."[11] But it did not explicitly endorse the actual solution. In another letter, signed by 11 former heads of both antitrust agencies from the last four Administrations, reaching back 25 years, the effort to "clarify historical allocations of industries and products between the agencies, and introduce clear procedures for processing those few matters that do not clearly fall within existing allocations" was characterized as "desirable objectives" that could be "a real contribution to good government."[12] But they too did not explicitly endorse the specific solution. In my view, this was almost solely the result of agency alumni parochialism—they could not be against the concept, because it so obviously made sense, but they were not going to endorse a solution that many of the staffers they dealt with thought was not "fair," whatever the meaning of that term in this context could be.

Finally, the business community, who one would think would see themselves as most directly affected by the historical failures of the process and thus would be enthusiastic about its improvement, was also only generally supportive. The nation's leading business organizations (the Business Roundtable, the National Association of Manufacturers, and the U.S. Chamber of Commerce) issued a joint letter saying that "It is universally recognized that this [existing clearance] process is not an example of good government. It wastes the time and resources of both the agencies and the merging parties." [13] The letter urged the FTC and DOJ to "work together to resolve problems with 'clearance' that too often impair the most efficient use of scarce antitrust enforcement resources," and concluded that an "agreed process for resolving clearance disputes and an agreed allocation of particular industries between the agencies would represent an exercise in 'good government,' be far more efficient than the current system, and also provide certainty to the business community, bar and the agencies." But here too, no explicit endorsement of the specific solution, which frankly is consistent with the historical failure of the business community to actually put many chips on the table when there are debates about antitrust, no matter how much individual businesses railed against individual actions. Unlike taxes or many other kinds of regulation, antitrust is only an episodic problem for most businesses, and they choose (perhaps rationally) to spend their political energy on more comprehensive problems.

Still, while the support was less fulsome than would have been desirable, there was no real opposition from any objective and knowledgeable observer. This effort had about as close to universal acceptance as you could imagine in the circumstances, which I (perhaps immodestly) believe was at least in part a perception that the solution was well-designed to deal with the problem. Despite this fact, this new solution to an old problem did not survive the political attacks that, frankly, those of us involved in trying to fix the problem just did not foresee.[14] The resulting firestorm, led by Senator Ernest Hollings (who fortunately has long since left government service, with this as only one of the embarrassing entries on his particular record of "government service") eventually led the DOJ to abandon the new program, under the threat of continued harassment by its congressional appropriators, and the agency agreement collapsed.[15]

Of course, the fear of losing political contributions was never mentioned by Senator Hollings (a man of whom some of his colleagues said that he had been with them and against them, and it was hard to tell the difference). This would not have been a palatable explanation for his opposition; notwithstanding that it was the truth. Senator Hollings got excited because the groups that supported him politically got excited, not because he gave a damn about the subject. And those groups were almost exclusively driven by the fact that the new clearance process, and the new commodity list division between the two agencies, gave jurisdiction over media issues to the DOJ.

VI. The Importance of Happenstance

As it happened, the most visible media merger in a long time, maybe forever at that time, was AOL/ Time Warner ("TW"),[16] which had been reviewed by the FTC because the then-FTC Chair, Bob Pitofsky, had insisted on it and the ATD had, inexplicably, allowed him to take it, despite the fact that the DOJ had historically reviewed most media transactions. Pitofsky had a particular interest in media mergers, and really, really wanted to have a say on this one, which at the time was also the biggest merger in history. Somehow, despite the DOJ's historical record of reviewing virtually all media mergers before this, Chairman Pitofsky managed to get the DOJ to defer to him on this one. While the transaction was eventually permitted to proceed with only very minor remedies, it took a long time to get there and opponents had extraordinary access to the FTC to argue their case. I was representing AOL, and met with Pitofsky seven times on that transaction (more than on any other transaction I have ever been involved in), and he met with lawyers representing third parties opposing the transaction multiples of that; I used to bump into them coming out when I was going in. And so while the outcome was ultimately not any different than it likely would have been if the deal had been reviewed by the DOJ, the process certainly was more accommodating to the deal's opponents. The result was a belief among media activists (who typically oppose most media mergers) that the FTC would likely be more amenable to their concerns about future media mergers than would the DOJ. Given this, the fact that the DOJ would resume its historical role once this new system was put in place was enough to energize them to oppose it.

VII. Do Not Be Fooled into Thinking the Merits Matter in Political Debate

Of course, most of the arguments the opponents of the new clearance agreement made were either demonstrably wrong or silly. For example, they asserted that media mergers are different, but it was never clear why this was so. Where do the antitrust laws distinguish media mergers from any others? What exactly are the different standards that should be applied? What statute do these different standards come from? How are they to be tested? If the First Amendment is the basis, shouldn't that mean less regulation rather than more?

They argued that this was a secret back-room deal. But the clearance process had been in place for more than 40 years. It has never been a secret. The only things that have been opaque are the actual processes and standards the agencies use to make decisions. The main difference in the new modifications was that they were actually announced to the public and set forth as a public description of how the process was going to work in the future, while other agreements over the years were in fact secret back-room deals.

There had been a public commodity list that divides up commodities between the FTC and the DOJ for decades. But over time, it had become essentially unusable, with obscure distinctions and the accumulated weight of many years of disputes and compromise. The new list was remarkable only for its clarity—which would normally be desirable but in the political climate of the time turned out to be a detriment. The great benefit of a clear commodity list is that the parties would know in advance, in the vast majority of situations, which agency will handle that matter; this would eliminate (or at least minimize) the forum shopping, confusion and delays that characterized the clearance process for decades. To most people, these would be good things.

Another argument was that the FTC would be tougher on media mergers, and that would be a good thing. At that time, the FTC had reviewed exactly two—count them, two—significant media mergers in recent memory: TW/Turner[17] and AOL/TW. I was directly involved in both. The other common thread was Bob Pitofsky, the FTC's Chairman when both deals were done. As a result of the latter fact, both matters were characterized by the vigorous and lengthy exploration of very creative theories of liability, mostly having nothing at all to do with the facts. This was NOT indicative of a core difference between the FTC and the DOJ; instead, it reflected Bob Pitofsky's personal approach and perspectives, not institutional ones. Does anyone really believe that Jim Miller or Dan Oliver or Tim Muris or Debbie Majoras (all former FTC Chairs appointed by Republican Presidents) would have approached these transactions in the same way that Bob Pitofsky did? The notion that the FTC is uniformly and institutionally tougher than the DOJ was nonsense then, just as it is now. The people in charge are political appointees, and can be more or less aggressive and have various agendas. The agency staff will respond to that leadership, but there is nothing institutional that makes one agency tougher or milder than the other.

In addition, I defy anyone to explain to me what exactly was "tough" about the FTC's handling of TW/Turner or AOL/TW, other than the seemingly interminable process itself. Here is a News Flash: The Deals Went Through! Notwithstanding the rhetoric, the FTC finally conceded that any competitive issues were marginal, and demanded only very marginal relief. As a result, the deals were consummated with very few conditions and none that went to the core of the transaction. Of course, history has made it very clear that even this very mild set of constraints was completely useless and unjustified. It did not take long for it to become perfectly obvious that not only did TW's acquisition of AOL not produce any market power, it was also one of the most costly and least successful acquisitions in history (at least for TW shareholders).[18] Looking back, now that TW has spun off AOL and the latter is struggling to become relevant and perhaps to stay viable, Pitofsky's concerns are obviously even less valid than they appeared then, which is hard to imagine for those who lived through this process, but true.

Some argued that the FTC has a broader statutory mandate, and thus was better suited to review important mergers. The FTC does have another statute it can enforce, the infamous FTC Act. And its language does indeed seem to leave more room for FTC discretion than the Clayton Act does. But there are at least three problems with this argument:

(1) The last time the FTC tried to argue that the FTC Act gave it greater discretion in the antitrust area than did the Sherman and Clayton Acts, it almost got disbanded. This was in the Mike Pertshuck era of the 1970's, when the FTC earned the name "National Nanny" by its expansive readings of its authority to tell everyone else what they could and could not do—all in the name of the "public interest."[19] Now, it is one thing to attempt to use the FTC Act in non-merger contexts, which some at the Commission today would like to do; while the wisdom of such an effort is itself highly questionable, any such standards that became part of the existing jurisprudence would at least (presumably) be applied to all industries, much like criminal penalties are universally enforced by the DOJ. Thus, there would not be a different standard applied to merger transactions in different industries simply because of which agency is assigned the enforcement responsibility. But to have some mergers evaluated by the DOJ under the Clayton Act, and some others by the FTC under the FTC Act, would likely revive the calls for reform that were

generated by the last effort to use the elastic language of the FTC Act as, in effect, a way to unilaterally extend the reach of the primary antitrust laws.

(2) If it wants to get a transaction enjoined, the FTC has to go to court—just like the DOJ, and it must do so using essentially the same substantive legal standards as the DOJ would have to use.[20] This is the principal difference between the FTC and the EU, and is the main factor (other than general good judgment, which is too highly variable to be a reliable restraint) that constrains all American antitrust enforcers. Judges are, as a group, not inclined to allow the government to stop otherwise normal business behavior without a persuasive showing that the public interest is going to be adversely affected if the transaction goes forward. Put yourself in the judge's shoes: the FTC comes into court, and says "We don't have a good case under the Clayton Act (the anti-merger statute that both we and the DOJ normally use), but here's a theory under the FTC Act, that prohibits not anticompetitive mergers but: "unfair methods of competition." Please enjoin (and as a practical matter kill) this merger, or if the parties want to go forward, we can go back to our administrative hearing sandbox and play around for a couple of years with some new, not-quite-antitrust theories of why this merger is bad for the 'public interest'." Do you really think there would be competition within the FTC staff for the speaking role in this case?

(3) Finally, we already can see some indications of what the world would be like if the FTC and the DOJ applied truly different standards in merger cases—so that the outcome depends not on the facts and the law but on the bureaucratic roll of the dice that decided, on whatever criteria, which agency would review the transaction. Because of the statutory terms of FTC Commissioners, changes in administration that can make a significant change in the policy approach of the ATD will frequently have less immediate impact on the FTC. The result has been, on too many occasions in the past, some fairly dramatic policy differences between the two agencies. It is unfortunately true that which agency reviews a particular transaction can have a significant effect on the outcome. At the time of the clearance contretemps, that was more a possibility than a reality, but even as that, it was obviously not a desirable outcome. In recent years, the gulf between the two agencies in terms of policy and approach has periodically been very wide, and this is a terrible thing. To have the two federal agencies taking dramatically different positions on important policy issues should be embarrassing, but as noted earlier, both agencies have developed very high embarrassment thresholds.

The U.S. antitrust laws are already screwed up enough, with two federal agencies, state AGs, and specialized agencies like the FCC, the DOT, and the FERC.[21] If the two federal enforcement agencies actually started using really different rules, thus producing different outcomes based not on the facts but merely because of the identity of the agency, that would be a disaster that should immediately generate pressure for a fix. Indeed, this reality is no doubt the reason why not only Bill Kovacic but also a recent head of the Antitrust Division, Christine Varney, have called for a rethinking of the issues that are generated by the existence of two merger review agencies in the U.S.[22]

Finally, there was the argument that somehow it was improper for the agencies to seek advice from private practitioners. The most common attack was that it was outrageous that Muris and James asked private practitioners for their advice, and did not ask Senator Hollings, or the heads of various special interest groups, or maybe Madonna (today it would be Lady Gaga) for all I know. This was portrayed as somehow avoiding scrutiny or finding a way to do something secret and nefarious. In fact, of course, they asked us and not any of those others because we actually had something to contribute to solving the problem— experience both in and outside the agencies, a resulting understanding of the clearance process and the agencies, and a collective reputation based on that experience and knowledge that would presumably provide some credibility to any recommendations we made. Whatever their other accomplishments, those that were complaining the loudest about not being asked for their views did not share those attributes.

VIII. Lessons Learned

Notwithstanding the silliness of the various arguments made, the ultimate outcome of this imbroglio was unfortunately predictable—a determined politician with power and little to lose can have disproportionate weight in the Washington process. Good government has no heroes in Washington, and damn few defenders. For both agencies, having to spend precious time on stuff like this is a real cost. But on the list of priority issues for the entire DOJ, it is unfortunately true that improving the antitrust clearance system was not high on the list. When international and domestic terrorism are on your plate, the allocation of industries between the FTC and DOJ is likely to get little attention, and to justify spending few chips. And so the DOJ caved, and this effort died.

IX. Whither the Future?

What does this tell us about what makes sense today? It tells me that depending on bureaucracies to reform themselves is a fool's errand. This is probably not a revelation to most sentient creatures. It also tells me that Bill is probably right—the odds of fixing even this little piece of the problem are pretty low. Here we had a bi-partisan and highly informed group, agency heads that were willing to take some heat from their staff, and a general consensus on the solution, but it still failed to survive what were blatantly political attacks. I can tell you that there are many experienced antitrust practitioners who, in private conversation, will concede that the current system makes no sense, but who are not willing to come out and say so because of the fear of adverse reactions from the regulators before whom they must practice. And I can also tell you that it is not an imaginary fear, based on the reaction we got from the relatively minor proposed change to the *status quo* we recommended.

But even given all that, those of us who know what they are talking about should be willing to speak out and advocate for improvements to what is, in my view, an indefensible *status quo*, so here is my contribution on that front: we should either eliminate one of, or rationalize the scope of both of, our federal antitrust agencies.

There are several ways this could be done. We could remove antitrust jurisdiction from the FTC, and leave it with just its consumer protection responsibility, perhaps augmented to fill what some see as real holes in the FTC's reach and jurisdiction. We could eliminate the ATD, move its criminal enforcement responsibility to either the Criminal Division of the DOJ or the various U.S. Attorney's offices (for constitutional reasons, all criminal enforcement must remain in the Executive Branch of government in the U.S.) and leave the FTC as the sole federal antitrust enforcement agency. We could create a new federal agency that combines all the civil antitrust enforcement responsibilities of the two agencies, again leaving all criminal work in the DOJ; this new agency could be part of the Executive Branch, like the EPA, or an independent agency like the FTC. Or we could take a more modest step, focusing on the most indefensible aspect of the current system, and consolidate all merger authority in a single federal agency.

Any of these options would be an improvement over the *status quo*, which in my view has nothing to recommend it. If I had my druthers, I would chose either the first or second of my proposed solutions, either of which would consolidate what should be a single federal enforcement effort. But the most realistic option is probably the last—to simply consolidate merger enforcement. In fact, this is the most screwed up part of dual enforcement today. With arguably different legal standards in seeking preliminary injunctions and periodically different institutional and policy approaches, the stage is set for bad results. The notion that a merger result should be subject to the whim and fortuity of which agency happens to be able to convince the other to give it jurisdiction—whether, like in AOL/TW, that makes sense or not—is absurd. My personal view is that merger policy should be part of an Administration's economic policy, and thus it makes more sense to have this lodged in the Executive Branch, but frankly we also would be better off than we are today if all mergers were handled by the FTC, so long as they had to go to federal court with any challenges.

It is interesting that people as diverse as Bill Kovacic and Christine Varney—a Republican and a Democrat, a "do no harm" person and a "can we help" person in terms of antitrust philosophy—both see their experience with this process leading them to the same conclusion. It is, in my humble opinion, impossible to argue against this on the merits. But as history has shown, the merits might sometimes be relevant but are never determinative when you are dealing with Washington. So this suggestion, like most other good government suggestions, will probably accomplish nothing more than filling up a few pages of this esteemed *Festschrift*. Hoping for more is probably at best Sisyphean.

NOTES

*   I benefited from the help of several colleagues and friends in producing this article, but for obvious reasons, they will remain nameless. I am responsible for any errors or unpersuasive ideas.

1   Maybe there is something in the Jones Day water, since another of the more prominent antitrust couples is Debbie and John Majoras, the former the Chief Legal Officer and Secretary of Procter & Gamble and a former Jones Day partner and FTC Chair, and the latter a senior Jones Day antitrust litigation partner.

2   William E. Kovacic, *U.S. Antitrust Policy: The Underperforming Federal Joint Venture*, Concurrences No 4-2011, 65-69 (2011).

3   As Bill Kovacic has noted, "The number of smash-ups in the clearance process is relatively small, given the total volume of matters that the agencies clear to each other, but the individual smash-ups are costly to the parties . . . and they demand effective cooperation between the agencies." *Interview with William E. Kovacic, Chairman, Federal Trade Commission*, Antitrust Source (Aug. 2008).

4   Kovacic, *supra* footnote 2, at 69.

5   *Id.*; *see also* William E. Kovacic, *Congress and the Federal Trade Commission*, 57 Antitrust L.J. 869, 887 (1989) (discussing rent-seeking model of FTC-Congressional relations, "In the rent-seeking model, legislators seek to generate electoral resources (chiefly votes, and campaign contributions) by influencing the FTC's choice and disposition of specific enforcement initiatives").

6   *See* Lauren Kearney Peay, *The Cautionary Tale of the Failed 2002 FTC/DOJ Merger Clearance Accord*, 60 Vand. L. Rev. 1307 (2007).

7   *See* Timothy J. Muris, Comments on the FTC-DOJ Clearance Process Before the Antitrust Modernization Commission 3-4 (2005), *available at* http://www.amc.gov/commission_hearings/pdf/ Muris_Statement.pdf (recognizing "deficiencies" and "deterioration" in the clearance process).

8   *Id.* at 4-5.

9   Letter from Kevin Arquit, Bill Baer, Joe Sims and Steve Sunshine to Timothy Muris, Chairman, FTC and Charles James, Assist. Atty. General for Antitrust Division of U.S. Department of Justice (Dec. 21, 2001), *available at* http://www.ftc.gov/opa/2002/02/clearance/clearideas.htm.

10   *See* Memorandum of Agreement Between the Federal Trade Commission and the Antitrust Division of the U.S. Department of Justice Concerning Clearance Procedures for Investigations 8-11 (Mar. 5, 2002), *available at* http://www.ftc.gov/opa/2002/02/clearance/ftcdojagree.pdf (setting forth the final negotiated division). Under this agreement, the FTC was given jurisdiction over mergers in the following industries, among others: airframes; autos and trucks; building materials; chemicals; computer hardware; energy; healthcare; munitions; retail and grocery stores and grocery manufacturing, including distilled spirits and tobacco; pharmaceuticals and biotechnology; professional services; satellite manufacturing and launch; and textiles. The Antitrust Division was given authority over the following industries, among others: agriculture and associated biotechnology; avionics, aeronautics, and defense

electronics; beer; computer software; cosmetics and hair care; financial services/insurance/stock and option, bond, and commodity markets; health insurance; industrial equipment; media and entertainment; metals, mining and minerals; missiles, tanks, and armored vehicles; naval defense products; photography and film; pulp, paper, and lumber; telecommunications; travel and transportation; and waste. *Id.*

11   ABA Section of Antitrust Letter to FTC/DOJ (Jan. 23, 2002), *available at* http://www.ftc.gov/opa/2002/02/clearance/aba.pdf.

12   Letter to FTC/DOJ from Former Antitrust Enforcement Officials (Feb. 4, 2002), *available at* http://www.ftc.gov/opa/2002/02/clearance/multiletters.pdf.

13   Letter to FTC from the Business Roundtable, the National Association of Manufacturers and the U.S. Chamber of Commerce (Feb. 25, 2002), *available at* http://www.ftc.gov/opa/2002/02/clearance/ brt.pdf.

14   *See* Philip Shenon, *Plan to Split Up Antitrust Oversight Stalls*, N.Y. Times, Jan. 18, 2002, at C2.

15   Charles A. James, *Statement Regarding DOJ/FTC Clearance Agreement* (May 20, 2002), *available at* http://www.usdoj.gov/opa/pr/2002/May/02_ag_302.htm ("[I]n view of the opposition expressed by Sen. Hollings, Chairman of the Commerce, Justice, and State Appropriations Subcommittee, to the agreement and the prospect of budgetary consequence for the entire Justice Department if we stood by the agreement, the Department will no longer be adhering to the agreement").

16   In the Matter of America Online/Time Warner, 131 FTC 829 (Apr. 17, 2001).

17   In the Matter of Time Warner, et al., 123 FTC 171 (Feb. 3, 1997).

18   *See, e.g.,* Nina Munk, Fools Rush In: Steve Case, Jerry Levin, and the Unmaking of AOL Time Warner (HarperBusiness 2004); Alec Klein, Stealing Time: Steve Case, Jerry Levin, and the Collapse of AOL Time Warner (Simon & Schuster Paperbacks 2004); Kara Swisher, There Must Be a Pony in Here Somewhere: The AOL Time Warner Debacle and the Quest for the Digital Future (Three Rivers Press 2003).

19   *See* William E. Kovacic, *The Federal Trade Commission and Congressional Oversight of Antitrust Enforcement*, 17 Tulsa L.J. 584, 662-67 (1982).

20   The issue of whether there are or should be different preliminary injunction standards for the FTC and the DOJ is beyond the scope of this article. But it is relevant to note that the FTC argues that it has to meet a lesser standard in order to justify an injunction than does the DOJ. Since a district court injunction is frequently the death of a deal, this means that if the FTC is right there are already different standards for merger enforcement today, and thus the fate of your deal may depend on the fortuity of which agency reviews it. This banana republic approach should be unacceptable in an advanced economy.

21   This was highlighted by the February 16, 2012 FERC announcement that it would not revamp its merger procedures for utility mergers to reflect the changes resulting from the 2010 DOJ/FTC Horizontal Merger Guidelines. Order Reaffirming Commission Policy And Terminating Proceeding, 138 FERC ¶ 61,109 (Feb. 16, 2012), *available at* http://www.ferc.gov/whats-new/comm-meet/2012/021612/E-2.pdf.

22   Brent Kendall and Thomas Catan, *Antitrust Chief Urges a New Look at Merger Reviews*, Wall St. J., July 13, 2011, at B4.

Grading the Professor: Evaluating Bill Kovacic's Contributions to Antitrust Engineering

D. Daniel Sokol*

sokold@law.ufl.edu
Associate Professor of Law, University of Florida Levin College of Law

Christine Wilson**

christine.wilson@kirkland.com
Partner, Kirkland & Ellis, LLP

Joseph S. Nord

joseph.nord@kirkland.com
Associate, Kirkland & Ellis, LLP

Abstract

It is with two parts gumption and one part trepidation that we seek to turn the tables on Bill Kovacic in a way that his students might find amusing. In this chapter, we propose to use Bill's own metrics, laid out in his article *How Does Your Competition Agency Measure Up?*, to grade Bill's contributions to the field of "competition policy engineering" over time. These contributions span many decades as a practitioner, academic, enforcer, and consultant to other governments, so we can but scratch the surface. We nonetheless conclude that Bill Kovacic has passed with flying colors the work-study program of Antitrust Engineering by examining his academic writing and policy contributions both domestic and international.

I. Introduction

In discussing competition policy development and law enforcement,[1] Bill Kovacic frequently has used metaphors drawn from the field of flight. Thus, we thought it fitting to begin our article about Bill with an anecdote about a storied aircraft, the *Transaereo*, designed by Count Giovanni Caproni of Italy. Caproni developed a reputation for producing the largest warplanes outside Tsarist Russia, and built hundreds of large-scale bombers for the Italian air force during World War I. After the war drew to a close, Caproni dreamed of applying his skills in building large-scale bombers to the creation of large-scale commercial aircraft that could carry dozens of passengers across the North Atlantic. His plan began with a 77-foot houseboat named *Transaereo* that boasted a deluxe interior outfitted for 100 passengers. To the boat, Caproni affixed three sets of identical triplane wings, eight 400 hp Liberty V12 engines, and two pontoons intended to stabilize the aircraft. In The World's Worst Aircraft, Bill Yenne describes the maiden—and the only—flight of the *Transaereo* on March 4, 1921: "Somehow, the 3200 horses managed to drag the 23-ton monstrosity 60 feet out of the water before the ballast scudded into her nose, the center wing section crumpled and the [*Transaereo*] plummeted back into the lake in a hail of broken and splintering wood."[2]

Lest readers think that we are comparing Bill Kovacic's career trajectory to the brief and disastrous flight of the *Transaereo*, we hasten to note Bill's comparisons of substantive competition policy to physics, and the implementation of substantive policy to engineering. He noted that "the physics of regulation consists of intriguing questions of doctrine and its supporting conceptual framework," while "the engineering of policy making involves basic questions of implementation."[3] Continuing this analogy, Bill cautioned, "[i]t is one thing for the policymaking aerodynamicist to conceive a new variety of aircraft. It is another for the policy engineer to design and build it."[4] In other words, Bill noted that "to have elegant physics without excellent engineering is a formula for policy failure."[5]

Bill has devoted his professional career, both as a policy-maker and an academic, to analyzing how excellent competition policy engineering—and, consequently, excellent competition law enforcement—can be achieved. His writings over the years have explored in great detail the elements of an effective competition institution. Time and time again, Bill has reminded his readers that "skill in implementation and the quality of institutional arrangements shape policy results."[6] Take, for example, his 1997 article praising the contributions of Betty Bock to the field of antitrust, *Creating Competition Policy: Betty Bock and the Development of Antitrust Institutions*. He emphasized that "the value of infant and mature antitrust systems hinges on . . . not only competent enforcement authorities and courts but also a reservoir of critical inquiry, information networks to circulate ideas and developments, and mechanisms for synthesizing the insights of various substantive disciplines, including economics and law."[7] Without these attributes, Bill warned, "[n]o antitrust system can function effectively and wisely."[8]

A truism in business management that applies well to assessing competition policy development is that what gets measured is what gets done. Bill is acutely aware of this phenomenon; his writings convey clearly the concept that talking at length about developing strong institutions is meaningless without also identifying the right metrics to apply in determining whether, indeed, the resulting institutions are strong. Bill rejects equating activity with accomplishment, and eschews assessing an agency's success solely on the basis of how many cases it has initiated or prosecuted. This type of metric creates an incentive for agency heads to launch high-profile lawsuits against Fortune 100 companies—lawsuits that undoubtedly will garner significant media attention but that may or may not, in the long run, prove to enhance consumer welfare. Instead, Bill has sought to develop metrics that emphasize "investments in achieving superior institutional design and enhancing agency capability," the types of "long-term capital investments that provide the foundation for the identification and execution of successful programs."[9] Over time, Bill has identified several metrics to apply in determining whether an agency is functioning properly and performing well.

Bill recently left the Federal Trade Commission and returned to his professorship at George Washington University. It is with two parts gumption and one part trepidation that we seek to turn the tables on Bill in a way that his students might find amusing. In this article, we propose to use Bill's own metrics, laid out in *How Does Your Competition Agency Measure Up?*,[10] to grade Bill's contributions to the field of "competition policy engineering" over time. These contributions span many decades as a practitioner, an academic, an enforcer, and a consultant to other governments, so we can but scratch the surface. We nonetheless conclude that Bill Kovacic has passed with flying colors the work-study program of Antitrust Engineering.

First, we begin with our grading methodology. As with any grading assignment, before disclosing our grades, we suggest a theory of why we grade the way we do. The best way to do this is to introduce the evolution of Bill's own thinking about institutions in the past 20 years.

In a sense, Bill's international adventures helped to refine Bill's thinking about U.S. antitrust institutions as his international work and scholarship has served as a laboratory of natural experiments regarding institutional design. These experiments have allowed Bill to think through ideas that he might advocate in the U.S. setting. In a sense, Bill's domestic and international work have had a mutually reinforcing purpose. Both the domestic and international experiences have allowed him to reformulate and modify his thinking of what does and does not work within antitrust and under what conditions success could be defined and accomplished given various institutional factors.

Bill was among the academic pioneers to write about competition law in a developing world context. He based his writing upon experiences in the early 1990s providing technical assistance and capacity building across many countries. His initial writing in this area was shaped by his analysis of competition law and policy and its institutional structure within the United States.[11] However, Bill understood that many of the assumptions in the United States, with a history of limited government regulation and a dearth of state ownership, did not provide a direct analogy to emerging competition regimes in Central Europe,[12] Latin America,[13] Africa,[14] and Asia.[15]

As the U.S. competition agencies and other providers of technical assistance faced an increasingly liberalized world in the 1990s, they were confronted by countries who wished to introduce competition laws and set up enforcement agencies based on a set of realities very different from those found in more mature jurisdictions. These new competition regimes lacked a history of secure property rights[16] and contractual enforcement,[17] but had high levels of corruption,[18] overly burdensome taxes,[19] significant regulatory barriers that created problems for entry of new firms,[20] limited credit markets within a highly concentrated financial sector,[21] trade restrictions,[22] a history of state ownership,[23] family firms that wielded significant economic and political power,[24] government sponsored cartels,[25] and in a number of cases, a large informal economy.[26]

New competition regimes also faced limited human resources.[27] Within the university context, there had not been a law and economics movement in these countries to prepare agency leadership and staff for the issues of economic analysis that might emerge in competition law. Similarly, in many countries, a tradition of teaching the economics of industrial organization broadly or competition economics specifically was largely absent.[28]

Bill's immense value to the development of international competition law and policy was that he spent time to learn the specifics about a particular country's political, economic, and social institutions. Understanding this context allowed Bill to provide targeted advice that feasibly could be implemented and that could allow for successful outcomes in terms of institutional design, agency prioritization, and case selection. In both his formal and informal consulting capacities as an academic and practitioner, he cautioned against "one size fits all" policy prescriptions. Instead, he suggested advice that was more attuned to the pulse of a given country and its political economy. In a context in which the administrability of competition law and policy matters, Bill worked hard both as an academic and as a government official to ensure a positive impact. A few vignettes of his academic and policy work provide some insights on his thinking.

In 1995, the DePaul Law Review published Bill's article *Designing and Implementing Competition and Consumer Protection Reforms in Transitional Economies: Perspectives from Mongolia, Nepal, Ukraine, and Zimbabwe*.[29] Bill began the article with reflections of his 1992 trip to Mongolia and his discussion of safe harbors under competition law for market shares. The article was the first of its kind in the legal academic literature in the United States or Europe. It was novel because it treated the issue of transplanting competition law in a sophisticated manner, emphasizing that assumptions about legal, political, and economic institutions that are so familiar in the United States do not hold in transitional and developing world economies.[30]

Yet, in spite of potential limitations for competition law and policy in countries transitioning to market-based systems, Bill made a strong case for the implementation of competition law. He wrote, "[t]he first [reason for the implementation of competition law] deals with government activities that smother or distort market processes. It is important not to underestimate the hostility or skepticism among some elected officials, ministry leaders, and citizens' groups in many transitional economies to market-oriented reforms."[31] The concept that government restraints could be as deleterious to competition as private restraints drew from Bill's public choice related scholarship during the 1980s and 1990s.[32] From that experience, Bill understood that public restraints had a significant effect on economic growth and development in transitional regimes by raising the cost of capital and erecting barriers to business entry and exit. In fact, the harm to consumers as a result of government restraints in certain ways exceeded that of private restraints. When the government bestows monopoly power on a market participant, that monopoly power often is more durable. It is this experience in the developing world that served as a reminder of the dangers of public restraints in the U.S. context and that later prompted Bill, as FTC General Counsel, to provide significant input to the FTC's work on public restraints, including the State Action and *Noerr-Pennington* Task Forces formed during Chairman Muris' tenure.[33]

A second major theme of the DePaul article, further developed in later policy and scholarly work, was that competition law could "deal with private efforts to undermine market processes."[34] Since that article, Bill has written on monopolistic practices in the antitrust-intellectual property interface[35] as well as cartels.[36] In these writings, Bill challenged some of the conventional thinking about the interface between competition law and IP. (As we discuss later herein, Bill was active in the FTC's work in the antitrust-IP interface.) Bill also promoted a new approach to cartel detection, one which destabilized the traditional cartel because of the possibility of whistleblowers within the firm. This insight on whistleblowing (since adopted in Korea and the United Kingdom) emerged from Bill's teaching and scholarship on government contracts. His work on plus factors for agreements has pushed the envelope of policy considerations and scholarship.

The third major theme reflected in the DePaul article was that "institutions . . . provide actual and symbolic assurance to the public and their elected officials that the move to a market system does not leave citizens at the mercy of market failures."[37] In his scholarship, Bill made central the importance of creating competition institutions that worked at the "retail" level and that could gain popular support. Without popular support and recognition of competition law and policy efforts, even a well-designed competition system would fail in providing "deliverables" to improve social welfare. In various speeches, Bill suggested that cartel enforcement, for example, should focus on basic foodstuffs or in the construction sector to have the greatest impact in the developing world. Likewise, Bill focused his policy work on legitimating antitrust institutions within the United States. This played into Bill's thinking on evaluation criteria pertaining to formulating and clearly communicating well-specified goals to relevant constituencies.

In Bill's 1997 article *Getting Started: Creating New Competition Policy Institutions in Transition Economics*, he took to task much of the antitrust community that had imitated broader macro-economic liberalization trends and created competition law "shock therapy," in which an entire competition law regime was immediately imposed upon a country.[38] In contrast, Bill suggested a sort of competition gradualism "by which the country enacts a small number of legal commands and focuses early implementation efforts on building the new competition policy agency, conducting education and publicity programs, and performing case studies. Only after these activities were well underway would the new agency begin a modest program of law enforcement."[39] History has proven Bill's approach to be the one that works best in both creating and sustaining effective competition regimes around the world. There are countless regimes that started off strong with lots of activity and a charismatic initial leader but that have faltered as institutional inertia and societal pushback against the competition regime began in earnest because of the lack of gradualism. These observations played into Bill's criteria regarding the importance of formulating well-specified goals, establishing and refining internal planning mechanisms to devise strategies for accomplishing those goals, emphasizing the recruitment and retention of skilled agency staff, and making regular and substantial capital investments in building knowledge and collaborating with other key entities at home and abroad. In many situations, new agencies were active without a long-term plan and without a long-term investment in staff and institutional building. As we will discuss herein, issues of long-term investment, well articulated goals and retrospectives on what has worked and what has not also played a role in his U.S. policy work at the FTC.

Bill next tackled mergers in a developing world context in 1998 with his article *Merger Enforcement in Transition: Antitrust Controls on Acquisitions in Emerging Economies*.[40] In that article, Bill outlined the similarities and differences among merger competition issues in transition economies. Rereading the work shows how many of the insights from the article are still relevant in countries such as India and China that have recently rolled out merger control systems.

One of Bill's articles that was particularly important in its timing and its influence was the 2001 Chicago Kent Law Review article, *Institutional Foundations for Economic Legal Reform in Transition Economies: The Case of Competition Policy and Antitrust Enforcement*.[41] In that article, Bill outlined key issues the International Competition Network discussed in its first decade. The article focused on the initial conditions in which new competition regimes operate and how these initial conditions fundamentally affected the effectiveness of competition law and policy. Learning from the initial set-up of such regimes, Bill suggested lessons that could be learned in the provision of technical assistance and capacity building programs.

We focus on these articles because they predate Bill's more recent tenure as policy-maker at the FTC. We believe that these articles helped to shape the criteria that Bill himself developed to measure the success of competition agencies, as we explain below.

II. The Grading Scale

In his recent article *How Does Your Competition Agency Measure Up?*, Bill and his co-authors Hugh Hollman and Patricia Grant remind the reader that "[i]n engineering, the transformation of theoretical insights into applications of practical utility places a premium on the measurement of a specific design's effect."[42] Unfortunately, the authors observe, "[c]ontemporary discussions about competition policy suffer from the lack of well-defined, broadly accepted standards for determining how to evaluate a competition agency."[43] Instead, measurements of an agency's performance typically are based on the volume of an agency's outputs, without regard to how the busy work of today may impact consumer welfare tomorrow. Bill has long contended that this approach is flawed: cases based on unsound policy count as outputs while detracting from consumer welfare, and important research, policy development and other non-case activities may contribute to long-run consumer welfare while being left uncounted. In lieu of this flawed metric, Bill and his co-authors propose six specific characteristics of good agency process that, applied consistently, will inevitably lead to enhanced consumer welfare in the form of increased productivity, lower prices, and heightened innovation.[44]

The six characteristics identified by Bill and his co-authors form the grading scale for our Antitrust Engineering class, and include:

- Formulating and clearly communicating well-specified goals to relevant constituencies

- Establishing and refining internal planning mechanisms to devise strategies for accomplishing those goals

- Employing a problem-solving approach that uses the agency's full range of policy tools to address policies and practices that otherwise would decrease the well-being of consumers

- Emphasizing the recruitment and retention of skilled agency staff

- Making regular and substantial capital investments in building knowledge and collaborating with other key entities at home and abroad

- Engaging in data collection to assess the impact of the agency's work and disclosing that data to facilitate external review and comparative study

In the remainder of this article, we apply this grading scale to Bill's "course work." In Section III, we discuss Bill's activities in the domestic arena. In Section IV, we evaluate Bill's contributions to the international field of antitrust engineering, in what may be characterized as the "Study Abroad" portion of this hypothetical report card.

III. Assessment of Domestic Course Work

1. Agency Goals: Formulating and Clearly Communicating Well-Specified Goals to Relevant Constituencies

A mission statement answers the central question of the purpose of an organization.[45] In the same vein, Bill observed in his introduction to the The Federal Trade Commission at 100: Into Our 2nd Century—The Continuing Pursuit of Better Practices that "[a] fundamental characteristic of a good institution is the clarity with which it understands its purpose and defines its 'mission.'"[46] To be effective, agency leaders "must clearly articulate the agency mission so that staff and external constituencies have a firm grasp of what the agency is trying to achieve."[47] In the strategic plan in place at the issuance of the FTC at 100, the FTC defined its mission as "[preventing] business practices that are anticompetitive or deceptive or unfair to consumers; [enhancing] informed consumer choice and public understanding of the competitive process; and [accomplishing] these missions without unduly burdening legitimate business activity."[48]

There is no question that Bill fulfilled his role as an FTC leader by promoting the gospel of competition with truly unmatched zeal. During his tenure as General Counsel and as an FTC Commissioner and Chairman, he published dozens of articles and speeches that, to varying degrees, discussed the mission of U.S. competition law enforcement and how best to achieve its goals.[49] Moreover, Bill gave countless talks to various constituencies of the agency both within the U.S. and abroad. But there is one role Bill played in the domestic arena that stands out as particularly noteworthy, especially given Bill's admonition that "for an agency to thrive, its mission should enjoy support from key internal and external constituencies over time."[50] This role entailed cultivating support from Members of Congress, industry and consumer interest groups, and the general public for the FTC's approach to competition in the petroleum industry.

It is inevitable that an inch of snow will shut down Washington, DC for at least a day. It is just as inevitable that increases in gasoline prices lead to heightened Congressional scrutiny of the FTC's enforcement initiatives in the petroleum industry.[51] Irate constituents flood the phone lines of their Congressional representatives, who in turn hold hearings and demand that the FTC take enforcement action. But repeated industry investigations, detailed studies of industry dynamics, retrospectives of oil and gas mergers, and daily monitoring of gas and diesel prices in hundreds of cities have confirmed a principle that the student of economics learns in his first week of class: prices increase when supply constricts, and fall when supply expands. In the absence of anticompetitive conduct that falls within the scope of the Sherman Act or the FTC Act, the Commission declines to take enforcement actions when prices spike.

When Bill served as General Counsel, the task of explaining this market-oriented approach to Members of Congress frequently fell to Bill.[52] On several occasions, Bill strove to cultivate Congressional support for the mission of the FTC by enhancing Congressional members' and the public's understanding of the competitive process within the petroleum industry that resulted in higher prices, and explaining the FTC's policy of promoting competition and avoiding imposing undue burdens on legitimate business activity. In the spring of 2004 alone, Bill testified three times before Congress on this topic. Bill knew these events were more about political theater than objective fact-finding, but was always willing to devote time and energy to educating Congress and the public.

2. Sound Planning: Establishing and Refining Internal Planning Mechanisms to Devise Strategies for Accomplishing the Agency's Goals

Bill and his co-authors note that "a good strategy does not consist of mechanically repeating what the agency has done before."[53] Emerging market distortions may warrant a shuffled set of enforcement priorities; new learning in the field of economics may drive refinements in substantive policies; and changed circumstances with respect to a given issue may call for revisiting the types of tools employed to address it. In an earlier article, Bill wrote that a vital criterion of good agency leadership is "the demonstrated capacity of the regulatory authority to account for new commercial, political, and social phenomena and to adapt the agency to address them."[54] A cursory review of the press releases issued during Bill's tenure as FTC Chairman reveals that Bill launched an aggressive campaign not only to identify the areas most likely to require (and benefit from) the attention of the FTC, but also to insure that the FTC was well-equipped to address those issues. Here, too, Bill rises to the head of the class.

During his chairmanship, Bill led several workshops to identify areas in which the FTC could use its resources to enhance consumer welfare in the field of heath care. In April 2008, for example, the FTC held a workshop on innovations in health care delivery.[55] Panelists drawn from business, government, and academia discussed competition and consumer protection issues relating to limited service clinics, price and quality transparency, and electronic health records.[56] In October 2008, the FTC held a workshop focused on the different types of information that health care purchasers (e.g., consumers, employers, insurers, and physicians) must have at their fingertips to facilitate quality-based competition among providers and treatment options.[57] And in November 2008, the FTC held a third health care workshop on the development of an abbreviated regulatory pathway for follow-on biologic drugs that could deliver benefits similar to those delivered by Hatch Waxman in the field of branded and generic small-molecule products.[58] This roundtable capitalized on the substantial expertise of the Commission in "examining likely models of competition and likely competitive effects from particular regulatory schemes."[59]

These workshops built on the health care hearings that the FTC and the Antitrust Division of the Department of Justice ("DOJ") jointly sponsored during 2002 and 2003, and to which Bill contributed during his tenure as FTC General Counsel. These earlier hearings examined the state of the health care marketplace and the role of competition, antitrust, and consumer protection in satisfying the preferences of Americans for high-quality, cost-effective health care.[60] A major impetus for these hearings was the cost of health care in the United States: in 2002, 14 percent of U.S. GDP, or $1.6 trillion, was spent on health care services alone.[61] Notably, federal, state, and local governments paid for almost 45 percent of this sum.[62] The hearings included testimony from approximately 250 panelists and generated almost 6,000 pages of transcripts.[63] In 2004, the FTC and DOJ jointly issued Improving Health Care: A Dose of Competition, which reported on the hearings and provided recommendations on improving the balance of competition and regulation in health care.[64]

While FTC Chairman, Bill also focused the FTC's energies on competition issues in the field of intellectual property. In November 2008, the FTC announced a series of hearings designed to explore the evolving market for intellectual property.[65] The first hearing, held in December 2008, focused on the emergence of new business models involving the buying, selling and licensing of patents; recent and proposed changes in remedies law, their impact on innovation and consumers, and the use of economic analysis in determining remedies; and recent changes in legal doctrines affecting the value and licensing of patents.[66] This first hearing was followed by four additional hearings, three in 2009 and one in 2010. The fifth hearing, announced during the tenure of Chairman Jon Leibowitz, examined the intersection of patent policy and competition policy and its implications for promoting innovation. A report based on the fifth hearing, released in July 2011, recommended improvements to policies affecting patent notice and remedies for patent infringement.[67]

The IP hearings held during Bill's tenure as FTC Chairman built upon joint FTC/DOJ hearings held in 2002, to which Bill contributed while he was General Counsel. The earlier hearings, which focused on the interplay between competition and patent law and policy, involved more than 300 panelists.[68] These hearings were motivated by the recognition that, while both patent and competition laws are intended to promote innovation, invention, and consumer welfare, errors or biases in the interpretation and application of the rules of one body of law can harm the effectiveness of the other body of law.[69] The central findings of the hearings were published in the 2003 report, To Promote Innovation: The Proper Balance of Competition and Patent Law and Policy. This 315 page report, together with a similar one published by the National Academy of Sciences in 2004,[70] provided the impetus for competition-enhancing reforms to the patent system.

To insure the ability of the FTC to enhance competition not only in the areas of intellectual property and health care, but also in other areas characterized by either market or government failures, Bill launched an agency self-assessment initiative while at the helm of the FTC. His desire to conduct this institutional self-assessment grew while watching one overseas jurisdiction after another asking basic questions about institutional design and effectiveness that the U.S. agencies likely would view as asked and answered. Yet Bill knew that a "central characteristic of good regulatory design and performance . . . is a norm that emphasizes continuous improvement," which includes "identifying relevant commercial phenomena on a regular basis, upgrading the knowledge base of the agency on a routine basis, and always asking questions about what the appropriate institutional design should be."[71] For this reason, Bill became increasingly convinced that the FTC needed to conduct a self-assessment to prepare itself for future challenges.

Conducted over a period of seven months during Bill's tenure as FTC Chairman, the self-assessment relied on a mix of internal discussions and external consultations with practitioners, academics, and roughly 30 foreign agencies to answer two key questions: what must the FTC do to continue the valuable work that it performs today, and what steps must the FTC take to do still better in the future? By conducting this self-assessment, Bill expected not only to answer these immediate questions, but also to encourage adoption of a norm of periodic self-assessment. The findings of this self-assessment and Bill's recommendations for future action are embodied in The FTC at 100, issued in January 2009. This effort was augmented by Bill's work with Marc Winerman on the history of the FTC, which resulted in two articles examining the early years of the FTC and assessing the implications of those early years for the FTC today.[72]

Given a choice between eating one marshmallow now or two in fifteen minutes, many children choose to eat one immediately.[73] Political appointees similarly struggle with a tendency to consume today instead of making investments in tomorrow. Instead of eating marshmallows, though, consumption consists of engaging in activities that generate readily observable events for which a political appointee can claim credit, while investments consist of making enhancements in institutional infrastructure that tend to generate returns beyond the political appointee's tenure.[74] It is to Bill's immense credit that he ignored the siren call of consumption and instead invested the time and talent of some of the agency's best and brightest people on the types of projects described in this section—workshops, an extensive self-assessment, reports—that are destined to provide significant long-term benefits to the FTC and the field of competition policy more broadly while generating little immediate glory for Bill or the FTC.

3. Effective Resource Allocation: Employing a Problem-Solving Approach that Uses the Agency's Full Range of Policy Tools

In The FTC at 100, Bill emphasized that "[a]n agency's allocation of its scarce resources undoubtedly is one of the most significant determinants of its ultimate success."[75] He observed that, after identifying a desired outcome, "a successful agency will make optimal use of its tools to achieve that outcome."[76] Beyond law enforcement, the FTC benefits from having an extensive array of arrows in its quiver, including rulemakings; competition advocacy; guidelines; advisory opinions and amicus briefs; policy research and development; hearings, conferences and workshops; administrative litigation; partnership with domestic and foreign agencies; consumer and business education; and the encouragement of industry self-regulation. Bill's strategic and creative use of a wide cross-section of tools while at the FTC demonstrates that once again, Bill sets the curve.

The numerous merger challenges undertaken during Bill's tenure as Chairman indicate that, not surprisingly, he made full use of the law enforcement authority of the Commission.

With Bill at the helm, the FTC obtained several significant consent orders, including those which required Teva to divest generic drug assets in 29 product markets before consummating its $8.9 billion acquisition of Barr Pharmaceuticals;[77] Reed Elsevier to divest ChoicePoint's AutoTrackXP and CLEAR electronic public records services before consummating its $4.1 billion acquisition of ChoicePoint;[78] Hexion to divest its specialty epoxy business before consummating its $10.6 billion acquisition of rival chemical manufacturer Hunstman Corp.;[79] and Pernod to end its distribution agreement with the owners of Stolichnaya before consummating its $9 billion acquisition of V&S Vin and Sprit, the makers of Absolut Vodka.[80] Though Kovacic was no longer the Chair when CCC-Mitchell was decided, he was at the helm at the time the Commission voted out the complaint. That case was the first FTC merger preliminary injuction win in a long time and also influenced the structure of merger adjudication for FTC cases.

The Commission also employed litigation to obtain its goals during Bill's tenure as Chairman. In September 2008, the FTC issued an administrative complaint alleging that Polypore International's acquisition of Microporous decreased competition in the market for four types of battery separators.[81] The complaint also alleged that Polypore maintained a monopoly in certain battery separator markets through anticompetitive means.[82] An administrative law judge agreed with the FTC's findings, and in late 2010, by a vote of 5-0, the Commissioners ordered Polypore to divest the Microporous assets, constructively unwinding the deal.[83] In another high-profile litigation matter, the Kovacic Commission filed a lawsuit in federal district court challenging as unlawful Ovation Pharmaceuticals' January 2006 acquisition of the drug NeoProfen, alleging that the merger eliminated Ovation's only competitor for the treatment of a deadly congenital heart defect affecting premature babies.[84]

The Kovacic Commission also brought to a close an administrative litigation matter initiated during Bill's tenure as FTC General Counsel. In October 2001, the FTC filed an administrative complaint challenging as unlawful the consummated acquisition of certain assets of Pitt Des Moines by Chicago Bridge & Iron Company.[85] The complaint alleged that the transaction decreased competition in four separate markets involving the design and construction of certain specialty and industrial storage tanks.[86] The matter wound its way up to the Fifth Circuit which, in January 2008, affirmed the findings of the Commission and ruled the acquisition unlawful.[87] In November 2008, the Kovacic Commission approved the divestiture of assets necessary to create two separate, stand-alone divisions capable of competing in the four relevant markets.[88]

Bill's use of administrative litigation to achieve FTC goals was not limited to his time as Chairman. While General Counsel, Bill contributed to several noteworthy Part III matters, including *Polygram* (the "Three Tenors"), which clarified the Commission's analytical approach in rule of reason cases;[89] the initiation of two notable standard setting cases, *Union Oil Company of California* (which challenged Unocal with committing fraud in connection with regulatory proceedings before the California Air Resources Board)[90] and *Rambus* (which alleged that Rambus lied to an industry standards-setting body to ensure that its random access memory chips would be used as the industry standard);[91] careful analysis of two cases involving consummated mergers, *MSC Software* (involving the market for advanced computer-aided engineering software)[92] and *Aspen Technology* (involving the market for process engineering simulation software); and the initiation of a case involving the state action doctrine, *South Carolina State Board of Dentistry*,[93] in which the FTC challenged Board policies restricting the ability of dental hygienists to provide preventive dental service to children in South Carolina schools.[94]

Beyond engaging in important enforcement activities, the Kovacic Commission employed a variety of other policy tools to enhance consumer welfare. One noteworthy category of activity involved competition advocacy with both federal and state agencies. In September

2007, the FTC submitted a comment to the Federal Energy Regulatory Commission on wholesale electric power markets.[95] The comment stressed the importance of acknowledging that, even when wholesale energy prices increase, consumer demand does not decrease, and suggested tailored reforms to address this fact.[96] In June 2008, the FTC commented on a congestion management rule that the Federal Aviation Agency proposed for LaGuardia Airport.[97] The FTC comment supported the FAA's proposal to auction a limited number of slot pairs for a ten-year ownership period, and urged the FAA to consider congestion pricing as an additional option.[98]

With Bill at the helm, the FTC also engaged in extensive competition advocacy at the state level. At the request of then Florida Governor Charlie Crist, the FTC submitted testimony on health care competition and Florida's certificate-of-need laws to the Florida State Senate.[99] The testimony advocated for the elimination of certain certificate-of-need requirements, which placed regulatory hurdles on the establishment of hospitals and other types of health care facilities.[100] The FTC, in conjunction with the DOJ, issued a similar statement advocating for the repeal of certificate-of-need laws in September 2008 to the Illinois Task Force on Health Planning Reform.[101] The FTC and DOJ submitted another joint letter in April 2008 to the Supreme Court of South Carolina regarding proposed guidelines relating to the practice of law involving real estate transactions.[102] The letter noted that while permitting both non-attorneys and attorneys to perform functions in real estate transactions promotes efficiency and competition, with respect to the performance of certain specialized tasks, legal training is necessary to protect consumers' interests.[103] And in December 2008, the FTC filed a comment with the Pennsylvania Public Utility Commission ("PA PUC") regarding the PA PUC's implementation plan for its Energy Efficiency and Conservation Program.[104] The comment recommended framing policies in terms that allow consumers to take advantage of dynamic pricing and demand response programs.[105]

The Kovacic Commission also effectively employed the tool of rulemaking. In May 2008, the FTC issued an advance notice of proposed rulemaking regarding the prohibition of market manipulation in the petroleum industry.[106] The notice pertained to the scope and implementation of newly enacted requirements for wholesale petroleum markets pursuant to the Energy Independence and Security Act ("EISA"). This new law required the FTC to police market manipulation in these markets, focusing particularly on whether members of the wholesale petroleum industry were providing false or misleading information in their business transactions. The initial notice focused on discrete issues such as the definition of market manipulation, the applicability of precedent from other agencies that police market manipulation (e.g., the SEC, CFTC, and FERC), and potential overlaps between the FTC's jurisdiction and that of other agencies that oversee similar conduct.[107] The Commission received numerous public comments in response to this request, and it decided to engage in several additional rounds of comment on the scope of this rule, and to hold a public workshop, before issuing a final rule. These comment periods permitted the Commission to refine the scope of the proposed rule, to consider implementation issues, and to try to limit unintended consequences.[108] The FTC issued a final rule in August 2009 that prohibits fraud or deceit in wholesale petroleum markets and omissions of material information that are likely to distort pricing and supply in wholesale petroleum markets.[109]

The Kovacic Commission employed other policy tools, as well. As discussed elsewhere in this article, the FTC conducted numerous workshops and hearings on a variety of topics, including competition in the health care industry, competition and intellectual property issues, resale price maintenance, and Section 5 of the FTC Act. Another tool frequently employed pertains to consumer and business education. The consumer protection initiatives in this arena are too numerous to count; with respect to the competition mission of the FTC, the agency unveiled an online resource, the *FTC Guide to the Antitrust Laws*, that uses "plain language" to explain the antitrust laws to consumers and business people.[110] And with Bill at the helm, it will come as no surprise that the FTC interacted extensively with its foreign counterparts and with international organizations on policy issues and enforcement matters. These activities are discussed in Section IV, *infra*.

Although the Kovacic Commission issued no guidelines, as General Counsel and as a Commissioner, Bill encouraged the issuance of guidelines to provide transparency regarding the circumstances in which the FTC would use its enforcement authority in areas in which that authority was largely untested. While Bill was General Counsel, for example, the FTC issued guidance on the use of disgorgement as a monetary remedy for competition cases for FTC Act and HSR Act violations. The statement identified three factors to be considered in determining whether to seek disgorgement or restitution in a given case: (1) whether the underlying violation is based on clear precedent; (2) whether there is a reasonable basis for calculating the amount of remedial payment; and (3) whether there are other remedies available in the matter.[111]

While a Commissioner, Bill urged the FTC to issue guidelines explaining the circumstances under which it would challenge actions as anticompetitive under Section 5 of the FTC Act if those actions would not also be actionable under the Sherman Act. This suggestion was prompted by the Commission's overreaching with respect to Section 5 enforcement untethered from the Sherman Act in the 1970s and early 1980s.[112] During that period, the FTC sustained three resounding defeats in U.S. Courts of Appeal involving Section 5 cases. In *Competition Policy and the Application of Section 5 of the Federal Trade Commission Act* Bill and co-author Mark Winerman cautioned that future Section 5 enforcement should be based on a strategy that reflects an accurate diagnosis of past Section 5 enforcement failures and corrects them.[113] In addition to issuing guidelines to establish standards for Section 5 enforcement, the article also suggested the use of other policy tools to address this complex issue. For example, the article suggested that the FTC construct a framework that articulates the similarities of Section 5 to, and its differences from, the other antitrust laws.[114] In addition, the article suggested that the FTC use "research, workshops, reports, and related policy instruments to signal to the courts that the FTC has a sound basis for specific proposed applications of Section 5."[115]

4. Agency Resources: Emphasizing the Recruitment and Retention of Skilled Administrative Staff, Attorneys and Economists

Bill recognizes that "the success of a competition agency in achieving its mission depends fundamentally on the capabilities of the managers and staff who implement the agency's programs."[116] An increase in the capabilities of an agency's staff likely will lead not only to an improvement in the quality of the agency's performance, but also to an enhanced ability to assume increasingly complex tasks. Thus, investing in the training and retention of existing staff, and recruiting additional talented professionals from outside the agency, should be a perennial priority of an agency's leaders.

At least in the U.S., though, the ability to attract and retain highly talented professionals is made more challenging by the disparity in compensation between the public and private sectors. Indeed, Bill once observed that the U.S. has made the "deplorable" decision to pay its skilled administrative staff, economists, and attorneys "astonishingly less than competing rates in the private sector."[117] Accordingly, Bill has recommended that the FTC "engage Congress in a discussion about the possibility for augmenting the existing federal pay scale to enable the FTC to make salary-based departures to the private sector less frequent."[118] It is unlikely, though, that complete compensation parity will ever be achieved. For this reason, it is even more important to provide excellent training and fulfilling opportunities for staff.

Throughout his tenure at the FTC, Bill consistently practiced what he preached in this area. First, he sought to provide excellent training opportunities for FTC staff. While FTC Chairman, for example, Bill conducted an inaugural roundtable on microeconomics and its application to the mission of the FTC that since has become an annual event. The first event provided FTC staff with access to leading microeconomics scholars grappling with cutting-edge issues from across the nation. He built bridges between the FTC and experts in a variety of other areas, as well. Sometimes he encouraged those experts to come speak informally with Commission staff; on other occasions, he sought to have the FTC employ them. Indeed, Bill routinely sought to draw to the FTC the best and brightest from academia, in-house jobs, and private practice.

In addition, Bill sought to build bridges among members of the FTC community. He wrote about the benefits of having the consumer protection and competition missions housed in the same agency, observing that the Commission's "capacity to meld expertise in economics, competition and consumer protection is a conscious element of its institutional design and a major reason for its existence."[119] To obtain these benefits, though, cross-pollination of ideas and concepts across enforcement bureaus and other offices is imperative. To facilitate this beneficial flow of information, Bill encouraged cross-pollination both in formal and informal settings. While these efforts undoubtedly helped individuals perform their jobs more effectively, it is also likely that having a better sense of "the big picture" made those same individuals feel more tightly woven into the fabric of the agency, boosting retention efforts.

Bill also fostered loyalty among agency personnel by explaining why their contributions were not only necessary but appreciated. Bill conveyed clearly to each FTC employee with whom he interacted the importance of his or her contributions to the mission of the agency. When Bill met with incoming lawyers or paralegals, he took pains to explain how their work would further the broader goals of enhancing consumers' welfare. It is said that each person leaving one of those orientation sessions felt that he or she had a vital role to play in the work of the FTC. As Chairman, Bill also authored memoranda every few weeks celebrating jobs well done by various Commission personnel. Moreover, he celebrated the significant anniversaries of agency staff, calling to congratulate those who were passing major milestones in their FTC tenure. When Bill received the Miles W. Kirkpatrick Award, his former Chief of Staff, Sarah Mathias, stated in her remarks that Bill "knew the name of almost every single person here and he knew that he couldn't do his job without each of us doing our job. He values all of us. Isn't that a great thing to come to work and know each and every day?"[120]

Bill invested not only in current practitioners, but also those considering whether to make competition their chosen field. There is an anecdote that reflects not only this concept, but also Bill's understanding that it is necessary to take the long view (e.g., to plant trees while others are gathering low-hanging fruit). Asked to serve as a guest lecturer in one of the author's classes, Bill delivered his formal talk and then spent two hours discussing careers in competition law and seminal developments in the academic writing in this area. The entire class listened with great enthusiasm. It did not matter that these were not senior government officials or senior academics; Bill focused on the group with whom he could have the greatest impact. Indeed, Bill ran late for a reception in his honor because he spent so much time with the students. We do not think he would have preferred it differently.

5. Long-Term Investments: Regular and Substantial Capital Investments in Building Knowledge

Bill has observed that "[n]o input to a competition agency's work is more important than knowledge. To maintain its proficiency, an agency must stay attuned to state-of-the-art developments in economic theory, empirical work, legal analysis, major economic trends and the implementation of superior techniques in other competition agencies."[121] To accomplish this task, continued Bill, the agency must make "ongoing investments in competition policy research and development—outlays that make the agency smarter by ensuring that it sustains in-depth understanding about specific sectors, broader economic phenomena and advances in theory."[122] Bill's contributions in this area at home (discussed below) and abroad (discussed in Section IV) give him high marks.

As discussed in Section II.B., *supra*, the Kovacic Commission conducted hearings and workshops designed to illuminate competition issues involving specific sectors, including health care and high technology (intellectual property). The Kovacic Commission also invested heavily in refining the agency's thinking with respect to both its enforcement tools and its substantive policies. In October 2008, for example, the FTC held a workshop to examine the scope of the prohibition of "unfair methods of competition" under Section 5.[123] Panelists discussed the history of Section 5, a range of possible legal interpretations of this section, and the possible application of these interpretations to various instances of business conduct.[124]

Addressing another contentious topic, the FTC in 2009 posted four staff working papers relating to unilateral conduct. The papers were based on the proceedings of the FTC/DOJ joint hearings held in late 2006 and early 2007 to discuss the conduct properly proscribed by Sherman Act Section 2.[125] The papers discussed the effort to develop clear and administrable unilateral conduct rules, together with attendant error costs; reviewed the legal and policy issues raised by the use of Section 2 to challenge abuses of government processes (so-called "cheap exclusion"); examined the definition of monopoly power and the types of evidence that may demonstrate the existence of monopoly power; and analyzed the leading tests for evaluating single-firm conduct.[126]

In November 2008, the FTC hosted a two-day conference on microeconomics that brought together scholars working in areas related to the FTC's antitrust, consumer protection, and public policy missions.[127] Topics included developments in demand estimation and the use of demand estimation in merger cases, the economics of privacy and Internet behavior, and the economics of networks. A resounding success, this first microeconomics roundtable began a tradition of annual microeconomics conferences that has continued well past Bill's tenure as Chairman. In November 2011, the FTC held its fourth annual iteration of the event. These workshops have pushed the frontier of economics in terms of both theoretical and empirical economics, and have led to interactions and understandings that have helped to shape the FTC's policy.

6. Data Collection and Disclosure: Engaging in Data Collection to Assess the Impact of the Agency's Work and Disclosing that Data to Facilitate External Review and Comparative Study

Instead of using activity levels to assess agency performance, Bill long has advocated measuring the extent to which agency actions have enhanced economic performance and improved consumer welfare. In this vein, Bill noted that "[c]entral to the assessment of an agency's contributions to improved economic performance is the evaluation of its work," which may be facilitated by the collection of data "that recounts the agency's activities and measures their impact."[128] He further notes that collection of the data alone is insufficient; "[d]isclosure of this information is necessary to facilitate external review and comparative study."[129] In this final metric, Bill's "course work" is once again exemplary.

During Bill's tenure as Chairman, the FTC engaged in activities related to the collection and issuance of data that would allow the impact of its actions to be examined and assessed. In February 2009, for example, the Bureau of Economics published an issues paper discussing the role of efficiencies in FTC merger analyses.[130] The paper, entitled Merger Efficiencies at the Federal Trade Commission 1997-2007, authored by Malcolm Coate and Andrew Heimert, examined the role played by efficiencies in 186 mergers reviewed by the

FTC following the release of the 1997 Horizontal Merger Guidelines. The paper scrutinized (1) the types of efficiencies arguments made by merging parties to the FTC, and (2) the types of efficiencies arguments that the FTC was willing to accept.[131] The paper found that while FTC staff are just as likely to accept fixed-cost savings arguments as they are to accept variable-cost savings arguments, they are more likely to accept dynamic efficiencies and more likely to reject generic efficiency claims than other types of efficiencies.[132]

In addition, in December 2008, the FTC updated its ongoing horizontal merger investigation data report.[133] The 2008 data release built upon the original release of horizontal merger data in 2004 during Bill's tenure as General Counsel. The update expanded the coverage of mergers in the agency's database and contained data relating to investigations in 1,154 markets from 210 different merger investigations.[134] The market statistics included pre- and post-merger HHIs and the number of significant competitors in a given market. In addition, for investigations involving three or fewer markets, the update tabulated the Commission's enforcement decisions based on the presence or absence of "hot documents," "strong customer complaints," and "entry conditions" as identified by staff during each investigation.[135] These data provide important information about enforcement trends and facilitate transparency in merger enforcement, benefitting all constituencies of the FTC.

Another way to evaluate the effectiveness of an agency's actions lies in conducting retrospectives. In *Evaluating Antitrust Experiments: Using Ex Post Assessments of Government Enforcement Decisions to Inform Competition Policy*, Bill presented "the case for having government competition authorities develop programs for performing regular evaluations of their law enforcement decisions."[136] He recognized that, as a general rule, "[m]aking sound decisions about future public policy issues requires efforts to assess the wisdom of past choices."[137] He noted that this principle applies with special force in the competition sector, given several unique characteristics of this field: the uncertainty accompanying many antitrust enforcement decisions, which gives competition policymaking an experimental quality; the strong link between competition law and industrial organization economics, which requires policy adjustments that reflect evolving understandings of business practices; the frequency of settlements (as opposed to litigated cases resulting in judicial opinions), which typically offer inadequate insight into the rationales for intervention; and the exercise of overlapping authority within and across jurisdictions.[138]

While serving at the FTC, Bill on several occasions applied his recognition that "evaluations of past enforcement decisions can help establish whether an agency's assumptions and analytical methods require adjustment." The first occasion arose in 2002 when the FTC launched a series of retrospectives analyzing the competitive effects of consummated hospital mergers.[139] This project had two objectives: (1) to allow the FTC to "consider bringing enforcement actions against consummated, anticompetitive hospital mergers," and (2) "to update [the FTC's] prior assumptions about the consequences of particular transactions and the nature of competitive forces in health care."[140]

The retrospective analyzed four consummated hospital mergers, and revealed that one of the four had resulted in post-merger price increases and other anticompetitive effects. Thus, while Bill was General Counsel, the Commission issued an administrative complaint alleging that the 2000 acquisition of Highland Park Hospital by Evanston Northwestern Healthcare Corporation violated Clayton Act Section 7.[141] During Bill's tenure as an FTC Commissioner, the Commission in August 2007 affirmed an October 2005 ruling by an administrative law judge concluding that the acquisition was anticompetitive and violated federal antitrust law.[142] And while Bill was FTC Chairman, the Commission issued its final opinion and order laying out the specific requirements for the remedy that the Commission had ordered in its August 2007 liability decision.[143]

The second set of retrospectives launched during Bill's tenure as General Counsel involved the politically charged topic of petroleum mergers, and dovetailed with Bill's task of providing Congressional testimony on several occasions regarding the FTC's enforcement framework in this industry.[144] The FTC released a report in August 2004 that analyzed its enforcement history with respect to mergers in the petroleum industry, and responded to criticisms that the FTC had engaged in lax enforcement efforts.[145] The report concluded that mergers of private oil companies had not significantly affected worldwide concentration in crude oil; despite some increases over time, concentration at most levels of the petroleum industry remained low to moderate; and intense, thorough FTC merger investigations and enforcement had helped prevent further increases in petroleum industry concentration and avoid potentially anticompetitive problems and higher prices for consumers.[146]

IV. The Study-Abroad Program: Bill's International Contributions

In addition to making significant contributions to the U.S. competition regime, Bill has been active on international competition policy and scholarship for over twenty years. We begin with a quick review of his EU- related scholarship as a way to establish the context for his work as it relates to the ICN. As an ardent advocate of the ICN, his work in connection with this institution will serve as one of Bill's enduring legacies. Some of Bill's early comparative writing focused on divergences between the competition policies of the United States and Europe. During this period, the divergence was far more significant than whatever disagreements may exist at present. At that time, the European approach was far less focused on competition economics. The case law, as it had devel oped, had given the European Commission wide latitude for heavier handed enforcement than had been the case in the United States since the Chicago revolution of the 1970s. What many academics and practitioners in the United States may not have fully appreciated is that the theoretical underpinnings of European competition law were distinct from those of the United States because of path dependence. The initial focus of the European system was in integrating the economies of the Member States. Moreover, competition policy in Europe had a more distributive flavor than its American counterpart, as competition policy in the U.S. by this time embraced efficiency as the primary touchstone. There was far more concern about choices for consumers, even if preserving choice translated into enforcement policies that disfavored more efficient competitors.[147]

The divergence between the two great antitrust powers became a recurring theme in Bill's writing[148] and his later policy work. From this perspective, one of the most attractive features of the ICN was its ability, in the long run, to prevent significant trans-Atlantic eruptions such as *GE/Honeywell* or *Boeing/McDonald Douglas* from reoccurring. In this sense, the ICN has been a profound success. While General Counsel and later as Commissioner and Chairman, Bill worked within the ICN framework to help harmonize approaches both on substance and procedure. The ICN has been able to find areas of "soft" convergence based upon international best practices between the two great powers of competition policy largely because of the ICN's effective institutional design.

Bill not only has spent time in designing the various inputs and outputs of the ICN. He also has studied how the ICN has been able to affect the global governance of competition law and policy. [149] The ICN is a "soft law" network of competition agencies and non-state actors. The network is soft in the sense that the commitment is based on non-binding best practices that rely upon voluntary compliance by various competition regimes.[150] The first institutional difference between the ICN and other soft law networks is in its participation. That is, the active role of non-state actors is different from either the OECD or UNCTAD. These non-state participants from both the developed and developing world include academics, private-sector attorneys and economists, and civil society groups. Because of the non-state actor participation, the ICN has had greater buy-in by the various stakeholders in the global competition enterprise.

A second factor has aided the ICN in improving the overall global system and improved the capacity of many of its members. As a virtual institution that lacks a physical headquarters and dedicated permanent staff (agency officials from existing antitrust authorities and private sector participants volunteer their time to the various working groups), the ICN is effective precisely because of the lack of permanent staff. There are more contact points for norm diffusion among the various participants in ICN meetings who have a more direct stake in the success of the organization. Moreover, the virtual nature of the ICN prevents mission creep that a more permanent staff might encourage. The ICN does not try to do too much. What it does it does effectively because of narrowly tailored assignments and deadlines.

Bill spent a significant amount of time and resources within the ICN in getting the capacity building element of the organization to focus on those issues that would be most beneficial to younger competition agencies. This effort involved producing reports on industry sectors, surveying the effectiveness of capacity building, and creating various training manuals and workshops to improve agency capacity.

The ICN work falls most closely into the categories of establishing and refining internal planning mechanisms to devise strategies for accomplishing an agency's goals and employing a problem-solving approach that uses the agency's full range of policy tools to address policies and practices that otherwise would decrease the well-being of consumers. Many of the outputs from ICN projects were long term bets that better prioritization and agency design would ultimately yield to better outcomes. Although good quantifiable metrics to measure "success" remain somewhat elusive, anecdotal work suggests that the deep thinking that Bill encouraged has, at least on the margins, improved the performance of competition agencies around the world. This is true not merely among young agencies but for more mature agencies as well.

In terms of grading Bill's international work, he practiced on the international side what he did on the domestic side. In 2008, Bill helped organize a joint DOJ/FTC workshop on technical assistance in antitrust[151] to take stock of what worked and what did not in the provision of capacity building and technical assistance. Moreover, as a result of a reorganization within the FTC, the FTC compartmentalized its various international resources within a single office to better create synergies and efficiencies in the international work of the agency.

V. Conclusion

Bill's criteria to judge the effectiveness of an institution were forged in the fires of his "study abroad" work. That work in the international arena enabled him to make remarkable contributions to antitrust engineering back at home in the United States and once again in the international arena. Both in terms of inputs and outcomes, at home and abroad, Bill has been incredibly effective in strengthening the institutions of antitrust. Had the *Transaereo* been a nascent antitrust regime with the benefit of Bill's insights, it undoubtedly would have enjoyed a far more successful maiden voyage.

NOTES

*   Bill is a dear friend and mentor.

**   Christine Wilson first met Bill Kovacic when he spoke at an Antitrust Practice Group Retreat for Collier, Shannon, Rill & Scott in the 1990s. She subsequently had the privilege of serving with (and learning from) Bill at the FTC during his tenure as General Counsel.

1   In this paper, we have focused on Bill Kovacic's contributions to the issues associated with competition policy development and have not assessed his many contributions to other areas, including consumer protection.

2   BILL YENNE, THE WORLD'S WORST AIRCRAFT at 48-49 (2001).

3   William E. Kovacic, *The Digital Broadband Migration And the Federal Trade Commission: Building the Competition And Consumer Protection Agency of the Future*, 8 J. TELECOMM. & HIGH TECH. L. 1, 5 (2010) [hereinafter Kovacic, *The Digital Broadband Migration and the Federal Trade Commission*].

4   *Id.*

5   *Id.*

6   *Id.* at 6.

7   William E. Kovacic, *Creating Competition Policy: Betty Bock and the Development of Antitrust Institutions*, 66 ANTITRUST L.J. 231 244-245 (1997).

8   *Id.* at 245.

9   William E. Kovacic, *Rating the Competition Agencies: What Constitutes Good Performance?*,16 GEO. MASON L. REV. 903, 906 (2009) [hereinafter Kovacic, *Rating the Competition Agencies*].

10   William E. Kovacic, Hugh M. Hollman & Patricia Grant, *How Does Your Competition Agency Measure Up?*, 7 EUR. COMPETITION L.J. 25 (2011) [hereinafter Kovacic, Hollman & Grant, *How Does Your Competition Agency Measure Up?*].

11   *See e.g.*, William E. Kovacic, *Comments and Observations on the Sherman Act: The First Century*, 59 ANTITRUST L.J. 119 (1990); William E. Kovacic, *Failed Expectations: The Troubled Past and Uncertain Future of the Sherman Act as a Tool for Deconcentration*, 74 IOWA L. REV. 1005 (1989); William E. Kovacic, *Public Choice and the Public Interest: Federal Trade Commission Antitrust Enforcement during the Reagan Administration*, 33 ANTITRUST BULL. 467 (1988); William E. Kovacic, *The Federal Trade Commission and Congressional Oversight of Antitrust Enforcement*, 17 TULSA L.J. 587 (1982).

12   Mark A. Dutz & Maria Vagliasindi, *Competition Policy Implementation in Transition Economies: An Empirical Assessment*, 44 EURO. ECON. REV. 762 (2000); JOHN FINGLETON, ELEANOR FOX, DAMIEN NEVEN & PAUL SEABRIGHT, COMPETITION POLICY AND THE TRANSFORMATION OF CENTRAL EUROPE (1996).

13   ELEANOR M. FOX & D. DANIEL SOKOL, COMPETITION LAW AND POLICY IN LATIN AMERICA (2009).

14   Frederic Jenny, *Cartels and Collusion in Developing Countries: Lessons from Empirical Evidence*, 29 WORLD COMPETITION L. & ECON. REV. 1 (2006).

15   R. IAN MCEWIN, INTELLECTUAL PROPERTY, COMPETITION LAW AND ECONOMICS IN ASIA (2011); DAVID GERBER, GLOBAL COMPETITION LAW: LAW, MARKETS AND GLOBALIZATION (2010); Eleanor M. Fox, *An Anti-Monopoly Law for China— Scaling the Walls of Government Restraints*, 75 ANTITRUST L.J. 173 (2008).

16   HERNANDO DE SOTO, THE MYSTERY OF CAPITAL: WHY CAPITALISM TRIUMPHS IN THE WEST AND FAILS EVERYWHERE ELSE (2000).

17   MICHAEL TREBILCOCK, THE LIMITS OF FREEDOM OF CONTRACT (1993).

18   Anne O. Krueger, *The Political Economy of the Rent-Seeking Society*, 64 AM. ECON. REV. 291 (1974).

19   GEETA BATRA, DANIEL KAUFMANN & ANDREW H. W. STONE, INVESTMENT CLIMATE AROUND THE WORLD: VOICES OF THE FIRMS FROM THE WORLD BUSINESS ENVIRONMENT SURVEY (2003).

20   WORLD BANK, DOING BUSINESS REPORT (2011).

21   R. S. Khemani, Competition Policy and Promotion of Investment, Economic Growth and Poverty Alleviation in Least Developed Countries 1 (The World Bank, Occasional Paper No. 19, 2007).

22   KYLE BAGWELL & ROBERT W. STAIGER, THE ECONOMICS OF THE WORLD TRADING SYSTEM (2002).

23   D. Daniel Sokol, *Competition Policy and Comparative Corporate Governance of State Owned Enterprises*, 2009 BYU L. Rev. 1713.

24   Yishay P. Yafeh & Tarun Khanna, *Business Groups in Emerging Markets: Paragons or Parasites?*, 45 J. ECON LIT. 331 (2007).

25   D. Daniel Sokol, *What Do We Really Know About Export Cartels and What is the Appropriate Solution?*, 4 J. COMPETITION L. & ECON. 967 (2008).

26   Eleanor M. Fox, *Economic Development, Poverty and Antitrust: The Other Path*, 13 SW. J.L. & TRADE AM. 211 (2007).

27   D. Daniel Sokol, *The Development of Human Capital, in* COMPETITION LAW AND POLICY IN LATIN AMERICA (Eleanor M. Fox & D. Daniel Sokol eds. 2009).

28   William E. Kovacic, *Institutional Foundations for Economic Legal Reform in Transition Economies: The Case of Competition Policy and Antitrust Enforcement*, 77 CHI.-KENT L. REV. 265 (2001).

29   William E. Kovacic, *Designing and Implementing Competition and Consumer Protection Reforms in Transitional Economies: Perspectives from Mongolia, Nepal, Ukraine, and Zimbabwe*, 44 DEPAUL L. REV. 1197 (1995) [hereinafter Kovacic, *Designing and Implementing*].

30   Not mentioned in the article is an anecdote that Bill shared with us a number of years ago. He was in Mongolia in the middle of winter and the bottle of vodka that someone brought froze on the short distance between one building and the next.

31   *Id.* at 1202.

32   William E. Kovacic, *Public Choice and the Origins of Antitrust Policy, in* THE CAUSES AND CONSEQUENCES OF ANTITRUST: THE PUBLIC CHOICE PERSPECTIVE (Fred S. McChesney & William F. Shughart III eds., 1995); William E. Kovacic, *Public Choice and the Public Interest: Federal Trade Commission Antitrust Enforcement During the Reagan Administration*, 33 ANTITRUST BULL. 467 (1988).

33   FEDERAL TRADE COMMISSION, REPORT OF THE STATE ACTION TASK FORCE (2003); FEDERAL TRADE COMMISSION, ENFORCEMENT PERSPECTIVES ON THE NOERR-PENNINGTON DOCTRINE (2006).

34   Kovacic, *Designing and Implementing* at 1202.

35   William E. Kovacic, *Intellectual Property Policy and Competition Policy*, 66 N.Y.U. ANN. SURV. AM. L. 421 (2011); William E. Kovacic & Andreas P. Reindl, *An Interdisciplinary Approach to Improving Competition Policy and Intellectual Property Policy*, 28 FORDHAM INT'L L.J. 1062 (2005).

36   William E. Kovacic et al., *Plus Factors and Agreement in Antitrust Law*, 110 MICH. L. REV. 393 (2011); William E. Kovacic, *Criminal Enforcement Norms in Competition Policy: Insights from U.S. Experience, in* CRIMINALISING CARTELS: CRITICAL STUDIES OF AN INTERNATIONAL REGULATORY MOVEMENT 45, 66-67 (Caron Beaton-Wells & Ariel Ezrachi eds., 2011); William E. Kovacic, *An Integrated Competition Policy To Deter and Defeat Cartels*, 51 ANTITRUST BULL. 813 (2006); William E. Kovacic et al., *Lessons for Competition Policy from the Vitamins Cartel, in* THE POLITICAL ECONOMY OF ANTITRUST (Vivek Ghosal & Johan Stennek eds., 2007); William E. Kovacic et al., *Bidding Rings and the Design of Anti-Collusion Measures for Auctions and Procurements, in* HANDBOOK OF PROCUREMENT (Nicola Dimitri et al. eds., 2006); Cécile Aubert et. al, *The Impact of Leniency and Whistleblowing Programs on Cartels*, 24 INT'L J. INDUST. ORG. 1241 (2006); William E. Kovacic, *Private Monitoring and Antitrust Enforcement: Paying Informants to Reveal Cartels*, 69 GEO. WASH. L. REV. 766 (2001).

37   Kovacic, *Designing and Implementing* at 1202.

38   William E. Kovacic, *Getting Started: Creating New Competition Policy Institutions in Transition Economics*, 23 BROOK. J. INT'L L. 403 (1997).

39   *Id.* at 405-06.

40   William E. Kovacic, *Merger Enforcement in Transition: Antitrust Controls on Acquisitions in Emerging Economies*, 66 U. CIN. L. REV. 1075 (1998).

41   William E. Kovacic, *Institutional Foundations for Economic Legal Reform in Transition Economies: The Case of Competition Policy and Antitrust Enforcement*, 77 CHI-KENT L. REV. 265 (2001).

42   *Id.* at 26.

43   *Id.*

44   The "right" result is not always certain at the initiation of a policy choice. Thus, inputs (processes) matter as much as outputs. Bill has written that "[i]n golf, the logic of hiring a good swing coach is that improving swing technique increases the likelihood that the player will become more proficient in directing the ball in the desired direction. Similarly, using good processes over time leads to a greater likelihood of producing superior outcomes." Kovacic, *Rating the Competition Agencies* at 915.

45   WILLIAM AND CULLEY & JAMES D. LAZER, MARKETING MANAGEMENT: FOUNDATIONS AND PRACTICES (1983).

46   THE FEDERAL TRADE COMMISSION, THE FEDERAL TRADE COMMISSION AT 100: INTO OUR 2ND CENTURY –THE CONTINUING PURSUIT OF BETTER PRACTICES ii (2009) [hereinafter, FTC AT 100].

47   *Id.*

48   *Id.* at ii-iii.

49   *See* Federal Trade Commission, Speeches, Articles, and Statements by William E. Kovacic, *available at* http://www.ftc.gov/speeches/kovacic.shtm.

50   FTC AT 100 at iii.

51   For an excellent historical analysis, see Timothy J. Muris & Bilal K. Sayyed, *Policy, Petroleum, and Politics at the Federal Trade Commission*, 85 SO. CAL. L. REV. (2012) 843.

52 *See, e.g.*, Prepared Statement of the Federal Trade Commission Before the United States Senate Judiciary Committee (February 1, 2006) *available at* http://www.ftc.gov/speeches/kovacic/testimonyrepetroleumindustryconsolidation.pdf.

53 Kovacic, Hollman & Grant, *How Does Your Competition Agency Measure Up?*, at 32.

54 Kovacic, *The Digital Broadband Migration at the Federal Trade Commission*, at 6.

55 Federal Trade Commission Press Release, FTC to Host Workshop on Innovations in Health Care Delivery (Mar. 10, 2008), *available at* http://www.ftc.gov/opa/2008/03/hcd.shtm.

56 *See id.*

57 Agenda, FTC Roundtable on the Competitive Significance of Healthcare Provider Quality Information (Oct. 30, 2008), *available at* http://www.ftc.gov/bc/workshops/hcbio/agenda/hcqagenda.pdf.

58 Federal Trade Commission Press Release, FTC Announces Workshop and Roundtable on Emerging Health Care Competition and Consumer Protection Issues (Aug. 27, 2008), *available at* http://www.ftc.gov/opa/2008/08/hcissues.shtm.

59 FEDERAL TRADE COMMISSION, EMERGING HEALTH CARE ISSUES: FOLLOW-ON BIOLOGIC DRUG COMPETITION iii (2009), *available at* http://www.ftc.gov/os/2009/06/P083901biologicsreport.pdf.

60 FEDERAL TRADE COMMISSION & DEPARTMENT OF JUSTICE, ANTITRUST DIVISION, IMPROVING HEALTH CARE: A DOSE OF COMPETITION (July 2004).

61 *Id.* at 2.

62 *Id.*

63 *Id.* at 1.

64 *See generally id.*

65 Federal Trade Commission Press Release, FTC Announces First in Series of Hearings on Evolving Intellectual Property Marketplace (Nov. 6, 2008), *available at* http://www.ftc.gov/opa/2008/11/ipmarketplace.shtm.

66 *See id.*

67 FEDERAL TRADE COMMISSION, THE EVOLVING IP MARKETPLACE: ALIGNING PATENT NOTICE AND REMEDIES WITH COMPETITION (2011).

68 FEDERAL TRADE COMMISSION, TO PROMOTE INNOVATION: THE PROPER BALANCE OF COMPETITION AND PATENT LAW AND POLICY 3 (2003).

69 *See id.* at 1.

70 STEPHEN A. MERRILL, RICHARD C. LEVIN & MARK B. MYERS, U.S. NAT'L RESEARCH COUNCIL, A PATENT SYSTEM FOR THE 21ST CENTURY (2004).

71 Kovacic, *The Digital Broadband Migration at the Federal Trade Commission*, at 6.

72 Marc Winerman & William E. Kovacic, *The William Humphrey and Abram Myers Years: The FTC from 1925 to 1929*, 77 ANTITRUST L.J. 701 (2011); Marc Winerman & William E. Kovacic, *Outpost Years for a Start-Up Agency: The FTC from 1921-1925*, 77 ANTITRUST L.J. 145 (2010).

73 *See generally* Yuichi Shoda, Walter Mischel & Philip Peake, *Predicting Adolescent Cognitive and Self-Regulatory Competencies from Preschool Delay of Gratification: Identifying Diagnostic Conditions*, 26 DEVELOPMENTAL PSYCHOLOGY 978 (1990).

74 Kovacic, *The Digital Broadband Migration at the Federal Trade Commission*, at 6.

75 FTC AT 100, at xv.

76 FTC AT 100, at xv; *see also* Kovacic, Hollman & Grant, *How Does Your Competition Agency Measure Up?*, at 32 ("Central to the formation of a strategy to implement the competition agency's priorities is the determination of the mix of policy tools whose application will best solve specific competition policy problems.").

77 Federal Trade Commission Press Release, FTC Intervenes in Teva Pharmaceutical Industries' Proposed $8.9 Billion Acquisition of Barr Pharmaceuticals (Dec. 19, 2008), *available at* http://www.ftc.gov/opa/2008/12/tevabarr.shtm.

78 Federal Trade Commission Press Release, FTC Challenges Reed Elsevier's Proposed $4.1 Billion Acquisition of ChoicePoint, Inc. (Sept. 16, 2008), *available at* http://www.ftc.gov/opa/2008/09/choicepoint.shtm.

79 Federal Trade Commission Press Release, Commission Order Requires Divestiture of Specialty Epoxy Business and Certain Conduct Restrictions to Preserve Competition (Oct. 2, 2008), *available at* http://www.ftc.gov/opa/2008/10/hexion.shtm.

80 Federal Trade Commission Press Release, FTC Challenges Pernod Ricard's Proposed Acquisition of V&S Vin & Sprit (July 17, 2008), *available at* http://www.ftc.gov/opa/2008/07/pernod.shtm.

81 Federal Trade Commission Press Release, FTC Orders Polypore International to Divest Rival Manufacturer it Acquired in 2008 (Dec. 13, 2010), *available at* http://www.ftc.gov/opa/2010/12/polypore.shtm.

82 *See id.*

83 *See id.*

84 Federal Trade Commission Press Release, FTC Sues Ovation Pharmaceuticals for Illegally Acquiring Drug Used to Treat Premature Babies with Life-Threatening Heart Condition (Dec. 16, 2008), *available at* http://www.ftc.gov/ opa/2008/12/ovation.shtm. The District of Minnesota found for defendants in this case, holding that the FTC had failed to appropriately define a relevant market. *FTC v. Lundbeck, Inc.*, CIV. 08-6379 JNE/JJG, 2010 WL 3810015, at *21-22 (D. Minn. Aug. 31, 2010). The Eighth Circuit upheld the lower court's ruling. *See FTC v. Lundbeck*, 650 F.3d 1236, 1243 (8th Cir. 2011).

85 Federal Trade Commission Press Release, Federal Appeals Court Rules in Favor of FTC in Case Against Chicago Bridge & Iron Co. (Jan. 25, 2008), *available at* http://www.ftc.gov/opa/2008/01/cbi.shtm.

86 *See id.*

87 *Id.*

88 *See id.*

89 Federal Trade Commission Press Release, FTC Finds Vivendi Subsidiaries Violated Antitrust Laws In Distribution of Three Tenors CDs (July 29, 2003), *available at* http://www.ftc.gov/opa/2003/07/vivendi.shtm. For analysis *see* Timothy J. Muris, *A Response to Professor Goldberg: An Anticompetitive Restraint by Any Other Name*, 1 REV. L. & ECON . 65 (2005).

90 Federal Trade Commission Press Release, FTC Charges Unocal with Anticompetitive Conduct Related to Reformulated Gasoline (March 4, 2003), *available at* http://www.ftc.gov/opa/2003/03/unocal.shtm.

91 Federal Trade Commission Press Release, FTC Issues Complaint against Rambus, Inc. (June 19, 2002), *available at* http://www.ftc.gov/opa/2002/06/rambus.shtm.

92 Federal Trade Commission Press Release, FTC Challenges MSC Software's Acquisitions of Its Two Nastran Competitors (Oct. 10, 2001), *available at* http://www.ftc.gov/opa/2001/10/msc.shtm.

93 Federal Trade Commission Press Release, FTC Charges South Carolina Board of Dentistry (Sept. 15, 2003), *available at* http://www.ftc.gov/opa/2003/09/socodentist.shtm.

94 Federal Trade Commission Press Release, FTC Charges Aspen Technology's Acquisition Of Hyprotech, Ltd. was Anticompetitive (Aug. 7, 2003), *available at* http://www.ftc.gov/opa/2003/08/aspen.shtm.

95 Federal Trade Commission Press Release, Commission Approves Comments to the FERC on the Wholesale Electric Power Market (Sept. 18, 2007), *available at* http://www.ftc.gov/opa/2007/09/fyiwholesale.shtm.

96 *See id.*

97 Federal Trade Commission Press Release, FTC Submits Staff Comment to FAA on Proposed Congestion Management Rule for LaGuardia Airport (June 19, 2008), *available at* http://www.ftc.gov/opa/2008/06/laguardiafyi.shtm.

98 *See id.*

99 Federal Trade Commission Press Release, FTC Submits Testimony to Florida State Senate Regarding Bill That Would Amend State's Certificate-of-Need Laws (Apr. 17, 2008), *available at* http://www.ftc.gov/opa/2008/04/ florida.shtm.

100 *See id.*

101 Federal Trade Commission Press Release, Federal Trade Commission, Department of Justice Issue Joint Statement on Certificate-of-Need Laws in Illinois (Sept. 12, 2008), *available at* http://www.ftc.gov/opa/2008/09/illcon.shtm.

102 Federal Trade Commission Press Release, FTC/DOJ Submit Letter to Supreme Court of South Carolina on Proposed Guidelines Regarding the Practice of Law in Real Estate Transactions (Apr. 17, 2008), *available at* http://www.ftc. gov/opa/2008/04/scletter.shtm.

103 *See id.*

104 Federal Trade Commission Press Release, FTC Files Comment with Pennsylvania Public Utility Commission about Retail Electricity Pricing and Customer Participation (Dec. 23, 2008), *available at* http://www.ftc.gov/opa/2008/12/ papuc.shtm.

105 *See id.*

106 Federal Trade Commission Press Release, FTC Seeks Public Comment on Rulemaking to Prohibit Market Manipulation in the Petroleum Industry (May 1, 2008), *available at* http://www.ftc.gov/opa/2008/05/anpr.shtm.

107 *See id.*

108 Federal Trade Commission Press Release, FTC to Host Public Workshop on Petroleum Market Manipulation Rulemaking (Aug. 26, 2008), *available at* http://www.ftc.gov/opa/2008/08/pmmrwksp.shtm.

109 Federal Trade Commission Press Release, New FTC Rule Prohibits Petroleum Market Manipulation (Aug. 6, 2009), *available at* http://www.ftc.gov/opa/2009/08/mmr.shtm.

110 *See* Federal Trade Commission Press Release, New FTC Online Resource Answers Questions about U.S. Antitrust Laws (July 14, 2008), *available at* http://www.ftc.gov/opa/2008/07/bcwebfyi.shtm.

111 Federal Trade Commission Press Release, FTC Issues Policy Statement on Use of Monetary Remedies in Competition Cases (July 31, 2003), *available at* http://www.ftc.gov/opa/2003/07/disgorgement.shtm; *see also* FEDERAL-TRADE COMMISSION, POLICY STATEMENT ON MONETARY EQUITABLE REMEDIES IN COMPETITION CASES (2003), *available at* http://www.ftc.gov/os/2003/07/disgorgementfrn.shtm.

112 William E. Kovacic & Mark Winerman, *Competition Policy and the Application of Section 5 of the Federal Trade Commission Act*, 76 ANTITRUST L.J. 929 (2010) [hereinafter Kovacic & Winerman, *Application of Section 5*].

113 *See* Kovacic & Winerman, *Application of Section 5*, at 944.

114 *Id.*

115 *Id.*

116 Kovacic, *How Does Your Competition Agency Measure Up?* at 33; *see also* FTC AT 100 at vii (how an agency approaches "recruiting, training, and retention of talented and competent personnel bears significantly on the agency's ultimate success").

117 Interview with William E. Kovacic, Chairmain, Federal Trade Commission, THE ANTITRUST SOURCE, at 7 (Aug. 2008).

118 FTC AT 100, at 180. Other parts of government are not on the GS pay scale, such as the Federal Reserve.

119 FTC AT 100, at v.

120 Sarah M. Mathias, Remarks at the Miles W. Kirkpatrick Award Ceremony (Oct. 25, 2011) (on file with the authors).

121 Kovacic, Hollman & Grant, *How Does Your Competition Agency Measure Up?*, at 33.

122 *Id.* at 34.

123 Federal Trade Commission Press Release, Commission Announces Workshop to Explore Scope of the Prohibition of Unfair Methods of Competition under Section 5 of the FTC Act (Aug. 28, 2008), *available at* http://www.ftc.gov/opa/2008/08/section5.shtm.

124 Agenda, Federal Trade Commission, Workshop on Section 5 of the FTC Act as a Competition Statute (Oct. 17, 2008) *available at* http://www.ftc.gov/bc/workshops/section5/agenda.pdf.

125 Federal Trade Commission Press Release, FTC, DOJ Seek Comments for Upcoming Hearings on Single-Firm Conduct (Mar. 30, 2006), *available at* http://www.ftc.gov/opa/2006/03/unilateral.shtm.

126 Federal Trade Commission Press Release, Staff Working Papers on Section 2 Posted on Federal Trade Commission Web Site; FTC Publishes Notice on Proposed Rule Regarding Depository Institution Disclosure Requirements; FTC Extends Public Comment Period Related to Endorsement Guides Review (Jan. 16, 2009), *available at* http://www.ftc.gov/opa/2009/01/section2.shtm.

127 Agenda, Federal Trade Commission and Northwestern University, First Ever Microeconomics Conference (Nov. 6-7, 2008), *available at* http://www.ftc.gov/be/workshops/microeconomics/2008/agenda.pdf.

128 Kovacic, Hollman & Grant, *How Does Your Competition Agency Measure Up?* at 36.

129 *Id.*

130 Federal Trade Commission, Press Release, Bureau of Economics Releases Economic Issues Paper on Treatment of Efficiencies in Merger Matters (Feb. 6, 2009), *available at* http://www.ftc.gov/opa/2009/02/bemergers.shtm.

131 *See id.*

132 MALCOLM B. COATE & ANDREW J. HEIMERT, FED. TRADE COMM'N, MERGER EFFICIENCIES AT THE FEDERAL TRADE COMMISSION 1997–2007 vi (2009). On merger efficiencies analysis more generally, *see* D. Daniel Sokol & James A. Fishkin, *Antitrust Merger Efficiencies in the Shadow of the Law*, 64 VAND. L. REV. EN BANC 45 (2011).

133 Federal Trade Commission Press Release, FTC Issues New Update of Horizontal Merger Investigation Data Report (Dec. 2, 2008), *available at* http://www.ftc.gov/opa/2008/12/horizmerger.shtm.

134 *See id.*

135 FEDERAL TRADE COMMISSION, HORIZONTAL MERGER INVESTIGATION DATA, FISCAL YEARS 1996-2007 1 (2008).

136 William E. Kovacic, *Evaluating Antitrust Experiments: Using Ex Post Assessments of Government Enforcement Decisions to Inform Competition Policy*, 9 GEO. MASON L. REV. 843, 844 (2001).

137 *Id.* at 843.

138 *See generally id.*

139 FED. TRADE COMM'N, BUILDING A STRONG FOUNDATION: THE FTC YEAR IN REVIEW 9 (2002), *available at* http://www.ftc.gov/os/2002/04/ftcyearreview.pdf.

140 Timothy J. Muris, Fed. Trade Comm'n Chairman, Prepared Remarks Before the 7th Annual Competition in Health Care Forum, Everything Old is New Again: Health Care and Competition in the 21st Century 19-20 (Nov. 7, 2002), *available at* http://www.ftc.gov/speeches/muris/murishealthcarespeech0211.pdf.

141 Complaint, *In the Matter of Evanston Northwestern Healthcare Corp.*, Docket No. 9315 (FTC Feb. 10, 2004).

142 Opinion of the Commission, *In the Matter of Evanston Northwestern Healthcare Corp.*, Docket No. 9315 (FTC Aug. 6, 2007).

143 Final Order, *In the Matter of Evanston Northwestern Healthcare Corp.*, Docket No. 9315 (FTC Apr. 24, 2008).

144 *See, e.g., Market Forces, Anticompetitive Activity, and Gasoline Prices: FTC Initiatives to Protect Competitive Markets*, Prepared Statement of the Federal Trade Commission before the Subcommittee on Energy Policy, Natural Resources and Regulatory Affairs, Committee on Government Reform, United States House of Representatives, July 7, 2004.

145 FEDERAL TRADE COMMISSION, THE PETROLEUM INDUSTRY: MERGERS, STRUCTURAL CHANGE, AND ANTITRUST ENFORCEMENT (2004).

146 *Id*. at 2-3.

147 William E. Kovacic, *Transatlantic Turbulence: The Boeing-McDonnell Douglas Merger and International Competition Policy*, 68 ANTITRUST L.J. 805 (2001).

148 *Id*.

149 Hugh M. Hollman & William E. Kovacic, *The International Competition Network: Its Past, Current, and Future Role*, 20 Minn. J. Int'l L. 274 (2011); William E. Kovacic, Hugh M. Hollman & Patricia Grant, *How Does Your Competition Agency Measure Up?*, 7 EURO. COMPETITION J. 25 (2011).

150 *See generally*, D. Daniel Sokol, *Explaining the Importance of Public Choice for Law*, 109 MICH. L. REV. 1029 (2011); D. Daniel Sokol, *Monopolists Without Borders: The Institutional Challenge of International Antitrust in a Global Gilded Age*, 4 BERKELEY BUS. L.J. 37 (2007).

151 http://www.justice.gov/atr/public/workshops/techassist2008/agenda.html.

William Kovacic on Competition Law and Economic Development

DAVID J. GERBER

dgerber@kentlaw.iit.edu

Professor of Law, Chicago-Kent College of Law, Chicago

Abstract

This brief contribution to the Festschrift for Professor Kovacic highlights one aspect of his professional career that has perhaps been overshadowed by his many other accomplishments and writings—his work relating competition law to economic development. Until very recently, very few scholars in the United States and Europe paid serious attention to the role of competition law in the economic development of countries described as "developing" or "emerging," but here as in so many areas Kovacic has made important contributions on both the scholarly and policy levels. In my view, this area of his work also provides a key to understanding and appreciating his effectiveness on both levels. For example, I suggest that his success in helping to launch and effectively support the International Competition Network ("ICN") in the twenty-first century rests squarely on his experiences dealing with competition law and development in the 1990s. I here look briefly at Kovacic's writings in the area and their significance for the evolution of competition law on the global level.

Some scholars are known for their insights, some for their productivity, and some for the thoroughness of their analysis. Some administrators are known for their efficiency, others for their creativity and still others for their management skills. William Kovacic is known for all of the above and more. Scholars and administrators are often also noted for much less positive characteristics such as deviousness, inefficiency, laziness and so on. To my knowledge, no such negative images are associated with Bill Kovacic. He has combined the best of scholarship—such as profound insights, thorough study and penetrating analysis—with the best of administration (for example, effectiveness, leadership and creative problem-solving). He is not only a productive and successful scholar, but a world-renowned leader in competition law circles. This Festschrift celebrates a truly remarkable career that, we hope, will continue to be available to serve all for many more years.

This brief contribution to the Festschrift for Professor Kovacic highlights one aspect of his professional career that has perhaps been overshadowed by his many other accomplishments and writings—his work relating competition law to economic development. Until very recently, very few scholars in the United States and Europe paid serious attention to the role of competition law in the economic development of countries described as "developing" or "emerging," but here as in so many areas Kovacic has made important contributions on both the scholarly and policy levels. In my view, this area of his work also provides a key to understanding and appreciating his effectiveness on both levels. For example, I suggest that his success in helping to launch and effectively support the International Competition Network ("ICN") in the twenty-first century rests squarely on his experiences dealing with competition law and development in the 1990s. I here look briefly at Kovacic's writings in the area and on their significance for the evolution of competition law on the global level.

I. Contexts

Kovacic's writings that deal specifically with the role of competition law in economic development date primarily from the 1990s, and the issues raised there have been part of his agenda ever since. At the time, "globalization" was giving new importance to the role of competition in structuring societies.[1] For many, the idea was new and potentially alien. Many developing countries, particularly those in Africa, had long envisioned a "socialist" path to economic development, receiving "encouragement" and significant financial support from the Soviet Union in their economic development plans. Countries within the Soviet "bloc" had also had little acquaintance, at least recently, with the idea that competition should be the basic means of organizing economic activity. They had had little choice but to follow the Soviet model of a state-planned economy and to base their policies on the belief that this was the preferred road to economic development. In both arenas, the idea that law could be used to protect and enhance competition's role in structuring societies was virtually unknown. Even in the United States and Europe, many leading commentators had also supported the idea that government should play the central role in economic development.

The disintegration of the Soviet Union and the economic boom of the 1990s changed the discussion radically and rapidly. State socialist economic planning and the Soviet model of economic development had been discredited. The model had left the Soviet Union and its satellites with non-competitive economies, massive environmental degradation and poor populations. In addition, developing countries could no longer look to the Soviet Union for economic aid and support. The focus was now on competition—the market—as the path to economic development. Moreover, economic development funds now had to come primarily from the United States, Europe and international institutions such as the World

Bank. Advice and economic support from these institutions called for encouraging economic development through market mechanisms.

Virtually all relevant voices in the West supported the idea that competition law—i.e., a law designed to combat restraints on competition—should be part of this policy mix, but little was known about how it might work in a developing-country setting and what form or forms it should take in such a context. Predictably, most Western observers sought merely to export their own conceptions of competition law rules, methods and institutions to regimes now seeking to create market economies. Moreover, the temptations and pressures to follow a U.S.-centered approach were strong. The wave of enthusiasm for "the market" tended to obscure potential roles for governments in relation to economic development, and many commentators in "the West" assumed that releasing the market from state controls would automatically lead to the desired economic development.

Kovacic decided to go further and to ask questions that few others were asking. He asked more fundamental questions about how competition law might be expected to contribute to economic development under these new circumstances. Viewing globalization as a process that created new challenges and called for new responses, he began to explore in earnest competition law's potential roles in the process of economic development in post-Socialist and other countries emerging from state-oriented economies. Since then, he has paid significant attention to Eastern Europe as well as to a variety of newer entrants into the competition law world such as Mongolia and Zimbabwe.[2] As I read him, he was and is committed to the centrality of the market and to the values and objectives that have dominated "U.S." views of competition law in recent decades, but he has approached the developing country context with an open mind about how these goals could be achieved in these very different contexts.

II. Central Themes

Kovacic's writings about competition law and economic development reflect a wide range of concerns, interests and investigations. I mention here some themes in these works that seem to me to be particularly central. Each relates in one way or another to the role of "context" in thinking about competition law and economic development, and each reflects a pragmatic desire to "get things done—to make competition law work." [3]

1. Beyond the Moment

One element of the "context" theme relates to time. It has two components. One is the importance of locating competition law decisions temporally—that is, viewing them in relation to the factors of change and stability in which they must operate. Kovacic emphasized, for example, that thinking about, creating and implementing competition law in developing countries in the 1990s was subject to influences that were specific to the time period, and he argued that recognizing these influences was critical to achieving success. He noted, for example, the ways in which decades of state economic controls were distorting decisions about competition law, and he analyzed the ways in which these experiences impeded competition law progress.[4] He showed how officials steeped in the culture and practices of state planning had great difficulty approaching competition law from perspectives similar to those in the West.

Time is also important in another sense in Kovacic's writings about competition law and development. Kovacic emphasizes that strategies for the promotion of competition law in developing countries need to have a relatively long time-frame.[5] Many discussions of competition law in developing countries overlook the many adaptations that developing countries must make in order to construct an institutional basis for an effective competition law system. Kovacic argues that it is critically important not to move too rapidly. He uses his deep study of U.S. antitrust history to urge the value of allowing time for competition law systems to develop. He points out the dangers and harms of expecting too much, too soon. He notes that it took decades for U.S. antitrust law to develop effective and generally reliable standards and procedures, and this was in a political and legal context in which many key ingredients of an effective competition law—such as broad societal support for competition—were already present. Developing countries seldom, if ever, have such advantages.

2. Beyond Appearences

The broad "context" theme is related to—and implies—another more specific theme: The need to look beyond surface appearances when dealing with competition law in developing and transition contexts. Kovacic emphasizes the need to look at how legal institutions function in these countries. He notes a tendency of Western advisers merely to export their own statutes and assume that the words of the statute will generate outcomes in the developing country context that resemble the outcomes they generate in the United States or Europe. This necessarily leads advisers and developing country officials alike to overlook the specifics of the recipient country's situation. Courts in these countries may not operate as U.S. or European courts operate. Their institutions may have the same names as their Western counterparts, but they may have relatively little in common with them when the issue is how they function. As I have noted elsewhere, competition law contexts vary widely, and failure to recognize these specifics can only lead to mistakes that may retard rather than support achieving the desired goals.[6] Kovacic notes how the heady, confident mentality of the 1990s and beyond led many Western advisors to propose solutions without understanding either the problems they were intended to solve or the likely consequences of advocating such solutions.

3. The Need to Adapt

The first two themes lead directly to a third—a focus on the need to adapt thinking about competition law in emerging markets. These countries are not "the West." Kovacic recognizes that competition law there has to be understood differently from competition law in the United States and Europe and that, as a result, the prescriptions that have been successful in the United States and Europe may not be appropriate for developing countries. Harare (Zimbabwe) and Kiev (Ukraine) are neither Brussels nor Washington, DC, and Kovacic emphasizes many of the differences that tend to impact competition law development there. Developing countries have different traditions, different expectations, different economic structures and problems and very different institutional structures from their counterparts in the United States and Europe. As a consequence, the norms and institutions of competition law must correspond to the circumstances if they are to be effective. It is not enough for analysts and advisers to acknowledge differences, but then proceed to advocate the same competition law prescriptions that they developed or received in their home countries to the very different circumstances of the countries that are supposed to use them. It is necessary to think hard and creatively, adapting prescriptions to the circumstances. Merely noting differences is not sufficient. Effective policy requires adapting thinking to the differences.[7]

4. Technical Assistance: Institutions and Actors

Each of these themes relates to the provision of "technical assistance"—i.e., the activities of Western country "experts" in assisting and advising developing countries. Throughout his writings in the area Kovacic refers to his own experience as a Western technical advisor to competition law agencies in emerging countries. His numerous experiences in this role in countries as diverse as Zimbabwe, Ukraine and Mongolia have provided him with a wealth of examples and insights into what works and what does not in providing technical assistance to emerging market institutions. He assesses with often great insight some of the limitations and weaknesses of the way technical assistance relating to competition law was and often still is provided to developing countries. His experience and learning allow him to recognize and identify the difficulties and temptations of that role. His studies of this component of competition law dynamics on the global level are invaluable, replete as they are with valuable insights into the roles played by such advisors and into the obstacles to performing those roles effectively.[8]

He notes, for example, that Western competition law "advisors" often write about their experiences from a self-congratulatory perspective. The objective of the writing sometimes seems to be to show the importance of what the advisor has done more than it is to identify, let alone analyze, the actual issues and problems that remain after the advisor has left. Enactment of a statute with particular Western-sounding words and concepts is often presented as evidence of the advisor's "success." Such advisors appear not to be aware that in competition law, in particular, the wording of statutes is of limited value in achieving the desired results. In competition law, the real issues are often institutional rather than statutory.

Moreover, Western advisors often start from the assumption that by transmitting information about U.S. or other Western law they have performed a "noble" service. They may recount the difficulties they have had in drafting statutes: "people don't understand Western concepts," conditions are "primitive," officials are poorly trained officials and so on. This may be thought to further emphasize the "nobility" of their service. Kovacic shows that this approach is generally of little value and may in fact impede competition law progress. He emphasizes the importance of thinking carefully about the role of the technical advisor and about the ways in which such advisors can provide valuable services to the institutions, countries and people they have been sent to assist.

5. Values, Models, and Ultimate Goals

The emphasis on context in Kovacic's writings related to emerging competition law systems should not obscure his convictions about key elements of the U.S. approach to competition law and their potential value for competition law development elsewhere. As I read him, he is convinced that there is much to be learned from the U.S. experience with competition law and that certain of the lessons learned in that context should be central to thinking about competition law everywhere. What distinguishes Kovacic's writing about these issues from the writings of so many other U.S. writers, especially those writing about their experience as technical advisors, is that he reaches these conclusions on the basis of well-developed analysis and that he thinks carefully about how these competition law elements can actually be made to function effectively in an emerging market setting. He does not just seek to "export" U.S. antitrust law, but rather to make its tools, lessons and experiences available to and useful for those in developing countries who stand to benefit from them.

Two elements of this experience are central to his view. One is the role of economic analysis in competition law. Despite his emphasis on the differing contexts of competition law in developing countries and emerging markets, for example, he urges that economic analysis be central to the assessment of competition law issues. This is the basic lesson of the U.S. turn to economics as the core element of competition law analysis since the 1970s. It is important to distinguish here between two roles of economics in competition law: the descriptive and the normative. Economics performs a descriptive function. It tells competition law decision makers what has happened and what is likely to happen in the future as a result of conduct now.

The normative function is very different. In this role, economics determines whether conduct violates the law. It determines the norms of competition law. Failure to distinguish these two roles is a source of endless confusion in discussions of competition law, and the distinction bears directly on issues of competition law and development.[9]

With regard to the descriptive function, Kovacic recognizes the value to a developing country competition regime to have as much economic data as the government can reasonably afford, but he also recognizes that developing countries have limited resources and cannot be expected to spend large amounts on generating the kind of detailed factual analysis that has become the norm in developed countries, particularly in U.S. antitrust law. Many Western commentators overlook this critically important factor in the operation of a competition law system. They simply transpose U.S. and/or European principles onto developing countries, without taking into account the fact that in these countries this descriptive function must necessarily be more limited in its scope and depth. In advocating a level of economic analysis comparable to Western countries, such advisors and commentators risk appearing naive and/or unrealistic to their developing country listeners and readers. In contrast, Kovacic acknowledges the value of descriptive analysis, but notes that the costs of such analysis must be appropriate to the economic means of the country involved.

The normative function of economics raises quite distinct issues. Kovacic is convinced that legal institutions should intervene in markets through the use of competition law only in cases where economic harm can be identified with reasonable clarity. This credo of the U.S. antitrust "revolution" is central to his comments. If there is no identifiable economic harm, competition law should not intervene. Needless to say, the term "clarity" leaves much room for debate, but his basic point is firm. Competition law should not be used where there is no "economic harm." It should not be used to change social relations, rectify social inequality, protect state interests and other such interests. This significantly circumscribes the role of competition law, but Kovacic refers to the lessons of U.S. antitrust evolution to underscore the need for such constraints. Without them, as he sees it, competition law runs the risk of creating more harm than good.

A second element of U.S. experience that Kovacic emphasizes as critical to the success of competition law in developing countries is the "rule of law." This concept also obviously has a variety of meanings, but for Kovacic it seems to refer primarily to the (at least relative) independence of competition law officials from political and economic influences.

Kovacic urges the importance of developing institutions that can withstand external pressures and temptations and apply legal principles in a predictable and dependable way. He recognizes that for many developing countries such independence is remote, but he argues that moving toward it is necessary if competition law in a developing country is to be a useful tool of economic policy.

6. Communication

Implicit in and linked with the themes just discussed is a theme that I will call "the primacy of communication." On one level, this is a banal point, but closer inspection reveals that it can have far richer content. The point here is not just that people should talk to one another, but that the process of communication itself is critical to success of competition law in developing countries. Effective communication can provide developing countries with the kinds of information and experience that can be invaluable for them in building competition law. In order for this to be relevant and useful, however, technical advisors must listen. They must seek to understand the needs of those to whom they are giving advice. They are likely to be most effective where they engender confidence in those with whom they are dealing. For their part, developing country officials must take an active part in communication, explaining their own needs and circumstances rather than seeking merely to please Western commentators or portraying their own situations as more "advanced" (and thus similar to the West) then they actually are. Kovacic often refers to the difficulties of communication, and he recognizes that the effective transfer of knowledge and experience require that this be given much attention. His commitment to the International Competition Network reflects his belief in the importance of this communication factor for the evolution of competition law in developing countries.

III. Tools and Approaches

Kovacic's writings are based not only on broad reading and study, but also on extensive hands-on experience as an advisor in developing and post-Socialist countries. In various advisory capacities, he has gone to many such countries. He has been part of teams asked to draft competition laws and support their implementation, and he has been asked to evaluate the circumstances and evolution of competition law regimes there. This practical experience has combined with his deep knowledge of U.S. antitrust law development and his wide-ranging intellectual background to provide an exceptionally valuable set of approaches to the issues there and tools for analyzing them. Others have had extensive advising experience, but have maintained a relatively narrow set of perspectives on competition law development—based either on theory or on ideology or on confidence that one's own system could and should be exported to others—often all three together. Kovacic approaches the issues of competition law and development with three central perspectives and tools.

1. Openness and Curiosity

One part of the approach is its intellectual openness and modesty. Kovacic approaches the circumstances and conditions in the countries as much as possible on their own terms. He seeks to understand the issues from the perspective of those who will make the decisions about competition law and its development. What are their interests? What are their thoughts about the issues. I do not suggest for a moment that he views all ways of doing competition law as somehow equal or appropriate! He most certainly does not. Openness here refers to being willing to listen to the claims and questions of others and to seek to provide advice related specifically to those needs. His willingness to subject U.S. antitrust law to criticism on the basis of his experience in developing countries further reflects the open and critical approach that he takes to these issues.[10]

2. Value-Informed Pragmatism

This openness is closely associated with what might best be described as "value-laden pragmatism." His willingness to be open to the views of competition law officials and scholars in developing countries informs and is informed by a focus on the questions of "what works" and "what can we reasonably expect to work?" It is a highly pragmatic view that is more difficult to find in the literature in this area than one might expect. It differs fundamentally from the mindset of a Western advisor who focuses on his/her ability to convince others that they should follow a particular model of competition law developed in the West. In this latter view of the task of the advisor, the answers are givens, and the task is to promulgate them and to find followers. For Kovacic, only the basic principles are givens. The specifics have to be developed pragmatically. The specific elements of Western competition law systems cannot be expected to function effectively in developing countries.

This pragmatism compels a focus on institutions.[11] Effective competition law can become a reality only as a result of effective institutional structures. The structure, competence and morale within institutions will determine what kinds of decisions are made and the extent to which business decision makers adjust their conduct to more closely correspond to competition law norms. Kovacic focuses on how institutions work. He has less interest in the substantive provisions than in the institutional arrangements that generate actual competition law decisions. His experience in various roles at the United States Federal Trade Commission and as an adviser to many new competition law regimes has given him uniquely differentiated views and especially valuable insights into these institutional issues.

3. The Cross-Fertilization between Scholarship and Experience

The third central component of his approach to competition law in developing countries is the conscious interaction and cross-fertilization between theoretical and historical knowledge, on the one hand, and practical experience, on the other. I can think of no other competition law scholar who combines such an extraordinary range of experiences with such deep historical and theoretical knowledge, and this cross-fertilization adds enormously to the value of his writings on competition law and development. He intertwines these two elements in ways that are unique and valuable. In particular, he uses his deep knowledge of the history of antitrust law in the United States to call into question assumptions made by both Western advisers and developing country advice recipients. The value of Kovacic's deep knowledge of U.S. antitrust history can hardly be overemphasized in assessing his approach to the evolution of competition law in developing countries.[12] For example, he often notes the temptation to use competition law for purposes other than those of economic improvement.

IV. Some Consequences and Implications

This brief review of the themes of William Kovacic's writings on competition law and development can have value in many contexts. First, it adds, I hope, to an understanding of the work and importance of an exceptionally important figure in both U.S. and global competition law. Second, and at least as important, is its potential value for those seeking to understand the dynamics of competition law on the transnational level during the decades bracketing the turn of the twenty-first century. Kovacic has devoted much attention to competition law in developing countries because they are a key to the future development of competition law on the global level. For example, the analysis here points to some of the key factors in the evolution of the ICN and aids in understanding the role of the ICN. Kovacic played key roles in the creation of the ICN, and his experience with competition law in developing countries has greatly contributed to the effectiveness of that institution. Finally, and perhaps most fundamental, we have seen here the potential value of Kovacic's writings for identifying the challenges that developing countries face in moving toward more effective competition laws and more effective market structures. His writings could well be used as basic texts for decision makers in these countries, because they not only identify these obstacles, but they also show how some of these challenges can be more effectively met. Competition law officials and others seeking to develop competition law in these circumstances can do no better than to look carefully at Bill Kovacic's writings in the area.

A leading scholar and competition law official from a major European country (and a person not known for exaggeration or flattery) told me in the early 2000s that "Bill is a hero." I knew Kovacic was important, but "hero," I asked, how so? The official responded that Bill had played a key role in convincing European scholars and officials of the need to change the direction of competition law in Europe and to learn from the mistakes as well as the successes of U.S. antitrust history. A key factor in his effectiveness in doing this was the courage to listen to his European colleagues rather than preach to them and to relate these lessons to their needs. He has performed the same role with regard to competition law and developing countries. When I mentioned this to Bill, he did not accept the label of "hero", but I suspect that many would agree that it is appropriate.

NOTES

1   I discuss this evolution in detail in DAVID J. GERBER, GLOBAL COMPETITION: LAW, MARKETS AND GLOBALIZATION (Oxford U. Press, 2010, pbk, 2012) [hereinafter GERBER, GLOBAL COMPETITION].

2   For an example of the range of his comparative discussions, *see* William E. Kovacic, *Designing and Implementing Competition and Consumer Protection Reforms in Transition Economies: Perspectives from Mongolia, Nepal, Ukraine and Zimbabwe*, 44 DePaul L. Rev. 1197 (1995) [hereinafter Kovacic, *Designing and Implementing Competition and Consumer Protection Reforms in Transition Economies*].

3   *See, e.g.*, William E. Kovacic, *Getting Started: Creating New Competition Policy Institutions in Transition Economies*, 23 BROOKLYN J. INTL L. 403 (1997) [hereinafter Kovacic, *Getting Started*].

4   *See, e.g.*, William E. Kovacic, *The Competition Policy Entrepreneur and Law Reform in Formerly Communist and Socialist Countries*, 11 AM. U. J. INTL L. & POLICY 437 (1996) and Kovacic, *Designing and Implementing Competition and Consumer Protection Reforms in Transition Economies*, *supra* note 2.

5   *See, e.g.*, Kovacic, *Antitrust in Developing Countries, ibid.* at 1218-24.

6   GERBER, GLOBAL COMPETITION, *supra* note 1, at 262-9.

7   For discussion of comparative issues in competition law, *see* David J. Gerber, *Comparative Antitrust Law* in THE OXFORD HANDBOOK OF COMPARATIVE LAW 1193-1224 (M. Reimann and R. Zimmermann, eds., Oxford University Press, 2007).

8   *See, e.g.*, Kovacic, *Getting Started, supra* note 3.

9   Kovacic does not himself identify this distinction, but in my view it clarifies his analysis. For discussion, *see* David J Gerber, *Competition Law and the Institutional Embeddedness of Economics*, in ECONOMIC THEORY AND COMPETITION LAW 20-44 (Josef Drexl, ed., Cheltenham, UK, 2008).

10 *See, e.g.*, William E. Kovacic, *Lessons of Competition Policy Reform in Transition Economies for U.S. Antitrust Policy*, 74 ST. JOHN'S L. REV. 361 (2000).

11 *See, e.g.*, William E. Kovacic, *Creating Competition Policy: Betty Bock and the Development of Antitrust Institutions*, 66 ANTITRUST L.J. 231 (1997).

12 *See, e.g.*, William E. Kovacic, *The Modern Evolution of U.S. Competition Policy Enforcement Norms*, 71 ANTITRUST L.J. 377 (2003) and William E. Kovacic & Carl Shapiro, *Antitrust Policy: A Century of Legal and Economic Thinking*, 14 J. ECON. PERSP. 43 (1997).

Grading Antitrust Agency Performance: Bill Kovacic's Contribution and Commitment*

JAMES F. RILL

james.rill@bakerbotts.com
Senior Counsel, Baker Botts, LLP

JOHN M. TALADAY

john.taladay@bakerbotts.com
Partner, Baker Botts, LLP

Abstract

This article describes the leadership and continuing efforts by William Kovacic to focus attention on the desirability of retrospective analysis of the efficiency of government enforcement actions to stimulate and support realistic empirical analyses of these outcomes. His advocacy of undertakings to secure this result is described in the article. The article also cites some illustrative examples of analyses and addresses the challenges facing the attempt to secure realistic results. Such results do no merely serve as an agency "report card," but can provide a useful guide for future enforcement. In particular, the article contends that the "four Cs" hurdle (cost, complexity, confidentiality, and confession of error) should not deter the pursuit of the goal of reliable retrospective review. To paraphrase the words of Bill Kovacic, it is more important to know how the aircraft landed than to count how many took off.

I. Introduction

There are many dimensions of antitrust to which Bill Kovacic has contributed substantial, lasting, and continuing leadership. Noteworthy, for example, are his roles in fostering harmony and convergence of global competition policy and his scholarship in evaluating the trends of antitrust enforcement that transcend time, distinct presidential administrations, and enforcement agency heads. While it would be perhaps impossible to single out Chairman Kovacic's greatest contribution to antitrust, one particular subject that rightfully continues to attract intense focus in the world of competition policy is whether decisions to challenge, or not to challenge, individual matters result in a positive or negative effect on consumer welfare. Chairman Kovacic was a pioneer in advocating the need to evaluate not just the *number* of enforcement actions brought, but the *impact* of those actions. Or, to paraphrase Chairman Kovacic, it is more important how many airplanes land, than how many take off. As he put it succinctly:

> Debates about the U.S. federal competition agencies have revealed a serious need to return to the basic question of what is good performance . . . There is strikingly limited knowledge of what the federal agencies have done, there is no widely-accepted understanding of what competition agencies ought to do, and, even where criteria are expressly identified and applied, they tend to be unacceptably incomplete or to equate activity with accomplishment.[1]

His efforts to promote a correct standard for the evaluation of agency performance and his continued advocacy for the hard work such measurement requires are a very important part of his ongoing legacy. This brief article summarizes some of Chairman Kovacic's contributions to *ex post* agency performance evaluation and considers certain past agency efforts which indicate that this objective is attainable.

II. Evaluation by Significance

One commonly promoted measurement of an enforcement agency's performance is the extent to which an action generates headlines and, thereby, deemed "successes" in the public perception. Chairman Kovacic has questioned this metric and argued that the assessment should be based on the lasting impact of agency action rather than the immediate public display. He demonstrates this distinction by asking whether the highly visible, but essentially unsuccessful government attacks on IBM, the cereal industry, and the petroleum industry of the 1970s can be said to have the lasting embedded influence of the much less noted, at the time, *Otter Tail* and *Lorain Journal* antitrust actions.[2] He adds to this doctrinal assessment an evaluation of the immediate consumer welfare successes illustrated by the Federal Trade Commission's (or "FTC") challenges to Unocal and Bristol Myers.[3] In short, Chairman Kovacic evokes a longer view to grade the enforcement agencies, not a focus on the splashy "big case" action. As he summarizes the point, "Two suitable criteria would be economic impact and doctrinal significance. How did the case improve the economic well-being of consumers? Did the case address issues of importance to the development of antitrust law?"[4]

Chairman Kovacic supplements his fundamental approach with additional observations. He urges that an agency's own performance standards involve sufficient flexibility to take account of the dynamics of economic learning in the continuously evolving field of industrial organization.[5] As a corollary, he wrote, "Regular outlays for research and analysis serve to address the recurring criticism that competition policy lags unacceptably in understanding the commercial phenomena it seeks to address."[6] In addition, he explains that the doctrinal contribution of an agency is enhanced not merely by the cases it initiates, but by the studies and policy statements it produces. He offers as an interesting example, the FTC's report on interstate sales of wine, which he notes was cited more than twenty times by the Supreme Court in its decision overturning state sales restrictions.[7]

In sum, Chairman Kovacic has been the leading advocate for a principled assessment of agency performance based on the doctrinal and economic importance of its activities, not on a case count. The question that arises, of course, is how these activities can be measured by empirical research. Chairman Kovacic addresses that question as well.

III. The Need for Empirical Retrospective Analysis

The first apparent in-depth exhortation by Chairman Kovacic for systematic analysis of past enforcement efforts appears to have been published in 2001, prior to his becoming General Counsel of the Federal Trade Commission. He began his analysis with the position that:

> Making sound decisions about future public policy issues requires efforts to assess the wisdom of choices past. Understanding the effects of previous government initiatives can give public institutions valuable insights about designing future policies. Assuming as a matter of faith that chosen public policies produce beneficial outcomes is an unacceptable substitute for empirical testing.[8]

He expanded his recommendation by observing that competition issues are particularly well-suited for *ex post* analysis in light of the uncertain predictive nature of the field of antitrust and the dynamic influence of continued evolution of economic theory.[9]

As FTC General Counsel, he persisted in the effort to stimulate retrospective analyses, writing an exhaustive rebuttal of the "pendulum theory" of antitrust enforcement. In his conclusion he observed, "Among the most important vehicles for the federal agencies to promote policy improvements is to embrace a norm favoring *ex-post* assessment of outcomes."[10] Two years later, then-General Counsel Kovacic wrote, "[W]e must regard the analysis of past outcomes and practices as a natural and necessary element of responsible public administration. Even if definitive measurements are unattainable, there is considerable room for progress in determining whether actual experience bears out the assumptions that guide our acts."[11]

He expanded on the need for retrospective analysis in an interview while serving as Chairman of the Federal Trade Commission. The challenge, he explained, is to develop the techniques for identifying the criteria of performance and the correct methodology for measuring the achievement of the standards selected. He called for a substantial resource commitment for empirical studies in this effort.[12] Acknowledging the difficulties of evaluating the question of effective performance, he wrote, "Answering that question can force one to face very difficult methodological challenges, but getting convincing answers to those questions and tackling the hard methodologies issues are indispensible to resolving so many of the policy debates that take place today in a empirical vacuum."[13]

He reiterated his call for progress in identifying the mechanisms for retrospective performance evaluation in his 2009 George Mason Law Review article. There he called for a substantial resource commitment for the establishment of a database to provide a foundation for empirical performance review and analysis and once again underscored the need to undertake that evaluation.[14]

In short, Chairman Kovacic has been fully aware of the information shortfall and methodological challenges facing an analysis of whether an agency's performance has measured up to an acceptable level of contribution to antitrust doctrine and consumer welfare.

IV. Investing in the Continuing Effort

Chairman Kovacic has continued to foment interest and work in the area of accurate evaluation principles and methodology since his return to George Washington ("GW") University Law School. He reports that this topic will provide a major focus for the Competition Law Center at GW. Already, some outreach for private sector support is taking place.

Over the time that Chairman Kovacic has focused attention on the need for principled objective and empirical measurement, the Federal Trade Commission Bureau of Economics, outside economists and other antitrust authorities have conducted some retrospective merger studies, a few of which we will explore briefly in Section V. The work that has been done, however, is episodic and somewhat short of the systematic, broad-reaching empirical analysis called for by Chairman Kovacic.[15]

Perhaps the leading inhibition to tackling this work stems from the perceived magnitude of the task. Indeed, a number of threshold questions need to be addressed in facing the challenge of retrospective studies. First, is the effort worth undertaking? Stated a different way, is the learning to be derived from a retrospective study of sufficient value to justify the effort? The empirical work, in some cases, may need to be conducted a sufficient period of time after the original initiative such that the impact of the enforcement decision (i.e., action or inaction) can be measured. Take, for example, an analysis that might be done concerning the impact of the Supreme Court's *Leegin* decision.[16] There, the FTC and the U.S. Department of Justice ("DOJ") jointly filed an *amicus* brief arguing the Court should overrule *Dr. Miles* and subject resale price maintenance to a rule of reason—a recommendation that the Court adopted.[17] In the wake of that decision, a number of state antitrust enforcers announced that resale price maintenance agreements would continue to be considered a *per se* violation of state antitrust law, notwithstanding the *Leegin* decision's rule of reason application under the Sherman Act. Although this decision conceivably could have a vast impact on consumer welfare, it seems premature at this stage to determine how the rule of reason will actually play out in resale price maintenance cases.

On the other hand, undertaking a retrospective analysis a considerable period of time after the enforcement event raises two additional impediments to accurately evaluating the agency's initiative. Most apparently, the passage of time often introduces a plethora of intervening, extrinsic events that make an effective assessment of the agency action difficult to isolate, and subject to false evaluation of the action's impact on firm and business customers. Second, with the passage of time, legal and economic learning can evolve to such an extent that a challenge, or non-challenge, that might have seemed—or even been—appropriate at the time becomes tarnished by the evolution of learning. One can question the value of using a retrospective assessment to guide future agency conduct where the grade given agency performance may change in light of the intervening forces of economic and legal learning.

Nevertheless, Chairman Kovacic makes a persuasive case for undertaking the effort. Invoking Chairman Kovacic's suggestion to maintain a constant effort to empirically analyze past matters would help to smooth out some of these distortions, the same way that a financial investment in the stock market spread over time will moderate the volatility of the market. The work that can be achieved through consistent application will promote at least thoughtful analysis of agency priorities and enforcement efforts for the future, even with some inevitable shortcomings in the individual results.

The second question that arises is whether the work is worth doing in light of the methodological hurdles that arise in addition to the difficulties discussed above. These methodological hurdles can be addressed as "the four Cs": complexity, cost, confidentiality, and confession of error.

The first, complexity, has been considered above. As noted, the fact that the effort is difficult and that evolving facts and economic learning can clutter the landscape is not reason to reject the investment in retrospective evaluation. Some additional knowledge will be gained and consistent application, along with continuing improvements in methodology, can reduce the error rate. The evaluative process itself will evolve over time, through iteration and technical advancement, reducing the level of complexity and improving the reliability of results.

The second "C" factor is cost. The basic outreach, fact gathering and analytical evaluation would take not only time, but substantial financing. Whether the work is undertaken by the government agencies, the private sector, or a combination of both, the economic and legal skills that would need to be brought to bear for a quality product would be high. The expense would include both out-of-pocket costs as well as opportunity cost for the alternate use of those resources. The cost of inaction, however, currently is incalculable. What are the welfare costs to consumers of potentially misplaced decisions on mergers, horizontal agreements, joint venture policies, intellectual property licensing, statutory exemptions, etc.? At present, the answer is entirely unknown. Perhaps initial efforts at retrospective analysis would bear out past enforcement and policy decisions, demonstrating that they were correct. In that case, the work would not only have borne the fruit of historical self-assurance, but may well inform future policy refinements as the pace of business and technology marches forward and society demands further guidance. If past decisions, however, prove to have been off-base, agencies could quickly adjust to remedy (to the extent possible) past missteps and avoid ongoing or future errors. From this perspective, in either case the cost associated with the retrospective evaluation has the potential to create impacts that are high-value, far-reaching and welfare enhancing. It would be informative, albeit beyond the reach of this paper, to know what internal and out-of-pocket costs were involved in major projects that have been undertaken, such as the FTC's petroleum market studies. But when viewed in the broader perspective, the cost of undertaking such analysis is well justified.

The third "C" is confidentiality. The government agencies are confronted with statutory hurdles,[18] although those should erode with the passage of time in relation to any particular evaluation. Businesses whose data and particular internal documents might be sought legitimately could be concerned with the exposure of confidential trade information or business strategies, wholly apart from the question of time and cost involved in collecting and reviewing materials. This reluctance to provide internal information, for example, was a difficulty that confronted the authors of the Wood-Whish report on cross-border merger issues performed for the OECD in 1994.[19] But not all cases would present such challenges. The scope of publicly available information continues to expand. The internet makes access to much of this information easy and inexpensive. Third-party consultants and analysts specialize in collecting and assessing the information in many industries and their reports frequently are available at reasonable rates. Certain companies, and certain industries, may well have an incentive to help the agencies identify non-confidential information in support of these efforts. Thus, while some doors may be closed because of confidentiality, many others will be open.

Finally, the fourth "C" is confession of error, which can be a significant hurdle especially in the case of the enforcement agencies. Agencies may be reluctant to acknowledge past mistakes and may not want to be viewed as being critical of the efforts of prior administrations. This consideration, however, should be no more than a small pebble in the road. The agencies have confronted this issue in prior studies and have gone forward with the work. A regularized system of retrospective evaluation for the purpose of policy improvements would remove much of the stigma of identifying past missteps. What must be emphasized is the need for the agencies to overcome concerns with "confession" that would cause them to shield the work from the external world. A great portion of the value of the exercise is the extent to which the output is transparent and open for review, analysis, and debate by all stakeholders in the competition community. The role of business and business organizations, as well as consumer and labor organizations, and management professionals would be an important element of retrospective analysis. The nongovernmental community needs to be convinced that systemic retroactive analysis will promise a sufficient contribution to sound antitrust enforcement principles and practice to warrant a commitment of time and effort.

In sum, although these impediments to useful and accurate work cannot be overlooked, they should not stand in the way of both government and business embarking on the effort. So long as these shortcomings, such as they are, are acknowledged and accounted for, the product of retrospective evaluation should lead to a better understanding of the benefits of antitrust enforcement, or non-enforcement, initiatives.

Notably, the United States is well positioned to lead the effort to embrace the benefits of retrospective analysis. With an enforcement history extending beyond 100 years, the notion that antitrust laws are necessary to protect consumers has long had credibility in the U.S. As such, the U.S. agencies enjoy support and sustainability that is lacking in some other jurisdictions, for example, antitrust enforcement authorities in developing jurisdictions where they are still working to justify the existence of antitrust laws. A self-critical effort by the U.S. could add to the credibility of U.S. antitrust enforcement generally and help foreign agencies promote the benefits of competition law enforcement. The initiative could be further enhanced by the international cross-fertilization of results. The proliferation of antitrust regimes around the world and the desire of newly created agencies functioning under recently adopted statutes to study the experience of more established jurisdictions can be served by studies as urged by Chairman Kovacic. Indeed, the older jurisdictions could themselves profit by *ex post* empirical analyses of matters considered by the newer agencies.

V. Past Efforts at Retrospective Analysis

Despite the above challenges, in recent years there have been a number of studies aimed at analyzing the competitive effects of past merger decisions. Those conducting the studies have approached the analysis from different perspectives. Some studies have looked to the impact of merger decisions in individual cases or industries. In other instances, enforcement agencies have taken more of an across-the-board approach, with the aim of providing a broad self-assessment of the agency's merger enforcement record. Still another method has been to approach the analysis from a quantitative basis. While none of these efforts has approached the kind of comprehensive, ongoing retrospective evaluation advocated by Chairman Kovacic, they demonstrate that it is possible to scope out an empirical initiative that will achieve broader objectives of conducing retrospective analysis, and also support the principle that the results justify the investment.

1. Retrospective Evaluation of Individual Cases or Specific Industries

A. Whirlpool/Maytag Merger

Following the U.S. DOJ's oft-criticized decision to allow the merger of appliance manufacturers Whirlpool and Maytag, there have been attempts to determine whether the merger resulted in anticompetitive effects, as some critics outside of DOJ feared.[20] One such attempt was an empirical evaluation entitled "The Price Effects of a Large Merger of Manufacturers: A Case Study of Whirlpool-Maytag."[21] The authors relied upon data from the NPD Group to estimate the price effects of the merger in the four major appliance categories where the change in market concentration was highest: clothes washers and dryers (which was the focus of DOJ's investigation), refrigerators and dishwashers.[22]

The study concluded that there had been modest price increases for dishwashers and somewhat larger price increases for dryers, where post-merger prices increased approximately 7% and 14%, respectively.[23] The study did not reveal systematic price increases for refrigerators or washers. The authors concluded that "the factors cited by the DOJ [as likely to prevent anticompetitive effects] do not appear to have been sufficient to maintain pre-merger price levels for either clothes dryers or dishwashers."[24] The authors also indicated that they were somewhat surprised to see a large and systematic price increase in dryers but not in washers, given the similar pre-merger market shares for the two product types. They postulated that this may be due to the fact that the parties were less successful in the growing category of front-loading washers; their strengths both rested with traditional top-load varieties where demand is decreasing. The study also revealed a large reduction in the number of SKUs post-merger, particularly in washers and dryers, leading the authors to suggest that a reduction in variety may have followed the merger.[25] It is difficult to assess the robustness of the study or to determine whether the analysis properly isolated price-related effects of the merger from other (e.g., cost-related or quality-adjusted) influences. A retrospective review reflecting different findings was conducted by the Antitrust Division of the U.S. Department of Justice in close proximity to the consummation of the transaction. The study, conducted by the Economic Analysis Group, noted the increasing costs of important materials used in the manufacture of laundry machines, BLS data showing that laundry machine prices dropped in the two years since the merger, the costs associated with increasing machine energy efficiency, and featured prices at major retail outlets for machines of quality comparable to premerger offerings.[26] Thus, we cite these studies not for the reliability of the conclusions reached, but rather as examples of a retrospective merger analyses designed to evaluate both the specific outcome of a merger as well as the underlying basis for the agency's decision.

B. Hospital Mergers

In response to a string of failed attempts to challenge proposed hospital mergers in the late 1990s, the U.S. FTC announced in 2002 plans to increase scrutiny of past hospital mergers to determine whether the mergers benefitted patients or allowed hospitals to raise the cost of care.[27] That same year, the agency established a task force responsible for reviewing consummated hospital mergers to identify potential anticompetitive price increases.[28]

One of the consummated transactions reviewed by the taskforce was the 2000 merger of Evanston Northwestern Hospital Corporation, which owned Evanston Hospital and Glenbrook Hospital, with Highland Park Hospital.[29] As a result of its retrospective study, the

FTC concluded that the merger had anticompetitive effects and filed a complaint alleging that the transaction had substantially lessened competition for acute-care, in-patient hospital services sold to private payors in the hospitals' suburban Chicago location.[30] At trial, the Administrative Law Judge ("ALJ") held that the merger had in fact substantially lessened competition in the product and geographic markets defined by the FTC, in violation of Section 7 of the Clayton Act.[31] The FTC Commissioners unanimously affirmed the ALJ's finding, but chose a non-structural remedy rather than the divestiture sought by the Commission staff before the ALJ.[32] The order required the hospitals to maintain separate payor negotiating teams (one for Evanston and Glenbrook and another for Highland Park), restricted the teams' ability to demand equal terms or prices for the hospitals' separate contracts, and called for the establishment of a firewall to prevent the sharing of contract terms between the two teams.[33]

The FTC's Bureau of Economics published a retrospective case study of the Evanston/Highland merger in January 2009.[34] The study concluded that the econometric evidence "strongly suggests" that the transaction led to increased market power for the merged entity, "giving it the ability to negotiate higher prices"—a conclusion which the study described as "consistent with the majority of non-econometric evidence presented [at] trial."[35] The FTC's work provides a useful example of retrospective merger analysis and re-evaluation of past outcomes that led to corrective efforts through enforcement action. It also is likely to guide future agency decision-making in hospital mergers.

2. Self-Evaluation of Agency Programs

A. Canada

In August 2011 the Canadian Competition Bureau ("CCB") completed a several-year long study aimed at improving the effectiveness and implementation of merger remedies.[36] As part of its Merger Remedies Study, the CCB reviewed all cases between 1995 and 2005 in which remedies were ordered and implemented. The CCB did not conduct an independent analysis of market conditions following the implementation of a remedy, but instead relied upon input gathered from various participants in the affected markets. CCB staff members conducted a total of 135 interviews divided among four constituent groups. The four groups included: (1) merged entities; (2) customers; (3) purchasers of divested assets or other market participants impacted by the remedy (e.g., licensees of IP); and (4) third-party market participants (e.g., suppliers).[37] In its summary of the study the CCB explained that, given the number of interviews and individual viewpoints conveyed, it did not attempt to draw conclusions about the overall effectiveness of merger remedies, noting that the study made clear that remedies have been extremely effective at restoring competition in some cases, while less effective in other cases. Instead, the CCB explained that "[t]he major contribution of the study has been to assist the Bureau in identifying factors that tend to improve the effectiveness of remedies, as well as those factors that tend to detract from their effectiveness."[38]

In discussing the methodology, the CCB was rather candid about some of the limitations it faced in conducting the study. For example, cases after 2005 were excluded to ensure that adequate time had passed to enable an accurate assessment of the merger remedy. And of those cases within its target timeframe, the CCB had to eliminate some cases because the agency was unable to collect sufficient information from market participants to analyze the effectiveness of the remedy in those instances. For example, in those matters where remedies were ordered in several geographic markets, agency staff did not always have the ability to interview an adequate number of market participants in each geographic market and, as such, the CCB excluded those markets from the study.[39]

Despite these limitations, the CCB's summary suggests the study was still a valuable and successful exercise that will assist the agency in future matters requiring remedies. "The remedies study has been of significant value in confirming that many of the Bureau's existing policies and procedures relating to the design and implementation of merger remedies are effective, and in identifying areas where such policies and procedures could be more effective."[40] The CCB also plans to use the knowledge gained from the study to update the agency's *Information Bulletin on Merger Remedies in Canada* which describes "the general principles applied by the Bureau when it seeks, designs, and implements remedies."[41] Although this effort falls short of the objective empirical evaluation envisioned by Chairman Kovacic, it is important for its scope as it reflects a long-term, broad-ranging effort to capture the results of a significant number of agency enforcement actions and the effect of those actions on outcomes.

B. European Union

The European Commission's DG Comp also carried out a remedies study, the results of which it published in October 2005.[42] The stated objective of the study "was to review with the benefit of hindsight the design and implementation of commitments offered and accepted by the Commission in previous cases so as to identify areas where further improvements to the Commission's existing merger remedies policy and procedures may be necessary in future."[43] To that end, "[t]he focus of the study was to identify what factors and/or processes may have positively or negatively influenced the effective design and implementation of merger remedies."[44]

The study analyzed 40 decisions adopted by the Commission in the five-year period 1996 to 2000. This accounted for slightly less than half, or 44%, of the merger decisions involving remedies during that time period.[45] These 40 cases included a total of 96 required remedies which DG Comp classified into four categories depending on the intended competitive effect of the remedy: (1) commitments to transfer a market position (e.g., divestitures or long-term exclusive licensing); (2) commitments to exit from a joint venture; (3) commitments to grant access (e.g., to infrastructure of technical platforms); and (4) a small number of "other" remedies (e.g., removing a brand from the market).[46] In selecting cases for inclusion in the study, the agency made an effort to have a balanced sampling of remedies with respect to three criteria, including the type of remedy, the number of remedies accepted in Phase I versus Phase II, and the industrial sectors involved.[47] For the 40 cases included within the study, members of DG Comp conducted a total of 145 interviews, the bulk of which were divided amongst the committing parties or sellers, licensors, or grantors; the buyers, licensees or grantees; and the trustees.[48]

As with the CCB's study, DG Comp was candid about the limitations of its study's methodology, citing three limitations in particular.[49] First, for certain remedies it was difficult to make a comprehensive determination of the market outcome in the absence of a new in-depth investigation of the market. Second, external factors sometimes contributed to market changes, making it difficult to determine whether the external factors or the ordered remedy had a relatively greater impact on market conditions.[50] Third, to analyze the effect of a remedy, the study tried to compare actual market developments with the developments that likely would have occurred absent the remedy (i.e., the counter-factual scenario), which necessarily required some level of speculation.

Notwithstanding these methodological limitations, the agency felt the study met its goal of helping DG Comp to identify those remedies that were most effective, as well as identifying remedies which require further improvement in their design or implementation. Commenting on the success of the study, then-Competition Commissioner Neelie Kroes remarked that the study would provide guidance for future cases: "The findings of this important study will influence our future action in the field of merger remedies. It demonstrates the Commission's commitment to evaluate critically and transparently its past policy and practice in order to draw lessons from it."[51]

C. United Kingdom

The UK's Office of Fair Trading ("OFT") and Competition Commission ("CC") have conducted a number of interesting retrospective merger studies. The reports are a hybrid of the individual case study approach and the programmatic approach.[52] We focus here on the study with the largest number of cases examined, the 2005 report entitled "*Ex post* evaluation of mergers."[53] The study was conducted by PricewaterhouseCoopers on behalf of the OFT, the CC and the Department of Trade and Industry ("DTI").

The scope of the report included ten individual case studies. Each of the ten cases was among the 29 mergers from 1991 to 2002 that the CC cleared without remedies after a second phase review.[54] The agencies commissioned the report, believing the findings would be useful in three respects. One, the study tested the CC's belief that the merger would not substantially lessen competition. Two, where there has been no substantial lessening of competition, it tested whether this was due to factors cited by the CC, or whether other competitive constraints were paramount. Three, if there has been a lessening of competition, it revealed how, and how quickly, market participants responded. A goal of the study was that these findings would help the CC "to learn more about how markets respond to a significant increase in market concentration. Such information can be extremely useful in helping competition authorities improve their assessment of the competitive effects of mergers."[55] The authors implemented this study using an approach similar to that used in both the CCB and DG Comp studies: they interviewed various market participants for each case. This study was particularly focused on customer feedback, and also included interviews of the merged parties, their competitors, and industry experts (including regulators).[56] The evaluation found that qualitative evidence suggested that there were no long-term competition concerns that arose after the CC's clearance decisions. The study concluded that the CC's forecasts about entry and expansion were "generally sound, but that the CC had found it more difficult to predict the circumstances where buyer power was likely to act as a significant competitive constraint."[57]

This report, too, cited limitations to the study, including the small sample size. The report also acknowledged the fact that the chosen cases may be an unrepresentative sampling since they did not include mergers cleared by the OFT without reference the CC, nor did it include mergers that the CC determined were against the public interest.[58] Here again, in spite of these limitations, the authors concluded that the "study is capable of making an important contribution to the understanding of how markets respond to large increases in concentration, and how this information might be used by competition authorities to improve their analysis of mergers."[59]

In addition to the above study, the OFT also takes another approach to attempting to measure the impact of merger enforcement. The OFT regularly consults merger case teams to estimate *ex ante* the impact of Phase I merger decisions. The OFT estimates the "impact of its work in the areas of competition law enforcement, merger control, consumer protection enforcement, and market investigations in terms of monetary savings (or direct financial benefits) to consumers."[60] It publishes these estimates in its annual report and in its Positive Impact notes. For the 2008 to 2011 period, the OFT estimates that its work in the area of merger control resulted in average annual consumer savings of £90 million.[61]

3. Qualitative Policy-Oriented Analysis

The Commentary on the Horizontal Merger Guidelines, jointly issued by the U.S. DOJ and FTC in March 2006, offered yet another approach to *ex post* merger review.[62] Rather than conducting a quantitative review, the report provides a qualitative assessment by looking to past mergers and examining how the agencies apply the Guidelines in particular investigations. The purpose of the report was "to enhance the transparency of the analytical process by which the Agencies apply the antitrust laws to horizontal mergers."[63]

After providing an overview of the fundamental legal principles that govern the agencies' merger enforcement, the Commentary looks to the various elements identified by the Guidelines as relevant to merger analysis, including market definition and concentration; the potential adverse competitive effects of mergers, i.e., coordinated interaction and unilateral effects; entry conditions; and efficiencies. Following each topic, there is a summary of a related merger investigation conducted by one of the agencies, and a discussion of how the Guidelines' principles were applied in each of those cases.

By examining prior mergers in this fashion, the benefit of this retrospective analysis is a more thorough understanding of how antitrust agencies apply merger law. As Thomas Barnett, then-Assistant Attorney General in charge of DOJ's Antitrust Division remarked, "The business community can see how the agencies have applied the Horizontal Merger Guidelines to a wide range of specific factual circumstances."[64]

VI. Conclusion

Difficult though the challenge may be, good public policy requires that regulators endeavor to evaluate the impact of their decisions, including efforts to conduct empirical analysis of the outcomes that have resulted from agency action or inaction. As the above examples of retrospective analysis suggest — and Chairman Kovacic has long asserted — the challenges reflected in the "four Cs" are not insurmountable, particularly when the scope and objectives of the *ex post* review are defined properly. At the same time, the efforts to date have fallen well short of the required standard for a variety of reasons, not the least of which is a lack of commitment to make retrospective analysis part of enforcement agencies' core mission. A catalog of past undertakings and the methodologies used would at least be a start. It is understood that this review is likely to be one of the projects of the Competition Law Center under the leadership of Chairman Kovacic.[65]

Chairman Kovacic has been and continues to be the leading advocate of exploring the impact of where we have been to cast a bright light on where we are going. He carries this effort forward in his current position at George Washington University. The path he advocates and the strong exhortation he has expressed makes a convincing case for support and collateral efforts. The thirst for knowledge about how the airplanes have landed will be an important part of Bill Kovacic's legacy.

NOTES

*   The authors would like to gratefully acknowledge and thank Stacy Turner, Donna Loop and Jane Antonio for their assistance with this article.

1   William E. Kovacic, *Rating the Competition Agencies: What Constitutes Good Performance*, 16 Geo. Mason L. Rev. 903, 904 (2009).

2   *Id.* at 908, 912-13. For an extended discussion of the significance of the "small case," with a focus on *Otter Tail*, *see* William E. Kovacic, *The Modern Evolution of U.S. Competition Policy Enforcement Norms*, 71 Antitrust L.J., 377, 453-55 (2003).

3   Kovacic, *supra* note 1, at 912.

4   *Id.* at 913.

5   *Id.* at 919.

6   William E. Kovacic, *Achieving Better Practices in the Design of Competition Policy Institutions*, 50 Antitrust Bull. 511, 515 (2005).

7   Kovacic, *supra* note 1, at 921 (citing Granholm v. Heald, 544 U.S. 460 (2005)).

8   William E. Kovacic, *Evaluating Antitrust Experiments: Using Ex Post Assessments of Government Enforcement Decisions to Inform Competition Policy*, 9 GEO. MASON L. REV. 843, 843 (2001) (citations omitted).

9   *Id. passim.*

10 Kovacic, *supra* note 2, at 475.

11 Kovacic, *supra* note 6, at 513. The same year, he wrote, "One noteworthy element of the research agenda ought to be the examination of the consequences of past enforcement decisions, both to prosecute and not to prosecute. Retrospective assessments of enforcement choices are necessary to test the wisdom of past interventions and to guide future policy development." William E. Kovacic, *Measuring What Matters: The Federal Trade Commission and Investments in Competition Policy Research and Development*, 72 ANTITRUST L.J. 861, 866 (2005) (citation omitted).

12 *Interview with William E. Kovacic, Chairman, Federal Trade Commission*, ANTITRUST SOURCE (Section of Antitrust Law, American Bar Association) Aug. 2008, at 7, 17, *available at* http://www.americanbar.org/content/dam/aba/publishing/antitrust_source/Aug08_FullSource8_6f.authcheckdam.pdf.

13 *Id.* at 7.

14 Kovacic, *supra* note 1, at 924.

15 A fair amount of legal articles on this topic have been published, a good cross section of which has been identified by Kovacic. *See generally*, 68 ANTITRUST L.J. 1-237, 621-1061 (2001).

16 Leegin Creative Leather Products, Inc. v. DSKS, Inc., 551 U.S. 887 (2007).

17 *See* http://www.justice.gov/atr/cases/f221000/221027.pdf.

18 *See e.g.*, Hart-Scott-Rodino Antitrust Improvements Act of 1976, § 7A(h), 15 U.S.C. § 18a(h); Antitrust Civil Process Act of 1976, 15 U.S.C. § 1313; Federal Trade Commission Act, §§ 6(f), 21, 15 U.S.C. §§ 46(f), 57b-2.

19 RICHARD WHISH & DIANE WOOD, MERGER CASES IN THE REAL WORLD – A STUDY OF MERGER CONTROL PROCEDURES (OECD, 1994).

20 One of the authors, James Rill, acted as lead antitrust counsel to Whirlpool in this transaction.

21 Orley C. Ashenfelter, Daniel S. Hosken and Matthew C. Weinberg, *The Price Effects of a Large Merger of Manufacturers: A Case Study of Whirlpool-Maytag* (NATIONAL BUREAU OF ECONOMIC RESEARCH, Working Paper No. w17467 Oct. 2011) ("NBER Case Study of Whirlpool-Maytag").

22 NPD Group collects its data from "a nationally representative sample of national and regional major appliance retailers." *Id.* at 7.

23 *Id.* at 22.

24 *Id.* In its statement announcing its decision to allow the merger to proceed, the DOJ discusses the primary competitive factors influencing its decision. U.S. Department of Justice Antitrust Division, Statement on the Closing of Its Investigation of Whirlpool's Acquisition of Maytag (Mar. 29, 2006) *available at* http://www.justice.gov/atr/public/press_releases/2006/215326.htm.

25 NBER Case Study of Whirlpool-Maytag, *supra* note 21, at 22.

26 Address by Assistant Attorney General Thomas O. Barnett, Lewis Bernstein Memorial Lecture, 14-19 (June 26, 2008).

27 New York Times, U.S. to Step Up Antitrust Enforcement on Health Care (Aug. 2, 2002), *available at* http://www.nytimes.com/2002/08/09/business/us-to-step-up-antitrust-effort-on-health-care.html (reporting on interview with then-Chairman Muris who stated that "I've always thought it made sense for the government to go back and look at its work."). *See also* Everything Old is New Again: Health Care and Competition in the 21st Century, Remarks of Chairman Muris, Federal Trade Commission delivered at The Seventh Annual Competition in Health Care Forum, Chicago, Illinois, November 7, 2002, *available at* http://www.ftc.gov/speeches/muris/murishealthcarespeech0211.pdf.

28 FTC Press Release, Federal Trade Commission Announces Formation of Merger Litigation Task Force (Aug. 28, 2002), *available at* http://www.ftc.gov/opa/2002/08/mergerlitigation.shtm.

29 The FTC's Bureau of Economics conducted two other retrospective studies of hospital mergers. *See* Aileen Thompson, *The Effect of Hospital Mergers on Inpatient Prices: A Case Study of the New Hanover-Cape Fear Transaction* (Federal Trade Commission, Bureau of Economics, Working Paper No. 295 Jan. 2009), *available at* http://www.ftc.gov/be/workpapers/wp295.pdf, Steven Tenn, *The Price Effects of Hospital Mergers: A Case Study of the Sutter-Summit Transaction* (Federal Trade Commission, Bureau of Economics, Working Paper No. 293 Nov. 2008), *available at* http://www.ftc.gov/be/workpapers/wp293.pdf. For a discussion of other *ex post* reviews of hospital mergers, *see also* ANTITRUST, Merger Retrospective Studies: A Review, Vol. 23, No. 1 (Fall 2008), at 39-40. The Bureau of Economics also has conducted retrospective merger reviews for other industries. *See, e.g.*, Federal Trade Commission, Bureau of Economics, The Petroleum Industry: Mergers, Structural Change, and Antitrust Enforcement: A Report of the Staff of the Federal Trade Commission Bureau of Economics (Aug. 2004), *available at* http://www.ftc.gov/os/2004/08/040813mergersinpetrolberpt.pdf.

30 In the Matter of Evanston Northwestern Healthcare, Complaint, 2004 WL 1124294 (FTC) (Feb 10, 2004), *available at* http://www.ftc.gov/os/caselist/0110234/040210emhcomplaint.pdf.

31 In the Matter of Evanston Northwestern Healthcare, Initial Decision of Stephen J. McGuire, Chief Admin. L. Judge, 2005 WL 2845790 (FTC) (Oct. 20, 2005), *available at* http://www.ftc.gov/os/adjpro/d9315/051021idtextversion.pdf.

32 In the Matter of Evanston Northwestern Healthcare, 2007 WL 228195 (FTC) (Aug. 6, 2007), *available at* http://www.ftc.gov/os/adjpro/d9315/070806opinion.pdf. *See also* Commission Order, 2007-3 Trade Cases P75814, 2007 WL 2286196 (Aug. 6, 2007), *available at* http://www.ftc.gov/os/adjpro/d9315/070806order.pdf.

33 In the Matter of Evanston Northwestern Healthcare, Opinion of the Commission on Remedy, 2008 WL 1991995 (FTC) (Apr. 28, 2008), *available at* http://www.ftc.gov/os/adjpro/d9315/080428commopiniononremedy.pdf.

34 Deborah Haas-Wilson & Christopher Garmon, *Two Hospital Mergers on Chicago's North Shore: A Retrospective Study* (Federal Trade Commission, Bureau of Econ., Working Paper No. 294, Jan. 2009), *available at* http://www.ftc.gov/be/workpapers/wp294.pdf.

35 *Id*. at 21.

36 This was an internal study because confidentiality provisions of the Competition Act prohibit the CCB from releasing much of the information gathered as part of the agency's review. The CCB did, however, publish a summary of the study which is available on its website. Competition Bureau Merger Remedies Study (Aug. 2011) ("CCB Merger Remedies Study"), *available at* http://www.competitionbureau.gc.ca/eic/site/cb-bc.nsf/eng/03392.html.

37 *Id*. at 2.

38 *Id*. at 4.

39 *See generally* Section 2 of the CCB Merger Remedies Study for a discussion of study methodology, as well as the limitations noted above.

40 *Id*. at 8.

41 Canadian Competition Bureau, Information Bulletin on Merger Remedies in Canada (Sept. 2006), *available at* http://www.competitionbureau.gc.ca/eic/site/cb-bc.nsf/eng/02170.html.

42 DG Comp, European Commission, Merger Remedies Study, Public Version (Oct. 2005) ("EU Merger Remedies Study"), *available at* http://ec.europa.eu/competition/mergers/legislation/remedies_study.pdf. DG Comp noted at the outset of its report that there are virtually no public retrospective merger studies from any competition regime worldwide. It cited the "pioneering work" of the U.S. Federal Trade Commission and that agency's attempt to lessen this void with its 1999 divestiture study. *See* Federal Trade Commission, Bureau of Economics, A Study of the Commission's Divestiture Process (Aug. 1999), *available at* http://www.ftc.gov/os/1999/08/divestiture.pdf. DG Comp indicated that its own study was intended to build on the FTC's work and to contribute to the merger debate.

43 EU Merger Remedies Study, *supra* note 42, at 11.

44 *Id*.

45 *Id*. at 11-12.

46 *Id*. at 17-19.

47 *Id*. at 12.

48 *Id*. at 14-15.

49 *Id*. at 16-17.

50 For example, in one case, a remedy to transfer a market position was followed by the entry of a significant competitor two years later. The report notes that even a full-fledged market investigation would not resolve with certainty which factor had the greatest impact. *Id*.

51 Press Release, European Commission, Mergers: Commission analysis of past merger remedies provides guidance for future cases (Oct. 21, 2005), *available at* http://europa.eu/rapid/pressReleasesAction.do?reference=IP/05/1327.

52 The OFT and CC also have conducted other retrospective merger studies. *See* Competition Commission, Evaluation of the Commission's past cases (Jan 2008), *available at* http://www.competition-commission.org.uk/assets/bispartners/competitioncommission/docs/pdf/non-inquiry/our_role/analysis/evaluation_report.pdf (a study of four cases conducted by the CC as a follow-up to the 2005 report discussed above). Deloitte, Review of merger decisions under the Enterprise Act 2002 (Mar. 2009), *available at* http://www.competition-commission.org.uk/assets/bispartners/competitioncommission/docs/pdf/non-inquiry/our_role/analysis/review_merger_decisions.pdf. Deloitte conducted this study which analyzed eight mergers on behalf of the CC, OFT, and the Department for Business, Enterprise and Regulatory Reform. Lear Consulting, The Ex-Post Evaluation of Two Merger Decisions (Sept. 2011), *available at* http://www.competition-commission.org.uk/assets/bispartners/competitioncommission/docs/2011/11_09_20_ex_post_evaluation_of_two_merger_decisions.pdf. *See also* Organization for Economic Cooperation and Development, Directorate for Financial and Enterprise Affairs Competition Committee, Roundtable on Impact Evaluation of Merger Decisions, Note by the Delegation of the United Kingdom ("OECD Roundtable - UK Note") (Jun. 2011) (further discussing the UK's attempts at retrospective merger reviews).

53 PricewaterhouseCoopers LLP, Ex post evaluation of mergers: A report prepared for the Office of Fair Trading, Department of Trade and Industry, and the Competition Commission (Mar. 2005) ("PWC"), *available at* http://www.oft.gov.uk/shared_oft/reports/comp_policy/oft767.pdf.

54 *Id*. at 1.

55 *Id.* at 1, 5.

56 *Id.* at 2.

57 OECD Roundtable - UK Note, *supra* note 52, at 6 (discussing conclusions reached by PWC in 2005 study).

58 *See* PWC, *supra* note 53, at 9-10 for a fuller discussion of the study's limitations.

59 *Id.* at 10.

60 OECD Roundtable - UK Note, *supra* note 52, at 5, fn 15.

61 OFFICE OF FAIR TRADING, Positive Impact 10/11, Consumer benefits from the OFT's work (July 2011) at 5, *available at* http://www.oft.gov.uk/shared_oft/reports/Evaluating-OFTs-work/OFT1354.pdf. The U.S. DOJ issues a similar report on the annual fines earned through cartel enforcement, but neither of the U.S. antitrust agencies attempts to quantify consumer savings brought on by merger enforcement.

62 FEDERAL TRADE COMMISSION AND U.S. DEPARTMENT OF JUSTICE, Commentary on the Horizontal Merger Guidelines (2006), *available at* http://www.ftc.gov/os/2006/03/CommentaryontheHorizontalMergerGuidelinesMarch2006.pdf. The Commentary provided additional clarification on how the agencies applied the analytical framework laid out in the agencies joint publication, The 1992 Horizontal Merger Guidelines, later updated with the 2010 Horizontal Merger Guidelines, *available at* http://www.ftc.gov/os/2010/08/100819hmg.pdf.

63 *Id.* at v.

64 Press Release, Federal Trade Commission, FTC, DOJ Issue Joint Commentary on the Horizontal Merger Guidelines (Mar. 27, 2006), *available at* http://www.ftc.gov/opa/2006/03/mergercom.shtm.

65 At least one effort to stimulate nongovernmental analysis has been launched by Edwin Rockefeller and some colleagues in the formation of the Antitrust Research Foundation. "Economic Studies: New Research Foundation Will Study, Evaluate Results of Antitrust Enforcement," 101 ANTITRUST & TRADE REG. Rep. (BNA) No. 2522, at 531 (Oct. 28, 2011).

The Next Generation of Global Competition Law

SPENCER WEBER WALLER[*]

swalle1@luc.edu

Professor and Director, Institute for Consumer Antitrust Studies, Loyola University Chicago School of Law

Abstract

Bill Kovacic has played a key role in helping us move from the world of 1991 to the world of the present where over one hundred twenty jurisdictions have some recognizable form of competition law. This has been the one of the principal, but by no means the only, topic of his work as an academic, then as general counsel, commissioner, and chairman of the FTC, and now back in academia. Kovacic has studied competition systems around the world, advised many of them, traveled relentlessly to dozens of these jurisdictions, and represented the FTC and his universities in interacting with these jurisdictions in countless public and private fora for these same two decades. This essay focuses on the insights that Kovacic brought back from his travels and embodied in his scholarship. I also focus on how his work has both documented and affected transition economies enacting and enforcing competition law for the first time, their advisors from more experienced jurisdictions, and the more mature competition jurisdictions themselves. Finally, I offer a brief outline of a research agenda to help evaluate how well both old and new jurisdictions have applied these insights over the past twenty years and suggestions for the next twenty years.

The Soviet Union dissolved on December 26, 1991. This accelerated a trend toward both the development of market economies and competition law to protect those economies. No one could have predicted that within twenty years most of the world's trading economies would have adopted recognizable forms of competition law including the former nations of the Soviet Union, the centrally planned economies of Central and Eastern Europe, a host of transition economies in Africa, South America, and Asia, and such emerging economic giants as Brazil, China, and India.

Bill Kovacic has played a key role in helping us move from the world of 1991 to the world of the present where over one hundred twenty jurisdictions have some recognizable form of competition law. This has been the one of the principal, but by no means the only, topic of his work as an academic,[1] then as general counsel, commissioner, and chairman of the FTC, and now back in academia. Kovacic has studied competition systems around the world, advised many of them, traveled relentlessly to dozens of these jurisdictions, and represented the FTC in interacting with them in countless public and private fora for these same two decades.

He came back from these travels with both great insights and great stories. My favorite Kovacic story goes like this:

> In early February 1993, I stood in a queue of fellows Americans gathered in the offices of Mongolia's State Commission for Privatization, a major advocate of economic reform. As a member of a team from the University of Maryland's Center for Institutional Reform and the Informal Sector (IRIS), I was there to help draft a new antitrust law for Mongolia. I watched as another group of American consultants gave a Privatization Commission official whom I knew a foot thick pile of paper containing laws and regulations for the securities industry in the United States. The American securities experts, who had been in Mongolia for all of a week, explained that the materials could serve as models for establishing a new Mongolian securities regulation system.
>
> My Mongolian acquaintance laboriously leafed through the documents, examining almost every page. He then looked up at securities experts, smiled, and said: "These materials are clearly of high quality and will be very helpful to us. We will put them to good use." Pleased with this favorable reaction, the Americans quickly added that they could supply more model statutes and regulations if desired. The Mongolian official replied that he would welcome more materials and asked that they be printed on one side only, like the paper he had just reviewed. The American said they easily would provide one-sided copies, shook hands, and headed for the airport, buoyed by what seemed to be a most productive week in Ulaanbaatar.
>
> As I entered the privatization official's office, I asked what he would do with the securities documents, which seemed hopelessly complex for a country whose newly created stock exchange was open one day per week and traded shares in only a few companies. "In Mongolia we have a shortage of paper," he explained. "These advisors have given us high quality paper printed on one side. We will make copies on the other side. These materials are very useful. I hope they send more." After a pause he added: "Do you know how many Mongolians have the background to comprehend these laws and regulations? Maybe a handful. New laws must be suited to our capabilities, experiences, and circumstances. If new laws are to succeed, Mongolians will have to carry out the new laws. Do not forget the human dimension of reform."[2]

This essay focuses on the insights that Kovacic brought back from his travels and embodied in his scholarship. I also examine how his work has both documented and affected transition economies enacting and enforcing competition law for the first time, their advisors from more experienced jurisdictions, and the more mature competition jurisdictions themselves. Finally, I offer a brief outline of a research agenda to help evaluate how well both old and new jurisdictions have applied these insights over the past twenty years and suggestions for the next twenty years.

I. Getting Started

Kovacic suggests a strategy of gradualism for most new jurisdictions. His writings suggest gradualism in three distinct senses. The first is that the statutory scheme need not necessarily embrace the full array of prohibitions that one finds in more developed jurisdictions, such as vertical restraints, price discrimination, and pre-merger notification. One strategy would be to start with the basics of horizontal restraints and add the additional powers as the competition agency gains confidence, competence, and credibility.[3]

The second type of gradualism deals with institutional design. Given limited human capital and limited resources what does a new competition agency need and what should it do? Kovacic's articles are replete with stories from the early 1990s of small staffs, inadequate training, large turnover, miniscule salaries, inability to pay the overworked civil servants on a regular basis, lack of basic telecommunications and computer equipment (and sometimes reliable heat and electricity), poorly educated judges, potentially corrupt judicial systems, hostile state enterprises and recently privatized firms, an uniformed general public, lack of compulsory process, and other hurdles that can barely be conceived of in the United States and the European Union before its expansion eastward.[4]

Against this background, important decisions have to be made as to how to best utilize the seriously outgunned competition enforcers. Should resources be split between competition and consumer protection or integrated into a single agency? Should the competition authority have the power to prohibit conduct subject to appeal or have to seek enforcement in the courts? Should enforcement or appeal be before specialized tribunals or courts of general jurisdiction? Should resources and people be concentrated in a central office or spread across multiple regional offices? Should criminal penalties be sought which normally require access to a judiciary that lacks experience, expertise, and sometimes interest in such case? How many of these issues are unique to the early 1990s and how many are still with us today? Perhaps most, importantly, how can these choices be made in a way that is consistent to the greatest degree possible with the existing political, legal, and social institutions of the country?[5]

The competition agency also must make hard choices as to what kind of cases to pursue and whether to pursue cases at the expense of other non-litigation strategies to enhance the legitimacy and overall impact of competition enforcement. Kovacic suggests that it will often make sense in the early years to pursue educational campaigns, outreach to stakeholders, establishing effective internal organization procedures and training, research and publication, competition advocacy, and building relationships with foreign competition authorities and donors as major priorities before undertaking broad campaigns of case investigation and enforcement.[6] Even then, the initial group of cases has to be carefully selected to ensure successful outcomes and minimize the chances of backlash from public and private actors who suffer from the growth of a more competitive private sector. What is striking about these eminently sensible suggestions is that they apply to a striking degree to competition agencies in jurisdictions large and small, both new and well-established.

II. Advising New Jurisdictions

Apart from presumably well-intentioned, but clueless, foreign advisors who leave behind "high quality" paper, the task of an adviser to a new or developing competition law jurisdiction is a complicated one. Distilling Kovacic's many writings and experiences suggests a number of themes that should inform on-going future efforts.[7] The good news is that we seemed to have moved past the early days of the 1990s when too often advice for the new competition jurisdictions in Central and Eastern Europe appeared to consist of photocopies of the applicable U.S. antitrust statutes and guidelines.[8]

The first is simply humility. No one person, set of rules, history, institution, or system has all the answers for everyone else. The second is the need for careful study of the history, law, institutions, language, culture, and needs of the jurisdiction before offering any recommendations. The third is the need to avoid whenever possible short-term antitrust tourism in favor of longer term advisors. The fourth is the need for active, rather than passive, learning. Lectures, seminars, presentations, and position papers are fine, but pale in comparison to workshops, problem solving, and other team exercises that require active application of the key principles. Fifth, is the need for follow-up. Most studies of teaching and learning suggest that students understand and apply key concepts only after repeated exposure. Sixth is the need for a two-way street. U.S. and EU advisers should not just be working in the new jurisdictions, but key personnel from the newer jurisdictions can benefit even more from short-term and long-term assignments being seconded back to the adviser's jurisdiction, whether in the enforcement agencies or the private sector for hands-on training and experience which they can apply when they return home.

III. Applying the Lessons Back Home

Looking abroad also can bring important insights into how to reform institutions at home.[9] Kovacic noted early on that answering questions from officials in transition economies about the peculiarities of the United States honestly was a prerequisite to being able to effectively offer advice to others.[10] This experience abroad, and his experience in government service at the FTC, has led to an equally interesting body of scholarship applying lessons from abroad to questions of institutional design and the structure of U.S. competition law enforcement.

The major institutional quirk in the U.S. competition law system is the dual and overlapping enforcement of the federal antitrust statutes by the Antitrust Division and the Federal Trade Commission. Other important issues are the relationship between the federal competition agencies and the federal sectoral regulators, the relationship between federal and state antitrust law and enforcement, the effective immunity of anticompetitive governmental regulations at the state and local level under the state action doctrine, and the treble damage remedy and the predominance of private enforcement within the United States.[11]

The conventional view is two-fold. First, our system is certainly odd but functions well enough most of the time that making fundamental changes is not worth exploring.[12] The second is that if it were ever politically feasible to explore ending dual enforcement, that the FTC is the more obvious institution to be eliminated, or folded into the surviving federal enforcer.[13]

Kovacic has challenged both of these assumptions. At one time, he appeared to see a more primary role for the Antitrust Division if the question of dual enforcement were ever resolved.[14] In recent speeches and articles, those views have evolved and grown skeptical of the conventional wisdom. He is certainly correct that there is no natural, historical, or policy to favor the abolition of the FTC, if the two agencies were ever consolidated.[15] In fact, there are strong arguments that any consolidation should run in the opposite direction of a single independent agency with both competition and consumer powers with a strong commitment to research, education, and *ex post* evaluation of enforcement initiatives governed by traditional administrative law procedures and protections.[16]

Much of the case for such an outcome comes from the foreign experience of the past two decades. But given the realities of U.S. electoral and bureaucratic politics, Kovacic has also shrewdly focused on the more pragmatic issues of how to improve the existing federal joint venture and how to increase the effectiveness of federal competition advocacy and reform the gaping hole in U.S. competition policy by the state action doctrine.[17]

IV. Making the Grade

Comparative competition law is, or at least should be, a form of empiricism.[18] We now have approximately one hundred twenty jurisdictions with competition law systems, most with at least ten years or more of enforcement to study. Some have been studied intensively through the peer review processes of such entities as the Organization for Economic Cooperation and Development and the International Competition Network.[19] Others have been the subject of both descriptive and evaluative academic scholarship and study in the private sector. A number of jurisdictions have made important changes to the substance and enforcement of their laws making before and after comparisons possible for the first time.

Virtually all jurisdictions now have websites with a wealth of publicly available information that was unimaginable a generation ago at the dawn of the contemporary competition law era (and the internet).[20] We are on the verge of an era where a combination of quantitative and qualitative empirical research techniques can begin to draw tentative conclusions of the key criteria that Kovacic has offered for the formation and operation of competition law in transition economies.[21] Space limitations barely allow for the articulation of what some of those studies would be, let alone conduct them. But the challenge remains to study and analyze some of the issues set forth that Kovacic has so eloquently championed.

One challenge is that data may be difficult to gather to measure the effect of initial design choices and to disentangle a host of competing factors and explanations for progress or lack thereof. In other areas data on budgets and human capital may be available, but may not offer more than very tentative conclusions about how such resources translate into effectiveness. While traditional multi-factor regression analysis will be difficult, it appears that more rudimentary data sets are available that would at least allow for the comparison of comparable groups of jurisdictions, the formulation of basic theses, and the eventual drawing of tentative conclusions.

1. Gradualism Versus the Big Bang

One set of studies should focus on the key thesis that jurisdictions will be more effective if they take a gradual approach to their tasks rather than attempt to create and enforce a full-blown western style competition law all at once. Another set of studies could look at whether jurisdictions have been more effective if they choose to forego the blandishments of competition policy entrepreneurs selling a version of their own systems and embarked on the more arduous, but more meaningful, task of drafting an indigenous set of laws and institutions better suited to the new jurisdiction's history, institutions, and capabilities. Again, I suggest the study of roughly comparable competition authorities where the jurisdictions took different paths at their creation, rather than a rigorous econometric or control group study.

2. Institutional Design

Perhaps most interesting is the question of institutional design. Serious study is needed to determine how well jurisdictions have fared with the choice between:

1. Competition only missions compared to combined competition and consumer jurisdiction.

2. Civil enforcement power versus combined criminal and civil enforcement.
3. Administrative versus judicial control.
4. Specialized versus general courts.
5. Central offices only versus networks of regional offices plus headquarters.
6. The creation of dual or multiple competition enforcers versus unitary enforcement.
7. The allocation of jurisdiction between national and state and local authorities in federal systems.
8. The allocation of jurisdiction between the competition enforcer(s) and sectoral regulators.

While some jurisdictions conduct retrospective studies of individual initiatives, it is not apparent that many have done a serious study of their own institutional design and the success or failure of the choices made. Political considerations and resource issues may make it impossible for insiders or the agencies themselves to undertake this fascinating, but painstaking, research agenda. Twenty years of experience may now have given us enough natural experiments to compare the before and after within jurisdictions which have changed their institutional design and between comparable jurisdictions in the same region which have made different design decisions and enacted substantial amendments.

3. Resource Constraints

Kovacic has detailed so eloquently the extreme resource disadvantages that many new competition agencies have had to overcome. These range from tiny budgets, abysmally low salaries (when they are paid), rapid staff turnover, and the lack of heat, basic phone systems, computer resources, and even office supplies. One example is Ukraine whose total budget in its early years was a grand total of $263,000 for its headquarters and twenty-four regional offices.[23] Another example is the Republic of Georgia where in the early days sixty-five staff rotated in and out of a single unheated central office. Up to date comprehensive budget and staffing data are hard to come by, but are available for certain jurisdictions through commercial and governmental sources.[24] For example, as of 2009 the Antimonopoly Committee of Ukraine had an astonishing 924 employees, with 260 in the central body and 664 in the regional offices.[25] The current budget of the Ukrainian Antimonopoly Committee appears to be in the neighborhood of 65 million Ukrainian Hryvnia (approximately $8 million) spread over the many employees and offices.[26] It is hard to imagine how these resources are sufficient but it is equally hard to imagine how they are not an improvement over the early years. Every jurisdiction wants, and need more, to do their job effectively, but we finally can begin to study these questions with the benefit of time and data.

4. Human Capital

At the dawn of the competition law era, there was a woeful shortage of agency heads, managers and staff with relevant legal and/or economic experience. Many came from state run enterprises with experience in the very different processes of state planning. Many came from engineering or science backgrounds. Others came from other government ministries with very different mandates, often price control responsibilities. Some came in good faith, some came to develop skills to take to the private sector, and still others came with grave reservations of, or even opposition to, the protection of competition in the transition to a functioning market economy. Many jurisdictions were fortunate to have a first generation of competition agency heads that were phenomenally talented and dedicated to the tasks at hand despite many daunting obstacles.[27]

As in the budget area, we have some data available that can shed some light on what the second generation of competition enforcers looks like. Sources like the Global Handbook of Competition Enforcement Agencies and publicly available data from agency web site and peer review studies can reveal much about the education and professional backgrounds of key agency personnel, how long they remain with the agency, and where their careers take them after government service. Here too, we now have a full generation of data to draw preliminary conclusions about the "human dimension" that lies behind successful competition enforcement.

5. The Growth of Private Sector Support Institutions

In several of his articles and speeches, Kovacic has highlighted the need for a vibrant, non-governmental and private sector to support the growth of a competition culture and the work of the government competition enforcers.[28] He has identified universities and relevant curriculum, knowledgeable academic communities, a private competition bar, non-governmental organizations with a focus on competition and consumer issues as key participants in this process. In addition, there is the need for officials and staff to interact with each other in intergovernmental settings, regional and bilateral cooperation, academic conferences, and more informal gatherings to support each other, even when such support is lacking internally within their own jurisdiction. Other commentators have furthered identified the need for a vigorous press covering the work of the agencies, competition advocacy, and private litigation to further build a more vibrant culture of competition.[29]

Here the data are available, but their significance remain elusive. Enforcers in the newer jurisdictions can interact with each other in a broad range of public and private settings to develop best practices and promote the culture of competition within their jurisdiction and between jurisdictions. At the multilateral level, there are the annual and other meetings of the Organisation for Economic Co-operation and Development ("OECD"), United Nations Conference on Trade and Development ("UNCTAD"), and the International Competition Network ("ICN") and the related private meetings and conferences held in conjunction with those more official and formal intergovernmental meeting.[30] These multilateral meetings are supplemented with meetings of the various regional competition bodies. Diverse private academic and policy bodies ranging from Fordham University, Loyola University Chicago, the American Antitrust Institute, George Washington University, Chatham House, the Max Planck Institute, ASCOLA, Consumer Unity & Trust Society ("CUTS"), and other groups throughout the developed and developing world now offer regular programs focusing on the needs of newer competition jurisdictions. Even if private rights of actions are in their infancy outside of a small handful of jurisdictions, a far larger number of jurisdictions have a meaningful competition bar, often with sophisticated counsel who advise both the victims of competition violations as well as defend the accused. With sufficient diligence, one can identify the Universities and colleges which are now teaching meaningful competition related courses in their law, economic, and business faculties. Some programs and initiatives are available on-line, particularly the ICN curriculum project which Kovacic was instrumental in establishing.[31]

And yet, it would be difficult to argue that competition law is a vibrant part of the fabric of civil society in that many jurisdictions (either old or new). This area of the law usually lacks political salience or a high degree of public awareness for its potential to empower consumers and promote economic justice. For far too much of the globe, competition policy is still a luxury and not a necessity, and perhaps properly so given other pressing social and political priorities.

V. A Global Training Opportunity

Let me close with a suggestion that can make a modest contribution to training what will be the third generation of competition enforcers and advocates in many of these jurisdictions. It is time to explore the creation of a comprehensive on-line program for competition lawyers, and, equally importantly, non-legal staff and professionals whether economic, business, or governmental administrators originally from other areas.

For lawyers that could encompass an LL.M. or a related degree. For non-lawyers, it could involve a shorter Masters of Jurisprudence program for those who seek substantial training in competition law and economics but who are not interested or able to pursue comprehensive legal training.[32] The potential audience is the worldwide competition community whether in government service, private practice, or academia.

Faculty could be drawn from many jurisdictions. Courses could be in a combination of limited real time and mostly, asynchronous offerings to deal with the realities of students and faculty in up to twenty-four different time zones. While start-up costs would be significant, running costs would not. Fees could be scaled based on the modules taken and with students from wealthier jurisdictions paying more than students from developing jurisdiction. Much of the content could be free and/or licensed through open source licensing terms so that users could customize the materials to their own needs.[33] Resources permitting, capstone workshops, workshops, and thesis presentations could be held on-site in a network of cooperating universities, NGOs, and/or enforcement agencies geographically close to a critical mass of the students involved. If done right, imagine the benefits of harmonization with the creation of a low-cost common platform of knowledge and training within a given agency, between the public sector and private sector within a given jurisdiction, and between jurisdictions.

VI. Conclusion

It is important to think boldly in moving forward on the international competition front. It is relatively easy to demonstrate that the last twenty years have produced much more competition law and more sophisticated public and private sector actors who participate in the enforcement of competition law. It is much harder to demonstrate that there is much greater competition or consumer benefit. Documenting outputs is simply harder than documenting the growth of inputs in terms of people, resources, and know-how which are a legitimate source of optimism. However, the past twenty years have taught us much about how to go about that process and it is now our task to do so.

NOTES

*   Thanks to Andre Fiebig, Andrew Gavil, Matthew Sag, Maurice Stucke, and Alex Tsesis for their comments on this essay and to Ismael Salam for his research assistance.

1   A full list of Kovacic's publications can be found at http://portal.law.gwu.edu/Bibliography/Bibliography. asp?uid=1731. His work on the FTC embraced the full range of competition and consumer issues within the jurisdiction of the Commission.

2   William E. Kovacic, *The Competition Policy Entrepreneur and Law Reform in Formerly Communist and Socialist Countries*, 11 AM. U.J. INT'L & POL'Y 437, 437-39 (1996) (notes omitted) [hereinafter Kovacic, *Competition Policy Entrepreneur*].

3   William E. Kovacic, *Competition Policy, Economic Development, and the Transition to Free Markets in the Third World: The Case of Zimbabwe*, 61 ANTITRUST L.J. 253, 260 (1992) [hereinafter Kovacic, *Zimbabwe*]; William E. Kovacic, *Getting Started: Creating New Competition Policy Institutions in Transition Economies*, 23 BROOK. J. INT'L L. 403, 444-46 (1997) [hereinafter Kovacic, *Getting Started*]; William E. Kovacic, *Capitalism, Socialism, and Competition Policy in Vietnam*, 13 ANTITRUST 57, 59-60 (Summer 1999); William E. Kovacic, *Institutional Foundations for Economic Legal Reform in Transition Economies: The Case for Competition Policy and Antitrust Enforcement*, 77 CHI-KENT L. REV. 265, 293-96 (2001) [hereinafter Kovacic, *Institutional Foundations*].

4   *Ukraine*, 31 GEO. WASH. J. INT'L L. & ECON. 1, 16-18 (1997) [hereinafter Kovacic, *Ukraine*].

5   Kovacic, *Zimbabwe, supra* note 3, at 261.

6   Kovacic, *Getting Started, supra* note 3, at 430-41; Kovacic, *Institutional Foundations, supra* note 3, at 282-84.

7   Kovacic, *Competition Policy Entrepreneur, supra* note 2; Kovacic, *Getting Started, supra* note 3; William E. Kovacic, *Designing and Implementing Competition and Consumer Protection Reforms in Traditional Economies: Perspectives from Mongolia, Nepal, Ukraine, and Zimbabwe*, 44 DePaul L. Rev. 1197, 1215-20 (1995); Kovacic, *Institutional Foundations, supra* note 3, at 310-12.

8   *See e.g.*, Spencer Weber Waller, *Neo-Realism and the International Harmonization of Law: Lessons from Antitrust*, 42 U. Kan. L. Rev. 558, 569-71 (1994).

9   William E. Kovacic, *U.S. Antitrust Policy: The Underperforming Federal Antitrust Venture*, Concurrences No. 4-2011, 65; William E. Kovacic, *Rating the Competition Agencies: What Constitutes Good Performance*, 16 Geo. Mason L. Rev. 903-926 (2009); William E. Kovacic, *Lessons of Competition Policy Reform in Transition Economies for U.S. Antitrust Policy*, 74 St. John's L. Rev. 361 (2000).

10 Kovacic, *Competition Policy Entrepreneur, supra* note 2, at 461-63.

11 *See generally*, Symposium, *Designing Better Institutions to Enforce Competition Law*, 41 Loy. U. Chi. L.J. 411-586 (2010).

12 Antitrust Modernization Commission, Report and Recommendations 129-32 (2007).

13 *Current Antitrust Enforcement and its Critics: Recent Proposals for Reform and Restructure in the Antitrust Division, the FTC and the Courts*, 40 Antitrust L.J. 341, 360-87 (1971); Milton Handler, *Reforming the Antitrust Laws*, 82 Colum. L. Rev. 1287, 1318 (1982); Ernest Gellhorn et al., *Has Antitrust Outgrown Dual Enforcement? A Proposal for Rationalization*, 35 Antitrust Bull. 694 (1990).

14 William Kovacic, *Downsizing Antitrust: Is it Time to End Dual Federal Enforcement?*, 41 Antitrust Bull. 505 (1996).

15 *See* Daniel A. Crane, The Institutional Structure of Antitrust Enforcement 48 (2011).

16 Criminal enforcement would, of necessity, remain in the Justice Department presumably in an Antitrust Group within the Criminal Division of the Justice Department much like the Organized Crime Strike Force following its reorganization in the 1990s. Spencer Weber Waller, *Prosecution by Regulation: The Changing Nature of Antitrust Enforcement*, 77 Or. L. Rev. 1383, 1439 n. 250 (1998).

17 James Cooper & William E. Kovacic, *Antitrust and the Obama Administration: U.S. Convergence with International Competition Norms: Antitrust Law and Public Restraints on Competition*, 90 Boston U.L. Rev. 1555 (2010). *See generally* ABA Antitrust Section, State Action Practice Manual (2d ed. 2010). Another interesting exercise would address the Justice Department's controversial plans to eliminate certain regional field offices from the perspective of jurisdictions that included large number of regional offices and their contributions to effective competition enforcement.

18 Spencer Weber Waller, *Comparative Competition Law as a Form of Empiricism*, 23 Brook. J. Int'l L. 455 (1997).

19 Country reviews of competition policy frameworks, *available at* http://www.oecd.org/document/43/0,3746, en_2649_37463_2489707_1_1_1_37463,00.html; Peer review on competition law and policy, *available at* http://www.unctad.org/templates/Page.asp?intItemID=3845&lang=1. While there are important reasons that such exercises are carefully couched exercises in diplomacy, rather than hard hitting critiques, they nonetheless constitute an important and growing body of information for comparative competition law analysis.

20 Many of these web sites can be accessed at Antitrust Sites Worldwide, *available at* http://www.justice.gov/atr/contact/otheratr.html.

21 *See also* D. Daniel Sokol, *Designing Antitrust Agencies for More Effective Outcomes: What Antitrust Can Learn from Restaurant Guides*, 41 Loy. U. Chi. L.J. 573 (2010) (proposing annual reputational rankings of enforcement agencies).

22 Kovacic, *Ukraine, supra* note 4, at 16 n. 27.

23 Kovacic, *Getting Started, supra* note 3, at 419.

24 *See generally* Global Competition Review, The Handbook of Competition Enforcement Agencies (2011), *available at* http://www.globalcompetitionreview.com/handbooks/35/the-handbook-competition-enforcement-agencies-2011/. 2009 budgets in dollars range from $1.4 million for Argentina ((94 staff), $200,000 for Jordan; $1.5 million for Mauritius (21 staff); $46,700 for Senegal (9 staff); and $22 million for the 2010 budget for Turkey (327 staff). *Id.* at 15, 170, 193, 254, and 295.

25 *Id.* at 302. In contrast, the combined 2013 budget for the FTC was $300 million and the Antitrust Division was $165 million. The DOJ antitrust budget was up 3.2 percent from 2012, while the FTC's 2013 budget represents a drop from last year's allotment of approximately $310 million. *See* http://www.law360.com/articles/309169/2013-budget-trims-ftc-boosts-doj-s-antitrust-division.

26 *See* http://www.amc.gov.ua/amc/control/uk/publish/article?art_id=199017&cat_id=199016.

27 Kovacic identifies Ana Julia Jatar, Gesner Oliveira, Beatriz Boza, Anna Fornalyczk, the top leadership in Ukraine, and others as just some of this remarkable group of initial agency heads. Kovacic, *Lessons of Competition Policy Reform*, *supra* note 9, at 368.

28 Kovacic, *Institutional Foundations*, *supra* note 4, at 270-73.

29 Andreas Stephan, *Survey of Public Attitudes to Price-Fixing and Cartel Enforcement in Britain*, 5 COMP. L. REV. 123 (2008). Michael Hausfeld & Vincent Smith, *Competition Law Claims – A Developing Story*, THE EUROPEAN ANTITRUST REVIEW 2010 *at 39;* Albert A. Foer, & Jonathan W. Cunro, *Toward an Effective System of Private Enforcement*, in THE INTERNATIONAL HANDBOOK ON PRIVATE ENFORCEMENT OF COMPETITION LAW 590 (Albert A. Foer & Jonathan W Cuneo eds., 2010); Albert A. Foer, *International Consumer Advocacy for Competition Policy: Learning from the AAI Model*, BOLETIN LATINO AMERICANO DE COMPETENCIA 62 (Feb. 2009).

30 For example in 2012, the Academic Society for Competition Law (ASCOLA) is holding its annual meeting prior to the ICN annual meeting in Brazil. In addition, the International Development Research Centre (IRDC) holds a research conference aimed at developing country enforcement officials the day before the ICN annual meeting the past several years.

31 International Competition Network Curriculum Project, *available at* http://www.internationalcompetitionnetwork. org/about/steering-group/outreach/icncurriculum.aspx; SPENCER WEBER WALLER, COMPETITION POLICY IN THE GLOBAL ECONOMY: AN ON-LINE CASEBOOK, *available at* http://www.luc.edu/law/academics/special/center/antitrust/online_ case_book/index.html.

32 Loyola University Chicago runs similar web-based programs in the health law and family law areas. *See* http:// onlinemj.luc.edu/aboutMJ.html. Other law schools have various on-line LL.M. programs in different fields. To my knowledge there is nothing available anywhere in the world in the competition law area or that encompasses the global training mission outlined above.

33 *See* WALLER, COMPETITION POLICY IN THE GLOBAL ECONOMY, *supra* note 31.

Bill Kovacic and the Global Evolution of Antitrust

Theodore L. Banks

tbanks@scharfbanks.com
Partner, Scharf Banks Marmor, LLC
Adjunct Professor of Law, Loyola Univeristy Chicago School of Law
President of Compliance & Competition Consultants, LLC

Abstract

Bill Kovacic helped make enforcement of competition laws as near universal part of the world economy, and helped push for integrity and excellence in the administrative process behind antitrust. The discipline, competence, and consistency of enforcement agencies are key to an effective antitrust policy. Enforcement agencies can help the economy by providing positive guidance, and not just prosecuting wrongdoers.

I. Introduction

I always looked forward to programs when I saw that Bill Kovacic was on the agenda.[1] I knew that I would get an interesting, insightful, and honest discourse on whatever subject he was talking about. This would be true, unlike most other antitrust luminaries, whether he was talking while in the government or out. I never felt like he had asked a junior staff member to put together a bland 20-minute talk on the subject of the day, careful not to step on any political toes. But I was hearing the product of his intellectual and experiential processes. And his articles, over the course of a career, have added to our understanding of how competition law operates–and should operate–in conjunction with other aspects of our national and global economies.

So, I grabbed a sampling of his articles and took at a look at the wide-ranging subjects he has illuminated. I reflected on how they had impacted on my understanding of antitrust, particularly since my point of view came, starting in the mid-1970s, form inside a company, always wondering how to comply with the legal requirements for competition and the business requirements for corporate success. I was interested in how his analysis of antitrust law and enforcement utilized principles from business or could be applied to other areas of law. I was particularly interested in how these principles would parallel the learnings in corporate compliance and ethics.

II. Global Competition and Global Competition Enforcement

Over the last 35 years, antitrust has become a fixture of the legal regimes of industrialized countries. But it was not always that way. Apart from the United States, Canada, the European Union, and a few others, when I started competition laws did not exist in many countries, or if they did exist, were only enforced as a revenue-raising device.[2] But since that time, antitrust has become more accepted, due to the evangelistic efforts of Bill and a few others to convince countries that the benefits of a competition law regime were one of the keys to the economic development of their country.

Bill recognized that while competition theory was sound, it meant nothing when it was not implemented properly.[3] It is important to distinguish the volume of matters handled—or the amount or revenue raised—from the economic value of its activities. Bill correctly points out that that focus on prosecution takes the focus away from other activities, such as preparing reports that analyze aspects of the economy. I know from experience that much of an agency's work comes from the quiet conversations that don't result in a case filed or a second request. A deal that the agency believes to be anticompetitive that is abandoned without lengthy proceedings, as long as the agency's analysis is sound, is a much more efficient way to implement competition policy than litigation.

So, in addition to asking "What are you doing?" is it proper for an agency to be able to answer the question "Why are you doing that?" The goal of a competition agency is to provide benefits for consumers, not to put notches in its litigation belt. The investment in a high quality staff, whether in career or political positions, is extremely important. While there may be disagreements about the outcome of agency decisions, there should be confidence in the process. Almost always, when bringing a corporate executive in to the FTC to talk about a transaction, or even when sharing information as a third party in a telephone interview, my clients came away with a positive reaction. They were usually impressfed by the intelligence of the lawyers or economists with whom they spoke, and, although initially annoyed to have their schedule disrupted for the conversation, were ultimately happy to have had the chance to interact with the folks who were charged with implementing, and sometimes making, our competition policy.

This creation of an "excellent brand" is the same as in every other area of our economy. An agency rides on its reputation, as does a product. Within a corporation, much gets done based on the reputations of the individuals. For lawyers or compliance officers, this can be particularly important. If a person commands respect, the rest of the organization is likely to follow that person's guidance. A recommendation from a lawyer who is known as one who is excessively conservative, rigid under all circumstances, and not willing to listen to others, will find that his or her advice may be ignored, or perhaps he or she just won't hear about things that they should hear about.

The same factors impact on how an agency is perceived. If an agency is known as never litigating its positions, it will find that the entities it regulates are more willing to challenge its positions. If an agency is found to be excessively rigid and unrealistic, it will find that it loses its political support, as the outlet for frustration is realized through the political process, and efforts are organized to undercut the resources, or the mission, of the agency.

In some cases, recognition of this factor has the unfortunate effect of resulting in a very short-term orientation, or responses to political pressure. As in the corporate world, this can have a very negative impact. A company focused on the short-term (such as the price of the stock tomorrow) may ignore investments for the future, cheapen its products, or reduce its staff–all to get a quick financial bounce. It may often do so in response to large shareholders who want a better return on their investment. There are those who will argue that this is both normal and good, and it may be. But while a corporation may not have a fixed mission to guide its activities, an antitrust enforcement agency does. Replace the large shareholders with political forces, and one sees the challenge for the agency to balance the short-term pressures from politicians against the long-term mission of enhancing consumer welfare.

This may be inevitable in a democracy, where the challenge is to respond to the majority while not allowing the long-term goals to get lost. Sometimes, the "democratic" impetus is reflected in the combination of a tendency to litigate and obtain maximum publicity, if the enforcer has political ambitions rather than a professional commitment to an antitrust goal.[4] Trying to establish antitrust enforcement policy based on what the public wants or expects is both good and bad. Should a price increase or large transaction be challenged just because it looks wrong to the man (i.e., voter) on the street when an examination of the markets impacted by the deal shows that there really is not an impact on competition that rises to a level that should attract the attention of the enforcer?[5] Yet there is an almost irresistible attraction to filing suit against a big company, and garner the approval of the masses (elected officials and voters), regardless of policy considerations.

We have enough challenges getting our antitrust enforcement straight in the United States, and it is difficult to imagine the challenge of getting enforcement established with a degree of consistency in countries where there is no tradition of competition, and certainly none of antitrust enforcement. But there may be ways to help build this type of program. Bill correctly notes that formulating clear goals to the staff and external groups is very important to establishing credibility. While we cannot expect that every country will follow the U.S. approach to antitrust, the worst results can come from the enactment of a statute and then having "surprise" enforcement that seems to be guided by nothing other than caprice.[6] The willingness of agency staff to communicate with others in articles or public fora, and participation in multinational networks provided by ICN, OECD, and UNCTAD, helps extend the competition message. As Bill suggested, combining an examination of the output of the agencies with peer review that examines the output based on the impact over time, international agencies may be able to better understand their own performance, and better communicate their mission to those who may be regulated.

III. The U.S. Dual (or Dueling) Antitrust Enforcement Agencies

There is a lot of complaining about the dual civil antitrust enforcement of the Antitrust Division and the FTC. Critics talk about differences in enforcement philosophy, and wastes of government resources. How did it look to an inside counsel? No big deal. The worst aspect about it was the delay in starting the merger review process as the agencies dueled over who would get to review a particularly sexy deal. Only one time in my career was a deal cleared to one agency and then switched to the other agency. That did not leave us a lot of time if we hoped to answer any questions of the agency before time ran out and they issued a second request just for "jurisdictional reasons" to buy them more time. But the differences in approaches to merger review of the two agencies, except to the nuance-seeking antitrust practitioners in Washington, were not substantively significant to the clients of the inside-the-Beltway folks, who were only interested in whether a deal would go through or not.[7]

Obviously, there are differences in approach between the agencies, as well as different jurisdictions. The FTC's inability to pursue a criminal case is actually useful, since they have shown that there are many situations where a criminal antitrust prosecution was not appropriate (or impossible), but there was a clear violation that was deserving of sanction. Enter the FTC with its authority to use Section 5, and its various monetary penalty provisions that can be extremely painful even without the prospect of jail. The FTC's role to study various aspects of the economy also could prove very useful in adapting (i.e., improving) antitrust enforcement to reflect our evolving society and learnings about economics.[8] There should be no shame in recognizing that "[w]hat seems to be wisely conceived policy in one era might be proven to be unwise in a later period."[9]

In looking at the history of enforcement, Bill has noted the relatively modest role played by Section 5 in the history of monopoly enforcement, due (at least in part) to the expansive interpretation that courts had given to Section 2 of the Sherman Act, that obviated the need for Section 5 enforcement.[10] But judicial decisions have retrenched the expansive view of the Sherman and Clayton Acts, in view of concerns about overdeterrence of competitive behavior (particular with private litigation), new learning about the economic impact of certain conduct, and the capability of federal enforcers to administer antitrust policy. As a private party subject to antitrust enforcement, the main concern with an expansive approach to Section 5 enforcement is the surprise factor. Conduct that you thought was acceptable all of a sudden becomes illegal. This approach does nothing to enhance the image of the enforcement agency–or of the lawyers who need to deliver the bad news to their clients (Why didn't you warn us?). So, the articulation of a policy, perhaps through rulemaking, that would indicate what conduct was unacceptable before actual enforcement occurs would give potential enforcement targets the ability to mend their ways before engaging in litigation.[11] The FTC might also follow the SEC practice of starting out slowly when beginning a new type of enforcement.

One reason that it makes sense to focus on the FTC enforcement is that in an increasingly interconnected and interdependent world, the FTC enforcement model can be harmonized (or maybe already is harmonized) with the administrative enforcement model of the European Union.[12] Except for a unique EU requirement of "free movement of goods," the general approach is the same (e.g., focus on consumer welfare). The specific implementations by the European Union in some areas that diverge from the United States (e.g., abuse of dominance)[13] may be easier to manage since the European Union tends to express its policy positions very explicitly. It may be more difficult to change some of the U.S. positions, to the extent they are solidified in Supreme Court decisions,[14] whereas the administrative model of the European Union tends to rely on the expertise of the Commission. But the increased communication between the EU, the U.S. antitrust authorities, and antitrust enforcers in other countries may allow for some convergence as the enforcers consult with regard to a specific enforcement action.

Both enforcement agencies should be concerned about providing maximum benefits to consumers by encouraging compliance with law. One way to do this is to prosecute violators and impose severe punishment. This certainly happens in many cases. The Antitrust Division's focus on criminal prosecution has seen the development of an amnesty program that encourages members of a cartel to confess their sins, by providing complete amnesty to the first party that comes to the Justice Department to disclose their violations. This program, the antitrust version of the "prisoner's dilemma," has resulted in the discovery and prosecution of many cartels that might never have been discovered by other means. Many jurisdictions in addition to the United States use an amnesty program, and it seems to be a "best practice" among enforcement agencies.[15]

But an amnesty program only deals with one small aspect of antitrust compliance–deterrence based on fear that a cartel member will have an incentive to leave the cartel to escape punishment. Complete amnesty to a cartel participant creates a perverse incentive to focus resources not on preventing a violation, but on monitoring for indications that the cartel is about to break up, and then being the first in the door to confess. Incentives to whistleblowers might also play a helpful role (as in the *qui tam* actions that might be available to a whistleblower under certain U.S. statutes), but these are not part of the usual antitrust enforcement regime.[16] The encouragement of compliance requires a number of tools, and merely rewarding the first guilty party to confess is hardly adequate. The forces that would drive someone to violate the law (i.e., collude), and then perhaps to confess to a violation, are only partially explained by a profit motive. Attempting to explain the impact of the amnesty program through a mathematical approach makes the same error as economists make by attempting to explain market behavior through the Chicago-school lens. Yes, the forces that drive the profit motive can explain some, and perhaps even much, of the behavior. But when dealing with human motivation, one needs to examine the psychological and sociological forces that drive an individual or a company to violate a law.

Why would people violate a law? Here are some of the reasons discussed in the literature: dire financial straits (often caused by medical problems or drug abuse), dislike of management (often a desire to "get back" at a mean boss), an atmosphere of sloppiness ("they'll never know its missing"), intense pressure on an individual, department, or company to hit an unreasonable financial target, a feeling that one is smarter than everyone else and the normal rules don't apply, or the individual won't get caught, ignorance of the law, a weak personality that won't resist what a corrupt boss instructs, fear of retaliation, etc.

With all of these reasons that impact on the individual and corporate motivations to violate the law, focusing attention on one tool, amnesty, is clearly inadequate. What is needed, if an agency is to encourage compliance with the law, rather than just punishment, is a complete set of tools to help people comply with the law, not just punishment for violations. The Antitrust Division compounds its narrow-minded approach by going a step further and stating that it will not consider corporate compliance programs to be available to mitigate the punishment of a possible violation. Alone among all of the federal criminal laws enforced by the Department of Justice, the Antitrust Division has excepted itself from the principles of the Sentencing Guidelines published by the U.S. Sentencing Commission that seek to encourage compliance by providing guidance on how to achieve an effective compliance program, and by granting credit to companies who demonstrate a good faith attempt to comply with the law.

The FTC is a little better here. The FTC has a much more nuanced enforcement policy, and has shown a willingness to listen to respondents outline the details of a compliance program that was in place, even if imperfect.[17] But more can be done. The FTC website does provide some explanation of the laws that the FTC enforces, but does not really talk about how a company can implement a compliance program. The FTC often imposes compliance requirements as part of consent decrees, which, in addition to a "do not violate the law" provision, may contain requirements for training programs or other ways to communicate the requirements of the law and the terms of the consent decree to affected parties, sometimes supervised by a monitor appointed by the Commission.[18] But many times these requirements are like blunt objects; an order that directs a company to distribute a copy of a consent decree to customers or employees does not really ensure compliance with anything other than the physical distribution of the order. Does anything ensure that employees will read and understand the order? Does a requirement of "live" training ensure that it will be more effective than computer-based training?[19] In keeping with a mission to help enforce the laws, both the FTC and Antitrust Division should have a staff of compliance experts,[20] whose mission is to help companies establish programs to comply with the law.

Amnesty programs, if implemented incorrectly, undermine the efforts of a sincere compliance program that has, as its foundation, a commitment to ethical business conduct. This concept usually includes the assumption that if you do wrong you will be punished. An amnesty program that allows a violator to escape the consequences of its actions undermines this basic ethical assumption. However, an amnesty program tied to a compliance requirement may work very well. For example, if implementation of a compliance program resulted in a company discovering that it was violating the antitrust law, and immediately notifying the authorities, that conduct should be applauded—and even rewarded. But if an amnesty program merely holds out an award for the first malefactor to rush in, and does not consider whether a compliance program was in place or require the company to implement a compliance program is devoid of any moral content. This somewhat cynical approach to enforcement would be understandable to lawyers who want to get the best deal for their client, but how does one explain this to an employee? How can we expect them to do the right thing when there is no incentive for trying to do the right thing? At the very least, an amnesty grant should be coupled with a requirement to implement a compliance program, with the risk of losing amnesty should violations recur.[21]

But, as I noted, this is an area where the FTC does somewhat better than the Antitrust Division. Its efforts should be commended—but they should be expanded, in keeping with the FTC mission as an antitrust policy leader, and not just as one of the antitrust policemen on the beat.

IV. The Purpose of Antitrust Enforcement

From his perspective as staff member, General Counsel, and Commissioner of the FTC, Bill could observe both the development and execution of competition and consumer protection policy. From those vantage points, one could stop and think about the purpose of "competition policy," of which antitrust is but one part. Americans, notwithstanding their pronouncements to the contrary, have always had ambivalence about competition in general.[22] Americans like choice and low prices, but they may like convenience more—until they get tired of the monopolist. Historically, there was a preference for a unified communications system (AT&T), at least partly because it offered higher quality than its early competitors. But, the lack of competition may stifle innovation.[23] Reading the biography of Steve Jobs shows that he had no desire whatsoever for competition. Jobs tried simultaneously to portray himself and his company as the rebels, while demanding absolute compliance from someone who would utilize Apple products (and absolute obedience from Apple employees).[24] Americans (and people in other countries, too, of course) went along because at the same time they were being asked to do things his way and only his way, they didn't mind because his way usually worked better. The Apple consumer could (and can) buy into the fiction that they are independent from Big Brother, merely because the options (e.g., Microsoft) is big, not because it is restrictive.

So even while most Americans may talk about their preference for small, local businesses, they freely free ride at those local dealers and then go purchase from Amazon or some other Internet vendor. While there are situations where the network efficiencies may justify a regulated monopoly (how many cable TV systems, with separate wires, do you need in your city?), convenience will always seem to provide a convenient basis to overlook monopoly for most Americans. But just as there are policy arguments as to why an economy may want to forego some of the efficiencies of monopoly to gain diversity and competition, there are policy reasons to encourage monopoly in certain situations. We must remember that antitrust is a political creature. In the American iteration, it is designed to balance off the two principles enshrined in our political documents: freedom and equality. The antitrust laws attempt to insert these values into our economy. The notion of economic freedom is reflected in the general distaste for regulations, notwithstanding the thousands we have. Americans still fancy themselves as the rugged pioneers, self-sufficient and able to operate with the government's help. So, our economic freedom includes the ability to relatively easily start a business, make a lot of money—or fail completely. We balance this freedom with the notion of equality, that everyone should have an opportunity to compete. So, in the interest of providing maximum benefits to consumers (and not just to competitors), and allowing companies of different size and shape to participate in the economy, the antitrust laws provide some rules of behavior. There is certain conduct that is considered too intrusive into the functioning of our economy to go unregulated. What are those behaviors? Well, we sort of know, but the precise bounds of our thinking vary over time. They vary with economic learning about the way markets operate, and they vary with political changes in administration. It may be an oversimplification, but it may be useful to think of the Republican administrations leaning toward the freedom value and the Democratic administrations leaning toward the equality value.

Looking at total transactions, the data show a steady drop in the issuance of second requests from the Reagan through George W. Bush administrations—with second requests stabilizing in the low 3% range from 1993-2008. Among transactions that cleared to one of the agencies, the trend similarly shows a decline from Reagan through George W. Bush, although with a slight uptick under Clinton and a sharper decline under George W. Bush. By each measure, the Obama administration in its first two years reversed that trend, increasing the rate of second requests among total reported transactions to 4.3% and to 20.5% among transactions that cleared to one agency or the other. While the increase under Obama might be worth noting by parties currently contemplating a merger in the United States, these data do not show a systematic political correlation; indeed, note the decline under Clinton among total transactions and the very slight increase under Clinton among cleared transactions. Moreover, in themselves, these data say nothing about the nature of the investigations or whether the change is due to the particular pool of transactions or to the agencies' use of a more aggressive standard for launching second requests.

Regardless of politics, there is a remarkable degree of agreement on the benefits of competition, and conduct like price-fixing gets enthusiastic enforcement from administrations of all political leaning. But when the question is not so easy, the antitrust policy becomes a little more murky. One of those areas of murkiness is the conundrum known as patent-antitrust. We all know the reasons why patent holders are granted some insulation from competition, but a blind application of antitrust immunity in all cases is certainly not appropriate. By the same token, overeager elimination of patent protection may pose a grave danger of stifling the incentives for innovation that seem to have worked well for many years. As Bill noted,[25] the FTC had recognized[26] that patents of questionable quality, being either improperly invalidated or too broad, can distort competition and harm innovation. Overly broad extension of patent coverage can discourage follow-on innovation, and improperly granted patents will increase costs through litigation or payment of royalties to march through the patent thickets. The FTC recommended reform of the patent process to allow the process to work more effectively, and recent legislation did introduce some reforms.

But the patent system still faces the problem of the "trolls" or "nonpractising entities," the plaintiffs that picked up a patent somewhere along the line (i.e., without inventing anything), and do not use the patent to make anything. But they do make lawsuits, deter innovation, and impose significant costs on the economy.[27] The recent patent reform act addressed many issues, and in the reform of the False Marking Claim provision,[28] by limiting the private right of action to those who have suffered a competitive injury, a very important concept from the antitrust laws was utilized. Language also makes it clear that sanctions may be imposed for violations of criminal or antitrust laws, and specifically Section 5 of the FTC Act for unfair methods of competition.[29] Here some enhanced enforcement would be a boon to competition, perhaps by expanding the patent misuse doctrine to those who did not invent and are not manufacturing but only seek to enforce a patent right they purchased. While patent purists may argue that patent law gives an individual the right not to use it, and the right to sell or license it, the concept of abusive non-use certainly deserves more exploration, particularly since there is no argument that protecting this right provides any benefit to society that government should support.

V. A Parting Thought

I've noticed over the years that there seemed to be various attempts to denigrate the activities of the FTC in comparison to those of the Antitrust Division. I never understood that. I will freely admit that throughout the course of my career, I had relatively less contact with the Department of Justice, but isn't that the way it should be? As I emphasize to my students today, as they dream about being trial lawyers, it is a much nobler calling to help clients do the right thing in the first place, rather than trying to clean up a mess afterwards. The FTC helps companies do that. Both in the consumer protection and competition roles, it tries to help consumers by guiding companies in the right direction—and correcting those that go astray. Not every company or individual that goes astray needs to be indicted, they just need to be directed. Bill Kovacic for many years has helped provide that direction, to the great benefit of consumers—and companies—everywhere

NOTES

1   I am only saying this in the past tense with reference to Bill's prior government service at the FTC I certainly look forward to hearing him in the future, whether in government or speaking as a "mere" antitrust professor.

2   Such as in countries, who shall remain nameless, where premerger filings were encouraged since the filing fee was tied to the size of the transaction (so, the larger, the better), but where substantive review was cursory if performed at all.

3   William E. Kovacic, Hugh M. Hollman & Patricia Grant, *How Does Your Competition Agency Measure Up?*, 7 EUROPEAN COMP. J. 25 (April 2011).

4   This can be a painful outcome, as I personally experienced, by being subject to state antitrust litigation after federal clearance was received. This is one of the dilemmas of our federal system, where state and federal antitrust policy can diverge. Unfocused state policy can result in enforcement being dependent on political aspirations of an attorney general, or where transactions are evaluated based on impact on local employment or investment, and not on impact on competition.

5   Antitrust may be behind some price increases, but not all. Every time the price of gasoline goes up, there are demands for investigations, and criticism of the enforcement agencies when their investigations do not yield a violator that can be prosecuted in the United States, even though everyone has heard of OPEC.

6   The Chinese Antimonopoly Law does have elements of this. The amount of deference to state decisions that is explicit in the text of the statute at least puts everyone (foreign investors particularly) on notice that certain decisions will not necessarily follow principles of competition, but will reflect a state decision as to how it wishes to manage its economy at a given moment.

7   But as much as I respect the antitrust practitioners who spend every day immersed in the arcane world of the FTC or DOJ, sometimes their own expertise morphs into arrogance. My boss at Kraft Foods for many years was Calvin Collier, who had a distinguished career as a staff member and commissioner of the FTC Most lawyers in the United States are trained to be advocates, the gladiators who are unafraid to leap into battle to defend their clients. Cal emphasized the importance of listening, rather than talking (particularly when someone from an enforcement agency was talking), and this approach actually worked. You have a better chance of convincing a decision-maker by addressing his or her concerns, instead of spending all your time talking about your theories. When there were problem facts, instead of burying them and hoping they wouldn't be found, you surfaced them at the outset, and addressed the questions they raised. A consistent approach of respect and openness could still be combined with advocacy, but would enable one to advocate for one's client with credibility. Unfortunately, on several occasions I wanted to hide under the table as distinguished Washington counsel (representing the party on the other side of the deal) would tell a hardworking FTC staffer that they were, in effect, stupid for not grasping the theory they presented. That staffer, earning a fraction of the salary of the big-firm lawyer, would invariably politely listen–and remember. The staff was usually very open about their questions, and if they were not answered to their satisfaction, one could imagine the recommendation that would result. Smart lawyers knew that these staffers had the power of life or death over their deals, and respected them accordingly. Arrogant lawyers seemed to forget that these staffers would be around for a while, and they might be looking at a future deal–and would remember.

8   William E. Kovacic, *The Modern Evolution of U.S. Competition Policy Enforcement Norms*, 71 ANTITRUST L.J. 377 (2003).

9   William E. Kovacic, *Rating the Competition Agencies: What Constitutes Good Performance?*, 16 GEO. MASON L. REV. 903 (2009).

10   William E. Kovacic & Marc Winerman, *Competition Policy and the Application of Section 5 of the Federal Trade Commission Act*, 76 ANTITRUST L.J. 929 (2010).

11   For example, when consumers and manufacturers in the United States began to show more of an interest in recycling and recycled packaging, there was confusion about how to communicate recycled content and recyclability. So, the "Green Guides" were developed to provide a common baseline for those claims. Today, as recycling is a more common occurrence, the FTC can respond to current environmental issues by focusing on energy-savings claims.

12   William E. Kovacic, *Competition Policy in the EU & US: Convergence or Divergence?*, Presentation at FIDE, Madrid (Feb. 17, 2009).

13   William E. Kovacic, *Competition Policy in the European Union and the United States: Convergence or Divergence in the Treatment of Dominant Firms?*, COMPETITION POLICY INTERNATIONAL 9 (Oct. 2008), noting the more restrictive policy of the European Union with regard to abuse of dominance. Bill posits that the expansive use of the private right of action in the United States may have resulted in the tendency of U.S. courts to raise the bar for monopolization cases to offset excesses of private plaintiff claims, and absent the history of private litigation, the U.S. model might have evolved to look more like that of the European Union.

14   Bill identifies the dominance of the Chicago school of economics in the United States, which sometimes results in decisions that may look good on a spreadsheet, but do not reflect actual human behavior. The European Union has moved beyond a slavish following of Chicago-school theories, and a growing understanding of behavioral economics in the United States may assist in taking a more nuanced look at transactions or other antitrust-sensitive behavior to understand the real impact on consumers and their welfare.

15   Cécile Aubert, Patrik Rey & William E. Kovacic, *The Impact of Leniency and Whistleblowing Programs on Cartels*, 24 INT. J. OF INDUSTRIAL ORG. 1241 (2006).

16   Legislation was introduced on July 31, 2012 in the United States Senate to provide protection to antitrust whistleblowers, entitled the "Criminal Antitrust Anti-Retaliation Act."

17   The Sentencing Guidelines make it clear that perfection is not expected, and a company can still show due diligence in establishing a program to prevent and detect violations of law even if an employee ignored corporate instructions and chose to violate the law.

18   The author serves as a corporate monitor appointed by the FTC.

19   Interestingly, the Italian antitrust authority, in announcing that it would give some credit for antitrust compliance programs when formulating its penalties, noted that it would not credit computer-based training programs, since it did not think they could be effective as off-the-shelf presentations.

20 Of course, the FTC does have a dedicated staff who oversee compliance with orders, and that group's role could be expanded by adding staff with expertise in areas other than legal enforcement. Such expertise might include adult educational specialists, psychologists who understand the motivations for malfeasance, corporate organization experts who can assist in targeting programs for the antitrust risks in specific jobs or departments, electronic media experts who can help develop effective training courses and presentations, and financial experts who could develop a compelling case as to why an investment in compliance yields a high rate of return. A rotating position could be established to attract leaders in the corporate or academic compliance world, the way that the Bureau of Economics attracts the highest caliber of economists who are willing to devote several years of their career to public service. The Bureau of Economics might also create a position devoted to behavioral economics to understand more about why people do what they do, which would help understand actual (as opposed to theoretical) effects on competition of a merger, as well as help to provide guidance on compliance programs. Having an official commission staff position (or group) encouraging compliance would help all of the lawyers and compliance personnel who struggle to adequate resources to implement an effective program.

21 As might be found in a deferred prosecution agreement sometimes used by the Department of Justice. The French antitrust authority, in its recent guidelines on compliance, created a system to grant credit against a penalty based on the implementation of a compliance program as part of the settlement of a case.

22 *See, e.g.*, Tim Wu, *The Love of Monopoly*, THE NEW REPUBLIC (May 19, 2011), review of Richard R. John, *Network Nation: Inventing American Telecommunications* (2011).

23 Notwithstanding the inventions of AT&T over the years, I remember being adamantly told by an AT&T representative in the 1970s that an electronic switchboard for my law firm was out of the question. The traditional analysis would posit that AT&T would have had no incentive to innovate, since no competitors were pushing them. So what drove them to have Bell Labs? Corporate conscience? Remains a mystery to me.

24 WALTER ISAACSON, STEVE JOBS (2011).

25 William E. Kovacic, *Intellectual Property Policy and Competition Policy*, 66 N.Y.U. ANN. SUR. AM. L. 421 (March 2011).

26 U.S. FEDERAL TRADE COMMISSION, TO PROMOTE INNOVATION: THE PROPER BALANCE OF COMPETITION AND PATENT LAW AND POLICY (Oct. 2003).

27 James E. Bessen, Jennifer Laurissa Ford, and Michael J. Meurer, *The Private and Social Costs of Patent Trolls* (Boston University School of Law Working Paper 11-45, 2011), *avaialble at* http://www.bu.edu/law/faculty/scholarship/workingpapers/Bessen-Ford-Meurer-troll.html. The authors conclude that patent troll may have resulted in $500 billion in lost wealth to defendants from 1990 through 2010, mostly from technology companies. Very little of this loss represented a transfer to small inventors, but it did serve as a reduction in the incentives to innovate.

28 35 U.S.C. § 292.

29 35 U.S.C. § 257.

Part II
New Frontiers of Antitrust

Avoiding the "Robin Hood Syndrome" in Developing Antitrust Jurisdictions[*]

Alden F. Abbott

alabbott@rim.com

Director Global Patent Law and Competition Strategy, Research in Motion
Former Deputy Director for Special Projects, Office of International Affairs, U.S. Federal Trade Commission

Seth Sacher

ssacher@ftc.gov

Economist, Bureau of Economics, U.S. Federal Trade Commission

Abstract

It has been our observation that in many developing jurisdictions, competition agencies intervene in what are essentially regulatory or contracting matters or even law enforcement matters. Sometimes this is done of their own volition, but it is frequently in response to requests from regulators or other enforcement agencies, possibly due to shortcomings in these agencies' own enforcement capabilities. We call this tendency of competition enforcers in developing jurisdictions to shoulder responsibilities beyond antitrust enforcement the "Robin Hood Syndrome." While the lines between antitrust, regulation and contract law may not always be definitively drawn, and all competition agencies struggle with the appropriate boundaries, we argue that competition enforcers in newer agencies should be particularly mindful of the distinction. Undertaking such roles can undermine good competition enforcement as well as hinder the development of an effective regulatory regime and undermine the rule of law. Competition agencies have a vital role to play in advancing social welfare in developing economies by focusing on enforcing competition law and promoting market-oriented reforms. To avoid undermining their effectiveness, they should stick to this role, and avoid pressures or temptations to engage in activities beyond their core competencies.

I. Introduction

Bill Kovacic has spent a good part of his career promoting the sensible application of antitrust principles in developing economies. Much significant progress has been made and Bill deserves no small share of the credit.[1] However, there is still work to be done and this paper focuses on one such area.

Competition law enforcement generally encompasses at least three major areas: (1) agreements among firms that harm the competitive process (the most egregious of which are hard core cartel and price-fixing arrangements); (2) merger enforcement policies; and, (3) behavior by dominant firms that may create or enhance monopoly power. A fourth non-enforcement role that many competition agencies have assigned to them is advocacy, which refers to actions aimed at providing a perspective on how competition may be affected by various regulatory or legislative initiatives.[2] However, it has been our observation that competition agencies in various jurisdictions (particularly agencies that are relatively new) are frequently called on, or simply assume, roles beyond the four areas mentioned above, including intervening in what appear to be matters that would more appropriately be handled by regulators and what may be better characterized as contract disputes.

This article seeks to highlight the problems that may arise when competition authorities go beyond their core responsibilities and stray into areas unrelated to competition concerns. We argue that undertaking such roles can undermine good competition enforcement. It can also hinder the development of an effective regulatory regime and undermine the rule of law. As explained more fully below, we call this tendency of competition enforcers in developing jurisdictions to take on roles beyond antitrust enforcement the "Robin Hood Syndrome."[3]

II. Dangers of Overextending the Responsibilities of Competition Agencies

1. General

The most obvious problem with having competition agencies investigating and enforcing matters outside the traditional purview of antitrust is that the limited resources of the competition agencies are strained. Additionally, there are costs of duplication as more than one agency becomes involved in investigating and prosecuting a matter. Further, error costs, and, in particular, harm stemming from false positives, may loom particularly important when a competition agency ventures into new areas.

Another danger is that the legitimacy of the competition agencies can be undermined. As it will be explained more fully below, taking on regulatory roles can drive the competition agencies into continuing relationships with certain entities. While the issue of the "capture" of regulatory agencies is well known,[4] this phenomenon may also apply to competition agencies that assume regulatory roles.

The reasons for maintaining the perceived integrity of a competition agency within a jurisdiction are obvious. The perception of integrity has assumed even greater significance in a world where business practices and transactions are increasingly international in scope, and multiple competition agencies must, therefore, cooperate on a regular basis. Building a reputation for integrity may pose particularly difficult challenges for newly minted competition agencies, which are just "learning the ropes" and deciding how to interact with established public and private institutions and interest groups.

Decreasing the perceived legitimacy of antitrust agencies, as well as creating conditions for capture, can be especially dangerous during times such as the recent financial crisis. There are undoubtedly special interests that will seek to use such crises to enact competitive constraints that will have nothing to do with the crisis at best and will exacerbate it at worst.[5] The competition agencies are well situated to expose the true nature of such anti-competitive proposals through their advocacy functions. Moreover, advocacy can be a particularly important role for many competition agencies in newly emerging market economies, whose governments are seeking to privatize various formerly state-owned enterprises or other protected monopolies. Anything that undermines the legitimacy of the competition agency can hinder its effectiveness when engaging in advocacy. Indeed, if it is truly captured, it may not even engage in advocacy when needed.

As we will explain, having the antitrust agencies involved in matters beyond their traditional roles also has effects on agencies and institutions other than the competition agency itself. Thus, if regulatory agencies, other enforcement organizations, or the courts, turn to the competition agency because of their own shortcomings, this can impede the proper development of such institutions. For these reasons, it may be advisable for relatively new competition agencies to be especially circumspect about extending their activities beyond traditional antitrust roles, even into gray areas between the boundaries of antitrust and other areas of regulation and law enforcement. Finally, as developed more fully in the next section, imposing the possibility of a second set of penalties on activities already covered by other areas of law enforcement can have chilling effects on legitimate efficiency-enhancing endeavors.[6]

2. The Problem of Overdeterrence

The concept of underdeterrence appears easy to grasp. Underdeterrence refers to the fact that since some violations of the law may not be detected, some individuals will go ahead and attempt to violate the law if the perceived benefits are large enough.[7]

More difficult to grasp though is that there can also be overdeterrence. The potential for overdeterrence is broadly recognized in both the legal and economic realms and the costs can be very real. Overdeterrence occurs when the prospect of being held liable deters individuals from engaging in socially productive activity. For example, stepping in to break up a fight might be misinterpreted by the police arriving later at the scene. To avoid this risk, a bystander may refrain from getting involved even if the intervention would potentially be conducive to the public good. Examples of overdeterrence in antitrust might be firms avoiding contacts with other firms to initiate legitimate collaborative relationships because such contacts might be misconstrued as price fixing, or abstaining from innovative pricing arrangements that might be misconstrued as some form of abusive vertical behavior.

Overdeterrence is somewhat related to the issue of false positives and both have similar effects. However, whereas false positives go more to the issue of the incorrect detection of a violation, overdeterrence goes more to the issue of the chilling effects from overly harsh punishment for a violation.[8] As noted above, it is also the case that by imposing a second level of review, and a level of review that may be less expert than the primary level, the likelihood of false positives is also increased when competition agencies step into the areas of regulation and contract law.

Overdeterrence may be of more concern when antitrust oversteps into the contracting area rather than the regulatory area. Thus, in the regulatory area, either because of the nature of the industry (i.e., it may be a "natural monopoly") or regulatory fiat, there is often only one firm (or very few firms) in the industry. In such cases, the chilling of horizontal relationships and entry may be of little importance. On the other hand, as explained more fully below, in the contracting area some contracts may not be written for fear of incurring antitrust liability and efficient relationships either may not be created or may take on inefficient forms. This is not to say that there could not be any negative overdeterrence effects in the regulatory area either, as even regulated firms will engage in, or avoid, certain efficient behaviors, when double punishment is an issue. Examples are considered more fully below.

Another key argument for limiting the role of competition agencies in non-competition matters is that taking on such responsibilities may have other deleterious effects, as regulators may be led to believe they can shirk their responsibilities. In a sense, this may mitigate some of the concerns with overdeterrence. That is, if the regulator believes the competition agency will handle matters on its behalf, it may not start an investigation or impose a penalty. However, this is hardly a refutation of our overall arguments for avoiding the "Robin Hood Syndrome," since the other deleterious effects remain and are still significant.

III. Issues when Competition Agencies Investigate and Enforce Regulatory Matters

1.General

Although antitrust is sometimes thought of as a form of regulation, it is distinct from most other forms of regulation that involve a continuing relationship between the firms being regulated and the regulator(s). Antitrust is meant to be an infrequent intervention so that markets can more nearly achieve certain social objectives on their own.

The continuing relationship between regulators and the regulated often leads to what is called "regulatory capture." Thus, regulators are frequently lobbied by the very firms they are meant to regulate. Further, regulatory agency officials are routinely chosen from among participants in the particular industry since this is where the industry expertise lies. Moreover, regulated firms may have a vested interest in the industry they regulate because their budgets may be tied to the health of the regulated industry.

Given the lack of regular contact between antitrust enforcers and particular market participants, competition agencies are less susceptible to capture. Since the regulators may not be able to overcome various pressures, it has been our observation that in many developing jurisdictions regulators will depend on competition agencies to "rescue" them. Thus, regulators will often look to the antitrust agencies to act as "Robin Hood" on their behalf. Of course, Robin Hood did not always wait to be asked to perform the role of hero and so it is with the competition agencies as they will sometimes step in to non-antitrust areas even without receiving a request. We argue that such behavior is not actually heroic and can actually have a deleterious effect on both the regulatory and competition agencies and the firms potentially involved.

The detailed industry-specific knowledge that gives rise to capture also may give the regulatory agency informational advantages over the competition authority. (In the case of regulated industries, industry-specific knowledge often relates to a particular firm). Thus, the competition agency will often not be adding to the expertise of the regulator and could also be undermining the legitimacy of both agencies.[9]

While we have made much of the possibility of regulatory capture, this is not to say anti-trust agencies can never be susceptible to outside political pressures. If competition agencies are subject to such pressures, our concerns about competition agency involvement in regulatory matters apply with even greater force. Adding an additional layer of incorrect politically-inspired enforcement will only exacerbate the problems referred to herein, and inhibit the ability of the competition agency to correct itself or be corrected by outside forces.

2. Distinguishing between Regulatory and Competition Matters

A. Cases where the Distinction Is Debatable

While drawing clear boundaries between the responsibilities of regulators and competition agencies appears to be a sound principle, this does not mean there are not areas of legitimate antitrust intervention in regulated industries. Indeed, all competition agencies struggle with the boundaries between antitrust and regulation at times. Nevertheless, as noted above, newer competition agencies should be particularly mindful of these boundaries, especially because of the possible impact on the healthy development of the regulatory agencies themselves.

Broadly speaking, the majority of industries in even the most liberal economies are regulated to some extent, such as with respect to safety issues. Clearly competition agencies should not eschew intervention in industries on the basis of such regulations. We are referring to the type of regulation that is meant to displace competition, usually because the structure of an industry or technology is such that competition is not feasible. Nevertheless, even here, firms can be involved in violations of the competition laws, and situations where antitrust may have to become involved in regulated industries abound.[10]

For example, firms may try to use various forms of regulation in an anticompetitive manner, through "raising rivals' costs"[11] or creating entry barriers. Thus, in the *Unocal* matter, the FTC alleged that a company misrepresented its patent position to a state regulatory authority (the California Air Resources Board) during rulemaking proceedings.[12] The FTC asserted that those misrepresentations should bar the company from enforcing its patents that applied to standards (and thus conferred market power upon the firm) adopted as a result of those proceedings. Nevertheless, such situations may require a difficult balancing with patent rights and the right of firms to petition the government.[13] However, even if firms have certain rights to petition the government for anticompetitive regulations, this does not mean there is not a role for the competition agency to use its advocacy function. Further, there can be a role for antitrust if firms abuse the regulatory and legal processes as a tactic for raising rivals' costs and delaying their date of effective entry, a form of behavior referred to as "sham litigation."[14]

It might be argued that the appropriate yardstick for determining whether antitrust liability is appropriate when the conduct at issue is already covered by another set of laws is the marginal benefit of such liability. However, in thinking about this principal, it may be useful to draw a distinction between the marginal benefit of antitrust liability and the marginal benefit from involvement by the competition agency. Often, what we are referring to here is not the extension of antitrust liability to fuzzy areas, but rather the involvement of the competition agency in matters for which there is little or no intersection with antitrust. There may be a marginal benefit from involvement of the competition agency in that the agency appears to be able to sanction or discontinue some kind of problematic behavior while other institutions face constraints in doing so; however, in so acting, the competition authority is not necessarily applying antitrust principles.

B. Cases where the Distinction Is Clearer

The aforementioned areas are by no means an exhaustive list of the possible intersections between antitrust and regulation. We are not taking a position here on the correct approach in such matters, but merely noting that there are many areas where antitrust forbearance due to regulation is not obvious and the marginal benefit of antitrust liability may not be insignificant. However, despite the absence of bright lines, there are areas in which limiting principles may be identified.

On the one hand, there may be cases where intervention by a competition agency into the regulatory sphere appears highly appropriate.[15] For example, regulation may be used to mask a cartel. Thus, a cartel consisting of politically powerful firms might be able to induce a legislature to regulate them so that they could avoid antitrust scrutiny, if there were too strict a barrier between competition law and regulatory law.[16]

On the other hand, there are some situations that very clearly should be the bailiwick of regulation, and competition law would have little to add. For example, if a firm simply charges a price higher than that explicitly set by the regulator, there appears to be little marginal benefit from antitrust intervention.[17] While this should clearly be a matter for the regulator,[18] we have seen competition agencies intervene in such matters.[19]

Consider a decision by one competition authority with respect to an electric utility.[20] In this matter, the utility tried to collect payments owed to it by a customer who had absconded, by cutting off power to the former landlord of the absconded customer. That is, the utility either hoped to collect the debts from the landlord or force the landlord into the role of a collection agency. This appears to have been a course of action explicitly forbidden by the regulatory regime. The authority in question submitted a statement of objections to the regulator, arguing the electric utility had abused a dominant position. The utility agreed to terminate the conduct under the rules established for energy and water regulation. The competition agency nevertheless imposed sanctions, holding that its basis for imposing sanctions could not depend on a remedy that is subject to another body. Further, the competition agency held that the remedy proposed by the defendant under the regulatory statutes not only would not lead to elimination of that conduct, but actually would increase the chance of its happening again.[21]

The utility's behavior does not appear to have been in the nature of an antitrust violation. Although it is a dominant firm, that appears to have done something "abusive" in a colloquial sense, this does not appear to have been an "abuse of dominance" within the meaning of competition law. Nothing in its attempt to collect an unpaid debt, however untoward, appears to either preserve or extend a dominant position. (Indeed, a dominant position does not appear to be necessary to engage in such behavior as even firms with the smallest of market shares engage in similar, if not more egregious, forms of behavior to collect bad debts.) The violation, in this case, appears to have been a violation of regulations.[22] There appears to have been some kind of shortcoming in the regulations that may have increased the chance of the behavior, but the simple fact of a regulatory shortcoming should not generally fall within the purview of competition law enforcement.

Another example involves alleged abuses of dominance by an international airport. There the competition authority sanctioned the airport for refusing to allocate a competing jet fuel supplier *more* space in the fuel storage facilities, and a parking space for its fuel supply vehicle. The transportation ministry already had the power to regulate such conduct, but the competition agency nevertheless imposed a fine on the airport.

Both of these instances of involvement by the competition agency appear to raise the potential harms to which we refer. In the first instance, the competition agency appears to have gotten involved because the remedies available to the regulator were deemed to be inadequate. While there may have been a gap in the regulations in terms of how the utility could seek to handle bad debts, this gap does not appear to have implicated a competition issue. While there may have been some marginal benefit by having the competition agency involved, it was not competition principles that were providing any marginal benefit. This involvement arguably may have hindered the full development of the regulatory agency, in that it may have felt less pressure to remedy the gap in its rules. [23]

In the second example, the competition agency appears simply to have imposed a second penalty. The regulator's power over such behavior does not appear to have been in any way limited. In addition to the aforementioned concerns, there is also the threat of overdeterrence. Perhaps due to concerns about overdeterrence, the airport will withdraw from, or open access to, other firms for other airport services such as security or catering services to the airplanes. It is entirely plausible such vertical disintegration can reduce efficiency due to a loss of scale or scope economies.

IV. Issues when Competition Agencies Step into Contracting Matters

We have also observed that sometimes competition regulators in some jurisdictions get involved in what are better characterized as contracting cases rather than antitrust cases. Just as was the case with regulation, sometimes the boundaries between antitrust and contracting matters can be controversial and all jurisdictions struggle with where to place the boundaries. For example, antitrust observers have debated whether the *Kodak* case, [24] which was adjudicated under antitrust law, was really a matter for contract law. In this matter, a group of aftermarket service organizations for Kodak copiers and micrographic equipment sued Kodak for certain policies that limited the availability of replacement parts. Some have maintained that if buyers had fully understood Kodak's aftermarket policies, they could only have been exploited if Kodak had changed those policies after they had made sunk investments in Kodak equipment. A change in those policies would have represented more of a breach of contract than an abuse of dominance. Arguably, problems of this type would be better remedied by contract law, either by encouraging buyers to obtain additional contractual protections before entering into such relationships, or by holding sellers accountable for the representations they make about aftermarket terms and conditions when selling their equipment.

It is our observation that relatively new competition agencies sometimes appear to find themselves embroiled in contracting disputes. As was the case with the electric utility discussed above, just because a firm is dominant and appears to be doing something that, in a colloquial sense, may appear abusive, this does not necessarily imply it is an abuse of dominance in an antitrust sense. Nevertheless, at times competition enforcers appear to intervene in matters simply because a firm is large and appears to be behaving in an inappropriate (i.e., abusive) manner regarding competitors or customers. Another reason competition agencies get involved in such matters may be similar to those given in the regulatory area more generally; that is, third parties (or the competition agency itself) will look to the agency to act as "Robin Hood" to help them overcome the enforcement deficiencies of others.

Many of the harms from antitrust involvement in the contracting area are the same as with regulatory involvement. First, the resources of the competition agency are stretched thin. Second, the legitimacy of the antitrust agency, as well as other institutions, such as the courts, may be damaged in the eyes of many stakeholders. Third, there will be the costs of duplicative effort, as multiple institutions deal with these questions. Fourth, when a competition agency intervenes in a matter that should properly have been adjudicated as a contracting dispute, and where it lacks expertise, it is possible that error costs will be higher, particularly the risk of false positives.

Furthermore, the social welfare benefits of the contracting process itself may be undermined when antitrust steps into the contracting realm. In the contracting area some contracts may not be written for fear of incurring antitrust liability. As explained more fully below, this could lead to too much vertical integration or too little trade. It could also lead to overly rigid contracts being written.

One important decision firms must make is the extent of vertical integration. Over 70 years ago, Ronald Coase explained that a firm and a market are substitute means of organizing economic activity.[25] Coase emphasized that firms can undertake certain tasks or manufacture certain inputs internally or use other entities (i.e., the "marketplace") to achieve those tasks. Nevertheless, both internal governance and the use of the marketplace entail costs. The extent of vertical integration is an attempt to balance these costs (sometimes referred to as a "make or buy" decision). When the cost of using the marketplace is artificially increased, as it might be if firms would face both antitrust and contractual liability for various relationships, then this tips the balance in favor of more vertical integration. While many times increased vertical integration is efficient, excessive vertical integration decreases efficiency. For example, excessive vertical integration may make firms more difficult to manage, increase the extent of shirking within a firm, or simply cause firms to undertake certain activities internally for which they do not have a comparative advantage, which decreases the overall amount of economic activity.

Another area in which antitrust involvement in the contracting area can chill efficient contracting behavior is in what is called *contractual incompleteness in the face of transaction specific assets*. Transaction-specific assets are assets that cannot be deployed outside a particular relationship without a loss of value (i.e., they are "sunk"). For example, a parts manufacture may decide to invest in dies to produce parts that can only be used by one downstream equipment manufacturer. In such situations, the parties may become vulnerable to opportunistic behavior by their trading partner. Thus, the parts manufacturer would have no customers if the downstream equipment manufacturer decided to stop purchasing from it. One response may be to write contracts that limit the potential for such opportunistic behavior. However, it may be complicated and extremely costly to specify all possible contingencies. The threat of opportunism due to contractual incompleteness may chill investment in transaction specific assets.[26]

Various protective safeguards against *ex post* opportunism may be adopted by exchanging parties when detailed explicit contracts cannot prevent all opportunistic behavior. These governance structures include displacing bilateral negotiation with common ownership (i.e., vertical integration), but they also include informal agreements and investments, such as reputational bonding mechanisms. For example, a downstream manufacturer may need various upstream suppliers to make asset specific investments in order to supply it with other parts. Such a downstream firm will be constrained from dealing opportunistically with any one upstream input supplier, in order to maintain its reputation for dealing fairly. This reputation is key to convincing other upstream suppliers to make necessary investments in the production of the other parts it requires. Under this scenario, simple reputational safeguards may be sufficient to yield efficient and non-opportunistic contractual outcomes.

Thus, in addition to leading to more vertical integration, excessive competition law liability for contracting matters could tip the balance in favor of more explicit and detailed contracts and away from such informal mechanisms. This could make inter-firm relationships more rigid and inflexible than would be warranted without such liabilities.

Just as regulators have advantages over competition enforcers in certain areas, contract law may also have advantages over antitrust. Thus, contract law often recognizes that circumstances can change in ways unforeseen by the parties that may require good faith renegotiation of terms. Competition law as applied in many jurisdictions may not possess this flexibility. Further, imperfectly informed antitrust authorities may carry out market power type assessments in reviewing contract disputes that potentially could be flawed. For example, the competition agency might mistakenly focus solely on the current (*ex post*) exercise of market power, rather than assessing such exercise in light of the situation as it existed when the firms initially agreed to contractual terms (*ex ante* analysis).

Two cases from one jurisdiction illustrate situations where the competition authority appears to have been involved in what should have been adjudicated as a contracting matter. One involved two companies that were spun off from the former state-owned petrochemical company. One company retained the oil refining assets while the other produced downstream petrochemical materials (e.g., rubber, fertilizers, coating materials, etc.). It was not feasible for the downstream petrochemical company to obtain petroleum inputs from another company.[27] When the parties were unable to come to an agreement on prices, the upstream petroleum supplier stopped delivery to the petrochemical producer for a period of approximately 39 hours. The jurisdiction's competition agency imposed a fine on the refiner on the basis of a refusal to deal theory.

There appears to have been a great deal of asset specificity between the parties in this matter. As noted above, in such situations firms usually have a number of tools at their disposal to prevent opportunism, including long-term contracts, vertical integration and various informal mechanisms. To the extent the petrochemical firm did not establish such protections, this was without doubt largely due to its founding, as the result of a privatization, rather than freely choosing to locate near the petrochemical plant. It was probably entitled to protections beyond those afforded a firm that chooses to freely enter into such an arrangement. However, this lacuna does not appear to have been a competition issue, but rather a shortcoming of the contractual guarantees established in the initial privatization. There were no indications the dispute was of a nature where the refinery was trying to extend or protect its dominant position. Nevertheless, trying to remedy this shortcoming through competition law can chill efficient contracting, as other firms that may have to make asset specific investments may choose less efficient mechanisms for deterring opportunism, since they may now believe they face, or are able to bring, antitrust actions in the case of such disputes. A much more beneficial approach to this dispute would have been to seek to remedy the situation through changes in the relevant contractual terms.

The second case involved a bus station in a particular city. In this matter, the competition authority concluded that the bus station abused its dominant position by denying the use of its facility to a particular bus line that provided transportation between that city and the jurisdiction's capital, even though several other companies used the facilities to provide transportation on the same route. Again, it is hard to see an abuse of dominance here since other companies were able to use the bus station to provide transportation on this route and it does not appear that denying access by this particular company to its facility either enabled the bus station to protect its monopoly in bus station provision or extend it to other markets. We believe it would have been healthier to resolve this matter through the contractual process. Characterizing this as an abuse of a dominant position can lead to inefficiencies, such as creating congestion at the station due to contracting with too many carriers.

V. Exceptional Cases

We noted above that the lines between antitrust, regulation and contracting law are not always easily drawn. Nevertheless, in areas that appear to be primarily regulatory or of a contract law nature, it is advisable for the newer competition authorities to encourage other institutions to handle the violations, both to promote efficient resource allocation and to encourage the healthy development of all agencies involved. This will also enhance the reputation of the competition agency in international dealings and in its advocacy roles.

Nevertheless, there may be cases when behavior is so egregious that, even though there are no antitrust violations, antitrust enforcers may decide that they need to act, perhaps when public safety is an issue.[28] Even in such situations, to the extent possible, competition agencies should strive to address such concerns through their advocacy functions, rather than get involved as *de facto* regulators or law enforcers. In cases where involvement is unavoidable, competition agencies should be explicit that they are undertaking an intervention that should be handled by other authorities and emphasize the limited nature of the intervention. This should limit the chilling effects of the intervention and may even encourage regulators or other enforcers to undertake appropriate actions on their own when similar situations arise again.

VI. Concluding Remarks

Competition agencies should resist the "Robin Hood Syndrome," whereby they intervene in what are essentially regulatory or contracting matters or even law enforcement matters. While the lines between antitrust, regulation and contract law may not always be definitively drawn, and all competition agencies struggle with the appropriate boundaries, competition enforcers in newer agencies should be particularly mindful of the distinction. When problems are brought to their attention that are not necessarily antitrust abuses, they would be better advised to coordinate with relevant government agencies or institutions to avoid conflicts and unnecessary administrative costs. In the long run, we contend that this approach would make them more effective in handling competition issues and encourage the healthier development of other institutions in their societies as well.

In sum, by focusing on enforcing competition law and promoting market-oriented reforms (particularly, through advocacy), competition agencies have a vital role to play in advancing social welfare, particularly in developing countries, where market institutions are not well-established. To avoid undermining their effectiveness, they should stick to this role, and avoid the temptation to engage in activities beyond their core competencies.

NOTES

* The views expressed in this paper are solely attributable to the two authors. They do not represent the views of the U.S. Federal Trade Commission, any individual Commissioner, or any other member of the FTC staff.

1 For an entertaining description by Kovacic of the challenges involved in promoting market-oriented policies in developing countries, *see* William E. Kovacic, *Lucky Trip? Perspectives from a Foreign Advisor on Competition Policy, Development and Technical Assistance*, 2 EUROPEAN COMP. J. 319 (2007). In this article, we use the terms "antitrust" (the American term) and "competition law" (the most generally used foreign term) interchangeably.

2 We also note that some competition agencies are empowered by law to bring actions against "exploitative" abuses, in particular, against excessive pricing by dominant firms. Certain agencies have exercised that authority, which they may deem a core function. Although we are not enthusiastic about such enforcement initiatives (in our view they risk inappropriately entangling competition agencies in regulatory endeavors for which they typically are ill

suited), we acknowledge that some competition agencies may view actions against exploitative abuses as a key part of their mission. Some jurisdictions may assign additional responsibilities to their competition agencies. For example, the European Union has prohibitions on State Aid that are enforced by competition agencies. The discussion of such additional obligations is, however, beyond the scope of this article.

3   We were inspired to use this moniker by the comment of a foreign official who referred to a competition agency as playing "Robin Hood" when it strayed beyond its core mission to "rectify" a perceived harmful situation, although this may be a strained analogy. After all, Robin Hood was an outlaw, not an arm of government. The analogy does capture the notion of a crusading entity that seeks to "do good" by straying beyond its assigned responsibilities to "rescue" other actors.

4   For some of the seminal works on regulatory capture, *see* JAMES M. BUCHANAN & GORDON TULLOCK, THE CALCULUS OF CONSENT (1962); DANIEL A. FARBER & PHILIP P. FRICKEY, LAW AND PUBLIC CHOICE (1991); Richard A. Posner, *Theories of Economic Regulation*, 5 BELL J. ECON. & MGMT. SCI. 335 (1974); George J. Stigler, *The Theory of Economic Regulation*, 2 BELL J. ECON. & MGMT. SCI. 3 (1971).

5   The economic crisis of the 1930s initially led to a severe curtailment of antitrust enforcement in the United States that many believe exacerbated the crisis. *See* CARL SHAPIRO, COMPETITION POLICY IN DISTRESSED INDUSTRIES (speech, ABA Antitrust Symposium: Competition as Public Policy, May 13, 2009), *available at* http://www.usdoj/atr/public/speeches/245857.htm.

6   A focus on core competition activities would also facilitate development of performance measures that would help governments evaluate the effectiveness of national competition agencies, thereby promoting greater accountability to the public. As Bill Kovacic has stressed, "[w]ithout consistent, meaningful performance measures, it is difficult to make sound judgments about agency quality and to compare agency performance across different time periods, or to benchmark agencies with their counterparts in other jurisdictions. This obstacle impedes the identification of useful improvements in agency design or operations, and frustrates efforts to assess the efficacy of any single reform." William E. Kovacic, Hugh M. Hollman, and Patricia Grant, *How Does Your Competition Agency Measure Up?*, 7 EUROPEAN COMP. L.J. 25, 26 (2011).

7   For a fuller discussion of this concept, *see* A. Mitchell Polinsky and Steven Shavell, *The Economic Theory of Public Enforcement of Law*, 37 JOURNAL OF ECONOMIC LITERATURE 45, 47-48 (2000). Underdeterrence may be rational given that detection is not costless. That is, it may not be optimal to devote so many resources to detection that every criminal act or civil violation is detected and punished.

8   In jurisdictions such as the United States, with treble damages and class action suits, overdeterrence may prove particularly costly.

9   To the extent there is particular expertise residing in the competition agency, such as a particularly knowledgeable staff member, this expertise can be shared without involving the entire competition agency as a redundant investigator and/or prosecutor.

10   The U.S. Department of Justice case that led to the dismantling of AT&T is the most cited recent American application of antitrust to a pervasively regulated industry. *See* United States v. AT&T, 552 F. Supp. 131 (D.D.C. 1982), *affirmed mem. sub nom.*, Maryland v. United States, 460 U.S. 1001 (1983). In Europe competition law is regularly applied to combat anticompetitive behavior in regulated industries. *See, e.g.*, Nellie Kroes, THE INTERFACE BETWEEN REGULATION AND COMPETITION LAW (Apr. 28, 2009), *available at* http://europa.eu/rapid/pressReleasesAction.do?ref erence=SPEECH/09/202&format=HTML&aged=0&language=EN&guiLanguage=en (remarks of former European Competition Commissioner on this topic).

11   *See generally* David Scheffman and Steven Salop, *Raising Rivals Costs*, 72 AM. ECON. REV. 267 (1983). A raising rivals' costs strategy would seek to promote the adoption of regulations that impose relatively greater costs on rivals than on the firm seeking the regulations.

12   *In re* Union Oil Co. of Cal. (*Unocal*), 138 FTC 1 (2004).

13   In U.S. jurisprudence, under the the the *Noerr–Pennington* "petitioning immunity" doctrine, antitrust laws cannot be applied to prohibit competitors from petitioning the government for changes of law, even anticompetitive changes. *See generally* HERBERT HOVENKAMP, FEDERAL ANTITRUST POLICY 746-766 (4th ed. 2011). Since Unocal allegedly made statements that misrepresented its willingness to invoke its patent rights, the FTC argued that its speech was deceptive and should not be protected by the *Noerr* doctrine.

14   The U.S. Supreme Court has suggested that petitioning that is a mere "sham" would fail to qualify for petitioning immunity. *See* California Motor Transport Co. v. Trucking Unlimited, 404 U.S. 508 (1972).

15   A possible gray area would involve regulatory evasion, such as when firms "tie" the sale of a competitively produced good with a regulated monopoly service to evade the price regulations. For example, suppose a telephone monopolist sold price-regulated phone services and also sold other unregulated services provided in competition with other suppliers. If the telephone company were able to shift accounting costs from its unregulated division to its regulated division, it might be able to fool the regulator into believing that its regulated profits were below the accepted rate of return and thus be authorized to charge a higher price for its regulated offerings. Overall profits could be increased through such a strategy (this is referred to as Baxter's law. *See, e.g.*, Joseph Farrell and Philip J. Weiser, *Modularity, Vertical Integration, and Open Access Policies: Towards a Convergence of Antitrust and Regulation in the Internet Age*, 17 HARV. J.L. & TECH. 85 (2003)). If there were no explicit regulations forbidding a regulated monopolist from entering competitive industries, there might be scope for the competition agency to be involved. In order to avoid a blurring of roles in such a situation, however, we would urge that the competition agency be explicit that it was simply undertaking a targeted intervention aimed at countering an anticompetitive distortion and thereby, ultimately enhancing the efficacy of the regulator.

16   Many competition regimes have established laws to stop such abuses of the regulatory process. For example, in the United States, the *state action doctrine* is meant to prevent such outcomes. Thus, under this doctrine, a state legislature can displace competition only if it clearly articulates its intent to displace market completion and engages in active supervision of the institution(s) used to supplant competition. *See generally* Hovenkamp, *supra* note 13, at 793-814. There have been antitrust challenges to regulations in case where these criteria have not been met (*see, e.g.*, FTC v. Ticor Title Insurance Co., 504 U.S. 621 (1992), in which the FTC challenged a state rule that allowed competitors to collectively agree on the rates they would charge for title insurance which the state then simply adopted by default).

17   This is not to say that a regulated firm cannot "game" pricing regulations, perhaps by tying its regulated sales with unregulated goods, or through vertical integration with unregulated businesses, or by pricing in such ways that its "rate base" is artificially increased. There might be a role for targeted antitrust enforcement in such situations, as indicated in note 16 above. (We also recognize, of course, that some competition agencies have been authorized to prosecute "exploitative abuses" such as "overly high" prices, but argue as a matter of principle that competition authorities should seek to avoid such interventions, to the extent they can consistent with their legal obligations. *See* note 3, above.)

18   One of the authors was made aware of one such example involving a regulated bread purchaser, which was presented at an OECD conference he attended in Budapest in 2009.

19   This would be distinct from a case where the regulator may have set too high a tariff because of the various capture pressures discussed above. In that case, whether or not the competition agency should be involved is less clear-cut. However, given the dangers to the proper development of antitrust and regulatory agencies in such jurisdictions, we would argue against direct action by the competition agency to challenge the tariff. Advocacy would be a more effective and benign path.

20   This and subsequent examples are drawn from real cases, but the parties and authorities are not identified.

21   The reason for this was not explained.

22   Under other regimes, this might also be seen as a breach of contract in that the utility did not have the right to seek payment for bad debts through suppliers or customers of the debt holder. (Another relatively new competition authority had a similar case against a public water utility, which was presented at a Budapest OECD conference attended by one of the authors in 2009.)

23   Some might argue that antitrust liability is appropriate when a regulated firm does not fulfill its obligations to the detriment of competition. Indeed, the *Trinko* case may have had such elements. *See* Verizon Communications Inc. v. Law Offices of Curtis V. Trinko, LLP, 540 U.S. 398 (2004) (telephone company's violations of Federal Communications Commission regulations concerning the sharing of company's network with competitors did not violate the Sherman Antitrust Act). We note that in *Trinko* the U.S. Supreme Court held that antitrust liability should not apply, because the mere violation of a regulatory agency's regulations did not involve conduct that independently violated antitrust norms. Although various commentators have taken issue with the *Trinko* holding, *Trinko* type arguments against additional liability may apply with particular force to newly established competition agencies because of the various potential problems with fostering the development of sister enforcement agencies discussed in the text. The utility case discussed in the text appear to have involved very particular violations of regulations (*e.g.*, was there *enough* parking for the competitor, *enough* storage space, etc.), which seem best left to a regulator or other authority, especially when these responsibilities have already been assigned to them.

24   Eastman Kodak Company v. Image Technical Services, Inc., 504 U.S. 41 (1992).

25   Ronald H. Coase, *The Nature of the Firm*, 4 ECONOMICA 386 (1937).

26   Seminal works in the extensive economics literature on firm behavior when there is asset specificity and incomplete contracts include Benjamin Klein, Robert G. Crawford & Armen A. Alchian, *Vertical Integration, Appropriable Rents, and the Competitive Contracting Process*, 21 J.L. & ECON. 297 (1978); Oliver J. Williamson, *Transaction-Cost Economics: The Governance of Contractual Relations*, 22 J.L. & ECON 233 (1979); Benjamin Klein & Keith B. Leffler, *The Role of Market Forces in Assuring Contractual Performance*, 89 J. POL. ECON. 615 (1981).

27   It is unclear whether the upstream refiner could sell its product to other customers.

28   For example, at a conference in Budapest, one of the authors was informed of a billing dispute between a utility and a city in a particular jurisdiction. When the utility disconnected the power supply for the entire city, the competition agency imposed sanctions for an abuse of dominance, even though competition law principles were not implicated.

Striving for Better Competition Enforcement

Thomas Barnett

tbarnett@cov.com

Co-chair of the global competition practice, Covington & Burling, LLP

Kristin Shaffer

shafferk@cov.com

Associate, Covington & Burling, LLP

Abstract

As competition enforcement becomes an increasingly global undertaking, Prof. Kovacic's teaching that "[t]he *best* practice in competition policy is the relentless pursuit of *better* practices" has become even more salient. In this article, the authors react to some of the comments and recommendations made by Prof. Kovacic. For example, they highlight the need to evaluate not just the agencies charged with competition enforcement, but also the tools that are at their disposal. By recognizing the limitations of evaluation methods, commentators and agencies can improve their enforcement decisions. The authors discuss the benefits of increased interaction between the U.S. DOJ and FTC as well as between each of them and other competition enforcement agencies around the world. Additionally, the authors discuss the importance of transparency and predictability in enforcement and the opportunities that globalization presents for agencies to learn from—and potentially adopt or adapt—the policies and procedures of other jurisdictions.

I. Introduction

For more than four decades, William Kovacic has challenged and improved the way we think about and apply the principles of competition law. His legacy includes countless books and articles published around the world as well as students who are better attorneys today due to his teaching. Bill has made an untold number of appearances at competition law events and has tirelessly dedicated personal hours to meeting with individuals from competition agencies around the world. Moreover, we have all benefited from his commitment to public service—one that has led him to serve in multiple roles at the Federal Trade Commission, most recently as a Commissioner and as Chairman.

It is an honor to contribute to this project. Bill's observations in his article *U.S. Antitrust Policy: The Underperforming Federal Joint Venture*[1] are, as always, well-grounded and thought provoking. Whether you ultimately agree or disagree with his conclusions, Bill continues to push us to re-evaluate our approach to competition law policy and enforcement. As only he can put it, he challenges us to adhere to one of his best adages: "The *best* practice in competition policy is the relentless pursuit of *better* practices."[2]

II. Defining Better Practices

1. Importance of the Task

As Bill observes, there is a tendency in the press and by some commentators to measure the success of antitrust enforcement by counting enforcement actions initiated by the Department of Justice (DOJ) and Federal Trade Commission (FTC), with contested enforcement actions receiving far greater weight than consent decrees. This method of defining success, however, is fundamentally flawed. Focusing as Bill does on mergers and acquisitions as an illustration, there is a broad consensus that most mergers either benefit competition or do not threaten harm to competition. Such transactions can generate cost savings and improve innovation that benefits consumers, and therefore should not be the subject of enforcement actions. As a result, antitrust enforcement agencies strive to separate those transactions that threaten harm to competition (to avoid Type II errors or false negatives) from those that that do not (to avoid Type I errors or false positives), and to do so as quickly and efficiently as possible.

Put another way, the goal should not be more antitrust enforcement actions for their own sake or fewer antitrust enforcement actions, but better antitrust enforcement.[3]

A misguided focus on the number of contested enforcement actions distorts analysis and disserves the business community, which needs guidance on likely enforcement actions in order to enable better decision making. For example, after the DOJ entered into consent orders in the Ticketmaster/Live Nation[4] and Comcast/NBC Universal[5] transactions, some commentators suggested that the Antitrust Division might not be willing to litigate to block a merger.[6] The unreliability of such an undue inference became readily apparent when the DOJ successfully sued to block the proposed H&R Block/2SS Holdings Inc.[7] and AT&T/T-Mobile[8] transactions. In the wake of these actions, resulting commentary quickly engaged in a discussion of the Justice Department's "newfound toughness."[9]

The point is not to comment on the merits of any of these enforcement actions. Rather, it is to underscore that every enforcement decision is based upon a careful analysis of the particular facts in each proposed transaction. Further, the result in a particular case should not be over-read as a general barometer of either what the agency is likely to do in the next transaction or whether the agency is achieving the goal of better antitrust enforcement. Such a judgment requires a far more extensive, nuanced, and deliberate assessment.

As we consider critiques of the ways in which the agencies perform their duties, we should, as Bill does, keep this point firmly in mind.

2. Consensus on Fundamental Goals of Antitrust Enforcement

While the finer points of what constitutes better enforcement will always be debated, we have achieved a broad consensus on the key goals of antitrust enforcement and the basic framework of analysis. As Robert Pitofsky has observed:

> The period from 1970 to the present—roughly a third of a century—has witnessed profound changes in the quality of regulation at the Federal Trade Commission and a remarkable convergence of antitrust enforcement policy between left and right, and between primarily legal as opposed to primarily economic approaches. With respect to substantive law, areas of intellectual debate and uncertainty remain, but viewpoint differences that existed between the 1960s and the 1980s are today vastly reduced.[10]

Key areas of convergence, which have become so familiar that they risk being taken for granted, include the following:

1. Competition law protects competition, not individual competitors;
2. Competition law seeks to promote economic efficiency and growth;
3. Strong cartel enforcement should be a priority;
4. Transparency and predictability improve the effectiveness of competition enforcement; and
5. Increasing the efficiency as well as the effectiveness of the investigatory process is important.

The final report and recommendations of the Antitrust Modernization Commission, a bipartisan commission charged with the task of examining the state of antitrust law and recommending proposals to modernize policies, bears out this view.[11] After a thorough review of the laws and their application, soliciting opinions from experts and the public alike, the Commission released a more than 500 page report. One of the most notable features of this undertaking was the finding that the laws and policies themselves were still sound in our new economy and did not require major revision.[12]

These principles should guide the formation of the goals of antitrust enforcement as well as assessments of the effectiveness of the agencies in furthering those goals. However, as the discussion that follows illustrates, applying these accepted principles to specific cases is far from easy and often engenders a lively debate.

3. Finding Right Answers

Measuring whether individual merger enforcement decisions are "right" is a difficult task. While the *ex post* analysis that Bill has suggested, both in his Concurrences article and elsewhere,[13] can be an important tool, it also has important limitations that should be understood. A lack of meaningful data often presents the first hurdle to effective *ex post* merger analysis. While the FTC has the authority to undertake studies unrelated to enforcement actions,[14] it rightfully exercises that authority only in limited circumstance given the enormous burden that it can impose on the subject business community.

Additionally, even were the agency able to capture all of the data available without regard to burdens, such data only relates to the road that was traveled. By definition, there is no data on the road not taken. Further, interpreting the data and determining causation as opposed to just correlation can be difficult as well. Nominal prices might increase or decrease after a transaction, but whether the change was the result of the transaction or an exogenous change in market conditions is often difficult to determine.

We can, however, acknowledge this complexity without coming to the conclusion that we must simply throw up our hands and walk away from the task of seeking to measure whether the agencies are furthering their goals. The lesson to draw from these observations is to be careful about how the analysis is performed and cautious about drawing too firm or too broad a conclusion from the results.

Dennis Carlton has suggested one approach to an assessment of merger analysis that is consistent with this lesson. He suggests that the agencies systematically compare pre- and post-merger conditions on discrete issues with the outcomes that the agencies had predicted in their assessment during the investigation.[15] This approach would require the agencies to record summaries of a reasonable number of their merger analyses. Such summaries could then be compared to actual outcomes in the relevant market, with efforts to adjust, of course, for exogenous changes.[16] The sharing of such results between the DOJ and FTC could help assure that the enforcement approaches of the agencies are consistent. Further, this process would provide an opportunity for the DOJ and FTC to engage their merger staffs in regular communication, as Bill has recommended.[17]

Such an approach would still face complications, however. In addition to the data and causation issues discussed above, selection bias can skew the results. When it is impossible for the agency to study all aspects of all merger decisions, the choice of what transactions to evaluate in this manner will limit the degree to which findings can be extrapolated to draw broader conclusions about agency enforcement actions.

For these and other reasons, evaluation as an "Achilles heel of merger policy and competition law enforcement"[18] is a legitimate concern that cannot be easily remedied. While Bill has effectively drawn our attention to the need for building a "common framework to assess the consequences of past enforcement decisions,"[19] we also should exercise caution and not use case studies, or any other single tool, as the yardstick against which to measure enforcement effectiveness. Rather, we should recognize the limitation of the tools at our disposal and use them in a manner consistent with those limitations.

4. Process Evaluation

Process is important for two reasons. First, good process ensures that the agency is able to collect and evaluate the information necessary to assess a transaction. Second, the investigatory process itself imposes costs on businesses and the economy, as well as on the agency. Thus, the goal is to focus on the right transactions, to collect the information needed, and to minimize the burdens (including time) of the investigation.

Evaluation of the efficiency of agency processes also presents challenges, although some basic measures seem feasible to implement. For example, the percentage of second requests (or, more generally, second-phase investigations) for the agencies that result in enforcement actions should, in theory, be high in an effective regime. If the agency has put in place policies to quickly identify transactions unlikely to harm competition, then the agency should be moving to a second-phase investigation only for transactions that are likely to threaten competition. If so, second-phase investigations should have a high correlation to eventual agency action. Such efficiency pays dividends not only in allocating limited agency resources to those transaction that genuinely threaten competition in the marketplace, but also in the market itself, as companies are relieved of the burden of a more in-depth investigation where there is no competitive harm.

Therefore, as the agencies self-assess their effectiveness, they should seek to reduce the false positive (or Type I error) rate for second-phase investigations. Once again, however, there are complications. For example, there could be a temptation for an agency to seek "cheap consents" from companies in order to keep their statistics high,[20] and the agencies should actively guard against pressures to do so.

Additional efficiency gains also can be made by looking at the process by which the agencies collect information. For example, in August 2011, the DOJ and FTC issued a new premerger notification form under the Hart-Scott-Rodino Act.[21] The agencies sought to simplify the filing process and increase its effectiveness by eliminating certain sections of the form, which called for information the agencies had found over time was rarely needed. At the same time, the form added requests for other information that the agencies had found more likely to be useful early in a review and not unduly burdensome to produce.

As another example, the FTC recently has taken a comprehensive look at its adjudicative process and modified its rules to expedite the prehearing, hearing, and appeal phases.[22]

Transparency is also an important part of the efficiency of enforcement. If private parties can better predict enforcement actions, they can better conform their behavior and avoid the need for lengthy, and costly, investigations or enforcement proceedings.[23] As Bill has explained, the revised Horizontal Merger Guidelines (HMG) are a helpful step in this process.[24] They represent a recent undertaking in a long history of the DOJ and FTC working together to provide greater guidance to market participants. For example, the 2006 Commentary on the HMG provided significant information about the new analytical tools used by the agencies, much of which has now been incorporated in the 2010 Guidelines.[25] In addition, the DOJ and FTC use speeches, data releases, closing statements, and competitive impact statements to provide greater insight into agency decisions.[26] The agencies use each of these tools to increase the transparency of the decision making process and allow market participants to anticipate future agency action.[27]

5. Interagency Relationship

As Bill explains, an important ingredient in increasing the effectiveness and transparency of the DOJ and FTC is the continued fostering of a collaborative relationship between them. Increased harmony between the agencies can help them to improve each other's decision making, provide greater confidence in the agencies by the public, and enable the agencies to engage more effectively in the global dialogue that now takes place in the international competition community.

Bill's suggestions for increasing interaction between the agencies, particularly at the staff level, make good sense. Joint sessions to discuss the application of the HMG, as well as training that includes staff from both agencies, would undoubtedly be useful as the DOJ and FTC seek to assure their interpretations are consistent. Additionally, the agencies might consider forming working groups to discuss such subjects as the standard to be applied in issuing a second request in a merger investigation, the types of documents that have proved particularly helpful or unhelpful in investigations, or each agency's experience with merger simulations or critical loss analysis.

Part of the motivation for Bill's suggestions in this regard is to improve and strengthen the relationship between the DOJ and FTC. Here, it bears mention that disagreements between the DOJ and FTC should be kept in perspective. Not only are the majority of investigations seamlessly allocated between the agencies, but the agencies have successfully interacted on a wide-variety of policy matters. Without trying to be exhaustive, the following examples illustrate the point: (i) the joint release of the 2010 HMG and the 2006 Commentary on the HMG; (ii) joint hearings conducted by the agencies on topics of mutual interest; (iii) routine submission of joint papers to the Organization for Economic Cooperation and Development and the International Competition Network; (iv) bilateral discussions between the DOJ and FTC, on the one hand, and other agencies, on the other hand; and (v) successful negotiations of memorandums of understanding with international bodies, as illustrated by the DOJ/FTC Memorandum of Understanding with the Chinese agencies, which was signed in the Summer of 2011.[28]

Nevertheless, there is no doubt room for improvement, and it is hard to argue with Bill's admonition that we should strive for better interagency interactions at both the staff and senior management levels.

6. Globalization

As Bill has articulated better than anyone, successful implementation of antitrust policy requires a constructive relationship among the more than 100 competition enforcement agencies around the world. This perspective is well recognized by both the DOJ and the FTC. In fact, Bill's observations that the FTC has a more extensive working relationship with the Director-General for Competition of the European Commission than it does with the DOJ[29] may be seen as evidence of the success the agencies have had in forging international relationships.[30]

In the international arena, a key priority should be for the United States agencies to recognize areas of consensus. The agencies should communicate these points of consensus in a coherent and consistent manner. Necessarily, this first requires coherence and consistency between the DOJ and FTC themselves. In this regard, for all of the ink spilled over the differences between the DOJ and FTC, it should not be lost that the two agencies have always seen eye-to-eye on the vast majority of issues in recent years. "While there will always be forceful advocates calling for far more or far less enforcement, a substantial consensus has emerged, consigning much of antitrust to a common middle ground."[31]

The "common middle ground" has become so well accepted that there is a tendency in the United States to take it for granted while focusing on areas of continued debate, which are more at the margin but make for more interesting press or debates at conferences. The agencies should remind themselves and others of the common ground so that they can speak with one voice on these issues and provide more effective input in the international dialogue surrounding them.

At the same time, the United States should keep an open mind in assessing the successful innovation of others. For example, leniency programs in other jurisdictions provide some consideration for those companies or individuals who are second or third in line in reporting their own misconduct.[32] The United States should consider whether it can draw any lessons from this experience. As another potential example, the European Commission imposes far less burdensome requests for documents than do the United States agencies in conducting merger reviews. While there are understandable reasons for this difference, the United States should consider whether it could learn from the EU process and reduce the burdens of its document requests. In short, a willingness to consider adopting the successful practices of enforcement agencies in other jurisdictions is part of a healthy international discussion and can lead to benefits both here and abroad.

III. Conclusion

Consumers around the globe could have no better and no more effective advocate for their welfare than Bill Kovacic. Fortunately, his dedication and boundless energy continue unabated, so we call all look forward to being pushed, prodded, cajoled, and challenged to strive to improve competition law and enforcement for many years to come.

NOTES

1   William E. Kovacic, *U.S. Antitrust Policy: The Underperforming Federal Joint Venture*, 4 CONCURRENCES 65 (2011).

2   William E. Kovacic, then General Counsel, FTC, Remarks Before the Seoul Competition Forum: Achieving Better Practices in the Design of Competition Policy Institutions (Apr. 20, 2004), *available at* http://www.ftc.gov/speeches/other/040420comppolicyinst.pdf.

3   *See* David Meyer, then Deputy Assistant Attorney General, Remarks before the 11th Annual Symposium on Antitrust, George Mason University Law Review: We Should Not Let the Ongoing Rationalization of Antitrust Lead to the Marginalization of Antitrust (Oct. 31, 2007), *available at* http://www.justice.gov/atr/public/speeches/227399.pdf.

4   *See* United States v. Ticketmaster Entertainment, Inc., No 1:10-cv-00139 (D.D.C. July 30, 2010) (final judgment).

5   *See* United States v. Comcast Corp., No. 1:11-cv-00106 (D.D.C. Sept. 1, 2011) (final judgment).

6   *See, e.g.*, Jia Lynn Yang, *AT&T Deal Draws High Profile Suit by Justice Department*, WASH. POST (Aug. 31, 2011), *available at* http://www.washingtonpost.com/business/economy/atandt-deal-draws-high-profile-suit-by-justice-department/2011/08/31/gIQAjNAzsJ_story.html; Josh Silver, *Comcastrophe: Comcast/NBC Merger Approved*, HUFFINGTON POST (Jan. 18, 2011, 12:06 PM), *available at* http://www.huffingtonpost.com/josh-silver/comcastrophy-comcastnbc-m_b_810380.html.

7   *See* United States v. H&R Block, Inc., No. 11-cv-00948 (D.D.C. filed May 23, 2011).

8   *See* United States v. AT&T, Inc., No. 11-cv-01560 (D.D.C. filed Aug. 31, 2011).

9   Thomas Catan & Brent Kendall, *AT&T Case Shows Antitrust Mettle*, WALL ST. J. (Dec. 21, 2011), http://online.wsj.com/article/SB10001424052970204058404577110963826534228.html.

10   Robert Pitofsky, *Past, Present, and Future of Antitrust Enforcement at the Federal Trade Commission*, 72 U. CHI. L. REV. 209, 209 (2005).

11   ANTITRUST MODERNIZATION COMMISSION, REPORT AND RECOMMENDATIONS (2007).

12   *Id.* at ii.

13   *See, e.g.*, William E. Kovacic, *Evaluating Antitrust Experiments: Using Ex Post Assessments of Government Enforcement Decisions to Inform Competition Policy*, 9 GEO. MASON L. REV. 843 (2001).

14   15 U.S.C. §§ 46, 49.

15   Dennis W. Carlton, *Why We Need to Measure the Effect of Merger Policy and How to Do it*, 5 COMPETITION POL. INT'L 77 (2009).

16   *Id.* at 83.

17   Kovacic, *supra* note 1, ¶¶ 15-18.

18   *Id.* ¶ 18.

19   *Id.*

20   Faced with the potential of a lengthy and costly defense against an enforcement action, companies may be willing to consent to limited divestiture or other measures in order to secure agency clearance of a merger, even though the companies believe such action is unwarranted. Likewise, during periods of heightened merger activity, the agencies may be more willing to reach settlements quickly rather than challenge a transaction broadly. *See* Timothy J. Muris, *Facts Trump Politics: The Complexities of Comparing Merger Enforcement Over Time and Between Agencies*, 22 ANTITRUST 37, 37 (2008).

21   FTC, PREMERGER NOTIFICATION; REPORTING AND WAITING PERIOD REQUIREMENTS, 76 FED. REG. 42,471 (July 19, 2011).

22   *See, e.g.*, FTC, RULES OF PRACTICE, 77 FED. REG. 3,191 (Jan. 23, 2012); FTC, RULES OF PRACTICE, 76 FED. REG. 52,249 (Aug. 22, 2011); FTC, RULES OF PRACTICE, 74 FED. REG. 20,205 (May 1, 2009).

23 Anticipatory conformity with antitrust rules by companies further counsels against measuring agency effectiveness by counting the number of enforcement actions. When agencies have coupled a pattern of correct decision-making with transparency regarding the process, one would expect to have a very low rate of enforcement actions, as the incentive for companies to conform their behavior would be strong and a failure to do so would be associated with high costs.

24 Kovacic, *supra* note 1, ¶¶ 5, 7-8.

25 *Compare* DOJ & FTC, Horizontal Merger Guidelines (Aug. 19, 2010), *available at* http://www.justice.gov/atr/public/guidelines/hmg-2010.pdf *with* DOJ & FTC, Commentary on the Horizontal Merger Guidelines (Mar. 2006), *available at* http://www.justice.gov/atr/public/guidelines/215247.htm.

26 Such communications are available on the websites of both agencies. *See, e.g.*, DOJ, Closing Statements, http://www.justice.gov/atr/public/closing/index.html; DOJ, Speeches, http://www.justice.gov/atr/public/speeches/index.html; FTC, Commission Cases and Documents, http://www.ftc.gov/os/filing_types.shtm.

27 Bill suggests that the agencies expand their use of closing statements by committing to issuing such statements after each instance where an agency engages in a significant inquiry and decides not to intervene. Kovacic, *supra* note 1, ¶ 21. His focus is on mergers, where the existence of a transaction and at least the possibility of an agency investigation is frequently public knowledge. It is important to note, however, that not all investigations undertaken by the agencies are public, particularly outside the merger context. Therefore issuing a closing statement may not be appropriate in all instances. Nevertheless, it is certainly a laudable goal to for the agencies to seek to issue more closing statements.

28 Memorandum of Understanding on Antitrust and Antimonopoly Cooperation Between the United States Department of Justice and Federal Trade Commission, on the One Hand, and The People's Republic of China National Development and Reform Commission, Ministry of Commerce, and State Administration for Industry and Commerce on the Other Hand (July 27, 2011), *available at* http://www.ftc.gov/os/2011/07/110726mou-english.pdf.

29 Kovacic, *supra* note 1, ¶ 10.

30 In some respects, it is easier for the DOJ and FTC to forge working relationships with agencies in other jurisdictions because they frequently investigate the same matters, while the FTC and DOJ virtually never work on the same matter. The DOJ and FTC, therefore, need to take more proactive steps, which is what Bill advocates in his article.

31 Pitofsky, *supra* note 10, at 212.

32 Under current DOJ policies, a corporation or individual must be the first reporter in order to be eligible for the leniency program. *See* DOJ, Frequently Asked Questions Regarding the Antitrust Division's Leniency Program and Model Leniency Letters, Nov. 19, 2008, *available at* http://www.justice.gov/atr/public/criminal/239583.pdf. In contrast, leniency policies in the European Commission offer reduced leniency to both the second and third reporters as well. *See* Commission Notice on Immunity from fines and reduction of fines in cartel cases, 2006 O.J. (C 298) 11, 20, *available at* http://eur-lex.europa.eu/LexUriServ/LexUriServ.do?uri=OJ:C:2006:298:0017:0022:EN:PDF.

Market Data and Participants' Views in Horizontal Merger Analysis

JOSEPH FARRELL*

farrell@econ.berkeley.edu
Professor of Economics, University of California, Berkeley

Abstract

Merger review at the U.S. antitrust agencies considers, as their 2010 Merger Guidelines put it, "any reasonably available and reliable evidence."[1] The Guidelines' Section 2 illustrates the variety of such evidence. Of course one could divide the kinds of evidence in various ways; this article stresses one such broad division. We draw inferences from market data such as prices, costs, quantities, demand estimates, and the like, using our own analytical apparatus and doing our own modeling or calculations; we also draw inferences from the testimony, documents, and views of market participants, which might in turn rest on their formal or (more often) informal analysis of facts, data, experience, and judgment. These methods should be viewed as complements, not as rivals.

I. Inferences from Market Data

When useful data are available, we use a range of techniques that might be described as an "outside" competitive assessment. I interpret this quite widely to include, for instance,

- Calculating how the merger can be expected to change firms' competitive incentives; this in turn could include one or more of:
    - Calibrating an oligopoly model and undertaking a merger simulation;
    - Evaluating the "value of diverted sales" and gauging upward pricing pressure;
    - Intermediate calculations such as the "illustrative price rise" used e.g. by UK competition authorities;
    - Considering how firms' incentives might be affected by circumstances such as vertical integration, and whether/how the merger changes that;
    - Considering how, if at all, the merger would affect conjectural variation or the tendency to engage in "coordinated conduct";

- Defining a market and measuring concentration or change in concentration; this in turn potentially includes such things as:
    - Evaluating substitution patterns, margins, and other factors bearing on market definition; considering implications of different plausible markets;
    - Counting competitors pre- and post-merger;
    - Grouping competitors by size or other indicators of significance, and counting (for instance) "major competitors";
    - Examining how shares, concentration, etc., have changed over time;
    - Calculating the Herfindahl index of concentration, and how it would change with the merger;

- Attempting to predict the likelihood of entry and how that likelihood would be affected by the merger; this might in turn include:
    - Analysis of costs relative to prevailing or hypothesized post-merger prices, perhaps with particular emphasis on sunk costs;
    - Historical experience with entry and exit;
    - Analysis of incentives for customers or complementors to enter or sponsor entry;
- Using "natural experiments" to gauge the merger's likely effect.

I want to stress two things about how these techniques are used in practical merger analysis, that I fear are not sufficiently reflected in the academic industrial organization literature on antitrust merger review.

First, it can be tempting to organize one's thoughts in terms of evaluating the reliability of analytical approach A "versus" approach B. In particular, this is the tone of a fair amount of debate about inferences from concentration and market shares "versus" inferences from analysis of incentives. But most of the time, in practical merger review, if one is lucky enough to have the data to use two different reasonable analytical frameworks, one would want to weigh both of them; and if they do point in opposite directions, one uses that fact to probe on each of them, rather than deciding in advance that one trumps the other. Yes, sometimes one must decide what to do when framework A suggests that a merger is problematic and B suggests the opposite; and sometimes it's relatively easy to decide which framework is more compelling; but often it's not, or shouldn't be. One should really evaluate the usefulness of each kind of evidence in the light of other evidence, not in isolation and not compared to another kind of evidence in isolation. This point is significant here, within this section on modes of formal economic analysis, but more importantly as between that cluster of techniques and the rather different cluster discussed in the next section.

Second, if one is fortunate enough to participate in a large number of merger reviews, one learns that industries and their participants are endlessly and richly idiosyncratic. A standard framework will seldom fit perfectly without custom tailoring. To mention just a handful of idiosyncrasies, some firms may be non-profit; some may be vertically integrated; some may be fast-growing; some may be based abroad; some may have a business model that relies more than others on follow-on sales such as spare parts or the development of customer relationships. Another set of issues concerns the level of analysis. Data-intensive techniques often most naturally focus on competition among particular existing products, which is important, but so is considering the possibility of broader effects: for instance, do shares of a broader "market" indicate firms' relative ability to introduce successful new products in a category? Similarly, if one has a lot of price variation data that's recent enough to seem fresh, it will tend to illuminate short-run responses more than long-run. All in all, any analytical framework, especially one capable of being applied in a limited time, has to abstract from at least some, usually many, of the rich details of a particular industry.

This fact does not make standard frameworks based on economic models unhelpful: on the contrary, we humans cope with complexity by simplifying it. In my experience, those who most complain about omitted complexities in the application of a simple standard framework are often implicitly seeking to apply another, often even simpler, standard framework. In particular, I don't think it is legitimate to complain that incentives analysis omits industry nuances and to claim that therefore a concentration-based approach must obviously be better: any concentration-based approach omits a lot of nuances too. However, when we apply standard frameworks we shouldn't forget that, almost always, we are simplifying.

II. Practitioners' Summarizing Views

These observations about the use of our own analytical frameworks as applied to industry data provide one possible context for understanding another broad category of evidence and inference that's heavily used in merger review: the use of information and views from market participants and sophisticated longtime observers of the market. These include documents and testimony of the merging parties, and the insights and views of customers, sometimes competitors, likely potential entrants, industry consultants, and complementors. Unlike the 1992 Guidelines, the 2006 Guidelines Commentary and the 2010 Guidelines acknowledge the role of this kind of evidence.

In the broadest terms, one might expect this kind of evidence to be less systematic and less transparent than the agency's or the parties' own data-driven economic analysis, but to have the potential to incorporate "soft" information, experience, intuitions, and evidence in a way that a formal analysis might not. To some degree, thoughtful and well-informed participants' views and intuitions based on experience might capture, albeit probably imperfectly, a broader set of those complexities and nuances that it's difficult or impossible for a formal analysis to incorporate with the limited time and resources available. I'm not suggesting that this is "better" evidence than an economics-based analysis: it has a variety of downsides, some of them discussed below, and in any event, as stressed above, the issue is not which is better but whether this "soft" information is valuably complementary with a more formal "outside" analysis.

III. Time and Resources in the U.S. Merger Review Process[2]

Most—though not all—merger antitrust review in the U.S. takes place before the merger is consummated. Under the Hart-Scott-Rodino (HSR) Act, most mergers above a threshold value (currently about $65 million) must be pre-notified to the FTC and DOJ, with a limited initial information submission. If the proposed merger raises questions, then one of the agencies (normally guided by which has more closely relevant experience and expertise) will review it, using the information submitted, public information, and other sources, often including talking to customers. While other federal agencies (such as the FCC or FERC) sometimes review mergers, and while state attorneys general and private parties sometimes also intervene, this article focuses on prospective HSR review by the FTC and DOJ.

Under the Act, the agency has a limited initial period, usually 30 days, to either allow the merger to proceed, or issue a "second request" for further information from the merging firms (the agency can also subpoena information from parties other than the merging firms). Complying with a second request often takes months.[3] After the firms "substantially comply" with the second request, the agency has a further limited period under the Act, again usually 30 days, to challenge the transaction prior to consummation.

These statutory rights and responsibilities are often the default or basis for negotiation. In particular, under the game as specified by the Act, in order to fulfill its responsibilities the agency would be pushed toward issuing a second request in more cases, and toward making that request relatively broad, since the agency only gets one "second request" and it is often not clear 30 days into an investigation what information will be available and useful.[4] That may involve costs and delays for the firms, so it is common to negotiate voluntary timing agreements and phased production of information; sometimes firms withdraw their HSR filing and refile it, restarting the clock. In such ways, investigations can be streamlined (an area of common interest between the parties and the agency) and second requests can be better focused. Thus DOJ has reported that "[a]lmost every matter with sufficiently difficult competitive questions as to merit a meeting between the parties and the [Antitrust] Division's Front Office now has a scheduling agreement in place . . . regarding how the investigation will proceed, and when it will end."[5]

In recent years, generally over a thousand mergers have been HSR-notified each year.[6] In Fiscal 2010, 1128 were notified, of which 149 were cleared to the FTC and 73 to the DOJ.[7] Compared with those 222 mergers that were cleared to an agency, 46 got second requests, although as noted above this is not a perfect measure of how many initial reviews raised continuing concern.[8]

In the same theme of negotiation in the shadow of a formal framework, many more mergers lead to divestitures or other negotiated settlements ("consents") under which the merger proceeds with modifications to protect competition, than are simply blocked or litigated.[9] For example, during fiscal 2010 the FTC "challenged 22 transactions, leading to 19 consent orders, and three transactions that were abandoned after the parties learned of the Commission's concerns."[10] Similarly DOJ "challenged 19 merger transactions. Consent decrees resolved ten of these challenges, one [led to] litigation, and eight transactions were abandoned or restructured"[11] Some transactions are abandoned early enough that they don't make it into the second-request data; for the reasons sketched above, this isn't only if they are abandoned in the first 30 days.

Finally, it is helpful to give a sense of the resources available for agency review. The FTC's Bureau of Economics has about 50 professional economists working on antitrust (another

20-plus work on consumer protection economics), and merger review is their biggest time commitment but by no means their only responsibility. Typically one or two staff economists will work on a merger, actively overseen by a mid-level manager, with "front-office" review of work product mostly, but by no means entirely, near the end of the review process. If a case appears headed for litigation the staff will often be augmented, and a potential testifying expert identified. There are normally substantially more lawyers than economists working on each case.[12] Similar statements could be made about review at the Antitrust Division of the Department of Justice.

The FTC's 2008 public report, "Horizontal Merger Investigation Data, 1996-2007"[13] gives statistics concerning various samples associated with the 384 second requests issued by the FTC during that period.[14] The data are extracted from staff's memos to the Commission recommending whether or not the Commission should challenge the merger—data on *what FTC staff believed* about proposed mergers—and on whether or not the Commission decided on antitrust *enforcement action*. This is meant to illuminate some aspects of the internal decision process. It is not data on actual marketplace results of mergers; as readers may know, such data is regrettably scant.[15]

The 2008 report discusses measures of concentration (Herfindahl indices, nominal changes in the Herfindahl, and number of significant competitors), and also statistics on "hot documents," customer complaints, and entry conditions.[16] While one could comment from many angles, this article stresses how the "views" evidence from documents and customers complements "data" evidence and arguably comparably "hard" evidence on entry conditions.

IV. Measures of Concentration

The older IO literature and the antitrust literature, including the 2010 Horizontal Merger Guidelines, give concentration (and the change in concentration) plenty of ink as an indicator of competitive effects.[17] For the purposes of this article my point is that one can view this as one representative, in the 2008 Report, of the broader category of quantitative data-driven analysis. The Report prominently features market concentration statistics: reporting concentration in multiple bands, and cross-tabulating it with each of the other variables separately, while the other variables are binary and not cross-tabulated with one another. The interaction of "data-driven" and other kinds of evidence is complex and nuanced.

V. Hot Documents

"Hot documents" are business documents of the merging firms that indicate plans or predictions that the merger will be anticompetitive. For example, the FTC found that Whole Foods' CEO advised his Board that acquiring their close rival Wild Oats would "avoid nasty price wars . . . which will harm . . . margins and profitability."[18]

Antitrust is well accustomed to the idea that intent matters—not primarily as such (outside attempted monopolization), but as a guide to an informed party's prediction of likely effect. The 2010 *Horizontal Merger Guidelines* explicitly recognize this source of information.

The academic economist's instinct, I think, is not to stress that kind of informal prediction by industry insiders. This is partly because in academic work one seldom has access to those documents. Perhaps it is also partly because academics want to see whether they can contribute an independent analysis; and if they can't, they may feel they don't have much to say.

Since a significant number of IO economists have been exposed to this melding and its second component, one might ask why talking to participants has not grown into a more widely used technique in IO. For example, when the National Bureau of Economic Research and the Alfred Sloan Foundation sponsored some studies using this source of information, they described it as "relatively unusual."[19] Or perhaps economists use this technique more than one might glean from their publications: for instance, they may use conversations with participants to formulate initial hypotheses but feel that once they have completed a more "objective" analysis it is no longer crucial to describe the source of the hypothesis.

Be that as it may, the FTC's data (Tables 5.1 and 5.2) show 22 out of 25 investigations resulting in enforcement when "hot documents" are identified, versus 109 out of 173 when they are not. The ratios are noticeably but not dramatically different (22/25=88%; 109/173=63%). The agencies do treat "hot documents" as "highly informative," as the 2010 Merger Guidelines confirm.[20] It is less clear that one can quantify this inference through the 2008 report's statistics, in part because even if the documents didn't much sway the agencies' internal evaluations, they could affect their perceived prospects in litigation, and hence the likelihood of effective enforcement action.

With strong caveats, one might view those statistics as a starting point for discussing the extent to which staff treat the views of the merging firms as a reliable predictor of the effect of the merger. Among the caveats must be that not all hot documents are sober high-level predictions. Still, it prompts the question of how reliable business participants' own predictions are, relative to practicable data- and theory-driven predictions "from the outside". What can be said about the degree to which business plans are good predictors—compared to, or more relevantly in conjunction with, more standard IO-like analyses? We don't yet know as much as we should about this question.

VI. Customer Complaints

In many horizontal mergers, the direct customers are not final consumers, but may themselves be sophisticated firms. Talking to such customers is often among the first tasks in a merger investigation. This is partly so as to understand the products and the industry, and partly in order to gauge customers' ability to substitute among products in and out of potential "antitrust markets."[21] But customers' views on the likely effects of a merger—in particular, customer complaints—are strongly correlated with enforcement action. Thus in the FTC's 2008 report, Tables 7.1 and 8.1 show 83 cases of enforcement and only 2 closings when there are "strong customer complaints;" Tables 7.2 and 8.2 show 37 cases of enforcement and 55 closings when there are not. Again, one would expect customer complaints to be correlated with other (observable to customers and/or to staff, but not necessarily reported in the tables) predictors of likely harm, so even this strong correlation doesn't show causation; but it would be consistent with public discussions of the role of customer complaints.[22]

One can ask much the same methodological questions about customers' predictions of merger impact as one can about the merging firms.' See for instance the cautious discussion in the FTC's and DOJ's 2006 *Commentary on the Merger Guidelines*.[23] The Oracle-People-Soft merger decision controversially suggested that customer testimony would be reliable only if based on quantitative studies, which is not how customer complaints are generally gathered. Of course one would like testimony to be as well-informed as possible; but the agencies are capable of doing their own quantitative studies (and in this instance the Antitrust Division had done so); my argument here is that customer testimony should cross-check and complement such studies with the more impressionistic predictions of those who live and breathe the industry. Insisting that customer testimony be based on quantitative studies might risk insisting that it be more correlated with other available evidence, and thus quite likely making the entire portfolio of evidence less informative.

To expand a little on that last point: if one were to evaluate a merger based on customer testimony alone, one would want the customers to have considered formally economic or data-driven kinds of evidence and analysis. But if one is bringing those sources of evidence to bear separately through the agencies' and parties' own analyses, then the theory of statistical inference suggests that one wants customer testimony to best bring out and evaluate those sorts and sources of evidence that the formal economic data-driven analyses *don't* incorporate. Trying to make customer evidence more like economist evidence might well be a good thing if we didn't also have economist evidence, but is much less apt to be a good idea when we do.

A second question is the following. It is very common for some direct customers to tell us that a proposed merger will be anticompetitive, and for others to tell us the opposite.[24] Indeed, the DOJ was also criticized for not showing that its customer testimony against the Oracle merger was representative of all customers; see also Sungard.[25] This diversity of views would be a puzzle if the merger would either be very simply anticompetitive—harming all customers, as for instance by raising "the price"—or very simply procompetitive—benefiting all customers, as for instance by lowering "the price". Most academic IO models of mergers, and most academic antitrust discussion, do in effect assume some version of that simple common-impact model.[26]

One possible answer starts by noting that, often, direct customers compete with one another downstream, perhaps selling to final consumers. The more competitive that interaction is, the more the direct customers' interests depend on their costs *relative to one another*, rather than on whether all of their costs have risen or fallen. As an extreme example, if direct customers face different costs (including prices paid to upstream suppliers), and compete as undifferentiated Bertrand competitors with inelastic market demand, then profits depend only on cost *differences* and not on common cost shocks. With softer competition, both differences and common level matter, though sometimes in surprising ways.[27]

If (or when) that's roughly the right way to think about the problem, how should an agency or a court evaluate the different views of different direct buyers? Is there a good summary statistic? For instance, should the views of large buyers get a lot more weight than those of small buyers? How would this depend on other aspects of the market—for instance, the strength of competition among direct buyers?

A different issue is raised when customers say that they believe a merger is anticompetitive but are reluctant to testify because they fear retaliation from their suppliers. Intuitively, when customers compete downstream, a supplier with market power can impose sharp punishment by varying relative prices among its customers, with relatively little impact on its own total sales or profits.[28] Conversely, some customers might be tempted to "hold up" a merger by threatening to tell enforcers (incorrectly) that they thought it would be anticompetitive.

VII. Entry Conditions

Tables 9.1 and 10.1 of the FTC's 2008 report show 36 investigations closed and none leading to enforcement where staff described entry as easy, while Tables 9.2 and 10.2 show 131 leading to enforcement and 31 closed where staff described entry as difficult.

In my experience one often cannot comfortably describe (timely and sufficient) entry either as "easy" or as "difficult." Entry is usually possible; yet in most markets where antitrust enforcement would be contemplated it is not really very easy or an everyday event.[29] The

1992 Guidelines seemed to propose a kind of "shadow business plan" approach to entry, in effect evaluating whether and at what prices stand-alone entry would become profitable. But while the

antitrust analysis of entry could very much benefit from additional work (I think it is fair to say that the volume of academic work on how existing oligopolists compete has not been matched by work on entry into competitively problematic or marginal markets[30]), I also think we have learned that a large fraction of competitively significant entry comes from adjacent players, suggesting the modestly different investigational strategy proposed in the 2010 Guidelines.

We often hear that a major barrier to entry, or to significant expansion by entrants and small firms, is access to effective distribution. Distributors may prefer to deal only with a limited set of suppliers, or expect that dominant suppliers will disfavor them if they show disloyalty. In some cases this is described as the principal barrier to effective entry or expansion out of specialized niches.

Whether downstream competition among direct buyers affects the risk of exclusion through exclusive dealing has been discussed in the exclusive dealing literature.[31] But as far as I know the effects of exclusive dealing on merger analysis have not been academically studied. If it's important in a particular industry, one can address it, but inevitably given the time and resource constraints, nobody can address everything. Thus impressionistic testimony from thoughtful and experienced customers, entrants (successful, failed, or potential), and others can help complement the best available economic analysis.

VIII. Conclusion

Real-world antitrust merger review is a variegated activity, with some investigations awash in data, others the reverse; some in simple and familiar markets, others obscure or institutionally confusing; some decisions where we feel confident, whatever litigation risks may remain, and others where we must make our best guess. It is also a challenging task, usually conducted under time pressure, so we do well to draw on all reasonably available and reliable sources of evidence. This very often includes both objective "outside" economic analysis of market data and of incentives, and the sober predictions and views of thoughtful and well-informed observers and participants. Setting up an either/or atmosphere in which these vie for hegemony misses the point; so does trying to force either to be like the other. There is strength in diversity of evidence, if intelligently understood and exploited.

NOTES

* The author was Director of the Federal Trade Commission's Bureau of Economics from June 2009-June 2012. Views expressed here are my own and do not purport to represent the Commission or any Commissioner. I am grateful to Elizabeth Callison, Malcolm Coate, and Marian Bruno for helpful comments, but they are not responsible for my views. This article was first written for a presentation to academic economists at the American Economic Association annual meeting, January 2012.

1 U.S. Dep't of Justice & Fed. Trade Comm'n, Horizontal Merger Guidelines § 2.0 (2010).

2 This is just my informal summary. A more official narrative explanation (still not the official rules) is at http://www.ftc.gov/bc/hsr/introguides/guide1.pdf. Lawyers can track down the official rules.

3 I am not aware of systematic public data on the timing. However, two former enforcement officials studied "an admittedly non-scientific sample" from 2000 and 2005 and found average elapsed times from announcement of a deal to conclusion, for cases involving second requests, varying from 5.4 to 11.4 months. Steven C. Sunshine & David P. Wales, Testimony before the Antitrust Modernization Commission (Nov. 17, 2005), *available at* http://govinfo.library.unt.edu/amc/commission_hearings/pdf/Sunshine_Statement.pdf. Separately, DOJ reported that its average review time fell from 93 days to 57 days, with the average duration of second request investigations falling from 248 days in 2001 to 134 days in 2005. *See* U.S. Dep't of Justice, Background Information on the 2006

AMENDMENTS TO THE MERGER REVIEW PROCESS INITIATIVE (Dec. 14, 2006), *available at* http://www.justice.gov/atr/public/220241.pdf. Former FTC Chairman Deborah Majoras described second request investigations as taking "a substantial amount of time, often ranging from six to nine months." REFORMS TO THE MERGER REVIEW PROCESS (Feb. 16, 2006), *available at* http://www.ftc.gov/os/2006/02/mergerreviewprocess.pdf).

4   Moreover, part of the initial waiting period is sometimes consumed in the "clearance process" of deciding which agency will review the merger.

5   BACKGROUND INFORMATION, *supra* note 3.

6   33 HART-SCOTT-RODINO ANN. REP. app. B tbl.1 (2010) (showing annual totals by year, 2001-2010). Only in 2009 was the total below 1,000; twice it was over 2,000.

7   *Id.* at exh. A tbl.II.

8   Because reporting is of filings and actions in a given year, actions may concern mergers filed the previous year, and the numbers could be disproportionate if the process is far from steady state. Of course these lags are less of a potential issue with second requests, which normally follow within 30 days of a filing.

9   When a settlement is a court order settling (often very promptly settling) litigation to block the merger, the FTC issues an "Analysis to aid public comment," or the DOJ issues a "Competitive Impact Statement." These are often among the most insightful public official documents to emerge from what is mostly a confidential process.

10 HART-SCOTT RODINO ANN. REP., *supra* note 6, at 1-2.

11 *Id.* at 2.

12 The Bureau of Competition, primarily antitrust lawyers and their support staff, has nearly 300 staff, well over three times the portion of the Bureau of Economics dealing with competition matters.

13 *See* FED. TRADE COMM'N, HORIZONTAL MERGER INVESTIGATION DATA, FISCAL YEARS 1996-2007 (2008), *available at* http://www.ftc.gov/os/2008/12/081201hsrmergerdata.pdf.

14 The counts are a bit complex. Data points for the findings of hot documents, etc., are markets of potential concern, rather than mergers, each of which may well involve multiple markets. However, mergers with more than three identified markets are excluded from these data tabulations.

15 This is the topic of the "merger retrospectives" literature. *See* for instance the meta-analysis by John Kwoka and Daniel Greenfield, *Does Merger Control Work?: A Retrospective on U.S. Enforcement Actions and Merger Outcomes* (Nov. 4, 2011), *available at* http://ssrn.com/abstract=1954849.

16 Malcolm Coate, *Transparency at the Federal Trade Commission: Generalities and Innovations in Merger Analysis,* CPI ANTITRUST CHRONICLE (Dec. 16, 2009), *available at* https://www.competitionpolicyinternational.com/an-overview-of-transparency-at-the-federal-trade-commission-generalities-and-innovations-in-merger-analysis; a similar version is at http://ssrn.com/abstract=1111687.

17 I will briefly observe that concentration depends on market definition, which is often controversial; and that when a horizontal merger is likely to induce a hefty price rise, the merging firms and any rivals "between" them will usually together constitute an antitrust market in the Guidelines sense, so one would expect some correlation between predictions of harm and concentration measures through versions of that mechanism even if—implausibly in my view—there were no causal link running from highly concentrating mergers in exogenously defined markets to declines in market performance.

18 Complaint at 1-2, Fed. Trade Comm'n v. Whole Foods Market, Inc., 502 F. Supp. 2d 1 (D.D.C. 2007) (No. 07-cv-01021), *available at* http://www.ftc.gov/os/caselist/0710114/070605complaint.pdf.

19 *See* Severin Borenstein et al., *Inside the Pin-Factory: Empirical Studies Augmented by Manager Interviews,* 46 J. INDUS. ECON. 123 (1998).

20 HORIZONTAL MERGER GUIDELINES, *supra* note 1, at § 2.2.1.

21 This line of enquiry leads to "antitrust market definition" and to inferences about likely effects of a merger based on pre- and post-merger concentration.

22 *See* Darren Tucker et al., *The Customer is Sometimes Right: The Role of Customer Views in Merger Investigations,* 3 J. COMPETITION L. & ECON. 551, 552 n.1 (2007) (multiple quotes).

23 *See id.*; U.S. DEP'T OF JUSTICE & FED. TRADE COMM'N, COMMENTARY ON THE HORIZONTAL MERGER GUIDELINES 9-10 (2006), *available at* http://www.ftc.gov/os/2006/03/CommentaryontheHorizontalMergerGuidelinesMarch2006.pdf.

24 This customer issue, among others, is noted in the Merger Guidelines, *supra* note 1, at § 2.2.2.

25 United States v. SunGard Data Systems, 172 F. Supp. 2d 172 (DDC 2001).

26 As a very informal summary statistic, the 74-page chapter on horizontal mergers in Michael Whinston's (2004) excellent *Lectures on Antitrust Economics* finds no discussion of different impacts on different customers; I think this reflects the general state of the economics literature, although see Sheldon Kimmel and others (cited below). However, some retrospective studies of hospital mergers have explicitly found very different impacts on different direct customers (health insurers). *See, e.g.,* Deborah Haas-Wilson & Michael Vita, *Mergers Between Competing Hospitals: Lessons from Retrospective Analysis,* 18 INT'L J. ECON. BUS. 1 (2011).

27 *See* Sheldon Kimmel, *Effects of Cost Changes on Oligopolists' Profits,* 40 J. INDUS. ECON. 441 (1992). Other relatively recent discussions by economists include Joseph Farrell, *Listening to Interested Parties in Antitrust Investigations* 18 ANTITRUST 64 (2004), and Ken Heyer, *Predicting the Competitive Effects of Mergers by Listening to Customers,* 74 ANTITRUST L.J. 87 (2007). The classic, and far ahead of its time, cite is Oliver E. Williamson, *Wage Rates as a Barrier to Entry: The Pennington Case in Perspective,* 82 Q.J. ECON. 85 (1968).

28 For calculations showing (in a different context) how little it costs a seller with even moderate market power to price somewhat above its profit-maximizing level for some buyers and below that level for others, *see* Severin Borenstein, *Settling for Coupons,* 39 J.L. & ECON. 379 (1996). Borenstein's calculations assumed independent demand from different buyers; I believe that when buyers compete downstream, the results will be stronger.

29 Gregory Werden & Luke Froeb, *The Entry-Inducing Effects of Horizontal Mergers,* 46 J. INDUS. ECON. 525 (1998) (questioning easy-entry arguments in what they argue is the likely relevant range of entry costs).

30 For a recent study and literature review, *see* Daniel Hosken et al., *Dynamics in a Mature Industry: Entry, Exit, and Growth of Big-Box Retailers* (Fed. Trade Comm'n, Working Paper No. 308, 2011), *available at* http://www.ftc.gov/be/workpapers/wp308.pdf.

31 *See* Chiara Fumagalli & Massimo Motta, *Exclusive Dealing and Entry, when Buyers Compete,* 96 AM. ECON. REV. 785 (2006); John Simpson & Abraham Wickelgren, *Naked Exclusion, Efficient Breach, and Downstream Competition,* 97 AM. ECON. REV. 1305 (2007); Jose Miguel Abito & Julian Wright, *Exclusive Dealing with Imperfect Downstream Competition,* 26 INT'L J. INDUS. ORG. 227 (2006).

Antitrust:
Time for a Tear-Down?

HARRY FIRST

harry.first@nyu.edu
Charles L. Denison Professor of Law, New York University School of Law

Abstract

This article addresses an issue that has been an important part of William Kovacic's scholarship, as well as his public enforcement efforts: What is the appropriate institutional design for antitrust enforcement? Kovacic has recently argued that the current U.S. structure is deeply flawed and has indicated that he would prefer a major restructuring were it politically feasible. In this article I argue to the contrary. We should retain the current system of decentralized antitrust enforcement because it is superior to a more centralized one that we might put in its place. I make the argument in three parts. First, I describe how our system has evolved, from its origins in 1890 in the United States to today's global system operating in more than 100 jurisdictions, and how this diverse system is managed today. Next, I set out a theoretical case for decentralized enforcement, arguing that such a system fosters policy diversity and innovation, maximizes enforcement resources, and mirrors constitutional structure. In addition, decentralization provides competition in law enforcement that can help check enforcement discretion. Finally, I conclude with some thoughts on why restructuring U.S. federal enforcement agencies might produce less effective antitrust enforcement in the United States.

I.

I live in Larchmont, New York, a very nice suburban community immediately north of New York City. Larchmont was first developed residentially in the 1890s. Situated on Long Island Sound, it was an attractive spot for wealthy New Yorkers to build summer homes to escape the oppressive heat of the City. Builders put up large Victorian mansions near the Sound, a small railroad station was added, a few hotels sprung up.

As the population of New York grew, demand for housing in Larchmont grew. Streets were platted where farms had been, more residential housing was built (albeit not as grand as the original mansions), and the population spread out from the original concentration near the Sound. The new houses, built mostly over the first half of the twentieth century, were individually built. No large tract developments, each one of its own design, almost no duplicates. Of course, they each followed certain general styles (mostly "Tudor" and "colonial") and they were all single-family dwellings (although there were some apartment houses as well). Still, no one "designed" Larchmont. It grew organically.

Several years ago a new phenomenon took hold in Larchmont—the tear-down. The first one I noticed was down the block from my house. One day I walked past this house and saw bulldozers in front of it. The old house was not a grand house, but it was nice enough–a four-bedroom home in what appeared to be decent condition and which must have been sold to its new owners for a decent sum of money. Yet there were bulldozers tearing it down and, eventually, builders there to put up a new home, a larger one to be sure, built in a vaguely new style.

The second tear-down in my neighborhood was just two blocks away. This house was well-maintained, fairly large, with a swimming pool in the back, and no doubt expensive to buy. Down it went. In its place came two houses, both large ones, each a bit different than the other. Two families now live where there had only been one before.

When I think about why people might buy perfectly good houses in Larchmont, tear them down, and then build new ones, I try to imagine the choices they have if they live in Larchmont. It used to be that people who bought homes in Larchmont would remodel, improving their homes in various ways—adding a bedroom or a family room, redoing the kitchen and the bathrooms. These new owners, though, have decided to start from scratch. Maybe the flaws in the old home were too overwhelming to fix, or maybe they just want something brand-new and up to date, better suited for life in the twenty-first century. Or maybe they think that two separate houses are more valuable than one. In any case, these new owners have decided that the tear-down and rebuilding is worth doing.

In a recent speech to the New York State Bar Association, William Kovacic—former chairman and commissioner of the Federal Trade Commission—likened antitrust to a Victorian house. Originally built long ago in what is now a recognizably quaint design, added to over the years in odd ways (including that "modern" addition that doesn't quite fit), it really looks strange now, with an interior that is clearly behind the times and doesn't work well. Still, it's our house and we love it.

The implication of Kovacic's analogy was that we need to think seriously about this house and not just tolerate its quaintness and live there without complaint. Kovacic did not quite put it this way, but his remarks led me to wonder whether he thinks it is time for an antitrust tear-down. Are we beyond the remodeling stage in antitrust, ready to tear it down and build something new?

Before I tackle this rhetorical question, I should set Kovacic's challenge in the context of his long interest in the architecture of antitrust enforcement. I can think of no one—either in the academy or in government—who has paid more-sustained or deeper attention to the institutions of antitrust enforcement.[1] So, it is not surprising that his attention to institutional design would lead him to question the intelligence of that design and to at least suggest that it is time to rethink the wisdom of its basic structure.[2]

II.

I approach my rhetorical question with an analogy slightly different than Kovacic's. I don't view antitrust as a Victorian house. I view it as a neighborhood, indeed, one much like the neighborhood in which I happen to live. Like Larchmont, my antitrust neighborhood started in the 1890s and has grown organically, with some planning but not a whole lot. Like Larchmont, I like it, and I like it because it works.

It is a commonplace to say that no one would have designed the U.S. antitrust enforcement system that we have today. It looks crazy. We have two major federal antitrust enforcement agencies, the Antitrust Division of the Justice Department and the Federal Trade Commission, each with somewhat overlapping authority but each with its own area of exclusive responsibility (criminal enforcement for the Justice Department, "unfair methods of competition" for the FTC). We then have a number of significant sectoral agencies—in banking, telecommunications, energy, transportation—each with pieces of antitrust authority involving either mergers or various business practices. Added to this are fifty-five separate state enforcement agencies (fifty states, four territories, and the District of Columbia), each with authority to enforce federal antitrust law in federal court, plus, of course, authority to enforce their own state antitrust laws in state court. Topping it all off is private antitrust enforcement, done through litigation for money damages or injunctions. As many have pointed out, the amount of private antitrust litigation actually far outstrips the amount of public antitrust litigation, and has for more than half a century.[3]

There is a reason why the system looks like no one designed it. No one did. The antitrust enforcement system was not designed, top-down, all at once. Rather, it is the product of organic growth, often responsive to the needs of a particular time and then changed by those who are affected by it and who have to manage it.

Start with the beginning. When the Sherman Act was passed in 1890 a key innovation was to create a system of public enforcement. Prior to that time, "competition law" was mostly a common law enterprise, invoked by private parties seeking to avoid contractual obligations by arguing that enforcement of a particular contract term would restrain trade and hence was void as against public policy. Congress did not eliminate private enforcement when it passed the Sherman Act, though. Instead it federalized it by creating a private right of action for damages, intended to compensate the victims of antitrust violations. Thus, our system of multiple antitrust enforcement was born.

At the time the Federal Trade Commission was being considered in 1914, Congress saw a system with weak federal government enforcement, modest private litigation, and fairly robust state litigation by states suing "trusts" under their own state antitrust statutes. If anything, it is state enforcement that told Congress what is possible in terms of antitrust enforcement.

By 1900, twenty-seven states and territories had antitrust statutes; at least thirty-five had them by 1915.[4] Between 1890 and 1902, twelve states had brought twenty-eight antitrust suits; the United States Department of Justice had brought nineteen.[5] The total fines imposed in Justice Department antitrust suits by the end of 1914 was $619,965; by contrast, in one suit brought by Texas in 1906 a subsidiary of Standard Oil was fined $1.6 million for violating Texas antitrust law.[6] By 1914 state enforcers had sued many of the same companies that the federal government sued for antitrust violations, including the major trusts of the day—the Standard Oil trust, the sugar trust, the beef trust, and the tobacco trust.[7] On June 8, 1914, five days before Commerce Committee reported its bill giving the new FTC power to prescribe unfair methods of competition, the Supreme Court decided two state antitrust enforcement cases, brought by Missouri and Kentucky, against the International Harvester company.[8] International Harvester had also been a target of federal antitrust action in a suit the Justice Department brought in 1912, filed after Missouri's action and based on the same grounds as the successful state suit.[9] Congress was aware of the Supreme Court's decision in the Missouri case because Senator Reed (a proponent of strong antitrust enforcement) had the decision immediately printed and circulated. In fact, state antitrust enforcement was substantial enough that Senator Reed offered an amendment during the debates over the proposed Clayton Act to permit states to bring antitrust cases in the name of the United States if the Attorney General did not act, an amendment which failed, after vigorous debate, by a vote of 21-39.[10]

It is no wonder that when Congress created the FTC in 1914 it was not overly concerned with having more than one enforcement agency. We already had multiple enforcement. In fact, in the four months during which Congress had the FTC Act under consideration, Congress strengthened the future Commission's powers, changing it from an agency that would have been "hardly more than an adjunct of the Department of Justice" when the bill passed the House to one with more substantial enforcement powers that could, so far as the statute indicated, investigate the same conduct at the same time as the Justice Department.[11]

Despite this potential for overlapping enforcement, the Commission that Congress established was also intended to operate differently and to do different things than the Justice Department. The Justice Department would continue to litigate in federal court (including criminal cases); the FTC would work administratively. The Justice Department would concentrate on big cases and deal with monopoly "as established fact"; the new agency could "check monopoly in the embryo" and stop unfair methods of competition by a corporation of "no conspicuous size."[12] In fact, the FTC was given power to monitor the Justice Department, by investigating court orders entered in Justice Department antitrust cases and reporting its findings to Congress, for Congress was worried about Justice Department "laxity."[13]

The institutional story of 1914, therefore, was an embrace of diversity in antitrust enforcement. Congress explicitly understood that organizational structure could make a difference in enforcement approaches. Congress also showed a wariness about the adequacy of the efforts of what was then the sole federal antitrust enforcement agency. Congress knew that state antitrust enforcers were sometimes out ahead of their federal counterpart in attacking large-scale combinations, but was uncertain about giving the states the power to represent the United States in antitrust proceedings. And finally, Congress was aware of the importance of private suits and took steps to strengthen the private action in the companion Clayton Act, for example, by giving private parties the right to sue to enjoin violations of the antitrust laws.

It is true that Congress did not design the new institutions in great detail, but I take that as good fortune. Conflicts that were possible turned out not to materialize, at least initially. Prior to 1950, for example, the Justice Department rarely filed suit under the Clayton Act's provisions dealing with mergers or exclusive dealing, despite the grant of dual jurisdiction in 1914; the FTC, on the other hand, filed a substantial number of complaints. Both agencies handled civil pricing conspiracies (the FTC being slightly more active); Justice had the monopoly on criminal prosecutions.[14] It was not until 1938 that the FTC and the Department entered into an informal agreement to determine which agency should handle a particular investigation, an agreement not formalized until 1948.[15]

Problems with coordination became more acute after the passage of the Hart Scott Rodino Antitrust Improvements Act in 1976, requiring parties to large mergers to provide premerger notification simultaneously to both federal agencies. Congress did not specify which agency would get to investigate which merger, nor did it concentrate all merger enforcement in one of the agencies, both of which could have done it. Instead, Congress relied on the agencies themselves to decide which mergers each would investigate. This led the agencies to improve their liaison procedures, an effort that has proven problematic at times despite ongoing attempts to agree on a method to allocate cases efficiently.[16] But, again, we should be glad that Congress did not try to write into law how the agencies should divide their work. Try to imagine what sort of rules Congress could have put in place in 1976 that would have decided which agency would handle the AOL/Time Warner merger a quarter of a century later or the Google/AdMob merger a decade after that. If the idea is to allocate mergers to the agency with the most expertise, only an organically supple institutional design could meet the challenge of making that decision in the face of changing industrial boundaries and the emergence of new technologies.

Further complicating the difficulties of institutional design is the globalization of antitrust. Although the first wave of modern antitrust legislation came in the immediate post-war period—Japan in 1947, the United Kingdom in 1948, Germany and the European Community in 1957—the most spectacular increase in antitrust legislation began in the 1990s. By the end of 1996, seventy countries had some form of competition law; sixty-one percent of these laws were adopted in the 1990s.[17] By the early 2000s, the number of jurisdictions with antitrust laws had risen to approximately eighty-five. By the end of the decade the number had risen to approximately 110, as both China and India adopted modern competition law regimes.[18]

Globalization matters to institutional design not only because there are more competition law regimes, but because competition problems increasingly cross jurisdictional boundaries. Not only are transnational mergers frequent, but the effects of business practices by firms based in one country are often felt in others. This has led virtually every competition law regime to recognize some form of extraterritoriality to allow enforcement of competition law against companies located outside the jurisdiction but whose anticompetitive conduct has effect within the jurisdiction. The United States led the way in this development in the *Alcoa* case, where the Sherman Act was applied to a cartel of non-U.S. firms whose conduct could have affected U.S. commerce.[19] Other regimes have now come to do nearly the same, most significantly, the European Union.[20]

Just as with the potential for conflicts between the Department of Justice and the FTC, the potential for conflicts among national competition enforcement agencies over international competition matters has been addressed organically. First came the 1991 bilateral agreement between the United States and the European Union to set out principles for coordinating on enforcement matters; agreements with other countries followed.[21] Next came the establishment of the International Competition Network ("ICN") in 2001. Not a traditional bricks-and-mortar international agency, with a permanent building and staff, the ICN is a form of virtual organization, designed to bring together representatives of enforcement agencies, along with private parties from NGOs and the bar, to develop non-binding recommendations on best practices regarding enforcement, which individual agencies are then free to implement or not.[22] The result has been a variety of reports setting out "guiding principles" and "recommended practices" for merger notification and review, manuals relating to "good practices" in cartel enforcement, and a movement to enunciate substantive legal rules.[23]

Parallel to this organizational effort has been coordination among competition authorities in various countries on individual merger reviews and on cartel investigations and enforcement in specific cases. "'Pick up the phone'" cooperation now occurs on a daily basis.[24]

Of course, in this complicated multi-enforcer system things do not always run smoothly, to say the least. On the international level, there have been occasional public disagreements over a few high-profile mergers.[25] In the United States, disagreements between the DOJ and the FTC have sometimes come into public view, as they did in 2011 when the agencies not only argued over particular mergers, but also over whether one of them would get exclusive power to review "Accountable Care Organizations" (newly-forming associations of hospitals and physicians pursuant to the Patient Protection and Accountable Care Act) and which agency would get to review Google's business practices for antitrust violations. The disputes were substantial enough, and public enough, that a group of eleven Senators wrote to the Assistant Attorney General in charge of the Antitrust Division and the Chairman of the FTC urging them to be more cooperative. In fact, then-Commissioner Kovacic was reported as believing that the FTC "had a better working relationship with the European Union than it did with the Justice Department, just two blocks away."[26]

III.

Living in the antitrust neighborhood is not always easy. Still, despite occasional dust-ups, it can be done. The deeper question, though, is whether it should be done. Is there good reason to have so many different houses? Or, turning from metaphor to real-world institutional design, should we move toward more centralization in the institutions of antitrust enforcement or should we retain the model of decentralized antitrust enforcement?

I think that decentralization is the better model. Decentralization offers three major benefits: it fosters policy diversity and innovation, maximizes enforcement resources, and mirrors constitutional structure. In addition, decentralization allows for competition in law enforcement, and competition can help check enforcement discretion. Taken together, the result should be better enforcement than would be produced by a more centralized system.

The first benefit of decentralized enforcement agencies is policy diversity. Policy diversity is more likely with decentralized enforcement because different agencies will likely reflect different interests and constituencies, along with different institutional approaches. Different agencies can also develop different specializations (whether by knowledge of different industries or different remedial approaches), which can then provide comparative advantage in dealing with particular competition problems. True, different policies can be hashed out internally in a single agency, but "not invented here" and other bureaucratic obstacles can transform diversity into unwelcome dissent and reduce the chances that different policies will emerge and be adopted. By structuring a system that makes policy diversity more likely, we are then more likely to reduce the risk that antitrust violations will go undetected or unremedied.

The U.S. experience with the Antitrust Division and the Federal Trade Commission bears out these predictions. Operational control over the two agencies is structured differently (a single head for the Division, five Commissioners for the FTC) and the two agencies determine policy direction separately (with the Antitrust Division more closely tied to White House direction and the goals of other Cabinet agencies). The antitrust enforcement agencies have tended to split enforcement responsibilities based on industry knowledge, particularly in mergers, promoting specialization. Political control in Congress is even different, leading to oversight by different Committees.

This diversity was intended from the beginning. It has produced some important differences in enforcement interests (intellectual property being a particularly important example in recent years, where the FTC was active while the Justice Department was not),[27] has allowed the airing of different views in ways that would not have occurred were there only one agency (the disagreement over unilateral conduct being an important recent example),[28] and may have even produced some differences in merger enforcement during the Bush Administration, when the Justice Department was felt to have become too non-interventionist in merger policy.[29] Even the different structure of the two agencies has mattered, because the FTC's multiple-commissioner model has provided a legitimate way for dissenting commissioners to air publicly their disagreements over cases that the Commission has chosen not to bring.[30]

Many have argued not just that decentralization can produce diversity in policy, but also that institutional diversity is important for producing and testing innovations in government policies. The argument, developed in the context of the 1930s debate over the desirability of allowing the states to experiment with legislation to cure the ills of industrialization and the Depression, was most famously articulated by Justice Brandeis in 1932: "It is one of the happy incidents of the federal system that a single courageous state may, if its citizens choose, serve as a laboratory; and try novel social and economic experiments without risk to the rest of the country."[31]

Policy diversity and innovation may be particularly important in antitrust, where views of what constitutes optimal antitrust policy necessarily shift over time. Not only does antitrust reflect political values that are subject to change (views on corporate size and economic concentration being important examples), but the economic theories that support antitrust are also subject to constant empirical testing and re-evaluation. We should not expect the social science of economics to be more fixed than the natural sciences of physics or biology, all of which rely on experimentation and are subject to evolution. Nor should we expect to converge on an unchanging policy equilibrium in antitrust any more than we should expect (or want) unchanging scientific "truths." Diversity in the institutions of antitrust enforcement helps test orthodoxy and is an important mechanism for insuring antitrust's continuing evolution.[32]

A second argument for decentralization is that decentralization can increase the resources available for enforcement. Different agencies are likely to face different budgetary constraints, even within the same system of government, but certainly if they are in different governmental systems. Having different agencies involved in enforcement can mean that there will be more antitrust enforcement at any given time, or that through collaboration more resources can be brought to a given task than any single agency might be able to muster. In the U.S. system, for example, the Justice Department and FTC have different amounts budgeted for their antitrust enforcement missions.[33] State enforcement budgets vary on a state-by-state basis, both in absolute amounts and in the ways in which states fund their enforcement efforts; occasionally, separate federal funding has been made available to augment these resources.[34]

A third argument for decentralization is constitutional structure. Today's enforcement system reflects core structural aspects of our political system. Although state antitrust enforcement, and even state antitrust law, could likely be preempted by Congress, efforts to centralize antitrust enforcement in the federal government would need to contend with the politics and structure of federalism, an effort with ramifications for areas beyond antitrust, such as the regulation of financial institutions and the environment. Indeed, even though the Antitrust Modernization Commission began with a mandate to assess the proper role of the states in antitrust enforcement, the Commission ended up making very limited recommendations for changes in state enforcement practice, in part because the Commission recognized that "principles of federalism and practical political concerns" counseled in favor of deference to state interests.[35]

The political immutability of decentralized antitrust enforcement is even clearer on an international level. When the U.S. economy changed in the post-Civil War period, and business conduct began affecting many states, the obvious solution was to use the power of the federal government to deal with national economic problems. This approach was followed in areas as diverse as fraud, railroad regulation, and antitrust. But this approach is not available on an international level. With the failure of the effort to give the WTO some modest competence in transnational antitrust matters, there is little choice but to continue the current pragmatic networking effort to connect independent national agencies, an effort which tries to combine the strengths of diversity with the strengths of cooperative mechanisms.[36]

Decentralization is not without its costs. First, there are the transactions costs in coordinating action and dividing responsibility among agencies. Second, diversity can impose costs on the businesses that are subject to different enforcement approaches. Compliance costs may increase if multiple enforcers have different views of competition policy. Different enforcement views might lead companies either to adapt to the most interventionist agency's approach or alter their business practices from jurisdiction to jurisdiction to stay within "the law."[37] Third, decentralized enforcement can invite forum shopping. With a single decision-maker, parties must present all their arguments to a single decision-maker that they cannot end-run. With multiple enforcers, parties can look for a more sympathetic enforcer, something that could be of particular concern in antitrust where the complainant might be a losing competitor trying to get the government to bring it the success that the marketplace has denied.

It is hard to deny that a decentralized system imposes some higher costs than would a fully centralized one, but the concern for regulatory capture would not go away even in a world where there was only one enforcement agency. Sectoral regulation is usually done by having a single agency in charge of regulating an industry, but we are still concerned about capture. In antitrust, however, capture has generally been of lesser concern, in part because the enforcement agencies are not in charge of any one industry and in part because the agencies are very aware of the potential for capture and are capable of discounting complaints to be certain that they are not protecting competitors when taking action. Having more than one agency should not alter this calculus.

At bottom, however, the cautions about diverse institutions reflect a concern that diverse policies and multiple enforcement agencies will lack the coherence that centralized enforcement can produce, leading to too much enforcement and bad results. Put otherwise, the fear is that institutional differences will lead to a race to the bottom, not a race to the top.

Competition among enforcement agencies, however, should produce a race to the top, not the bottom, because the process of institutional competition itself can constrain enforcement agency abuse in much the same way that marketplace competition can constrain improper business behavior. It is true, of course, that government agencies do not compete in the same way that businesses do, but there are some particular aspects of the competitive process in government enforcement that act to check what might otherwise be self-interested behavior, leading, instead, to action that serves the broader public interest.

The first way in which institutional competition can check enforcement abuse comes from the concept of yardstick competition. Yardstick competition occurs when one agency's performance is used to measure another's. The idea is a familiar one in the public utility regulatory context, where regulatory agencies have compared the rates and performance of different firms as a way to test whether requested rates are "just and reasonable" and should be approved.[38] In the antitrust area, judgments about the quality of government enforcement decisions need to be made by legislators who fund these agencies and, ultimately, by voters who elect these legislators. These judgments are very difficult to make, however, even for professional observers. Yardstick competition, by providing comparisons of enforcement performance, can help decision-makers form more accurate judgments, thereby disciplining or rewarding antitrust regulatory agencies for comparatively poorer or better performance.

The second check can come from regulatory competition. The idea here is that jurisdictions seek to attract mobile factors of production so as to improve the economic welfare of their citizens. One way to do this is to provide attractive regulatory regimes.[39] Applying this theory to antitrust, we can see both general and specific aspects of antitrust enforcement that can make economies stronger or weaker, and more or less attractive to investment. For example, antitrust rules can protect competitors or, instead, provide a more open market system that protects competition; antitrust rules can favor consumer welfare or producer welfare; antitrust rules can give manufacturers a free hand in arranging their distribution systems or can protect discount retailers from termination for price-cutting; antitrust rules can be permissive or intolerant of cartel activity. Regulatory competition provides pressure to adopt whichever of these approaches works better and produces economic benefit for the citizens of a particular jurisdiction.

The third way that competition checks enforcement agency behavior—particularly the behavior of dominant agencies—is maverick competition. In the industrial world a maverick is a firm with some incentive to deviate from the consensus within an industry—it is "an observably disruptive force."[40] Economists have pointed out that monopoly firms have incentives to protect the *status quo* and avoid disruptive technologies that will undercut their current products. In the world of government antitrust enforcement, dominant enforcement agencies may similarly be inclined to the conventional wisdom; non-dominant enforcement agencies can provide similar disruptive force. For example, developing countries can remind enforcers in developed countries that antitrust can have distributive effects that developed countries might ignore. Private enforcers suing for damages on behalf of injured consumers can remind public enforcers that consumer welfare means paying attention to practices that injure consumers.

Dominant agencies will not necessarily respond to maverick enforcers, but the existence of mavericks at least provides some external prod that may lead dominant agencies to consider approaches that they otherwise might not have.

The final disciplining force that comes from enforcement agency competition is norms competition. Norms are consensus views of correct group behavior. Scholars have long pointed out that social norms extend beyond strict legal requirements to encompass customs and standards that groups adopt and apply to themselves and which help to control the behavior of the members of the group.[41]

From the very beginning of antitrust in the United States there has been a tradition of vigorous policy debate over the propriety of various antitrust enforcement norms.[42] This debate in part reflects the open-textured language that Congress consciously chose when enacting the Sherman Act in 1890, but it also reflects the fact that political views regarding the core values of antitrust law—our concerns about monopoly, concentrated economic power, and the role of the state in the economy—are constantly changing.

The norms of antitrust enforcement at any particular time can be shaped by this policy debate. The report of the Antitrust Modernization Commission, for example, can be seen as a way to articulate and shape current enforcement norms (even though the report resulted in no changes in U.S. antitrust legislation). Similarly, the effort of the International Competition Network is consciously directed at articulating "best practices" in various enforcement areas in the context of an international legal regime that lacks any transnational antitrust enforcement agency. In these cases and others, antitrust enforcement agencies, along with interested scholars and lawyers, contend over the correct approach to antitrust rules and enforcement practices, in an effort to gain legitimacy for their views. Some views get marginalized and others become the consensus norms, to be tested through actual enforcement practice.

Not every institutional competitive effect applies to every example of inter-agency competition and not every effect is equally strong. Yardstick competition could be very important, but it depends on whether those who oversee institutional performance actually compare different results, in the way that state regulatory agencies often do.[43] Regulatory competition does not apply within the U.S. federal system, either between the Antitrust Division and the FTC, or between the federal agencies and the states, but it could be operative on the international level. Maverick competition can be particularly important where smaller agencies operate within a larger national system, as is the case in the United States. Norms competition is internal within the world of antitrust policy-making, but this competition can have some bite when enforcers need to convince other decision-makers—like courts—that their policies are correct.

Nevertheless, there are good examples of each type of competitive effect. Yardstick competition is implicated when Congressional oversight hearings separately examine the record of the two enforcement agencies.[44] Regulatory competition is a way of understanding the general spread of antitrust in the 1990s, as well as the increasing intolerance of cartels shown by enforcers in jurisdictions such as Europe and Japan. Policy-makers saw that antitrust law generally, and cartel enforcement specifically, could lead to more robust economies with lower prices, to the advantage of both producers and consumers. Many countries wanted the economic benefits of these policies. Maverick competition has come from state antitrust enforcers, consciously so during the Reagan Administration when it cut back on merger enforcement but also in the context of specific enforcement actions, such as the remedies proceeding in *Microsoft*.[45] And norms competition has been apparent in many areas, perhaps none more so than in merger enforcement where the federal agencies have consciously used the Horizontal Merger Guidelines as a way to advance their policy views both nationally (particularly in the absence of any legislative changes in substantive merger law for more than sixty years and no Supreme Court involvement for more than thirty) and internationally (where the U.S. agencies have been quite successful in moving other jurisdictions much closer to U.S. analytical approaches).[46]

It would be overly Panglossian to say that the competitive process in government enforcement always drives enforcement to the "right result," any more than we can say the same for product market competition. Market failures will always occur. Still, we should be careful to compare the imperfections of a competitive process in government enforcement with the imperfections that we might see were there to be a highly centralized system. Looked at this way, I think that the arguments for institutional competition are compelling and the advantages that diverse institutions bring are persuasive. Institutional decentralization, not monopoly, should be the default position.

IV.

My neighbors in Larchmont who have torn down their houses have replaced them with newer, bigger ones. What would we do if we decided to tear down our antitrust house? Assuming that we can't tear down all the antitrust houses around the world, and that it would be difficult to tear down the "state" antitrust houses (although some critics would like to[47]), and that those private houses are still a good idea (although some could do without them as well[48]), maybe we could just tear down the "federal" house. If we did that, what would the new design look like?

The institutional design most common around the world is a single competition law agency that handles all competition enforcement except for criminal prosecutions. We could duplicate this approach by repealing those parts of the Sherman and Clayton Acts that give jurisdiction to the United States to enforce those statutes through civil process and concentrating all civil enforcement in the FTC. This would end the current merger clearance process that has caused so much angst, but would we get better overall enforcement?

Putting aside the general arguments for decentralization in federal antitrust enforcement, one major effect of this redesign would be to split civil and criminal enforcement. There is something to be said for doing this. Presumably, criminal enforcement would be done by the career prosecutors in the Criminal Division of the Justice Department. Career criminal prosecutors will likely have different backgrounds and experience than antitrust lawyers who do criminal prosecutions; fulltime criminal prosecutors might very well be more aggressive enforcers. Indeed, this has turned out to be the case in some jurisdictions that have taken this approach, Brazil being an important example.[49]

The institutional unknown in such a redesign is whether a general public prosecutor will be as committed to criminal antitrust enforcement as a specialized antitrust agency, like the Antitrust Division. In terms of absolute numbers of cases brought, criminal antitrust enforcement ranks far below other federal crimes, such as immigration and narcotics.[50] How will prosecutors allocate their enforcement resources if they have to rank their priorities with antitrust in mind? Even more to the point, would we have expected a non-specialized antitrust public prosecutor to come up with the major innovation in criminal antitrust enforcement that the Antitrust Division has pioneered, the amnesty program, an innovation that has propelled criminal antitrust enforcement in the United States and has been adopted in jurisdictions around the world? There is no way to answer this question for certain, except to say that the amnesty tool is unique in the Justice Department to antitrust. No other federal criminal prosecutors use it. Did it take a specialized enforcement agency both to understand the importance of prosecuting cartel behavior and to understand that the way to destabilize cartels was to formalize the prisoners' dilemma game and create a race to the prosecutor's office?

Finally, perhaps curiously, coordination problems would not vanish with this new restructuring. Instead of coordinating on antitrust enforcement generally, the new FTC would now have to coordinate with the Justice Department on criminal referrals and amnesty decisions. It is not impossible to coordinate on these decisions, as jurisdictions outside the United States have found, but the coordination process may affect the incentives that the FTC would have with regard to pursuing cases that might end up as criminal matters. Would we then have fewer collusion cases generally? More civil collusive practices cases and fewer criminal ones? It is hard to predict.

The other approach is to repeal the FTC's unfair methods of competition jurisdiction under Section 5 of the FTC Act and concentrate enforcement in the Justice Department's Antitrust Division. This would avoid the split of civil and criminal enforcement, but it would end any administrative-agency approach to antitrust and would eliminate the possibility of moving public antitrust enforcement beyond the confines of the Sherman Act.[51] Again, this is not an impossible structure to build, but it does entail costs that go beyond the loss of diversity in federal government antitrust policy.

V.

The idea of consolidating all federal government antitrust enforcement into one institution is an idea that has periodically surfaced in antitrust debate.[52] It has generally been set aside as too institutionally difficult and not worth doing, although likely a superior institutional design if we could start from scratch. This is the position that the Antitrust Modernization Commission took in 2007,[53] albeit over the dissents of three Commissioners who recommended consolidating enforcement in the Justice Department.[54] Kovacic now appears to concur with the AMC majority, but based more on the political difficulty of getting one of the relevant Congressional committees to give up oversight responsibility.[55] To return to my original metaphor, a new house might be great, but the moving costs are impossibly high.

My case against the antitrust tear-down, however, does not assume that we should never have designed two antitrust enforcement agencies in the first place. To the contrary, I think that antitrust policy has been well-served by having potentially competing enforcement agencies with different outlooks and procedures. Unlike some, I do not view the inevitable disagreements between the Justice Department and the FTC as "bickering" or "squabbling."[56] Rather, I view them as necessary contesting over competition policy. Efforts to make the current system work better, to joint venture more efficiently, as Kovacic argues, are certainly worth doing.[57] But I would not want to lose the independent centers of decision-making that we have now.[58] Decentralized antitrust decision-making has served us well in the past. Theory and history predict it will serve us well in the future.

NOTES

1   A partial listing includes: *Using Ex Post Evaluations to Improve the Performance of Competition Policy Authorities*, 31 IOWA J. CORP. L. 503 (2006); *Measuring What Matters: The Federal Trade Commission and Investments in Competition Policy Research And Development*, 72 ANTITRUST L.J. 861 (2005); *Toward a Domestic Competition Network*, in COMPETITION LAWS IN CONFLICT: ANTITRUST JURISDICTION IN THE GLOBAL ECONOMY 316 (Richard A. Epstein & Michael S. Greve, eds., 2004) [hereinafter COMPETITIONS LAWS IN CONFLICT]; *The Quality of Appointments and the Capability of the Federal Trade Commission*, 49 ADMIN. L. REV. 915 (1997); *The Federal Trade Commission and Congressional Oversight of Antitrust Enforcement: A Historical Perspective*, in PUBLIC CHOICE AND REGULATION: A VIEW FROM INSIDE THE FEDERAL TRADE COMMISSION 63 (Robert J. Mackay, James C. Miller III & Bruce Yandle eds. 1987). Perhaps most significantly, Kovacic spearheaded the most comprehensive self-study ever undertaken by the FTC, with the stated goals of encouraging acceptance of a norm of periodic self-assessment, creating a template for the agency to engage regularly in an analysis of its performance, and identifying approaches for improvement over both the short and long term. *See* THE FEDERAL TRADE COMMISSION AT 100: INTO OUR 2ND CENTURY — THE CONTINUING PURSUIT OF BETTER PRACTICE (Jan. 2009), *available at* http://www.ftc.gov/ftc/workshops/ftc100/docs/ ftc100rpt.pdf.

2   In fact, Kovacic anticipated many of the ideas I discuss in this essay, although we reach different conclusions. See William E. Kovacic, *Downsizing Antitrust: Is It Time To End Dual Federal Enforcement?*, 41 ANTITRUST BULL. 505 (1996) (offering a "preliminary assessment" that the costs of having two federal antitrust enforcement agencies likely exceed the benefits and that the Justice Department is the "appropriate candidate" to be the surviving agency).

3   For data on private enforcement, *see* Stephen Calkins, *Perspectives on State and Federal Antitrust Enforcement*, 53 DUKE L.J. 673, 699-700 (2003) (comparing numbers of U.S. government and private case filings, along with private antitrust class actions); B. Zorina Kahn, *Federal Antitrust Agencies and Public Policy Toward Antitrust and Intellectual Property*, 9 CORNELL J.L. & PUB. POL'Y 133, 137 fig.1 (1999); Richard A. Posner, *A Statistical Study of Antitrust Enforcement*, 13 J. L. & ECON. 365, 366-71 (1970).

4   *See* James May, *Antitrust Practice and Procedure in the Formative Era: The Constitutional and Conceptual Reach of State Antitrust Law*, 1880-1918, 135 U. PA. L. REV. 495, 499 (1987). Other commentators have different counts. *See, e.g.*, Stanley Mosk, *State Antitrust Enforcement and Coordination with Federal Enforcement*, 21 A.B.A. ANTITRUST SECTION 358, 363 (1962) (twenty-one states had antitrust laws at time Sherman Act was adopted).

5   *See* May, *supra* note 4, at 500-01.

6   *See id.* at 502. The Supreme Court upheld the fine against constitutional challenge in *Waters-Pierce Oil Co. v. Texas*, 212 U.S. 86 (1909).

7   *See* May, *supra* note 4, at 501.

8 *See* Int'l Harvester Co. v. Kentucky, 234 U.S. 216 (1914) (holding that a Kentucky antitrust law prohibiting fixing a price that was "greater or less than the real value of the article" violated the Fourteenth Amendment); Int'l Harvester Co. v. Missouri, 234 U.S. 199 (1914) (holding that Missouri antitrust laws did not violate the Fourteenth Amendment). In the Missouri case, the Missouri State Supreme Court pointed out that International Harvester combined firms that had between eighty and ninety percent of the market in Missouri, *see* State *ex. rel.* Major v. Int'l Harvester Co., 237 Mo. 369, 384 (1911), and the U.S. Supreme Court wrote: "The purpose of such [antitrust] statutes is to secure competition and preclude combinations which tend to defeat it . . . . There is nothing in the Constitution of the United States which precludes a State from adopting and enforcing such policy. To so decide would be stepping backwards." Missouri, 234 U.S. at 209.

9 *See* United States v. Int'l Harvester Co., 214 F. 987, 999-1000 (D. Minn. 1914) (combination of five companies, holding eighty to eighty-five percent of the market, was an unreasonable restraint of trade, in violation of Sections 1 and 2 of the Sherman Act), *appeal dismissed*, 248 U.S. 587 (1918).

10 For discussion of Reed's amendment, *see* 51 Cong. Rec. 14,513-14 (1914). Proponents of the amendment argued that federal enforcement had been lax, that the amendment would put "46 watchdogs on guard," and that the "best enforcement" had actually come from state attorneys general acting under more limited state law. Critics were concerned about "divided responsibility" in the enforcement of federal law and the "temptation" for state attorneys general to "get more publicity" by taking up the "larger matters" of federal enforcement. *See, e.g., id.* at 14,515, 14,519. For a description of Senator Reed's role in the enactment of the Clayton and FTC acts, *see* Marc Winerman, *The Origins of the FTC: Concentration, Cooperation, Control, and Competition*, 71 Antitrust L.J. 1, 70-71 (2003). For the reprinting of the Supreme Court's decision in *International Harvester v. Missouri, see* S. Doc. No. 63-498 (ordered to be printed, June 13, 1914). The district court decision in *United States v. International Harvester, see supra* note 8, was also reprinted, on the day that the Senate debated Reed's amendment. *See* S. Doc. No. 63-569 (ordered to be printed, Sept. 1, 1914); 51 Cong. Rec. 14,514 (1914).

11 Gerard C. Henderson, The Federal Trade Commission: A Study in Administrative Law and Procedure 25-26 (1924).

12 *See* Winerman, *supra* note 10, at 68, 74.

13 *See* 51 Cong. Rec. 8845 (1914) (remarks of Rep. Covington). The provision is codified at 15 U.S.C. § 46 (c). The Commission used this power in its early days, attempting to prod the Justice Department to enforce previously entered decrees. *See* Thomas C. Blaisdell, Jr., The Federal Trade Commission: An Experiment in the Control of Business 183-258 (1932) (investigations of meat-packing, steel, tobacco, oil, aluminum, and radio). These efforts "received slight consideration by the Department of Justice." *Id.* at 255.

14 For enforcement data on the pre-1940 period, *see* Gilbert H. Montague, *The Commission's Jurisdiction Over Practices in Restraint of Trade: A Large-Scale Method of Mass Enforcement of the Antitrust Laws*, 8 Geo. Wash. L. Rev. 365 (1940) (FTC and Justice Department).

15 *See* Report of The Attorney General's National Committee to Study the Antitrust Laws 376 & n. 53 (1955).

16 The liaison process, as it operated by the 1970s, is described in Robert A. Katzmann, Regulatory Bureaucracy: The Federal Trade Commission and Antitrust Policy 193-94 (1980). The process was formally modified in 1993, *see* 65 Antitrust & Trade Reg. Rep. (BNA) 746 (1993), and in 1995, *see* 68 Antitrust & Trade Reg. Rep. (BNA) 403 (1995). For information about an aborted effort to modify the liaison agreement in 2002, *see* Memorandum of Agreement Between the Federal Trade Commission and the Antitrust Division of the United States Department of Justice Concerning Clearance Procedures for Investigations (Mar. 5, 2002), *available at* http://www.ftc.gov/opa/2002/02/clearance/ftcdojagree.pdf. For the current liaison agreement, *see* U.S. Dep't of Justice, Antitrust Division Manual § 7.A.1 (4th ed. 2008), *available at* http://www.justice.gov/atr/public/divisionmanual/chapter7.pdf.

17 *See* Mark R.A. Palim, *The Worldwide Growth of Competition Law: An Empirical Analysis*, 43 Antitrust Bull. 105, 109 (1998).

18 As of 2011, the membership of the International Competition Network, discussed *infra* notes 22-23 and accompanying text, consisted of competition authorities from 106 jurisdictions. Email to Author from ICN Secretariat (July 25, 2011) (on file with author). This figure does not include China, which is not an ICN member.

19 United States v. Alum. Co. of Am., 148 F.2d 416, 443-44 (2d Cir. 1945).

20 *See* Joined Cases 89/85, 104/85, 114/85, 116/85, 117/85 and 125-129/85, Ahlström Osakeyhtiö v. Comm'n, [1988] ECR 5193. The defendant was the Pulp, Paper and Paper Board Export Association of the United States, formerly the Kraft Export Association, which was exempt from U.S. antitrust law under the Webb-Pomerene Act. *See* Commission Decision 85/202 of 19 December 1984 in case IV/29.725, Wood pulp, [1985] OJ L 85/1. The period of infringement started in 1974; the Commission started its investigation in 1977 and initiated proceedings in 1981.

21 *See* Agreement Between the Government of the United States of America and the Commission of the European Communities Regarding the Application of Their Competition Laws, U.S.-E.C., Sept. 23, 1991, 30 I.L.M. 1487, *available at* http://www.usdoj.gov/atr/public/international/docs/0525.htm. Other cooperation agreements are posted at http://www.justice.gov/atr/public/international/int-arrangements.html.

22 For a brief history of the circumstances surrounding the founding of the ICN, *see* Harry First, *Evolving Toward What? The Development of International Antitrust*, in The Future of Transnational Antitrust: From Comparative to Common Competition Law 23 (Josef Drexl, ed., 2003) [hereinafter First, *Evolving Toward What?*].

23 For ICN reports, *see* http://www.internationalcompetitionnetwork.org/index.php/en/library. The OECD and UNCTAD are also involved in efforts to increase international antitrust enforcement. For a discussion of UNCTAD's role, *see* Ioannis Lianos, *The Contribution of the United Nations to Global Antitrust*, 15 TUL. J. INT'L & COMP. L. 415 (2007).

24 Rachel Brandenburger, Special Advisor, International, U.S. Dep't of Justice, Antitrust Div., *Twenty Years of Transatlantic Cooperation: the Past and the Future* at 5 (Oct. 14, 2011), *available at* http://www.justice.gov/atr/public/articles/279068.pdf. The formal and informal relationships among enforcement agencies are mapped in FIRST, *Evolving Toward What?*, *supra* note 22, at 23, 25-33.

25 The most dramatic examples of conflict in merger enforcement between the U.S. and E.U are the GE/Honeywell and Boeing/McDonnell Douglas mergers; in both the Commission found anticompetitive effects but U.S. enforcement agencies did not. *See* Commission Decision 2004/134 of 3 July 2001 in case COMP/M.2220, General Electric/Honeywell, [2004] OJ L 48/1; Commission Decision 97/816 of 30 July 1997 in case IV/M.877, Boeing/McDonnel Douglas, [1997] OJ L 336/16. *Compare* Statement of Chairman Robert Pitofsky and Commissioners Janet D. Steiger, Roscoe B. Starek III and Christine A. Varney in the Matter of The Boeing Company/McDonnell Douglas Corporation, File No. 971-0051 (July 1, 1997), http://www.ftc.gov/opa/1997/07/boeingsta.htm (separate statement of four FTC Commissioners providing reasons for not opposing merger). Not all disagreements cause controversy, however, nor do all disagreements involve cases where the Commission acts but the U.S. does not. *Compare* Commission Decision of 16 October 2002 in case IV/M.2867, UPM/Kymmene/Morgan Adhesives (labelstock), [2002] OJ C 284/4 (clearing merger) *with* United States v. UPM-Kymmene Oyj, 2003-2 Trade Cas. (CCH) ¶ 74,101 (N.D. Ill. 2003) (enjoining merger as likely violative of Section 7 of the Clayton Act).

26 Thomas Catan, *This Takeover Battle Pits Bureaucrat vs. Bureaucrat*, WALL ST. J., April 12, 2011, at A1.

27 For example, in 2002 the FTC and the Justice Department held joint hearings on the patent system and its effect on competition and innovation, but a 2003 report on those hearings was issued only by the FTC, *see* TO PROMOTE INNOVATION: THE PROPER BALANCE OF COMPETITION AND PATENT LAW AND POLICY (2003), *available at* http://www.ftc.gov/os/2003/10/innovationrpt.pdf (critiquing the patent system); a joint FTC/DOJ report was not issued until 2007, *see* U.S. DEP'T OF JUSTICE & FTC, ANTITRUST ENFORCEMENT AND INTELLECTUAL PROPERTY RIGHTS: PROMOTING INNOVATION AND COMPETITION (2007), *available at* http://www.usdoj.gov/atr/public/hearings/ip/222655.pdf. The FTC and the Justice Department also disagreed on whether to seek Supreme Court review of an unfavorable decision involving "reverse payments"; the FTC eventually filed its own (unsuccessful) petition seeking review while the Justice Department filed an amicus brief in opposition to review. For further discussion of this case and the divergence in enforcement interest between the FTC and Justice Department, *see* Harry First, *Controlling the Intellectual Property Grab: Protect Innovation Not Innovators*, 38 RUTGERS L.J. 365, 391-95 (2007).

28 The dispute between the Justice Department and the FTC over how to analyze single-firm conduct resulted in the Justice Department issuing a report in 2008 with which three of four FTC Commissioners publicly disagreed. *Compare* U.S. DEP'T OF JUSTICE, COMPETITION AND MONOPOLY: SINGLE-FIRM CONDUCT UNDER SECTION 2 OF THE SHERMAN ACT (Sept. 2008), *available at* http://www.usdoj.gov/atr/public/reports/236681.pdf *with* U.S. FEDERAL TRADE COMM'N, STATEMENT OF COMMISSIONERS HARBOUR, LEIBOWITZ, AND ROSCH ON THE ISSUANCE OF THE SECTION 2 REPORT BY THE DEPARTMENT OF JUSTICE (Sept. 8, 2008), *available at* http://www.ftc.gov/os/2008/09/080908section2stmt.pdf. Kovacic, as Chairman, issued a separate statement calling for more empirical work regarding the issues raised in the Justice Department's report. *See* http://www.ftc.gov/os/2008/09/080908section2stmtkovacic.pdf. The Justice Department in the Obama Administration subsequently withdrew the report, but did not issue a new one in its place. *See* Press Release, U.S. Dep't of Justice, Justice Department Withdraws Report on Antitrust Monopoly Law (May 11, 2009), *available at* http://www.usdoj.gov/atr/public/press_releases/2009/245710.htm. For a fuller discussion, including differences between U.S. and European Commission views, *see* Alden F. Abbott, *A Tale of Two Cities: Brussels, Washington, and the Assessment of Unilateral Conduct*, 56 ANTITRUST BULL. 103 (2011).

29 *See* JONATHAN B. BAKER & CARL SHAPIRO, *Reinvigorating Horizontal Merger Enforcement*, in HOW THE CHICAGO SCHOOL OVERSHOT THE MARK 247-48 (Robert Pitofsky ed. 2008) (reporting survey results showing that lawyers involved in merger reviews saw the Justice Department as "more lax" than the FTC and felt that their clients' interests "would be better served" by DOJ review).

30 For examples, *see* Press Release, FTC Closes its Investigation of Genzyme Corporation's 2001 Acquisition of Novazyme Pharmaceuticals, Inc. (Jan. 13, 2004), http://www.ftc.gov/opa/2004/01/genzyme.shtm (with links to statements by Chairman Muris and Commissioner Harbour, and dissenting statement of Commissioner Thompson); In the Matter of Royal Caribbean Cruises, Ltd./P&O Princess Cruises plc and Carnival Corporation/P&O Princess Cruises plc (Oct. 4, 2002), http://www.ftc.gov/os/caselist/0210041.shtm (with links to FTC Statement and dissenting statement of Commissioners Anthony and Thompson).

31 New State Ice Co. v. Liebmann, 285 U.S. 262, 386-87 (1932) (Brandeis, J., dissenting). The idea that state governments, moved by local concerns and knowledge, should be free to experiment without Supreme Court veto had earlier been advocated by Felix Frankfurter. Frankfurter drew on Justice Holmes' dissent in *Truax v. Corrigan*, where the Court had struck down, as a violation of the Due Process clause, a Washington state statute forbidding the granting of labor injunctions. *See* Felix Frankfurter, The Public & Its Government 49 (1930) ("government means experimentation"); Truax v. Corrigan, 257 U.S. 312, 344 (1921) (Holmes, J., dissenting) (the Supreme Court should not prevent "the making of social experiments"); *see also id.* at 357 (Brandeis, J., dissenting) ("The divergence of opinion in this difficult field of governmental action should admonish us not to declare a rule arbitrary and unreasonable merely because we are convinced that it is fraught with danger to the public weal, and thus to close the door to experiment within the law.").

32 For discussion of the theory that developments in competition law require continuous learning, *see* WOLFGANG KERBER & OLIVER BUDZINSKI, *Competition of Competition Laws: Mission Impossible?*, in COMPETITION LAWS IN CONFLICT, *supra* note 1, at 31, 37-39. For a full discussion of the argument that pluralism in approaches to competition policy is both inevitable and desirable, *see* Oliver Budzinski, *Pluralism of Competition Policy Paradigms*

and the Call for Regulatory Diversity (October 1, 2003) (Philipps-University of Marburg Volkswirtschaftliche Beitraege No. 14/2003), *available at* http://ssrn.com/abstract=452900. For a discussion of the development of U.S. antitrust policy, stressing "the evolutionary and experimental quality of competition policy making," *see* William E. Kovacic, *The Modern Evolution of U.S. Competition Policy Enforcement Norms*, 71 ANTITRUST L.J. 377, 470 (2003).

33 For example, in FY 2011, the FTC's budget was $129 million; the Antitrust Division's was $163 million. *See* ANTITRUST DIV., CONGRESSIONAL SUBMISSION FY 2013 PERFORMANCE BUDGET at 19, *available at* www.justice.gov/ jmd/2013justification/pdf/fy13-atr-justification.pdf; FTC, PERFORMANCE SNAPSHOT, http://www.ftc.gov/opp/ gpra/2011snapshotpar.pdf. For historic data comparing the two agencies, *see* DANIEL A. CRANE, THE INSTITUTIONAL STRUCTURE OF ANTITRUST ENFORCEMENT 31 (2011).

34 For federal appropriations for state antitrust enforcement, *see* Crime Control Act, Pub. L. No. 94-503, § 309, 90 Stat. 2415 (1976) (codified at 42 U.S.C. § 3739) ($21 million in "seed money" for distribution to the states to strengthen their antitrust enforcement efforts).

35 ANTITRUST MODERNIZATION COMM'N, REPORT AND RECOMMENDATIONS 273 (2007). For a review of the Antitrust Modernization Commission's decisions on state antitrust enforcement, *see* Harry First, *Modernizing State Antitrust Enforcement: Making the Best of a Good Situation*, 54 ANTITRUST BULL. 281 (2009).

36 Although proposals for some sort of international enforcement agency or enforcement process have been made since the end of World War II, including recent efforts to use the WTO, none has succeeded. *See, e.g.*, Jae Sung Lee, *Towards a Development-Oriented Multilateral Framework on Competition Policy*, 7 SAN DIEGO INT'L L.J. 293 (2006) (discussing failed WTO efforts in the Doha Round); Eleanor M. Fox, *International Antitrust and the Doha Dome*, 43 VA. J. INT'L L. 911 (2003) (examining alternative models for international antitrust).

37 An example of this might be resale price maintenance, where state antitrust enforcers maintain a stricter enforcement view of the practice while federal enforcers take a very hands-off view.

38 *See* KERBER & BUDZINSKI, *Competition of Competition Laws: Mission Impossible?*, *supra* note 32, at 36-37. A regulatory example of the yardstick function was the use of the Tennessee Valley Authority's electricity rates to measure the efficiency and pricing of private electric power companies regulated by state and federal agencies. *See* ALFRED E. KAHN, THE ECONOMICS OF REGULATION: PRINCIPLES AND INSTITUTIONS 104-05 (1971). For a general discussion of the theory, *see* Andrei Schleifer, *A Theory of Yardstick Competition*, 16 RAND J. ECON. 319 (1985) (application to performance of regulated firms).

39 For discussion of the application of regulatory competition to antitrust, *see, e.g.*, Eleanor M. Fox, *Antitrust and Regulatory Federalism: Races Up, Down, and Sideways*, 75 N.Y.U. L. REV. 1781, 1788-96 (2000) (international competition among antitrust regimes); Frank H. Easterbrook, *Antitrust and the Economics of Federalism*, in COMPETITION LAWS IN CONFLICT, at 189 (discussing competition among states relating to economic regulation); Kerber & Budzinski, *supra* note 32, at 46-49 (discussing whether regulatory competition involving antitrust law is likely). For a useful general review of the theory of regulatory competition, as well as its application in a number of different areas, *see* REGULATORY COMPETITION AND ECONOMIC INTEGRATION: COMPARATIVE PERSPECTIVES (Daniel C. Esty & Damien Geradin, eds., 2001).

40 *See* Jonathan B. Baker, *Mavericks, Mergers, and Exclusion: Proving Coordinated Competitive Effects under the Antitrust Laws*, 77 N.Y.U. L. REV. 135, 163 (2002).

41 *See, e.g.*, ROBERT C. ELLICKSON, ORDER WITHOUT LAW: HOW NEIGHBORS SETTLE DISPUTES (1991).

42 For a discussion of the importance of norms in antitrust enforcement, *see* William E. Kovacic, *The Modern Evolution of U.S. Competition Policy Enforcement Norms*, 71 ANTITRUST L.J. 377 (2003).

43 Kovacic has urged competition authorities "in one jurisdiction to benchmark their operational procedures with their counterparts," arguing that "diversification in approaches provides numerous comparative yardsticks by which an agency can evaluate the soundness of its own organizational choices and procedures." William E. Kovacic, *Using Ex Post Evaluations to Improve the Performance of Competition Policy Authorities*, 31 IOWA J. CORP. L. 503, 513 (2006).

44 For example, both agencies submit separate annual reports to Congress. *See* FTC PERFORMANCE AND ACCOUNTABILITY REPORT FISCAL YEAR 2011, *available at* http://www.ftc.gov/par; ANTITRUST DIV., CONGRESSIONAL SUBMISSION FY 2013 PERFORMANCE BUDGET, *supra* note 33.

45 *See* New York v. Microsoft Corp., 224 F. Supp. 2d 76 (D.D.C. 2002) (rejecting separate remedial requests from non-settling plaintiff states), *aff'd*, 373 F.3d 1199 (D.C. Cir. 2004). For discussion of the contribution that the state plaintiffs made to the district court's supervision of the remedies decree, sometimes in opposition to the Department of Justice, *see* First, *Modernizing State Antitrust Enforcement*, *supra* note 35, at 297-99.

46 Kovacic makes this point in *U.S. Antitrust Policy: An Underperforming Joint Venture*, CONCURRENCES No. 4-2011 65 ¶ 5 (2011).

47 *See* Richard A. Posner, *Federalism and the Enforcement of Antitrust Laws by State Attorneys General*, in COMPETITION LAWS IN CONFLICT, *supra* note 32, 260-62 (states should be stripped of their authority to bring antitrust suits under either state or federal law, or, at least, Congress should preempt state antitrust law insofar as it might affect interstate or foreign commerce).

48 *Cf.* William H. Page, *Antitrust Damages and Economic Efficiency: An Approach to Antitrust Injury*, 47 U. CHI. L. REV. 467, 475 (1979) (arguing that the private remedy should not reach "inefficient levels of deterrence").

49 *See* OECD, Competition Law and Policy in Brazil: A Peer Review 18-19 (2010) (in a "few short years" Brazil developed a program that is "one of the most active" in the area of criminal competition law enforcement; criminal violations prosecuted by public prosecutor under Economic Crimes Law) (discussing number of dawn raids, investigative detentions, and convictions between 2002 and 2009), *available at* http://www.oecd.org/dataoecd/4/42/45154362.pdf.

50 *See* Sourcebook of Criminal Justice Statistics Online, Criminal Cases filed in U.S. District Courts, Table 5.10.2010 (cases filed for FY 2010: 28,046 immigration violations; 15,785 drug violations; 26 antitrust violations), *available at* http://www.albany.edu/sourcebook/pdf/t5102010.pdf.

51 *See* Crane, *supra* note 33, at 135-41 (arguing for the development of Section 5 of the FTC Act somewhat independent of the requirements of Sections 1 and 2 of the Sherman Act).

52 A 1989 American Bar Association report noted that despite persistent questions about the FTC's antitrust jurisdiction, the case for abolishing the FTC's antitrust jurisdiction "has not been made." The Report is printed in 56 Antitrust & Trade Reg. Rep. (BNA), No. 1410 (Special Supplement), April 6, 1989; 58 Antitrust L.J. 42 (1989). *See* also Ernest Gellhorn, Charles James, Richard Pogue, & Joe Sims, *Has Antitrust Outgrown Dual Enforcement? A Proposal for Rationalization*, 35 Antitrust Bull. 695 (1990). In its 2001 Report, the ABA relegated the issue of dual federal enforcement to a footnote, *see* American Bar Association, Section of Antitrust Law, The State of Federal Antitrust Enforcement 2001 at 9 n.4 (This is a topic that continues to be debated, but the Task Force does not perceive any political or policy consensus to revisit this issue, so we do not discuss it in this Report.).

53 AMC Report, *supra* note 35, at 129-30 ("Although concentrating enforcement authority in a single agency generally would be a superior institutional structure, the significant costs and disruption of moving to a single-agency system at this point in time would likely exceed the benefits.").

54 *Id.* at 129 n. *. Note that two of the three dissenting Commissioners are former heads of the Antitrust Division.

55 *See* Kovacic, *An Underperforming Joint Venture*, *supra* note 46, at ¶ 28 ("Given the political phenomenon described above, it is difficult to imagine what form of exogenous shock would be necessary to induce Congress to revisit the dual federal enforcement agency structure and either consolidate federal government responsibility in one agency or redistribute authority between DOJ and the FTC.").

56 *See* Crane, *supra* note 33, at 44-46 (arguing that the "squabbling" and "bickering" over Supreme Court positions and the unilateral conduct report, *see supra* notes 27, 28 and accompanying text, diminishes the influence of positions taken by the antitrust enforcement agencies).

57 *See* Kovacic, *The Underperforming Federal Joint Venture*, *supra* note 46, at ¶¶ 15-19 (advancing proposals to increase policy coherence in merger enforcement, including more information sharing among agency case handlers and more programs to educate agency staff).

58 *See* American Needle, Inc. v. NFL, 130 S.Ct. 2201, 2209 (2010).

Designing Private Rights of Action for Competition Policy Systems: The Role of Interdependence and the Advantages of a Sequential Approach[*]

Andrew I. Gavil[**]

agavil@law.howard.edu

Professor of Law, Howard University School of Law

Abstract

There is an abundance of commentary on the institutional design challenges associated with the crea-tion of public competition enforcement agencies. Less attention has focused on the challenges of inte-grating private rights of action into already operative public enforcement systems. This article des-cribes how the interdependence of competition policy systems should influence the design of private rights in such circumstances. It argues that the kind of sequential approach being followed by the EC is not only defensible, but is consistent with the U.S. experience. The U.S. private right of action evolved over decades in response to many developments within and without antitrust law, and it continues to evolve. The article also explains how perceived excesses in private enforcement have led U.S. courts to constrain substantive antitrust doctrine, which in turn can limit the ability of public enforcers to protect competition. It concludes, however, that backlash of the kind experienced in the U.S. is far less likely in Europe and offers some recommendations for tracking the developments of private actions, so the success of reforms can be studied and evaluated over time.

I. Introduction

The spread of competition policy enforcement systems over the last two decades has spawned extensive commentary on institutional design. Given the initial focus of reforms on public enforcement, it is not surprising that much of that literature focused on the choices faced in defining the substantive scope of the law, establishing enforcement agencies, defining their powers, and integrating them into existing administrative, regulatory, and judicial systems.[1] Newly formed agencies looked to the more established jurisdictions, such as the European Union, United States, United Kingdom, Canada, and Australia, both for their examples and, more actively, for guidance in drafting statutes and guidelines. Through a multitude of technical assistance programs, these jurisdictions also provided various forms of training. Donor agencies also interjected themselves, funding technical assistance projects around the globe. As a consequence of this burst of activity, today the International Competition Network ("ICN")—which itself is just over a decade old—boasts more than a hundred members. The competition policy systems that have emerged combine substantive and institutional features from the more established jurisdictions, adapted to local cultures and conditions. There is convergence, but also divergence, in this still-evolving and vibrant global competition policy community.[2]

While new competition policy regimes were sprouting in some parts of the world, other more established ones were maturing. That maturation process included significant reforms to substantive prohibitions and institutions, but also consideration of greater reliance on private rights of action to supplement the private enforcement system. Private rights of action served other goals, too. For example, the European Commission viewed the private right of action as a way of promoting public awareness of the values of competition and facilitating the development of a broader "competition culture."[3]

As is true for public enforcement, the success of private rights of action is deeply dependent upon the existence of conditions that generally favor rule of law, and more particularly, an established, well-functioning judicial system. Given modern competition policy's focus on economic analysis, private rights of action for competition law infringements also require an infrastructure that can support and manage complex litigation, including highly differentiated legal and economic expertise.[4] Moreover, private rights of action must be "integrated" into the larger *public* competition policy system, which may require re-calibration to take into account the effects of the private right. Private rights also must be considered in light of the features of the general litigation system, such as rules of procedure and evidence. Even well-defined rights of action may have little effect on the level of enforcement if the procedural infrastructure and litigation culture are insufficient to support them.

Beginning with the *Green Paper* issued in 2005,[5] the European Commission opened a dialogue on the wisdom of, and challenges of, facilitating wider use of private rights of action for damages attributed to competition law infringements. The *Green Paper* was followed after comment by the *White Paper* in 2008.[6] Whereas the *Green Paper* sought merely to identify issues that would need to be addressed in connection with the establishment of a more robust private right of action, the *White Paper* moved toward specific policy recommendations that would facilitate their evolution. From February to April 2011, the Commission also held a public consultation on collective redress, initiating the latest stage of the dialogue on facilitating private rights of action.[7] The public consultation on collective redress was followed in June 2011 by a public consultation on quantification of damages.[8]

In this essay, I will discuss the efforts to promote private rights of action in Europe and how those efforts can take account of the larger goal of integrating private rights into existing public enforcement systems. First, I will emphasize the "interdependence" of competition policy systems generally, and, more particularly, the interdependence of the various components of public and private enforcement regimes. To illustrate these points, I will discuss the interdependence of: (1) the private right of action for indirect purchasers (often consumers); (2) the availability of a mechanism for collective redress; and (3) access to economic evidence. As I will argue, and as some observers including the Commission staff have observed, indirect purchaser rights have little independent value without a procedural device for enforcing them, such as collective redress. Yet, given the substantive prohibitions of European competition law, a procedural device for collective redress is itself unlikely to be effective without the means to collect and present the evidence now required to establish an infringement, especially economic evidence. Does that mean more comprehensive and fully integrated reforms are needed?

Second, I will examine how, given the interdependence of various elements of the private rights "system," jurisdictions can best approach the task of introducing and integrating reforms designed to remove or reduce identified impediments to private rights of action. Two paths to reform will be considered: "holistic" and "sequential." Contrary to what might be perceived as the case, I will examine the U.S. experience and show that private rights of action developed *sequentially* over decades, not all at once, and that their development continues today in the U.S. in the courts and legislative bodies. From this experience, I conclude that there is much to commend the sequential approach now being followed by the European Commission. Despite the interdependence of various components of a successful system of damages actions, a more holistic approach to reform—trying to address all of the pieces of the system at once—is not required and is likely to lead to unintended, unanticipated, and likely undesirable consequences.

Finally, I will turn to the role of public enforcement agencies in assisting—and monitoring—the evolution of private damages rights. I will conclude that the public system has an important role to play in birthing the private system, and that like any good parent it needs to nurture, monitor, and even occasionally intervene to insure the well-being of this new child until it reaches maturity. If public enforcers do not remain attentive to the development of private damages actions, the salutary goals of the private action—providing an added source of deterrence, an effective means for securing compensation, and promoting a deeper culture of competition in Europe—are less likely to be realized. Moreover, if the U.S. experience is replicated, the potential price for lack of active engagement may be undesirable, judicially imposed limitations on the law that unduly constrain public as well as private enforcers. If courts view private damage actions as abusive, they may adjust the content of competition law in response, as, for example, by imposing more demanding burdens of economic proof. I will conclude, however, that the relevance of the U.S. experience in this regard—and hence the risk of a similar kind of backlash to private damages actions in the courts of the EU—is limited given significant differences between the U.S. and European litigation systems that are likely to endure.

II. System Interdependence

Competition laws do not exist in isolation and are not self-executing. The commands and prohibitions contained in competition law statutes and regulations are but a single component of larger "competition policy systems." Whether the laws are effective depends on their goals, the specific features of that system, and how effectiveness is measured. Typical systems are comprised at a minimum of (1) prohibitions, (2) a public enforcement agency or agencies with investigatory powers, a (3) remedial scheme that specifies the consequences of infringements, and (4) a judicial system that, under specified and standardized rules of procedure and evidence, reviews the actions of the agency and, when private actions are authorized, evaluates civil actions by individuals claiming injuries attributable to an infringement.

Theses various elements, however, are highly interdependent. If prohibitions are not well-specified, even expert agencies will be challenged to enforce them in a consistent manner. Conversely, a well-specified law is unlikely to be effective without a well-functioning enforcement agency. The same will be true of a prohibition that lacks effective sanctions, be they criminal or civil. Additional institutional features like leniency programs seek to boost effectiveness by increasing detection rates. Agencies and private plaintiffs alike also need means of obtaining access to the information necessary to prove infringements. And courts must have the independence and institutional expertise necessary to review and intelligently evaluate the economic evidence presented to them.

The three most typically identified goals of competition systems are deterrence, compensation, and remediation. Deterrence is often the primary goal of public enforcement systems. But public and to a larger degree private enforcement systems also may seek to provide compensation for victims, something that governments do not always do, even if they have a system of civil fines or disgorgement. A third goal is often remediation—providing means for not only halting offensive conduct, but perhaps correcting for its adverse competitive effects, as with proscriptive equitable and injunctive relief.[9] As is discussed in the next section, one of the complicating factors in calibrating the private right of action in Europe is that it has some distinct, additional goals related to promoting a culture of competition.

Calibrating the various components of a system to realize its goals is a complex process that is informed by each system's specific goals as well as "decision theory." Decision theory has come to exert significant influence on how we think about system design and evaluate system performance. It prompts us to inquire about both error costs and direct or administrative costs. Assuming that no system is flawless, all systems will have some incidence of error and there will be varying consequences associated with those errors. Decision theory demands that we examine the potential rate of and likely consequences of errors in specifying prohibitions and calibrating the system. Given any specific design, what will be the incidence of false convictions (false positives) and false acquittals (false negatives)? Although it sometimes receives less attention, decision theory also demands that we consider the direct costs of enforcing any specific prohibition. What will it take for the parties and institutions to resolve a dispute given the prohibition and other features of the system? If, for example, a lenient burden of proof provides relatively greater certainty of condemnation but raises concerns about false positives, one possible cure might be to raise the burden of proof by, perhaps, demanding greater economic proof of competitive harm. In that event, however, it is also fair to ask whether the benefit from the reduction of false positives will be outweighed by the cost of lost certainty *and* the increased processing costs that may follow from using a more demanding standard of proof. Similarly, if a kind and quantity of evidence is required as a matter of law to establish an offense or defense, it is also fair to ask whether the litigation system provides adequate, cost-effective means for gathering and presenting that evidence to decision-makers. If it does not, specification of a demanding burden of proof may in effect lead to an increase in false negatives.[10] Failure to undertake such an economic analysis of economic evidence can mask an underlying normative preference for more or less interventionist competition rules.

These are not mere theoretical issues. Over the last thirty years, the antitrust decisions of the U.S. Supreme Court have exhibited deep concern about false positives and the over-deterrence they can cause.[11] The Court has also openly expressed its concern that the antitrust private right of action may coerce defendants into settling even unmeritorious claims to avoid the costs and risks associated with complete adjudication.[12] To diminish the occurrences of false positives, it has largely relied on two techniques: limiting the standing of private parties[13] and imposing more demanding burdens of pleading, production, and proof.[14] But the Court has expressed almost no concern for the loss of certainty that had been associated with now abandoned per se rules and lenient burdens of proof. Neither has it been concerned with the possibility that the incidence of false negatives could increase due to cost and lack of access to the necessary proof. In effect, the Court has presumed that the benefits of a lower incidence of false positives outweigh the possible costs of these other effects. In part, that belief was animated by an unspoken assumption that markets will be self-correcting and hence false negatives will not be as costly to competition as false positives.[15] Yet, in a seeming contradiction, courts and commentators are also expressing concern about the costs of administering competition law systems. For example, in the U.S. increased expectations for precise economic evidence have significantly boosted the cost of litigating antitrust cases. While that has benefited the large economic consultancies, it has likely made it far more costly on average to resolve antitrust claims and made their outcome less, not more certain.

The interdependent nature of competition policy systems and the experiences in the U.S. with the private right of action suggests a framework for evaluating optimal methods of integrating private rights of action in Europe and elsewhere. The issues can be helpfully divided into three areas of inquiry that might be denoted "foundations," "mismatch," and "backlash."[16]

Reflecting an appreciation for the first concern of interdependency, the *Green Paper* focused largely on "foundations" and asked whether the building blocks—the prerequisites—for a successful private action for damages existed within the context of the legal systems of EU member states.[17] Hence, it identified various impediments to private damage actions, such as access to evidence, fault and causation requirements, standing, costs of litigation, and jurisdictional rules, and posed various reform options for each.[18] After further study and consultation, the *White Paper* took the next step, suggesting specific solutions for some of the impediments that had been discussed in the *Green Paper*.

But the *Green Paper* and *White Paper* also demonstrated sensitivity to the problem of "mismatch"—a primary concern in calibration of the private enforcement component of a competition system. For example, the *White Paper* observed that under the European Court of Justice's *Courage and Crehan* and *Manfredi* decisions, the right of victims to seek compensation is guaranteed and that right includes the right of indirect purchasers to sue for damages.[19] As a practical matter, however, it also acknowledged that the procedural components necessary to enforce those rights were lacking. One can argue convincingly that indirect purchaser rights have little value without some kind of procedural mechanism for collective redress. Many indirect purchasers will be consumers and their individual injuries from a cartel, for example, or from abuse of dominance, might be small. Yet the collective financial harm to consumers can be very substantial. This, of course, is one of the principal justifications for creating collective redress.[20]

A further premise of the *Green Paper* and *White Paper* was that there now exists an established body of European Union-wide competition law that is ready to be enforced by private parties. The content of that law, however, has evolved towards greater economic sophistication. In fact, in a series of merger cases in the early 2000s reversals in the courts attributable to a lack of economic support in part led the Commission to create the Office of the Chief Competition Economist in 2003.[21] If those same substantive standards are applied to other kinds of competition law cases and also to private actions, will plaintiffs, including indirect purchasers allied together through a collective redress mechanism, be in a position to prevail without access to business records and strategic planning documents from the defendants they choose to sue? In short, if indirect purchaser rights are to have substance, does Europe not only need a means of collective redress, but also—at least to some degree—means for conducting what is called "discovery" in the U.S. system? Again, the *White Paper* addressed this mismatch problem, calling for a greater degree of access to the evidence necessary to evaluate competition law infringements.[22] But the Green Paper declined to endorse the use of testifying expert witnesses in favor of court-appointed experts, which may prove to be a significant continuing impediment for private damages actions, both in establishing liability and in proving damages.[23] In private damages actions, who will fill the role of the Chief Competition Economist?

As discussed here, "mismatches" of expectations and means can undermine the effectiveness of reforms, such as private rights of action. If cases prove difficult to win, parties and lawyers alike will abandon the effort. More broadly, however, mismatches can corrode public confidence in the rule of law and, in the case of competition law, public understanding of and commitment to the underlying principles of a market-based economy. Quality calibration, therefore, is an essential goal of any reform effort intended to integrate private rights of action in to a competition policy system.

There is likely no single, optimal way to calibrate every system. Many combinations of prohibitions, penalties, remedies, and institutional design are possible, and differently calibrated systems may achieve different mixes of deterrence, compensation, and remediation.[24] While some have proven to be objectively ineffective (for example, agencies that lack autonomy and prohibitions in countries with weak traditions in terms of rule of law tend to be ineffective), "optimal design" is likely to remain mostly a relative not an objective aspiration.

III. Integrating Private Rights of Action: Holistic and Sequential Approaches

With the *Green Paper* and *White Paper*, and now the examination of collective redress and damage calculations, the European Commission has embarked upon what might be described as a "sequential" approach to reform. Having identified a set of impediments to private actions, it has elaborated on specific proposals for addressing them that, as noted in Part I, evidence appreciation for the interdependence of the various elements of its competition policy system. But it has not done so with the expectation that a comprehensive, European-wide solution will be instantly adopted or that even a significant number of member states will embrace wide-ranging reforms. It has chosen more of an incremental approach, relying primarily on its role as an advocate for competition policy reform.

One might be inclined to criticize such an approach in light of what has already been said here of interdependence and the collective list of impediments identified in the *Green Paper*. Why not seek a comprehensive, EU-wide reform based on the *White Paper's* recommendations?

First, even if that option was politically feasible, there are significant dangers associated with trying to simultaneously implement multiple, complex reforms. Precisely because of interdependence, it is difficult to predict in advance how multiple reforms will interact with other new and existing elements of the system. For example, as the *White Paper* acknowledged, it is important to ask what effect amplification of the private right of action will likely have on leniency applications. If leniency currently improves detection, but fear of private suits inhibits firms from coming forward in the future, an increase in private damages actions could have the unintended consequence of undermining cartel detection and reducing cartel prosecution.[25] Similarly, since collective actions by indirect purchasers are a likely candidate for addressing cartels and would expose them to greater damages exposure, would the combination of improved private damages actions *and* collective actions acutely undermine the leniency program? On the other hand, will the threat of effective private actions provide additional deterrence, reducing the incidence of cartel formation and hence the importance of the leniency program? With too many new parts in motion, it might be difficult to isolate cause and effect to answer these kinds of questions.

Moreover, even if the perfect solution could be known in advance, as the saying goes, "the perfect should not be the enemy of the good." In other words, even if a sequential approach is a practical concession to political reality, it may be a defensible one and it may move the system in the right direction. A decided advantage of sequential change over system-wide calibration is that it permits observation and assessment, such as in a controlled experiment, of the impact of each step. Over-and under-correction can more easily be observed, diagnosed, and addressed.

Does the U.S. experience suggest otherwise? Perhaps surprisingly, the clear answer is "no." It is easy to demonstrate that the U.S. followed a sequential, not a holistic, approach to developing its private right of action—and that it evolved over many decades. That process of evolution and calibration continues daily in the courts and before the antitrust enforcement agencies.

First, while it is true that the current statutory authorization of a treble damages private right of action for persons injured by an antitrust violation originated in the Sherman Act of 1890,[26] it would be inaccurate to say that the private right *as it exists today* originated in 1890. Such a view disregards the "systems" nature of the private right of action. Like any field of law, to flourish competition law requires a complete infrastructure and such infrastructures take time to evolve. Although created in 1890, private treble damage antitrust actions were not common in the United States until the 1960s—seventy years after the private right of action was created.[27] What was missing before then?

First, antitrust as a field of study and legal practice was slow to develop. The broad-based educational, legal, and economic infrastructure necessary to nurture and then monitor the field simply did not exist before the 1950s. Although there were some early scholarly articles about antitrust that appeared in law reviews at the turn of the twentieth century, and William Howard Taft authored an important early study of the field in 1914,[28] the first antitrust casebook for use in law schools was not published until 1931.[29] Not surprisingly, therefore, the Antitrust Section of the American Bar Association was not established until 1952, when it held its first "annual meeting."[30] In addition, the development of the field of industrial organization economics accelerated significantly following World War II at mid-century and for the first time began to focus intently on antitrust.[31] Yet the most comprehensive expressions of the principal, economically-rooted schools of criticism of antitrust law came even later in the 1970s.[32]

Second, the field of *complex litigation* did not develop until the middle of the twentieth century. Until 1938, there were no uniform federal rules of civil procedure and the modern class action rule was not promulgated until 1966, followed by the basic framework for the modern discovery rules in 1970. Similarly, there were no uniform federal rules of evidence until 1975. Indeed, despite the presumed enticement of treble damages and attorneys' fees, there were few if any private antitrust cases filed in the federal courts until the 1960s.[33] Only then did all of the preconditions to a fully functioning antitrust system coalesce so that the incidence of private antitrust civil actions became significant.[34] The 1960s also spawned the phenomenon of multiple, related civil antitrust cases, filed in various jurisdictions. The government's investigation of a price fixing conspiracy among electrical equipment manufacturers led to the filing of over 2000 private treble damages actions. A direct and important further procedural consequence of those cases was the creation in 1968 of the Judicial Panel on Multi-district Litigation, which facilitated the coordination of multiple, related antitrust cases filed in different federal districts around the country.[35] Before the *Electrical Equipment* antitrust cases, the phenomenon of large volume, multiple, related follow-on antitrust cases was simply unknown.

The private right of action in the U.S., therefore, did not sprout in its fullest form the day the Sherman Act became law. There was no "system" to support it. That system, including a trained bar and an interested academy, took decades to form and many of its pieces, such as class actions and modern discovery rules, developed without any specific focus on antitrust, even though it was collaterally and profoundly affected by them. Collectively, therefore, the construction of the modern U.S. private right of action is correctly understood as having been *sequentially* developed—over decades.

Second, although the U.S. private antitrust system certainly has its excesses, those excesses can be easily exaggerated—and often are.[36] It is very difficult and very expensive today for plaintiffs to successfully bring private antitrust cases.[37] Like running the hurdles, plaintiffs must establish their standing,[38] and vault over demanding pleading standards,[39] screens for necessary expert testimony,[40] increasingly demanding standards for class certification,[41] and heightened burdens of production[42] and proof.[43] These are not cases lightly instituted for "quick settlements" as is frequently suggested by irate defendants, their lawyers, and their economists. As a result, the number of private civil cases filed in the federal courts has steadily declined on average over the last forty years and is now less than half of what it was in the 1970s despite an otherwise burgeoning federal civil docket. Over the last five years, on average there have been less than 1,000 private civil cases filed in the federal court system out of a total civil docket of roughly 270,000 cases. The numbers have been declining, however, and in 2010 there were only 544 new federal private antitrust cases filed, a 33% decrease from the previous year.[44] In truth, of course, focusing on the number of cases filed can understate the magnitude of the cases, which can be very large, long-lasting, and challenging to litigate and resolve. In addition, focusing solely on federal statistics understates the number of private antitrust cases actually filed each year. Because a majority of states have rejected *Illinois Brick* as a matter of state antitrust law, indirect purchaser cases can be filed in significant numbers in state courts. Even with these caveats, however, would the European Commission be troubled if the volume of private cases filed throughout the member states in say 2020 was 500? It seems unlikely.

IV. Nurturing Private Rights: The Continuing Role of Public Agencies

As noted earlier, public competition enforcement agencies may have to live with the consequences of poorly conceived private actions. If a "market" develops for private actions—if parties and lawyers alike perceive that they are economical to pursue—it will be hard to predict which kinds of cases will be initiated. If courts do not view the cases brought favorably, they may respond as courts have in the U.S., by elevating standards of pleading and proof, imposing screens that require very specific kinds of proof that may not always be reasonably available, and generally developing skepticism about the wisdom of competition law as a mechanism for regulating corporate behavior. In short, unleashing a private market for private rights of action could trigger "backlash" that would very much defeat the purposes of promoting them in the first place. As former FTC Chairman and Commissioner William E. Kovacic has cautioned, "an expansion of private rights could lead judicial tribunals to adjust the doctrine in ways that shrink the zone of liability," which may "encumber public prosecutors" enforcing the same prohibitions.[45]

Andrew I. Gavil

Therefore, if for no reason other than self-interest, the agencies will want to monitor the development and use of private actions. On the other hand, as noted above, the risk of backlash in the EU can be overstated if based on the U.S. experience. It is evident that in limiting the scope of U.S. antitrust law, the U.S. Supreme Court has been influenced not merely by the treble damage remedy, but by its perception—right or wrong—of the specter of protracted and costly discovery and the threat of class action damages coercing unwarranted settlements. The often-criticized U.S. litigation "toxic cocktail" consists of contingency fee arrangements, the right of prevailing plaintiffs to recover their attorneys' fees, treble damages, broad discovery, class actions, and jury trials. This mix of ingredients simply does not exist in Europe and is unlikely to be replicated—certainly not to the same degree—from the reforms being considered.

Beyond self-interest, however, lies the greater importance of developing competitive economies. In their role as advocates of that goal, public agencies will want courts and private parties to get the economics right in private competition cases. The incentives of the private rights market and the litigation system, however, may not always support that result—indeed, it may not even be the chief aim of the litigants. Plaintiffs and defendants alike may be inclined to seek any advantage they can through legal process, even at the price of distorting the ultimate result for competition. Agency intervention, therefore, may be critical, especially in the early days of development. As Bill Kovacic has observed, "[a]n expansion of private rights in the EU and the Member States . . . is likely to alter the way in which public competition agencies spend their resources."[46] Agencies will not be well advised to be bystanders as private rights develop.

Agency intervention might take many forms. Here are four ways that agencies might encourage thoughtful and productive development of the private right of action beyond advocating reforms that facilitate the filing of damages actions.

Monitoring Private Action Activity. There will be no effective way to evaluate the quantity or quality of private actions if they are not tracked in some form. Because it will generally be more difficult to identify and study competition law cases retrospectively, a competition case tracking system could be implemented that would build a database of information designed to assist statistical as well as qualitative analyses of private cases. The first order of business will be to accurately identify them. Because such actions will be filed in the courts of member states, a successful monitoring program would likely require partnering arrangements with National Competition Authorities (NCAs). It would be useful to know, for example, not just how many cases are filed, but the general nature of the alleged infringements (e.g., cartels, abuse of dominance, dealer restraints), the specific conduct being challenged (e.g., price fixing, refusals to deal, bundled rebates, resale price maintenance), and the remedy being sought (e.g., damages or injunctive relief). Together, the Commission and the NCAs could share the task of tracking and evaluating the private cases. And from the broader set of cases, subsets could be identified for further study. This kind of tracking could also aid in determining whether various types of interventions would be advisable.

Case Intervention. One of the more obvious devices available to the Commission and the NCAs would be an *amicus curiae* brief program. This has long been a staple of agency advocacy in the U.S. and has often been used to rein in poorly conceived private antitrust cases. Less frequently, it has also been used to support plaintiffs being confronted with unreasonable interpretations of law or demands for elevated standards of proof. Intervention might also be especially valuable with respect to the design of remedies.[47] Finally, the agencies might want to offer their views if defendants urge courts to adopt other calibrating devices, such as limits on evidence or standing.

Direct Assistance. Monitoring private activity might suggest a need for more aggressive intervention. Just as was true in the early days of agency development in the wake of the collapse of the Soviet Union and the expansion of competition agencies in Central and Eastern Europe and elsewhere in the world, the EC and the NCAs might find it advisable to offer a form of "technical assistance" to private lawyers, economists, and advocacy groups interested in pursuing private litigation. This would not likely take the form of specific case support. Rather, the agencies might play the role of teacher, offering instruction on competition law requirements and perhaps even assistance in prospective case evaluation, helping parties to identify "good" and "bad" cases for challenge and advising on possible remedial solutions.

Trust But Verify. If the level and nature of competition actions give rise to concerns—if the cases brought do not appear to have merit and threaten to inhibit rather than promote competition—a more aggressive type of intervention could be considered. Although not common in competition law, in other areas of regulation private parties can be required to seek and receive pre-approval from the appropriate government agency to initiate a civil action. In the U.S. for example, private cases alleging employment discrimination are screened by a federal agency and cannot be initiated unless the government issues a "right to sue" letter.[48] This provides the government with a very direct way of screening and ensuring the threshold merit of specific, proposed civil suits.

Between the *White Paper* and now the public consultation on collective redress, the European Commission has assumed a leadership role in exploring the need for more private damages actions, identifying impediments to their use, and proposing solutions for facilitating their future growth. Having assumed that role, the Commission may also want to plan for concrete steps to monitor the progress of any reforms.

V. Conclusion

Intra- and inter-system calibration is a continuing challenge for all competition policy systems. In the case of private rights of action, jurisdictions will need to carefully consider the need for private enforcement as a complement to public enforcement, the goals sought to be achieved, and the receptivity of the judicial system to the needs of competition cases.

Although the success of private rights ultimately will turn on many different factors, it is not necessary, and might even be counter-productive, to undertake broad-based reform efforts all at once. While a sequential approach may not fully succeed in the short run, it will permit careful integration and perhaps avoid judicial and political backlash. Markets will play an important role in the process, but public agencies also must keep a watchful eye and play an important role.

NOTES

*   Copyright 2012, Andrew I. Gavil. This essay is adapted from remarks presented at the 16th Annual EU Competition and Policy Workshop, *Integrating Public and Private Enforcement of Competition Law: Implications for Courts and Agencies*, sponsored by the European University Institute, Fiesole, Italy, 17-18 June 2011. A version of this essay will appear in Philip Lowe & Mel Marquis, Eds, Integrating Public and Private Enforcement in Competition Cases: Implications for Courts and Agencies (forthcoming, Oxford: Hart Publishing).

**   Professor of Law, Howard University School of Law. The author would like to thank Varnitha Siva for her valuable research assistance. The preparation of this article was supported by the Howard University School of Law and a gift from Google Inc., which is not responsible for its content. After this article was completed, Professor Gavil was appointed as the Director of the Office of Policy Planning at the U.S. Federal Trade Commission.

Andrew I. Gavil

1   *See, e.g.*, Eleanor M. Fox, *Antitrust and Institutions: Design and Change*, 41 Loy. U. Chi. L.J. 473 (2010); William E. Kovacic, *Rating the Competition Agencies: What Constitutes Good Performance?*, 16 Geo. Mason L. Rev. 903 (2009); William E. Kovacic, *Institutional Foundations for Economic Legal Reform in Transition Economies: The Case of Competition Policy and Antitrust Enforcement*, 77 Chi.-Kent L. Rev. 265 (2001); D. Daniel Sokol, *Antitrust, Institutions, and Merger Control*, 17 Geo. Mason L. Rev. 1055 (2010); Philip J. Weiser, *Towards an International Dialogue on the Institutional Side of Antitrust*, 66 N.Y.U. Ann. Surv. Am. L. 445 (2011).

2   For a recent article critically evaluating the desirability and achievability of convergence, *see* Thomas K. Cheng, *Convergence and its Discontents: A Reconsideration of the Merits of Convergence of Global Competition Law*, 12 Chi. J. Int'l L. 433 (2012).

3   *See* Commission of the European Communities, *White Paper on Damages Actions for Breach of the EC Antitrust Rules*, COM (2008) 165 Final, at 3 ("A competition culture contributes to better allocation of resources, greater economic efficiency, increased innovation and lower prices.") [hereinafter *White Paper*], *available at* http://eur-lex.europa.eu/LexUriServ/LexUriServ.do?uri=COM:2008:0165:FIN:EN:PDF.

4   *See generally* Andrew I. Gavil, *The Challenges of Economic Proof in a Decentralized and Privatized European Competition Policy System: Lessons from the American Experience*, 4 J. Comp. L. & Econ. 177 (2008). For a discussion of how the specific features of a procedural infrastructure can influence how economics becomes "embedded" in the substantive antitrust law, *see* David J. Gerber, *Convergence in the Treatment of Dominant Firm Conduct: The United States, The European Union, and the Institutional Embeddedness of Economics*, 76 Antitrust L.J. 951, 957-58 (2010).

5   Commission of the European Communities, *Green Paper on Damages Actions for Breach of the EC Antitrust Rules*, COM (2005) 672 Final [hereinafter *Green Paper*], *available at* http://eur-lex.europa.eu/LexUriServ.do?uri=COM:2005:0672:FIN:EN:PDF. *See also* Commission Staff Working Paper, *Annex to the Green Paper on Damages Actions for Breach of the EC Antitrust Rules*, SEC (2005) 1732, *available at* http://ec.europa.eu/competition/antitrust/actionsdamages/sp_en.pdf.

6   *White Paper*, *supra* note 3. *See also Commission Staff Working Paper Accompanying the White Paper on Damages Actions for Breach of EC Antitrust Rules*, SEC (2008) 404, *available at* http://eur-lex.europa.eu/LexUriServ/LexUriServ.do?uri=SEC:2008:0404:FIN:EN:PDF.

7   *See* Commission Staff Working Document Public Consultation: *Towards a Coherent European Approach to Collective Redress*, SEC (2011) 173, *available at* http://ec.europa.eu/justice/news/consulting_public/0054/ConsultationpaperCollectiveredress4February2011.pdf.

8   *See* European Commission, DG Competition, *Draft Guidance Paper on Quantifying Harm in Actions for Damages Based on Breaches of Article 101 or 102 of the Treaty on the Functioning of the European Union* (Public Consultation) (Jun, 2011), *available at* http://ec.europa.eu/competition/consultations/2011_actions_damages/draft_guidance_paper_en.pdf.

9   For a more comprehensive discussion of the range of goals that may be served by a private right of actions, *see* Edward D. Cavanagh, *The Private Antitrust Remedy: Lessons from the American Experience*, 41 Loy. U. Chi. L.J. 629 (2010).

10 For a more complete discussion, including citations to some of the relevant literature, *see* Andrew I. Gavil, *Burden of Proof in U.S. Antitrust Law*, *in* I ABA Antitrust Section, Issues in Competition Law and Policy 125, 129-31 (2008) [hereinafter Gavil, *Burden of Proof in U.S. Antitrust Law*].

11 *See, e.g.*, Matsushita Elec. Indus. Co., Ltd. v. Zenith Radio Corp., 475 U.S. 574, 594 (1986) ("mistaken inferences in cases such as this one are especially costly, because they chill the very conduct the antitrust laws are designed to protect."); Verizon Commc'ns, Inc. v. Law Offices of Curtis v. Trinko, LLP, 540 U.S. 398, 414 (2004) (limiting the scope of the U.S. prohibition of monopolization citing concerns about "[m]istaken inferences and the resulting false condemnations" and "[t]he cost of false positives").

12 *See, e.g.*, Bell Atl. Corp. v. Twombly, 550 U.S. 544, 559 (2007) ("the threat of discovery expense will push cost-conscious defendants to settle even anemic cases.").

13 *See* Brunswick Corp. v. Pueblo Bowl-O-Mat, Inc., 429 U.S. 477, 489 (1977) (requiring private plaintiff to demonstrate "antitrust injury"); Ill. Brick Co. v. Illinois, 431 U.S. 720 (1977) (barring indirect purchasers); Associated Gen'l Contractors of Cal., Inc. v. Cal. State Council of Carpenters, 459 U.S. 519 (1983)(limiting standing for remote injuries not proximately caused by defendant's conduct). *But see* Reiter v. Sonotone Corp., 442 U.S. 330, 343 (1979) (concluding that overcharges attributable to an antitrust violation constitute injury to a consumer's "property"); and Blue Cross Blue Shield of Va. v. McCready, 457 U.S. 465, 472 (1982) (acknowledging consumer standing to challenge reduced competition flowing from exclusionary conduct).

14 *See* Gavil, *Burden of Proof in U.S. Antitrust Law*, *supra* note 10, at 132-37.

15 *See, e.g.*, Frank H. Easterbrook, *The Limits of Antitrust Law*, 63 Tex. L. Rev. 1(1984) (arguing that false positives are a greater concern than false negatives because markets will tend to correct for any market power that results from false negatives).

16 The problem of backlash is addressed in discussion, *infra* Part III.

17 Another specific area of interdependency discussed by the *White Paper* was the interaction of leniency programs and private damages actions against cartels. *See White Paper*, *supra* note 3, §2.9.

18 *See generally Green Paper*, *supra* note 5.

19 *See White Paper, supra* note 3, at 2, 4 (*citing* Case C-453/99, Courage and Crehan, [2001] ECR I-6297, and Joined Cases C-295–298/04, Manfredi, [2006] ECR I-6619). The overwhelming majority of states in the US now agree and grant indirect purchasers the right to sue for antitrust violations under state antitrust law, but as is widely understood today, under the Supreme Court's decision in Ill. Brick Co. v. Illinois, 431 U.S. 720 (1977), those same indirect purchasers are barred from suing under the federal antitrust laws. *See generally* Andrew I. Gavil, *Thinking Outside the* Illinois Brick *Box: A Proposal for Reform*, 76 ANTITRUST L.J. 167 (2009); Andrew I. Gavil, *Antitrust Remedy Wars Episode I:* Illinois Brick *from Inside the Supreme Court*, 79 ST. JOHN's L. REV. 553 (2005).

20 *See White Paper, supra* note 3, at § 2.1.

21 *See* ANDREW I. GAVIL, WILLIAM E. KOVACIC & JONATHAN B. BAKER, ANTITRUST LAW IN PERSPECTIVE: CASES, CONCEPTS AND PROBLEMS IN COMPETITION POLICY 555-56 (2d ed. 2008).

22 *See White Paper, supra* note 3, at § 2.2.

23 *Green Paper, supra* note 5, at §2.9. *See also* Gavil, *supra* note 4, at 201-04 (analyzing *Green Paper*'s approach to expert witnesses).

24 *Illinois Brick*, for example, can be understood as prioritizing deterrence over compensation. Faced with the challenges of calculating pass-on, the Court concluded that concentrating all rights of action in the hands of direct purchasers would maximize the incentive to challenge illegal conduct and achieve maximum deterrence, even though it might not be the optimal rule from the point of view of compensation, because it barred indirect purchasers from suing even though pass-on surely occurred in some, if not many, cases.

25 *White Paper, supra* note 3, at §2.9.

26 In 1914 it was relocated to Section 4 of the newly adopted Clayton Act, 15 U.S.C. §15.

27 *See* Douglas H. Ginsburg & Leah Brannon, *Determinants of Private Antitrust Enforcement in the United States*, 1 COMPETITION POL'Y INT'L 29, 32 (2005) (Figure 1 shows level of private and public antitrust cases filed in U.S. federal courts from 1945-2000).

28 WILLIAM H. TAFT, THE ANTI-TRUST ACT AND THE SUPREME COURT (1914).

29 *See* Andrew I. Gavil, *Teaching Antitrust law in its Second Century: In Search of the Ultimate Antitrust Casebook*, 66 N.Y.U. L. REV. 189, 198 (1991) (discussing early history of antitrust casebook development).

30 For a timeline showing the history of the founding and evolution of the Antitrust Section, *see Special Insert, ABA Section of Antitrust Law 50th Year Milestones 1952-2002*, ANTITRUST, Summer 2002 (following page 46).

31 For one of the more influential early treatises, *see* CARL KAYSEN & DONALD F. TURNER, ANTITRUST POLICY: A LEGAL AND ECONOMIC ANALYSIS (1959).

32 For two of the most influential reflections of Chicago School thinking, *see* ROBERT H. BORK, THE ANTITRUST PARADOX (1978) and RICHARD A. POSNER, ANTITRUST LAW: AN ECONOMIC PERSPECTIVE (1976). The first edition of what is often associated as the "Harvard School's" equivalent was published at the same time. *See* PHILIP AREEDA & DONALD F. TURNER, ANTITRUST LAW (1978). Collectively, these three works evidenced the intellectual maturing of the field as it transitioned to the modern era. For a more complete analysis of the intellectual history of U.S. antitrust law, see William E. Kovacic & Carl Shapiro, *Antitrust Policy: A Century of Economic and Legal Thinking*, 14 J. ECON. PERSPS. 43 (2000). *See also* William E. Kovacic, *The Intellectual DNA of Modern U.S. Competition Law for Dominant Firm Conduct: The Chicago/Harvard Double Helix*, 2007 COLUM. BUS. L. REV. 1.

33 *See* Ginsburg & Brannon, *supra* note 27, at 32.

34 *Id.*

35 *See* 28 U.S.C. § 1407. For a contemporaneous discussion of the cases, *see* Phil C. Neal & Perry Goldberg, *The Electrical Equipment Antitrust Cases: Novel Judicial Administration*, 50 A.B.A. J. 621 (1964).

36 *See, e.g.*, Cavanagh, *supra* note 9, at 640 (describing criticisms of U.S. private right of action as "harsh and misleading").

37 One study reported that defendants prevailed in rule of reason cases almost 100% of the time. *See* Michael A. Carrier, *The Rule of Reason: An Empirical Update for the 21st Century*, 16 GEO. MASON L. REV. 827, 830 (2009) ("plaintiffs almost never win under the rule of reason").

38 *See* note 13, *supra.*

39 *See, e.g.*, Bell Atlantic Corp. v. Twombly, 550 U.S. 544 (2007).

40 *See, e.g.*, Daubert v. Merrell Dow Pharm., Inc., 509 U.S. 579 (1993).

41 *See, e.g., In re* Hydrogen Peroxide Antitrust Litig., 552 F.3d 305 (3d Cir. 2008).

42 *See, e.g.*, Matsushita Elec. Indus. Co., Ltd. v. Zenith Radio Corp., 475 U.S. 574 (1986).

43 *See, e.g.*, Leegin Creative Leather Prods., Inc. v. PSKS, Inc., 551 U.S. 877 (2007) (resale price maintenance); Verizon Commc'ns Inc. v. Law Offices of Curtis V. Trinko, *LLP*, 540 U.S. 398 (2004) (refusals to deal); Brooke Group Ltd. v. Brown & Williamson Tobacco Corp., 509 U.S. 209 (1993) (predatory pricing).

44 This decrease in the number of new federal, civil antitrust actions has occurred despite a steady increase in the overall number of civil actions filed in the federal courts and continued in fiscal year 2011. Out of a total of 289, 252 civil actions filed, only 475 were antitrust cases. *See* ADMINISTRATIVE OFFICE OF THE UNITED STATES COURTS, JUDICIAL BUSINESS OF THE UNITED STATES COURTS: ANNUAL REPORT OF THE DIRECTOR, at 126 tbl C-2A (2011), *available at* http://www.uscourts.gov/uscourts/Statistics/JudicialBusiness/2011/JudicialBusiness2011.pdf.

45 *See* William E. Kovacic, Gen Counsel, Fed. Trade Comm'n, *Private Participation in the Enforcement of Public Competition Laws* (May, 15, 2003), *available at* http://www.ftc.gov/speeches/other/030514biicl.shtm. *See also* Howard A. Shelanski, *The Case for Rebalancing Antitrust and Regulation*, 109 MICH. L. REV. 683 (2011).

46 *Id.*

47 *Id.* ("Competition agencies may need to spend more time preparing *amicus curiae* submissions in private cases to guide the courts in their treatment of substantive doctrinal issues and, in some instances, the proper design of remedies.")

48 *See* 42 U.S.C. §2000e-5(f)(1).

Antitrust Settlements: The Culture of Consent*

Douglas H. Ginsburg

dginsburg@nyu.edu

Professor of Law, New York University School of Law
Senior Circuit Judge, United States Court of Appeals for the District of Columbia Circuit

Joshua D. Wright

jwrightg@gmu.edu

Professor, George Mason University School of Law and Department of Economics

Abstract

The beginning of a shift toward a more regulatory and less litigation-oriented regime of antitrust enforcement was observable by the mid-1990s, if not earlier. The transition toward this more bureaucratic approach by antitrust enforcement agencies is the subject of our analysis. Consent decrees create potential for an enforcement agency to extract from parties under investigation commitments well beyond what the agency could obtain in litigation—commitments that may impair rather than improve competition and thereby harm consumers. The consequences of such consent decrees, that is, are borne not only by the parties that are subject to them, but also by consumers and by non-parties who glean the agency's enforcement position from the terms of those decrees. Moreover, consent decrees signal to foreign competition authorities that such commitments are appropriate and, consequently, the FTC and the Division lose the ability they might otherwise have to convince other agencies to minimize their own departures from the appropriate standard. We proffer that the culture of consent at antitrust agencies both in the United States and abroad has had an untoward effect upon the agencies' selection of cases to bring and, more certainly, upon the remedies the agencies obtain in settlement agreements.

I. Introduction

The Antitrust Division's first entered into a consent decree in a case in *United States v. Otis Elevator Company* in 1906.[1] By the 1950s, 87 percent of all civil antitrust cases brought by the Division were settled by consent decrees. By the 1980s, 97 percent of civil cases filed by the Division resulted in a consent decree, and that percentage remained relatively constant at 93 percent in the 1990s.[2] This trend has continued, with the Division resolving nearly its entire antitrust civil enforcement docket by consent decree from 2004 to present.[3] The Federal Trade Commission has experienced a similar increase in the use of consent decrees as a proportion of enforcement activity. FTC consent decrees more than tripled in number from 1992 to 1995.[4] Since 1995, the FTC has settled 93 percent of its competition cases.[5]

The beginning of a shift toward a more bureaucratic and less litigation-oriented regime of antitrust enforcement was observable by the mid-1990s, if not earlier.[6] The transition to a new, more regulatory approach to enforcement appears now to be complete. This significant shift in the nature of antitrust enforcement institutions—and its effects—is the subject of our analysis. We have undertaken this analysis in tribute to William E. Kovacic, teacher, scholar, public servant extraordinaire and, we are proud to say, our friend, who has prompted and led a generation of scholarship on the institutions of antitrust law.

Some tradeoffs between moves along the continuum toward the regulatory model and away from what might be described as a "law enforcement" model are well known. The regulatory model brings greater reliance upon the consent decree as the principal means of enforcement—and in turn, the benefits of economizing on scarce agency resources—at the cost of potentially stunting the development of the common law arising through adjudication. The regulatory model also focuses more intensely upon the remedy than the underlying violation and thus, unsurprisingly results in consent decrees tending to place the agency in the position of monitoring or supervising the firm's compliance with remedial obligations or imposing conditions that extend beyond what the agency would likely be able to obtain after successful litigation.

We focus upon less well-recognized consequences of the institutional shift toward a culture of consent in the antitrust enforcement agencies. Part I outlines the direct welfare costs of antitrust settlements. Part II focuses upon the less direct but nonetheless significantly deleterious effects of the shift toward the culture of consent. Part III briefly concludes, and the Appendix catalogs the antitrust settlements analyzed and other examples of noteworthy settlements both in the United States and in other jurisdictions.

II. Materially Adverse Welfare Effects

Antitrust settlements subvert the purposes of antitrust law when they depart from the welfare standard adopted by most jurisdictions—whether progress toward that purpose is measured by the consumer welfare or by the total welfare standard. The most obviously harmful antitrust settlements are those with a substantive provision that directly reduces consumer welfare. There can be reasonable disagreement as to whether certain settlement provisions further consumers' interests; however, a non-trivial number of recent antitrust consents in the United States and other jurisdictions include settlement provisions that will likely make consumers worse off. We denominate these settlements, running as they do, directly counter to the goals of antitrust law, as "abuses" of power by the antitrust enforcement agency. Common examples of abuses include settlement provisions imposing restrictions upon the merging firms' employment decisions,[7] requiring the settling firm to make charitable contributions unrelated to compensating victims of an antitrust violation,[8] and extracting concessions irrelevant to the potential antitrust concerns under review.[9]

Consent decrees placing the agency in the role of monitoring competition can also have materially adverse consequences for consumers, even when the decree is targeted at conduct that might reasonably be viewed as reducing consumer welfare. We denominate "misuses" of the settlement process consent decrees containing provisions that potentially further the goals of antitrust law by preventing arguably welfare-reducing conduct but that do so by placing the enforcement agency in a position of monitoring and supervising competition for an extended period of time. A consent decree with such a provision rises to the level of an abuse, however, if the remedy exceeds what the agency could reasonably have anticipated obtaining in litigation. A paradigmatic example of a recent misuse is the FTC's consent decree with Intel Corporation.[10] That decree restricted Intel's ability to offer certain discounts to its customers, but those provisions at least arguably serve consumer welfare according to the FTC's economic theory of the case. More to the point, the settlement also contains a provision—among others arguably placing the FTC in a significant supervisory role—prohibiting Intel, until the decree expires in 2020, from making any change in the design of its microprocessors or graphics processing units that does not "provide an actual benefit" to the products and degrades the performance of a rival product.[11]

The adverse welfare consequences of abusive settlements are not bounded by the transaction-specific costs imposed upon the parties to the consent decree and upon their customers. An abusive settlement can also have a chilling effect upon non-parties, whether in the same or other industries, who glean the agency's enforcement position from the terms of the settlement. Recent examples include the aforementioned FTC settlement with Intel as well as its settlement in *N-Data*. In *Intel*, the FTC not only acquired a role in supervising the product design, innovation, and engineering decisions of a firm engaged at the center of the fast-changing technology sector of the economy.[12] The FTC also communicated its willingness to rely in a future case upon the uniformly disfavored standard for assessing bundled discounts that the Third Circuit had adopted in *LePage's*.[13] Non-parties counseling clients with regard to potential antitrust exposure must pay close attention to the substance of consent decrees that communicate valuable information concerning how the agency is likely to view and seek to remedy certain forms of business conduct. A consent that communicates the agency's willingness to challenge procompetitive or competitively innocuous business arrangements will have a detrimental impact upon consumer welfare; similarly, an agency's endorsement of a legal standard generally recognized to deter competition, such as the standard in *LePage's*, almost certainly will harm consumers.[14]

The settlements into which the FTC or the Antitrust Division enter also communicate information to state and foreign competition authorities. Like other non-parties to settlements, state and foreign competition authorities pay close attention to the content of the FTC's and the Division's antitrust settlements. To the extent those settlements depart from the objective of protecting consumer welfare, they signal to other competition authorities that such considerations are appropriate. Consequently, the FTC and the Division lose the ability they might otherwise have to convince other agencies to minimize their own departures from the appropriate standard.[15]

III. The Culture of Consent

An antitrust agency, or indeed any law enforcement agency, resolving a case by entering into a civil consent decree with a person or firm accused of having violated the law, may be able to extract more favorable terms by agreement than it could reasonably or perhaps even lawfully obtain after litigating its accusations to judgment in a court. The agency's ability to obtain concessions, whether up to or beyond the remedies it might obtain at law, reflects the defendant's comparison of the costs and benefits of litigating as opposed to the costs and benefits of acquiescing in the terms sought by the agency.

In all material respects, the civil antitrust defendant's calculus mirrors that of a criminal defendant, whether in an antitrust or other case, weighing the relative merits of putting the prosecution to its proof versus entering into a plea bargain. Among the major considerations are, of course, the relative strength of the parties' arguments and evidence, the cost of litigation, and the uncertainty attending the outcome.[16] Just as the vast majority of criminal cases, for antitrust violations as for other crimes, are resolved by a plea bargain,[17] so too are the great majority of antitrust agency civil matters resolved by a settlement agreement. The agreement will be entered as a court judgment if the agency must bring its enforcement actions in court or, as in the case of the FTC, will take the form an agreement settling an administrative complaint brought pursuant to Part III of the Federal Trade Commission Act.

As discussed, both the FTC and the Antitrust Division have settled more than 90 percent of the civil cases they have brought in the last twenty years, following a steady increase in the settlement rate over the decades prior.[18] Indeed, trials have long been a thing of extreme rarity in the experience of FTC and Antitrust Division lawyers, including those of the so-called litigation staff; the Division's 2011 case against H&R Block Inc.'s proposed acquisition of the maker of TaxAct tax preparation software was its first matter to go to trial since 2004.[19] As a consequence, the work of the agencies is devoted much less to actual litigation—the presentation of evidence and arguments in a trial-type forum—or even to preparation for trial, than it is to investigation and negotiation.[20]

The culture of an agency is inevitably affected by the tasks it predominantly performs. For an antitrust agency that settles the great majority of the cases it brings, most staff time is devoted to investigation. Whether a matter is destined for litigation or for settlement, the necessary investigative skills are the same but it may become apparent, whether at the outset or in the course of an investigation, the agency's case is sufficiently strong, or the defendant's resources sufficiently limited, that settlement is a virtual certainty. A more thorough investigation of the sort needed in anticipation of litigation can be substantially truncated in such a case. Indeed, insofar as the agency is able to find easy cases, that is, cases almost certain to be settled, it will neither need nor acquire nor cultivate more sophisticated forensic skills. In short, a degree of laxity if not sloppiness may come to infect an agency's investigations that are heading inevitably toward resolution by consent.

Insofar as the agency is in a position readily to extract settlements from potential defendants, it might not limit itself to extracting terms of the sort or degree that it could obtain from a defendant in a contested case in court. On the contrary, the agency might well seek to settle upon terms that serve its bureaucratic interests.[21] These include broadening the agency's goals and responsibilities, a vector well-expressed by the phrase "mission creep,"[22] benefitting a politically influential interest group, and accumulating power over the regulated community in general and over the consenting firms in particular.

Consider, for example, *Nevada v. UnitedHealth Group*,[23] in which a state Attorney General obtained, as a condition of approval for a merger of insurance companies, an agreement that the merged company would "donate" $15 million to support various health-related activities, including the nursing program at the state university and funding for five years "one position within the Governor's Consumer Healthcare Assistance program for small employer education and advocacy."[24] A properly notorious example is the recent agreement between the Competition Commission of South Africa and Wal-Mart as a condition of that company's acquiring Massmart, which the Competition Appeal Court approved with seeming reluctance under its "public interest" standard.[25] Although the lower court had found the "merger raise[d] no competition concerns" and "the likely consumers [would] benefit" from lower prices, the agreement provided there would be no layoffs for two years and the company would invest at least R100 million within three years.[26] None of the conditions in either of the two cases is even plausibly related to the preservation of competition but rather each serves some other agency interest.

The bureaucratic imperative may also cause an agency in negotiating a settlement to seek concessions that make it easier for the agency to assure the defendant's continuing compliance with the settlement or, indeed, with antitrust law in general. For example, the Antitrust Division negotiated a 33-page consent decree with Google as a condition of approving its acquisition of ITA, a developer of software for the online purchase of airline tickets.[27] The consent decree required the companies to allow the Division to inspect its documents and interview its officers and employees concerning their continuing compliance with the substantive terms of the decree, which prohibited Google from restricting its competitors' access to certain software and committed the company to continue both improving that software and developing a new search product that ITA had started.[28] Quite apart from the objection that the settlement gave the Antitrust Division a continuing role in monitoring the merged business, the Antitrust Division also obtained a means of access to documents and testimony under terms even less demanding than would ordinarily apply to its issuance of a Civil Investigative Demand ("CID").[29] Indeed, if this provision of the settlement had not made it easier for the Antitrust Division to investigate the firm's post-merger compliance than did the ordinary process of the law, then the provision would not have been worth negotiating.

This is not to suggest that an agency routinely would seek or enter into settlements that called for it or the defendant to do things that are facially antithetical to its proper, lawful mission. The goals of antitrust law, however, have been subject to notoriously broad and changing interpretations, more so than perhaps any other body of law. Although it is now generally understood that the sole appropriate goal of antitrust law enforcement is to enhance consumer welfare, that goal can be (and in our view should be) understood narrowly to justify only remedial steps that clearly thwart efforts to restrict competition. The antitrust laws are still, however, understood by some enforcement agencies, as reflected in the cases discussed above and epitomized in the Appendix to this article, to include a variety of other interventions that are not relevant to enhancing competition, or that may even tend to frustrate it, notwithstanding their appearance of aiding consumers.

Another consequence of an agency bringing cases primarily with an eye to settlement is to change the agency's case selection criteria. In addition and to some extent in lieu of the criteria that would otherwise make a case attractive, such as the benefit to consumers from terminating an anticompetitive business practice, the probability and ease with which the case will settle become part of the mix. That is, instead of pursuing the cases that advance most the agency's law enforcement mission, it will tend to pursue cases with the best prospect for settlement, cases that will consume few investigative resources, settle quickly, and are more likely to result in a consent decree that provides a continuing role for the agency. To the extent that case selection is altered by the prospect of obtaining an easy settlement, the agency is positioned more like a private plaintiff doing a cost-benefit analysis. To that extent also, the agency does not have any special claim to exemption from the constraints placed upon private antitrust plaintiffs in cases such as *Trinko* and *Credit Suisse*, notwithstanding the Commission's call "for Congress to clarify that neither [case] prevents public antitrust agencies from acting under any of the antitrust laws when they conclude that anticompetitive conduct would otherwise escape effective regulatory scrutiny."[30]

IV. Conclusion

We submit that the culture of consent at antitrust agencies both in the United States and abroad has had an untoward effect upon agencies' selection of cases to bring and, more certainly, upon the remedies the agencies obtain in settlement agreements. The Appendix further documents examples of the abuses and misuses to which antitrust law has been put in consent decrees and settlement agreements.

Appendix: Cases of Antitrust Abuse and Misuse

I. Antitrust Abuse

1. United States

A. Google / Motorola; Apple, Microsoft, & RIM / Nortel; Apple / Novell[31]

The DOJ issued a closing statement on February 13, 2012, regarding its investigation of (1) Google Inc.'s acquisition of Motorola Mobility Holdings Inc.; (2) Apple Inc., Microsoft Corp., and Research in Motion Ltd.'s ("RIM's") acquisition of patents from Nortel Networks Corp.; and (3) Apple Inc.'s acquisition of patents from Novell Inc. The acquisitions involved patents that would assist the acquiring firm(s) in the development of cellular phone technology, including smart phones and operating systems for those phones. The DOJ had expressed concern that the acquiring companies would use patents essential to various technological standards (called standard essential patents or "SEPs") they obtained to hold up rivals and harm competition and innovation.

Upon investigation, the DOJ concluded that none of the acquisitions was likely substantially to lessen competition. In determining it was proper to close its investigations, the DOJ "took into account the fact that during the pendency of these investigations, Apple, Google and Microsoft each made public statements explaining their respective SEP licensing practices." Specifically, Apple and Microsoft agreed not to seek injunctions for licensing violations. Google's commitment was "less clear" to the DOJ, giving it reason to "continue[] to have concerns about the potential inappropriate use of SEPs to disrupt competition." Concluding its analysis, the DOJ emphasized its role, at the intersection of intellectual property and antitrust, of balancing the "rightful exercise of patent rights" against "the anticompetitive use of those rights." Notably absent from this statement was an indication that the DOJ sought to use the antitrust laws to determine the proper balance. Rather, the DOJ focused upon what it perceived to be the dangers of injunctive relief with little discussion of the potential competitive benefits in the SSO context.

B. Providence Health System, Inc. / North Central Pennsylvania Health System[32]

Pennsylvania entered into a settlement agreement with Providence Health System, allowing the hospital's acquisition of North Central to go forward but prohibiting the merged entity from employing more than 40 percent of physicians practicing in certain fields in Lycoming County. The settlement also required the merged hospital to make at least 20 percent of available operating room scheduling times available on a first-come, first-served basis, and it prohibited exclusive contracts with health plans.

C. Altoona Hospital / Bon Secours Holy Family Regional Health System[33]

In 2004, the federal district court for the Western District of Pennsylvania accepted approved a consent decree in a state case challenging a merger between two hospitals. The consent decree required the merged hospital to notify the Pennsylvania Attorney General thirty days prior to hiring additional doctors.

D. UnitedHealth Group / Sierra Health Services[34]

In 2008, the Nevada Attorney General entered into a settlement agreement with the insurance companies UnitedHealth Group and Sierra Health Services in conjunction with their merger. Pursuant to the settlement, the defendants agreed to make $15 million in charitable contributions to "health care programs" chosen by the Attorney General. The defendants also agreed to assist in creating a Physician Council with the purposes of "discuss[ing] issues of concern to Nevada physicians, and [of] establish[ing] goals and benchmarks for voluntary compliance relating to the physician-payor relationship and the quality and delivery of health care to Nevada consumers." The defendants agreed in addition to cooperate with the Governor's Office for Consumer Healthcare Assistance in developing and expanding its Healthcare Advocacy and Assistance Program by, among other things, assisting with promulgating guidelines and with preparing and submitting reports concerning relevant healthcare issues.

E. Kenosha Hospital and Medical Center, Inc. / St. Catherine's Hospital, Inc.[35]

The state of Wisconsin reached a settlement with Siena, the hospital formed by the merger of Kenosha and St. Catherine's, prohibiting Siena from employing more than 30 percent of the physicians who practiced certain specialties within a twenty-mile radius of the Kenosha County. The settlement contained an exception allowing Siena to employ up to the same percentage as did any rival hospital. The settlement also authorized the state Attorney General to exempt Siena from the employment limitation when justified by market conditions.

F. Leominster Hospital / Burbank Hospital[36]

To consummate a merger between Leominster Hospital and Burbank Hospital, the hospitals entered into an agreement with the Attorney General of Massachusetts according to which they committed the merged hospital to increase spending on community health outreach programs by $600,000 over a four-year period. The agreement also required the hospitals to commence a demonstration project evaluating the impacts of the merger and to seek public input prior to closing any emergency facilities.

2. Outside the United States

A. Coca-Cola[37]

Distri-One, a competitor of Coca-Cola Enterprises Belgium (CCEB), complained in 1998 to Belgian competition authorities about CCEB's alleged scheme of discriminatory rebates and other distribution practices. In 2005, Belgium's Competition Council dropped its investigation after CCEB agreed to curtail its challenged practices, and the Coca-Cola Company (CCEB's parent) reached a related settlement with the European Commission. Coca-Cola agreed to refrain from entering into exclusive contracts with customers; from entering into tying arrangements; and from conditioning rebates upon purchase thresholds, growth rates, shelf-space commitments, or the purchase of other beverage products.

B. Wal-Mart / Massmart[38]

In May 2011, South Africa's Competition Tribunal approved a merger between the US-owned superstore, Wal-Mart, and a South African retailer, Massmart. The Tribunal placed several conditions upon the merger even though Wal-Mart had no presence in retail markets in South Africa. Wal-Mart thereby agreed to freeze job cuts for two years, to honor existing collective bargaining rights, to give preference to rehiring Massmart employees who had previously lost their jobs due to retrenchment, to address concerns that it would switch procurement from local manufacturers to imports, and to set up a R100 million ($13.3 million) fund with the purpose of assisting local suppliers and manufacturers. After a challenge to the merger by a union and several government ministries, the South African Competition Appeal Court in 2012 affirmed the decision and approved the acquisition subject to the conditions already imposed by the Tribunal. The Court further ordered three experts to conduct a study and advise the court on the fund's operation.

C. Coca-Cola / Huiyuan[39]

In early 2009, China's Ministry of Commerce (MOFCOM) rejected Coca-Cola's acquisition of Huiyuan, a Chinese fruit juice producer. MOFCOM cited harm to competition, including the potential leveraging by Coca-Cola of its dominant position in market for soft drinks to gain market power in the market for juices, as a reason for blocking the merger. At the same time it indicated the more protectionist concern that smaller domestic juice producers would be unable to compete effectively with the merged firm.

II. Antitrust Misuse

1.United States

A. Intel Corp.[40]

The FTC undertook a regulatory role and placed limits on Intel's freedom to discount in its settlement with Intel in 2010 regarding the company's patent cross-licensing agreement with Advanced Micro Devices, Inc. The settlement contains a provision that prohibits Intel from making engineering design changes to its computer-related products that do not "provide an actual benefit to" the products, thereby giving the FTC the job of overseeing the ongoing design changes Intel will make to its products. The settlement also exempts Intel from liability for "winning all of a Customer's business, so long as [Intel] has not bid for more business than a Customer has asked to be bid." The FTC also implemented restrictions upon the terms on which Intel could deal with its customers, including prohibitions upon applying a percentage discount across all units purchased when the customer purchases a number of units beyond a given threshold and upon the bundling of discounts across purchases of several products if, when all discounts are attributed to one product, the price of that product falls below a specified measure of incremental cost. Thus, the FTC can become involved in particular transactions and opine upon the nature of Intel's dealing with its customers.

B. Google Corp. / ITA Software Inc.[41]

The DOJ, Google, and ITA Software recently consented to entry of a final judgment following the DOJ's filing of a complaint challenging Google's proposed acquisition of ITA, a producer of software designed for online purchases of airline tickets. The DOJ's concern with the merger was that Google would restrict licensing of QPX, a software product many airlines, travel agents, and travel search sites use to provide flight search functionality to consumers. The final judgment prohibited Google from restricting its competitors' access to the software, and it required Google to continue improvement of QPX and development of a new search product ITA had begun to develop.

Google and ITA agreed to allow the DOJ to inspect documents and to interview officers and employees in order to ensure compliance. Google and ITA also agreed to submit written reports and respond to interrogatories upon the DOJ's request. The compliance provisions required the DOJ to play an ongoing monitoring role outside the scope of its normal antitrust enforcement responsibilities.

C. Ciba-Geigy Ltd. / Sandoz Ltd.[42]

In *Ciba-Geigy Limited*, the FTC placed itself in an ongoing regulatory role by requiring approval of royalty rates, royalty terms, and patent licensees. After an investigation, the FTC commenced a challenge of a proposed merger between two pharmaceutical companies, Ciba-Geigy and Sandoz. Thereafter, the FTC and the companies entered into a consent agreement that required compulsory licensing of various technology and patent rights to other pharmaceutical companies that requested licenses. The order also stipulated that, in licensing certain patents, the merged company had to seek Commission approval of the licensee and of the terms of the license. The FTC also set a maximum rate at which the company could license certain patents.

D. Transitions Optical, Inc.[43]

In its settlement with Transitions Optical, Inc., the FTC drastically limited Transitions's ability to enter into exclusive or nearly exclusive contracts with its customers. The FTC had alleged that Transitions used such contracts to foreclose its rivals from access to important downstream distribution channels, thereby harming competition. In its analysis to aid public comment, the FTC explained the provision would keep down entry barriers and would allow competition to be restored. It concluded there were no efficiency justifications for the exclusive agreements; e.g., they did not prevent free riding because Transitions' promotional efforts were brand specific, eliminating any interbrand free-riding concern. The FTC did not acknowledge other justifications for exclusive contracts unrelated to free-riding, such as providing retailers with the incentive to increase promotional efforts.

E. McCormick & Co.[44]

The FTC has both taken on an ongoing regulatory role and restricted potentially procompetitive conduct in markets for spice and seasoning products. In its settlement with McCormick, the largest spice and seasoning supplier in the country, the FTC prohibited McCormick from engaging in price discrimination. The Commission's majority reasoned that McCormick's price discrimination harmed its disfavored customers. Price discrimination, however, is often either procompetitive or competitively neutral, and McCormick was thus prohibited from engaging in potentially welfare-increasing conduct. Additionally, the FTC cast itself in an ongoing regulatory role by requiring McCormick to document for the next ten years all relevant information relating to price discrimination it determines is justified by the "meeting competition" defense of the Robinson-Patman Act.

F. Pool Corp.[45]

The FTC recently proposed a consent agreement with Pool Corporation (PoolCorp), a distributor of swimming pool products, in which PoolCorp would agree to refrain from refusing to deal with manufacturers that deal with PoolCorp's rivals. The Commission found PoolCorp had, by foreclosing access to essential inputs, prevented potential rivals from entering the market and competing effectively. Although the consent order discusses the potential for such threats to raise rivals' costs and harm competition, it acknowledges that new distributors were able to realign supply contracts in order to avoid potential exclusion. Evidence presented in the settlement, moreover, suggests manufacturers did not honor PoolCorp's demands, no exclusion actually occurred, and there was little or no actual injury to consumers.[46] Such an enforcement action, in the absence of solid evidence of anticompetitive behavior or effect, runs the risk of chilling potentially procompetitive activities by other market participants.

G. Ticketmaster Entertainment, Inc. / Live Nation Inc.[47]

In early 2010 the Division entered into a settlement agreement with Ticketmaster Entertainment Inc., a ticketing-service provider, approving the company's merger with Live Nation Inc., a concert promoter, subject to various conditions. The agreement required Ticketmaster to license its ticketing software to the second-largest U.S. concert promoter for up to five years. The agreement also forbade the merged firm from retaliating against customers who leave to use a competitor's ticketing services. The Division determined the agreement would facilitate entry of competitors, and thereby increase competition in the market for ticketing. Requiring the merged entity to enter into an arrangement to license its ticketing platform to a competitor, however, is fraught with the well-known competitive risks associated with imposing a duty upon firms to assist their rivals.

H. General Motors Corp.[48]

In 1984, General Motors and Toyota entered into a consent agreement with the FTC regarding a joint venture between the automobile manufacturers. The FTC agreed not to challenge the joint venture on the condition that the venture exist no longer than twelve years and produce no more than 250,000 new automobiles per year. Although such an output restriction appears to be harmful to consumers, the Commission justified it by reference to a concern that the joint venture would reduce "GM's incentives to continue alternative production of small cars." In the decade following the consent agreement, industry changes including significant entry and expansion by competitors eliminated the need for the output and duration limits on the joint venture, and the FTC reopened and set aside the order.

2. Outside the United States

A. CATVP - TV Cabo Portugal / TVTel - Comunicações[49]

The Portuguese Competition Authority placed itself in a regulatory role with its Phase I clearing of a merger between two subscription television providers. The Authority required divestiture of half the acquired firm's cells in geographic areas where the merging parties' service overlapped, with the intent of facilitating entry of competitors in the distribution of cable television. The Authority also required the merged entity to make a national wholesale satellite television offer available to third parties to use in offering subscription television services without the need for a network infrastructure. The Competition Authority appointed an independent trustee to ensure compliance with these conditions.

B. Walcheren Hospital/Oosterschelde Hospitals[50]

The Netherlands Competition Authority approved a hospital merger upon condition that the merged entity "make its facilities available to all parties that wish to offer specialist medical care [and] apply normal charges for the use of its facilities, in line with national market norms." The Authority also imposed a price ceiling, saying "[i]n principle, the price ceiling will apply indefinitely." In a footnote, the Authority indicated it would review and revise the decision if market conditions changed and the parties submitted a "reasoned request."

NOTES

*   We thank Angela Diveley and Daniel Haar for research assistance.

1   1 CCH, Decrees & Judgments in Federal Anti-Trust Cases 107 (N.D. Cal. 1906).

2   Joseph C. Gallo et al., *Department of Justice Antitrust Enforcement, 1995-1997: An Empirical Study*, 17 REV. INDUS. ORG. 75, 111-12 (2000); George Stephanov Georgiev, *Contagious Efficiency: The Growing Reliance on U.S.-Style Antitrust Settlements in EU Law*, 2007 UTAH L. REV. 971, 1006-07 (2007).

3   Department of Justice Antitrust Division, Congressional Submission FY 2012 Performance Budget 27.

4   A. Douglas Melamed, *Antitrust: The New Regulation*, ANTITRUST, Fall 1995, at 13.

5   FEDERAL TRADE COMMISSION COMPETITION DATABASE (last visited Oct. 19, 2011), http://ftc.gov/bc/caselist/index.shtml.

6   Harry First, *Is Antitrust "Law"?*, ANTITRUST, Fall 1995, at 11 (observing a similar "shift on the policy continuum toward bureaucratic regulation"); Georgiev, *supra* note 2, at 1026 ("Settlements further the bureaucratic regulation model because they focus not on the actual past violation of the law (indeed, they are purposefully silent on this question), but rather on the future remedies that would best address what the regulator perceives as a market failure."); Melamed, *supra* note 4, at 13 (describing antitrust enforcement as having "moved markedly along the continuum from the Law Enforcement Model toward the Regulatory Model").

7   *See, e.g., Providence Health System, Inc. / North Central Pennsylvania Health System*, Case II.B.3 in the Appendix.

8   *See, e.g., UnitedHealth Group / Sierra Health Services*, Case I.A.4 in the Appendix.

9   *See, e.g., Leominster Hospital / Burbank Hospital*, Case I.A.6 in the Appendix.

10   *See, e.g., Intel Corp.*, Case II.A.1 in the Appendix.

11   *Id.*

12   Analysis of Proposed Consent Order to Aid Public Comment, 75 Fed. Reg. 48343 (Aug. 10, 2010). The FTC Rules of Practice set forth a procedure for accepting consent decrees that requires the agency to publish the proposed consent for public comment with an explanation of the provisions in the order. 16 C.F.R. § 2.34(c) (2010).

13   LePage's Inc. v. 3M Co., 324 F.3d 141 (3d Cir. 2003) (en banc).

14   ANTITRUST MODERNIZATION COMM'N, REPORT AND RECOMMENDATIONS 94 (2007) ("[T]he Third Circuit's decision is likely to discourage firms from offering procompetitive bundled discounts and rebates to consumers.").

15   *See* William E. Kovacic, *The Modern Evolution of U.S. Competition Policy Enforcement Norms*, 71 ANTITRUST L. J. 377, 477 (2003) (discussing the sensitivity of the development of antitrust law in transition economies to developments in the United States).

16   *See generally* Robert D. Cooter & Daniel L. Rubinfeld, *Economic Analysis of Legal Disputes and Their Resolution*, 27 J. ECON. LIT. 1076 (1989) (surveying the economic literature on the decision to litigate or settle).

17   From 1996 to 2006, 307 of 367 (84 percent of) criminal antitrust defendants in the United States pled guilty. *See* F. Joseph Warin et al., *To Plead or Not to Plead? Reviewing a Decade of Criminal Antitrust Trials*, ANTITRUST SOURCE, July 2006, at 2. The DOJ reports the settlement rate in criminal cases over the past twenty years to be "over 90 percent." *See* Ann O'Brien, Cartel Settlements in the U.S. and EU: Similarities, Differences and Remaining Questions, Remarks by Senior Counsel to the Deputy Assistant Attorney General for Criminal Enforcement before the 13th Annual EU Competition Law and Policy Workshop (June 6, 2008), *available at* http://www.justice.gov/atr/publicspeeches/235598.htm.

18   Comparable data are not available for state or foreign antitrust enforcement authorities but, based upon daily reporting of antitrust developments worldwide, we believe they are generally similar in nature and degree.

19   Sara Forden & Jeff Bliss, *U.S. Antitrust Enforcers Add Litigators to Bolster Odds at Trial*, BLOOMBERG NEWS, Feb. 3, 2012, *available at* http://mobile.bloomberg.com news/2012-02-03/u-s-antitrust-enforcers-add-litigators-to-bolster-odds-at-trial.

20   Another significant use of agency resources is policing compliance with negotiated settlements. The FTC Bureau of Competition Compliance Division currently has a staff of thirteen. *See* BUREAU OF COMPETITION, FED. TRADE COMM'N, INSIDE BC 22-23 (2012), *available at* http://www.ftc.gov/bc/BCUsersGuide.pdf.

21   *Cf.* MILTON FRIEDMAN, WHY GOVERNMENT IS THE PROBLEM 9 (1993) ("The general rule is that government undertakes activity that seems desirable at the time. \Once the activity begins, whether it proves desirable or not, people in both the government and the private sector acquire a vested interest in it. If the initial reason for undertaking the activity disappears, they have a strong incentive to find another justification for its continued existence.").

22   "Mission creep refers to an organizational phenomenon in which entities inadvertently, over time, stray from their fundamental mission by engaging in activities or behaviors less closely related to the core . . . purpose." Gary W. Jenkins, *Who's Afraid of Philanthrocapitalism?*, 61 CASE W. RES. L. REV. 753, 805 n.212 (2011); *see also* William E. Kovacic, *Lessons of Competition Policy Reform in Transition Economies for U.S. Antitrust Policy*, 74 ST. JOHN'S L. REV. 361, 385 (2000) (Antitrust consent decrees specifically offer "a valuable opportunity for enforcement officials to portray their work as path-breaking and innovative, and thereby distinguish it from the accomplishments of previous management").

23   *UnitedHealth Group / Sierra Health Services*, Case I.A.4 in the Appendix.

24 *Id.* Sched. A, Ex. C.

25 *See S. Afr. Commercial, Catering & Allied Workers Union v. Wal-Mart Stores Inc.*, Case I.B.2 in the Appendix.

26 *See* Devon Maylie, *Wal-Mart Gets Nod in Africa*, WALL STREET J., June 1, 2011, *available at* http://online.wsj.com/ article/SB10001424052702303657404576357132239525222.html.

27 *See United States v. Google Inc.*, Case II.A.2 in the Appendix.

28 *Id.* at 30.

29 A CID is subject to "the standards applicable to discovery requests under the Federal Rules of Civil Procedure." 15 U.S.C. § 1312(c)(1)(B) (Department of Justice Antitrust Division); *id.* § 57b-1(c)(1) (requiring "reason to believe" a person has information regarding a violation of antitrust law (Federal Trade Commission)).

30 *Is There Life After Trinko and Credit Suisse? The Role of Antitrust in Regulated Industries: Before the Subcomm. on Courts & Competition Policy of the H. Comm. on the Judiciary*, 111th Cong. 14 (2010) (Statement of The Federal Trade Commission); *see also* J. Thomas Rosch, Commissioner, Federal Trade Commission. Rewriting History: Antitrust Not as We Know It . . . Yet, Remarks Before the ABA Antitrust Section 2010 Spring Meeting 17-19 (Apr. 23, 2010).

31 DOJ, Statement of the Department of Justice's Antitrust Division on Its Decision to Close Its Investigations of Google Inc.'s Acquisition of Motorola Mobility Holdings Inc. and the Acquisitions of Certain Patents by Apple Inc., Microsoft Corp. and Research in Motion Ltd. (Feb. 13, 2012), *available at* http://www.justice.gov/atr/public/ press_releases/2012/280190.pdf.

32 Pennsylvania. v. Providence Health Sys., Inc., No. 4:CV-94-772, 1994 WL 374424 (M.D. Pa. May 26, 1994).

33 *Antitrust Multistate Litigation Database*, NAT'L ASS'N OF ATT'YS GEN., *available at* http://app3.naag.org/antitrust/ search/viewCivilLitigation.php?trans_id=466 (last visited Mar. 11, 2012).

34 Nevada v. UnitedHealth Grp. Inc., No. 2:08-CV-00233-JCMRJJ, 2008 WL 5657751 (D. Nev. Oct. 8, 2008).

35 Wisconsin v. Kenosha Hosp. & Med. Ctr., No. 96-C-1459, 1996 WL 784584 (E.D. Wis. Dec. 31, 1996).

36 *Antitrust Multistate Litigation Database*, NAT'L ASS'N OF ATT'YS GEN., http://app3.naag.org/antitrust/search/view-CivilLitigation.php?trans_id=252 (last visited Mar. 11, 2012) (summarizing the agreement).

37 *The Belgian Competition Council Accepts Commitments in Order to Improve Competition on the Soft Drink Market*, CONCURRENCES (Nov. 2005), http://www.concurrences.com/article.php3?id_article=389&lang=fr; Press Release, European Commission, Competition: Commission Makes Commitments from Coca-Cola Legally Binding, Increasing Consumer Choice (June 22, 2005), *available at* http://europa.eu/rapid/pressReleasesAction.do?reference =IP/05/775&format=HTML&aged=0&language=EN&guiLanguage=en; Proposed Commitments Case Comp/39.116/B-2 – Coca-Cola, EUROPEAN COMMISSION (Oct. 19, 2004), http://ec.europa.eu/competition/antitrust/ cases/dec_docs/39116/39116_5_6.pdf.

38 S. Afr. Commercial, Catering & Allied Workers Union v. Wal-Mart Stores Inc., 110/CAC/Jul11 (2012), *available at* http://www.comptrib.co.za/assets/Uploads/110111CACJun11-Walmart-judgment.pdf; Press Release, South Africa Competition Tribunal, Tribunal Statement on the Conditional Approval of the Merger Between Wal-Mart Stores Inc. and Massmart Holdings Limited (May 31, 2011), *available at* http://allafrica.com/stories/201105311240.html; *see* Mike Cohen & Robert Brand, *Wal-Mart Wins South African Lawsuit Contesting Massmart Deal*, BLOOMBERG (Mar. 9, 2012, 10:12 AM), http://www.bloomberg.com/news/2012-03-09/south-africa-appeal-court-dismisses-case-against-wal-mart-s-massmart-deal.html.

39 FRESHFIELDS BRUCKHAUS DERINGER, CHINA'S MOFCOM PROHIBITS COCA-COLA'S ACQUISITION OF HUIYUAN 1 (2009), *available at* http://www.freshfields.com/publications/pdfs/2009/mar09/25486.pdf.

40 *In re* Intel Corp., FTC Docket No. 9341, 2010 WL 4542454 (FTC Nov. 2, 2010).

41 Final Judgment, United States v. Google Inc., No. 1:11-cv-00688 (D.D.C. Oct. 5, 2011); Competitive Impact Statement at 6, United States v. Google Inc., No. 1:11-cv-00688 (D.D.C. Apr. 8, 2011).

42 *In re* Ceiba-Geigy Ltd., 123 F.T.C. 842 (1997).

43 *See In re* Transitions Optical, Inc., 2010 WL 1804580 (Apr. 22, 2010); FTC, ANALYSIS TO AID PUBLIC COMMENT: IN THE MATTER OF TRANSITIONS OPTICAL, INC. 7 (Mar. 3, 2010), *available at* http://www.ftc.gov/os/caselist/0910062/10 0303transopticalanal.pdf.

44 Complaint, *In re* McCormick & Co., 2000 WL 264190 (FTC 2000); Statement of Chairman Robert Pitofsky and Commissioners Sheila F. Anthony and Mozelle W. Thompson, *In re* McCormick & Co., 2000 WL 264190 (FTC 2000).

45 Order, *In re* Pool Corp., 2011 WL 5881164 (FTC 2011); Complaint, *In re* Pool Corp., 2011 WL 5881164 (FTC 2011).

46 *See* Dissenting Statement of Commissioner Rosch, *In re Pool Corp.*, 2011 WL 5881164, at *1-2 (FTC 2011) ("This case presents the novel situation of a company willing to enter into a consent decree notwithstanding a lack of evidence indicating that a violation has occurred. The FTC Act requires that the Commission find a 'reason to believe' that a violation has occurred and determine that Commission action would be in the public interest any time it issues a complaint. 15 U.S.C. § 45(b). In my view, the same standard applies regardless of whether the Commission is seeking a litigated decree or a consent decree for the charged violation.").

47 United States v. Ticketmaster Entm't, Inc., No. 1:10-cv-00139 (D.D.C. July 30, 2010); DOJ, *Justice Department Requires Ticketmaster Entertainment Inc. to Make Significant Changes to Its Merger with Live Nation Inc.*, Jan. 25, 2010, http://www.justice.gov/opa/pr/2010/January/10-at-081.html.

48 *In re* Gen. Motors Corp., 103 F.T.C. 374, 375 (1984); *In re* Gen. Motors Corp., 116 F.T.C. 1276, 1284-85 (1993).

49 *See The Portuguese Competition Authority Clears a Merger in Phase I in the Pay-TV Market Subject to Remedies*, CONCURRENCES, Nov. 2008, *available at* www.concurrences.com/article.php3?id_article=26663. For the Competition Authority's decision in Portuguese, *see* Autoridade da Concorrencia, *Decisions Search*, www.concorrencia.pt/vEN/ Mergers/Decisoes/Pages/pesquisa.aspx#top (last visited Jan. 5, 2012).

50 Netherlands Competition Authority, *Decision of the Board of the Netherlands Competition Authority, Within the Meaning of Section 41 of the Competition Act*, NEDERLANDSE MEDEdingingsautoriteit (Mar. 2009), available at http:// www.nma.nl/en/images/6424BCV_UK23-154012.pdf.

Antitrust Enforcement in a Rent-Seeking Society

JOHN D. HARKRIDER

jdh@avhlaw.com

Partner, Axinn Veltrop & Harkrider LLP

Abstract

Over the last few decades there has been a debate as to whether one *should* expect a change in antitrust enforcement if one political party or the other gains control of the White House. A theme that has emerged from this debate is that antitrust enforcement falls during Republican Administration and increases during Democratic administration. Commissioner Kovacic has long criticized these efforts to compare the antitrust activity between different administrations arguing that there is a political component to antitrust that necessarily "robs it of legitimacy." This paper sets forth a public choice perspective as to why one should expect to see a change in antitrust enforcement priorities and why this change does not mean that consumers are less well off during Republican administrations. This article concludes that the fact that Republicans and Democrats have different views as to the ability of government to correct market failure does not, as Commissioner Kovacic suggests, rob the system of its legitimacy, but rather helps legitimize the variability in antitrust enforcement that one observes.

I. Introduction

Over the last few decades there has been a spirited debate—usually during a Presidential campaign—as to whether one should expect a change in antitrust enforcement if one political party or the other gains control of the White House. A theme that has emerged from this debate is that antitrust enforcement falls during Republican Administration and increases during Democratic administration.[1]

Commissioner Kovacic has long criticized these efforts to compare the antitrust activity between different administrations as "unsupportable,"[2] "unreliable,"[3] and "superficial."[4] He criticizes both a broad historical view of the swings in antitrust enforcement as well as more narrowly focused comparisons of antitrust enforcement levels or case studies of particular mergers. Moreover, he criticizes any effort to draw normative conclusions about "specific levels of enforcement activity"[5] noting that it is not possible to determine whether more or less enforcement at a particular time would be efficient. Indeed, Commissioner Kovacic goes so far as to argue the very argument that there is a political component to antitrust necessarily "robs it of legitimacy."[6]

The purpose of this paper is not to argue that antitrust enforcement necessarily increases or decreases when the political party in charge of the White House changes. Rather it is to set forth a public choice perspective as to why one *should* expect to see a change in antitrust enforcement priorities and why this change does not mean that consumers are less well off during Republican administrations. Specifically, Republicans are generally skeptical about both the ability of Government to identify and correct market failure. That is especially true in antitrust where much of the evidence as to the likely effects of a merger or agreement is likely to be in the hands of competitors engaging in rent-seeking activity. In contrast, Democrats tend to have greater confidence in the ability of the Government to identify both market failure as well as rent-seeking activity. The fact that Republicans and Democrats have different views as to the ability of government to correct market failure does not, as Commissioner Kovacic suggests, rob the system of its legitimacy, but rather helps legitimize the variability in antitrust enforcement that one observes.

II. The Pendulum Narrative

Commissioner Kovacic rejects the pendulum narrative—which holds that the level of antitrust enforcement swings wildly from aggressive antitrust enforcement during Democratic administrations apathetic enforcement during Republican Administrations. Commissioner Kovacic criticizes this narrative both for being hyperbolic as well as glossing over the continuity in the views of antitrust regulators with respect to merger analysis, especially as exhibited in the Merger Guidelines.

Specifically, Commissioner Kovacic argues that proponents of the pendulum narrative believe that the Clinton era on the 1990s was "just right" in terms of merger enforcement, and that this period was preceded by wild swings in the 1960s, where "trust busting zealots... saw evil in every big company or merger," the 1970s, which was a period of "tremendous activism," and the 1980s, which was a period during which federal antitrust enforcement "ceased" and "ground to a halt."[7] The 1990s were then followed by "an extraordinarily low level of government merger enforcement" under the Bush Administration in the 2000s, which was then followed by a promise of significantly more vigorous antitrust enforcement under the Obama Administration.

Although there is no question that some of these authors may have engaged in hyperbole in describing the antitrust enforcement policies of various administrations, most acknowledge differences in antitrust priorities between administrations.[8] For example, Rick Rule acknowledged in one paper that "budget constraints and the Reagan administration's hands-off approach to business sharply limited antitrust enforcement," noting that the number of full-time antitrust employees dropped in half by the time he left office.[9] Similarly, Commissioner Kovacic himself predicted a retrenchment in Section 2 enforcement during the Bush Administration[10] and further has noted a substantial increase in criminal enforcement activity between 1981 and 1990, which fell significantly between 1991 and 2000.[11]

Moreover, is not correct to suggest that there is a consensus that the Clinton era was "just right," and the Bush and Reagan eras were lawless and devoid of reason. For example, Clinton's first Antitrust Division head Anne Bingaman was described by Rick Rule as somebody with a "shoot first, ask questions later" approach, a view few would characterize as balanced.[12] Similarly, not all commentators criticized Reagan's antitrust enforcement priorities. For example, Joseph Bower of Harvard wrote that Reagan's "tolerance for mergers . . . and the possible elimination of treble damages all speak to a more enlightened view."[13]

On the other hand, it is hard to deny that Democratic administrations anticipated bringing more cases given that Clinton decided to appoint a plaintiff's attorney as his first Antitrust Division chief, and Obama's antitrust policy statement made clear that he intended to substantially increase the level of antitrust enforcement,[14] and, in fact, his first few years in office found a number of litigators added to the Front Office of both the DOJ and the FTC. Given all of this, it seems odd to dispute the fact that there is a political component to antitrust enforcement.

That said, Commissioner Kovacic is certainly correct that the extreme versions of the pendulum narrative fail to take due account of the continuity and growth in the analysis of mergers as set forth in the Merger Guidelines. For example, for the past 30 years, antitrust regulators have used the HHI as a measure of concentration, steadily increasing the thresholds used to determine whether a market is unduly concentrated during both Republican and Democratic administrations.[15] Similarly, there has been an increased use of unilateral effects in both Republican and Democratic administrations, starting with the 1992 Merger Guidelines, which was consistently applied by both Republican and Democratic administrations.[16]

In addition, both Democratic and Republican administrations have increasingly used quantitative methods to evaluate the likely impact of mergers, including game theory and merger simulation, reflecting the general tendency of all administrations to adopt current economic thinking as part of their methodology. Such a tendency includes not only quantitative methods, but also a lack of emphasis on enforcement on certain practices, including vertical price fixing, price discrimination, conglomerate and vertical mergers, all of which saw steady decline in enforcement over different administrations. But of course, academic views progress in sometimes strange (or dialectic) ways and some practices that were once thought to rarely raise antitrust concerns (e.g., vertical mergers) are once again subject to significant enforcement levels. Again, this seems to reflect the views of the academic community, for example, the scholarship on raising rivals' costs, and should not purely be considered in partisan terms.

III. Normative Conclusions

One of Commissioner Kovacic's central points is that statistics on how often agencies issue Second Request or intervene to block or modify mergers do not "tell us anything about [whether] public merger enforcement [has] affected economic performance."[17] And, in particular, that "[a]ctivity levels say nothing about whether an agency's work has positive or negative economic effects."[18]

This is a significant and valid criticism. Merger enforcement involves both Type I and Type II errors, namely, the risk that an efficient merger is terminated or inefficiently modified (Type I) or an inefficient merger is consummated (Type II). Higher levels of antitrust enforcement lead to more Type I errors, while lower levels of antitrust enforcement lead to more Type II errors. It is difficult to determine *a priori* which type of error has a greater negative impact on the economy.

Moreover, it is important to note that heightened enforcement also has two additional effects. First, there are the significant transaction costs caused by merger review, which may impose tens of millions of dollars in legal fees, not to mention the cost of distracted management that is not focused on bringing innovative products to the market. In some cases these costs may outweigh the postulated beneficial post-merger impact. Second, there is the risk that potentially efficient mergers do not occur because of concerns over both transaction costs and completion risk.

Beyond the theoretical risks, it is very difficult to empirically test the proposition that a particular administration had too much or too little antitrust enforcement. Even if we could go back and measure the increase in price caused by the merger, we would still need to factor in the possible decreases in price in markets for which there was no overlap. We would also need to consider the potential efficiencies that would have resulted from mergers that were improperly stopped. Simply put, the exercise is very difficult for any given merger, and most certainly impossible for all mergers that were stopped or should have been stopped over an Administration.

IV. Public Choice and the Role of Government in Correcting Market Failure

Although Commissioner Kovacic's argument that it is impossible to determine whether a given administration engaged in too much or too little antitrust enforcement is most certainly correct, his argument that we should not engage in the exercise is certainly incorrect. Not only does the exercise help practitioners advise their clients, especially in drafting merger agreements in anticipation of a change in the political composition of an Administration, but the exercise helps us understand the different views of the proper role of Government in correcting market failure.

Most economists would agree that markets do not inherently allocate resources in an efficient manner. To the contrary, a number of market imperfections can result in inefficient outcomes, namely, (i) individual or collective market power that enables either a single firm or a collection of firms to raise price or restrict output; (ii) barriers to entry that force new entrants to incur costs not born by incumbents; (iii) information asymmetries that systematically prevent buyers or sellers from evaluating the utility of a given course of action; and (iv) externalities whereby the benefits (positive externalities) or costs (negative externalities) of a transaction are not fully born (and therefor taking into account) by contracting parties.

Modern antitrust jurisprudence and agency practice across Democratic and Republican administrations, however, recognizes that the government should not attempt to correct every market imperfections. For example, Section 2 of the Sherman Act does not make it unlawful to obtain market power through natural growth or even to exercise it in terms of higher prices or restricted output, but rather makes it unlawful to maintain it through exclusionary practices. Similarly, Section 7 of the Clayton Act does not make it unlawful for a firm to organically obtain market power, but rather proscribes increases in market concentration that are likely to lead to the exercise of market power. More significantly, perhaps, while antitrust analysis takes account of barriers to entry, information asymmetries,[19] positive and negative externalities, it does not make any effort to correct these market conditions.

There are at least two reasons market intervention is limited. First, there are serious questions as to whether regulators are competent to fix market imperfections. Markets are complex and every action has a reaction that cannot necessarily be predicated in advance. What's more, there is often a paucity of empirical evidence or natural experiments that help us understand whether a particular intervention is likely to make the problem better or worse. Furthermore, government mandates are difficult for market forces to correct. As a result, intervention may not only make the problem worse (or create a different problem) but also might make it more difficult for market forces to self-correct. This natural caution is at least one reason for the preference by regulators for structural as opposed to conduct remedies.

Public choice theory, which attempts to model the conduct of firms in the political process in terms of their rational self-interested behavior, also provides insight into why one should be concerned about Government intervention in the economy. In particular, public choice theory looks at political participation as a function of the costs of participation, including transaction costs, and the benefits of participation, as a result of Government action (or inaction).

In the context of antitrust, public choice theory would focus on the costs lobbying the government, which includes the costs of hiring a lawyer to complain about a transaction, and the costs of gathering information that may be useful to the government, including data, documents and declarations. For competing firms, the benefits that may flow from government action (or inaction) would include avoiding lost profits (or increased investment) that would result from competing with a more efficient competitor. For consumers, the benefits that may flow from government action would include avoiding paying higher prices for goods of equal or less quality.

Public choice theory would predict that antitrust enforcement may in fact permit firms to engage in rent-seeking behavior. This is true because the costs for consumers to petition an antitrust agency may frequently outweigh the benefits that they receive, especially when transaction costs are considered. Specifically, although consumers as a group may have a significant amount to gain from a properly functioning market, the cost to any specific individual in petitioning (or organizing a group to petition) the government may exceed the gain any given individual would receive from Government intervention.[20] Further, even if a particularly invested consumer could solve the collective action problem, consumers are without useful things like data, documents or declarations to give the government. Indeed, all they could give the government would be their prediction that prices were likely to rise, which, even if in the form of a declaration, would carry little evidentiary weight.[21]

In contrast, a competitor who fears that a horizontal or vertical merger is likely to cause them to lose profits to a more efficient firm has enough to gain that they are willing to internalize the costs of petitioning the government.[22] Indeed, given that there are no economic profits in competition, it would be rare for any competitor to petition the government to restore a market to a purely competitive state. In other words, the entities that have the capital to spend in influencing government behavior are most likely to be those who are earning supracompetitive profits in the status quo as a result of some sort of market imperfection. This is the source of the aphorism that any time a competitor complains about a merger it is likely the merger is good for competition.[23]

This is not to say that regulators are entirely blind to this problem. For this reason, competitors disguise their concerns—preferring to talk in terms of "raising rival's costs," "exclusionary conduct," and "predation"—instead of simply admitting that they fear they will lose rents as a result of a proposed merger. Even more perniciously, competitors subsidize consumer proxies to champion their causes, who are then willing to lobby the government given their costs of doing so are now in line with their expected return.

In this way, the move towards sophisticated quantitative analysis may actually exacerbate the public goods problem. For example, econometric analysis is both expensive and requires access to proprietary data. As a general matter, only competitors of the merging firm have access to that data, and only firms with millions to gain by the result of the Governments' intervention have the incentive to perform their own econometric analysis. Put another way, econometric analysis not only increases the cost of lobbying the antitrust agencies but also creates an information asymmetry that necessarily favors the group that has the greatest incentive to engage in rent-seeking activity.

Although Republicans and Democrats generally have different views on the role of Government in correcting market failure, there is, in fact, a general consensus between the parties that antitrust enforcement is important. This is to be contrasted with other forms of regulation. For example, there was a far more significant decline in Environmental Protection Agency enforcement than in antitrust enforcement during Republican administrations, with some going so far as to recommend abolishing this agency.[24] Nobody has seriously suggested abolishing federal oversight of mergers, though there have been calls for consolidation of the two agencies. Nor has anybody seriously suggested that antitrust enforcement should be brought to zero.

Public choice theory again helps explain why one would expect to see less variability in antitrust enforcement than in other regulatory enforcement actions. In particular, there is no permanent community of interest in favor of lower (or higher) antitrust enforcement. This is to be contrasted with the rather stable regulatory views of most industries that grow from a consistent community of interests. That is to say, in most industries, firms are permanently in one position—a utility company is always a utility company—a bank is always a bank. As a result, they are able to determine their regulatory interest with some level of precision and then lobby for those regulatory changes as an industry. For example, a utility provider almost always wants less regulation of its emissions; and an employer generally wants less regulation of its hiring practices. Their industry groups then collectively lobby for those changes.

In contrast, most firms are at once both producers and consumers. In other words, they buy things and they sell things. When they are selling things (producers) they generally like higher prices and lower output and therefore favor less antitrust enforcement. When they are buying things (sellers), they generally prefer lower prices and lower output and therefore prefer more antitrust enforcement. To add an additional level of complexity, firms are also competitors, and so while they may want their own mergers or practices to go forward, they generally don't want their competitors to enjoy the same ability (especially when they lead to a more efficient competitor). These varying factors make it difficult for firms to categorically prefer low or high levels of antitrust enforcement and especially prevent the formation of homogenous industry coalitions, which, in turn, leads to a relative consistency in antitrust analysis.

V. Conclusion

The fact that Democrats and Republicans have different views as to the ability of government to solve market imperfections goes to the core of the differences between the parties. It is the reason that one party may think that Government subsidized national health care is able to solve the market imperfections in our healthcare system and another party believes that government intervention will just make the problem worse, not only because this is a complex problem perhaps beyond the competency of any regulator to fix, but also because any intervention is likely to reflect the economic views of firms engaging in rent-seeking activity.

Similarly, differences in the antitrust enforcement priorities are also shaped by different views as to the ability of government to correct market imperfections. For example, a regulator with doubts as to the ability of government to identify and fix market imperfections, one might focus, as the Republicans have, on hard-core cartels where there is clear evidence of unlawful activity and a negative impact on the economy. Similarly, a regulator with confidence in the ability of government to identify and fix market imperfections, might seek to use Section 2 of the Sherman Act to fundamentally change a successful firm's business practice, ignoring the risk that its rivals want to free ride the larger firms' innovations rather than invest in innovations of its own. Again, this is why we see more monopolization enforcement during Democratic administration.

But the fact that there is a change in enforcement activity does not rob the FTC or DOJ of their legitimacy. More to the point, there is no reason to be shy about the fact that elections matter. One would normally expect that Democrats would want to expand the regulatory state and that Republicans would want to shrink it (it is, in fact, the core of the difference between the parties) and concerns about legitimacy of antitrust should not cause us to blind ourselves to reality. In sum, it is most certainly true that no single methodology tells the whole story of comparative shifts in levels of antitrust enforcement. And it is also true that effort to capture the story will have some flaws—perhaps even important ones. And finally, it is true that the normative judgment as to the optimal level of antitrust enforcement is most certainly beyond our capability. But none of these truths should stop us from undertaking the exercise, though with the modesty and caution that Commissioner Kovacic suggests.

NOTES

1   *See generally* John D. Harkrider, *Antitrust Enforcement During the Bush Administration - An Economic Estimation,* ANTITRUST (Summer 2008); John D. Harkrider, *Risk-Shifting Provisions and Antitrust Risk: An Empirical Examination,* ANTITRUST (Fall 2005); Malcolm B. Coate, *A Test of Political Control of the Bureaucracy: The Case of Mergers,* 14 ECONOMIC AND POLITICS 1 (2002); Jonathan B. Baker & Carl Shapiro, *Detecting and Reversing the Decline in Horizontal Merger Enforcement,* ANTITRUST (Summer 2008); Deborah L. Feinstein, *Recent trends in U.S. Merger Enforcement: Down But Not Out,* ANTITRUST (Summer 2007).

2   William E. Kovacic, *Rating the Competition Agencies: What Constitutes Good Performance?,* 16 GEO. MASON L. REV. (2009), at 910.

3   William E. Kovacic, *The Modern Evolution of U.S. Competition Policy Enforcement Norms,* 71 ANTITRUST LAW JOURNAL 2 (2003), at 467 [hereinafter Kovacic, *The Modern Evolution of U.S. Competition*].

4   William E. Kovacic, *Assessing the Quality of Competition Policy: The Case of Horizontal Merger Enforcement,* 5 COMPETITION POLICY INTERNATIONAL 1 (2009), at 138 [hereinafter Kovacic, *Assessing the Quality of Competition Policy*].

5   *Id.*, at 131.

6   *Id.*, at 137.

7   *See* Kovacic, *Assessing the Quality of Competition Policy, supra* note 4, at 135.

8   *See*, Malcolm B. Coate & Andrew N. Kleit, *Does it Matter That the Prosecutor is Also the Judge? The Administrative Complaint Process at the Federal Trade Commission*, 19 MANAGERIAL & DECISION ECONOMICS 1 (1998) ("The coefficient on the party affiliation variable, Republican, has expected sign and is statistically significant, indicating that the political composition of the commission affects merger decisions. In particular, as Republicans replace Democrats, the commission becomes relatively less likely to enjoin a transaction that has been challenged.").

9   *See* Lisa Wirthman, *Antitrust's Odd New Frontiers: Is Gov't Catching Bad Guys Or Punishing Success*, INVESTOR'S BUSINESS DAILY, March 25, 1999 [hereinafter Wirthman, *Antitrust's Odd New Frontiers*].

10 *See* William E. Kovacic, *How next president will handle technology*, POLITICS & TECHNOLOGY (Nov. 7, 2000), *available at* http://www.politechbot.com/p-01477.html (last visited Aug. 11, 2012).

11 Kovacic, *The Modern Evolution of U.S. Competition, supra* note *3*, at 419.

12 Wirthman, *Antitrust's Odd New Frontiers, supra* note 9.

13 Joseph L. Bower, *The Case For Building More I.B.M.'S*, N.Y. TIMES, § 3, p. 2, Col. 3 (Late City Final Edition), Feb.16, 1986.

14 *See* Sen. Barack Obama, Statement for the American Antitrust Institute (Feb. 20, 2008), *available at* http://www.antitrustinstitute.org/files/aai-%20Presidential%20campaign%20-%20Obama%209-07_092720071759.pdf.

15 *See* John D. Harkrider, *A Return to Von's Grocery?*, 10 ANTITRUST SOURCE 1 (October 2010).

16 *See* U.S. DEPARTMENT OF JUSTICE & FEDERAL TRADE COMMISSION, HORIZONTAL MERGER GUIDELINES (1992, rev. 1997), *available at* http://www.justice.gov/atr/public/guidelines/hmg.pdf; *see also* U.S. DEPARTMENT OF JUSTICE & FEDERAL TRADE COMMISSION, HORIZONTAL MERGER GUIDELINES (2010), *available at* http://www.ftc.gov/os/2010/08/100819hmg.pdf; *see also* U.S. DEPARTMENT OF JUSTICE & FEDERAL TRADE COMMISSION, COMMENTARY ON THE HORIZONTAL MERGER GUIDELINES (2006), *available at* http://www.ftc.gov/opa/2006/03/mergercom.shtm.

17 Kovacic, *Assessing the Quality of Competition Policy, supra* note 4, at 139.

18 *Id.*

19 Conduct that takes advantage of information asymmetries to mislead consumers, however, may violate § 5 of the FTC Act.

20 *See generally* MANCUR OLSON JR., THE LOGIC OF COLLECTIVE ACTION: POLITICAL GOODS AND THE THEORY OF GROUPS (Harvard University Press 1965).

21 *See* United States v. Oracle Corp., 331 F. Supp. 2d 1098 (N.D. Cal. 2004). ("If backed by credible and convincing testimony of this kind or testimony presented by economic experts, customer testimony of the kind plaintiffs offered can put a human perspective or face on the injury to competition that plaintiffs allege. But unsubstantiated customer apprehensions do not substitute for hard evidence."); *see also* FTC v. Arch Coal, Inc., 329 F. Supp. 2d 109, 146 (D.D.C. 2004). ("Plaintiffs rely heavily on testimony from utility customers expressing concern about the increased consolidation in the SPRB market that will result from the proposed transaction . . . . In many contexts, however, antitrust authorities do not accord great weight to the subjective views of customers in the market. Furthermore, while the court does not doubt the sincerity of the anxiety expressed by SPRB customers, the substance of the concern articulated by the customers is little more than a truism of economics: a decrease in the number of suppliers may lead to a decrease in the level of competition in the market. Customers do not, of course, have the expertise to state what will happen in the SPRB market, and none have attempted to do so. The court therefore concludes that the concern of some customers in the SPRB market that the transactions will lessen competition is not a persuasive indication that coordination among SPRB producers is more likely to occur."); *see also* United States v. Engelhard Corp., 126 F.3d 1302, 1304 (11th Cir. Ga. 1997). ("In fact, in response to the Government's contention that the district court had rejected the 5-10% test, the court explicitly stated that '[i]n light of the inadequacies in breadth and scope of the plaintiff's inquiries to consumers, the Court could not hold that gel quality attapulgite constituted a relevant market even under the plaintiff's 5 to 10 percent standard.").

22 Ernest C. Pasour discusses this phenomenon by focusing on the example of the U.S. Sugar Program. Using public choice theory, Pasour explains that although the program is harmful to the public at large, high earning sugar producers have the financial means to influence legislators to maintain the program in place. Therefore, the market failure at hand does not persist because it is beneficial to consumers, but rather because information and incentive problems in the collective choice process lead to perverse results. *See* Ernest C. Pasour Jr., *Economists and public policy: Chicago political economy versus conventional views*, 74 PUBLIC CHOICE 2 (1992). A similar conclusion is reached by Buchanan and Vanberg who explain that political influence over the market and the tendency of players to influence the legislative and regulatory process to their own advantage are likely to lead to market failure. *See* James M. Buchanan & Viktor J. Vanberg, *The Politicization of Market Failure*, 57 PUBLIC CHOICE 2 (1988).

23 *See* Malcolm B. Coate & Andrew N. Kleit, *Art of the Deal: The Merger Settlement Process at the Federal Trade Commission*, 70 S. ECON. J. 4 (2004) ("The FTC's preferences, although somewhat difficult to establish, indicate that when it has the opportunity, the Commission is more likely to prefer that efficient acquisitions be abandoned rather than move forward with a compromise settlement. This result is compatible with a capture theory of the bureaucracy and perhaps suggests that the FTC should be more critical of competitor complaints.").

24 *See* Amanda Griscom, *A look back at Reagan's environmental record*, GRIST MUCKRAKER (June 11, 2004) http://grist.org/politics/griscom-reagan/ (last visited Aug. 11, 2012); *see also* Bruce Barcott, *Changing All the Rules*, N.Y. TIMES, April 4, 2004; *see also* Environmental Integrity Project, Press release, EPA taking 75% fewer polluters to court, major polluter cases down 90% (October 12, 2004), *available at* http://www.environmentalintegrity.org/news_reports/archives.php; *see also* Rena Steinzor, Testimony Before the Subcommittee on Fisheries, Wildlife, and Water of the U.S. Senate Regarding Implementation of the Clean Water Act (September 16, 2003), *available at* http://www.progressivereform.org/articles/EPA_Enforcement_Testimony_091603.pdf; *see also* Colin Provost, Brian J. Gerber & Mark A. Pickup, *Enforcement Dynamics in Federal Air Pollution Policy* (Paper presented at the Meeting of the European Consortium of Political Research, Pisa, Italy, September 6-8, 2007), *available at* http://regulation.upf.edu/ecpr-07-papers/cprovost.pdf.

The Danger of "Fairness": Section 5 of the FTC Act and the Propagation of the "Unfairness" Standard

STEPHEN HARRIS

stephen.harris@bakermckenzie.com
Partner, Baker & McKenzie

JOHN FEDELE

john.fedele@bakermckenzie.com
Associate, Baker & McKenzie

The United States has long viewed itself as being at the forefront of the development of antitrust law. However, as highlighted in William Kovacic's article, *U.S. Antitrust policy*: The underperforming federal *joint venture*, there are flaws within the United States model that have long stood unaddressed and should give pause to the architects of other jurisdictions' competition law regimes. Common critiques of the United States antitrust enforcement regime include the inefficiencies and uncertainties consequent to the existence of two primary federal antitrust enforcement agencies, their different procedures and their sometimes divergent substantive views. To a substantial degree, this tension is rooted in the differences between the two organizations, the most obvious example of which may be said to be the FTC's exclusive authority to enforce Section 5 of the Federal Trade Commission Act, which, with respect to competition law, broadly prohibits "unfair methods of competition." This article argues that the ambiguous scope of the FTC's Section 5 power renders it a dangerous regulatory power that is largely unnecessary and has limited useful application. We discuss that Section 5 "unfair conduct" is poorly defined, allows considerations other than maximizing competition to influence enforcement decisions, and does not provide sufficient guidance to market participants seeking to make decisions regarding their conduct. We then explain that the concept of "fairness" in Section 5 of the FTC Act has been adopted as part of the competition laws of a number of other jurisdictions, particularly in Asia, typically with no more limiting principles than exist under the U.S. statute. We conclude that Antitrust enforcement should be directed towards producing predictable outcomes based on the notion of maximizing consumer welfare through the protection and enhancement of allocative efficiency.

I. Introduction

The United States has long viewed itself as being at the forefront of the development of antitrust law with over a century of experience and leading global enforcement agencies committed to reducing the incidence of anticompetitive conduct, based on the latest teachings of economics. Indeed, the United States has envisioned its antitrust agencies and the work in which they are engaged as a model for the rest of the world. However, as highlighted in William Kovacic's recent article, *U.S. Antitrust policy: The underperforming federal joint venture*, there are flaws within that model that have long stood unaddressed and should give pause to the architects of other jurisdictions' competition law regimes that have been designed, to one extent or another, upon the U.S. model.

As described in Kovacic's article, common critiques of the United States antitrust enforcement regime include the inefficiencies and uncertainties consequent to the existence of two primary federal antitrust enforcement agencies, their different procedures and their sometimes divergent substantive views. To a substantial degree, this tension is rooted in the differences between the two organizations, the most obvious example of which may be said to be the FTC's exclusive authority to enforce Section 5 of the Federal Trade Commission Act, which, with respect to competition law, broadly prohibits "unfair methods of competition."

The boundaries of Section 5 are unclear, though the FTC has generally presumed that they extend beyond those of the Sherman Act and the Clayton Act, the primary antitrust regulations in the United States, and the statutes enforced by the DOJ Antitrust Division. This article argues, as others have, that the ambiguous scope of the FTC's Section 5 power renders it a dangerous regulatory power that is largely unnecessary and has limited useful application. The primary danger of relying on Section 5 and principles of "fairness" is that it expands the scope of prohibited competitive conduct too broadly, and is unmoored from the general requirement that antitrust violations result in demonstrable anticompetitive effects. Relatedly, "unfair conduct" is poorly defined, allows considerations other than maximizing competition to influence enforcement decisions, and does not provide sufficient guidance to market participants seeking to make decisions regarding their conduct. As described below, these critiques are prevalent, yet the FTC continues to rely on its Section 5 powers.

Moreover, policing "fairness" under the rubric of enforcing competition law has become a significant U.S. antitrust export, both hurting the reputation of the U.S. as a model of antitrust policy of intervention only in cases of demonstrable harm, actual or likely, to the competitive process, and hampering the evolution of foreign competition regimes toward the establishment of rules and enforcement policies based on unambiguous, effects-based rules of conduct that provide clear guidance to market participants. Largely to the detriment of other competition regimes, the concept of "fairness" in Section 5 of the FTC Act has been adopted as part of the competition laws of a number of other jurisdictions, particularly in Asia, typically with no more limiting principles than exist under the U.S. statute. Invoking this concept of "fairness" under the broad rubric of antitrust, anti-monopoly, or competition law, enforcers in such jurisdictions have targeted many kinds of behavior that have not been shown to reduce allocative efficiency, apparently motivated by the desire to manage business conduct toward compliance with societal norms of "fairness" unrelated to any effects on competition. The emphasis on "fairness" has caused regulators to target behavior other than that which demonstrably harms efficiency and, in the name of competition law, to look more widely at other conduct that may or may not enhance social welfare, but perhaps offends other societal norms regarding "fairness." The failure of Congress to repeal or clarify the "unfair competition" provisions of the FTC Act, and the recent unwillingness of the U.S. courts and the FTC itself to impose empirical limiting principles on those provisions, as they have done for over a century with regard to the Sherman and Clayton Acts, have allowed this pernicious doctrine to take root and grow in both domestic and foreign soils.

II. Fairness and Section 5 of the FTC ACT

Under Section 5 of the FTC Act, the FTC is empowered to enjoin instances of "Unfair Methods of Competition."[1] For most of its history, this broad mandate has been interpreted by courts, and often by the FTC itself, as reaching only the limits of conduct prohibited by the Sherman and Clayton Acts. That is to say, agreements between competitors that unreasonably restrain trade; the acquisition, enhancement, or maintenance—or attempted acquisition—of monopoly power by exclusionary conduct; and transactions that may substantially lessen competition or tend to create a monopoly.

However, in the 1970s the Supreme Court suggested that Section 5 could extend beyond those limits,[2] emboldening the FTC to apply the statute to conduct not demonstrated to harm competition. In *Sperry v. Hutchinson*, the FTC brought a Section 5 action against S&H, a stamp trading company.[3] The FTC found that S&H had suppressed the operation of trading stamp exchanges and other "free and open" redemption of stamps.[4] S&H admitted to the findings, but argued that Section 5 could only reach practices that violate established antitrust laws.[5] The Fifth Circuit agreed with S&H and reversed the findings of the FTC.[6] The Supreme Court, however, reversed and found that Section 5 permitted the FTC to proscribe unfair practices regardless of their competitive effects.[7] The Court held that the "Federal Trade Commission does not arrogate excessive power to itself if, in measuring a practice against the elusive, but congressionally mandated standard of fairness, it, like a court of equity, considers public values beyond simply those enshrined in the letter or encompassed in the spirit of the antitrust laws."[8]

Relying on this decision, the FTC has since viewed its Section 5 powers broadly, though not without objection. Despite the proclamation of the Supreme Court, in many instances where the FTC has attempted to bring stand-alone actions under Section 5, such actions have met significant opposition.[9] The principal objection expressed by courts has been that a standard based on "unfairness" is too amorphous, does not clearly delineate legal activity from illegal and anticompetitive activity, and is not tied to a demonstration of anticompetitive effects.[10] If we operate from the assumption that antitrust law is intended to maximize efficiency and discourage only conduct demonstrated to harm competition, then these criticisms appear to be well founded.

In *Official Airline Guides v. FTC*, for example, the Second Circuit held that evidence of anticompetitive effects in a market outside the market in which the respondent competed could not constitute a violation of Section 5.[11] The court emphasized that allowing such a claim would not sufficiently limit the reach of Section 5.[12] It held that "enforcement of the FTC's order here would give the FTC too much power to substitute its own business judgment for that of the monopolist in any decision that arguably affects competition in another industry."[13]

Similarly, in *Boise Cascade v. FTC*, the Ninth Circuit rejected the FTC's theory that Section 5 allowed courts to presume the existence of anticompetitive effects.[14] The FTC alleged that anticompetitive effects could be presumed from evidence of parallel action by industry members to stabilize prices through use of an artificial pricing system.[15] The Supreme Court in rejecting the FTC's conclusions, found that there was a "complete absence of meaningful evidence in the record that price levels in the . . . industry reflect an anticompetitive effect."[16] It went on to reject the FTC's argument for the creation of a *per se* rule under Section 5 condemning industry-wide adoption of an artificial method of price-quoting.[17] It noted that the law in this area was already settled and that a different result was not warranted by the features of the FTC Act.[18]

Other courts have likewise noted the necessity of a limiting principle for Section 5. In *E.I. Du Pont De Nemours & Co. v. FTC* (*Ethyl*), the Ninth Circuit held that Section 5 unfairness authority must be circumscribed, explaining:

> [A]ppropriate standards must be adopted and applied to protect a respondent against abuse of power. As the Commission moves away from attacking conduct that is either a violation of the antitrust laws or collusive, coercive, predatory, restrictive or deceitful, and seeks to break new ground by enjoining otherwise legitimate practices, the closer must be our scrutiny upon judicial review. A test based solely upon restraint of competition, even if qualified by the requirement that the conduct be "analogous" to an antitrust violation, is so vague as to permit arbitrary or undue government interference with the reasonable freedom of action that has marked our country's competitive system.[19]

As such, the court held that before a court can find unfairness under Section 5, the minimum standard "demands . . . , absent a tacit agreement, at least some indicia of oppressiveness must exist such as (1) evidence of anticompetitive intent or purpose on the part of the producer charged . . . ."[20]

In light of these decisions, the FTC, at least initially, pulled back on claims that a Section 5 action could lie where there was no evidence of anticompetitive effects. In *General Motors Corp.*, the FTC held that although there could be cases where Section 5 allows the FTC to reach "the spirit" of the antitrust laws, *General Motors* was not such a case because there was no proof of anticompetitive effect.[21] Still, at least in certain cases the FTC has continued to endorse a position that no such showing is required. In *Coca-Cola*, for example, the FTC rejected an assertion by Coca-Cola that an unconsummated merger could not violate Section 5 because there was no evidence of anticompetitive purpose or effect.[22] Citing *Sperry* and holding *Boise Cascade* and *Ethyl* to be inapposite, the FTC concluded that a Section 5 violation had occurred.[23]

Despite the judicial criticism noted above, the FTC continues to pursue stand-alone Section 5 cases ungrounded in antitrust principles.[24] In 2008, in *In re Negotiated Data Solutions*, the FTC brought a stand-alone Section 5 claim against Negotiated Data Solutions ("N-Data").[25] In its complaint, the FTC alleged that N-Data, which had acquired a patent from a previous holder, now refused to honor the terms of an agreement between the original patent holder and the Institute of Electrical and Electronics Engineers (IEEE), a standard setting organization.[26] The previous patent holder had agreed to license its technology for a specified fee if the IEEE adopted its technology as the industry standard. However, N-Data, after acquiring the patent, sought a higher royalty for the license. The FTC's majority opinion found that N-Data's conduct constituted an unfair method of competition in violation of Section 5.[27] It noted that the Supreme Court had in the past endorsed a broad reading of the FTC's mandate to enforce unfair methods of competition, though the FTC paid homage to the decisions discussed above and acknowledged the need for certain limiting principles on its Section 5 power, including the need for some showing of an adverse affect on competition.[28] In this instance, because N-Data's royalties would undoubtedly rise after it rescinded its prior licensing commitment, the FTC summarily concluded that such an adverse impact existed.

In 2009, on the heels of the *Negotiated Data Solutions* settlement, the FTC once again asserted broad Section 5 authority by bringing Section 5 claims against Intel Corporation.[29] The FTC alleged that Intel undertook a course of conduct to destroy its competitors' ability to compete.[30] It alleged that Intel engaged in loyalty discounts, bundling, unilateral refusals to deal, and predatory pricing.[31] Although the FTC also brought Section 1 and 2 claims, Commissioner Rosch stated that one of the policy goals of the *Intel* case was to expand the FTC's Section 5 jurisdiction by use of stand-alone Section 5 claims.[32] In fact, Rosch explicitly dissented on the FTC's decision to bring Section 1 and 2 claims, arguing that Section 5 was sufficient.[33] Chairman Leibowitz and Commissioner Rosch issued a statement on the case arguing that Section 5 has the potential to protect consumers while also protecting companies from collateral consequences of treble damages in private antitrust enforcement.[34]

This recent reliance on Section 5, however, has not been without its critics, both internal and external. In the *N-Data* case both Commissioner Kovacic[35] and Chairman Majoras dissented from the opinion.[36] Chairman Majoras's strongly written dissent argued that the use of a stand-alone Section 5 claim in the case of N-Data was "not advisable as a matter of policy or prosecutorial discretion."[37] Specifically, she noted that in the past the FTC had cabined the use of Section 5 to instances where there was clear potential to harm competition although not rising to meet the requirements of Section 1 of the Sherman Act.[38] Majoras argued that this limitation of Section 5 was an acknowledgment that the Sherman Act is sufficiently broad to address all matters that properly warrant competition policy enforcement and that the courts have insisted that the Commission's discretion to enforce unfair competition be bound meaningfully.[39] Chairman Majoras conceded that the majority considered competitive effects, but concluded that such consideration was only perfunctory. Majoras maintained that the claim of an adverse impact on prices based on renegotiation was impossible to prove on the available evidence. Additionally, Chairman Majoras viewed N-Data's conduct as, at worst, an attempt to evade a contractual price constraint, a reasonable decision under certain circumstances.

In his *N-Data* dissent, Commissioner Kovacic similarly expressed concerns that the FTC had not clearly delineated the scope of its powers to deem conduct an "unfair method of competition."[40] He was concerned specifically that the FTC failed to rigorously and clearly explain its liability theory.[41] He noted that the Commission alleged both "unfair methods of competition," typically reserved for antitrust violations, as well as "unfair acts or practices," the provision of the FTC Act typically used to address conduct injuring consumers but not competition, but did not specify the individual contributions of each to the liability determination and thus left a muddled analysis with no clear guidance to business on the limits of acceptable behavior.[42] With respect to the allegation of an "unfair method of competition," like Chairman Majoras, Commissioner Kovacic found the FTC's assessment of competitive effects limited, at best. He noted that "the balancing of harm against legitimate business justifications would encompass the assessment of procompetitive rationales that is a core element of a rule of reason analysis in cases arising under competition law," yet no such balancing was done in the *N-Data* decision.[43]

Even those Commissioners who have supported the use of stand-alone Section 5 cases have acknowledged generally the need for limiting principles. Though Chairman Leibowitz and Commissioner Rosch supported the use of Section 5 in *Intel*, they acknowledged that: "Section 5 is clearly broader than antitrust laws, but it is not without its boundaries."[44] However, they failed to articulate what those boundaries are, merely stating that:

> Of course, even though the Commission has broad authority under Section 5, the Commission is well aware of its duty to enforce Section 5 responsibly. We take seriously our mandate to find a violation of Section 5 only when it is proven that the conduct at issue has not only been unfair to rivals in the market but, more important, is likely to harm consumers, taking into account any efficiency justifications for the conduct in question.[45]

Left without clear guidance of the contours of Section 5, several former and current FTC commissioners have commented on the appropriateness of expanding Section 5 beyond the scope of the Sherman Act and a demonstration of actual competitive effects.

While not everyone believes that the FTC's Section 5 authority is superfluous, there is a general consensus that limits must be placed on Section 5 power to ensure that over-enforcement does not occur, and that potentially procompetitive conduct is not stifled. In a recent paper, former Commissioner Kovacic argues in favor of certain applications for stand-alone Section 5 claims, but emphasizes that the FTC must be cautious in clearly articulating the boundaries of "unfairness."[46]

He notes that Section 5 was originally designed to be a broader enforcement tool than the Sherman Act at a time when the Sherman Act was prone to narrow construction.[47] However, because the Sherman Act evolved to be far more flexible than originally believed, the use for stand-alone Section 5 claims proved to be too small.[48] Now, however, he argues that courts have reigned in the liberal interpretation of the Sherman Act and, as such, there may be some useful applications of Section 5.[49]

Kovacic argues that there are several types of cases where Section 5 might be applied. First, it may be helpful in certain gap-filling cases, for example where the anti-competitive effect of an activity is clear, but where there is no concerted action or monopoly power.[50] Second, it may also be useful in so called "frontier" cases,[51] being those cases that ostensibly meet the requirements of the Sherman Act, but where there is no clear precedent making clear that the conduct at issue is a violation of the Sherman Act.[52] Thus, Section 5 could be used to prospectively announce a new principle under the Sherman Act, but without the risk of subjecting companies to the threat of follow-on private litigation.[53] In addition, the FTC's structure as a specialized tribunal may be a superior platform on which to elaborate competition policy.[54]

Significantly, both the "gap-filling" and "frontier" cases described by Kovacic would require some demonstration of competitive effects. Kovacic believes that there may be a place for stand-alone Section 5 actions, but only if the FTC self-regulates and establishes a clearly defined analytical framework for its implementation, supported by evidence that any enforcement actions are consistent generally with other antitrust statutes. He has argued that effective use of this tool must be based on a strategy resting upon an "accurate diagnosis of past Section 5 enforcement failures."[55] In addition, the FTC's construction of "unfair methods of competition" should be a "competition-based concept, in the modern sense of fostering improvements in economic performance rather than equating the health of the competitive process with the well-being of individual competitors. . . ."[56]

The history of the FTC's attempts to bring stand-alone Section 5 claims is a grim one. Courts have generally rebuked efforts by the FTC to bring claims that are not based on established Sherman Act doctrine. Thus, for Section 5 claims to be successful today and durable within the courts, Kovacic believes that the FTC must first articulate a clear policy statement on what constitutes an "unfair method," and how the agency will enforce its discretion.[57] Kovacic argues that it is imperative that the FTC "foster institutional competence by means of workshops, reports, and related policy instruments to signal to the courts that the FTC has a sound basis for specific proposed applications of Section 5."[58] The FTC policy statements would, he argues, thus provide assurances to courts that the steps the

Commission takes are wise and worthy of support as well as address courts' concerns of an unbounded FTC mandate.[59]

Other commentators in favor of some application of Section 5 have also echoed Kovacic's sentiment that reliance on Section 5 must be rooted in demonstrable anticompetitive effects. Like Kovacic, Professor Herbert Hovenkamp has argued that there remain gaps in Section 1 and 2 of the Sherman Act that could be filled by Section 5.[60] In his view, Section 5 would be applicable in cases where there is clear anticompetitive activity, but where the activity does not meet all the elements of the Sherman Act.[61] Notably, Section 5 actions could be brought in cases of incipient monopoly, cartel-like behavior where there is no conspiracy, and conduct analogous to abuse of dominant positions. Hovenkamp underscores, however, that the FTC must only condemn those practices that are actually anticompetitive "in a meaningful sense."[62]

Other commentators, however, have argued that the risk of an unbounded application of Section 5 is greatest in gap-filling cases.[63] Without more limiting guidelines, the FTC risks chilling legitimately competitive business activity.[64] Courts will not accept such limitless discretion, they argue, unless the FTC imposes stringent requirements.[65] One commentator has argued that the FTC's new position is 'hubristic' and in essence asserts that the FTC is not susceptible to errors of enforcement.[66] An expanded use of Section 5, he argues, is dangerous and risks substantial over-deterrence because the government has an incentive to develop and bring suits proposing novel theories of anticompetitive conduct.[67]

A related criticism is that Section 5 encourages experimentation with antitrust laws without sufficiently rigorous testing of these novel theories. Though scholars such as Kovacic have argued in favor of the use of Section 5 in "frontier cases," the risk of frontier cases is that they may too easily "become a means for the Commission to short-circuit asking the hard analytical questions imposed by the rigorous standards of the Sherman Act."[68] Frontier cases would be cases analyzing new forms of conduct, and these are precisely the cases that require that the court ask hard analytical questions to determine whether anticompetitive conduct exists. Thus, commentators suggest that in order for Section 5 to be meaningful in the frontier case context and for courts to accept the FTC's analysis, the Commission must analyze and litigate the case precisely as it would under the Sherman Act.[69]

Of course there are others like Judge Richard Posner who strongly disagree with any attempts to expand the use of Section 5.[70] Posner, noting the history of the Sherman Act, believes that the "Sherman and Clayton Acts have been interpreted so broadly that they no longer contain gaps that a broad interpretation of Section 5 of the FTC Act might be needed to fill."[71] Unlike Chairman Kovacic and others, Posner believes that the contracting scope of Section 2 is not an invitation to extend Section 5. Implicit in Posner's position is the belief that the contracting scope of the Sherman Act is a deliberate response to increased economic learning and is thus intentional and beneficial. Allowing Section 5 to now reach areas outside the scope of the Sherman Act would only revert to older standards discredited by economic learning.

These concerns were echoed by Chairman Majoras in *N-Data* as well as certain courts that sought to significantly curtail the stand-alone use of Section 5 in the early 1980s.[72] As one commentator has noted, the primary concern motivating these courts was the fear of a nebulous standard of unfairness and thus potentially arbitrary enforcement.[73] These courts worried that a vague standard would "blur the distinction between guilty and innocent commercial behavior," and unfortunately, these concerns persist.[74]

III. Exporting Unfairness

While the FTC's experience under Section 5 is sufficient illustration of the dangers of an "unfairness standard," the same "unfairness" principles have been adopted more widely. In the United States alone, the "unfairness standard" has been incorporated into numerous state laws targeted at anticompetitive conduct and known as "Little FTC Acts." These statutes are, as one would expect, modeled after the federal FTC Act and, as a result, many look to FTC jurisprudence for guidance.[75] But the reach of the FTC's "unfairness" standard also extends beyond the borders of the U.S. to numerous other countries—particularly in Asia—and has injected a lack of clarity into these antitrust regimes, undermining the establishment of normative competition regimes focused on the goal of allocative efficiency and requiring proof of anticompetitive effects of conduct deemed to constitute violations of the law.

1. JAPAN

Perhaps the best example of the influence of the FTC Act and the attendant challenges for the adopting country's antitrust law is the Japanese Antimonopoly Act ("JAA"), which in many respects parallels U.S. antitrust laws.[76]

The JAA Cartel Regulation is the analogue to section 1 of the Sherman Act, which prohibits concerted activity that unreasonably restrains trade. The JAA Monopoly Regulation corresponds to section 2 of the Sherman Act, which reaches single-firm conduct and prohibits monopolization or attempted monopolization. The JAA Merger Regulation targets the same conduct as Section 7 of the Clayton Act. And like the United States, Japan also has an Unfair Trade Practice Regulation—the equivalent of Section 5 of the FTC Act.

In the United States, justification for the existence of the FTC's power to police "unfair" conduct is often attributed to, among other things, the dual-agency antitrust enforcement structure. The U.S. Congress created the FTC as an independent agency designed to have antitrust expertise, but with fewer enforcement powers than its counterpart, the Antitrust Division of the Department of Justice. Accordingly, the threats posed by an agency with broad power to investigate "unfair methods of competition" were mitigated by the remedies available to that particular agency.

In Japan, however, there is only one antitrust agency, the Japan Fair Trade Commission ("JFTC"). Nevertheless, Japan saw fit to adopt the Unfair Trade Practice Regulation, which prohibits sixteen types of conduct: (i) concerted refusals to deal; (ii) other refusals to deal; (iii) discriminatory pricing; (iv) discriminatory treatment in transaction terms; (v) discriminatory treatment in a trade association; (vi) unjustly low price sales; (vii) unjustly high price purchasing; (viii) deceptive customer inducement; (ix) customer inducement by unjust benefits; (x) tie-in sales; (xi) dealing on exclusive terms; (xii) resale price maintenance; (xiii) dealing on restrictive terms; (xii) abuse of dominant bargaining position; (xv) interference with a competitor's transaction; and (xvi) interference with the internal operation of a competitor's company.[77]

Most of these practices, however, should be prohibited by the other elements of the JAA. It is this overlapping coverage of the Unfair Trade Practice Regulation that has been responsible for generating significant confusion as to the proper interpretation of Japanese antitrust law and raising questions concerning precisely what values the Unfair Trade Practice Regulation was intended to protect. While modern economic learning teaches that the appropriate goal of antitrust law to be the promotion of efficiency and thus the elimination of weak competitors, according to its plain language the Unfair Trade Regulation is supposed to protect those companies with weak bargaining positions. Holding a dominant bargaining position is clearly different than having market power or dominating a particular market. In nearly every transaction, there is a party with a superior bargaining position.

Indeed, these provisions are an excellent example of the elastic nature of a "fairness" standard allowing other interests to infiltrate a purported antitrust analysis. At least historically, the restrictions on firms with dominant bargaining positions were used to protect Japanese firms from contract terms imposed by foreign companies. For example, in international licensing agreements, a foreign licensor was presumed to have the dominant bargaining position and so in order to protect Japanese firms, the JAA includes licensee-friendly requirements regarding grant back provisions and other relevant terms.

The prohibitions against dominant firms were also used to protect suppliers transacting with large retailers. In these situations, the retailer was assumed to be the party with the superior bargain position and, in the interest of "fairness," and without regard to a need to prove anticompetitive harm, the JAA was used to protect suppliers. The JFTC issued guidelines that erected limitations on large retailers' abilities to return products, refuse to accept products, and reduce agreed upon prices.[78] Despite giving lip service to the general goal of the JAA being consumer welfare through enhanced efficiency, however, the JFTC has enforced these rules and guidelines to protect competitors, without regard to the effect on consumers.

Indeed, commentators have observed that Japan has traditionally enforced its antitrust laws with a goal of not only fostering "free" competition with an emphasis on the nature of transaction-related processes, but also "fair" competition, with instead a focus on "fairness" of outcomes. This focus on "fairness" can distort the interpretation of the antitrust laws, as it has with respect to the JFTC's enforcement of its Monopoly Regulation. A 1999 OECD study concluded that there had only been 15 monopolization cases pursued under the JAA despite the relevant provisions of the law having been enacted in 1947.[79] According to the report, the reason for the dearth of monopolization cases was that this type of anticompetitive conduct was more commonly addressed under the Unfair Trade Practice Regulation and remedied in a way that actually restricted competition. The OECD observed that "[t]he most common complaint that the JFTC receives is about excessive discounts, that is, competitors complaining about "too much competition."[80] The JFTC has been involved in a material number of cases concerning prices that are "unjustly low," "which is typically competitor complaints about rivals' price cutting."[81] Based on these observations, the OECD found that "[t]he surprisingly large number of JFTC actions about price cutting would not inspire confidence in consumers that competition enforcement is promoting their interests."[82]

The fact that allocative efficiency is less prominent in Japanese antitrust law and "fairness" among competitors receives greater emphasis is reflected even in the first article of the JAA. Article I of the JAA states that the law's overall objectives are "to protect the democratic and wholesome development of the national economy *as well as* to assure the interests of consumers in general."[83] The need to distinguish the "democratic and wholesome development" of the economy from the interests of consumers suggests that these are distinct concepts, and also conjures up notions of protecting national champions, even if not the most efficient market participants. By comparison, most contemporary antitrust commentators assume that maximizing consumer welfare will maximize overall economic welfare and that these are not divergent interests.

2. KOREA

The "unfairness" standards that exist in Japan are also found in Korea's antitrust laws.[84] Like Japan, Korea looks to two standards when determining the legality of competitive conduct: anticompetitiveness and unfairness.[85] Where conduct is deemed "anticompetitive," it is considered likely to result in reduced competition. "Unfair," conduct, does not necessarily result in reduced competition. Rather, it is the exploitation of a superior bargaining position, the effects of which may go beyond the pricing or quality of goods or services.

The "unfairness" standard in Korean antitrust law was adopted from Japan[86] that, as discussed above, borrowed from the prohibition of "unfair methods of competition" in the FTC Act. However, the emphasis on "unfairness" also reflects the traditional structure of the Korean economy. Historically, there has been a marked dichotomy between "highly competitive, export-oriented manufacturing and a much less dynamic, domestic demand-oriented sector."[87] The OECD has found that "the productivity gap between the manufacturing and service sectors in Korea is the largest in the OECD area.[88] Indeed, the Korean economy has been characterized by the presence of large conglomerates, known as chaebols. Other firms are at a significant disadvantage when transacting with these dominant entities. Given the disparity in the relative bargaining positions of the chaebols and the smaller market participants, it is not entirely surprising that there has been a desire to protect the weaker parties.

Of course, one solution would be to completely and effectively dissolve the chaebols, an exercise that has, in practice, proved politically impossible to date. The operation of these dominant conglomerates and the erection of barriers to entry is generally understood to have anticompetitive effects. Among other things, the chaebols have often engaged in intra-group transactions not conducted at arms length that have had the effect of sustaining chaebol members that, from an efficiency perspective, should more appropriately exit the market.[89] Yet the chaebols are allowed to continue to operate and instead the Korean Fair Trade Commission has elected to police the chaebols and maintain a socially acceptable level of concentration, responsible conduct, and "fairness." Maintaining only "fairness," however, likely leads to inefficient outcomes.

Reliance on "unfairness" principles over maximizing efficiency also allows poor competitors to survive in the Korean economy in other ways. Similar to Japan, rules exist which tend to have the effect of reducing promotional offers and dampening market competition. One observer has opined that in Korea, "regulation stymies efficiency gains by preventing large scale stores from driving the mom-and-pops out of business."[90]

All this said, in recent years—and despite the history of "unfairness" enforcement—Korea has been moving towards a greater reliance on analyzing competitive effects when assessing whether conduct is in violation of its antitrust laws. A recent study found that the KFTC had one of the largest staffs of economists in the world,[91] which would support this new enforcement direction. Nevertheless, even recent guidelines issued by the KFTC on the intersection of intellectual property rights and antitrust law continue to maintain the role of "unfairness" in its review of market behavior. Under the rubric of "unfairness," the recent guidelines condemn practices which include the exercise of intellectual property rights by a company that is in a superior bargaining position, or in a manner where the other parties to the transaction suffer "excessive disadvantage beyond customary trade practices."[92]

3. CHINA

China's decision to embrace antitrust law is much more recent than that of Japan and Korea. As such, one would expect its laws to more reflect the current antitrust emphasis on economic efficiency and protecting the interests of consumers, and indeed those goals are among the objectives of the Chinese Anti-Monopoly Law.[93]

Still, the role of "fairness" is something with which the drafters of the AML struggled. Commentators were concerned when the October 2002 Draft AML used the phrase "fair competition," when describing the interests the AML was designed to protect.[94] Observers questioned whether the term was intended to mean something short of "free competition" or whether it referred to consumer protection concerns, which would correspond with the meaning given to the phrase in the context of China's Anti-Unfair Competition Law.[95] During conferences, Chinese officials attempted to assuage any fears by providing assurances that there was no intention for "fair competition" to mean anything other than market competition, and this is reflected in the AML, as adopted, which makes clear that the law was enacted to protect "fair market competition."[96]

That the protection of "fairness" is not highlighted in the AML does not, however, mean that concept does not exist within Chinese antitrust law. Indeed, that is precisely what the 1993 Anti-Unfair Competition Law of the People's Republic of China was intended to do.[97] The AUCL regulates a broad range of conduct including advertising and misappropriation of trade secrets, only some of which is generally considered to be antitrust-related. This conduct includes exclusionary practices by public utilities; administrative monopolies; selling below cost to exclude competitors; tying; and bid-rigging. Much of this conduct is also addressed by the AML, but differences do exist between their treatment under the two statutes.

As in other countries, when China relies on a standard of "unfairness," it exhibits the potential to restrict competition in a manner that may hurt efficiency. One example of this propensity is the AUCL's prohibition on selling products below cost for the purpose of forcing out competitors, except under narrow circumstances.[98] This prohibition applies even if the company engaged in the practice does not have a dominant position. Similarly, Article 11 does not require the existence of a negative effect on competition. Thus, even if there is an overall procompetitive justification for a company's decision to sell at below cost, the company will not be permitted to do so as a result of the "unfairness" to competitors.

IV. Conclusion

Antitrust enforcement should be directed towards producing predictable outcomes based on the notion of maximizing consumer welfare through the protection and enhancement of allocative efficiency. To inject generalized notions of "unfairness" into antitrust analyses not only dilutes the focus of enforcers, but more importantly undermines the achievement of that primary goal of competition policy. When looking to remedy "unfairness," antitrust agencies inevitably fall into the trap of protecting competitors, not competition, or worse, sacrificing enhanced competition on the altar of fairness.

The experience of the FTC's enforcement of its Section 5 power demonstrates the problems with an "unfairness" standard and the manner in which it encourages over-enforcement. U.S. courts have recognized these problems, yet the FTC continues to seek to expand the exercise of its "unfairness" powers. And unfortunately, the FTC's model has spread across the world, particularly in Asia. As discussed above, Japan, Korea, and China have all—to varying degrees—incorporated the notion of "fairness" into their competition regimes. Other countries have also followed this model including Taiwan, Thailand, Indonesia,[99] and Vietnam,[100] and more are expected to follow.[101]

To restore confidence in its methodology, the FTC would be wise to adopt the suggestions of numerous commentators and establish clear criteria, rooted in anticompetitive effects, for the exercise of its Section 5 power. The only hope is that like the FTC's reliance on "unfairness," its hoped-for decision to circumscribe those powers will also be widely disseminated.

NOTES

1   15 U.S.C. 45(a)(1) (2012).

2   Federal Trade Commission v. Sperry & Hutchinson Co., 405 U.S. 233 (1972).

3   *Id.* at 234.

4   *Id.*

5   *Id.* at 235.

6   Sperry & Hutchinson Co. v. Federal Trade Commission, 432 F.2d 146 (5th Cir. 1970).

7   *Sperry,* 405 U.S. at 239.

8   *Id.* at 244.

9   *See e.g.,* Boise Cascade Corp. v. Federal Trade Commission, 637 F.2d 573 (9th Cir.1988).

10   *See* E. I. Du Pont de Nemours & Co. v. Federal Trade Commission (Ethyl), 729 F.2d 128, 137-138 (2d Cir. 1984).

11   Official Airline Guides v. Federal Trade Commission, 630 F.2d 920 (2d Cir. 1980).

12   *Id.* at 927.

13   *Id.*

14   *Boise Cascade,* 637 F.2d at 581-82.

15   *See id.*

16   *Id.* at 579.

17   *Id.* at 581-82.

18   *Id.*

19   *Ethyl,* 729 F.2d at 137.

20   *Id.* at 139.

21   *In re* General Motors, 103 F.T.C. 641, 131-132 (1984) (In *General Motors,* the FTC alleged that General Motors
Corporation violated section 5 of the FTC Act as well as the Robison-Patman Act by not making promotional allowances available to rental and leasing companies on proportionally equal terms. One method GM used to promote
its vehicles was to pay rental companies to include phrases in their advertisements such as, "We feature GM cars."
However, GM provided significant allowances only to large rental companies and not smaller competitors. The
Commission rejected a per se approach to a section 5 case and remanded for a trial on the competitive effects of
the activity).

22   *In re* Coca-Cola Co., 117 F.T.C. 795 (1994).

23   *Id.* at 213-214.

24   *See e.g., In re* Negotiated Data Solutions, Docket No.C4234, File No. 051-0094 (2008), *available at* http://www.
ftc.gov/os/caselist/0510094/index.shtm.

25   *In re* Negotiated Data Solutions, Docket No.C4234, File No. 051-0094 (2008) (complaint), *available at* http://www.
ftc.gov/os/caselist/0510094/080122complaint.pdf.

26   *Id.*

27   *In re* Negotiated Data Solutions, Docket No. C4234, File No. 051-0094 (2008) (decision and order), *available at*
http://www.ftc.gov/os/caselist/0510094/080923ndsdo.pdf.

28   *In re* Negotiated Data Solutions, Docket No. C4234, File No. 051-0094 (2008) (statement of the Federal Trade
Commission), *available at* http://www.ftc.gov/os/caselist/0510094/080122statement.pdf.

29   *In re* Intel Corp., Docket No. 9341, File no. 061-0247 (2009) (complaint), *available at* http://www.ftc.gov/os/adjpro/
d9341/091216intelcmpt.pdf.

30   *Id.*

31   *Id.*

32   *In re* Intel Corp., Docket No. 9341 File no. 061-0247 (concurring and dissenting statement of J. Thomas Rosch),
available at http://www.ftc.gov/os/adjpro/d9341/091216intelstatement.pdf.

33   *Id.* at 3-4.

34   *In re* Intel Corp., Docket No. 9341, File no. 061-0247 (statement of Chairman Leibowitz and Commissioner Rosch),
available at http://www.ftc.gov/os/adjpro/d9341/091216intelchairstatement.pdf.

35   *In re* Negotiated Data Solutions, Docket No.C-4234, File No. 0510094 (dissenting statement of Commissioner
William E. Kovacic), *available at* http://www.ftc.gov/os/caselist/0510094/080122kovacic.pdf.

36   *In re* Negotiated Data Solutions, Docket No. C-4234, File No. 0510094 (dissenting statement of Chairman Majoras), *available at* http://www.ftc.gov/os/caselist/0510094/080122majoras.pdf.

37   *Id.* at 2.

38   *Id.* at 3.

39   *Id.*

40   *In re* Negotiated Data Solutions, Docket No.C-4234, File No. 0510094 (dissenting statement of Commissioner William E. Kovacic), *available at* http://www.ftc.gov/os/caselist/0510094/080122kovacic.pdf.

41   *Id.* at 2-3.

42   *Id.* at 2-3 ("The Analysis here does not discuss why the Commission endorses separate UMC and UAP claims. The Analysis does not integrate the two theories of liability. A fuller effort to explain the relationship between the theories of liability in the Analysis would have led the Commission to confront anomalies in its exposition of the decision to prosecute.").

43   *Id.* at 3.

44   *In re* Intel Corp., Docket. No. 9341, File no. 061-0247, at 2 (statement of Chairman Leibowitz and Commissioner Rosch), *available at* http://www.ftc.gov/os/adjpro/d9341/091216intelchairstatement.pdf.

45   *Id.* at 2.

46   William E. Kovacic & Marc Winerman, *Competition Policy and the Application of Section 5 of the Federal Trade Commission Act*, 76 Antitrust L.J. 929 (2010).

47   *Id.* at 934-35.

48   *Id.*

49   *Id.* at 939.

50   *Id.* at 949.

51   *Id.* at 948.

52   *Id.*

53   *Id.*

54   *Id.* One advantage of relying on the FTC rather than the DOJ to bring so-called "frontier cases" is that, unlike the Sherman Act, the FTC Act does not include a private right of action. Accordingly, there is no risk of follow-on private litigation stemming from an adverse decision under the FTC Act. That said, Kovacic has pointed out that there is the possibility that the FTC precedent may be used to interpret state "little FTC Acts," some of which may be enforced by private citizens. *See id.* at 939, n. 54.

55   *Id.* at 944.

56   *Id.* at 945.

57   *Id.* at 944.

58   *Id.* at 950.

59   *Id.*

60   Herbert Hovenkamp, *The Federal Trade Commission and the Sherman Act*, 62 Fla. L. Rev. 871 (2009).

61   *Id.* at 878-882.

62   *Id.* at 878.

63   Susan Creighton & Thomas Krattenmaker, *Some Thoughts About the Scope of Section 5*, 2008 FTC Workshop: Section 5 (October 17, 2008), at 3, *available at* http://www.ftc.gov/bc/workshops/section5/docs/screighton.pdf.

64   Amy Marshak, *The Federal Trade Commission on the Frontier: Suggestions for the Use of Section 5*, 86 N.Y.U.L. Rev. 1121, 1143 (2011).

65   *Id.*

66   Geoffrey Manne, *The FTC's Misguided Rationale for the Use of Section 5 in Sherman Act Cases*, The CPI Antitrust Journal (February 2010), at 4, *available at* papers.ssrn.com/sol3/papers.cfm?abstract_id=1562489.

67   *Id.*

68   Creighton, *supra* note 63 at 4.

69   *Id.*

70   Richard A. Posner, *Federal Trade Commission 90th Anniversary Symposium: Article: The Federal Trade Commission: A Retrospective*, 72 Antitrust L.J. 761(2005).

71   *Id*. at 3-4.

72   Official Airline Guides Inc. v. Federal Trade Commission, 630 F.2d 920 (2d Cir. 1980); Boise Cascade Corp. v. Federal Trade Commission, 637 F.2d 573 (9th Cir. 1980); E.I. Du Pont De Nemours & Co. v. Federal Trade Commission (Ethyl), 729 F.2d 128 (2d Cir. 1984).

73   *Marshak, supra* note 64 at 1134.

74   *Boise Cascade*, 637 F.2d at 582.

75   In a recent survey, one researcher identified 29 states that incorporate the Commission's interpretation of Section 5 into their construction of their state FTC Acts. *See* Justin J. Hakala, *Follow on State Actions Based on the FTC's Enforcement of Section 5*, October 9, 2008, at 6, *available at* http://papers.ssrn.com/sol3/papers.cfm?abstract_id=1283261.

76   AKIRA INOUE, JAPANESE ANTITRUST LAW MANUAL: LAW, CASES AND INTERPRETATION OF JAPANESE ANTIMONOPOLY ACT (Kluwer Law Int'l 2007) (2007).

77   Japan Fair Trade Commission, Designation of Specific Unfair Trade Practices, *available at* http://www.jftc.go.jp/en/legislation_guidelines/ama/unfairtradepractices/index.html.

78   Japan Fair Trade Commission, Designation of Specific Unfair Trade Practices by Large Scale Retailers Relating to Trade with Suppliers, *available at* http://www.jftc.go.jp/en/legislation_guidelines/ama/pdf/dsutp.pdf.

79   POLICY BRIEF: COMPETITION LAW AND POLICY IN JAPAN, OECD OBSERVER, Sept. 2004, at 2, *available at* http://www.oecd.org/dataoecd/22/18/33723798.pdf.

80   *Id*.

81   *Id*. at 6.

82   *Id*.

83   *See* Law Relating to Prohibition of Private Monopoly and Securing Fair Trade, Art. 1, *translated in* General headquarters, Supreme Commander for the Allied Powers, 30 History of the Nonmilitary Activities of the Occupation of Japan 1945-1951, Promotion of Fair Trade Practices, App. 2, at 4 (cited in Harry First, *Antitrust Enforcement in Japan*, 64 ANTITRUST L.J. (1995), *also available at* http://www.jftc.go.jp/en/legislation_guidelines/ama/amended_ama09/01.html.

84   *See* Laws and Guidelines of Fair Trade Commission of Korea, *available at* http://eng.ftc.go.kr/legalauthority/recentlaw.jsp?pageId=0401.

85   Korea Fair Trade Commission, Guidelines for Review of Unfair Trade Practices, *available at* http://eng.ftc.go.kr/files/static/Legal_Authority/Guidelines%20for%20Review%20of%20Unfair%20Trade%20Practices(2005).pdf; *see* Dr. Youngjin Jung, *The KFTC's Foray into the Intersection between Competition Law and Intellectual Property Law: A Path Towards Convergence or Divergence?*, 7-2 COMPETITION LAW INTERNATIONAL 21 (November 2011).

86   Jung, *supra* note 85, at 2.

87   *See* Yongchun Baek, Randall S. Jones & Michael Wise, *Product Market Competition and Economic Performance in Korea* (OECD Economics Department Working Papers, No. 399, p. 5 OECD Publishing), *available at* http://dx.doi.org/10.1787/634035868056.

88   *Id*.

89   *Id*. at 17.

90   Hugo Restall, *Book Review: Getting More for Less, A Survey of Inefficiency . . . and What to Do About It*, THE WALL STREET JOURNAL, June 23, 2004, *available at* http://online.wsj.com/article/0,,SB108793937931244475,00.html.

91   GLOBAL COMPETITION REVIEW, vol. 7, issue 3, p. 26 (2004).

92   Korea Fair Trade Commission, Review Guidelines on the Undue Exercise of Intellectual Property Rights, *available at* http://eng.ftc.go.kr/files/static/Legal_Authority/Review%20Guidelines%20on%20Undue%20Exercise%20of%20Intellectual%20Property%20Rights.pdf.; *see* Jung, *supra* note 85, at 3.

93   *See* Anti-Monopoly Law of the People's Republic of China (2007), *available at* http://www.china.org.cn/government/laws/2009-02/10/content_17254169.htm.

94   H. Steven Harris Jr. et al., ANTI-MONOPOLY LAW AND PRACTICE IN CHINA 21 (Oxford University Press 2011) (2011).

95   *Id*. at 22.

96   *Id*.

97   *Anti-Unfair Competition Law of the People's Republic of China* (1993), *available at* http://en.chinacourt.org/public/detail.php?id=3306.

98   *See id*. at Article 11 (Article 11 of the AUCL allows below cost sales with respect to (1) sale of fresh or live products; (2) disposal of products whose period of validity is due to expire soon or other overstocked products; (3) seasonal price reductions; or (4) sale of products at reduced prices in order to satisfy debts or due to a change in the line of production or closure of business).

99 *See* Lawrence S. Liu, *In Fairness We Trust? — Why Fostering Competition Law and Policy Ain't Easy in Asia*, Oct. 19, 2004, at 4, *available at* http://papers.ssrn.com/sol3/papers.cfm?abstract_id=610822.

100 Mark Furse, Antitrust Law in China, Korea, and Vietnam, 306 n.2 (2009) (Noting that the Vietnam Law on Competition distinguishes between "competition-restricting acts" and "unfair competition acts," and that the scope of "unfair competition acts" may apply to conduct that would not violate "standard" antitrust regulations.).

101 All ASEAN countries have committed to enacting competition laws by 2015. Those countries that do not yet have general competition laws, such as the Philippines, are likely to adopt laws that mirror the laws of other Asian jurisdictions, including the adoption of a "fairness" component. *See* ASEAN Economic Community Blueprint § B1, *available at* http://www.aseansec.org/21083.pdf.

Merger Enforcement Across Political Administrations in the United States[*]

RONAN P. HARTY

ronan.harty@davispolk.com
Partner, Davis Polk & Wardwell, LLP

HOWARD A. SHELANSKI

has37@law.georgetown.edu
Director, Bureau of Economics, U.S. Federal Trade Commission
Professor of Law, Georgetown University

JESSE SOLOMON

jesse.solomon@davispolk.com
Associate, Davis Polk & Wardwell, LLP

Abstract

Bill Kovacic has written persuasively that the political rhetoric of antitrust has often been at odds with what the antitrust agencies have actually done and with any meaningful assessment of their performance. This article follows Kovacic by analyzing data from the FTC's and the DOJ's review of mergers over thirty years, from 1981 through 2011, for correlations to shifts in political administration. We analyze historical trends from one administration to the next with regard to five metrics: (1) agency budgeting, (2) the number of transactions reported under the Hart-Scott-Rodino Antitrust Improvements Act of 1976, (3) requests for and grants of early termination of the waiting period, (4) the issuance of second requests by the agencies, and (5) transaction challenges brought by the agencies. These data demonstrate some interesting, and at times counterintuitive, relationships between specific administrations and merger review and enforcement activity. On a more granular level, these data also demonstrate some trends regarding how merger review and enforcement statistics have been sensitive to changeover from one agency chief to the next within administrations. By some measures, enforcement activity appears to decline during Republican administrations and increase during Democratic governments. At the same time, there are other measures that contradict that pattern. Our analysis therefore supports Kovacic's skepticism about any simple relationship between antitrust enforcement and political administration and reinforces his call for moving beyond activity measures in judging the success of an administration's antitrust policies.

I. Introduction

New political administrations often come into office with assumptions, and sometimes clear statements, about how their approach to antitrust enforcement will differ from that of their predecessors. Thus, President George W. Bush took office in the wake of his statements that antitrust law "needs to be applied where there are clear cases of price-fixing" and that he would not see other roles for antitrust enforcement because "everything evolves into price-fixing over time."[1] Such radical sentiments stoked strong expectations that Bush administration appointees to the Antitrust Division of the U.S. Department of Justice (Antitrust Division or DOJ) and to the Federal Trade Commission (FTC) would greatly reduce antitrust enforcement. Indeed, during his campaign President Obama stated that antitrust enforcement under President Bush "may be the weakest" of "any administration in the last half century," signaling that there would be increased enforcement during an Obama administration. [2] Shortly after Christine Varney took over as President Obama's Assistant Attorney General (AAG) for antitrust, she delivered a speech promising a more aggressive approach to antitrust enforcement than that of her predecessors.[3] She also specifically withdrew a report, which the Bush DOJ had issued, that was viewed as establishing a less aggressive approach to alleged monopoly conduct.

Bill Kovacic has persuasively written that the political rhetoric of antitrust has often been at odds with what the antitrust agencies have actually done and with any meaningful assessment of their performance.[4] He is particularly skeptical of uncritical, activity-based measures of agency performance.[5] Kovacic notes that there is a basic lack of agreement or understanding of what level of activity in fact took place[6] as well as little critical assessment of the value of judging the agencies based on activity levels in the first place.[7]

In this article, we follow in Kovacic's line of thought by taking a preliminary look at data on merger review by the FTC and DOJ across political administrations from 1981 through 2011. Our goal is not to address Kovacic's important second question about the value of activity-based measures; it is instead to investigate, in the context of merger review, his basic point that antitrust activity levels cannot be assumed to correlate with the political party in power. In finding the available data to support Kovacic's skepticism about a simple relationship between politics and antitrust, we reinforce his arguments for measures of antitrust agency performance that transcend activity levels and join his call to focus not on case counts but on "progression toward a durable consensus on what constitutes good policy."[8]

II. Agency Budgeting

As we consider how merger review has evolved from administration to administration, one place to start is with a measure that would systematically affect the agencies' ability to enforce the antitrust laws at all: funding. In this regard, it is useful to look at both combined funding for the DOJ's and the FTC's antitrust missions and at the relative allocation of that budget between the agencies. One might imagine, for example, that an administration with a strong antitrust agenda one way or the other might not only change budgeting but allocate that budget away from the more independent and bipartisan FTC and toward the Antitrust Division, which is within the executive branch and under more direct presidential control.

The available evidence, however, suggests that neither the overall level of antitrust enforcement funding nor the allocation of that funding cycles significantly with administrations. In fact, the federal budget for antitrust enforcement has increased steadily and substantially since the first Bush administration, including strong growth during the second Bush administration.

The allocation of antitrust enforcement budgets between the FTC and the DOJ has varied somewhat, but not dramatically or predictably with political party. If we examine federal budget data back to the beginning of the Reagan administration in 1981,[9] the FTC's Bureau of Competition has historically received an allocated budget that is approximately 60% the size of the Antitrust Division's budget, which is not surprising given the large amount of criminal cartel and price-fixing enforcement done by the DOJ, an area over which the FTC has no jurisdiction. For example, during President George W. Bush's administration, the Bureau of Competition received an allocated budget that was, on average, 62.5% the size of the budget that the Antitrust Division received:

Fig. 1: Average Total Annual Budget Allocations for Antitrust Division and Bureau of Competition by Political Administration, 1989-2011[10]

Admin.	Total Budget for Antitrust Enf't ($M)	% Change	Antitrust Division Budget ($M)	% Change	Bureau of Comp. Budget ($M)	% Change	Bureau as % of Division Budget
Bush (1989-92)	65.8	–	41.3	–	24.5	–	59.5%
Clinton (1993-2000)	120.0	82.5%	87.9	113.0%	32.2	31.2%	36.7% [52.1% ('97-'00)][11]
Bush (2001-08)	218.5	82.0%	134.5	53.1%	84.0	161.1%	62.5%
Obama (2009-11)	286.7	31.2%	166.0	23.4%	120.7	43.7%	72.7%

As *Figure 1* shows, the 62.5% average allocation under President George W. Bush is slightly higher than the average allocation during President Clinton's second term (when the Bureau of Competition received a federal budget that was on average 52.1% of the size of the Antitrust Division's budget from 1997 to 2000) and comparable to the average allocation during the term of President George H.W. Bush (59.5% between 1989 and 1992).

The Obama administration, however, has departed to some degree from this historical trend. In the first three years of the Obama administration, the Antitrust Division's budget grew by an average of 2.6% annually, while the Bureau of Competition's budget grew by 6.7% — narrowing the gap between the agencies to some degree and providing the Bureau of Competition a budget that is, on average, 72.7% the size of the Antitrust Division's budget.

These budgeting patterns do not, however, correlate with the level of FTC enforcement. To the contrary, by at least some common measures the Bureau of Competition's rates of activity relative to the Antitrust Division's are slightly *lower* under President Obama than they were under President George W. Bush, when the Antitrust Division had a larger budget relative to the Bureau of Competition. Since the Obama administration began, the FTC issued 44.4% of second requests, down 6.4% from an average 50.8% under President Bush, and it accounted for 53.2% of transaction challenges, down 4.6% from an average 57.8% during the Bush administratio.[12] Moreover, the rate at which the FTC issues second requests declined slightly (from 14.6% average under President George W. Bush to 14.4% average under President Obama).

It is important to note that the federal funds allocated to the antitrust agencies approximate — but do not fully identify — all resources available to these agencies. Funding allocations from the annual federal budget are offset (and, potentially, supplemented) by fees collected from the premerger notification regime; the allocated budget figures therefore do not necessarily represent all funds available for agency expenditure over time.[13] President Clinton's first term provides a useful example: in 1996, the Bureau of Competition technically received no directly allocated federal funds.[14] However, the budget provided up to $48.3 million of offsetting collections derived from premerger notification fees for FTC expenditure, including but not limited to expenditures for the Bureau of Competition.[15] We do not know how much of this $48.3 million went to the Bureau of Competition, limiting the degree to which we can interpret the available data.

To the extent we can draw a lesson from these data, then, it is that merging parties should not assume that a particular administration will allocate funds in a way that would predictably affect either the level of overall antitrust enforcement or the relative levels of FTC versus DOJ enforcement activity. We turn next to data on that activity itself.

III. Reportable Transactions

The number of reported transactions per year, not surprisingly, tends to reflect periods of economic expansion or recession in the general U.S. economy far more than it correlates with political administrations. In fact, the high-water mark for reported transactions came during a Democratic administration (the Clinton administration), when the average number of reported transactions rose approximately 70% over what they had been during the Bush administration.

The number of transactions reported annually pursuant to the Hart-Scott-Rodino Antitrust Improvements Act of 1976 (the "HSR Act")[16] has tended to drop only during periods of economic downturn, such as 1982-83 (corresponding roughly to the January 1980–July 1980 and July 1981–November 1982 "double dip" recession), 1990-92 (corresponding to the July 1990–March 1991 recession), 2000-01 (corresponding to the March 2001–November 2001 burst of the late 1990s "bubble"), and 2008-09 (corresponding to the December 2007–June 2009 subprime mortgage collapse and the global financial crisis)[17]:

**Fig. 2: Total Number of Transactions
Reported under HSR Act, 1981-2011**

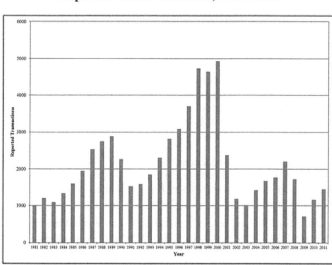

Notably, during these periods of economic recession or contraction, when the number of reportable transactions has declined, that reduction has tended to occur across all deal values; the distribution of low-value, medium-value, and high-value deals has not changed significantly. In most years, about 50-60% of transactions are valued at $1 billion or higher, about 10% of reported transactions are valued at $500 million to $1 billion, and the remainder are valued at below $500 million. This distribution tends not to change even during periods of recession, such as calendar years 2000-02 or 2007-09.

These data, of course, cannot capture the number of potentially merging parties that choose not to enter into a transaction due to concerns that, for example, the political administration in power will impose transaction costs, delays, or modifications that would undermine the efficiencies of a merger. We might expect merger and acquisition activity to be higher during Republican administrations that are said to champion more restrained intervention in the merger market than under Democratic administrations assumed to be more enforcement-minded. If there is anecdotal evidence of this phenomenon, however, it is not reflected in the data of reported transactions, which increased most during President Clinton's second term—precisely the time when the DOJ brought its monopolization case against Microsoft[18] and the FTC made several high-profile merger challenges.[19] Not surprisingly given the economic expansion and "tech boom" that occurred in the 1990s, President Clinton's administration saw the highest average level of annual transactions out of the five administrations that we consider here:

Fig. 3: Average Annual Number of Transactions Reported under HSR Act by Political Administration, 1981-2011

Administration	Transactions Reported (Avg.)	% Change
Reagan (1981-88)	1,682.9	–
Bush (1989-92)	2,065.8	22.8%
Clinton (1993-2000)	3,506.5	69.7%
Bush (2001-08)	1,671.9	-52.3%
Obama (2009-11)	1,110.7	-33.6%

Taken on its own, the decline in the number of reported transactions during the first three years of the Obama administration looks stark: a 33.6% decline in the number of transactions reported under the HSR Act during a period in which then-AAG Christine A. Varney called for more robust antitrust enforcement. When we place this decline in context, however, it is clear that it is less dramatic than the decline in the number of transactions reported under President George W. Bush (a 52.3% decline, or a decline 18.7% greater under a Republican president than a Democratic one). By contrast, the number of transactions increased 69.7% from President George H.W. Bush to President Clinton. These data suggest that, to the extent that transactions reported have fallen and remained low under President Obama, the reduced number of transactions is a reflection of general economic conditions more so than businesses' unwillingness to file under the HSR Act during a Democratic administration, even one that came in vowing stronger antitrust enforcement.

IV. Early Termination

To assess the rate at which different political administrations and different agency heads have granted early termination,[20] we must examine two figures: (1) the rate at which parties request early termination, and (2) the rate at which the agencies grant those requests.

On a macro level, the political affiliation of the administration does not appear to affect the rate at which parties request early termination. In fact, rates of request for early termination have been remarkably flat since the middle of the Reagan administration, reaching 80% by 1985 and remaining, since then, in the 80-90% range:

Fig. 4: Average Annual Requests for Early Termination by Political Administration, 1981-2011

Administration	Transactions Reported	Early Termination Requests	% of Transactions Requesting Early Termination
Reagan (1981-88)	1,682.9	1,197.4	71.2%
Bush (1989-92)	2,065.8	1,820.3	88.1%
Clinton (1993-2000)	3,506.5	3,152.8	89.9%
Bush (2001-08)	1,671.9	1,390.5	83.2%
Obama (2009-11)	1110.7	895.0	80.6%

The progression from President George H.W. Bush to President Clinton to President George W. Bush is perhaps surprising: the rate at which parties requested early termination rose almost 2% in a Democratic administration and then fell 6.7% under the following Republican administration. While it is true that requests for early termination have fallen 2.6% under President Obama, that drop is less than half the reduction of parties requesting early termination from President Clinton to President George W. Bush (a 6.7% reduction).

Not only does it appear that the rate at which parties request early termination does not correspond to the political affiliation of the administration, the rate at which the agencies grant requests for early termination does not appear to correlate with party politics, either. In fact, the nadir of early termination grants occurred during a Republican administration—71% under President George H.W. Bush:

Fig. 5: Average Annual Grants of Requests for Early Termination by Political Administration, 1981-2011

Administration	Early Termination Requests	Grants of Early Termination	% of Requests Granted
Reagan (1981-88)	1,197.4	928.5	77.5%
Bush (1989-92)	1,820.3	1,290.8	70.9%
Clinton (1993-2000)	3,152.8	2,373.4	75.3%
Bush (2001-08)	1,390.5	1,057.9	76.1%
Obama (2009-11)	895.0	662.7	74.0%

While grants of early termination rose from President Clinton to President George W. Bush, they did so by less than 1%. And if early terminations rose under President George W. Bush less than one might have expected, they also decreased under President Obama less than one might have expected. In the first three years of the Obama administration, 74.0% of early termination requests were granted—a higher rate than under President George H.W. Bush and only a 2.1% reduction from President George W. Bush. If we look to the Obama administration for increased antitrust enforcement, it does not appear to have increased scrutiny by significantly decreasing the rate of early terminations. It has, however, supplied increased scrutiny by raising the rates at which it issues second requests and challenges transactions, as we will explore below.

V. Second Requests

For almost every year since 1981, the range of second requests has been 2% to 5% of the total number of transactions reported to the agencies under the HSR Act. Among the subset of reported transactions that clears to one agency or the other,[21] second requests generally have been issued in 15% to 40% of cases. But the rate at which different administrations have issued second requests, as well as the relative activity of the FTC and the DOJ in issuing second requests within administrations, leads to several observations related to political administrations and to the agency chiefs within those administrations.

Among the total pool of transactions reported each year, the parties are typically eligible to receive a second request in approximately 95% of cases.[22] If we compare the rate at which administrations have issued second requests, the average rate of issuance peaked during the early years of the Reagan administration and then fell steadily until the Obama administration, which increased the rate of issuing second requests from 3.1% to 4.2% of reportable transactions by 2011:

Fig. 6: Average Second Requests Issued on an Annual Basis Out of Eligible Transactions, by Political Administration, 1981-2011

Administration	Second Requests Issued (Annual Average)	% of Eligible Transactions with Second Requests	% Change
Reagan (1981-88)	61.6	5.3%	–
Bush (1989-92)	65.3	3.7%	-30.3%
Clinton (1993-2000)	100.3	3.2%	-12.7%
Bush (2001-08)	48.5	3.1%	-4.1%
Obama (2009-11)	45.0	4.2%	37.1%

Looking only at transactions that cleared to one of the agencies for review—arguably representing the subset of transactions to which the agencies really pay attention—the rate at which second requests have been issued has generally fallen from administration to administration, with only a slight increase under President Clinton until a larger increase in the early Obama administration:

Fig. 7: Average Second Requests Issued on an Annual Basis Out of Cleared Transactions, by Political Administration, 1981-2011

Administration	Second Requests Issued (Annual Average)	% of Cleared Transactions with Second Requests	% Change
Reagan (1981-88)[23]	61.6	31.6%	–
Bush (1989-92)	65.3	24.3%	-23.0%
Clinton (1993-2000)	100.3	25.1%	3.2%
Bush (2001-08)	48.5	18.3%	-27.3%
Obama (2009-11)	45.0	21.3%	16.9%

Looking at total transactions, the data show a steady drop in the issuance of second requests from the Reagan through George W. Bush administrations—with second requests stabilizing in the low 3% range from 1993-2008. Among transactions that cleared to one of the agencies, the trend similarly shows a decline from Reagan through George W. Bush, although with a slight uptick under Clinton and a sharper decline under George W. Bush. By each measure, the Obama administration in its first three years reversed that trend, increasing the rate of second requests among total reported transactions to 4.2% and to 21.3% among transactions that cleared to one agency or the other.[24] While the increase under Obama might be worth noting by parties currently contemplating a merger in the United States, these data do not show a systematic political correlation; indeed, note the decline under Clinton among total transactions and the very slight increase under Clinton among cleared transactions. Moreover, in themselves, these data say nothing about the nature of the investigations or whether the change is due to the particular pool of transactions or to the agencies' use of a more aggressive standard for launching second requests.

Looking further at the data on second requests, they show that within a given administration, the FTC and the DOJ have varied in their comparative rates of issuing second requests. Since the administration of President George H. W. Bush, the data show relatively higher rates of FTC activity under Republican presidents and relatively higher rates of DOJ activity under Democratic presidents:

Fig. 8: Average Distribution of Second Requests between DOJ and FTC by Political Administration, 1981-2011

Administration	DOJ-Issued Second Requests	FTC-Issued Second Requests	Advantage
Reagan (1981-88)	55.6%	44.4%	DOJ (11.2%)
Bush (1989-92)	43.2%	56.8%	FTC (13.6%)
Clinton (1993-2000)	53.7%	46.3%	DOJ (7.4%)
Bush (2001-08)	49.2%	50.8%	FTC (1.6%)
Obama (2009-11)	55.6%	44.4%	DOJ (11.2%)

The above comparative data might appear to suggest a political dynamic in which, at least since 1989, the relatively independent, bipartisan FTC has been more consistent in enforcement than the more institutionally political DOJ, which one might predict to increase enforcement during Democratic administrations. (As we will see, the tendency for DOJ scrutiny to rise under Democratic administrations and fall under Republican administrations is also evidenced in data suggesting that merger challenges by the DOJ tend to fall under Republican administrations and rise under Democratic administrations.)

Interestingly, however, when one adjusts the rates at which the DOJ and the FTC issue second requests for the relative number of transactions that cleared to each agency, a somewhat different picture emerges. Compare Figure 9 and Figure 10, below:

Fig. 9: Average Rate of Issuance of Second Requests for Transactions Cleared to the DOJ by Political Administration, 1981-2011

Administration	Transactions Cleared to FTC (Annual Average)	Average Rate of DOJ Issuance of Second Requests for Transactions Cleared to DOJ	% Change
Reagan (1981-88)	79.5	42.5%	–
Bush (1989-92)	71.3	39.3%	-7.4%
Clinton (1993-2000)	162.4	34.1%	-13.2%
Bush (2001-08)	99.6	24.3%	-28.6%
Obama (2009-11)	74.3	34.1%	40.0%

Fig. 10: Average Rate of Issuance of Second Requests for Transactions Cleared to the FTC by Political Administration, 1981-2011

Administration	Transactions Cleared to FTC (Annual Average)	Average Rate of DOJ Issuance of Second Requests for Transactions Cleared to DOJ	% Change
Reagan (1981-88)	115.7	24.1%	–
Bush (1989-92)	197	18.9%	-21.5%
Clinton (1993-2000)	236.9	18.9%	0.2%
Bush (2001-08)	166.1	14.6%	-22.9%
Obama (2009-11)	136.7	14.4%	-1.4%

These data show that in every administration since Reagan's, when a transaction is cleared to the DOJ it is more likely (24-43%) to receive a second request than is a transaction that is cleared to the FTC (14-24%). The data also show that the DOJ steadily reduced the frequency of second requests from administration to administration until that of President Obama, whose administration oversaw a rise in the rate at which second requests were issued, from 24.3% under President Bush to 34.1% during the first three years of the Obama administration. The FTC data show a drop in second requests from the Reagan administration to the present. Notably, unlike the DOJ, which has increased the rate of second requests under Obama, the FTC has issued second requests slightly less frequently during the Obama administration than under the George W. Bush administration.

The data shown above make it difficult to draw overarching conclusions about FTC and DOJ activity from administration to administration. They do, however, reveal some interesting correlations between agency activity and the tenures of specific agency heads. Consider the following comparative distribution of second requests between the FTC and the DOJ from 1981 to 2011:

Fig. 11: Annual Distribution of Second Requests between FTC and DOJ, 1981-2011

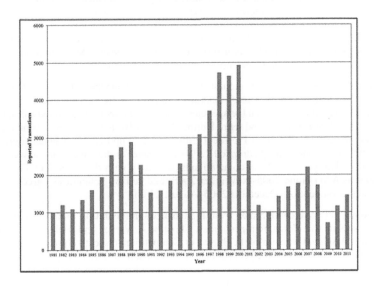

Importantly for any inferences tied to political administration that one might be tempted to draw, many—though not all—of the inflection points in *Figure 11*, above, coincide with notable shifts in agency personnel *within* administrations.

During the Reagan administration as a whole, the DOJ typically issued second requests more frequently than the FTC (55.6% to 44.4%). That overall figure, however, masks significant variation during the Reagan administration. In 1982, for example, that distribution changed dramatically, with the FTC issuing 60% of second requests in 1982—up from 49.3% in 1981. That nearly 11% jump coincides closely with Thomas J. Campbell's tenure as Director of the Bureau of Competition (October 1981–March 1983).[25] When Timothy J. Muris succeeded Campbell as Director of the Bureau of Competition, the FTC's share of second requests fell by nearly half to 35.3% and remained roughly in the 35-40% range during Muris' tenure. That trend is confirmed if we examine the rate at which the FTC issued second requests to transactions cleared to the FTC; in 1982, Campbell's Bureau issued second requests to 48.1% of transactions that cleared to the FTC; in 1983, Muris' Bureau issued second requests to 15.0% of its transactions.

In 1986, when Douglas H. Ginsburg served as AAG,[26] the pendulum swung back and the rate at which the DOJ issued second requests relative to the FTC dropped notably. While the DOJ continued to issue relatively more second requests than the FTC from 1985-87, the DOJ issued an approximately 10% to 15% greater share of second requests under Charles F. Rule in 1985 (64.2%) and in 1987 (69.0%) than it did during the bulk of Ginsburg's tenure in 1986 (54.9%).[27]

Beginning in 1996, we see a marked departure in distribution from the first three years of the Clinton administration, with the DOJ increasing its share of second requests by 21.0% in the space of one year (from 42.6% to 63.6%). This shift coincides roughly—if not exactly—with the tenures of Joel I. Klein as AAG (October 1996–September 2000) and William J. Baer as Director of the Bureau of Competition (May 1995–August 1999).[28] Such a dramatic shift in the middle of the administration—from a period of a relatively greater FTC share of second requests to a relatively greater DOJ share—may be explained by other factors (e.g., the relative mix of industries experiencing consolidation in the late 1990s), but the general correspondence to personnel changes is nonetheless striking. The result appears driven more by an increase in DOJ activity than a decrease in FTC enforcement. The DOJ issued second requests to 31% of transactions clearing to the DOJ during President Clinton's first term. Then, during the majority of AAG Klein's tenure in President Clinton's second term, the DOJ issued second requests in nearly 38% of transactions—an almost 22% change in rate from Clinton's first term to his second.

While the distribution of second requests between the DOJ and the FTC was relatively even during President George W. Bush's administration (49.2% by the DOJ and 50.8% by the FTC), the overall rate at which the agencies issued second requests declined substantially during President Bush's second term. During President Bush's first term, second requests actually *increased* 0.2% from President Clinton (3.2%) up to 3.4%, whereas during his second term, second requests dropped 2.7% on average for the three years between 2006 and 2008. The years 2006-08 coincide approximately with the tenures of Thomas O. Barnett as AAG (June 2005–November 2008) and Jeffrey Schmidt as Director of the Bureau of Competition (December 2005–August 2008).[29]

We do not yet have enough data from the Obama administration to know how second requests relate to enforcement personnel; Christine A. Varney and Richard A. Feinstein served as AAG and Director of the Bureau of Competition, respectively, during almost the entire period of the only three years of data we have available. After Congress confirms the next AAG, however, we may receive a better sense of how agency personnel affect the issuance of a second request in the Obama administration.

We do not present the data and discussion above to argue causality between personnel changes and patterns of enforcement activity, but instead to show that activity levels fluctuate as much or more within administrations as across them. These data also confirm that perceptions of antitrust activity from one administration to the next change depending upon which measures and comparisons one uses. These results should cast doubt on any inferences that one might draw from simple correlations between enforcement activity and political party, to the extent that such correlations appear.

VI. Transaction Challenges

The rate at which each administration has challenged reported transactions has increased steadily since the Reagan administration, with particular increases under President Clinton, President George W. Bush, and President Obama. Between the agencies, the FTC has historically challenged transactions more frequently than the DOJ, possibly because the FTC has administrative mechanisms for challenging a transaction that the DOJ does not and possibly because substantially more transactions clear every year to the FTC than clear to the DOJ (see *Figure 9* and *Figure 10*).

The data reflect a significant increase in the number of challenges brought over time, with the greatest increases during the Democratic administrations of Presidents Clinton and Obama, although there was a still-significant increase of 21.0% under President George W. Bush:

Fig. 12: Average Percentage of Reported Transactions Challenged by Political Administration, 1981-2011

Administration	% Challenged	% Change
Reagan (1981-88)	1.1%	–
Bush (1989-92)	1.2%	9.5%
Clinton (1993-2000)	1.7%	45.2%
Bush (2001-08)	2.0%	21.0%
Obama (2009-11)	3.3%	62.0%

Interestingly, when we consider the raw data underlying these rates, the absolute number of transactions challenged has not increased significantly under President Obama, with an average 36.3 annual challenges, up from an average 33.8 annual challenges under President George W. Bush. The difference, however, is that while there was an average of 1,672 transactions reported annually between 2001 and 2008, there was only an average of 1,111 transactions from 2009 to 2011.

These data show that the Obama administration has significantly increased the rate of transaction challenges over the previous administration. But the data also belie the notion that President George W. Bush diminished merger enforcement; to the contrary, the rate of enforcement actions increased approximately 20% from President Clinton to President George W. Bush.

It is notable that, in general, the FTC has historically challenged more transactions than the DOJ has, particularly during Republican administrations:

Fig. 13: Average Distribution of Challenges between DOJ and FTC by Political Administration, 1981-2011

Administration	DOJ Challenges	FTC Challenges	Advantage
Reagan (1981-88)	45.1%	54.9%	FTC (9.8%)
Bush (1989-92)	44.2%	55.8%	FTC (11.6%)
Clinton (1993-2000)	54.9%	45.1%	DOJ (9.8%)
Bush (2001-08)	42.2%	57.8%	FTC (15.6%)
Obama (2009-11)	46.8%	53.2%	FTC (6.4%)

The FTC's larger number of merger challenges is not surprising given that a significantly higher number of transactions clear to the FTC than to the DOJ each year. Indeed, when we adjust for the number of transactions that cleared to each agency, we see consistently higher rates of challenge at the DOJ across administrations, with particular increases in enforcement during Democratic administrations:

Fig. 14: Average Rates of Challenges by DOJ and FTC Out of Cleared Transactions, by Political Administration, 1981-2011

Administration	DOJ Annual Challenges	% of DOJ-Cleared Mergers Challenged	FTC Annual Challenges	% of FTC-Cleared Mergers Challenged
Reagan (1981-88)	8.0	13.0%	9.8	8.4%
Bush (1989-92)	10.5	14.9%	13.3	6.7%
Clinton (1993-2000)	32.1	19.9%	26.4	11.1%
Bush (2001-08)	14.3	14.2%	19.5	11.7%
Obama (2009-11)	17.0	23.7%	19.3	14.1%

The reasons for the different rates of challenge between the FTC and the DOJ reflected in *Figure 14* may be related to the nature of the industries reviewed by the respective agencies, the different administrative structure of the FTC, the comparative political independence of the FTC, or to other reasons.

Whatever the reasons for the different rates of challenge, one data point reflected in *Figure 13* and *Figure 14* is particularly striking. During the Clinton administration, between 1993 and 2000, the DOJ challenged significantly more mergers than the FTC. The increased share of challenges by the DOJ coincides with the 1996-2000 period in which the DOJ began to issue second requests more frequently than the FTC did. Notably, the comparative increase in DOJ challenges over FTC challenges is due less to reduced enforcement by the FTC than to increased enforcement by the DOJ. Indeed, the FTC challenged an average 29.2 transactions per year between 1996 and 2000, slightly above the average number of transactions challenged per year during the Clinton administration overall (26.4 challenges). By contrast, the DOJ averaged 20 challenges per year during President Clinton's first term, but averaged 44.3 challenges per year in his second term during the years that Joel I. Klein served as AAG.

As we have noted, the increase in merger challenges under AAG Klein appears to reflect a general trend toward increased rates of challenge by the DOJ during Democratic administrations and reduced rates of challenge by the DOJ during Republican administrations. This trend appears to hold true regardless of whether we examine DOJ challenges against the total number of transactions eligible for review or against only those transactions that cleared to the DOJ. Consider *Figure 15* and *Figure 16*, which show fewer DOJ challenges under President George W. Bush and more challenges by the DOJ under Presidents Clinton and Obama, using both the total number of transactions eligible for review as well as only those transactions that cleared to the DOJ:

Fig. 15: Average Rate of DOJ Merger Challenges of Total Eligible Transactions by Political Administration, 1981-2011

Administration	Average Rate of DOJ Challenge of Total Eligible Transactions	% Change
Reagan (1981-88)	0.6%	–
Bush (1989-92)	0.6%	-1.2%
Clinton (1993-2000)	1.0%	69.3%
Bush (2001-08)	0.9%	-8.6%
Obama (2009-11)	1.6%	78.1%

Fig. 16: Average Rate of DOJ Merger Challenges of Transactions Cleared to the DOJ by Political Administration, 1981-2011

Administration	Average Rate of DOJ Challenge of Transactions Cleared to the DOJ	% Change
Reagan (1981-88)	13.0%	–
Bush (1989-92)	14.9%	15.0%
Clinton (1993-2000)	19.9%	33.3%
Bush (2001-08)	14.2%	-28.5%
Obama (2009-11)	23.7%	66.1%

VII. Limitations and Unanswered Questions

In our analysis, we have sought to analyze public data to tease out correlations between agency activity on merger review and the governing administration. We note that there are some gaps in the data that the agencies provide to Congress each year on their activities under the HSR Act, which leave us with some unanswered questions.

For example, we cannot tell from the agencies' annual reports to Congress what happens to transactions that are not subject to specific agency action, such as a grant of early termination, the issuance of a second request, or a transaction challenge. Most of those probably just go forward after the waiting period expires. Of greater interest would be the fate of transactions that receive a second request but never receive a challenge. In many of those cases, the agency closes the investigation and allows the transaction to proceed. But in others the parties abandon the transaction during the review process. We know that the costs of complying with a second request can be significant for merging parties and, in some transactions, even fatal to a transaction. Because the agencies do not report the number of transactions abandoned during the review process—and how many of those transactions are abandoned as a result of an agency issuing a second request, notifying the parties that it plans to do so, or indicating serious concerns during the second request—it would require significant research beyond the reported data to understand the effect of agency activity and changes in political administration on parties' decisions to abandon or persist with a transaction.

VIII. Conclusion

This article has presented descriptive data that reinforce the conclusion that simple activity measures are of little help in understanding the ways that political administrations differ in antitrust enforcement or in assessing the performance of a given antitrust enforcement regime. Indeed, several important trends hold across administrations and other measures vary more with personnel changes within administrations. While by some measures enforcement by the DOJ declines in Republican administrations and increases during Democratic governments, this trend is contradicted by other measures and does not hold for antitrust enforcement overall.

To be sure, the data and analysis we present do not mean that there are no meaningful differences among administrations in how they enforce the antitrust laws. The Obama DOJ has been more aggressive in investigating vertical mergers than past administrations, while the George W. Bush administration was overtly more skeptical about single-firm anticompetitive conduct. What our results do show, in furtherance of Bill Kovacic's important work on the assessment of enforcement performance, is that activity counts neither capture important differences in enforcement nor do they say anything about the performance and social value of an administration's antitrust regime. Political rhetoric about levels of antitrust enforcement are thus unlikely to tell us much about a particular administration's seriousness about competition policy or to help us with the far more important goal that Kovacic identifies: the development of greater consensus about what constitutes sound competition policy and how the agencies should deal with novel and difficult cases. It is with an eye toward this latter objective that the research agenda on the measurement and evaluation of antitrust enforcement should move forward.

NOTES

* The authors wish to thank Kevin G. Danchisko for his excellent research assistance.

1 *See* Stephen Labaton, *The World Gets Tough on Fixing Prices*, N.Y. Times, June 3, 2001, http://www.nytimes.com/2001/06/03/business/the-world-gets-tough-on-fixing-prices.html?pagewanted=all&src=pm (last visited Aug. 11, 2012).

2 Sen. Barack Obama, Statement for the American Antitrust Institute (Feb. 20, 2008), *available at* http://www.antitrustinstitute.org/files/aai-%20Presidential%20campaign%20-%20Obama%209-07_092720071759.pdf

3 Christine A. Varney, Assistant Attorney General, Antitrust Division, U.S. Dep't of Justice, Vigorous Antitrust Enforcement in This Challenging Era, Remarks Prepared for the Center for American Progress (May 11, 2009), *available at* http://www.justice.gov/atr/public/speeches/245777.htm.

4 William E. Kovacic, *Rating the Competition Agencies: What Constitutes Good Performance?*, 16 Geo. Mason L. Rev. 903, 904 (2009).

5 *Id*. at 910-12, 918.

6 *Id*. at 911.

7 *Id*. at 918.

8 *Id*. at 926.

9 In our analysis, we track agency review and enforcement figures back to the beginning of the Reagan administration in 1981 rather than to 1977, the first year in which agency review was implemented. We do so primarily because using the Reagan administration as a starting point permits us to examine the data after several transitional years in which processes for merger review were implemented at the agencies.

10 *See* Budget of the U.S. Government, Fiscal Years 2003-2010, available at http://www.gpo.gov/fdsys/ (referencing actual expenditures for 2001-08). The Antitrust Division at the DOJ receives its own line item, while the Bureau of Competition is referenced in a line item for "Maintaining Competition." We have derived all budget calculations in our analysis from publicly available federal budgets, which are available online at http://www.gpo.gov/fdsys/ for Fiscal Years 1996-2013 and in print form for years prior to 1996. The federal budgets for the years of the Reagan administration (1981-88) do not clearly identify the allocated funds for the Antitrust Division and the Bureau of Competition, so we do not include these data here.

11 We must qualify the comparative data between the Bureau of Competition and the Antitrust Division for the first term of President Clinton's administration. From 1994 to 1996, the Bureau of Competition received either a minimal directly allocated budget ($18.7M in 1994 and $2M in 1995) or no directly allocated budget at all (the case in 1996), with the Bureau of Competition receiving funding through offsets of fees, as we discuss *infra*. Therefore, factoring in the anomalous years 1994-96 suggests that the Bureau of Competition received a budget only 36.7% of the size of the Antitrust Division's budget during the Clinton administration. If we look instead to President Clinton's second term (1997-2000), we see that the Bureau of Competition received 52.1% of the size of the Antitrust Division's budget – much closer to historical trends.

12 *See* FEDERAL TRADE COMMISSION, BUREAU OF COMPETITION, AND DEPARTMENT OF JUSTICE, ANTITRUST DIVISION, ANNUAL REPORT TO CONGRESS, FISCAL YEAR 2011, pursuant to subsection (j) of Section 7A of the Clayton Act, Hart-Scott-Rodino Antitrust Improvements Act of 1976, *available at* http://www.ftc.gov/bc/anncompreports.shtm. All percentage calculations and averages reported throughout are made simply by averaging and comparing the review and enforcement data included in these annual reports.

13 *See, e.g.*, BUDGET OF THE U.S. GOVERNMENT, FISCAL YEAR 2013, *available at* http://www.gpo.gov/fdsys/, at 774 (stating that allocated funds will remain available, provided that "fees collected for premerger notification filings . . . shall be retained and used for necessary expenses in this appropriation" and that the sum allocated in the general fund shall be reduced by offsetting collections received during the fiscal year).

14 *See* BUDGET OF THE U.S. GOVERNMENT, FISCAL YEAR 1998, *available at* http://www.gpo.gov/fdsys/, at 1062.

15 *See* BUDGET OF THE U.S. GOVERNMENT, FISCAL YEAR 1996, *available at* http://www.gpo.gov/fdsys/, at 998.

16 Hart-Scott-Rodino Antitrust Improvements Act of 1976, Pub. L. No. 94435, § 201, 90 Stat. 1390 (codified as amended at 15 U.S.C. § 18a), amending the Clayton Antitrust Act of 1914, Pub. L. No. 63-212, 38 Stat. 730. The regulations adopted by the FTC to implement the HSR Act appear at 16 C.F.R. §§ 801-03.

17 THE NATIONAL BUREAU OF ECONOMIC RESEARCH, U.S. BUSINESS CYCLE EXPANSIONS AND CONTRACTIONS, *available at* http://www.nber.org/cycles.html.

18 *See* United States v. Microsoft Corp., Civ. Action No. 98-1232 (CKK) (Nov. 12, 2002) (final judgment), *available at* http://www.justice.gov/atr/cases/f200400/200457.pdf.

19 *See* Press Release, Federal Trade Commission, FTC Wins Court Order Blocking Staples and Office Depot Merger (June 30, 1997), *available at* http://www.ftc.gov/opa/1997/06/stapdec.shtm; Press Release, Federal Trade Commission, FTC to Challenge Merger of Beech-Nut Nutrition Corp. and H.J. Heinz Co. (July 7, 2000), *available at* http://www.ftc.gov/opa/2000/07/heinz.shtm.

20 The HSR Act imposes an "initial waiting period" for agency review before the transaction can be completed, which, for most acquisitions, is 30 days. Filing parties may, however, request that the reviewing agency terminate the waiting period before the statutory period expires. A grant of early termination by an agency signals that the reviewing agency has determined not to take enforcement action against the merging parties during the waiting period. *See* FTC, Early Termination Notices under the Hart-Scott-Rodino Act, http://www.ftc.gov/bc/earlyterm/index.shtml.

21 Most transactions filed under the HSR Act are never "cleared", which is to say formally investigated, by one agency or the other. While the agencies will clear certain transactions that look like they warrant more than passing review to either the FTC or the DOJ, most filed mergers undergo only a preliminary review by FTC and DOJ staff and then either they are granted early termination or their waiting periods are allowed to expire. For example, in 2010, there were 1,166 transactions reported under the HSR Act and 1,128 eligible for agency review; of these, 222 were cleared to one agency or the other (149 to the FTC and 73 to the DOJ). The remaining 906 transactions eligible for agency review (or 80.3% of reported transactions) did not clear to either agency.

22 In the remaining 5% of reported transactions, the filings are incomplete, the transactions are exempt from reporting, or the transactions are simply non-reportable. *See, e.g.*, FEDERAL TRADE COMMISSION, BUREAU OF COMPETITION, AND DEPARTMENT OF JUSTICE, ANTITRUST DIVISION, ANNUAL REPORT TO CONGRESS, FISCAL YEAR 2011, Pursuant to Subsection (j) of Section 7A of the Clayton Act, Hart-Scott-Rodino Antitrust Improvements Act of 1976 (Thirty-Third Report), available at http://www.ftc.gov/bc/anncompreports.shtm, at Appendix A, n. 2 (stating that the adjusted figures in which the parties were eligible to receive a second request are calculated by omitting incomplete transactions, transactions reported pursuant to the exemption provisions of the HSR Act, and transactions that were found to be nonreportable).

23 The data provided for President Reagan exclude fiscal years 1981 and 1986, for which the number of transactions cleared to the agencies is unavailable in the annual HSR reports.

24 Several articles on the Stanford Law Review's website have recently picked up the debate over whether the Obama administration has "reinvigorated" antitrust enforcement, including merger enforcement, from both quantitative and qualitative perspectives. Daniel Crane argued that "merger statistics do not evidence 'reinvigoration' of merger enforcement under Obama," while Jonathan Baker and Carl Shapiro, both of whom served in the Obama administration, countered that "nothing in Daniel Crane's article seriously challenges our interpretation of the preliminary data as demonstrating that the necessary reinvigoration [under President Obama] has taken place." Daniel A. Crane, *Has the Obama Justice Department Reinvigorated Antitrust Enforcement?*, 65 STAN. L. REV. ONLINE 13, 16 (July 18, 2012), http://www.stanfordlawreview.org/online/obama-antitrust-enforcement; Jonathan B. Baker & Carl Shapiro, *Evaluating Merger Enforcement During the Obama Administration*, 65 STAN. L. REV. ONLINE 28, 34 (Aug. 21, 2012), http://www.stanfordlawreview.org/merger-enforcement-obama-administration (referencing Jonathan B. Baker & Carl Shapiro, *Reinvigorated Merger Enforcement in the Obama Administration*, Antitrust & Competition Pol'y Blog (June 25, 2012), http://lawprofessors.typepad.com/antitrustprof_blog/2012/06/reinvigorated-merger-enforcement-in-the-obama-administration.html); *see also* Daniel A. Crane, *The Obama Justice Department's Merger*

Enforcement Record: A Reply to Baker and Shapiro, 65 STAN. L. REV. ONLINE 41 (Sept. 6, 2012), http://www. stanfordlawreview.org/online/obama-merger-enforcement-response. We continue to believe, as Professors Crane, Baker, and Shapiro also acknowledge at various points in their exchange, that quantitative assessments of merger enforcement are—at their best—an insufficient metric for capturing the strength of a merger control regime.

25 *New FTC Chief Appoints Heads to Energy Bureau [sic.]*, WALL ST. J., Oct. 6, 1981; *FTC Appointments*, PLATTS OILGRAM NEWS, Oct. 8, 1981; *Muris Gets FTC Post*, ASSOCIATED PRESS, March 15, 1983.

26 Eileen V. Quigley, *Washington's Movers and Shakers*, THE NATIONAL JOURNAL, April 13, 1985; Nell Henderson, *New Antitrust Chief Prompts Uncertainties*, WASH. POST, Sept. 15, 1985; Nancy Lewis, *U.S. Lawyer Said to Lead Field for Appeals Bench*, WASH. POST, July 22, 1986; *Trust Busted*, AMERICAN BANKER WEEKLY REVIEW, Oct. 20, 1986; Ruth Marcus, *Rule Defends Antitrust Enforcement*, WASH. POST, Sept. 4, 1987.

27 As noted above, the agencies did not disclose how many transactions cleared to each agency in 1986; we therefore can compare issuances of second requests under AAG Ginsburg only on a comparative rather than absolute scale.

28 Eliza Newlin Carney, *Washington's Movers and Shakers*, THE NATIONAL JOURNAL, May 13, 1995; Rory J. O'Connor, *Senate Prepares to Confirm New Antitrust Chief*, SAN JOSE MERCURY NEWS, July 14, 1997; Mark Taylor, *Status Quo Expected from New FTC Director*, MODERN HEALTHCARE, August 9, 1999; John R. Wilke, *Klein to Step Down from Antitrust Unit in Washington*, WALL ST. JOURNAL, Sept. 21, 2000.

29 *Competition Director Susan Creighton to Leave FTC*, STATES NEWS SERVICE, Dec. 20, 2005; John R. Wilke, *New Antitrust Chief Has Full Plate*, WALL ST. J., Feb. 13, 2006; Press Release, Federal Trade Commission, Competition Director Jeffrey Schmidt to Leave FTC (Aug. 7, 2008), *available at* http://www.ftc.gov/opa/2008/08/bcchanges. shtm; Press Release, U.S. Department of Justice, Statement of Attorney General Michael B. Mukasey on the Resignation of Assistant Attorney General Thomas O. Barnett (Nov. 7, 2008), *available at* http://www.justice.gov/atr/ public/press_releases/2008/239277.htm; *Deborah A. Garza Acting Assistant Attorney General for Antitrust*, STATES NEWS SERVICE, Nov. 20, 2008.

Criminal Cartel Prosecution: Considerations on Attempts to Compensate Victims

ROXANN E. HENRY*

rhenry@mofo.com
Partner, Morrison & Foerster, LLP

Abstract

The United States has a long history of following criminal cartel prosecutions with private, civil, treble damage, and class actions. Around the world this model is under the microscope as various jurisdictions step up public enforcement and consider whether or how to compensate victims. Few, if any, see the U.S. system as a paragon of efficient redress. Much criticism focuses on the litigation process and its attendant burdens and expense, but it is also important to recognize that serious tensions arise between the private actions and public enforcement, and to examine the broader social welfare allocation results of the system. This paper notes some of the concerns that flow from the current system. It first analyzes the antitrust civil tremble damage class actions in the United States. It then explains the existing tensions between parallel criminal and civil actions and looks at potential alternatives to private enforcement in cases where the government has already devoted the resources to prosecute. Finally, it concludes that perhaps the time has come to debate the merits of handling victim claims for restitution as part of the U.S. criminal process and blocking private litigation purporting to accomplish victim redress on violations that are the subject of public enforcement.

I. Introduction

The United States has a long history of following criminal cartel prosecutions with private, civil, treble damage, and class actions. Around the world this model is under the microscope as various jurisdictions step up public enforcement and consider whether or how to compensate victims. Few, if any, see the U.S. system as a paragon of efficient redress. Much criticism focuses on the litigation process and its attendant burdens and expense, but it is also important to recognize that serious tensions arise between the private actions and public enforcement, and to examine the broader social welfare allocation results of the system. Moreover, judgments about deterrence all too often simply equate punishment with deterrent value and, thus, view increased punishment through private follow-on action as increased deterrence without further examination. This paper notes some of the concerns that flow from the current system and looks at potential alternatives to private enforcement in cases where the government has already devoted the resources to prosecute.[1] Perhaps the time has come to debate the merits of handling victim claims for restitution as part of the U.S. criminal process and blocking private litigation purporting to accomplish victim redress on violations that are the subject of public enforcement.

II. U.S. Antitrust Civil Treble Damage Class Actions

The situation involved in follow-on cartel class action litigation is very different from typical litigation involving dispute resolution between the parties or when a party seeks the protection of legal rights. By definition, a follow-on case is when the government does the work to establish a violation of law. It also may refer to private litigation commenced only upon the basis of the report of a government investigation. The key point is that the case depends upon the government. Even when the government concludes its prosecution, plaintiffs rely heavily on the existence of the government investigation to try to avoid dismissal and rely on the pressure of the government action to induce settlements. In these civil cases, plaintiffs' class action lawyers fight to take control over the litigation to garner a lucrative one-quarter to one-third of the settlement damage fund.[2] The lawyers, not the alleged victims, control the litigation process. The cases virtually never go to trial. The purported victims typically have no investment in the litigation, neither emotional nor pecuniary. They are not seeking to vindicate rights. As an inducement to be the named plaintiff in the representative action, the plaintiff lawyers typically ask the court for a bonus payment to the named plaintiff.

The court process takes a long time and cases may drag on for years until settled. It is well known that in private antitrust litigation typically high-priced experts digest and disgorge massive amounts of data to arrive at a calculation of the amount of damages. The experts hired by the defendants then offer their own massive amounts of data to rebut the findings of the expert or experts hired by the plaintiffs. The experts will undergo rigorous cross-examination. And, judges must review whether the experts are basing their conclusions on accepted scientific principles applied according to accepted scientific methods.[3] The extraordinary burden and expense of antitrust discovery have been recognized repeatedly, including by the U.S. Supreme Court.[4]

Many months, if not years, and many millions are spent in the civil litigation process. Yet, none of that money spent on the litigation process goes to the victims. The money goes to lawyers, experts, and supporting services, such as electronic database support that alone can cost well over a million dollars for a modest case. These costs do not even encompass the judicial resources and the time and burden on business executives that distracts from focusing on business.[5] Similarly, there are real foregone opportunity and business impairment costs to operating when a business is known to be facing the type of unquantified substantial potential liability that weighs on any defendant in the midst of treble damage antitrust class action litigation. These soft costs should not be underestimated and, because of the difficulty of quantification, are largely ignored.

III. Tensions between Parallel Criminal and Civil Actions

The government, plaintiffs, and defendants can lose important rights and protections when criminal and civil actions proceed in parallel. Similarly, some parties can seek to procure new advantages from the dual proceedings to which they otherwise would not be entitled.

One area where this tension has long been recognized is that the extraordinarily broad discovery rules in civil litigation can create interference with the criminal investigation. Indeed, it has not been uncommon for prosecutors to request a stay of some or all discovery in parallel civil proceedings. Sometimes plaintiffs do not object, as they would like the government to secure convictions that create a prima facia case in the civil litigation. But, sometimes the plaintiffs, especially after some convictions, would prefer the pressure of a faster time schedule to increase settlement pressure. In general, the government wins its request for stay. Last year, in a notable crack in the prosecutorial record of protecting its investigations, the court denied the government request in favor of plaintiffs continuing discovery against defendants.[6]

In another recent matter, last May, a judge in civil redress litigation pretrial proceedings regarding allegations of price fixing by three principal players in the packaged ice industry granted the direct purchaser plaintiffs' motion to compel the U.S. Department of Justice ("DOJ") to produce to them certain tape recordings made by the government during its investigation.[7] The government had enlisted the cooperation of certain individuals who agreed to participate in and tape record conversations with persons of interest, and the government had sole possession of the recordings. The government objected to the plaintiffs' subpoena to the government to procure the recordings. It argued sovereign immunity and various privileges, including the federal law enforcement privilege. The court rejected these arguments and forced the government's disclosure.

While in this instance, the government lost, from the perspective of the defendants, this case highlights a perplexing dilemma. Discoverability of government submissions in the context of cooperation on the government side presents a huge risk. In balancing the risks and rewards, the U.S. civil litigation weighs heavily *against* cooperating with government. As stated by some commentators, "[t]oday, targets of multijurisdictional investigations appear to face a dilemma: cooperate with governmental authorities or protect rights and defenses in U.S. Civil litigation."[8]

IV. Social Welfare Allocation Issues

A number of factors lead to questions whether the process and damages assessed through private cartel follow-on litigation result in a decrease or increase in social welfare. Are these actions helping or harming consumers? A strong case can be made that private cartel follow-on litigation merely penalizes the consumer once again.

In the United States, the rules in federal court provide that only the direct purchaser can recover damages. These corporate direct purchasers calculate their injury without regard to pass-on of any overcharge. Numerous state courts provide for indirect purchasers to sue also for damages. While indirect purchasers are often corporations, the possibility exists for consumer class-action litigation as well. Thus, the injured parties seeking damages recoveries are typically corporations with the not infrequent indirect consumer class action as well.[9]

The little examined secret in private follow-on class action distributions is how few of the alleged victims actually submit claims against the settlement funds created. Often plaintiffs' lawyers seek final approval of the settlements prior to completion of the claims process. This shields the disclosure of the paucity of claimants. But some judges insist upon reviewing this, and some data exists. In one recent settlement the claim response rate was 8.1% and that was measured only after shrinking the universe by those notices that were returned as undeliverable.[10] Plaintiffs' counsel noted that 8.1% is "well within the range of acceptability" as other settlements have 2%, 6.9% and 3.9% response rates.[11]

There simply is no basis to argue that antitrust class actions are the best way to provide consumer level redress. This point has been recognized repeatedly.[12] As consumers generally do not retain receipts or other proof of purchase, determining which consumers should receive how much is virtually impossible, even before taking into account other difficulties.[13]

With regard to the corporate plaintiffs and the corporate defendants, there are numerous reasons why these damage actions are neutral at best for social welfare and, more typically, affirmatively adverse. Judge Ginsburg has cogently explained that the punishment of shareholders, who likely are innocent of any conceivable wrongdoing and who may well have suffered as victims of it themselves, does not further social welfare. Similarly, and equally importantly, the author knows of no empirical research to support that the corporate recipients of these windfall damages use such monies in the furtherance of consumer benefits. And, there can be no question that the settlement amounts from the treble damage follow-on cases are viewed as windfalls to the corporate balance sheet.

The temporal disparity between when the wrongful activity occurred and when the costs and damages are paid also creates a number of issues. This is especially true for cartels that operated over a lengthy period. The injured direct purchasers likely long ago passed on overcharges, and the shareholders on either side are not the same as, respectively, the ones who benefited or were harmed. The wealth transfer goes from one hapless group of shareholders to a different, much happier group who suddenly finds itself enriched.

Moreover, if most all industry participants are finding themselves caught up in a cartel investigation, who truly bears the litigation and settlement costs? What happens when the cost of doing business goes up? Ultimately, it is hard to imagine that the consumers do not pay the price or at least bear a major part of the cost.

Perhaps the largest concern is whether the civil litigation affects the willingness of defendants to cooperate with governments. The highest price that consumers could pay for the purported benefits of private follow-on litigation is that fewer cartels are disclosed and prosecuted. While that would not be a result sought by government, plaintiffs' lawyers, or victims, the potential to kill the goose laying the golden eggs is real. No one today disputes the effectiveness of leniency programs and cooperation to robust government enforcement.

Many have claimed that higher fines and higher settlement amounts lead to greater deterrence. Yet, there is no support for a simplistic linear approach. No study of motivation has ever indicated any validity to the linear model. No empirical study supports the linear approach.[14] Moreover, for anyone who has spoken in depth with persons who have been conspirators in cartel activity regarding how and why they became involved, this model makes no sense.

First, it is important to consider that individuals ultimately need to make the decision whether to participate in a cartel. Corporations are composed of individuals. It is those individuals who make the decision whether to become a co-conspirator in a cartel. Few U.S. boards of directors have approved a corporation's participation in a hard-core cartel. Instead, each individual who facilitates a company's participation in a cartel must make an individual choice whether to do so. Some may do so at the behest of individuals in other companies and some at the request of individuals within their own company. Some may have originated the concept of a collusive arrangement and convinced others to join. In almost all instances of a U.S. corporation, the individual could choose not to participate and to report the request to counsel, to the government, or to the board of directors.

This begs the question of what is it that the corporate entity does and what the public interest would have it do. Corporations can mandate and monitor programs to educate officers and employees on the law and create a compliance culture. This type of activity can be viewed as a truly corporate act emanating from the board of directors. In many cases, a corporation that has been found guilty of cartel conduct had a policy in place demanding that officers and employees refrain from conspiring with competitors regarding prices or other competitively sensitive decisions. While a "policy" alone likely has little value without more, many companies expend a lot of resources to educate and monitor antitrust compliance. In some instances, the corporation has made extraordinary efforts to monitor activities of its officers and employees, sometimes only to see the individuals circumvent the efforts.[15] While such efforts may not always succeed in preventing individuals from going astray, the public interest is well served by such programs. Thus, one aspect of deterrence is to incentivize companies to make the effort and expend the resources to educate and monitor antitrust compliance.

While the linear model of increasing fines corresponding to increasing deterrence would not appear to be a rational methodology that is not to say that monetary payments play no role in deterrence. If the monetary penalty is truly small compared to the potential gain, a corporation is unlikely to expend resources on compliance efforts. Outside the United States, some cartel conduct that has surfaced is linked to historical cultures that accepted cartels as an acceptable business practice. High fines can be an important component to breaking this tradition. All this suggests that an important calibration of the monetary penalty needs to be implemented for effective deterrence.

The other side of effective deterrence needs to focus on the individual. In the recent AU Optronics trial, it has been reported that one of the key executives who pled guilty had his employer pay his fine, pay his salary while in prison and promised to save him his job immediately upon his return from the U.S. prison.[16] It is hard to imagine how this individual would view increasing monetary payments by the company as an effective deterrent. This scenario happens outside the United States on an unknown basis, but faced with potential shareholder suits and disclosure requirements, it is highly unlikely that such conduct occurs with any U.S. publicly held company, but, unfortunately U.S. companies still have been found guilty of cartel conduct. What this does dramatically illustrate is the concept that to affect individual decision-making requires something more than just money paid out by the corporation.[17]

V. Alternative Methods for Compensation and Deterrence

1. Fraud Claims

Virtually every jurisdiction already permits victims of fraud to sue for redress. The laws are clear, require specific causation, and focus on the specific relations between the parties to the claim. In a cartel situation, a buyer who knows of the cartel and accepts the price, knowing it to be one that has been agreed among competitors, cannot fairly be viewed as a "victim." This ability to seek fraud damages provides a safety net for instances where compensation should be provided. Admittedly, the recovery may not be the easy money of today, but a remedy exists.[18]

2. Fines and Consent Decrees

While deterrence is often cited as a reason to promote private civil damage actions, measuring the appropriate pecuniary amount to provide deterrence has never been a goal of private litigation, nor a by-product. Moreover, the notion of a need for private attorneys general simply does not apply in the context of today's follow-on cartel litigation. Years ago when this structure and concept were conceived, criminal fines were minimal, and the offense was only a misdemeanor. In that circumstance, an argument could be made that supplemental civil damages would further deterrence. Now, the government does the work to expose a violation and imposes huge fines. And when the action is brought merely on the basis of the report of a government investigation, it may well fall into the category of extortionate litigation that parties settle simply to avoid litigation costs.

On the other hand, the government has a range of options that provide it the ability to review all relevant circumstances and create an appropriate monetary penalty to meet the goals of deterrence, both individual and social.[19] The government may also insist upon the institution of compliance programs if specific deterrence is necessary. In the past, it was common for the U.S. government to enter into consent decrees along with plea agreements, which decrees required the company for a period of years to maintain a robust compliance program.

3. Criminal Restitution

The concept of handling victim recompense as part of the criminal sentencing process is not new. Today, the practice of combining redress and criminal punishment is frequently employed in the context of cartels affecting public procurement, albeit more typically through use of a supplemental settlement agreement than through court-ordered restitution. Perhaps more importantly, the concept is embedded into statutory sentencing requirements for federal crimes. Courts are required to impose a sentence mandating restitution unless the case falls into a specific statutory exception.[20]

Most criminal antitrust cases invoke the exception. Plea agreements with the Antitrust Division generally contain language similar to the following: "In light of the civil class action cases filed against the defendant, which potentially provide for a recovery of a multiple of actual damages, the United States agrees that it will not seek a restitution order for the offense charged in the Information."[21]

The prospect of handling victim claims as restitution has come to the forefront in two recent criminal cases. In the first case the prospect of restitution was simply raised by the court as a possibility; in the second, however, restitution was actually included in the settlement agreement between defendants and various government authorities, throwing a wrench squarely into civil plaintiffs' pursuit of a follow-on class action.

With regard to the first matter, Samsung SDI ("Samsung") agreed to plead guilty with regard to a price-fixing conspiracy related to color display tubes (CDTs).[22] The charging information alleged that Samsung participated in a conspiracy from at least January 1997 until at least March 2006, "to suppress and eliminate competition by fixing prices, reducing output and allocating market shares of CDTs to be sold in the United States and elsewhere." Pursuant to the agreement, Samsung agreed to pay a fine of $32 million.

Not surprisingly, Samsung SDI is also a defendant in various private civil case proceedings seeking trebled compensatory damages for price fixing of CDTs.[23] At the initial hearing on the criminal case, when the government and Samsung requested the court impose the sentence in accord with the plea agreement, the judge balked and raised the question whether he should impose a restitution requirement. He allowed the parties to reconsider the plea terms in light of his comments, and ultimately restitution was not required.[24] Nonetheless, the negative reaction of seemingly all parties except the judge to the prospect of handling redress for private antitrust victims as restitutionary relief in the context of criminal sentencing bears further attention.

The second matter pertains to the DOJ's investigation into anti-competitive conduct in the municipal bond market. In 2006, the Antitrust Division began an investigation into the competitive practices of providers and brokers of municipal bonds.[25] Soon thereafter multiple cities, states and other entities filed suits alleging price-fixing and bid-rigging in the municipal derivatives industry and seeking treble damages under the Clayton Act. The cases have since been consolidated into a single multidistrict litigation ("MDL") lawsuit.[26]

In December 2010, the DOJ entered an agreement with Bank of America, the amnesty applicant, under the terms of which Bank of America agreed to pay "restitution to federal and state agencies for its participation in a conspiracy to rig bids in the municipal bond derivatives market."[27] The DOJ has since entered into similar settlement agreements with UBS AG, JP Morgan, Wachovia, and GE Funding, requiring, among other conditions, that the parties pay restitution to persons or entities injured by their anticompetitive conduct in return for the DOJ's agreement not to prosecute.[28] Concurrently with their agreements with the DOJ, the parties entered into agreements with a number of government agencies and representatives, including a coalition of state attorneys general. The agreement with the latter specifically sets aside funds for restitution to municipalities harmed by the parties' anticompetitive conduct.[29] Under the terms of the agreement, persons and entities that seek compensation through the restitution fund cannot participate in the civil class action.

Immediately after the agreement was signed between the DOJ and Bank of America, plaintiffs' counsel in the civil class action complained to the court that the restitution agreement with the DOJ, which awards compensation directly to the purported victims, effectively circumvents the class action.[30] Unmentioned was the fact that the agreement also cuts plaintiffs' lawyers—and their compensation—out of the settlement. If the Antitrust Division reaches settlements with companies that include restitution, it erodes the class action plaintiffs lawyers' ability to recover large fees in these lawsuits.

Following the filing of various motions, the court ordered that before any notice of settlement was issued by the state attorneys general, the court would have to review and approve the notice, and that such notice must let claimants know that they may have rights under the class action.[31] Subsequent settlements have drawn similar criticism from plaintiffs' counsel and similar court orders.[32] The content of the notice was contentious, with state attorneys general indicating that class counsels' proposed language discouraged potential claimants from participating in the state attorney general settlement, while class counsel argued that the state attorneys general proposed notice did not sufficiently advise potential claimants of alternatives. After months of court filings and arguments, the final notice letter for the Bank of America settlement was issued in mid-November 2011.[33]

The relationship of civil treble damage litigation and restitution is not examined sufficiently often to understand entirely the interaction of the two. Arguably, if the court provided for restitution to victims as part of the criminal process, having no longer sustained injury to their business or property as a result of the violation, it is unclear whether the victims could continue to seek treble damages. As a matter of standing rules, it could be strongly argued that the victims no longer had standing to seek treble damages. In this manner, the use of treble damage class actions could be cut off in cases of follow-on cartel litigation while not affecting other types of civil antitrust litigation.[34] This procedure also would avoid the need for statutory reconstruction.

The extra burden on the government to request, quantify, and administer restitution to victims should not be taken lightly. On the other hand, the social welfare benefits may well justify the burden, and means may be found largely to privatize the burden through simplified procedures in the sentencing process.

VI. Conclusion

Whether the issue of victim compensation for criminal cartels could be handled in a manner that provided a far greater increase in social welfare than the current method of private civil follow-on treble damage class action litigation is a subject worth greater exploration. The potential for restitution proceedings as part of criminal sentencing may provide one alternative short of statutory reconstruction. In any event, as jurisdictions around the world contemplate systems for victim recompense, they would be well advised to scrutinize closely how well the U.S. system should be measured in terms of overall social welfare.

NOTES

* Ms. Henry would like to thank Sharon Connaughton, Associate at Cooley, LLP for her assistance. This paper builds on one earlier prepared for the ABA Antitrust Section's 2012 International Cartel Workshop.

1 This paper does not address the circumstances of private litigation, even in the cartel area, that is not based upon government proceedings. Nor does it address private litigation outside the cartel area even when the government may have taken enforcement action. Other considerations apply to both of those circumstances.

2 *See* R. Kriger, *Clash of the Class Action Law Firms*, LAW 360 (Oct. 3, 2011).

3 Daubert v. Merrell Dow Pharmaceuticals, Inc., 509 U.S. 579, 597 (1993).

4 Bell Atlantic Corp. v. Twombly, 550 U.S. 544, 558-560 (2007).

5 Nor do these costs reflect the potential that has been noted by Bill Kovacic and others that the perceived punitive excesses of the treble damage remedy may well affect judicial decision-making to alter liability rules in ways that make government enforcement more difficult. William E. Kovacic, *The Intellectual DNA of Modern U.S. Competition Law for Dominant Firm Conduct: The Chicago/Harvard Double Helix*, 2007 COLUM. BUS. L. REV. 1, 62; *see also* Stephen Calkins, *Summary Judgment, Motions to Dismiss, and Other Examples of Equilibrating Tendencies in the Antitrust System*, 74 GEO. L. J. 1065, 1088-98 (1986).

6 *In re* Optical Disk Drive Prods. Antitrust Litig., 3:10-MD-02143-RS (N.D. Cal. June 24, 2010). The court did indicate that it might reconsider on a case-by-case basis. *Id.*

7 *In re* Packaged Ice Antitrust Litigation, 2011 U.S. Dist. LEXIS 51116, Case No. 08-MD-01952 (E.D. Mich., Docket 363, filed May 10, 2011).

8 Joy Fuyuno & Jason K. Sonoda, *The Hidden Cost of Cooperation: Discoverability of U.S. and Foreign Governmental Submissions in Private Litigation*, 2008 International Cartel Workshop 2-3 (Jan. 30-Feb. 1, 2008).

9   Title III of the Hart-Scott-Rodino Act does grant *stats parens patriae* authority to sue under the Sherman Act on behalf of natural persons who reside in their respective state. 15 U.S. C. §§ 15c-15h. The state may sue to recover treble damages incurred by the natural persons as direct purchasers and may also recover the state's attorneys fees. The court may distribute the damages in its discretion or award to the state as a civil penalty "subject in either case to the requirement that any distribution procedure adopted afford each person a reasonable opportunity to secure his appropriate portion of the net monetary relief." *Id*. § 15c.

10   Plaintiff's Supplemental Memorandum of Law in Support of Motion for Final Approval of Proposed Settlement Agreements With (1) Virginia Harbor Services, Inc., Robert B. Taylor, and William Alan Potts; and (2) Gerald Thermos Board of Commissioners of the Port of New Orleans v. Virginia Harbor Services, Inc., No. SACV11-00437-GW (filed January 19, 2012).

11   This percentage is well within the range of acceptability for class action settlements. *See, e.g.*, Touhey v. United States, No. EDCV 08-01418, 2011 WL 3179036, at *7-8 (C.D. Cal. July 25, 2011) (finding a 2% response rate acceptable – 38 responses from 1,875 mailed notices); *In re* Cardizem CD Antitrust Litigation, 218 F.R.D. 508, 527 (E.D. Mich. 2003) (finding a 6.9% response rate acceptable – 1,800 responses from 26,000 mailed notices); *In re* New Motor Vehicles Canadian Export Antit. Litig., MDL no. 1532, 2011 WL 1398485, at *3 (D. Maine April 13, 2011) (finding favorable class reaction in a 3.9% response rate – 438,169 claims submitted from 11.3 million eligible claimants); La Count Decl. ¶ 18 (Based on my experience in cases where claims with documentation of purchases are required and involving the type of product at issue here, this response rate falls within an acceptable range). *Id*.

12   *See e.g.*, Albert A. Foer, *Enhancing Competition Through the Cy Pres Remedy: Suggested Best Practices*, 24 ANTI-TRUST 86 (2010).

13   *Id*.

14   Professors Lande and David purported to do an empirical study to assess whether private enforcement of the anti-trust laws serve the intended purposes and promote the public interest and provide an example of precisely this linear approach. R. Lande & J. Davis, *Benefits from Private Antitrust Enforcement: an Analysis of Forty Cases*, UNIVERSITY OF SAN FRANCISCO LAW RESEARCH PAPER No. 2010-07, *available at* http://ssm.com/abstract=1090661. What they did in the study was to look at the amount of money paid out in 40 large, recent private antitrust cases, choosing only those that had a successful outcome. They claim that "[t]he results of the Study [] showed that private litigation probably does more to deter antitrust violations than all the fines and incarceration imposed as a result of criminal enforcement by the DOJ. We do not know of any past study that has documented that private enforcement has such a significant deterrence effect as compared to DOJ criminal enforcement." Based only on the fact that more money was paid out in private cases than in criminal antitrust fines imposed during the same period, the professors boldly conclude that "private litigation provides more than four times the deterrence of the criminal fine." They make the same comparison comparing private case payments to criminal fines for only those cases that resulted in criminal fines or prisons sentences. Thereafter they note that "[r]egardless of which figure we use, we may safely conclude that the private cases provided far more deterrence than the criminal antitrust fines." The professors then take their analysis one step further and make an assumption pulled from thin air to conclude that they "believe that the deterrence effect of being sentenced to a year of confinement is likely significantly less than $5 million." They generously then note that even if they used "$10 million for the equivalent value of a year's imprisonment (an estimate we believe is much too high)", the result would be the same.

15   There is the instance of the general counsel who was duped by her officers when attending a trade association meeting through an elaborate fake first-time meeting of competitors who had been conspiring for years. Similarly, the stories abound of individuals using personal email accounts to avoid the company finding out about competitor communications. In one instance known to the author, the individual who engaged in collusion was aware that the company had fired other employees for communications with competitors in violation of company policy preventing such communications.

16   *See, e.g.*, Chunghwa Bribed Worker to Plead Guilty in LCD Case: AUO, LAW360 (Jan. 23, 2012).

17   Increasing the sense of likelihood that such conduct will be exposed is the most important deterrent for most individuals, and leniency programs are gaining ground in this effort. Prison acts as a strong to deterrent to most individuals in the social and employment milieu where they can affect a company's bidding or pricing if they believe there is the possibility of getting caught. Moreover, shaming, employment consequences and other collateral consequences, particularly from criminal proceedings, can have a dramatic impact. While all of these issues deserve greater exploration, this paper focuses on the monetary side of deterrence, particularly in terms of whether private claims are necessary to deter wrongful conduct.

18   There certainly seems no reason to incentivize the bringing of these cases given the alacrity of plaintiffs' lawyers leaping forward to bring them. Moreover, the notion of any need for treble damages to compensate for risks seems absurd when the government has established a violation.

19   In addition to imposing penalties and fines, the DOJ has recently added the equitable remedy of disgorgement to its arsenal of options to use in fashioning appropriate monetary remedies for Sherman Act violations. In United States v. KeySpan Corp., No. 10-cv-1415 (S.D.N.Y. Feb. 2, 2011), the court approved a DOJ settlement agreement under the terms of which the defendant, KeySpan Corporation, was required to disgorge profits resulting from anticompetitive activities. The DOJ complaint alleged that KeySpan entered into an agreement to restrain competition in the New York City electricity market. The court's holding was significant in that it was the first time the DOJ sought disgorgement in a civil suit for a Sherman Act violation. When making its decision, the court noted that the defendant's anticompetitive conduct had ceased, the derivative instrument used to manipulate the market had expired, no restitution to New York City consumers was available, and there were no assets that could be divested. Accordingly, the court recognized that failure to impose a disgorgement remedy would have "incentivized other generators to manipulate electricity markets using derivative instruments that expire in the short term, with

the understanding that they will be permitted to retain their earnings because restitution to consumers is unavailable." Investment bank Morgan Stanley has also agreed to disgorgement of profits for its participation in the electricity market manipulation agreement. United States v. Morgan Stanley, No. 11-civ-6875 (S.D.N.Y. filed Sep. 30, 2011).

20 18 U.S.C. § 3663A(c) provides for mandatory restitution to victims for certain crimes; for example, "in which an identifiable victim or victims has suffered a physical injury or pecuniary loss." § 3663A(c)(1)(B). There is one statutory exception to mandatory restitution for Title 18 property offenses where ˝(A) the number of identifiable victims is so large as to make restitution impracticable; or (B) determining complex issues of fact related to the cause or amount of the victim's losses would complicate or prolong the sentencing process to a degree that the need to provide restitution to any victim is outweighed by the burden on the sentencing process." 18 U.S.C. § 3663A(c)(3).

21 Plea Agreement, United States v. Akzo Nobel Chemicals International B.V., No. CR 06-0160 MMC (N.D. Cal. May 17, 2006), *available at* http://www.justice.gov/atr/cases/f216300/216369.pdf.

22 DOJ, Samsung SDI Agrees to Plead Guilty in Color Display to Price-Fixing Conspiracy, *See Press Release*, (Mar. 18, 2011), *available at:* http://www.justice.gov/opa/pr/2011/March/11-at-350.html. *See also* United States v. Samsung SDI Co., Ltd., No. 11-cr-00162-WHA-1 (N.D. Cal. Mar. 18, 2011), ECF No. 1.

23 *See In re* Cathode Ray Tube (CRT) Antitrust Litigation, MDL No. 1917, 3:07-cv-05944-SC (N.D. Cal. filed Nov. 29, 2007).

24 The court imposed its sentence on August 17, 2011, accepting the $32 million plea agreement with no restitution apparently based on in camera materials related to the defendant's substantial cooperation. *See* Pamela MacLean & Karen Gullo, *Samsung SDI's Plea Deal in Price Fixing Case Blocked*, Bloomberg, Apr. 20, 2011 *available at* http://www.bloomberg.com/news/2011-04-20/samsung-sdi-s-32-million-plea-deal-with-u-s-in-price-fixing-blocked.html. For the judgment, *see* United States v. Samsung SDI Company, LTD, 3:11-cr-00162 -WHA (N.D. Cal. Aug. 19, 2011).

25 *See* William Selway & Martin Z. Braun, *U.S. Subpoenas Muni Firms, Seizes Papers in Probe*, Bloomberg, Nov. 16, 2006, *available at* http://www.bloomberg.com/apps/news?pid=email_en&refer=home&sid=aDrqOJHmHQLQ.

26 *In re* Municipal Derivatives Antitrust Litigation, MDL No. 1950, Master Docket No. 08-2516 (VM) (GWG) (S.D.N.Y).

27 *See*, DOJ, Bank of America Agrees to Pay $137.3 Million in Restitution to Federal and State Agencies as a Condition of the Justice Department's Antitrust Corporate Leniency Program, Press Release (Dec. 7, 2010), *available at:* http://www.justice.gov/opa/pr/2010/December/10-at-1400.html.

28 DOJ, UBS AG Admits to Anticompetitive Conduct by Former Employees in the Municipal Bond Investments Market and Agrees to Pay $160 Million to Federal and State Agencies, Press Release, (May 4, 2011), *available at:* http://www.justice.gov/opa/pr/2011/May/11-at-567.html; DOJ, JPMorgan Chase Admits to Anticompetitive Conduct by Former Employees in the Municipal Bond Investments Market and Agrees to Pay $228 Million to Federal and State Agencies, Press Release, (July 7, 2011), *available at:* http://www.justice.gov/opa/pr/2011/July/11-at-890.html; DOJ, Wachovia Bank N.A. Admits to Anticompetitive Conduct by Former Employees in the Municipal Bond Investments Market and Agrees to Pay $148 Million to Federal and State Agencies, Press Release, (Dec. 4, 2011), *available at:* http://www.justice.gov/opa/pr/2011/December/11-at-1597.html ; DOJ, GE Funding Capital Market Services Inc. Admits to Anticompetitive Conduct by Former Traders in the Municipal Bond Investments Market and Agrees to Pay $70 Million to Federal and State Agencies, Press Release, (Dec. 23, 2011), *available at:* http://www.justice.gov/opa/pr/2011/December/11-at-1706.html.

29 Agreement Among the Attorneys General of the States and Commonwealths of Alabama, California, Connecticut, Florida, Illinois, Kansas, Maryland, Massachusetts, Michigan, Missouri, Montana, Nevada, New Jersey, New York, North Carolina, Ohio, Oregon, Pennsylvania, South Carolina and Texas and Bank of America Corporation dated December 7, 2010, *available at*: http://www.stateagmunisettlement.com/docs/BOA%20Settlement%20Agreement%20with%20scanned%20signatures.pdf.

30 Letter from Interim Co-Lead Class Counsel Michael D. Hausfeld of Hausfeld LLP to the Honorable Victor Marrero, (Doc. No. 1192), In re Municipal Derivatives Antitrust Litigation, MDL No. 1950, Master Docket No. 08-2516 (VM) (GWG) (S.D.N.Y. December 14, 2010).

31 Order, (Doc. No. 1253), *In re* Municipal Derivatives Antitrust Litigation, MDL No. 1950, Master Docket No. 08-2516 (VM) (GWG) (S.D.N.Y. Mar. 1, 2011).

32 Letter from Seth Ard of Susman Godfrey LLP to the Honorable Victor Marrero, dated May 9, 2011 (Doc. No. 1329), *In re* Municipal Derivatives Antitrust Litigation, MDL No. 1950, Master Docket No. 08-2516 (VM) (GWG) (S.D.N.Y.) (complaining regarding the UBS AG settlement); Letter from Elinor R. Hoffman, Assistant Attorney General, State of New York, to the Honorable Victor Marrero, dated July 12, 2011 (Doc. No. 1533) (responding to Interim Class Counsel's complaint regarding the JP Morgan settlement).

33 GE Funding Capital Market Services Inc. reached a similar arrangement in connection with municipal bond trading bid rigging allegations with a $70 million settlement including about $34 million to settle state disgorgement, and interest to be returned to municipalities who suffered the injury. The Antitrust Division of DOJ agreed not to prosecute based on GE's willingness to admit wrongdoing, its settlement commitments, the promise to take corrective measures, and cooperation. S.E.C. v. GE Funding Capital Market Services, Inc., Case No. 2:11-cv-07465 (D. N. J. (Dec. 23, 2011).

34 The concept of replacing private damages with a system of fines to "eliminate the perverse incentives and misinformation effects and reparation costs" inherent in the current treble damage system is not new. William Breit & Kenneth G. Elzinga, *Private Antitrust Enforcement: The New Learning*, 28 J.L. & Econ. 405, 440 (1985). That approach, however, ignored that restitution may, at times, be appropriate, and it would also require legislation that in the United States is not likely to happen.

The Quality of Mercy and the Quality of Justice: Reflections on the Discovery of Leniency Documents and Private Actions for Damages in the European Union

Clifford A. Jones

Clifford.Jones@outlook.com

Associate In Law and Lecturer, Center for Governmental Responsibility,
University of Florida Levin College of Law

Abstract

This article addresses the apparent increasing tensions between the Commissions leniency policy and the rights of private damages claimants under Article 101 TFEU to obtain some types of documents gathered in the course of Commission enforcement proceedings concerning cartels. It attempts to evaluate the extent to which private actions threaten public enforcement and how the courts should balance competing concerns. Several recent judgments of national courts in the UK and Germany as well as decisions of the General Court and European Court of Justice are considered, and an approach to disclosure of leniency documents is offered that seeks to support private damages claims without impeding cartel enforcement.

Portia: *"The quality of mercy is not strain'd,*
It droppeth as the gentle rain from heaven
Upon the place beneath: it is twice blest;
It blesseth him that gives and him that takes...."[1]

I. Introduction

As the European Union's approach to competition enforcement has evolved from its origins as a 'Commission-centric' administrative model with a monopoly on exemptions toward a more pluralistic system featuring enforcement activity by not only the Commission but also National Competition Authorities (NCAs), and increasingly, private actions for damages, the possible tensions created by parallel and/or sequential proceedings in national courts and NCAs have risen to the surface.[2] Two developments in particular have brought these heightened tensions into focus.

First, the efforts of the Commission to enhance enforcement of EU competition rules (Articles 101 and 102 of the Treaty on the Functioning of the European Union, TFEU, in particular) over several decades have increasingly begun to bear fruit in the form of an increase in private damages claims in national courts. The increase so far can be attributed to a combination of judgments of the European Court of Justice (ECJ) recognizing that private parties have rights to damages under EU law that national courts must protect,[3] the decentralization of enforcement under Regulation 1/2003,[4] changes in some national court systems meant to facilitate private damages claims, and the possible adoption of EU-wide rules facilitating collective redress for consumers in general and private damages actions under competition rules in particular.[5]

Second, the Commission's efforts to increase the effectiveness of its own enforcement efforts with regard to some of the most serious infringements of the EU competition rules have led the Commission (and many Member States) to adopt "leniency" policies in which undertakings who meet the specified conditions may exchange information and evidence for whole or partial immunity from Commission or NCA-imposed fines. These leniency policies, generally modeled after those first adopted by the USA's Department of Justice (DOJ) for criminal violations of the U.S. Sherman Antitrust Act, have been regarded as an unqualified success in promoting the identification and punishment of price-fixing and other cartel activity.

Both private actions and leniency policies broadly pursue the objectives of preventing, penalizing, or deterring infringements of the competition rules or compensating consumers who are victimized by them. There is thus no small irony in the fact that the Commission and NCAs now fear that the growth of private enforcement actions may threaten the effectiveness of their leniency policies in that victims of cartel activity such as price-fixing increasingly seek access to documents in the possession of the Commission, an NCA, or cartel members that were created or furnished in connection with the operation of a leniency policy administered by the Commission or an NCA for the purpose of obtaining compensation in a private damages action in national courts. The fear is that if firms engaged in cartel behavior think their evidentiary submissions will be available to cartel victims to prove damage claims against them, cartel members will be less likely to seek immunity or reductions in fines under the leniency programs, since financial savings in fines from assisting a competition authority enforcer might be reduced by having to pay private damages claims. Absent evidence induced by promises of mercy, competition authorities fear they will be unable to prosecute as many cartels or impose fines at a level sufficient to deter or punish cartel conduct effectively. In short, the EU Commission and its brethren NCAs fear that discovery of leniency documents will undermine their 'quality of mercy'.

The Commission and NCAs have responded to this perceived conflict by assuring leniency applicants that their submissions will not be made available to private litigants and resisting efforts by private plaintiffs to obtain them. In turn, private plaintiffs driven in part by the general inadequacy of discovery rules in most European national court systems, have sought to obtain leniency documents from the Commission, NCAs, and cartel members and even sometimes in the courts of the USA under the more liberal discovery provisions of the Federal Rules of Civil Procedure. Private plaintiffs fear that competition authorities' suppression of documents probative of cartel violations impairs their right to compensation under EU and national law and undermines the quality of justice.

In a trilogy of recent decisions, the European Courts have begun to address the extent to which documents possessed by competition authorities may be subject to disclosure to private claimants for use in claiming damages under EU and national law. This chapter analyzes the judgments of the ECJ in *Pfleiderer*[6] and *MyTravel*[7] and the General Court in *CDC Hydrogen Peroxide*[8] and attempts to assess their implications for both the future of leniency programs and private damages claims. I attempt to answer the question of whether there are genuine conflicts between the interests of EU and national competition authorities and those of private damages claimants, and how those interests ought to be balanced.

II. Leniency Programs in the EU and USA

The leniency programs in the EU drew their initial inspiration from the success of the program adopted by the U.S. Department of Justice Antitrust Division (DOJ), beginning in 1978, and substantially revised in 1993. The DOJ's original 1978 leniency policy was a qualified success in that it attracted an average of one applicant per month, but the 1993 revision aimed at clarifying the policy and offering more specific guarantees of lenient treatment proved enormously more successful. DOJ's Scott Hammond has noted that leniency applications increased 20-fold after the 1993 revision and that the leniency policy is now the most effective cartel detection and punishment tool available to the DOJ, more effective than all other tools combined.[9]

Enhancements to the DOJ leniency policy have included the adoption of a "marker" system by which a leniency applicant secures its place as first in the door to seek leniency while receiving a (limited) period of time to "perfect" its marker by providing details of cartel activity after further internal investigation when the applicant does not yet have full knowledge of conduct and documents at the time of initial application.[10] In addition, the DOJ's "Amnesty-Plus" program allows leniency applicants additional relief from punishment when the applicant who has participated in one cartel reveals the existence of one or more other cartels in different products or industries. Hammond estimates that fully fifty percent of the DOJ's international cartel investigations result from previously unknown cartels revealed through its Amnesty Plus program.[11]

The success of the DOJ's amnesty program has spurred other competition jurisdictions to adopt broadly similar programs to enhance detection and punishment of cartel behavior. While in 1978 only the DOJ operated a leniency program, today over fifty antitrust jurisdictions have such programs,[12] including the EU and twenty-five of its presently twenty-seven Member States.

The basic elements of the DOJ leniency program, in summary, are that the DOJ agrees not to prosecute an applicant who first provides the DOJ with information (Type A leniency) about the antitrust violation, cooperates fully in assisting the DOJ with proof of the violation, ceases to participate in the cartel, and was not the originator of the cartel activity and did not coerce others to participate.[13] Where possible, the amnesty applicant must make restitution to victims of the antitrust violation. In return, the applicant and its officers, directors, and employees receive complete immunity from prosecution, fines, or jail sentences and confidentiality as to their identity as informants. Only one firm can receive full leniency, and there is no partial immunity or reduction in fines available to the second firm in the door.

Type B leniency is available to the first applicant in those situations where the DOJ has already received information about the violation, and may even have begun an investigation, but the DOJ does not yet have enough evidence to sustain a conviction against the company, and the applicant is the first to come forward and apply for leniency. Other criteria are similar or identical to those applicable to Type A leniency, including the obligation where possible to make restitution. Only the first applicant can receive leniency; there is no reduction in fines for later applicants.

The DOJ's leniency program does nothing to protect any cartel participants from civil damages actions by victims; on the contrary, any court judgment obtained by the DOJ serves as prima facie proof of a violation in Federal court and may be used as the basis for private claims under the famous treble damages actions under the U.S. Sherman Antitrust Act regardless of whether leniency is given. Moreover, receipt of leniency obligates recipients to provide restitution to victims where possible. Under the Antitrust Criminal Penalties and Enforcement Reform Act (2004), a leniency recipient may apply for relief from a treble-damages verdict (e.g., limit the award to single damages without joint and several liability) if it satisfies the trial court in the civil trial that it has fully cooperated with the plaintiffs in the damages action, separate from any cooperation given to the DOJ.

1. A Brief History of the EU Leniency Program

The first official EU leniency program was adopted in 1996 in the form of a Commission 'Notice on the non-imposition or reduction of cartel fines',[14] and it was subsequently amended in 2002[15] and 2006.[16] Prior to the 1996 Notice, cartel cases had not been a priority effort of the Commission's enforcement caseload, representing only about one case per year.[17] The effect of the leniency policy on EU anti-cartel efforts is shown by the rise in cartel prohibition decisions from an average of one or two per year prior to the Notice to an average of seven or eight per year following the Notice. From 2002 through 2008, the Commission issued fifty-two statements of objections of which forty-six were derived from information provided by leniency applicants.[18] Although there is no doubt that there has been a genuinely significant increase in cartel detection and punishment under the various EU Leniency Notices, about half of leniency applications are derivative in the sense that the EU application was made by applicants who had previously decided to seek leniency from the DOJ with regard to an international cartel and sought complementary leniency in the EU.[19] It is likely that few of those applicants would have sought leniency from the EU in the absence of the more severe criminal sanctions on offer in the U.S.[20] Connor's recent examination of thirteen cartel fining decisions rendered by the Commission since the adoption of the 2006 Fining Guidelines indicates that twelve of the thirteen cartel decisions involved granting of whole or partial leniency to one or more applicants.[21]

2. Key Elements of Leniency Programs in the EU

Under the most recent EU Leniency Notice (2006), there are features similar to some but not all of the features of the DOJ program. Total immunity from fines is available to the first leniency applicant (only) who brings a previously undiscovered cartel to the attention of the E.C Commission. If the Commission has previously discovered or is already investigating the cartel, the first applicant may still obtain total immunity from fines if its evidence enables the Commission to prove the infringement. Other conditions including complete cooperation with the Commission, termination of infringement, non-disclosure of the leniency application, and non-coercion of other participants are also required to be met to benefit from immunity. The Commission does not impose any obligation to make restitution to victims of the cartel.

The Commission's Leniency Notice also provides for a partial reduction in fines to applicants who are not first to seek leniency, but only the first applicant receives total immunity. Second or later applicants who provide evidence not in the Commission's possession that provides "significant added value"—evidence that reinforces the Commission's ability to prove the infringement—may receive a reduction in a range determined by the order in which they apply to the Commission. The second applicant can receive a reduction in the fine which would otherwise have been assessed of 30-50 percent; the third firm can receive a reduction of 20-30 percent, and subsequent applicants can receive a 20 percent reduction in fine. Thus, when multiple cartel members receive whole or partial immunity, the amount of total fines assessed can be greatly reduced. The most extreme case noted by Connor under the 2006 Fining Guidelines was the *Sodium Chlorate* cartel, in which two of the four cartel members received 100 percent leniency and 50 percent leniency respectively, so that total actual fines awarded were relatively lenient.[22]

Generally speaking, an applicant initiates a leniency request under the EU Notice by submitting a "corporate statement" in writing or orally,[23] in which it describes the cartel and its participation in detail and submits relevant evidence in its possession. The evidence submitted with the statement generally consists of pre-existing contemporaneous documents evidencing the infringement. The duty of cooperation imposed on leniency applicants continues after the initial application throughout the administrative process. The duty of secrecy concerning the fact and content of the leniency application imposed on leniency applicants exists until such time as the Commission issues a Statement of Objections. The Commission does not make a final decision on immunity from or reduction of fines until the conclusion of the administrative process, at which time it sets the fine owed after accounting for a reduction in fine based on the leniency applicant's cooperation throughout the process. The Commission's final decision identifies those firms which received leniency and the percentage amount (100 percent to 20 percent) of reduction in fine allowed.[24]

3. The Definition and Scope of Leniency Documents in the EU

In order to examine in detail the issues raised by attempts to obtain leniency documents for use in civil damages claims, it is necessary to further define and identify exactly what documents are involved, as the weight of the various interests involved may vary according to the character of a particular document. The Commission's file includes several different types of documents that potential claimants have sought to discover, although not all are technically leniency documents. For purposes of this chapter, "leniency documents" may include the following:

1. The "Corporate Statement", whether written or oral and transcribed [Category A].

2. Pre-existing Documents supplied by the leniency applicant voluntarily, often submitted with or following the corporate statement [Category B].

3. Documents seized by the Commission in "dawn raids", whether from a leniency applicant or another alleged cartel member [Category C].

4. Internal memoranda of Commission DG Comp or Legal Service staff [Category D].

5. Indexes of documents in Commission file [Category E].

III. A 2011 Transparency Trilogy: Pfleiderer, MyTravel, CDC Hydrogen Peroxide

1. Pfleiderer

In *Pfleiderer v. Bundeskartellamt*, the Grand Chamber of the ECJ considered a preliminary reference from the Amtsgericht Bonn on whether Arts. 11 and 12 of Regulation 1/2003 dealing with cooperation and information sharing among the EU Commission and Member States precluded granting access to leniency documents obtained by the Bundeskartellamt (BKA) from leniency applicants after the closure of the proceedings. Germany operated a national leniency policy consistent with the EU's Model Leniency Policy. Pfleiderer was a purchaser of décor paper from price-fixing cartel members in an amount exceeding €60 million and desired to bring a damages claim for compensation. German law considered victims of the cartel as having a legitimate interest and rights of access to the BKA file, but the BKA objected to providing access to certain leniency documents, including corporate statements and documents submitted voluntarily in cooperation with the BKA [Category A and B documents]. The BKA also refused to provide access to documents seized in dawn raids from cartel participants [Category C] which presumably may have included copies of some documents falling into Category B as well.

Advocate General Mazák expressed the opinion that corporate statements under the leniency policy [Category A] should not be disclosed,[25] even though the ability of claimants to recover damages would be hindered, but that pre-existing documents [Category B and C] could not be shielded from disclosure since they were not prepared in anticipation of a leniency application.[26] However, the Advocate General also considered that in Member States such as Germany where the BKA infringement findings were binding on national courts in subsequent damages actions, access should not be given to documents voluntarily submitted in the course of the leniency procedure as they were unnecessary to an effective remedy and fair trial.[27]

While Advocate General Mazák took the view that the balance of EU interests in effective leniency programs favored non-disclosure of corporate statements prepared for a leniency application but that the claimants' interest in an effective remedy generally favoured disclosure of pre-existing documents, even if submitted together with a corporate statement, the Grand Chamber judgment of the Court of Justice did not adopt this categorical approach. Instead, the ECJ took the view that the EU interests involved had to be balanced by the national court on a case-by-case basis, provided that national rules on access to leniency documents had to provide equivalent remedies to those provided in national law and could not make it excessively difficult or practically impossible to protect EU rights. The key language of the Court's judgment states:

> 25. However, as maintained by the Commission and the Member States which have submitted observations, leniency programs are useful tools if efforts to uncover and bring to an end infringements of competition rules are to be effective and serve, therefore, the objective of effective application of Articles 101 TFEU and 102 TFEU.

> 26. The effectiveness of those programs could, however, be compromised if documents relating to a leniency procedure were disclosed to persons wishing to bring an action for damages, even if the national competition authorities were to grant to the applicant for leniency exemption, in whole or in part, from the fine which they could have imposed.

27. The view can reasonably be taken that a person involved in an infringement of competition law, faced with the possibility of such disclosure, would be deterred from taking the opportunity offered by such leniency programs, particularly when, pursuant to Articles 11 and 12 of Regulation No. 1/2003, the Commission and the national competition authorities might exchange information which that person has voluntarily provided.

28. Nevertheless, it is settled case-law that any individual has the right to claim damages for loss caused to him by conduct which is liable to restrict or distort competition (see Case C 453/99 Courage and Crehan [2001] ECR I 6297, paragraphs 24 and 26, and Joined Cases C 295/04 to C 298/04 Manfredi and Others [2006] ECR I 6619, paragraphs 59 and 61).

29. The existence of such a right strengthens the working of the Community competition rules and discourages agreements or practices, frequently covert, which are liable to restrict or distort competition. From that point of view, actions for damages before national courts can make a significant contribution to the maintenance of effective competition in the European Union (Courage and Crehan , paragraph 27).

30. Accordingly, in the consideration of an application for access to documents relating to a leniency program submitted by a person who is seeking to obtain damages from another person who has taken advantage of such a leniency program, it is necessary to ensure that the applicable national rules are not less favorable than those governing similar domestic claims and that they do not operate in such a way as to make it practically impossible or excessively difficult to obtain such compensation (see, to that effect, Courage and Crehan, paragraph 29) and to weigh the respective interests in favor of disclosure of the information and in favor of the protection of that information provided voluntarily by the applicant for leniency.

31. That weighing exercise can be conducted by the national courts and tribunals only on a case by case basis, according to national law, and taking into account all the relevant factors in the case.

32. In the light of the foregoing, the answer to the question referred is that the provisions of European Union law on cartels, and in particular Regulation No 1/2003, must be interpreted as not precluding a person who has been adversely affected by an infringement of European Union competition law and is seeking to obtain damages from being granted access to documents relating to a leniency procedure involving the perpetrator of that infringement. It is, however, for the courts and tribunals of the Member States, on the basis of their national law, to determine the conditions under which such access must be permitted or refused by weighing the interests protected by European Union law.

In my view, the most important implications of the *Pfleiderer* judgment are first, that EU law does not establish a hierarchy between enforcement of the competition rules by the Commission or Member State competition authorities and enforcement by private parties seeking damages; second, the assurances of confidentiality contained in Commission or Member State Leniency Notices or policies are not binding on the courts of the Member States; and, third, leniency policies may not a priori preclude the possibility of access to documents needed by private parties to effectively obtain a remedy in national courts. Rather, the interests on both sides must be weighed in the concrete on a case-by-case basis to determine when and to what extent access will be granted.

For leniency applicants, the refusal of the ECJ to categorically eliminate the possibility of private plaintiffs having access to leniency documents may have been disappointing, and some critics have complained about the lack of legal certainty which now may be present. However, it is difficult to see on what basis the ECJ could have ruled differently given the interests at stake and the absence of binding legislation at EU level. The Commission has suggested that it now intends to legislate in this area, but it remains to be seen how much time will pass before such legislation may be adopted, if ever. Moreover, as discussed in more detail below, the competing legitimate interests under EU law are multiple and do not lend themselves well to inflexible assessment.

Following the Grand Chamber judgment, the *Pfleiderer* case returned to the Amtsgericht Bonn for the national court to balance the respective interests involved. In somewhat of a turn-around in attitude, a new judge on the case substantially adopted the position of the BKA and denied the plaintiff access to the corporate statement [Category A] and the documents submitted voluntarily in connection with the leniency procedure [Category B], but allowed Pfleiderer access to documents seized from the cartel participants in dawn raids [Category C]. The Amtsgericht Bonn considered that the binding effect of the BKA decision on the national court meant that it would not be excessively difficult for Pfleiderer to obtain an effective remedy, that the leniency applicants had legitimate expectations that their submissions would not be disclosed, and that the purpose of inspections would be compromised if leniency submissions and document were disclosed. The Bonn Court considered that the purpose of inspections involved was the discovery and pursuit of anticompetitive practices, and that future, hypothetical leniency applicants might be deterred from applying for leniency if access were granted. The decision of the Amtsgericht Bonn on remand was welcomed by the BKA, which has also indicated the intent to amend the German competition law to provide binding measures consistent with its leniency policy.[28]

2. MyTravel (Sweden v. Commission)

In *MyTravel*, the ECJ reversed the judgment of the Court of First Instance (now General Court) refusing access to MyTravel of certain documents from the Commission's files under the Transparency Regulation (Reg. 1049/2001), which the CFI had considered exempt from disclosure. MyTravel was seeking to assert a claim against the Commission for compensation for the Commission's erroneous blocking of a merger in the well-known *Air Tours* case[29] in which the CFI had reversed the Commission's merger prohibition decision. In pursuit of its damages claim, MyTravel had sought documents from the Commission's file pertaining to the underlying decision blocking the merger. The General Court had allowed the Commission to assert exemptions from the disclosure requirements of the Transparency Regulation, Arts. 4(2), 4(3), and 4(6) for a variety of internal documents on the general and hypothetical grounds that disclosure of the documents might undermine the decision-processes of the Commission, might undermine the taking of legal advice, that it would force the Commission to defend its decisions against internal criticism from, for example, the Legal Service or would cause Commission staff to be reticent in expressing opinions. The General Court had accepted these claims of exemption in some cases without requiring a specific analysis of each document and an explanation of how in particular disclosure of each document might undermine Commission decisions. The ECJ rejected the argument that disclosure of documents in this proceeding might impair the success of future proceedings, even those in the same industrial market. The ECJ stressed the principles of openness and transparency in the EU Treaty and the consequent need to construe exceptions to disclosure obligations narrowly and not to shield documents from disclosure on the basis of general and hypothetical arguments without specifically addressing the content of the specific documents under consideration.

MyTravel, unlike *Pfleiderer*, involved the general obligations of document disclosure contained in the Transparency Regulation. The Transparency Regulation was not involved in *Pfleiderer* because the documents there were in Bundeskartellamt files, not Commission files, and because German law offered perhaps a more robust right of access to victims of a cartel than might be owed to the public at large. Nonetheless, it seems likely that the reasoning of the ECJ in *MyTravel* will be applied to private parties seeking disclosure of leniency documents from the Commission files. In particular, the emphasis by the ECJ on avoiding general and hypothetical grounds for refusing access to documents seems fully applicable to generalized claims that disclosure of leniency documents in one case might impair the operation of leniency policies in future cases. If the Commission insists that pre-existing documents submitted under leniency procedures must not be disclosed [Category B], the reasoning in *MyTravel* strongly suggests that such pleas may fall on deaf ears, as discussed more fully below.

3. CDC Hydrogen Peroxide v. Commission

The third case in our transparency trilogy is the judgment of the General Court in *CDC Hydrogen Peroxide*, in which the innovative Cartel Damages Claims undertaking, an assignee of claims for damages from victims of the Hydrogen Peroxide Cartel, sought to obtain a particular document from the Commission's case file on the basis of the Transparency Regulation, Regulation 1049/2001. The Commission had found a nine-member cartel and fined participants some €338 million. Interestingly, the document sought was not the corporate leniency statement, nor even evidence submitted voluntarily or obtained in dawn raids. Instead, CDC sought the index to the Commission's file, the contents of which, presumably, included a list of the documents in the file, including possible descriptions of evidentiary documents, dates, or perhaps the names of witnesses who had given statements.[30] Such a document might well be a road map for a private damages claim and would likely go far toward enabling counsel to frame discovery requests specific enough to satisfy a national court in the EU.

The Commission refused to supply the Index on the asserted grounds that the disclosing the Index would undermine the purposes of the investigation, impair the commercial interests of the cartel participants, and undermine the Commission's decision-making process, and thus was exempt from disclosure on the basis of Arts. 4(2) and 4(3) of Regulation 1049/2001. The General Court first determined that the document index (the Index) did not itself contain any commercial information belonging to the participants in the cartel, but the Commission argued that the Index if disclosed might be used to mount damages claims against the cartel participants, and having to pay damages or even just incur costs of defense of such actions would adversely affect the commercial interests of the cartel members. The General Court properly and resounding rejected the argument that cartel participants have a legitimate commercial interest in not paying damages to victims of their infringements, stating at Para. 49:

> In addition, even if the fact that actions for damages were brought against a company could undoubtedly cause high costs to be incurred, even if only in terms of legal costs, and even if the actions were subsequently dismissed as unfounded, the fact remains that the interest of a company which took part in a cartel in avoiding such actions cannot be regarded as a commercial interest and, in any event, does not constitute an interest deserving of protection, having regard, in particular, to the fact that any individual has the right to claim damages for loss caused to him by conduct which is liable to restrict or distort competition (Case C 453/99 Courage and Crehan [2001] ECR I 6297, paragraphs 24 and 26, and Joined Cases C 295/04 to C 298/04 Manfredi and Others [2006] ECR I 6619, paragraphs 59 and 61).

The Commission further argued that disclosing the Index would undermine the purposes of its investigations, on two grounds. First, that while the Hydrogen Peroxide cartel decision was final, appeals were pending that might have caused the matter to reopened, at least in part, if they resulted in annulment of parts of the decision. However, the General Court rejected this claim and considered that the investigation was final, and the contingency of possible reversal did not mean the investigation was not closed, especially since issues on appeal pertained only to limited questions such as duration of the cartel or responsibility of parent undertakings. Therefore, a closed investigation could not have its purpose undermined by disclosure of the Index.

Second, the Commission argued that the general purpose of its anti-cartel investigations might be undermined if disclosure of documents including the Index caused cartel undertakings not to make leniency applications or not to fully cooperate with the Commission in its investigations. The General Court was not persuaded by this general and hypothetical defense, finding it to be overly broad and legally erroneous, in paras. 69-72:

> 69. The Commission argues, in essence, that the exception based on that concept is independent of any specific procedure and may be relied on, in a general way, to refuse disclosure of any document likely to undermine the Commission's cartel policy and, in particular, its leniency program. In particular, if applicants for leniency had to fear that, as a result of the disclosure of documents which they submitted in the context of their application, that they would be the prime target of actions for damages brought by companies damaged by the cartel, they might refrain, in the future, from co-operating with the Commission, which would affect the effectiveness of the leniency program.

> 70. However, acceptance of the interpretation proposed by the Commission would amount to permitting the latter to avoid the application of Regulation No 1049/2001, without any limit in time, to any document in a competition case merely by reference to a possible future adverse impact on its leniency program. Moreover, the present case is an illustration of the broad application which the Commission wishes to give to that interpretation, inasmuch as it refuses here to disclose a document which was not itself submitted by an applicant for leniency and contains no information likely in itself to damage the interests of the companies which applied for leniency. In fact, the Commission merely states that certain information contained in the non-confidential version of the hydrogen peroxide decision could be put together with other information, contained in the statement of contents, so as to permit victims of anti-competitive practices to know which documents in the file could contain further evidence of the infringement.

> 71. It must be held that such a broad interpretation of the concept of investigation activities is incompatible with the principle that, by reason of the purpose of Article [sic] 1049/2001, set out in recital 4, namely, 'to give the fullest possible effect to the right of public access to documents', the exceptions laid down in Article 4 of that regulation must be interpreted and applied strictly (see the case-law cited in paragraph 36 above).

> 72. It must be stressed, in that regard, that nothing in Regulation No 1049/2001 leads to the supposition that EU competition policy should enjoy, in the application of that regulation, treatment different from other EU policies. There is thus no reason to interpret the concept of the 'purpose of the investigation activities' differently in the context of competition policy than in other EU policies.

The General Court in *CDC Hydrogen Peroxide* thus applied the reasoning of the ECJ in, inter alia, *MyTravel*, to reject a general hypothetical argument of the Commission that disclosure of any document in the file represented a threat to the Commission's leniency policy. The General Court's *CDC Hydrogen Peroxide* judgment is in some respects more profound than that of the ECJ in *Pfleiderer*, which only required a (national) court to engage in a balancing exercise without indicating how the interests implicated were to be weighed. The Commission's defense of its leniency policy has failed its first serious test, and the General Court's ruling in *CDC Hydrogen Peroxide* raises grave doubts about the validity of the judgment of the Amtsgericht Bonn in its remand in *Pfleiderer*. The Amtsgericht Bonn adopted exactly the same general, hypothetical argument rejected by the General Court in *CDC Hydrogen Peroxide*. While the context was different (index versus actual leniency documents), it is clear that the Commission will have to do a better job of justifying its refusal to disclose certain documents; a blanket nondisclosure position will not suffice.

IV. Weighty Matters: Balancing the Interests in Disclosure of Leniency Documents

1 .Why Leniency Programs Work

In order to properly balance the interests of competition authorities and others in effective leniency programs against the interests of private plaintiffs in pursuing damages actions, it is necessary to understand why such programs work in order to evaluate whether private plaintiffs seeking access to leniency documents are or are not a threat to their continued success. It is generally considered that leniency programs are a real-world application of that aspect of game-theory known as the "Prisoner's Dilemma" in which prisoners confess or don't confess to crimes depending on what they think their co-defendants will do.[31] Cartel members who think their cartel is likely to go undiscovered will likely not confess, but members who believe that their co-defendants are likely to confess will seek to confess first in order to strike the most favorable deal with the government. Leniency programs are structured to enhance the value of the first confession (100% immunity) so as to create a race to the competition authority among distrustful conspirators. What drives the success of leniency programs is the fear of discovery and punishment, sweetened by the opportunity to avoid government penalties by confessing first.

In the U.S. DOJ's leniency program, individual defendants fear most the threat of imprisonment,[32] since criminal violations by individuals often result in jail sentences, while the corporation itself can only be fined. The EU leniency program does not have the threat of imprisonment since at the present time only the undertaking can be fined for an infringement, and there are no prison sentences for officers or directors of undertakings involved in the infringements at EU level. The EU leniency program has benefitted from some applications prompted by the U.S. criminal penalties to a certain extent, but there does not seem to be much likelihood of criminal sanctions for individuals soon in the EU. However, some of the Member States have adopted criminal sanctions for cartel-type offenses, and to the extent more Member States may do so, criminal sanctions for individuals in the Member States may result in an increase in the risk of imprisonment, which in turn may benefit the EU leniency program.

2. The Impact of Private Actions on Leniency Decisions

In general terms, a participant in a cartel which is fined by the EU Commission can now expect, even in Europe, that it may well face damages claims from cartel victims and some of those damages claims may well be very large. This has not historically been the case in Europe, but this is changing, even while the Commission's proposal for EU-wide antitrust damages legislation has been pending since the Green Paper in 2005.

The Commission's (and NCAs') antipathy toward allowing access to leniency documents for private parties stems from the fear that access to such documents would discourage leniency applications since having to pay civil damages might reduce or negate the inducement of immunity from or reductions in the amounts of Commission or NCA fines. While the Commission's desire to protect its successful leniency program from any conceivable threat is understandable, it is respectfully submitted that this concern is misplaced. There is no reported evidence that the prospect of civil liability materially deters leniency applications, and there is considerable experience that indicates this is not the case.

The experience in the U.S. DOJ's leniency program contradicts this fear of the Commission. There has been a robust supply of private damages actions in the U.S. for decades, historically on the order of ten times the number of government enforcement actions, yet the DOJ's leniency program has been its most successful anti-cartel tool.[33] Moreover, the DOJ, unlike the Commission, insists leniency applicants make restitution where possible to victims as an express condition of receiving leniency. This means that an amnesty applicant in the U.S. "is precluded by the DOJ's Leniency Policy and a pleading defendant is collaterally estopped from denying the violation in civil litigation."[34] The contrast could not be more clear: The DOJ's successful leniency policy virtually assures that private victims will receive compensation, but the Commission's successful leniency policy paradoxically seeks to assure cartel participants that it will attempt to shield their evidence from private plaintiffs. At the least, this strongly indicates that civil liability concerns do not have a decisive deterrent effect on whether cartelists seek leniency.

Second, the Commission's leniency policy operates only at the conclusion of the Commission's administrative process. At that time, the Commission Decision names all participants in the cartel — including the leniency applicants — and shows which undertakings had their fines reduced under the leniency application by what percentage and in what monetary amounts. The Commission's decision is binding on national courts in private cases involving the same subject matter, so that the Commission decision naming all cartel participants binds leniency applicants to the same extent it binds non-cooperating cartel members. The Commission's Leniency Notice asserts that it intends to guard the submissions of Leniency applicants so that cooperating cartel members will be no worse off in private litigation for cooperating than they would be if they did not cooperate.[35] However, clearly the fact that leniency recipients are found to be infringers in Commission decisions is a negative consequence of applying for leniency as compared to not applying, so if fear of civil liability were a deterrent to leniency applications, they would already be deterred under current practice. The Commission's Leniency Notice also instructs leniency applicants, and rightfully so, that leniency cannot shield them from the civil consequences of their participation in the cartel. It seems to me that if fear of civil liability were a decisive consideration in making leniency applications, the Leniency Policy would not be enjoying its current level of success.

Third, in the *CDC Hydrogen Peroxide* case, CDC pointed out to the General Court that leniency applications have not been reduced in number notwithstanding that private damages claims are now more numerous in Europe than ever before.[36] Wils has opined that "There is no reason to assume that the probability of successfully being sued for damages in a national court on the basis of a Commission decision finding participation in an Article 81 [EC, now Art. 101 TFEU] infringement would be any higher for an enterprise which cooperated with the Commission, or even denounced the infringement in the first place, than for an enterprise which did not cooperate."[37]

To the extent that a cartel might remain undiscovered, the prospect of civil damages is obviously enhanced by a leniency application, but if a cartel member thinks the cartel will not be discovered, it is not likely to seek leniency anyway. If a cartel member thinks another member may confess to the cartel, or that the government may detect the cartel through screening or other methods, it then faces a choice between having to pay substantial government fines plus civil damages, or confessing and avoiding the fines, but still facing civil liability. In such circumstances, the prospect of civil damages is unlikely to be a deterrent.

The International Competition Network has investigated the possibility of enhancing civil damage remedies for cartel victims in the major (and newer) competition jurisdictions and one of the questions studied by its working group on cartels was whether private damages actions would adversely impact leniency programs. The Cartels Working Group report concluded that fear of civil damages actions was only one factor among many in deciding to apply for leniency

> In the discussion on the relation between private and public cartel law enforcement the question as to what extent private enforcement presents a disincentive for leniency applications often arises. The survey showed that the decision to seek leniency is first of all determined by financial aspects and that potential significant private follow-on claims are clearly a financial risk to consider.
>
> The companies put it as follows: The greater and less determinable the financial risks are, the less attractive a leniency program becomes. In this context, some companies voiced their concern that the attractiveness of leniency programs would be reduced if private litigation in cartel cases in their jurisdictions were characterized by treble or double damages, class actions and broad discovery rules. However, the vast majority of the NGAs and a few companies assess the risk of potential follow–on claims as only one factor among many others. In general, they experienced that the benefits of a leniency application outweigh the potential risk of a follow-on damage claim, especially since the latter can never be ruled out as another cartel member may make the first application for leniency, leaving the other cartel members exposed both to the risk of public penalties as well as compensation of damages. This applies especially to leniency applications where full elimination is granted whereas for applications for reduction the disincentives stemming from "excessive" private follow-up claims are considered to be more important.[38]

The EC Commission's announced policy of opposing use of leniency materials in damages claims may apply only to damages claims brought by parties other than itself. In the *Lifts and Elevator Cartel* decision, the Commission found a cartel with four company groups totaling 17 participants in the elevator and lifts market in four Member States and assessed fines of €962 million in fines, including fine reductions of 100% to Otis, Kone Belgium and Kone Luxembourg under the leniency notice. However the Commission then filed a damages claim against the four company groups in a Belgian commercial court seeking compensation of up to €10 million for overcharges on elevators purchased by the Commission and incorporated into Commission and other EU institution buildings in Belgium and Luxembourg. Are we expected to believe that the Commission as plaintiff ignored the leniency documents in its file obtained from Kone and Otis? I have been assured that this is the case by persons in the Commission who I have reason to trust, but I doubt that prospective cartel defendants will be convinced.

3. Beware of Crocodile Tears

It can be expected that in discussion with alleged cartelist members or their legal counsel, the Commission may well have received statements or comments suggesting to the Commission that cartel members are less likely to confess to cartel offenses if they have to incur the expense of private damages litigation or payment of judgments or settlements. Such statements may even be true in some cases, but it is more likely that these are intended as negotiating positions, and such claims must not be taken at face value. The Commission has taken the position that leniency applicants should not be placed in a worse position in national courts for having cooperated with the Commission, as noted above. However, this does not—and should not—create an obligation on the part of the Commission to affirmatively undertake to shield firms from damages claims.

In *CDC Hydrogen Peroxide*, the Commission argued that any release of documents that might damage the cartel participants should be disallowed, but the General Court found that protecting cartel profits was not a legitimate commercial interest. The Commission's argument put it perhaps unwittingly in the position of an advocate for cartelists against the interests of citizens' rights under the EU and TFEU Treaties, which is not a comfortable or appropriate place for the Commission. Such a posture for the Commission comes worryingly close to looking like a sort of regulatory capture where the Commission views cartelists as its clients to the exclusion of the interests of the cartel victims. I respectfully submit that the Commission should not lose perspective and go beyond the level of secrecy necessary to assure the proper functioning of the leniency program to become a shield for admitted cartelists.

4. Balancing EU Interests in Leniency Programs and Private Enforcement

The European courts have identified a number of specific EU interests served by private enforcement of the TFEU's competition rules, beginning with the fact that Arts. 101 and 102 have direct effect and the rights contained therein must be protected by national courts. In addition, since the coming into force of the Lisbon Treaty (December, 2009) private plaintiffs have an increased ability to rely on several fundamental treaty protections, including rights to a fair trial and effective remedy under Arts. 47 and 51 of the Charter on Fundamental Rights of the European Union and Art. 6(1) of the European Convention on Human Rights. Moreover, the Lisbon Treaty codified in Art. 19(1) TEU the obligation on Member States identified in earlier judgments of the ECJ to provide remedies sufficient to ensure effective legal protection of rights in fields covered by European Union law.

With regard to the specific interest of private litigants in obtaining discovery of evidence, the principle of effectiveness of national court remedies dictates that private parties are entitled to court orders requiring production of documents by opposing or third parties.[39] In addition, the Transparency Regulation, Reg. 1049/2001, is intended to implement the principle that decisions in the EU are to be taken as closely as possible to the citizen; the requirement of access to documents is related to the democratic nature of EU institutions; and the Regulation is intended to give the fullest possible effect to the right of access to the documents of EU institutions.[40] Accordingly, exemptions from disclosure are to be strictly construed.

However, all EU interests do not fall exclusively on the side of private enforcement. As important and weighty as these interests are, several of them are shared by leniency programs. Leniency programs to a certain extent further the EU interest in enforcement of Art. 101 TFEU, although care must be exercised to ensure that discounts on fines for cooperating cartelists do not cause overall fine levels to decrease.[41] In addition, it has been argued that secrecy with regard to leniency documents is essential to the ability of private plaintiffs to recover damages on the theory that private parties are only able to recover damages in follow-on actions because the competition authorities have discovered and fined the cartel.[42] The suggestion seems to be that any injury to private interests is not worth weighing because the private damages are merely derivative of public enforcement.

I find the derivative argument unpersuasive in its broad conception. This argument in fact says more about the paucity of discovery rights available to private parties in Europe than it does about the weighing of the interests of leniency programs versus the interests of private claimants. Private parties often trigger competition authority investigations of cartels and other anti-competitive arrangements with their complaints, whether or not cartel participants subsequently submit leniency documents. But the most significant point for the weighing of public versus private interests is that the Commission's view of the scope of leniency document protection goes far beyond what is reasonably needed to protect leniency programs. An appropriate balancing exercise must take into account the proportionality of the Commission's position on access to documents in the Commission's files.

As I understand the Commission's position argued in *Pfleiderer*, *MyTravel*, *and CDC Hydrogen Peroxide*, the Commission opposed the disclosure of corporate leniency statements [Category A], pre-existing documents submitted along with leniency statements [Category B], internal memoranda [Category D] and the Index of documents in the file [Category E]. It is not clear from the judgments in *Pfleiderer* whether the Commission also opposed disclosure of pre-existing documents seized in "dawn raids" [Category C], although the Amtsgericht Bonn apparently allowed this disclosure, and it has been reported that the Commission did not in its argument seek to protect such documents from disclosure.[43]

From the standpoint of the leniency program operation, there is no apparent overriding justification for denying a private plaintiff access to the Index to the Commission's file [Category E] or internal memoranda [Category D]. These are not prepared or submitted by leniency applicants and cannot be regarded as any sort of self-incrimination. There is no indication that leniency applicants have relied on the secrecy of documents prepared by others in deciding to confess. Indeed, it appears likely that such documents would be prepared at some time after the leniency submissions, and their secrecy therefore could not serve as part of the inducement to cartel members. The Commission's interest in protecting internal memoranda such as those protecting legal advice varies according to the time at which disclosure is sought; the ECJ in MyTravel found that such documents were not entitled to a blanket exemption from disclosure, at least where the underlying proceeding was closed, not to mention annulled. In any event, it seems clear that such documents may be entitled to exemption from disclosure under the Transparency Regulation only upon a showing of concrete harm specific to the facts of the case, and the justification for withholding them will not be found in the general and hypothetical justification of the leniency program.

With regard to other categories of documents, the analysis is somewhat different. The corporate leniency statement [Category A] has the best case for being shielded from disclosure; it is also the category of document which if disclosed would be most likely to deter future leniency applications. Corporate leniency statements, whether written or oral, are of a self-incriminating nature; are prepared specifically for the purpose of the leniency program; and are the only types of documents for which a persuasive claim can be made that applicants have relied on a legitimate expectation of secrecy. The Leniency Notice specifically recognizes (point 38) that the leniency policy creates legitimate expectations vis-à-vis the Commission. The corporate statement can be conceived of as analogous to a privileged attorney-client or work-product communication, but the best justification for preserving its secrecy from private plaintiffs is that it is prepared specifically for the leniency application and would not otherwise exist.

However, the case for non-disclosure of corporate leniency statements [Category A] is not free from doubt, especially taking into account the timing of the disclosure. The Commission, in its own interest and to protect the security of its investigations, initially prohibits disclosure of the fact or content of the leniency application even by the applicant. However, once the statement of objections is issued, applicants are free to disclose it. All members of the cartel receive access to the corporate statements once the Statement of Objections issues. Moreover, once the Commission has issued its decision, the identities of all cartel participants and their fines, as well as their participation in the leniency program becomes public information, even if the detailed evidence is not. Given that the Commission decision formally finds infringement of Art. 101 TFEU by the leniency applicants, even though fines are reduced or eliminated, it is clear that leniency applicants are guilty of infringement. It seems to me that after the Commission decision, the concept of protection from self-incrimination no longer applies. After the Commission has issued its decision, the leniency applicant has received the benefit of the bargain, and the Commission offers no assurances that leniency applicants will be shielded from civil liability. Finally, given than leniency statements may be discoverable in civil litigation in the USA[44] despite the Commission's best efforts, it can be doubted whether leniency applicants have a justified expectation of nondisclosure in perpetuity, especially after the Commission's formal decision.

With regard to other categories of documents, pre-existing documents submitted voluntarily along with or following leniency applications [Category B] and pre-existing documents seized in dawn raids [Category C], it is submitted that that refusing disclosure of these two categories of documents may not be justified past the point at which dawn raids are conducted, and certainly may not be justified at any point after the Statement of Objections has issued. Advocate General Mazák recognized in his opinion in *Pfleiderer* that pre-existing documents are not prepared for the purpose of leniency applications and exist at the risk of discovery whether or not the preparer intends to apply for leniency. If civil plaintiffs do not obtain Category B documents, it is only because of flaws in European discovery procedures, not because the leniency applicants have cooperated with the competition authority. The case for suppressing Category B documents collapses when it is considered that to do so exploits the asymmetry of information between plaintiffs and culpable defendants based only on the principle that truthful facts may be concealed because they can be, a principle which finds little in law, morality, or public policy to recommend it.

As to pre-existing documents seized in dawn raids [Category C], there is no apparent justification for suppressing their disclosure once dawn raids have taken place or the statement of objections has issued. They are not prepared for purposes of leniency applications, they exist at the risk of discovery without regard to any cooperation with the Commission, and they are not provided on a voluntary basis. In *Pfleiderer*, Category C documents apparently were disclosed to the plaintiff, but not Category B documents, even though both categories included pre-existing documents. It is likely that some of the same documents in Category C were duplicative of Category B documents but in the possession of cartel members who did not apply for leniency, and vice versa.

Advocate General Mazák suggested that in cases such as *Pfleiderer*, where the national court was bound by the infringement decision taken by the BKA, Category B documents need not be disclosed, whereas if the competition authority decision was not binding, they should be. This apparently influenced the Amtsgericht Bonn to deny disclosure of the category B documents. However, AG Mazák's explanation that in cases where the competition authority decision is binding it is not excessively difficult to bring private damages claims without the documents is not satisfactory. AG Mazák seemed to view the question as one of what minimum level of documents could be disclosed that would not completely prevent the plaintiff from being able to prove a case. Instead, the AG ought to have kept in mind that the possible deterrent effect on the leniency policy of disclosure of pre-existing documents is the same regardless of whether the competition authority finding is binding on a national court. Therefore, AG Mazak's proposed distinction is not justified on its face. Moreover, a competition authority finding may not be sufficient to enable a plaintiff to prove damages even if it establishes an infringement, because additional facts likely need to be adduced. The documents may provide some if not all of the additional required information in cases where the competition authority findings do not.

V. Conclusion

In summary, I propose that documents included in the Commission's file (or an NCA's file) be available to private plaintiffs for use in damages actions in accordance with the following guidelines. First, Category A documents, corporate leniency statements created expressly for the leniency application and which would not exist but for that application, should not be made available unless the leniency applicant has disclosed it to a third party or it has been disclosed pursuant to a court order elsewhere. This protects the expectations of the leniency applicant and allows the Commission to respect its assurances of confidentiality, thus preserving the central feature of the leniency policy—leniency with respect to government fines. This also protects the private plaintiff's right to an effective remedy for infringement of EU law rights without compromising the leniency program if the corporate statement has already been released, or if a defendant bargains with the plaintiff for the release.

Second, with regard to pre-existing documents, whether Category B or Category C, I propose that these be made available to private plaintiffs seeking to establish damages claims regardless of whether the NCA infringement finding is binding on a national court hearing the damages claim. Because these documents are pre-existing, their disclosure does not compromise the purpose or appeal of leniency programs. To the extent that access to such documents may be thought by some to place cooperating cartel members at a financial disadvantage in civil lawsuits by reason of their cooperation (e.g., because some documents were voluntarily furnished with corporate statements), I suggest that cartel defendants do not have a legitimate protectable financial interest in concealing the true facts of their conduct. If the Commission seeks to shield the profits of cartel members from civil damages claims by suppressing truthful pre-existing documents in its possession, it goes beyond that which is necessary to operate an effective leniency program and contradicts the Commission's warning to leniency applicants that cooperation will not shield it from the civil consequences of the infringement. It also represents an inappropriate exploitation by a EU institution of the weakness of national civil discovery rules to in effect subsidize the most serious infringements of the competition rules.

To the extent that the Commission fears that general growth in private damages actions by itself will negate the economic incentive for cartel members to confess, I suggest that a public policy that relies on limiting private plaintiffs' damages from violations of their directly effective EU rights to enhance the Commission's enforcement policy is conceptually and fundamentally flawed. Private enforcement, properly implemented and fully empowered, will significantly enhance a competition culture in the EU and vastly increase the deterrent effect of competition rules. Experience in the U.S. shows that discoverability of pre-existing documents does not unduly deter participation in leniency programs. In the long run, it is likely that private enforcement will have a greater deterrent effect on the formation of cartels than government prosecution.[45]

With regard to Category D documents (internal memoranda) and Category E documents (Indexes to file materials), I submit that access to these documents can take place routinely as far as the leniency program is concerned, because these are documents prepared by

Commission staff without regard to whether any respondent to a statement of objections has applied for leniency. That said, they may be exempt from disclosure if they otherwise meet the conditions applicable to the exemptions, e.g., Art. 4(2) or 4(3) of the Transparency Regulation, but the leniency policy provides no basis for generally preventing access.

Like the quality of mercy generally, the Commission's mercy in the form of its Leniency Notice is to be generally applauded if confined to its proportionate and appropriate role. But the quality of mercy ought not to be permitted to undermine the quality of justice in the form of protection of EU rights to bring private damages claims. In seeking to excessively shield cartel participants from the civil consequences of their conduct, the Commission has nearly lost its way out of fear that one of its most valuable tools in the public enforcement arsenal may be compromised. I submit guidelines for a proposed resolution that should preserve both the quality of mercy and the quality of justice.

Late 2012 Postscript: National Grid, EnBW, and Odile Jacobs

After the foregoing was written in early 2012, at least three other relevant court judgments were handed down by the UK High Court Chancery Division[46] (*National Grid*), the General Court[47] (*EnBW*), and the Third Chamber of the ECJ[48] (*Odile Jacobs*). Full commentary on these cases is not compatible with the time constraints of publishing this volume, but a few brief points should be noted.

In *National Grid*, Mr. Justice Roth applied *Pfleiderer* to a damages action against members of the Gas Insulated Switchgear cartel. He balanced interests and ordered substantial, if not complete, disclosure of a number of documents or parts thereof, including the Commission Decision (non-public version) containing extracts from some leniency documents. After receiving written comments from the Commission submitted in the case, Mr. Justice Roth ruled that *Pfleiderer* applied to the Commission's leniency policy and the national court could apply its disclosure rules. The Transparency Regulation did not appear to be considered.

In *EnBW*, the General Court considered the Transparency Regulation, Regulation 1/2003, and the Commission's leniency policy and other Regulations pertaining to file access in the context of EnBW's request for the entire Commission file concerning the Gas Insulated Switchgear cartel. The Commission had refused access to any documents, contending that there was a blanket protection for its entire file as well as a categorical claim of applicable exemptions to the Transparency Regulation. The Commission did not consider each document on a case-by-case basis, and its claim of excessive workload was not part of the contested decision but was only advanced in defense on appeal. EnBW was a potential plaintiff in a damages claim against the cartel. In sum, the General Court followed its *CDC Hydrogen Peroxide Cartel* reasoning and found that the Commission was required under the circumstances to evaluate each document individually for application of an exemption to disclosure under the Transparency Regulation and Regulation 1/2003.

Of particular note, the General Court in *EnBW* distinguished the ECJ's *Technische Glasswerks Ilmenau Gmbh* (*TGI*) judgment on the basis that the investigation in this case was closed notwithstanding pending appeals, that all access to the file was not forbidden by applicable Regulations (as was the case in *TGI*, a state aids case), and that even if applicable by analogy, the Commission could not rely on blanket or categorical exceptions ("general presumptions") for all documents in the file, but had to give reasons specific to the documents in the file. The General Court also noted the non-binding nature of the Leniency Notice and emphasized the importance of private damages actions to the enforcement of EU competition law.

Finally, and perhaps most importantly, in *Odile Jacobs* the Sixth Chamber of the ECJ applied the Grand Chamber's judgment in *TGI* in ruling that the Commission was entitled to refuse disclosure of its file documents in a merger case (the merger was found compatible) which Odile Jacobs (not a party to the merger) was seeking to annul in the General Court. The Sixth Chamber annulled the General Court's judgment annulling the Commission's non-disclosure decision on the basis of a "general presumption" arising from the Merger Regulation's specific rules governing treatment of information gathered. In such a case, the Sixth Chamber found that document-by-document examination was not required to justify non-disclosure. The Sixth Chamber considered that neither the Transparency Regulation nor the Merger Regulation had primacy but both should be construed as compatible through "coherent application." The Sixth Chamber considered that the application of such general presumptions was not dependent on the closed or open status of the merger for the Art. 4(2) Transparency Regulation exemption, unlike the Art. 4(3) (internal documents) exemption. However, the Court recognized that there might be reasons why the "general presumption" should not be applied and that a higher public interest might justify disclosure, as noted in Art. 4(2) of the Transparency Regulation and *TGI*.

Following the *Odile Jacobs* judgment, it may be that the General Court's approach to disclosure of cartel file documents in general and leniency documents in particular in *CDC Hydrogen Peroxide Cartel* and *EnBW* will not be sustained. In *National Grid*, Mr. Justice Roth declined to make a preliminary reference concerning his disclosure order on the grounds that the balancing under UK national law did not involve a question of EU law, and the doctrine of acte clair. A higher UK court might conceivably order a reference, but that is speculative at this writing. However, there are several reasons to think that *Odile Jacobs* is not inconsistent with the General Court's cartel documents disclosure approach.

To begin with, the Leniency Notice itself is not binding EU legislation comparable to the Merger Regulation or the state aids regulations, as was specifically noted by the Grand Chamber in *Pfleiderer*. Moreover, *Odile Jacobs* drew its general presumptions from the Merger Regulation, and *TGI* drew its general presumptions from the state aids regulations. In contrast, *EnBW* and *CDC Hydrogen Peroxide Cartel* involved Regulation 1/2003 and cartel matters visibly distinct from the Merger and state aids regulations. *Pfleiderer*, a Grand Chamber judgment, has already found that nothing in Reg. 1/2003 precludes a damages claimant from obtaining leniency documents where the national court balances interests under national law. It seems fairly clear that as the law now stands, that no general presumptions of the kind seen in *TGI* and *Odile Jacobs* arise from Regulation 1/2003. However, if the EU revises Regulation 1/2003 (unlikely very soon) or adopts a binding regulation on leniency policy or private damages actions, that situation could change to be more like *Odile Jacobs*. At this writing, the content of any possible additional binding legislation is too speculative to evaluate.

There also remains a reasonable possibility that the ECJ could find either that a general presumption should not be applied in the Arts. 101 and 102 TFEU context, or that a higher public purpose enables the Transparency Regulation to have primacy over leniency policy. This might derive from two related but somewhat distinct concepts. First, private parties have directly effective rights to seek compensation for infringements of Articles 101 and 102 TFEU; this is not the case either with respect to state aids (with one exception) or the Merger Regulation. Second, the ECJ has several times noted the beneficial effects on EU competition policy of private damages actions, and *Pfleiderer* establishes that public enforcement does not have primacy over private enforcement. Hence, private damages actions have a public purpose of deterrence and compensation that makes the competition rules more effective. This is not merely a private purpose. The balancing approach described in *Pfleiderer* makes it particularly inappropriate to apply the kind of blanket "general presumption" found in *TGI* and *Odile Jacobs*.

NOTES

1   WILLIAM SHAKESPEARE, THE MERCHANT OF VENICE (1596), Act 4, Scene 1.

2   Ingrid Vandenborre, *The Confidentiality of EU Commission Cartel Documents in Civil Litigation: The Ball is in the EU Court*, EUR. COMP. L. REV. 116 [2011].

3   Case 26/62, Van Gend en Loos v. Netherlands Inland Revenue Administration, [1963] ECR 5; Case 127/73, *BRT v. SABAM*, [1974] ECR 51, 313, Case C-453/99, Courage and Crehan [2001] ECR I-6297; Joined Cases C-295/04 to C-298/04, *Manfredi* [2006] ECR I-6619.

4   2003 OJ L1/1.

5   *See generally*, Commission of the European Communities, *Green Paper on Damages Actions for Breach of the EC Antitrust Rules*, COM(2005) 672 Final; Clifford A. Jones, *Nostradamus Strikes Again: A Premature U.S. Perspective on the EU's Green Paper on Private Enforcement*, in CARL BAUNDENBACHER (ED.), NEUESTE ENTWICKLUNGEN IM EUROPÄISCHEN UND INTER-NATIONALEN KARTELLRECHT — 12TE ST. GALLEN INTERNATIONALES KARTELLREECHTSFORUM 2005, (at 360 Helbing Lichtenhahn Verlag 2006); Commission, White Paper on Damages actions for breach of EC antitrust rules, COM(2008) 165 final (2.4.2008); Clifford A. Jones, *Toward Balanced Private Antitrust Enforcement in the EU: The White Paper on Damages Actions for Breach of the EC Antitrust Rules from an American Perspective*, in CARL BAUNDENBACHER (ED.), NEWEST DEVELOPMENTS IN EUROPEAN AD INTERNATIONAL COMPETITION LAW — FIFTEENTH ST. GALLEN INTERNATIONAL COMPETITION LAW FORUM 2008, at 213 (Helbing Lichtenhahn Verlag 2009).

6   Case C-360/09, Pfleiderer v. Bundeskartellamt (June 14, 2011).

7   Case C-506/08, Sweden v. European Commission (July 21, 2011) (*MyTravel*).

8   Case T-437/08, CDC Hydrogen Peroxide v. European Commission (Dec. 15, 2011).

9   Scott D. Hammond, The Evolution of Criminal Antitrust Enforcement over the Last Two Decades, Speech to the 24th National Institute on White Collar Crime, Miami, FL, (Feb. 25, 2010) at p. 3; Scott D. Hammond, Cracking Cartels with Leniency Programs, Speech to OECD Competition Committee, Paris, (Oct. 18, 2005), at p. 2.

10   Scott D. Hammond & Belinda A. Barnett, Frequently Asked Questions Regarding the Antitrust Division's Leniency Program and Model Leniency Letters (Nov. 18, 2008), at pp. 2-3.

11   Hammond, *supra* note 9, Cracking Cartels with Leniency Programs, at p. 12.

12   Scott D. Hammond, The Evolution of Criminal Antitrust Enforcement over the Last Two Decades, Speech to the 24th National Institute on White Collar Crime, Miami, FL (Feb. 25, 2010), at p. 3.

13   Hammond & Barnett, *supra* note 10, at pp. 4-5.

14   1996 OJ (C 207).

15   *Commission Notice on Immunity from Fines and Reduction of Fines in Cartel Cases*, 2002 OJ (C45/3).

16   *Commission Notice on Immunity from Fines and Reduction of Fines in Cartel Cases*, 2006 OJ C 298/17.

17   Alan Riley, *The Modernization of EU Anti-Cartel Policy: Will the Commission Grasp the Opportunity?*, CENTRE FOR EUROPEAN POLICY STUDIES SPECIAL REPORT, at p. 3, 5 (2010).

18   *Id.*, at p. 5.

19   Margaret Bloom, *Despite its Great Success, the EC Leniency Program Faces Great Challenges*, in CLAUS-DIETER EHLERMANN & ISABELLA ATANASIU (EDS.), EUROPEAN COMPETITION LAW ANNUAL 2006: ENOFRCEMENT OF CARTEL PROHIBITIONS, at p. 9 (Oxford/Portland: Hart 2007).

20   Bloom, *supra* note 19, at p. 9.

21   John M. Connor, *Has the European Commission Become More Severe in Punishing Cartels? Effects of the 2006 Guidelines*, [2011] 1 EUR .COMP. L. REV. 27-36, at p. 13.

22   Connor, *supra* note 21.

23   The Commission began allowing oral statements in an attempt to prevent corporate leniency statements from being discoverable in civil proceedings in, inter alia, courts of the USA. Oral statements are recorded by the Commission and the Commission prepares a transcript, which may be verified as to accuracy by the applicant. The transcript constitutes a document of the Commission to which access is only permitted on the premises of the Commission. Access is granted only to respondents who are the subject of a statement of objections, including the leniency applicant.

24   *See, e.g.*, the recent decision of the Commission in the *Window Mountings Cartel* in which nine undertakings participated and were collectively fined € 86 million. One undertaking received 100% immunity, one received a 45% reduction in fine, and one received a 25% reduction in fine (EC Commission Press Release IP/12/313, March 28, 2012.).

25   Case C-360/09, Opinion of Advocate General Mazák, at ¶ 46, 48 (16 December 2010).

26   *Id. at* ¶ 47, 48.

27   *Id. at* ¶ 47, note 25.

28 Andreas Mundt, President of BKA, Bundeskartellamt Press Release, Jan. 30, 2012.

29 Case T 342/99 Airtours v Commission [2002] ECR II 2585.

30 The reported case does not describe the contents of the index with particularity, but the General Court noted in ¶ 45 that the Index contained the origin, addressee, and description of documents. Based on general litigation experience, such an Index is likely to give such information as the date of the document, the name of its author, the names of one or more recipients, and perhaps a title or summary of the content. It may list the number of pages, or possibly even the legal issue or facts to which it pertains.

31 *See* Nicolo Zingales, *European and American Leniency Programs: Two Models Towards Convergence?*, [2008] Eur. Comp. L. Rev. 5, Vol. 1 at 9.

32 The DOJ maintains jail sentences for individuals are the most effective deterrent to cartel activity and the greatest incentive to self-report, and has pledged to "hold individuals, as well as corporations, responsible for engaging in criminal conduct." United States Department of Justice, Press Release, Former Qantas Airline Executive Agrees to Plead Guilty to Participating in Price-Fixing Conspiracy on Air Cargo Shipments (May 8, 2008) (emphasis added); *See* Scott D. Hammond, Recent Developments, Trends, and Milestones In The Antitrust Division's Criminal Enforcement Program, address before the ABA Section of Antitrust Law (Nov. 16, 2007) [hereinafter Hammond, Recent Developments I], Scott D. Hammond, The U.S. Model of Negotiated Plea Agreements: A Good Deal With Benefits For All, address before the Organization for Economic Co-operation and Development Competition Committee (Oct. 17, 2006) [hereinafter Hammond, Negotiated Plea Agreements]; Thomas O. Barnett, Criminal Enforcement Of Antitrust Laws: The U.S. Model, address before the Fordham Competition Law Institute (Sept. 14, 2006), at 3; Scott D. Hammond, Charting New Waters In International Cartel Prosecutions, address before the National Institute on White Collar Crime (Mar. 2, 2006) [hereinafter Hammond, Charting New Waters]; Scott D. Hammond, An Update Of The Antitrust Division's Criminal Enforcement Program (Mar. 2, 2006), at 1 [hereinafter Hammond, Criminal Enforcement Update], at 3; Scott D. Hammond, When Calculating The Costs And Benefits Of Applying For Corporate Amnesty, How Do You Put A Price On An Individual's Freedom?, address before the National Institute On White Collar Crime (Mar. 8, 2001) [hereinafter Hammond, Calculating the Costs and Benefits]; Gary R. Spratling, Negotiating The Waters Of International Cartel Prosecutions, address before the National Institute on White Collar Crime (Mar. 4, 1999).

33 The DOJ does not make corporate leniency statements available to private parties, but does not prevent disclosure of evidentiary documents supporting the statements, which are furnished to private plaintiffs through USA discovery rules or cooperating defendants.

34 Gary R. Spratling, former Assistant Attorney General for International Antitrust & D. Jarrett Arp, Making the Decision: What to Do When Faced with International Cartel Exposure, Speech to Competition Law Spring Forum, Toronto, CN (May 17, 2010), at p. 5.

35 2006 Leniency Notice, *supra* note 16, point 6.

36 *CDC Hydrogen Peroxide, supra* note 8, at ¶ 54.

37 Wouter P. J. Wils, The Optimal Enforcement of EC Antitrust Law, at 64 (Kluwer, 2002).

38 ICN Cartel Working Group, Interaction of public and Private Enforcement in Cartel Cases, Report to the International Competition Network Conference, at p.48 (May 2007).

39 Case C-526/04 Laboratoires Boiron, [2006] ECR I-7529, at ¶55:

> In those circumstances, in order to ensure compliance with the principle of effectiveness, if the national court finds that the fact of requiring a pharmaceutical laboratory such as Boiron to prove that wholesale distributors are overcompensated, and thus that the tax on direct sales amounts to State Aid, is likely to make it impossible or excessively difficult for such evidence to be produced, since inter alia that evidence relates to data which such a laboratory will not have, the national court is required to use all procedures available to it under national law, including that of ordering the necessary measures of inquiry, in particular the production by one of the parties or a third party of a particular document.

40 *MyTravel, supra* note 7 at ¶¶ 72-73.

41 See Wils, *supra* note 37, at p. 53; Connor, *supra* note 21.

42 Andreas Mundt, President of the Bundeskartellamt, after the remand decision of the Amtsgericht Bonn:

> Private claims for damages suffered from cartel law violations are an important supplement to public antitrust enforcement. But to be able to claim damages, the victims of cartel agreements depend on the competition authorities to uncover the cartel. If the leniency program does not function properly, significantly fewer cartels will be uncovered. This would not only hamper the punishment of the perpetrators, but also the compensation of the victims.

BKA Press Release (January 30, 2012).

43 Silke Heinz, *The District Court of Bonn denies access to leniency applications for third parties in cartel case (Pfleiderer)*, e-Competitions, No44741 (30 Jan. 2012).

44 *See, e.g.,* Vitamins Antitrust Litigation, *Re*, Rep. of Special Master (99-197) (TFH), 2002 U.S. Dist. LEXIS 26490 January 23, 2002 (D.D.C. 2002), denying motion to reconsider at Vitamins Antitrust Litigation, Re (99-197) (TFH), 2002 U.S. Dist. LEXIS 25815 December 18, 2002 (D.D.C. 2002); *but see,* Rubber Chemicals Antitrust Litig.486 F. Supp. 2d 1078 (N.D. Cal. 2007).

45 *See*, Robert H. Lande & Joshua P. Davis, *Comparative Deterrence From Private Enforcement and Criminal Enforcement of the U.S. Antitrust Laws* (University of San Francisco Law Research Paper 2010-17) (October 22, 2009), *available at* http://ssrn.com/abstract=1565693.

46 *National Grid Electricity Transmission v. ABB and Others* [2012] EWHC 869 (Ch) (Roth, J.).

47 Case T-348/08, *EnBW Energie Baden-Württemberg AG v. Commission* [2012] ECR-II-0000, decided June 8, 2012.

48 Case C 404/10 P, *Commission v.* Éditions *Odile Jacob SAS* [2012] ECR I-0000, decided June 28, 2012 (3rd Chamber).

Sorting Out the Analytical Mess: A Step-Wise Approach to Joint Venture Analysis after *Dagher* and *American Needle*

JAMES A. KEYTE*

James.Keyte@skadden.com

Partner, Skadden, Arps, Slate, Meagher & Flom, LLP

Abstract

This article proposes a step-by-step analysis of joint venture restraints in the wake of the Supreme Court decisions in *Texaco Inc. v. Dagher*, 547 U.S. 1 (2006) and *American Needle, Inc. v. NFL*, 130 S.Ct. 2201 (2010). The proposal is based on the Court in *Dagher* making a clear distinction between "inside" and "outside" venture restraints as well as the suggestion in *American Needle* that many venture restraints can be approved on a "quick look." The steps would include: 1) assessing whether the defendants have the capacity to conspire under *American Needle*; 2) assessing whether the restraint is "inside" the venture, in which case "ancillary restraints" analysis would *not* apply; 3) assessing whether the particular subject of the inside restraint can be viewed as "core" or facially necessary to the venture's activities; and 4) if an "outside" venture restraint, assessing whether the defendants have market power and, if so, whether the restraint is reasonably necessary to a legitimate venture objective. Only for the latter type of restraint would "less restrictive alternatives" come into play.

In the wake of *Dagher*[1] and *American Needle*,[2] there has followed understandable confusion as to how and when the rule of reason should apply to legitimate joint ventures.[3] *Dagher* signaled that "economically integrated" joint ventures should be treated like a "single firm" and, at a minimum, that the "internal" decisions of all legitimate joint ventures — especially "core" decisions concerning the venture's product — are not really restraints "in the antitrust sense."[4] Indeed, *Dagher*, albeit *in dicta*, relegated "ancillary restraints" analysis to agreements that restrict a venture member's conduct *outside* of the scope of the venture's activities, leaving practitioners legitimately to ask whether "inside" venture restraints — especially those relating to the production and sale of venture products themselves — should be deemed reasonable as a matter of law.[5]

Four years later, *American Needle* came along and threw cold water on the Seventh Circuit's view of single entity, starkly reminding practitioners that single-entity status is reserved for the circumstance in which the venture members are incapable of actual or potential competition for the particular product in question — in that case, NFL team-owned intellectual property ("IP"). Yet the Court emphasized that it was only enunciating single-entity principles. And not only did it leave some wiggle room for single entity to apply, it also declared that the NFL need not be "trapped" by the application of Section 1: under the rule of reason, even a restraint among joint venture "competitors" can be approved in the "'twinkling of an eye.'"[6] Hence, what the Court took away on single entity, it may have given back with a defendants'-oriented "quick look," at least for activities that facially appear to promote the joint venture's primary activities (e.g., producing and selling football rather than team-logo hats).[7]

Certainly, however, what *Dagher* and *American Needle* offer in the way of provocative dicta, they lack in terms of analytical clarity. Nowhere does the Court lay out an analytical framework for applying the rule of reason to legitimate joint ventures, let alone in the era of *Twombly* where businesses are not supposed to be harassed with sparse and speculative antitrust allegations.[8] Moreover, given the Court's various pronouncements that joint ventures deserve all of the judicial respect of other forms of businesses operating in the economy,[9] one would think that an analytical framework may have been forthcoming with one or both of these cases.[10] It was not, which is why that attempt is made here.

I. Setting the Stage: What Guidance Can Be Gleaned from Dagher and American Needle

A starting point for considering a stepwise approach to joint venture analysis is to consider what guidance can be gleaned from the Court's discussions in *Dagher* and *American Needle*. Certainly, in both, the Court emphasizes that joint ventures should not be penalized by their status as joint ventures; moreover, in each there are brief references to principles that are likely to influence future rule of reason analyses for legitimate joint ventures.

1. Dagher and "Inside" Venture Restraints

Dagher arose in the context of a *per se* challenge to a joint venture that coordinated the pricing of two formerly independent gasoline brands, Texaco and Shell. In 1998, Texaco and Shell, once direct competitors in the oil and gasoline markets, formed a joint venture called Equilon, which integrated their downstream operations in the western United States. Under the joint venture agreement, Shell and Texaco pooled their resources and agreed to share the risks and profits in connection with Equilon's operations. The Federal Trade Commission and four state attorneys general investigated and, subject to certain conditions in a consent decree, approved the formation of the joint ventures.

A class of Texaco and Shell service station owners brought suit in district court alleging that by setting common prices for the two brands, Shell and Texaco had engaged in *per se* price fixing under Section 1 of the Sherman Act. The district court granted summary judgment to Shell and Texaco, but the Ninth Circuit reversed, rejecting what it characterized as a request by Shell and Texaco for an "exception to the *per se* prohibition against price fixing."[11] Utilizing the same misguided approach it had employed in *Raiders*,[12] the court applied the "ancillary restraints doctrine" to Equilon's conduct, holding that the gas companies could avoid *per se* condemnation only by proving that the pricing decision was ancillary to the procompetitive justifications for the venture—i.e., that it was "reasonably necessary" to further the venture's admitted synergies and efficiencies and there was no less restrictive alternative available to achieve the same objectives.[13]

The Supreme Court granted certiorari "to determine the extent to which the *per se* rule against price-fixing applies to an important and increasingly popular form of business organization, the joint venture."[14] In a unanimous decision, the Court first reiterated that the rule of reason is the presumptively applicable mode of analysis in Section 1 cases. The Court then held that Equilon's pricing decision did not fall within the *per se* category of price fixing but would, if necessary, be subject to the rule of reason. The Court explained that this conclusion was justified in part "because Texaco and Shell Oil did not compete with one another in the relevant market—namely, the sale of gasoline to service stations in the western United States—but instead participated in that market jointly through their investments in Equilon."[15]

Moreover, the Court emphasized that a legitimate joint venture should receive the same scrutiny from an antitrust perspective as any single-entity firm when it comes to venture "activities." Therefore, characterizing Shell's and Texaco's role in the ventures as investors, not competitors, the Court stated that "[w]hen 'persons who would otherwise be competitors pool their capital and share the risks of loss as well as the opportunities for profit... such joint ventures [are] regarded as a single firm competing with other sellers in the market.'"[16] In turn, the Court described Equilon's pricing policy as "little more than price setting by a single entity—albeit within the context of a joint venture—and not a pricing agreement between competing entities with respect to their competing products."[17] The Court also pointed out that the plaintiffs had conceded the *per se* rule would not condemn the pricing practice had the gasoline been sold under one brand, leading the Court to find that, "[a]s a single entity, a joint venture, like any other firm, must have the discretion to determine the prices of the products that it sells, including the discretion to sell a product under two different brands at a single, unified price."[18]

Finally, the Court expressly rejected the use of an ancillary restraints analysis to scrutinize the "core activity" of legitimate joint ventures.[19] The ancillary restraints doctrine, the Court explained, only applies to restrictions external to—or outside—the venture, such as noncompetition restraints placed on venture participants.[20] Therefore, the doctrine was inapplicable where "the business practice being challenged involves the core activity of the joint venture itself—namely, the pricing of the very goods produced and sold by Equilon."[21]

Ultimately, however, there was no need for the Court to lay out an analytical framework that may have more fully captured what the Court had in mind in discussing these principles. Plaintiffs had relied on a *per se* theory of antitrust misconduct, which the Court rejected; a full discussion of the rule of reason's application to legitimate joint ventures would have to await another day.

2. American Needle and a Defendant's "Quick Look" for Joint Venture Restraints

That day would not come with *American Needle*, which held only that single-entity status could not apply to venture members that retained the economic ability to compete against each other in the marketplace—in this instance, the licensing of team-owned IP. Again, however, the Court offered dicta signaling that the traditional full rule of reason need not apply to the restraints of sports leagues and, presumably, other legitimate joint ventures.

The background of *American Needle* is well known. In 1963, the NFL teams formed a separate corporate entity, NFL Properties Inc. ("NFLP"), to license and market both the league- and team-owned IP and to advertise and promote the sport of football. After years of granting nonexclusive headwear licenses to numerous vendors, including American Needle Inc., NFLP declined to renew American Needle's license in 2001, instead granting an exclusive ten-year headwear license to Reebok International Ltd.

American Needle then filed suit against the NFL, NFLP, the individual teams, and Reebok, alleging violations of Sections 1 and 2 of the Sherman Act. The district court granted summary judgment to the NFL, and the Seventh Circuit affirmed, reasoning that the NFL qualified for single entity treatment in part because "only one source of economic power controls the promotion of NFL football," and "the NFL teams share a vital economic interest in collective [] promoti[on]."[22] The Supreme Court unanimously reversed and remanded.

The Court stated the issue on appeal as follows: "whether the NFL respondents are capable of engaging in a 'contract, combination . . . or conspiracy' as defined by § 1 of the Sherman Act, or... whether the alleged activity by the NFL respondents '*must* be viewed as that of a single enterprise for purposes of § 1.'"[23] In reversing, the Court emphasized the "'basic distinction'" between "concerted action" among actual or potential competitors and the "independent" (or unilateral) actions of a single firm, focusing on "a functional consideration of how the parties involved in the alleged anticompetitive conduct actually operate."[24] The Court then restated what it viewed as the guiding principle of *Copperweld*:

> The key is whether the alleged 'contract, combination . . . or conspiracy' is concerted action—that is, whether it joins together separate decisionmakers. The relevant inquiry, therefore, is whether there is [an agreement] amongst '*separate economic actors* pursuing separate economic interests,' such that the agreement 'deprives the marketplace of *independent centers of decision-making*,' and therefore of 'diversity of entrepreneurial interests,' *and thus of actual or potential competition*.[25]

Applying this principle from the perspective of consumers (potential licensees of NFL-team logos), the Court explained that "NFL teams do not possess either the unitary decisionmaking quality or the single aggregation of economic power characteristic of independent action."[26] Instead, the "teams compete with one another, not only on the playing field, but to attract fans, for gate receipts and for contracts with managerial and playing personnel."[27] Indeed, from the perspective of potential licensees of NFL-team logos, the Court held that NFL teams clearly compete in the market for IP, thus rejecting the NFL's argument that the member teams constitute a single entity.[28]

Importantly, however, the Court emphasized that for established legitimate joint ventures like sports leagues, application of the rule of reason need not require the kind of drawn out litigation that typifies antitrust cases. Instead, "depending upon the concerted activity in question," defendants may win early dismissal of meritless cases on a so-called quick look.[29]

As the Court explained:

> When restraints on competition are essential if the product is to be available at all, *per se* rules of illegality are inapplicable, and instead the restraint must be judged according to the flexible Rule of Reason. In such instances, the agreement is likely to survive the Rule of Reason. And depending upon the concerted activity in question, the Rule of Reason may not require a detailed analysis; it "can sometimes be applied in the twinkling of an eye."[30]

Hence, the Court effectively directed lower courts in these cases both to carefully assess the concerted activity in question and to consider whether, as a matter of law (or some other summary resolution), the conduct in question is legitimate, procompetitive conduct of the venture.

* * *

Like *Dagher* before it, *American Needle* provided a straightforward holding that can easily be applied on similar facts—the collective decisions of the thirty-two NFL teams regarding the joint licensing of team-owned IP constituted concerted activity under Section 1 of the Sherman Act. However, the Court also made a conscious decision not to explain the analytical contours for applying the rule of reason to legitimate collaborations. While some commentators have thus viewed *American Needle* as limiting or taking a step back from *Dagher*, the majority (and better) view is that *American Needle* did not and could not have undermined any part of *Dagher*.[31] A worthy task, therefore, is to try and translate the opaque guidance of *Dagher* and *American Needle* into a step by step analysis for assessing the restraints of legitimate joint ventures. What we see is not only that the "full" rule of reason need not come into play at all, but that many cases should be rejected at the pleading stage, just as *Twombly* suggested.

II. A Stepwise Approach to Joint Venture Analysis

The challenge for determining an appropriate and fair analytical framework for assessing the conduct of joint ventures lies in part with the history of the rule of reason. For example, while several courts have addressed whether certain conduct of a purported joint venture can be *condemned* as a matter of law or on a truncated record,[32] few cases have addressed the circumstances under which the activity of a joint venture can be *approved* either as "single entity" conduct (post-*American Needle*) or "reasonable as a matter of law."[33] Yet, *Dagher* and *American Needle*—especially in the wake of *Twombly*—suggest exactly this inquiry where plaintiffs cannot plead facts that warrant full rule of reason analysis. Accordingly, it is worthwhile to consider how courts should proceed, analytically, when faced with antitrust challenges to what appear to be legitimate joint ventures.

1. A Word on the Role of the Court

One of the fundamental challenges of a truncated rule of reason approach—for plaintiffs or defendants—is to consider the appropriate role of the court. In years past, especially before *Twombly*, the working assumption of many was that any rule of reason assessment of a challenged joint venture restraint would require litigation up through summary judgment, if not trial. And many joint venture cases no doubt slogged through years of discovery before a court ever seriously considered the substantive merits of the claim.

Under the light of *Twombly* and *American Needle*'s reference to a quick look for joint venture defendants, this paradigm needs to be adjusted. Certainly at the pleading stage, courts must now require plaintiffs challenging joint venture restraints to allege facts that support all of the substantive elements—including those that would demonstrate why single entity status for the restraint is inappropriate and why an otherwise internal business decision of the venture (e.g., a "core" decision under the *Dagher* parlance) may be challenged at all. Indeed, at least one court has found that at defendant's "quick look" can be applied at the pleading stage.[34] Further, in time, courts are likely to develop means by which these threshold or quick-look inquiries can be undertaken, if necessary, with minimal discovery. The process is now common for jurisdictional issues, and several courts have used the sequencing of discovery and potentially dispositive issues to manage complex litigation. Antitrust challenges to the decisions of legitimate joint ventures appear particularly well-suited to these efficient resolution mechanisms.

III. Step 1: Do the Defendants Have the Capacity to Conspire with Respect to the Restraint at Issue?

Given *American Needle*, the first step in any antitrust case challenging the conduct of a legitimate joint venture (i.e., not a sham) should be to determine whether the joint venture members have the capacity to conspire with respect to the restraint at issue. The inquiring has two subparts, as follows.

1. What is the Restraint?

First, as *American Needle* emphasized, one must understand precisely what restraint is at issue. While this will not be difficult most of the time, there does need to be a focus on what agreement, in particular, allegedly prevents competition from taking place. In fact, on close examination, it may be the case that the real gripe is with much earlier joint venture agreements that may go all the way back to venture formation, in which case the plaintiff may have more fundamental problems dealing with laches, the statute of limitations and perhaps basic causation. In any event, a clear understanding of the restraint at issue is essential to the single-entity inquiry that survived *American Needle*.[35]

2. Are the Parties Actual or Potential Competitors for the Product at Issue?

Second, one must consider whether the subject of the restraint (e.g., the product being sold or licensed, etc.) is an asset that the venture itself owns and controls as opposed to individual venture members. A strong argument could be made that single-entity status still holds for the restrictions on the manufacture, distribution and sale of *the venture products themselves*, even where the venture is not "economically integrated." As to these, no individual venture participant can be an *independent* economic actor or decisionmaker in the marketplace. For example, in *American Needle*, the venture owned the "NFL" logo-IP, and the Court's reasoning indicated that a restraint relating to that IP should be treated as that of a single entity.[36]

At least one court, for example, has invoked the single entity doctrine in light of *American Needle*. In *Washington v. NFL*, 2012 WL 3017961 (D.Minn. 2012), retired professional players brought an antitrust action based on the NFL's and teams' collective denial of rights to game footage and player images. In dismissing the complaint, the court found that under *American Needle*, the single-entity doctrine should apply: only the league owned NFL game footage and images or, at most, the NFL and teams owned them jointly. Accordingly, as a matter of law the alleged conduct was that of a single entity.

Likewise, one must consider whether, as to the specific restraint in question, the venture members are in fact "economically integrated." The Court in *Dagher* placed great weight on the fact that Shell and Texaco fully integrated their venture activities and "shared in the profits of Equilon's activities in their role as investors, not competitors."[37] In fact, even in *American Needle* the Court observed that this was a close call as to NFL Enterprises ("NFLE"), but ultimately found that as to licensing of team IP, the teams still retained ownership of the IP assets needed to participate in the market as potential licensors.[38] However, there are likely to be circumstances where a venture—*or the relevant aspects of a venture*—are in fact "economically integrated." For example, if the teams had previously transferred the IP to NFLE, the case likely would have been different. And one can imagine any number of circumstances where venture members simply do not have the contractual rights under the venture to be actual or potential competitors for the product in question.

IV. Step 2: Can the Reasonableness of the Restraint Be Determined as a Matter of Law or on a Truncated Record?

Assuming the existence of conspiratorial capacity, *Dagher* strongly suggests that the analytical framework for assessing the reasonableness of the restraint turns on whether the challenged conduct relates to "internal" or inside venture activities as opposed to restraints that affect a venture member's external or outside activities. Indeed, *Dagher*'s discussion of "core" venture activities, as well as its explanation of "ancillary restraints," is premised on just such a dichotomy.[39] And, of course, it makes sense if in fact legitimate joint ventures are not to be penalized merely because of the business structure they chose, which the Supreme Court emphasized in *Dagher* and *Trinko*.[40] Moreover, once that threshold methodological issue is determined, other established antitrust principles naturally guide the analysis.

1. Is the Restraint Inside the Scope of the Venture's Actvities?

Perhaps the most fundamental *factual* threshold inquiry for assessing joint venture restraints is to determine the scope of the venture itself. This not only means the venture as formed, but also the interation of the venture at the time the restraint is challenged. Indeed, as we have seen, where restraints are inside the venture, they may be viewed as not even restraints "in the antitrust sense."[41] By contrast, if restraints are outside the scope of the venture they, in theory, could be condemned either as unjustified,[42] or at least subject to the "reasonably necessary" inquiry of the ancillary restraints doctrine.[43]

The key for courts, of course, is to invoke *Twombly* or other mechanisms to make the parties deal with factual reality. For example, where a venture obviously includes the distribution and sale of the venture's output (or any part of it), certainly restraints that restrict such distribution and sale would be viewed as inside venture activities. For example, in *Bulls II*,

Judge Easterbrook recognized that "when acting in the broadcast market," the NBA is close to the core activity of the venture because the NBA's product is that "[i]t makes professional basketball."[44] Similarly, citing both *American Needle* and *Dagher*, at least one district court has recognized that "[t]he ancillary restraints doctrine cannot be applied to a joint venture's 'core activity.'"[45] By contrast, if parties truly only set up a R&D or production joint venture—e.g., as in *Yamaha* or (at first) in *Three Tenors*—then that venture would be subject to a different analysis under the ancillary restraints doctrine.

Importantly, courts must be able to make this determination either in the face of a complaint—for example by requiring *factual* support for why any alleged venture should be limited to the scope alleged—or perhaps by invoking a mechanism for determining that scope with early, targeted discovery. Either way, under the policy objections of *Twombly*, courts and parties should not be burdened with exhaustive antitrust litigations just because a plaintiff asserts in conclusory terms that a venture is for "production" when in reality the venture controls the distribution and sale of the venture's output.

Again, post-*Dagher* and *American Needle*, we see the use of the reasonable as a matter of law approach in both *Washington v. NFL*[46] and *Agnew*.[47] In each instance, the court was willing to look at the subject of the challenged restraint and determine as a matter of law, that the restraint was integral to the ventures activities, and therefore procompetitive.

2. Is the Restraint on "Parent" Competition with the Venture's Activities?

For inside venture restraints, one of the most fundamental joint venture principles that can be applied as a matter of law concerns restrictions on a venture parent's competition with the venture itself. For example, the Supreme Court in *Penn-Olin* explained that the "parents [of a joint venture] would not compete with their progeny [the venture itself]."[48] And, more recently in a suit between Madison Square Garden and the NHL, the court observed that "agreements among parents of a joint venture not to compete in the market in which a joint venture operates have generally been upheld."[49]

In the wake of *Dagher* and *American Needle*, this basic principle also should be quite easy to follow "in the twinkling of an eye." What could be more "core" to a venture than to prohibit its members from competing with the venture, especially *for the sale of venture products themselves*. Thus, if a complaint is premised on the notion that the plaintiff (whether a venture member or a potential customer) should be allowed to "compete" in the distribution and sale of products within the scope of the venture, then the case should be dismissed as matter of law. Otherwise, ventures of all types would be subject to the type of claims and costs that took *Dagher* all the way to the Supreme Court (and on a *per se* theory at that), and many would never have been formed in the first place.

3. Is the Restraint Permissible as a Matter of Law for "Single" Firm Conduct?

Another important question to consider in any truncated assessment of an inside venture restraint is whether antitrust courts have permitted the conduct from single firms or integrated joint ventures. The notion, as in *Dagher*, is that joint ventures should not be penalized in carrying out activities within the scope of the venture merely because of the "the context of a joint venture."[50] Hence, for core pricing, output or distribution decisions, assuming this is what is "restrained," courts should readily reject challenges to venture conduct that falls easily within the essentials of the economic activity of the venture itself.

Yet the principle should not be limited to the most obvious venture activities. Indeed, given that the underlying assumption of *Dagher*'s discussion of "core" conduct is that single firms obviously can make these essential basic business decisions, the same should hold for other economic activity within a venture's scope that would be perfectly permissible as a matter of law for a single firm. This would include, for example, refusals to deal,[51] the establishment of exclusive distribution territories,[52] and the allocation of customers or other non-price vertical restraints.[53] And while some may argue that the Court's reference to *Topco* and *Sealy* in *American Needle* precludes just this type of analysis,[54] the Court did not suggest that the NFL (or other ventures) were pretextual in their formation. In any event, to the extent the facts in those cases showed legitimate integrations, they would be decided differently today.[55] Going forward, courts can and should assess the internal restraints of ventures in as summary a fashion as possible—*Twombly* and *American Needle* suggest no less.

This position is supported by those in the academic community who have thought carefully about the rule of reason in light of *Dagher*. For example, Gregory Werden has explained that the Supreme Court's description in *Dagher* of "core" activities "recognizes that constraints joint venture participants place on the conduct of the venture itself, within the ambit of its operation, are quite different than constraints they place on their own conduct outside the venture."[56] Werden concludes that restraints such as the products a venture produces, the area in which it operates, the parties with whom it deals, and the prices it charges "are not collateral restraints; rather they are integral parts of the joint venture and cannot be separated from it."[57] In turn, *American Needle*'s acknowledgment of a defendant's quick look for restraints integral to a venture's activities only reinforces the position that courts should resolve these fairly straightforward challenges on the face of the complaint or, at most, with targeted discovery rather than a full-blown rule of reason analysis.[58]

V. Step 3: For "Outside" Venture Restraints, Can the Ancillarity of the Restraint Be Determined as a Matter of Law or on a Truncated Record?

Albeit in dicta, the *Dagher* Court also made clear that restraints that fall outside of venture activities are to be analyzed under the modern version of the so-called ancillary restraints doctrine.[59] That framework asks whether the restraint is "reasonably necessary" to a legitimate venture activity, and further, whether the same objective can be met through any materially less restrictive means.[60] In recent years, this inquiry has folded into the mix of a broader rule of reason analysis with little room for truncated review, at least absent a clear *lack* of ancillarity and either quick look or even *per se* condemnation.[61] The question, now, however, is whether it is advisable to have any truncated review of restraints that are assessed for their "ancillarity"? Indeed, Professor Gary Roberts anticipated this issue decades ago when he posed the following question: "The ultimate issue here is . . . whether or not the internal rules and decisions of leagues ought to be immune from case-by-case rule of reason review under section 1."[62]

1. Is the Restraint In Fact "Ancillary" to the Venture's Activities?

Certainly, a threshold question is whether, *factually*, the restraint is ancillary to a legitimate objective. But this inquiry may be tougher than it appears. For example, the court in *North American Soccer League v. NFL*, treated the NFL's rule prohibiting members of that league from making or retaining a capital investment in any member of another professional sports

league as a restraint that was outside the venture.[63] Yet, in dissenting from the Supreme
Court's denial of certiorari, Justice Renquist argued that the restraint nevertheless was so
ancillary to the legislative objective of not having venture members compete with the
venture (even from the "outside" with a different product) that he would have upheld the
restraint *as a matter of law*.[64] Similarly, in *Rothery Storage*, the court appeared to find—
again, as a matter of law under an ancillary restraints analysis—that it is always permissible
(under a free-riding theory) to prevent a venture member from using venture assets to open
a competing venture.[65]

Similarly, the NBA scored a victory using the ancillary restraints doctrine in a case addressing the NBA's prohibition on its players participating in basketball competitions outside
the NBA joint venture.[66] A company that wanted to sponsor a one-on-one competition
between Michael Jordan and Magic Johnson alleged that the prohibition violated the antitrust laws. Citing Justice Rehnquist's *NASL* dissent, the court granted summary judgment
for the NBA, holding that it is reasonable as a matter of law for the member teams of a
professional sports league to require their player-employees to remain loyal to the team
and the league and not work for any competing entity while they remain employed.[67]

Yet on the other side of the ledger, courts have not been hesitant to find that certain restraints plainly are not ancillary at all or are not guaranteed by *procompetitive* justifications.
For example, the court in *Yamaha* was faced with a joint venture between Yamaha and
Brunswick for, among other things, the production and sale of outboard motors.[68] The FTC
and the Eighth Circuit considered an agreement that precluded Yamaha from marketing
non-joint venture products anywhere but Japan. The FTC had determined that the challenged agreement was illegal because it was not "limited to those inevitably arising out of the
dealing between partners, or necessary (and of no broader scope than necessary) to make
the joint venture work."[69] The Eighth Circuit affirmed, condemning the territorial limitation
because the restriction could not "be termed 'reasonably necessary' to the purpose of the
joint venture."[70]

In a closer call, the court rejected a free-riding argument in *Three Tenors*.[71] In that case,
PolyGram and Warner each held the distribution rights to one previous concert of The Three
Tenors. In 1998, the two firms formed a venture to jointly distribute a third concert, subsequently agreeing to reduce marketing of the previous concerts so as not to compete with
the upcoming concert. The D.C. Circuit affirmed the FTC's holding that the joint venture
could not be used to justify a moratorium on promoting or discounting earlier Three Tenors
albums that were beyond the scope part of the joint venture. The court reasoned that "[a]n
agreement between joint venturers to restrain price cutting and advertising with respect to
products *not part of the joint venture* looks suspiciously like a naked price fixing agreement
between competitors, which would ordinarily be condemned as *per se* unlawful."[72]

2. Is There Room for Truncated Review of Ancillary Restraints?

While these factual and conceptual distinctions, on close inspection, may not be that difficult to parse, the *timing* of when a court should invoke such a review is another question.
Specifically, there is no reason that the "ancillarity" of outside venture restraints—good or
bad—cannot be assessed in the first instance on the pleadings or on a truncated record.
Indeed, this is how the inquiry was done in the days of *Addyston Pipe* and at common law.[73]
Moreover, where the fact of ancillarity matches up with a legally recognized procompetitive
justification—as in *Rotherey*, for example—there is no reason that this potentially dispositive inquiry should be muddled in the mix of the full rule of reason, just as a naked restraint should not either.

Perhaps the only time summary treatment would *not* be appropriate is where the restraint
does not appear ancillary, *but* also does raise the type of established or inherent risks to

competition that undertake *per se* or quick look condemnation. But if a restraint is either clearly "collateral" *and* anticompetitive *or* clearly ancillary to a procompetitive objective, the court should decide the case on a truncated record.

VI. Step 4: Apply the "Full" Rule of Reason if the Restraint Cannot Be Resolved as a Matter of Law or on a Truncated Record?

If and when a court determines that it cannot determine the competitive merits of the restraint in a truncated fashion—again, by way of pleading or through targeted discovery—then the court would permit the case to proceed to the "full blown" rule of reason with which we are all familiar. As to the subparts of that analysis, there is little dispute.

1. Define the Relevant Market and Apply a "Market Power" Screen

As a threshold matter, the court would apply a market power screen, which involves defining the relevant market and determining if the parties imposing the restraint at issue have market power within that market.[74] The underlying assumption is that "[i]f the relevant market is competitive, no participant will possess market power, and any appreciable procompetitive effect will be deemed sufficient to validate the contested restraint."[75] (Perhaps this, too, may be an inquiry that can be undertaken on a truncated record.)

2. Assess Whether There Are Likely Anticompetitive Effects, Including Injury to Competition

Next, even if a venture restraint involves defendants with real market power, a plaintiff must still prove that consumers are being harmed. In a full rule of reason, this requires empirical work as to efforts on output and price.[76] Again, the Supreme Court has required empirical evidence for this showing, and there is a significant body of law across the Circuits on this requirement, meaning that in many joint venture cases, plaintiffs simply cannot meet this burden.[77]

3. If Necessary, Assess Procompetitive Justifications

Finally, to the extent necessary, courts will assess procompetitive justifications, which are balanced against any demonstrable anticompetitive efforts. The Supreme Court in *American Needle* recognized "'that the interest in maintaining a competitive balance' among 'athletic teams is legitimate and important.'"[78] The Court similarly cited financial stability of the venture as a legitimate procompetitive justification,[79] and other courts have recognized that a venture's rules "can be procompetitive where they enhance the 'character and quality of the product.'"[80]

* * *

For those of us who have practiced antitrust law for many years, it is always surprising that analytical principles are rarely in full repose. This is now particularly true of joint venture analysis, which is long overdue for a step-wise analysis that would preclude legitimate joint ventures from being penalized merely because of the chosen form of collaboration.

NOTES

*   Thanks to David C. Weiss, an associate of the firm, who assisted in the preparation of this article.

1   Texaco Inc. v. Dagher, 547 U.S. 1 (2006).

2   American Needle, Inc. v. NFL, 130 S. Ct. 2201 (2010).

3   This refers to joint ventures that are understood to be legitimate, output-enhancing integrations in their formation. *See* FED. TRADE COMM'N & U.S. DEP'T OF JUSTICE, ANTITRUST GUIDELINES FOR COLLABORATIONS AMONG COMPETITORS 1 (2000) [hereinafter COLLABORATION GUIDELINES], *available at* http://www.ftc.gov/os/2000/04/ftcdojguidelines.pdf.

4   *Dagher*, 547 U.S. at 6–7.

5   *See id.* at 7 (explaining that the ancillary restraints doctrine is inapplicable where the restraint at issue is internal to the core activity of the venture).

6   *Am. Needle*, 130 S. Ct. at 2215–17 (quoting Nat'l Collegiate Athletic Ass'n v. Bd. of Regents of Univ. of Okla., 468 U.S. 85, 109, n.39 (1984)).

7   *See also* PHILIP E. AREEDA & HERBERT HOVENKAMP, ANTITRUST LAW, ¶ 1911c ("The 'quick look' approach is typically invoked when: . . . the defendant offers preliminary evidence suggesting that the challenged restraint is 'justified' in that it is reasonably necessary to some joint activity that in fact increases output or reduces price . . . .").

8   *See* Bell Atl. Corp. v. Twombly, 550 U.S. 544 (2007) (creating stricter pleading standards for plaintiffs alleging conspiracies in violation of Section 1 of the Sherman Act).

9   *See, e.g.*, *Dagher*, 547 U.S. at 5 (describing joint ventures as an "important and increasingly popular form of business organization").

10   *See* James Keyte & Paul Eckles, *Sports Leagues and the Rule of Reason: How to Assess Internal Venture Restraints*, GCP, May 2009, at 2–3, *available at* https://www.competitionpolicyinternational.com/file/view/5984.

11   Dagher v. Saudi Refining, Inc., 369 F.3d 1108, 1116 (9th Cir. 2004), *rev'd sub. nom*, Texaco Inc. v. Dagher, 547 U.S. 1 (2006).

12   L.A. Mem'l Coliseum Comm'n v. NFL (Raiders I), 726 F.2d 1381, 1395–97 (9th Cir. 1984).

13   *Dagher*, 369 F.3d at 1121.

14   *Dagher*, 547 U.S. at 5.

15   *Id.* at 5–6.

16   *Id.* at 6 (second and third alterations in original) (citation omitted).

17   *Id.*

18   *Id.* at 7.

19   *Id.* at 7–8.

20   *Id.*

21   *Id.* The Court also observed that had it applied the ancillary restraints doctrine, the alleged restraint clearly would have been considered ancillary. Quoting Judge Fernandez's dissent from the Ninth Circuit's opinion, the Court asked: "'What could be more integral to the running of a business than setting a price for its goods and services?'" *Id.* at 8.

22   Am. Needle, Inc. v. NFL, 538 F.3d 736 (7th Cir. 2008), *rev'd*, 130 S. Ct. 2201 (2010).

23   130 S. Ct. at 2208 (first alteration in original) (emphasis added) (citations omitted).

24   *Id.* at 2208–09.

25   *Id.* at 2212 (first alteration in original) (citations omitted) (emphasis added). In *Copperweld Corp. v. Independence Tube Corp.*, 467 U.S. 752, 777 (1984), the Court, of course, had held that a parent corporation and its wholly owned subsidiary could not conspire for purposes of Section 1.

26   *Am. Needle, Inc.*, 130 S. Ct. at 2212.

27   *Id.* at 2212–13.

28   *Id.* at 2213–14 (quoting *Copperweld* and explaining that the teams "are still separate, profit-maximizing entities, and their interests in licensing team trademarks are not necessarily aligned," and more importantly, the "justification for cooperation is not relevant to whether that cooperation is concerted or independent action" because the issue is whether the alleged agreement or activity "'deprives the marketplace of independent centers of decision making'").

29   *Id.* at 2216–17.

30   *Id.* (citations omitted).

31 *See* Gregory J. Werden, *American Needle and the Application of the Sherman Act to Professional Sports Leagues*, 18 Vill. Sports & Ent. L. J. 395, 405–06 (2011) (noting that "[s]even justices joined in the unanimous opinions in both *Dagher* and *American Needle*, including both authors, so no judge would read *American Needle* to undermine anything in *Dagher*").

32 *See* PolyGram Holding, Inc. v. FTC, 416 F.3d 29, 37 (D.C. Cir. 2005) ("Three Tenors"); Yamaha Motor Co. v. FTC, 657 F.2d 971, 981 (8th Cir. 1981).

33 *Cf.* Indep. Entm't Grp., Inc. v. NBA, 853 F. Supp. 333 (C.D. Cal. 1994) (holding that a the NBA's rule prohibiting its players from participating in basketball competitions outside the NBA joint venture was "reasonable as a matter of law").

34 *See Agnew v. NCAA*, 683 F.3d 328, 341 (7th Cir. 2012) (finding that certain NCAA bylaws could be upheld as procompetitive "'in the twinkling of an eye' . . . that is, at the motion to dismiss stage"). (Citations omitted).

35 *See* 130 S. Ct. at 2207 (describing the nature of the NFL's exclusive licenses).

36 *See id.* at 2215, 2217 (finding that the NFL was not a single entity for team IP in part because "[t]he 32 teams capture individual economic benefits separate and apart from NFLP profits as a result of the decisions they make for the NFLP" and emphasizing that the Court's holding was limited to "the marketing of the teams' *individually owned* intellectual property" (emphasis added)); Herbert J. Hovenkamp, *American Needle and the Boundaries of the Firm in Antitrust Law* 11 (Aug. 2010) (noting that "presumably the NFL's licensing of its own 'NFL' mark would be a unilateral act"), *available at* http://ssrn.com/abstract=1616625.

37 Texaco Inc. v. Dagher, 547 U.S. 1, 6 (2006).

38 130 S. Ct. at 2214 ("The question whether NFLP decisions can constitute concerted activity covered by § 1 is closer than whether decisions made directly by the 32 teams are covered by § 1.").

39 *See* 547 U.S. at 7–8 ("[T]he ancillary restraints doctrine has no application here, where the business practice being challenged involves the core activity of the joint venture itself—namely, the pricing of the very goods produced and sold by [the venture].").

40 Verizon Commc'ns Inc. v. Law Offices of Curtis V. Trinko, LLP, 540 U.S. 398 (2004).

41 *Dagher*, 547 U.S. at 6.

42 *See* PolyGram Holding, Inc. v. FTC, 416 F.3d 29, 37 (D.C. Cir. 2005).

43 *See Dagher*, 547 U.S. at 8 ("'Joint ventures and other cooperative arrangements are . . . not usually unlawful, at least not as price-fixing schemes, where the agreement on price is necessary to market the product at all.'" (quoting Broad. Music, Inc. v. Columbia Broad. Sys., Inc., 441 U.S. 1, 23 (1979) (alteration in original)); *see also* Yamaha Motor Co. v. FTC, 657 F.2d 971, 981 (8th Cir. 1981).

44 Chicago Prof'l Sports Ltd. P'Ship v. NBA, 95 F.3d 593, 599, 600 (7th Cir. 1996).

45 *In re* Sulfuric Acid Antitrust Litig., 743 F. Supp. 2d 827, 878 (N.D. Ill. 2010).

46 *See supra* ¶26.

47 *See supra* note 34.

48 United States v. Penn-Olin Chem. Co., 378 U.S. 158, 168 (1964).

49 Madison Square Garden, L.P. v. NHL, No. 07 CV 8455 (LAP), 2008 WL 4547518, at *13 (S.D.N.Y. Oct. 10, 2008) (citing United States v. Addyston Pipe & Steel Co., 85 F. 271, 280–81 (6th Cir. 1898)).

50 547 U.S. at 6.

51 *See, e.g.*, E & L Consulting, Ltd. v. Doman Indus. Ltd., 472 F.3d 23 (2d Cir. 2006) (affirming dismissal under Rule 12(b)(6) of claims of refusal to deal brought by terminated distributor).

52 *E.g.*, Electronics Commc'ns Corp. v. Toshiba Am. Consumer Prods., 129 F.3d 240, 245 (2d Cir. 1997) ("[E]xclusive distributorship arrangements are presumptively legal.").

53 *See, e.g.*, Cowley v. Braden Indus., Inc., 613 F.2d 751, 753, 755–56 (9th Cir. 1980) (affirming a district court decision finding territorial and customer restrictions reasonable despite 70% market share).

54 *See* Am. Needle, Inc. v. NFL, 130 S. Ct. 2201, 2214–15 (2010) (citing United States v. Topco Assocs., Inc., 405 U.S. 596, 609 (1972); United States v. Sealy, Inc., 388 U.S. 350, 352–354 (1967)).

55 *See Dagher*, 547 U.S. at 3.

56 Gregory J. Werden, *The Ancillary Restraints Doctrine After Dagher*, 8 Sedona Conf. J. 17, 20 (2007) (emphasis added).

57 *Id.*; *see also* 7 Philip E. Areeda & Herbert Hovenkamp, Antitrust Law, ¶ 1478b1 ("Because it would be senseless for antitrust law to take away with one hand what it gives with the other, approval [of a venture's formation] means that the subsequent realization of that which was foreseeable and judged reasonable at the time of creation *must also be legal*." (emphasis added)).

58 *See Am. Needle*, 130 S. Ct. 2216–17; *see generally* James A. Keyte, *American Needle: A New Quick Look for Joint Ventures*, 25 Antitrust 48 (2010).

59 547 U.S. at 7 (explaining that "the ancillary restraints doctrine . . . governs the validity of restrictions imposed by a legitimate business collaboration, such as a business association or joint venture, on nonventure activities").

60 *See, e.g.*, Rothery Storage & Van Co. v. Atlas Van Lines, Inc, 792 F.2d 210, 223, 227 (D.C. Cir. 1986) (holding that an attempt to counteract free riding from venture members was "reasonably necessary" to the joint venture); Collaboration Guidelines, *supra* note 3, § 3.2 (requiring that a joint venture restraint be "reasonably related to the integration and reasonably necessary to achieve its procompetitive benefits").

61 *See infra* notes 65-67.

62 Gary R. Roberts, *The Antitrust Status of Sports Leagues Revisted*, 64 Tul. L. Rev. 117, 119 (1989).

63 N. Am. Soccer League v. NFL, 670 F.2d 1249, 1258 (2d Cir. 1982) (noting that the cross-ownership ban did not relate to the production of NFL football but rather that the ban was "designed to restrain competition by NASL teams against NFL teams").

64 459 U.S. 1074, 1077–78 (1982) (Rehnquist, J., dissenting).

65 792 F.2d at 210, 223–24.

66 Indep. Entm't Group, Inc. v. NBA, 853 F. Supp. 333 (C.D. Cal. 1994).

67 *Id.* at 338.

68 Yamaha Motor Co. v. FTC, 657 F.2d 971 (8th Cir. 1981).

69 *In re* Brunswick Corp., 94 F.T.C. 1174, 1275 (1979).

70 657 F.2d at 981.

71 PolyGram Holding, Inc. v. FTC, 416 F.3d 29, 38 (D.C. Cir. 2005).

72 *Id.* at 37.

73 *See* United States v. Addyston Pipe & Steel Co., 85 F. 271, 280 (6th Cir. 1898) (Taft, J.) (describing the Sherman Act's codification of the common law by noting that at common law "[w]hen two men become partners in a business, although their union might reduce competition, this effect was only an incident to the main purpose of a union of their capital, enterprise, and energy to carry on a successful business, and one useful to the community. Restrictions in articles of partnership upon the business activity of the members, with a view of securing their entire effort in the common enterprise, were, of course, only ancillary to the main end of the union and were to be encouraged").

74 *See, e.g.*, PSKS, Inc. v. Leegin Creative Leather Prods., Inc., 615 F.3d 412, 418–19 (5th Cir. 2010) (holding that "[a] market-power screen is . . . compatible with [the Supreme Court's decision in] *Leegin* and [lower court] precedent"), *cert. denied*, 131 S. Ct. 1476 (2011).

75 New York v. Anheuser-Busch, Inc., 811 F. Supp. 848, 872 (E.D.N.Y. 1993) (citing Kevin J. Arquit, *Market Power in Vertical Cases*, 60 Antitrust L.J. 921 (1992); Douglas H. Ginsberg, *Vertical Restraints: De Facto Legality Under the Rule of Reason*, 60 Antitrust L.J. 67 (1991)).

76 *See, e.g.*, Marina Lao, *Comment: The Rule of Reason and Horizontal Restraints Involving Professionals*, 68 Antitrust L.J. 499, 503 (2000) ("In a full rule of reason case, this usually entails a detailed economic definition of the market and proof of market power, or actual proof of anticompetitive effect, such as evidence of higher prices or lower output.").

77 *See, e.g.*, Cal. Dental Ass'n v. FTC, 526 U.S. 756, 774 (1999) (requiring empirical evidence).

78 Am. Needle, Inc. v. NFL, 130 S. Ct. 2201, 2217 (2010) (describing competitive balance as "unquestionably an interest that may well justify a variety of collective decisions made by the teams" (quoting NCAA v. Bd. of Regents of the Univ. of Okla., 468 U.S. 85, 117 (1984)). Moreover, in *Board of Regents*, the Court explained that "[t]he hypothesis that legitimates the maintenance of competitive balance as a pro-competitive justification under the Rule of Reason is that equal competition will maximize consumer demand for the product." 468 U.S. at 119–20.

79 *Am. Needle*, 130 S. Ct. at 2216 (stating that "[t]he fact that NFL teams share an interest in making the entire league successful and profitable . . . provides a perfectly sensible justification for making a host of collective decisions.").

80 Deutscher Tennis Bund v. ATP Tour, Inc., 610 F.3d 820, 833 (3d Cir.) (quoting *Bd. of Regents*, 468 U.S. at 102), *cert. denied*, 131 S. Ct. 658 (2010).

The FTC Act in Merger Policy Integration

JOSEPH KRAUSS

joseph.krauss@hoganlovells.com
Partner, Hogan Lovells U.S., LLP

CHRISTIAN M. ROWAN

christian.rowan@hoganlovells.com
Associate, Hogan Lovells U.S., LLP

Abstract

Former Commissioner Kovacic's keynote address outlined several promising ways to promote merger policy integration, consistent enforcement, and a fair clearance process. However, he overlooked the growing gap in enforcement policy and practice between the FTC and DOJ resulting from the FTC's reliance on the FTC Act and administrative process in merger enforcement under the HSR Act. The FTC could promote merger policy integration by (a) adopting a policy of seeking both preliminary and permanent injunctions in federal court under Section 13(b) or Section 16 of the Clayton Act, much like the DOJ, (b) declining to file administrative complaints in HSR merger cases, or filing administrative complaints only in cases that are not time sensitive, and (c) asserting Section 5 claims only in exceptional cases that involve anticompetitive acts ancillary to an acquisition. Former Commissioner Kovacic's keynote address outlined several promising ways to promote merger policy integration, consistent enforcement, and a fair clearance process. However, he overlooked one important area—the growing gap in enforcement policy and practice between the U.S. Federal Trade Commission ("FTC") and the U.S. Department of Justice ("DOJ") resulting from the FTC's reliance on the FTC Act and administrative process in merger enforcement under the Hart Scott Rodino Act, 15 USC § 18A ("HSR Act"). Absent fundamental changes in the way that the FTC utilizes its unique statutory powers, coordination on merger enforcement policy between the agencies can only go so far in assuring the public that dual agency enforcement is consistent and fair.

I. FTC's Merger Enforcement Powers

The DOJ and FTC share enforcement powers with respect to Sections 7 and 7A of the Clayton Act. But from that common start, the agencies statutory framework for challenging mergers diverges sharply.

The FTC's key merger enforcement powers are found in Sections 5(a), 5(b), and 13(b) of the FTC Act, as well as Sections 7 and 7A of the Clayton Act.[1] Section 5(a) of the Act provides that "[u]nfair methods of competition in or affecting commerce, and unfair or deceptive acts or practices in or affecting commerce, are hereby declared unlawful."[2] Courts have interpreted Section 5(a) to be least as broad as Sherman Act Section 1 and Sherman Act Section 2.[3] Additionally, Section 5(a) may provide the FTC an alternative to Clayton Act Section 7 for merger review and enforcement, although the relationship between these two laws is not well settled.[4] Section 5(b) of the Act establishes the FTC's basic administrative complaint and review procedures, directing the FTC to issue an administrative complaint "[w]henever the Commission shall have reason to believe that [a person] has been or is using any unfair method of competition or unfair or deceptive act or practice in or affecting commerce, and if it shall appear to the Commission that a proceeding by it in respect thereof would be to the interest of the public."[5] Section 13(b) of the Act provides that the FTC may obtain a preliminary injunction "upon a proper showing that, weighing the equities and considering the Commission's likelihood of ultimate success, such action would be in the public interest."[6]

In contrast, the DOJ must rely upon Section 15 of the Clayton Act, 15 USC § 25, which does not include analogous language concerning the "public interest" or "weighing the equities." Furthermore, DOJ's procedural avenues to challenge a merger are limited to the preliminary and permanent injunction road since it has no equivalent administrative procedures. Finally the DOJ is limited in proving that a merger violates Section 7 of the Clayton Act, and it has no "unfair method of competition" enforcement statute analogous to Section 5 of the FTC Act. Thus, the DOJ is limited to federal court proceedings to permanently enjoin a transaction under the much stricter standard of the Clayton Act.

The FTC has the ability to bring pre-merger suits for preliminary and permanent injunctions that essentially mirror analogous suits brought by DOJ. Specifically, Section 13(b) not only empowers FTC to seek preliminary injunctions in federal court, as noted above, but it also provides "[t]hat in proper cases the Commission may seek, and after proper proof, the court may issue, a permanent injunction."[7] FTC may also seek preliminary and permanent injunctions under Section 16 of the Clayton Act, 15 USC § 26, "under the same conditions and principles as injunctive relief against threatened conduct that will cause loss or damage is granted by courts of equity." Thus, FTC does not need to resort to an administrative trial to seek a permanent injunction; it can pursue both preliminary and permanent remedies in federal court, as is the standard practice of DOJ under Section 15 of the Clayton Act, 15 USC § 25. Finally, as noted, FTC has the statutory power to file Clayton Act Section 7 claims and therefore does not need to file Section 5 claims in merger cases. Accordingly, the FTC could seek preliminary and permanent injunctions under the same procedures, under the same basic standards, and under the same substantive laws relied upon by DOJ.

Although the FTC *can* follow the same approach as DOJ, it has not pursued this policy. During the last ten years, the FTC has authorized staff to seek federal injunctions to prevent twenty-three mergers and acquisitions. Some mergers were abandoned before the FTC filed a complaint, and others settled before the FTC filed a complaint in federal court. Of the pre-merger cases where complaints were filed in federal court, all sought preliminary injunctions under FTC Act Section 13(b) *without* also seeking permanent injunctions under Section 13(b) or Section 16. In many cases, the FTC also filed administrative complaints concurrently, before, or shortly after filing complaints in federal court. In the cases were administrative complaints were not issued; the FTC retained the option to file such complaints until shortly after judicial disposition of the federal court cases.

In almost every case filed in federal court, including cases that resulted in settlements, the FTC asserted claims under both Clayton Act Section 7 and Section 5 of the FTC Act.

II. The Growing Gap in Merger Enforcement Due to the FTC Act

In *most* cases, the FTC's uses of administrative process and reliance on the FTC Act have had few significant consequences. For instance, courts have almost uniformly subsumed Section 5 claims into Section 7 claims.[8] FTC's filing of administrative complaints also traditionally has not resulted in administrative trials or substantive administrative decisions. Indeed, no pre-consummation case subject to the HSR Act has ever been litigated in an administrative proceeding after a preliminary injunction was granted by a federal court. Conversely, the FTC has opted to dismiss the administrative complaint in every case since 1995 where a preliminary injunction was not issued and sustained on appeal.[9] In recognition of this trend, courts generally have treated preliminary injunction hearings in cases brought by the FTC similar to trials consolidating preliminary injunction and permanent injunction proceedings in cases brought by the DOJ.[10]

The FTC's reliance on the preliminary injunction standard in Section 13(b) also *historically* has not created substantial differences between FTC and DOJ enforcement. While courts generally have paid lip service to the textual differences between Section 13(b) and Section 15 and have evaluated FTC motions for preliminary injunction on a sliding scale that diverges from the traditional equity standard for preliminary injunctions, the results typically have not been out of line with analogous enforcement actions brought by the DOJ. For instance, in *Heinz*, the DC Circuit acknowledged that "Congress intended [the 13(b)] standard to depart from what it regarded as the then-traditional equity standard."[11] Nonetheless, the court applied the analytical approach used in *Baker Hughes*, despite the fact that the case was decided at the merits stage under Clayton Section 15 as opposed to the preliminary injunctive relief stage under FTC Section 13(b).[12]

Heinz was an incremental victory for the FTC in relaxing the 13(b) standard, but nothing in the courts opinion except its initial citation of the sliding scale standard under 13(b) suggested that the court would have arrived at a different conclusion had the DOJ brought the case. The decisions in *Weyerhaeuser, Exxon, University Health*, and *Food Town Stores*[13] among other case, also acknowledged that Section 13(b) provides a nominally unique and more permissive standard than the typical preliminary injunction standard, but the cases were not decided under FTC-specific analytical frameworks or with substantially less evidence than contemporaneous cases brought by the DOJ.[14] Courts justified their refusal to adopt a substantially more relaxed approach to FTC 13(b) cases by noting that a grant of a preliminary injunction is effectively a death sentence in merger litigation, thereby cautioning against an overly permissive standard.[15]

In 2005 comments to the Antitrust Modernization Committee, then FTC General Counsel William Blumenthal also recognized that "there seems to be a general agreement that the outcome of the preliminary injunction motion will decide the fate of the majority of transactions."[16] He further argued that as a practical matter courts apply a relaxed "public interest" test rather than the "traditional equity test" to both FTC and DOJ, resulting in consistent enforcement between the agencies.[17] In 2007, Commissioners Garza, Jacobson and Kempf of the AMC agreed that the standards applied to the agencies were essentially the same and that legislation to ensure that the standards are identical is not necessary.[18]

In 2008, however, the notion that the agencies faced essentially the same preliminary injunction standard was significantly challenged. First, in hearings on the FTC's motion for a preliminary injunction to prevent the merger of Inova Health System Foundation and Prince William Health System, Inc. ("*Inova/Prince William*"), Judge Hilton of the Eastern District of Virginia ruled that he would decide the motion on the papers, with limited documentary evidence, and with no discovery beyond that permitted in parallel administrative proceedings.[19] In taking this novel approach, Judge Hilton accepted the FTC's argument that a full hearing on the merits of the case was unnecessary given FTC's parallel administrative proceedings. However, the case never proceeded to an administrative trial; the parties abandoned the merger about a week after Judge Hilton's decision.[20]

Shortly after the FTC's victory in *Inova/Prince William*, it won another substantial victory in *Whole Foods*.[21] In this matter, the FTC argued for a permissive preliminary injunction standard by stressing its adjudicative role in determining the legality of mergers through the administrative process, thereby drawing from the same arguments that prevailed in *Inova/Prince William*. Specifically, the FTC argued before the DC Circuit Court that 13(b) entitled it to a preliminary injunction if it could "show 'serious, substantial' questions requiring plenary administrative consideration."[22] In a similar vein, the FTC contended that a more stringent approach "effectively usurps the adjudicative role of the Commission." The FTC also cited legislative history stressing it was designed to "exercise power of a judicial nature."[23] Therefore, instead of hewing to Blumenthal's position before the AMC that government antitrust agencies are *all* entitled to an *equally* permissive standard, the FTC insisted that its unique adjudicative functions entitled it to a *uniquely permissive* standard.

Judge's Brown and Tatel, writing the opinion of the court and a concurrence, respectively, both appear to have endorsed FTC exceptionalism. Specifically, while conceding that "the district court applied the correct legal standard," Judge Brown opined that the FTC "does not need detailed evidence of anticompetitive effect at this preliminary phase," and that the district court could only correctly deny a preliminary injunction if the "decision . . . rested on a conviction the FTC entirely failed to show a likelihood of success."[24] Moreover, in directing the district court to balance the likelihood of the FTC's success against the equities, she cautioned that "[t]he equities will often weigh in favor of the FTC, since the public interest in effective enforcement of the antitrust laws was Congress's specific public equity consideration" in enacting the provision."[25] Judge Tatel's concurrence also endorsed a uniquely permissive standard under 13(b) that appears to have incorporated a presumption in FTC's favor.[26] Furthermore, Judges Brown and Tatel both premised their opinions regarding the 13(b) standard, in part, on the FTC's unique adjudicative role in the administrative process.[27] Judge Tatel went so far as to assume that there *would be* administrative proceedings ultimately evaluating the legality of the merger.[28] Predictably, the case did not proceed to an administrative trial; Whole Foods and the FTC settled shortly after the DC Circuit's decision.[29]

Unlike the nominally lesser standard adopted by the court in *Heinz*, the permissive standard adopted by Judges Brown and Tatel in *Whole Foods* created a substantial gap between the agencies' evidentiary burdens at the preliminary injunction stage. Specifically, the court ruled for the FTC even though a majority of the court seemingly agreed that FTC did not establish a likelihood that it would prove its market definition.[30] On the contrary, Judge Brown effectively concluded that even where the FTC premises its case on a certain market definition, a district court may grant the FTC's request for a preliminary injunction if there is merely *a chance* that it could prove that market definition as long as the equities weighed sufficiently in FTC's favor.[31]

Combined with Judge Brown's opinion that "the equities in a § 53(b) preliminary injunction proceeding will usually favor the FTC," the FTC in *Whole Foods* faced a radically different standard than has been applied to the DOJ. For example, in *Oracle*, the court rejected the DOJ's market definition and ultimately its entire case after holding that "[i]n order to sustain plaintiffs' product market definition the court must find, by a preponderance of the evidence, that plaintiffs' have shown an articulable and distinct product market."[32] In *H&R Block*, the court approved the DOJ's market definition, but it nonetheless recognized that DOJ bore the burden of proving its entire *prima facie* case and that "[d]efining the relevant market is critical in an antitrust case because the legality of the proposed merger[] in question almost always depends upon the market power of the parties involved,"[33] and while both of these cases were decided on permanent injunction standards, that fact is itself the result of inequities in FTC and DOJ enforcement, as the FTC has the ability and proclivity to avoid judicial permanent injunction proceedings in favor of an administrative trial (regardless of the extremely low likelihood that an administrative trial will actually occur).

After three and a half years, the ultimate effects of *Whole Foods* and *Inova/Prince William* are still unclear. Nonetheless, experience demonstrates that the FTC is pursuing a policy of expanding its powers under the FTC Act in order to acquire procedural and substantive advantages over private litigants, and indirectly over DOJ. In 2011, for instance, the FTC made arguments in *FTC v. Graco Inc.* that relied upon the FTC's administrative powers to marginalize the role judicial review in FTC enforcement.[34] In recent years, the FTC has also increasingly filed administrative proceedings simultaneously with or prior to filing its complaints. This serves the dual purposes of providing the FTC with an additional means of seeking discovery and reinforcing the FTC's position that administrative proceedings provide a viable alternative to thorough judicial review notwithstanding the fact that the FTC has not proceeded to the "completion of its administrative proceedings" in an HSR merger case for over fifteen years.

There have been no dramatic shifts in the FTC's approach to merger enforcement under Section 5 akin to recent shifts in Section 13(b) enforcement and jurisprudence, but the FTC's unusually expansive approach to Section 5 in other areas of the law could spill over to its merger enforcement practices. For instance, in *In the Matter of Negotiated Data Solutions LLC* ("*N-Data*") in 2008, the FTC charged Negotiated Data Solutions with stand-alone violations of Section 5 that did not include clear "exclusionary Conduct," such as deception, that would ordinarily be required to prove analogous Section 2 claims under the Sherman Act.[35] The FTC's approach in *N-Data* draws from decades-old jurisprudence from *Sperry & Hutchinson Co.* and other cases standing for the proposition that "the Federal Trade Commission does not arrogate excessive power to itself if, in measuring a practice against the elusive but congressionally mandated standard of fairness [enshrined in Section 5], it, like a court of equity, considers public values beyond simply those enshrined in the letter or encompassed in the spirit of the antitrust laws."[36]

Sperry & Hutchinson Co did not involve a merger or an acquisition, but the Court also did not limit its analysis to any specific antitrust laws. Additionally, in 1994 administrative proceedings, the FTC specifically held that Section 5 is an independent source of merger enforcement powers for the FTC that may exceed its enforcement powers under Clayton Act Section 7. In *Coca Cola*,[37] the FTC found that Coca Cola's proposed acquisition of Dr. Pepper would have substantially lessened competition in violation of Section 7 of the Clayton Act and Section 5 of the FTC Act, and its agreement to acquire Dr. Pepper also constituted an additional and *independent* violation of Section 5 of the FTC Act.[38] The Commission's holding rested on its opinion that "It is well established that certain practices that do not violate the Sherman and Clayton Acts . . . may nonetheless be "unfair methods of competition" that violate Section 5 of the FTC Act."[39]

Regardless of whether *N-Data* and older jurisprudence on Section 5 have any immediate significance on merger enforcement, the FTC's consistent assertion of Section 5 claims in addition to Clayton 7 claims in merger enforcement actions raises the specter that some transactions could be found unlawful under Section 5 when enforced by the FTC but not when enforced by the DOJ under Clayton Act Section 7. FTC staff has alluded to this possibility in recent pleadings in *Graco*.[40] In the FTC's opposition to a motion to transfer in *Graco*, FTC argued that "The standard of "unfairness" under the FTC Act . . . encompass[es] not only practices that violate the Sherman Act and the other antitrust laws, but also practices that the Commission determines are against public policy for other reasons. 15 USC § 45(a)(2)."[41] The FTC's goal in *Graco* was to establish that a seller in an asset acquisition was a proper defendant in a preliminary injunction case under Section 13(b) despite the fact that Clayton Act Section 7 is explicitly limited to "acquisitions" without also prohibiting "sales." The FTC's theory was that Section 5 provided it broader reach over sellers than Section 7, thus expanding the reach of Clayton Act Section 7.[42]

III. The FTC Can Unilaterally Promote Policy Integration and Consistent Enforcement and Fairer Clearance

The agencies cannot achieve full policy integration, consistent enforcement, and fair clearance while the FTC exploits a lower preliminary injunction standard that is effectively a permanent injunction standard, leaves the door open to a broader FTC-centric substantive standard under FTC Act Section 5, and seeks expanded jurisdiction beyond that available to the DOJ through FTC Section 5.

In 2007, the Antitrust Modernization Commission recognized many of these problems when it released its Report and Recommendations. In an effort to promote uniform and consistent enforcement between the agencies, the AMC report suggested that the FTC seek both preliminary and permanent injunctions in federal court for mergers under the HSR Act; that Congress should amend Section 13(b) of the Federal Trade Commission Act, 15 USC § 53(b), to prohibit the FTC from pursuing administrative actions in HSR merger cases; and that Congress should ensure that the same standard for the grant of a preliminary injunction applies to both the Federal Trade Commission and the Antitrust Division of the Department of Justice ("DOJ") by amending Section 13(b). Thus far, the FTC and Congress have not followed any of these suggestions, while the problems identified by the AMC report have only worsened during the last five years.

Even if Congress takes no action, the FTC can unilaterally adopt a policy of seeking both preliminary and permanent injunctions in federal court under Section 13(b) or Section 16 of the Clayton Act, as suggested by the AMC report; decline to file administrative complaints in HSR merger cases, or file administrative complaints only in cases that are not time sensitive;[43] and assert Section 5 claims only in exceptional cases that involve anticompetitive acts ancillary to an acquisition.[44]

We do not propose that the FTC abandon administrative challenges in all merger cases, and indeed, we recognize that the FTC has unique and valuable experience in challenges against consummated mergers that typically do not require final resolution in a matter of months.[45] Nonetheless, experience demonstrates that the three-step process that theoretically characterizes FTC suits in pre-merger litigation (a preliminary injunction in federal court, followed by a trial under an administrative judge on the merits, followed by review by the Commission) has effectively become a one-step process subject to an unusually permissive standard, because private litigants are not willing to continue to litigate a case in FTC's own administrative courts where FTC has an apparent—if not actual—conflict of interest, and an incentive to delay proceedings once a preliminary injunction has already been issued.[46]

None of these proposed actions would directly alter the standard under Section 13(b), but a permissive standard under Section 13(b) for preliminary injunctions would be irrelevant if the FTC simultaneously sought a permanent injunction. Additionally, one of the prevailing justifications for applying divergent standards to FTC and DOJ would evaporate if the FTC did not insist on pretending that the administrative process provides an effective forum for adjudicating permanent injunctions in time-sensitive mergers. Steps along these lines would complete Commissioner Kovacic's noble objective of closer integration of merger policy and enforcement between the DOJ and FTC and remove a schism that creates unnecessary and costly distortions in merger enforcement between the two agencies.

NOTES

1   These laws are codified at 15 U.S.C. §§ 45(a), 45(b), 53(b), 18, and 18A, respectively.

2   15 U.S.C. § 45(a).

3   *See, e.g.,* Neil W. Averitt, *The Meaning of "Unfair Methods of Competition" in Section 5 of the Federal Trade Commission Act,* 21 B. C.L. REV. 227, 239-242 (1980) (describing the relationship between the FTC Act, the Clayton Act, and the Sherman Act).

4   *See* Section II, *infra.*

5   15 U.S.C. § 45(b).

6   15 U.S.C. § 53(b).

7   *Id.*

8   *See, e.g.,* Federal Trade Commission v. Whole Foods Mkt., Inc., 548 F.3d 1028, 1036-37 (D.C. Cir. 2008) (applying only a Section 7 standard of review where the FTC charged violations of Section 5 of the FTC Act and Section 7 of the Clayton Act); Federal Trade Commission v. Weyerhaeuser Co., 665 F.2d 1072, 1090-91 (D.C. Cir. 1981) (applying only a Section 7 standard in affirming an order in an FTC action challenging a proposed merger under both Section 7 and Section 5); Federal Trade Commission v. Atlantic Richfield Co., 549 F.2d 289, 291-92 n.1 (4th Cir. 1977) (noting that no case has upheld the propriety of reaching mergers under Section 5); Federal Trade Commission v. PepsiCo, Inc., 477 F.2d 24, 28 n.6 (2d Cir. 1973) ("The particular significance of Section 5 of the Federal Trade Commission Act as a basis for relief here is not apparent either from an examination of the complaint or the brief of the Commission before us"); Federal Trade Commission v. Staples, Inc., 970 F. Supp. 1066, 1070 (D.D.C. 1997) (applying only a Section 7 standard in an FTC challenge to a proposed merger under both Section 7 and Section 5).

9   *See, e.g.,* Order Returning Matter to Adjudication and Dismissing Complaint, *In re* Lab. Corp. of Am., FTC Docket No. 9345 (April 21, 2011); Statement of the Commission, *In re* Arch Coal Inc., FTC Docket No. 9316 (September 10, 2004); Order Dismissing Complaint, *In re* Tenet Healthcare Corp., FTC Docket No. 9289 (Dec. 23, 1999); Order Granting Motion to Dismiss, *In re* Butterworth Health Corp., FTC Docket No. 9283 (Sept. 25, 1997); Order Dismissing Complaint, *In re* Freeman Hosp., FTC Docket No. 9273 (Nov. 30, 1995). In *Whole Foods,* the Commission stayed the administrative proceedings while it appealed the district court's denial of a preliminary injunction, but it later rescinded the stay when the case was remanded to district court. *See* Docket, *In re* Whole Foods Mkt., Inc., FTC Docket No. 9324, *available at* http://www.ftc.gov/os/adjpro/d9324/index.shtm.

10 *See, e.g.,* Federal Trade Commission v. Arch Coal, Inc., 329 F. Supp. 109, 109 (D.D.C. 2004) (noting that the court held two weeks of hearings featuring more than twenty witnesses and hundreds of exhibits), Federal Trade Commission v. Swedish Match, 131 F. Supp. 2d 151, 155 (D.D.C. 2000) (noting that the court held five days of hearings featuring more than eleven witnesses and hundreds of exhibits); *see also* J. Thomas Rosch, Commissioner, FTC, *A Peek Inside: One Commissioner's Perspective on the Commission's Roles as Prosecutor and Judge,* Remarks Before the NERA 2008 Antitrust and Trade Regulation Seminar, 13 (2008) *available at* http://www.ftc.gov/speeches/ rosch/080703nera.pdf (complaining that courts had "essentially turned proceedings on the Commission's application for a preliminary injunction into plenary trials on the merits").

11 Federal Trade Commission v. H.J. Heinz Co., 246 F.3d 708, 714 (D.C. Cir. 2001), *citing* H.R. Rep. No. 93-624 at 31 (1971) (opining that the traditional standard is not "appropriate for the implementation of a Federal statute by an independent regulatory agency where the standards of the public interest measure the propriety and the need for injunctive relief.")

12 United States v. Baker Hughes Inc., 908 F.2d 981, 715 (D.C. Cir. 1990).

13 Federal Trade Commission v. Weyerhaeuser Co., 665 F.2d 1072 (D.C. Cir. 1981), Federal Trade Commission v. Exxon Corp., 636 F.2d 1336, (D.C. Cir. 1980), Federal Trade Commission v. University Health, Inc., 938 F.2d 1206, 1217 (11th Cir. 1991), and Federal Trade Commission v. Food Town Stores, Inc., 539 F.2d 1339 (4th Cir. 1976).

14 *See supra* note 8 (describing the typical scope of preliminary injunction hearings for FTC cases). In some instances, courts have explicitly refused to adopt a different approach to FTC 13(b) cases. For instance, the court in *Tenet Health Care Corp.*, 186 F.3d 1045 (8th Cir. 1999) specifically declined to adopt the FTC's position that it needed only show a "fair and tenable chance of success on the merits" to prevail on a motion for a preliminary injunction.

15 *See, e.g.*, Federal Trade Commission v. Exxon Corp., 636 F.2d 1336, 1343 (D.C. Cir. 1980) ("[T]he issuance of a PI blocking an acquisition or merger may prevent the transaction from ever being consummated.").

16 William Blumenthal, General Counsel, FTC, *Observations on Federal Antitrust Enforcement Institutions*, 3-4 (2005).

17 *Id.* at 4-5.

18 ANTITRUST MODERNIZATION COMMISSION, REPORT AND RECOMMENDATIONS 141 (2007) ("2007 AMC REPORT").

19 Transcript of Hearing at 12-13, Federal Trade Commission v. Inova Health System Found., No. 1:08-cv-460 (E.D. Va., May 30, 2008).

20 In many respects, *Inova/Prince William* was an unusual case. The FTC had more than a year and a half to develop evidence prior to filing a complaint due to the parties' extremely slow compliance with the HSR clearance review process. *See* Plaintiffs' Memorandum of Points and Authorities in Opposition to Defendants' Motion for a Scheduling Order and an Expedited Status Conference at 5–6, *Inova/Prince William*, No. 1:08- cv-460-CMH/JFA (E.D. Va. May 20, 2008). Additionally, the FTC had taken extraordinary measures to demonstrate its intent to quickly and efficiently conduct an administrative trial by appointing Commissioner Rosch as the Administrative Law Judge ("ALJ") presiding over the trial and by declining to stay administrative proceedings during federal court proceedings.

21 Federal Trade Commission v. Whole Foods Market, Inc., 548 F.3d 1028 (D.C. Cir. 2008).

22 Proof Brief For Appellant Federal Trade Commission, at 27, FTC v. Whole Foods Market, Inc., Civ. No. 07-cv-Ol021-PLF (D.C. Cir., January 14, 2008).

23 *Id.* at 28.

24 Whole Foods, 548 F.3d at 1034, 1035.

25 *Id.* (internal citations omitted).

26 *Id.* at 1042, 1043.

27 *Id.* at 1035 ("in a § 53(b) preliminary injunction proceeding, a court is not authorized to determine whether the antitrust laws . . . are about to be violated . . . That responsibility lies with the FTC.) (internal citations omitted).

28 *Id.* at 1050 ("[I]f the district court concludes that the equities tilt in the FTC's favor, it will need to craft an alternative, fact-bound remedy sufficient to achieve section 13(b)'s purpose, namely allowing the FTC to review the transaction in an administrative proceeding and reestablish the premerger status quo if it finds a section 7 violation.").

29 *FTC Consent Order Settles Charges that Whole Foods' Acquisition of Rival Wild Oats was Anticompetitive*, Press release (March 6, 2009), *available at* http://www.ftc.gov/opa/2009/03/wholefoods.shtm.

30 Whole Foods, 548 F.3d at 1041 ("I cannot agree with the district court that the FTC would never be able to prove a PNOS submarket. This is not to say the FTC has in fact proved such a market, which is not necessary at this point. To obtain a preliminary injunction under § 53(b), the FTC need only show a likelihood of success sufficient, using the sliding scale, to balance any equities that might weigh against the injunction"); *id.* at 1052 (concluding that FTC failed to make "a sufficient showing that so-called organic stores constitute a separate product market.") (J. Kavanaugh, dissenting).

31 *Id.*

32 United States v. Oracle Corp., 331 F. Supp. 2d 1098 (N.D. Cal. 2004).

33 United States v. H&R Block, Inc. No. 11-00948 (BAH), 13-15 (D.D.C. Nov. 10, 2011).

34 Plaintiff Federal Trade Commission's Memorandum in Support of Motion for Temporary Restraining Order and Preliminary Injunction, F.T.C. v. Graco Inc., 1:11-CV-02239-RLW (D.D.C., Dec. 15, 2011).

35 ANALYSIS OF PROPOSED CONSENT ORDER TO AID PUBLIC COMMENT, NEGOTIATED DATA SOLUTIONS LLC, FTC File No. 051 0094 (Jan. 23, 2008) *available at* http://www.ftc.gov/os/caselist/0510094/080122analysis.pdf. *See also* Complaint, In re Intel Corp., FTC Docket No. 9341 (Dec. 16, 2009), *available at* http://www.ftc.gov/os/adjpro/d9341/091216intelcmpt.pdf. ("The Federal Trade Commission Act "was designed to supplement and bolster the Sherman Act and the Clayton Act . . . to stop in their incipiency acts and practices which, when full blown, would violate those Acts . . . as well as to condemn as 'unfair methods of competition' existing violations" of those acts and practices. The Act gives the Commission a unique role in determining what constitutes unfair methods of competition. "[L]ike a court of equity, the Commission may consider public values beyond simply those enshrined in the letter or encompassed in the spirit of the antitrust laws." Examples of conduct that fall within the scope of Section 5 include deceptive, collusive, coercive, predatory, unethical, or exclusionary conduct or any course of conduct that causes actual or incipient harm to competition." (citations omitted)).

36 Federal Trade Commission v. Sperry & Hutchinson Co., 405 U.S. 233, 244 (1972).

37 In the Matter of Coca-Cola Co., 117 Federal Trade Commission 795 (1994).

38 117 Federal Trade Commission at 961.

39 *Id.* at 913.

40 Federal Trade Commission v. Graco, Case 1:11-cv-02239-RLW (D.D.C. January 13, 2012).

41 Plaintiff's Supplemental Opposition to Defendant Graco's Motion to Dismiss or Transfer: Responses to the Court's Questions, *Federal Trade Commission v. Graco*, Case 1:11-cv-02239-RLW, 1 (D.D.C. January 13, 2012).

42 *Id.* at 4.

43 The FTC already effectively follows this policy inasmuch as it typically conducts administrative trials for post-merger Clayton Act Section 7 claims while its pre-merger Clayton Act Section 7 claims are usually resolved in federal court. However, the FTC continues to use the administrative process to avail itself of a favorable "prelimi-nary injunction" standard in federal court.

44 Some cases present issues that legitimately raise FTC Act Section 5 questions in addition to independent questions under Clayton Act. For instance, in Yamaha Motor Co. v. FTC, 657 F.2d 971 (8th Cir. 1981), the FTC charged defendants with independent violations of Section 5 for anticompetitive agreements not to compete with on another that were ancillary to an acquisition that the FTC alleged also violated Section 7.

45 *E.g., In re* Polypore International, Inc., FTC Docket No. 9327 (Dec. 13, 2010); *In re* Scott & White Healthcare, FTC File No. 091-0084 (Dec. 23, 2009); *In re* Carilion Clinic, FTC Docket No. 9338 (Oct. 6, 2009); *In re* Lubrizol Corp. and Lockhart Co., FTC Docket No. C-4254 (Feb. 26, 2009); *In re* Evanston Northwestern Healthcare Corp., FTC Docket No. 9315 (Aug. 6, 2007). In post-consummation merger cases, FTC typically does not start the admi-nistrative process with a preliminary injunction in-hand. In such cases, FTC has an incentive to quickly and effi-ciently conduct administrative proceedings given that continued post-merger integration makes designing and implementing a remedy increasingly difficult. Nonetheless, post-consummation administrative challenges cases can take years to resolve.

46 *See, e.g.,* Statement from Inova Health System and Prince William Health System about the Proposed Merger (June 6, 2008) (abandoning the Inova/Prince William merger because "unusual process changes by the Federal Trade Commission threatened to prolong completion of the merger by as much as two years.").

Standard Oil, the Origins of Dual Antitrust Jurisdiction in the U.S., and the Modern Justification for Unified Enforcement

GEORGE L. PRIEST

GEORGE.PRIEST@YALE.EDU

Edward J. Phelps Professor of Law and Economics and
Kauffman Distinguished Research Scholar in Law, Economics, and Entrepreneurship, Yale Law School

Abstract

Professor William Kovacic's spirited and articulate advocacy of unified and coordinated antitrust enforcement as between the dual U.S. antitrust agencies—the Justice Department and the FTC—gains force from a more complete historical understanding of the origins of the FTC and of the changes in antitrust understanding in the years since. Congress created the FTC in 1914, giving it independent antitrust enforcement authority, explicitly because it was disappointed in the antitrust efforts of the Justice Department, in particular with the outcome of the 1911 Standard Oil case, and wanted separate and more aggressive enforcement. In the years since the creation of the FTC, however, there has developed a consensus on the economic analysis of antitrust that eliminates the need for competing enforcement agencies, providing support for Professor Kovacic's recommendations.

I. Introduction

In his valedictory address, typically insightful, given as an inspiration for this volume and earlier published in this Journal,[1] my friend Bill Kovacic, though admitting some problems, emphasized the potential opportunities of the unique dual antitrust authority in the U.S. of the Justice Department and the Federal Trade Commission (FTC) according to which each agency possesses independent authority to bring antitrust prosecutions. Bill's article sought to rationalize this unusual administrative arrangement or, more precisely, to describe the many ways in which the arrangement might be better rationalized than it is at the present. The clear approach of his article (and of others that he has written on this subject) is that antitrust enforcement in the U.S. should possess a unified approach in terms both of underlying antitrust theory and of administration. An implication of his approach is that other countries should also adopt a unified approach, following the US as an exemplar, given that the U.S. has the longest antitrust tradition. As mentioned, Bill sets forth many valuable proposals involving interagency coordination and cooperation to achieve this end.

This article seeks to place the Kovacic analysis in context by reviewing in a summary way the origins of the creation in 1914 of dual antitrust enforcement authority in the U.S. as between the Justice Department and the FTC and by explaining how our understanding of antitrust principles has changed in the succeeding years. It explains that the origin of dual authority was motivated by the 1911 U.S. Supreme Court decision in Standard Oil Co. v. U.S.,[2] a decision whose 100th anniversary occurred within the past months. The Article shows that the Supreme Court's Standard Oil decision was widely unpopular among those advocating more aggressive antitrust enforcement and encouraged a movement to strengthen the laws regulating industrial competition. This reaction is somewhat unusual given that the Supreme Court had found Standard Oil — then the largest and most successful company in American history — guilty of monopolization in violation of the Sherman Act and ordered its dissolution. The Supreme Court's opinion, however, did not carefully address which practices of Standard Oil were or should be concluded to be illegal. Indeed, as will be explained, the Standard Oil opinion is more a corporate law, than an antitrust law, opinion. As a consequence, many viewed the opinion as creating great uncertainty as to what industrial practices were prohibited under the Sherman Act. Congress's creation of the FTC, its prohibition in the original FTC Act of "unfair methods of competition," and its nearly simultaneous prohibition in the Clayton Act of specific industrial practices were meant, first, to create a separate enforcement agency, independent of the Justice Department, to prosecute antitrust offenses according to a different and, designedly, more aggressive agenda and, second, to define, chiefly in the Clayton Act, but also through Section 5 of the FTC Act's prohibition of unfair methods of competition, a wide range of competitive practices, many characteristic of Standard Oil's rise, that the Supreme Court had not definitively condemned in its opinion, in its earlier opinion during the same term in Dr. Miles,[3] or in its opinion delivered short weeks after Standard Oil in American Tobacco.[4]

From an historical perspective, this account conflicts with Professor Kovacic's normative proposals in a central way. By my reading of the history of the origin of the FTC, Congress in 1914 deliberately wanted to establish a dual antitrust authority whose mission was to be independent of that of the Justice Department. The Congress's deliberation on this issue was clear and the outcome was intentional, expecting differences between the Justice Department and the newly created FTC over the understanding of what industrial practices should be prohibited. This original Congressional intent, in fact, is exactly opposite to Professor Kovacic's view of rationalized enforcement as between the agencies, each proceeding on common economic and legal grounds. To the contrary, the Congress in 1914 foresaw the FTC as a more aggressive antitrust agency — responsive to Congress, not, like the Justice Department, responsive to presidential politics. The original intent of the

Congress was for anti-coherence as between the agencies in antitrust, not the coherence proposed by Professor Kovacic.

Over the years since 1914, however, our understanding of antitrust policy has changed. Although this paper can only address these intellectual, economic and political changes summarily, there has emerged something of a consensus on the economic goals and the role of antitrust policy. This current consensus is quite different from the great divergence of views on antitrust policy at the time of the Standard Oil decision in 1911 or in 1914 with the enactment of the FTC and Clayton Acts. It is this current consensus that supports Professor Kovacic's endorsement of rationalized U.S. antitrust enforcement.

II. The Early Interpretation of the Sherman Act and the Movement to Standard Oil

As is well known, for almost a decade after the enactment of the Sherman Act in 1890, there was little attention given to enforcement of the Act. Most prosecutions were brought against unions. In 1895, the Supreme Court held in E.C. Knight[5] that acquisitions to monopoly in sugar refining did not constitute commerce within the jurisdiction of the Sherman Act, though that understanding was later quietly jettisoned. The first major decisions by the Supreme Court giving teeth to the Act were delivered in 1897 in Trans-Missouri Freight[6] and in 1898 in Joint Traffic Association.[7] Both decisions found pricing arrangements among railroads that competed over some range to be illegal in violation of the Act. But both were five-to-four opinions with the majority, led by Justice Peckham, emphasizing that the Sherman Act prohibited all contracts, conspiracies and combinations in restraint of trade, but with the dissent, led by Justice White, insisting that the Act had to be interpreted to prohibit only unreasonable restraints of trade. The five-to-four character of the decisions revealed the deep division on the Court over this central interpretive issue.

In an important Circuit Court opinion also delivered in 1898, Addyston Pipe & Steel,[8] Justice Taft crafted an interpretation alternative to both the majority and minority positions at the Supreme Court, holding that the Act prohibited restraints of trade central to the agreement in question, but not those ancillary to the agreement. The underlying agreement in question was an obvious collusive division of markets that would be condemned routinely given modern understanding. Taft's tortured reconciliation of the decision with earlier common law precedents again shows the tentative understanding of the role of the Sherman Act in this period. Taft's specific interpretation (which has received much modern attention because of its glorification in Robert H. Bork's influential book, The Antitrust Paradox)[9] is somewhat, but not exactly, similar to Justice White's advocacy of prohibiting only unreasonable restraints of trade: They are similar chiefly in that both standards allow defenses to claims of illegality, though Taft's standard is more precise as to which are available defenses. Taft's Circuit Court opinion was summarily affirmed by the Supreme Court, but without serious consideration of Taft's alternative standard.[10]

The next major antitrust case to reach the Supreme Court was Northern Securities in 1904 in which the Court invalidated joint ownership of the Northern Pacific and Great Northern railroads, which competed in part in transport from the Great Lakes to the Pacific Coast.[11] This decision, too, was a five-four opinion, though with different coalitions and for different reasons. Justice White again wrote the principal dissent, but this time joined by Justice Peckham, on the grounds that the Sherman Act should not be interpreted to interfere with the right to own property.[12]

Each of these strands of antitrust thought was implicated in the subsequent Standard Oil decision. The Justice Department brought suit against Standard Oil in 1906 under the Theodore Roosevelt presidency (Roosevelt was an ardent trust-buster). It was decided by the Supreme Court in 1911. The majority opinion, authored by now-Chief Justice White, found Standard Oil guilty of violating both Sections 1 and 2 of the Sherman Act on the grounds that Standard Oil's actions were unreasonable restraints of trade. The Court's opinion, thus, reversed the legal standard that had prevailed in Trans-Missouri Freight and Joint Traffic Assn., by adopting the Rule of Reason as the determinative legal standard for interpreting the Sherman Act.

III. The Peculiarity of Standard Oil as an Antitrust Precedent

The Supreme Court's decision in Standard Oil would have seemed to be a great success for antitrust enforcement. The Supreme Court affirmed an opinion finding the most successful company in American history guilty of restraint of trade and monopolization and ordered the Company dissolved. The opinion, however, was broadly viewed as a defeat by those advocating more aggressive antitrust enforcement. The basis for this view was the Court's ground for finding Standard Oil in violation of the Act, adopting the Rule of Reason, allowing a wide range of defenses to claims of antitrust violation, in place of the interpretation in the late-1890s of Trans-Missouri Freight and Joint Traffic Assn. that any restraint of trade violated the Act. There had been a vast change in Supreme Court personnel since the late-1890s. The division on the Court was no longer five to four. Only Justice Harlan, in the majority in Trans-Missouri and Joint Traffic, and who had authored the Northern Securities opinion, dissented from the adoption of the Rule of Reason in Standard Oil.

On reanalyzing the Court's opinion in Standard Oil, I believe that there is an additional basis that those interested in active antitrust control were disappointed in the opinion. The Court's opinion is entirely conclusionary. Although the opinion recites the particulars of the Justice Department's bill of indictment, which includes references to alleged illegal practices, it does so by rote; it equally recites the details of Standard Oil's defense.[13] The Court offers no commentary on any of the facts nor provides any guidance as to which industrial practices violate the Act or why.

One interpretation of the absence of discussion of details relating to restraint of trade or monopolization derives from the timing issues implicated by the suit. John D. Rockefeller and his associates created the Standard Oil monopoly over oil refining during the period 1871-79, more than a decade prior to the enactment of the Sherman Act.[14] As a consequence, the formation of the monopoly was not illegal at the time it occurred. To find illegality under the Sherman Act, the Court ruled 1) that the pre-Sherman Act monopolization constituted evidence of Standard Oil's intent to monopolize after enactment of the Sherman Act; and 2) that subsequent corporate reorganizations of the Company—most centrally, the 1899 transfer of the stock of the multiple Standard Oil Company affiliates to a holding company in New Jersey—were illegal under the Act. These were subtle grounds for decision; more bluntly, thin ice. Do actions by persons who form a monopoly when it is legal to do so demonstrate an intent to violate a statute enacted years later making it illegal to monopolize?[15] Does shifting the stock shares of a variety of companies acquired legally at one period into a different form of corporate organization at a later period demonstrate an illegal restraint of trade? The Standard Oil opinion cannot possibly be read as to embrace a general policy of deconcentration, as it did not: almost a decade later, the Court exonerated the US Steel merger to monopoly.[16] Indeed, the principal normative debate over the case, reflected in long passages in the Standard Oil opinion, generally ignored in excerpts read today, addresses not how Standard Oil's practices impaired competition, but how the Court's decision to dismember Standard Oil should not be read to contest the more central right to control of private property, a principle of the substantive due process Lochner school, the grounds for White's dissent in Northern Securities.

An alternative interpretation of the Court's opinion is that it simply found the underlying facts of the case too complicated for analysis. White begins the opinion by confessing that

The record is inordinately voluminous, consisting of twenty-three volumes of printed matter, aggregating about twelve thousand pages, containing a vast amount of confusing and conflicting testimony relating to innumerable, complex and varied business transactions, extending over a period of nearly forty years.[17]

After reciting the particulars of the indictment and defense, White excuses the Court from detailed discussion: "Without attempting to follow the elaborate averments on these subjects spread over fifty-seven pages of the printed record, ..."[18] The opinion later refers to the "jungle of conflicting testimony covering a period of forty years,"[19] and ultimately concludes that Standard Oil's "dominancy over the oil industry" was secured "not as a result of normal methods of industrial development, but by new means of combination which were resorted to in order that greater power might be added than would otherwise have arisen had normal methods been followed . . . ."[20]

There is some attention to Standard Oil's industrial practices. The Court states that the accusations against Standard Oil

may properly be grouped under the following heads: Rebates, preferences and other discriminatory practices in favor of the combination by railroad companies; restraint and monopolization by control of pipelines, and unfair practices against competing pipelines; contracts with competitors in restraint of trade; unfair methods of competition, such as local price cutting at the points where necessary to suppress competition; espionage of the business of competitors, the operation of bogus independent companies, and payment of rebates on oil, with the like intent; the division of the United States into districts and the limiting of the operations of the various subsidiary corporations as to such districts so that competition in the sale of petroleum products between such corporations had been entirely eliminated and destroyed; and finally reference was made to the "enormous and unreasonable profits" earned by the Standard Oil Trust and the Standard Oil Company as a result of the alleged monopoly; which presumably was averred as a means of reflexively inferring the scope and power acquired by the alleged combination.[21]

But the Court does not discuss in any serious way how these various practices should be concluded as having restrained trade and thus be illegal under the Act. For example, the "rebates, preferences and other discriminatory practices in favor of the combination" were, in the first instance, practices of the railroads, not of Standard Oil. Perhaps there is a hint of a Standard Oil monopsony here,[22] though it is not clearly explained. Similarly, control over the pipelines (here the Court is referring to local gathering pipelines from wells to gathering oil stations, for which there may have been some local monopoly issues, but not industry issues), again not explained. "[C]ontracts with competitors", not explained. "[L]ocal price cutting", not explained. "Espionage on the business of competitors", not explained; why shouldn't businesses learn from the success of their competitors? "[B]ogus independent companies"? Perhaps a deception issue; difficult to create a monopoly on deception. "[D]ivision of the United States into districts," limiting competition among them: an organizational issue not clearly addressed until decades later involving territorial distributional restraints. "[E]normous and unreasonable profits," a ground that never would become a basis of antitrust prosecution.

Put simply, there was no serious discussion in the Supreme Court's Standard Oil opinion of which industrial practices violated the Sherman Act and which did not. The outcome of the Standard Oil opinion was to conclude that Standard Oil had violated both Sections 1 and 2 of the Sherman Act, though without a clear delineation between the objectives of the two Sections. The Standard Oil opinion changed the basic interpretation of the Sherman Act, adopting the Rule of Reason as the dominant interpretive standard, prohibiting only unreasonable restraints of trade. But the opinion did not discuss in any detail which industrial practices were to be deemed unreasonable, except to the extent of those regarded as not "normal." To those in the society advocating a more aggressive antitrust policy, for the Court to insulate "normal" business practices from prosecution missed the point of the exercise entirely. Proponents of a more aggressive antitrust policy viewed normal industrial practices as constituting monopolization and restraint of trade. The abnormal practices prohibited by the Court were at the very end of the industrial practice distribution, obviously beyond the pale. Thus, the Standard Oil opinion was viewed as vastly reducing the scope of the Sherman Act.

The Supreme Court's opinion short weeks later in American Tobacco added some detail to the Sherman Act's prohibition of monopolization, but not satisfactorily. The Court added the point that American Tobacco's acquisition of competing manufacturers only to shut them down was evidence of restraint of trade, a slightly more detailed definition of restraint of trade, but not much more detailed.[23] The Court's earlier opinion during the same term in Dr. Miles had found manufacturer resale price maintenance to be illegal.[24] But still the Court had not provided a careful delineation of those specific industrial practices to be held illegal under the Act and, worse to those advocating an aggressive antitrust policy, had adopted a legal standard of interpretation—the Rule of Reason—that allowed multiple defenses to be raised to antitrust prosecution.

IV. The Movement to the FTC and Clayton Acts

After 1911, following the Standard Oil and American Tobacco decisions, there was substantial agitation for enhanced antitrust enforcement.[25] The Rule of Reason standard adopted by the Court in Standard Oil was viewed as creating great uncertainty as to which industrial practices were prohibited under the Act. Though President Taft, succeeding President Roosevelt, was regarded also as a trust-buster, he endorsed the Rule of Reason standard of the Supreme Court in Standard Oil.[26] As mentioned, the Rule of Reason standard is somewhat similar to the standard that Taft had proposed as a Circuit Court Judge in Addyston Pipe & Steel, prior to his election as President, distinguishing ancillary from central restraints.[27] But that was not sufficient for those advocating a more aggressive antitrust prosecution.

Taft's successor as President, Woodrow Wilson, was even a stronger proponent of active antitrust prosecution. (In fact, the platform of the Democratic Party, heavily influenced by William Jennings Bryan, was yet more aggressive on antitrust.)[28] Wilson, and the Democratic Congress, after much discussion, supported and enacted in 1914 the FTC Act and the Clayton Act, creating an independent antitrust enforcement agency—intentionally, an administrative agency with direct regulatory powers, not simply, though including, a separate prosecutorial office—with greater statutory authority to prohibit specific practices in restraint of trade. The adoption of Section 5 of the FTC Act, prohibiting "unfair methods of competition" and the adoption of the more specific prohibitions of industrial practices under the Clayton Act constituted a clear legislative repudiation of the Supreme Court's amorphous Rule of Reason in Standard Oil.

As mentioned, the FTC Act[29] created a separate antitrust prosecutorial agency, intentionally made independent of the Justice Department. Section 5 of the Act also prohibited "unfair methods of competition", meant to expand constraints on industrial practices.[30] The Clayton Act[31] prohibited specific practices, most implicated in the rise of Standard Oil, but not discussed directly by the Supreme Court in its Standard Oil opinion.

Section 2 prohibited price discrimination;

Section 3 prohibited exclusive dealing and tying arrangements;

Section 7 prohibited stock acquisitions whose effect was to substantially lessen competition;

Section 8 prohibited interlocking directorates among competing companies;

Section 14 extended liability to directors and officers.[32]

Again, most of the specific prohibitions of the Clayton Act were directed at actions of the Standard Oil monopoly that the Court had not specifically addressed as restraints of trade.[33] Section 2's prohibition on price discrimination is an obvious example. But Section 8's prohibition of interlocking directorates also derived from Standard Oil. A principal objection to the dissolution remedy ordered by the Court was that the various units of the former Standard Oil Company, purportedly separate after the dissolution, all had the same directors. Similarly, Section 7's prohibition of stock acquisitions whose effect is to lessen competition directly derives from the Standard Oil experience. Standard Oil created its monopoly in important part by acquiring the stock of competing companies, giving Standard Oil stock in return. Four decades later, the original Section 7's prohibition of only stock acquisitions was ridiculed upon the 1950 passage of the Celler-Kefauver Act, extending the prohibition to asset acquisitions, as if the Congress in 1914 had not known of or had not anticipated the potential anticompetitive effect of asset versus stock acquisitions. This criticism rests on an historical mistake. Standard Oil's monopoly resulted principally from stock acquisitions; the central action found violative by the Court was the transfer of stock into the Standard Oil of New Jersey holding company. Moreover, the acquisition of stock, rather than assets, did not implicate in the same way the principle of protection of private property ownership, central to the Court in Standard Oil, American Tobacco, and throughout the Lochner era.

The ambition of Congress with the enactment of the FTC Act and the Clayton Act, however, was to create an administrative agency, with prosecutorial authority as well as independent adjudicatory powers separate from the Justice Department. The intent of Congress was not coherence in antitrust enforcement. The Congress wanted more aggressive enforcement than had been achieved under the Taft administration or that might be achieved under subsequent presidential administrations. In the Clayton Act, the Congress prohibited a substantial number of specific industrial practices to achieve this end. In the FTC Act, it prohibited "unfair methods of competition," seeking to expand that authority. These Congressional actions were not taken at the sacrifice of antitrust coherence in theory or enforcement, but with the explicit rejection of coherence in antitrust theory and enforcement, intentionally establishing an approach separate from whatever the Justice Department might in the future determine as antitrust enforcement.

V. Sixty Years Later:
The Modern Antitrust Consensus

Over the years since 1914, much has changed in antitrust thinking and analysis. In the late 1930s and 1940s, the Supreme Court, on the urging of both the Justice Department and the FTC, developed per se prohibitions of various industrial practices, per se meaning without the opportunity of defense. Per se prohibitions were announced against all forms of price control starting with the per se prohibition of horizontal price fixing (Socony Vacuum Oil)[34] but extended to include the per se prohibition of resale price maintenance (reinterpreting the 1911 Dr. Miles opinion)[35] and maximum price limitations (Albrecht);[36] vertical territorial restrictions (Schwinn);[37] tying arrangements (Northern Pacific);[38] group boycotts (Fashion Originators' Guild);[39] and predatory pricing (Utah Pie);[40] among others. The Supreme Court also sanctioned what by any modern eye would be regarded as extreme limitations on mergers. In the 1966 Von's Grocery case,[41] the Supreme Court approved the prohibition of a merger of non-competing retail grocery companies in Los Angeles, each possessing less than 4 percent of the retail grocery market. This opinion signaled that the Court would sustain any challenge that the Justice Department brought against a proposed merger, leading the Department in 1968 to promulgate draconian Merger Guidelines that outlined its policy toward merger challenges, stifling future merger activity.

Beginning in 1977, however, responsive to a wealth of economic analysis showing the dysfunction of these rules, the Supreme Court changed its interpretation of the Sherman and Clayton Acts to largely adopt an economic approach to antitrust—promoted by the Chicago School, in particular by the work of Robert Bork building on the ideas of Aaron Director. According to this analysis, all forms of collusion among competitors should be prohibited and mergers to monopoly prohibited, but most other industrial practices, including most vertical practices should be interpreted as enhancing competition, not impairing it.[42]

In the now four decades since this change in law began, there is a new consensus over the economic goals of antitrust law that broadly embraces the economic approach to antitrust enforcement. Though there are some differences and remaining disputes, there is general agreement that the single goal of antitrust policy is to enhance consumer welfare, defined in terms of the lowest effective prices for competitively supplied goods and services. The goal of antitrust enforcement is not, as it had been in earlier periods, to benefit competitors over competition or to benefit small dealers over large but is, instead, to benefit consumers, chiefly in the form of providing products and services at the lowest prices.

It is this new consensus over the goals of antitrust law that supports the proposals of Professor Kovacic that the antitrust efforts of the Justice Department and the FTC be coordinated and unified, perhaps (though it would require legislation), administratively unified. In an era in which there existed fundamental normative differences over the role of antitrust law, as in the early decades of the 20th Century—an era before the development of serious economic analysis of antitrust issues—there was a reasonable case for separate and, perhaps, competing antitrust prosecutorial agencies. In fact, the history did not work out that way. The FTC, though making many contributions, never developed as a systematically more aggressive antitrust agency than the Justice Department, though it was systematically more aggressive as a consumer protection agency given its authority to prosecute under Section 5's "unfair methods of competition", later amended to prohibit "unfair or deceptive acts or practices."

Professor Kovacic's advocacy of a unified antitrust approach in theory and enforcement builds on and is supported by this new consensus. The separate antitrust enforcement authority of the Justice Department and FTC that he criticizes derived from discordant views over antitrust policy. These discordant views, with the benefit of economic analysis, have largely evaporated over time. There is good reason now to support Professor Kovacic's recommendations.

NOTES

1 U.S. Antitrust policy: The underperforming federal joint venture, CONCURRENCES No 4-2011—65-69.

2 221 U.S. 1 (1911).

3 Dr. Miles Medical Co. v. John D. Park & Sons Co., 220 U.S. 373 (1911).

4 United States v. American Tobacco Co., 221 U.S. 106 (1911).

5 United States v. E.C. Knight Co., 156 U.S. 1 (1895).

6 United States v. Trans-Missouri Freight Ass'n., 166 U.S. 290 (1897).

7 United States v. Joint-Traffic Ass'n., 171 U.S. 505 (1895).

8 United States v. Addyston Pipe & Steel Co., 85 F. 271 (6th Cir. 1898).

9 ROBERT H. BORK, THE ANTITRUST PARADOX: A POLICY AT WAR WITH ITSELF (1978).

10 Addyston Pipe & Steel Co. v. United States, 175 U.S. 211 (1899).

11 Northern Securities Co. v. United States, 193 U.S. 197 (1904).

12 Northern Securities included Justice Oliver Wendell Holmes notable dissent, "Great cases, like hard cases, make bad law. . . ." and his conclusion "I do not expect to hear it maintained that Mr. [J.P.] Morgan could be sent to prison for buying as many shares as he liked of the Great Northern and the Northern Pacific, even if he bought them at the same time and got more than half the stock of each road."

13 This was part of White's style. See his opinion in American Tobacco.

14 For a discussion of the formation of the Standard Oil refining monopoly, see G.L. Priest, Rethinking the Economic Basis of the Standard Oil Refining Monopoly: Dominance against Competing Cartels, 85 S. CAL. L. REV. 101 (2012).

15 What does this mean? Did Rockefeller have a legal duty to dismember Standard Oil upon enactment of the Sherman Act?

16 United States v. U.S. Steel Corp., 251 U.S. 417 (1920) (upholding merger to monopoly in steel industry involving no unusual practices).

17 Standard Oil, supra note 2, at 30-31.

18 Id. at 23.

19 Id. at 48.

20 Id. at 74.

21 Id. at 42-43.

22 In a separate paper, I argue, against the current dominant theory of the Standard Oil monopoly, Elizabeth Granitz & Benjamin Klein, Monopolization by "Raising Rivals' Costs": The Standard Oil Case, 39 J. LAW & ECON. 1 (1996), THAT THE REBATES WERE THE RESULT OF A STANDARD OIL MONOPSONY. See Priest, supra note 14.

23 American Tobacco, supra note 4, at 183.

24 Dr. Miles, supra note 3.

25 For an excellent discussion of this history from which much of this discussion is drawn, see Marc Winerman, The Origins of the FTC: Concentration, Cooperation, Control, and Competition, 71 ANTITRUST L.J. 1 (2003-2004).

26 Id. at 28-29.

27 Text at notes 8-9, supra.

28 Winerman, supra note 25, at 43 & n. 248.

29 38 Stat. 717 (1914).

30 Id. at 67.

31 38 Stat. 730 (1914).

32 There were other important provisions of the Act. Section 4 authorized private actions and Section 5 made a successful governmental action *prima facie* evidence of violation in a private action. Section 6, of course, introduced the labor exemption.

33 The prohibition of exclusive dealing and tying arrangements in Section 3 was not clearly motivated by actions of Standard Oil, but represented an overturning of the Supreme Court's opinion in Henry v. A.B. Dick Co., 224 U.S. 1 (1912), which had allowed a patent holder to tie the sale of ink to use of a patented mimeograph machine.

34 310 U.S. 150 (1940).

35 Dr. Miles Medical Co. v. John D. Park & Sons Co., 220 U.S. 373, 31 S.Ct. 376, 55 L.Ed. 502 (1911).

36 Albrecht v. Herald Co., 390 U.S. 145, 88 S.Ct. 869, 19 L.Ed.2d 998 (1968).

37 United States v. Arnold, Schwinn & Co., 388 U.S. 365, 87 S.Ct. 1856, 18 L.Ed.2d 1249 (1967).

38 United States v. Northern Pac. Ry. Co., 356 U.S. 1, 78 S.Ct., 514, 2 L.Ed.2d 545 (1958).

39 Fashion Originators' Guild of America v. F.T.C., 312 U.S. 457, 61 S.Ct. 703, 85 L.Ed. 949 (1941).

40 Utah Pie Co. v. Continental Baking Co., 386 U.S. 685, 87 S.Ct. 1326, 18 L.Ed.2d 406 (1967).

41 United States v. Von's Grocery Co., 384 U.S. 270, 86 S.Ct. 1478, 16 L.Ed.2d 555 (1966).

42 For an initial description of this history and of these changes, *see* G.L. Priest, *Advancing Antitrust Law to Promote Innovation and Economic Growth* in RULES FOR GROWTH: PROMOTING INNOVATION AND GROWTH THROUGH LEGAL REFORM (2011) at 209.

Antitrust Law Enforcement: What to Do About the Current Economics Cacophony?

J. Thomas Rosch[*]

Commissioner, U.S. Federal Trade Commission

Abstract

Rosch argues that we are on the brink of a moment where efforts to reconcile economic theories should be made (much as efforts to reconcile quantum mechanics and relativity theories were made in physics). He identifies four dominant economic theories. They include neoclassical (or "Chicago School) economics, Game School (or "post- Chicago School) economics, experimental economics (economic theories most closely associated with Joseph Farrell and David Teece), and behavioral economics. He urges that one way to reconcile these seemingly conflicting theories is to use structured rule of reason analysis that focuses on effects of the transaction or conduct rather than on how buyers or sellers behave (rationally, irrationally or experimentally). He argues that this may provide true convergence with the Treaty of Rome and the EC and that economists can play a key role in this analysis.

Good evening. My remarks tonight will focus on the proper intersection between economic theory, on the one hand, and antitrust doctrinal analysis, on the other. I have been giving this topic some thought for quite a while. Indeed, my attorney advisor, Mandy Reeves, was likely surprised in April when I called from an airport to say that a *New York Times* book review that I had just read on the origins of quantum physics should inform our thinking on this topic.[1] In that book, *The Age of Entanglement: When Quantum Physics Was Reborn*, the author explains that for more than half a century, physicists were of sharply different views as to whether general relativity or quantum mechanics should supply the organizing principle to describe the relationship between atoms and subatomic particles. But in the 1960s, the discord began to ebb with the contribution of a new generation of physicists who suggested that a modified version of quantum mechanics could sensibly coexist with a theory of relativity.

What does all of this have to do with antitrust? I believe that we are on the brink of a similar moment in the history of antitrust. While the orthodox Chicago School of economics has long been at the forefront of antitrust analysis, there are several other economic theories percolating under the surface that I believe supply a better understanding of how market participants—more specifically sellers and buyers—actually behave. But the fundamental issue for those of us responsible for enforcing the antitrust laws remains the same—when should the conduct of those firms be viewed as anticompetitive? While I remain far from having all or any of the answers, this evening I would like to offer you some initial thoughts on these topics. My remarks will proceed in three parts. First, I will explain my views on the proper role of economics in antitrust analysis. Second, I will describe what I perceive to be the four major and, to varying extents, competing schools of economic thought about how market participants behave. Third, I will sketch out an analytical framework for analyzing claims under Sections 1 and 2 of the Sherman Act and Section 7 of the Clayton Act that is not dependent on any of these schools, but can accommodate all of them. I will end with some concluding thoughts.

I.

Let me begin by dispelling a misconception about how I view economics and economists, attributable I fear to not making my views clear. More specifically, critics—overwhelmingly Chicago School apologists—have suggested that I am anti-economics and anti-economist and, indeed, that I doubt that economics should play a role in antitrust law enforcement.[2] Those are not my views. My views are as follows.

First, to be blunt, as I have freely admitted—perhaps too colorfully—even with 40-plus years of experience as an antitrust lawyer, I just do not understand complex economic formulae.[3]

Second, based on my experience as a trial lawyer who had limited success in communicating complex ideas to lay juries and generalist courts, I think economists who use complex formulae to express their conclusions respecting the economics considerations in antitrust cases are of little practical value. Indeed, it has long been my view that if I couldn't fully understand a message then I could not effectively communicate it, and, as I have noted, complex economic formulae have long been over my head and over the heads of any juries that I stood before. Third, I doubt that anyone other than someone with a Ph.D. in economics or other significant statistical training comprehends those formulae. It is no accident, for example, that there are few or no complex economic formulae in three of the most influential antitrust textbooks of our time—Judge Robert Bork's *The Antitrust Paradox*; Judge Richard Posner's *The Antitrust Laws*; and Professor Areeda's classic text, which he authored with several collaborators over the years.

J. Thomas Rosch

I am not the first to criticize the use of complex economic formulae. Indeed, other economists and businesspeople have criticized their use as well. Professor Nouriel Roubini of NYU and Warren Buffett, among others, have cautioned against falling victim to those formulae.[4] Likewise, economists who testify before judges and juries themselves insist on using words of one syllable to explain their conclusions. And with good reason: in a recent piece published by *Competition Policy International*, Judge Vaughn Walker, who presided over the Oracle trial, argued that generalist judges lack economic training (and often interest) and that, as such, if economic evidence is to be persuasive, it must be communicated in a way that a generalist can understand and must be consistent with other evidence.[5] Complex economic theories are simply not comprehensible to many specialists like myself, let alone to a generalist.

This is all to say that, while I think that economics are an important ingredient in applying the antitrust laws, they are no substitute for the laws themselves. In this regard, I find support not only in Judge Walker's views, but in Justice Breyer's comments in his dissenting opinion in *Leegin* when he opined that "economics can, and should, inform antitrust law. But antitrust law cannot, and should not, precisely replicate economists' (sometimes conflicting) views."[6] I think it is safe to say that I share that view.

II.

Next, I would like to discuss the role economic theory has played over the last forty years in antitrust analysis and highlight some strengths and weaknesses of the competing economic theories that already do or arguably should play a role in antitrust analysis.

To be sure, the most dominant school of economic thought in antitrust analysis is the orthodox Chicago School. As I see it, there are two fundamental premises that underlie that school: first, markets if not perfect, correct themselves quickly; and second, firms accordingly generally act rationally, which is to say that they generally act to maximize profits, instead of engaging in predatory behavior which will be nullified by market corrections.[7]

These principles, which have their origins in Friedrich von Hayek's and Milton Friedman's views, began bubbling to the surface in the late 1960s through, among other things, Nobel Prize winning economist George Stigler's 1964 article "A Theory of Oligopoly" in which he explained that it was improper to assume that firms in an oligopolistic market would find a way to agree to raise prices above competitive levels.[8]

The Chicago School came to the forefront of antitrust law in the late 1970s. During this period, the Supreme Court embraced the Chicago School way of thinking in its 1977 *GTE Sylvania* decision where the Court overturned its 1967 decision in *Schwinn* and held that non-price vertical restraints were subject to the rule of reason.[9] The Court cited then Professor Posner's 1976 book, *Antitrust Law: An Economic Perspective*, as support for the proposition that economists had identified several ways in which manufacturers use non-price vertical restraints to compete against other manufacturers.[10] The following year, Robert Bork penned *The Antitrust Paradox* which collected the Chicago School's basic tenets in one place and provided one of the most—if not *the* most—significant contributions to antitrust law in the 20th Century.[11] Bork asserted that many of the then current cases applying the antitrust laws were irrational and actually hurt consumers. He also argued that consumers were often beneficiaries of corporate mergers. With Ronald Reagan's victory in 1980 and Posner and Bork's appointments to the federal appellate bench in 1981 and 1982, respectively, the Chicago School's ascendancy as providing the predominant organizing principles for antitrust law was complete.

With the recent financial crisis, however, one has to wonder if the Chicago School's fundamental presumptions are still tenable. In a January speech before the New York Bar Association, I suggested that, in light of the economic crisis, the Chicago School was on life support if not dead. [12] As it turns out, other Republicans—including many who have embraced the Chicago School over the years at least as fervently as I—share this view. Alan Greenspan and former Secretary of the Treasury Henry Paulson are both Republicans who fully subscribed to the Chicago School theory before the crisis. But in his testimony before Congress last October, Alan Greenspan recanted his faith in the market and the rationality of business people, testifying that more government regulation of the financial sector was both necessary and proper.[13] Although Secretary Paulson was not so specific about market imperfections and irrational behavior, he intervened repeatedly to try to deal with perceived imperfections in that market.[14]

Yet perhaps most telling is Judge Posner's change in course. In his recent book on the financial crisis, Judge Posner declares that the "depression of 2008" (as he calls it) resulted from market failure. Judge Posner contends that there is a need for more active government regulation and that deregulation of the financial industry went too far by "exaggerating the resilience—the self-healing powers—of laissez-faire capitalism."[15] If Judge Posner is arguing that the markets failed to self-correct, it is safe to say that the Chicago School is indeed teetering on the edge of collapse.[16]

Apart from the current economic crisis, though, the more I read about alternative economic theories, the more I am certain that the Chicago School does not even accurately portray how buyers or sellers behave. The truth is—I doubt that there is any one economic theory respecting the way that buyers or sellers behave that accords with the real world. I have, however, identified three competing economic theories with various shades of grey in between them that do or should play some role in antitrust analysis.

The first of those theories—actually consisting of a group of theories—is what I have described as post-Chicago School theory but what others have called "game" theory. Game theorists may subscribe to the basic Chicago School tenets that markets are self-correcting (at least over the long run) and that sellers act rationally, which is to say that they engage in profit- maximizing conduct. But they contend that many practices that orthodox Chicago School theorists would consider predatory are in fact profit-maximizing in the real world (at least in some instances). Some examples are Salop's "raising rivals' costs" theories,[17] Whinston's "tying" theories,[18] and Creighton's "cheap exclusion" theories.[19] Although it's a closer call, I would also add to this list Einer Elhauge, in light of his recent thought-provoking article, *Tying, Bundled Discounts, and the Death of the Single Monopoly Profit Theory*, to the category of post- Chicago School theorists.[20] Although these theories do offer a more sophisticated, nuanced view of seller behavior than the orthodox Chicago School, the post-Chicago School theorists still principally subscribe to the view that profit-maximization is the organizing principle around which antitrust law should evolve.

The second economic theory is the one that Professor Joe Farrell, the FTC's new Director for the Bureau of Economics, has espoused in a piece called *Complexity, Diversity, and Antitrust* that appeared in the Spring 2006 issue of *The Antitrust Bulletin*.[21] I call his theory "experimentation" theory. Under that theory, which focuses on the sell-side of markets, most business firms do not engage in behavior that they consider profit-maximizing from the get-go. Instead, Farrell argues, firms engage in a trial-and-error process to identify which conduct will be profit-maximizing for themselves over the long run. Sometimes their experiments are successful, and sometimes they are not.

David Teece has also set forth a similar theory in the context of discussing the economics that underlie innovation.[22] Teece has argued that the concept of static competition, which looks only at price competition by rational agents for existing products, "reflects an intellectual framework" and "not a state of the world." In contrast, he argues, dynamic competition is driven by the trial and error efforts of innovators and institutional structures that support innovation. Again, speaking frankly, the theories that Farrell and Teece have posited are most consistent with my own real world experience. Perhaps that is because the behavior of most firms is determined by the decisions of middle managers, not senior executives, much less economists.

Third and finally, there are the behavioral economists, who contend that many, if not most, business firms, as well as consumers, behave irrationally or, at the very least, do not always behave in a perfectly rational manner. That literature has been gathered together by, among others, Professor Maurice Stucke.[23] Although behavioral economics bears some similarities to Farrell and Teece's experimentation theory in that it can inform understandings of behavior on the sell side, behavioral economics is arguably most useful in informing an analysis of the motives of parties on the demand or buy side of any given transaction.[24] Indeed, I think that one of the most significant insights from the behavioral economics literature is the suggestion that, because consumers will behave irrationally—which is to say that they will make decisions based on factors other than price and quality—when there is a situation with less or imperfect competition, the government should engage in consumer protection efforts in those cases rather than sitting back and waiting for a market to heal itself.[25]

Dennis Carlton has told me that while behavioral economics may be very useful in analyzing the behavior of individuals, it has little application to firm conduct. But I wonder about that distinction. After all, firms—and particularly the middle managers in firms—are just collections of individuals. There is recent literature that confirms that view. Economists George Akerlof and Robert Shiller of Berkeley and Yale, respectively, have just published *Animal Sprits*, in which they resurrect behaviorally-informed Keynesianism to show that free-market ideology is fundamentally incomplete because it fails to account for the fact that human irrationality infects human decision-making and, thus, decisions that govern how the market actually (as opposed to hypothetically) functions.[26] Likewise, in *Jones v. Harris*, a securities case which is now at the Supreme Court, Judge Posner himself has recently advanced a behavioral economics approach—and sharply rejected Chief Judge Easterbrook's free-market theory—in his dissent from the Seventh Circuit's denial of rehearing en banc.[27] Consistent with the behavioral economics literature, Posner observed that, in the absence of a competitive market, regulation is needed to protect consumers because market participants are not infallible.

Likewise, Carlton also has suggested to me that firms who behave irrationally will end up losing out to profit-maximizing firms in the long run. But that may take a very long time, and consumer welfare may suffer grievously in the meantime. And, if that is so, the complexity and uncertainty associated with identifying and regulating irrational conduct is of no comfort to the Commission as an antitrust law enforcement agency. To the contrary, it raises a number of questions about antitrust law enforcement. The most fundamental of those questions, however, is whether the complexity and uncertainty in this respect mean that the Commission should eschew antitrust enforcement for fear of making a mistake or should make a threshold decision about what kind of behavior by market participants is at issue and then analyze those practices or transactions differently, depending on that threshold determination.

III.

So where do we go from here? I would like to use the balance of my remarks to discuss an analytical approach that I suggest, by focusing chiefly on anticompetitive *effects* (as opposed to conduct) works regardless of which economic theory or theories one thinks best explains how sellers and buyers make decisions. That approach is a structured rule of reason analysis. My thesis is fourfold. First, structured rule of reason analysis provides an analytical framework that applies regardless of the real-world market, firm or customer behavior that is at issue, and it doesn't matter whether the challenge is made under the Sherman Act or under Section 7 of the Clayton Act. Second, that analytical framework is consistent with the antitrust case law in the United States. Third, it is also consistent with the Article 82 (now article 102 of the Treaty on the Functioning of the European Union) Guidance recently issued by the European Commission. And fourth, it is a mode of analysis in which economists do have a role to play, but not with complex formulae.

Structured rule of reason analytical framework is not new. Arguably it was introduced by former Chairman Tim Muris.[28] But it has been adopted by the Supreme Court in *Indiana Federation of Dentists*,[29] and by various regional courts of appeals, most notably in Judge Ginsburg's opinion in the *Three Tenors* decision of the DC Court of Appeals.[30] There are two essential ingredients of the analysis. The first ingredient is proof of a practice which, considered in context, is "inherently suspect" under the antitrust laws because it is likely to adversely impact consumer welfare. Some "inherently suspect" practices, such as the agreement not to compete challenged in *Three Tenors*, involve agreements among competitors and they chiefly implicate Section 1 of the Sherman act. Other practices, however, involve single firm conduct implicating chiefly Section 2 of the Sherman Act. In either event, it does not matter whether the practice is rational (in the sense that it is profit-maximizing), experimental, or just plain irrational. As long as the practice is likely to injure consumer welfare, the structured rule of reason analysis supplies a means to properly consider the legality of the practice.

In some instances, it is possible to determine whether a practice is likely to injure consumer welfare based on experience with the practice. In those instances, the Supreme Court has held that the practice can be deemed inherently suspect without determining whether the firm or firms engaging in the practices enjoy monopoly or near monopoly power in a relevant market. The Court's decisions in *NCAA v. Board of Regents* and *Indiana Federation of Dentists* are examples of those cases.[31] In other instances, however, experience with a practice does not teach that the practice is likely to injure consumer welfare. Then, it may be appropriate to look to circumstantial evidence of that probable effect, such as whether the practice was intended to have that effect;[32] or whether, in Section 2 cases, the practice is accompanied by other exclusionary practices.[33] Or, as in *California Dental Association*, it may be necessary to prove that the firm or firms engaging in the practice enjoy monopoly or near monopoly power.[34]

Otherwise, consumers can turn to alternative suppliers in order to avoid injury from the parties. Or, put differently, absent monopoly or near-monopoly power, the practice is not likely to have market-wide effects on prices, output, quality and/or innovation that are harmful to consumers. The fundamental point is that in any case, a practice can properly be considered to be "inherently suspect" because it is likely to injure consumer welfare, regardless of whether the practice is rational, irrational or experimental.

Efficiencies, however, are a second essential element in a structured rule of reason analysis. They may take many forms, including lower prices, superior quality, and enhancement of innovation. Again, moreover, whether the practice was rational, experimental or irrational is irrelevant. If it produces efficiencies that outweigh the likely consumer injury, the practice should not be condemned. That said, though, in order to rebut the presumption arising from proof that a practice is inherently suspect, the defendant must bear the burden of proving offsetting efficiencies.

Structured rule of reason analysis is consistent with U.S. antitrust case law generally. It is plainly consistent with the law in Section 1 cases. Indeed, it has its roots in the Section 1 case law. Section 1 of course also requires proof of an agreement, and as a technical matter, it may be argued that monopoly or near monopoly power will never exist in a Section 1 case because monopoly is a term of art that presupposes single firm conduct. But firms who are participants in a duopoly or a tight oligopoly market collectively enjoy power that is akin to monopoly power in the sense that that they have the power to increase prices and reduce output in the market as a whole. Thus, the fact that injury to consumer welfare is likely to flow from a collective exercise of monopoly or near monopoly power instead of from single firm conduct may be considered a distinction without a difference. That is probably why the analytical framework has been applied in Section 1 cases without any mention of the issue.

It may be argued that insofar as proof of collective monopoly or near-monopoly power is required, structured rule of reason analysis imposes on plaintiffs a higher burden of proof than they would bear in a traditional rule of reason case. I am not sure that is true. Absent proof that experience established that a practice is likely to injure consumer welfare, the regional appellate courts have generally required proof of that kind of power, reasoning that otherwise the practice is unlikely to adversely impact market-wide competition, which is what the antitrust laws were designed to prevent.[35] Moreover, the structured rule of reason framework certainly casts a lighter burden on plaintiffs than does a traditional unstructured rule of reason requirement, in which the plaintiff bears the burden of proof throughout the analysis, without the burden ever shifting to the defendant.[36]

Finally, it may be argued that if the firms engaging in the practice are behaving experimentally or irrationally, they cannot as a practical matter prove that the practice is efficient. But this does not follow. To be sure, their documents may not contain an efficiency story line. That does not mean, however, that they cannot prove that the practice has in fact resulted in offsetting efficiencies.

Structured rule of reason framework has not historically been used in Section 2 cases. However, there is no reason why it cannot be. To be sure, Section 2 expressly requires proof of monopoly or near-monopoly power before an attempt to monopolize or monopolization can be considered actionable. But as I have previously noted, that proof may be required in some Section 1 structured rule of reason cases too. Moreover, the Section 2 case law requires proof that a defendant has "willfully acquired or maintained" some power before a violation can be found.[37] That is plainly an effects-based requirement on its face.[38] There is ample support in the case law for considering illegal under Section 2 exclusionary practices by firms with monopoly or near-monopoly power that are likely to injure consumers by preventing rivals or would-be rivals from constraining the exercise of that power.[39] Finally, even when a practice is likely to have that effect, the practice can be justified by proof of efficiencies.[40] In short, there is nothing in the Section 2 case law that differentiates among kinds of exclusionary conduct based on whether it is rational, experimental or irrational. Structured rule of reason analysis has not been used historically in Section 7 cases.

Again, however, there is no reason it cannot be. Proof of a Section 7 violation requires proof that a transaction is likely to result in an exercise of monopoly power or a substantial lessening of competition. That is exactly the kind of effects-based proof of the kind I have described, except that it results from the transaction rather than a single firm practice or agreement.

Finally, it may be argued that under the case law proof of efficiencies is not permitted under Section 7. Courts have so held in merger cases.[41] However, since the 1992 Merger Guidelines, the agencies have permitted respondents to adduce offsetting efficiencies, just as they are under a structured rule of reason analytical framework.[42] Thus, use of a structured rule of reason analytical framework in Sherman Act cases is not inconsistent with Section 7 law enforcement.

Structured rule of reason analysis is also consistent with the European Commission's recent Article 82 Guidance.[43] Indeed, the major underlying theme in the Guidance is that Article 82 may be violated when a dominant firm engages in exclusionary practices that threaten consumer welfare by eliminating or crippling rivals or would-be rivals from constraining the dominant firm's exercise of its power.[44] That is one of the central concerns that is addressed in structured rule of reason analysis, and it would be squarely addressed by applying that analytical framework in Sherman Act Section 2 cases.

The Guidance is also quite clear that both direct and circumstantial evidence may be used to prove that this has occurred. More specifically, direct evidence in the form of evidence that the practice at issue has actually had that effect, as well as historical evidence respecting the likelihood that it will have that effect, may be adduced but it is not required. Circumstantial evidence may suffice instead.[45] For example, proof that that effect was intended or that the practice at issue was just one of multiple exclusionary practices employed may be used.[46] In the case of refusals to license or deal, proof that the practice represents an unexplained change in the defendant's course of dealing may be considered.[47] As I have discussed, the case law in the United States permits use of this kind of circumstantial evidence.[48] There is nothing in the case law applying structured rule of reason analysis to indicate that such circumstantial evidence would be excluded from that analytical framework.

Finally, the EC's Guidance permits defendants to prove that there are offsetting efficiencies.[49] However, as in structured rule of reason analysis, the efficiencies must be shown to outweigh the anticompetitive effects that make the practice inherently suspect in the first place.[50] Philip Lowe, the European Commission Director General for Competition has made it clear that although the Commission will generally consider whether the practice at issue has excluded competitors who are as efficient or more efficient than the defendant, it will take into account whether an excluded rival that is a less efficient rival is only that way because of the defendant's superior economies of scale or scope.[51] Again, however, there is nothing in the United States case law to rule out that kind of flexibility.

What role for economists is there in this analysis? I would suggest that it is very much the same role that economists have heretofore played in antitrust cases. Although market definition and market shares are not the only way to prove the existence of monopoly or near-monopoly power, like dominance in the EC, monopoly or near-monopoly power can be proved by evidence of actual anticompetitive effects.[52] As such, that is one way to prove or disprove its existence. In pricing cases, the proper measure of costs will continue to be debated. And whether there are offsetting efficiencies will remain a subject of controversy. In all of these areas, economists have traditionally made substantial contributions. There is no reason why they will not continue to do so. For this is essentially old wine in new bottles. The economic theories respecting the way that markets and business firms behave may have changed. But there is no need to change the legal framework in which business practices and transactions are evaluated under the antitrust laws. Indeed, arguably the proper legal framework is more generally applicable than we have supposed.

In sum, while I do not believe that antitrust law has yet to settle on the right economic theory (or group of theories as the case may be) to accurately account for the complexities of rational and irrational seller and buyer conduct, I think in the last few years, developments in economic thinking have brought us much closer to that objective. And just as in the 1960s, quantum physics was reborn stronger than ever, I am hopeful that as these ideas are incorporated into the mainstream thinking among members of the judiciary and the antitrust bar, we will soon see new life breathed into the antitrust laws through a doctrinal framework that can best identify and prevent anticompetitive conduct.

NOTES

* Remarks at the Bates White Antitrust Conference, Washington, D.C., June 1, 2009. The views stated here are my own and do not necessarily reflect the views of the Commission or other Commissioners. I am grateful to my attorney advisor, Amanda Reeves, for her invaluable assistance preparing this paper.

1 Peter Galison, *Sons of Atom*, N.Y. TIMES, Mar. 26, 2009 (reviewing Louisa Gilder, The Age of Entanglement: When Quantum Physics was Reborn (2009)).

2 *Truth on the Market* (Josh Wright), http://www.truthonthemarket.com/2008/07/03/commissioner-rosch-on-the-smaller-role-of-economists-in-antitrust-litigation/ (July 3, 2008, 11:07 p.m.); *Truth on the Market* (Josh Wright), http://www.truthonthemarket.com/2008/09/12/ inter-agency-scuffling-over-section-2-what-role-for-economists-and-economics-at-the-ftc-and- doj/ (September 12, 2008, 12:21 a.m.); *Truth on the Market* (Josh Wright), http://www.truthonthemarket.com/2008/10/07/commissioner-rosch-v-economics-again/ (Oct. 7, 2008, 10:40 a.m.).

3 *See, e.g.*, J. Thomas Rosch, *Litigating Merger Challenges: Lessons Learned*, Bates White Fifth Annual Antitrust Conference at 9–10 (June 2, 2008), *available at* http://www.ftc.gov/speeches/rosch/080602litigatingmerger.pdf.

4 In his annual letter to Berkshire Hathaway shareholders earlier this year, Warren Buffet harshly criticized the impenetrable mathematical formulae that were fashionable in business before the downturn. Investors are too easily seduced, Buffett said, by "a nerdy-sounding priesthood, using esoteric terms such as beta, gamma, sigma and the like. Our advice: Beware of geeks bearing formulas." David Segal, *In Letter, Warren Buffet Concedes a Tough Year*, N.Y. TIMES (March 1, 2009), *available at* http://www.nytimes.com/2009/03/01/business/01buffett.html?_r=1&hp.

5 Vaughn R. Walker, *Merger Trials: Looking for the Third Dimension*, 5 COMPETITION POLICY INTERNATIONAL 1 (Spring 2009).

6 Leegin Creative Leather Products v. PSKS, Inc., 127 S. Ct. 2705, 2729 (2007) (Breyer, J., dissenting) ("Law, unlike economics, is an administrative system the effects of which depend upon the content of rules and precedents only as they are applied by judges and juries in courts and by lawyers advising their clients. And that fact means that courts will often bring their own administrative judgment to bear, sometimes applying rules of *per se* unlawfulness to business practices even when those practices sometimes produce benefits.").

7 *See* J. Thomas Rosch, *The Common Law of Section 2: Is it Still Alive and Well?*, Remarks at George Mason Law Review 11th Annual Antitrust Symposium, Washington D.C. (Oct. 31, 2007) (discussing influence of Chicago School on Roberts Court antitrust decisions); J. Thomas Rosch, Implications of the Financial Meltdown for the FTC, Remarks at New York Bar Association Annual Dinner, New York (Jan. 29, 2009) (discussing relationship between financial crisis and Chicago School economic theory).

8 George Stigler, *A Theory of Oligopoly*, 72 J. POL. ECON. 44 (1964).

9 United States v. Arnold, Schwinn & Co., 388 U.S. 365 (1967), *overruled* by Continental T.V., Inc. v. GTE Sylvania, 433 U.S. 36 (1977).

10 *GTE Sylvania*, 433 U.S. at 54–55. The Court noted that

> Economists have identified a number of ways in which manufacturers can use such restrictions to compete more effectively against other manufacturers . . . Service and repair are vital for many products, such as automobiles and major household appliances. The availability and quality of such services affect a manufacturer's goodwill and the competitiveness of his product. Because of market imperfections such as the so-called "free rider" effect, these services might not be provided by retailers in a purely competitive situation, despite the fact that each retailer's benefit would be greater if all provided the services than if none did.

Id. at 55. Relying solely on economic theory, the Court found that a manufacturer's limitation of intrabrand competition actually aided that manufacturer in the interbrand market. *Id.* at 56.

11 ROBERT H. BORK, THE ANTITRUST PARADOX: A POLICY AT WAR WITH ITSELF (1978).

12 J. Thomas Rosch, *Implications of the Financial Meltdown for the FTC*, Remarks at New York Bar Association Annual Dinner, New York, NY (Jan. 29, 2009) (discussing relationship between financial crisis and Chicago School economic theory), *available at* http://www.ftc.gov/speeches/rosch/090129financialcrisisnybarspeech.pdf.

13 Edmund L. Andrews, *Greenspan Concedes Error in Regulation*, N.Y. TIMES, Oct. 23, 2008, *available at* http://www.nytimes.com/2008/10/24/business/economy/24panel.html (Greenspan stating that he is in a state of "shock and disbelief" at what has happened and that he has found a "flaw" in his ideology and is "very distressed by that fact.").

14 As I noted during my speech before the New York Bar Association, this is not to say that one size fits all when it came to Paulson's interventions. Secretary Paulson intervened in different ways at different times. For example, he intervened when he felt that some institutions were "too big to fail"—*e.g.*, Bear Stearns, Fannie Mae, Freddie Mac, and Citicorp—but did not do so when other institutions failed—*e.g.*, Lehman Brothers. Also, initially he intervened by purchasing (or standing behind) the distressed assets of financial institutions, and he initially considered using Troubled Asset Relief Program funds to do that exclusively. But, he ultimately intervened instead by buying equity in major financial institutions that were considered "too big to fail."

15 RICHARD A. POSNER, A FAILURE OF CAPITALISM: THE CRISIS OF '08 AND THE DESCENT INTO DEPRESSION (2009).

16 At least one Conservative overseas likewise shares Greenspan, Paulson, and Posner's views. In April, George Osborne, who is the "shadow" Chancellor of the Exchequer for David Cameron's Conservative Party in the United Kingdom "signaled that the Conservatives are breaking with the neo-liberal absolutism of the past 30 years to forge a new approach to the market economy." In a speech where Osborne lauded the benefits of a behavioral economics approach to understand market behavior, Osborne "repudiated laissez faire economics and the libertarian philosophy that licensed its practice." Philip Blond, *Let us put markets to the service of the good society*, Fin. Times (April 13, 2009), *available at* http://www.ft.com/cms/s/0/1f1541c4-2859-11de-8dbf-00144feabdc0.html.

17 *See, e.g.*, Thomas G. Krattenmaker & Steven C. Salop, *Anticompetitive Exclusion: Raising Rivals' Costs to Achieve Power Over Price*, 96 Yale L. J. 209 (1986); Michael H. Riordan & Steven C. Salop, *Evaluating Vertical Mergers: A Post-Chicago Approach*, 63 Antitrust L. J. 513, 519–22 (1995); Steven C. Salop & R. Craig Romaine, *Preserving Monopoly: Economic Analysis, Legal Standards, and Microsoft*, 7 Geo. Mason L. Rev. 617, 626–28 (1999).

18 *See, e.g.*, Michael D. Whinston, *Tying, Foreclosure, and Exclusion*, 80 Am. Econ. Rev. 837 (1990); Michael D. Whinston, *Exclusivity and Tying in U.S. v. Microsoft: What We Know, and Don't Know*, 15 J. Econ. Persp. 63, 79 (Spring 2001).

19 *See, e.g.*, Susan A. Creighton, et al., *Cheap Exclusion*, 72 Antitrust L.J. 975 (2005).

20 Einer Elhauge, *Tying, Bundled Discounts, and the Death of the Single Monopoly Profit Theory*, *available at* http://www.law.harvard.edu/programs/olin_center/papers/pdf/Elhauge_629.pdf. Although Elhauge takes a broader view of rational conduct on the supply-side, he arguably still views profit-maximization as the organizing principle.

21 *See, e.g.*, Joseph Farrell, *Complexity, Diversity, and Antitrust*, 51 Antitrust Bull. 165 (Spring 2006).

22 David J. Teece, *Favoring Dynamic Over Static Competition*, George Mason University/Microsoft Conference (May 15, 2008).

23 *See, e.g.*, Maurice E. Stucke, *New Antitrust Realism*, Global Competition Policy (January 2009); Maurice E. Stucke, *Behavioral Economics at the Gate: Antitrust in the Twenty-First Century*, 38 Loy. U. Chi. L.J. 513 (Spring 2007).

24 *See* Economics Roundtable, Global Competition Review (March 2009).

25 *Id.* ("We know that the competitive process will protect consumers even if they are myopic and don't realize what's going on. So if there is lots of competition, we should worry less about consumer protection. If there is less competition, then consumer protection policies are key.") (Comments of Jorge Padilla).

26 George A. Akerlof & Robert J. Shiller, Animal Spirits: How Human Psychology Drives the Economy, and Why it Matters for Global Capitalism (2009).

27 Jones v. Harris Assocs. L.P. ("*Jones II*"), 527 F.3d 728, 729 (7th Cir. 2008) (Posner, J., dissenting from denial of rehearing en banc). Writing for a unanimous panel, Chief Judge Frank Easterbrook had applied a stringent standard to hold that mutual fund shareholders could not sue their financial advisers for exacerbating their losses during the financial meltdown. Jones v. Harris Assocs. L.P. ("*Jones I*"), 527 F.3d 627 (7th Cir. 2008). In so holding, Easterbrook advanced a classical law-and-economics analysis that presumed a well-functioning market for investment advice, dismissed possibly irrational investor behavior, and concluded with a call for greater deregulation of the industry. In sharp contrast, Posner asserted in his dissent that Easterbrook's faith in the self-disciplining nature of market forces in the mutual fund industry is misplaced because "mutual funds are a component of the financial services industry, where abuses have been rampant." at 730. Finding an absence of healthy competition, Posner took the view that market regulation was needed to correct for disordered behavior.

28 Timothy J. Muris, *The New Rule of Reason*, 57 Antitrust L.J. 859, 861 (1989); Timothy J. Muris, *The Federal Trade Commission and the Rule of Reason: In Defense of* Massachusetts Board, 66 Antitrust L.J. 773 (1998); Timothy J. Muris, *The Rule of Reason After* California Dental, 68 Antitrust L.J. 527 (2000).

29 Federal Trade Commission v. Indiana Fed'n of Dentists, 476 U.S. 447 (1986).

30 Polygram Holding, Inc. v. F.T.C., 416 F.3d 29 (D.C. Cir. 2005). *See also* North Texas Specialty Physicians v. Federal Trade Commission, 528 F.3d 346, 370 (5th Cir. 2008).

31 NCAA v. Board of Regents, 468 U.S. 95, 109 (1984); Federal Trade Commission v. Indiana Federation of Dentists, 476 U.S. at 460–64.

32 *See* Chicago Board of Trade v. United States, 246 U.S. 231, 238 (1918); Aspen Skiing Co. v. Highlands Skiing Corp., 472 U.S. 585, 602 (1985).

33 *See, e.g.*, Le Page's Inc. v. 3M Co., 324 F.3d 141 (3d Cir. 2003) (en banc).

34 California Dental Association v. F.T.C., 526 U.S. 756, 778 (1999).

35 R.C. Dick Geothermal Corp. v. Thermogenics, Inc., 890 F.2d 139, 151, 153 (9th Cir. 1989) (en banc); Capital Imaging Assocs. v. Mohawk Valley Med. Assocs., 996 F.2d 537, 546 (2d Cir. 1993).

36 Schwinn, 388 U.S. at 374 n.5, *overruled on other grounds by GTE Sylvania*, 433 U.S. at 58–59 (1977); Worldwide Basketball & Sport Tours v. NCAA, 388 F.3d 955, 959 (6th Cir. 2004); Spanish Broad. Sys. v. Clear Channel Commc'ns., 376 F.3d 1065, 1072–73 (11th Cir. 2004).

37 Verizon Communications. v. Law Offices of Curtis V. Trinko LLP, 540 U.S. 398, 407 (2004) (noting that a Section 2 monopolization claim requires proof that the defendant (1) possesses monopoly power, and (2) has acquired, enhanced, or maintained that power by use of exclusionary conduct).

38 United States v. Microsoft Corp., 253 F.3d 34 (D.C. Cir. 2001).

39   *See, e.g.,* Aspen Skiing Co. v. Aspen Highlands Skiing Corp., 472 U.S. 575, 605 n.32 (1985).

40   *See, e.g.,* Multistate Legal Studies v. Harcourt Brace Jovanovich Legal and Prof'l Publications, Inc., 63 F.3d 1540 (1995).

41   Federal Trade Commission v. Procter & Gamble Co., 386 U.S. 568, 580 (1967) (rejecting efficiencies claims and declaring that "[p]ossible economies cannot be used as a defense to illegality") (citing Brown Shoe Co. v. United States, 370 U.S. 294, 244 (1962)); United States v. Mercy Health Servs., 902 F. Supp. 968 (N.D. Iowa 1995) (rejecting efficiencies defense to a claim that a merger was anticompetitive); *cf.* FTC v. Staples, Inc., 970 F. Supp. 1066 (D.D.C. 1997) (noting that in light of the 1992 Merger Guidelines, whether efficiencies "may be used to rebut the government's prima facie case is not entirely clear").

42   *See* 1992 Merger Guidelines, § 4 ("The Agency will not challenge a merger if cognizable efficiencies are of a character and magnitude such that the merger is not likely to be anticompetitive in any relevant market.").

43   European Commission Communication, *Guidance on The Commission's Enforcement Priorities In Applying Article 82 EC Treaty to Abusive Exclusionary Conduct By Dominant Undertakings* ("Guidance"), along with a press release, a list of questions and answers, the Commission staff working paper, and other useful citations, *available at* http://ec.europa.eu/comm/competition/antitrust/art82/index.html.

44   *Id.* at 7 (discussing "anticompetitive foreclosure" and noting that harm occurs where consumer welfare is harmed or where rivals are eliminated from competition).

45   *Id.* at 9 (noting that "if the conduct has been in place for a sufficient period of time, the market performance of the dominant undertaking and its competitors *may* provide direct evidence of anticompetitive foreclosure" but describing circumstantial evidence that the Commission will also find persuasive).

46   *Id.*

47   *Id.* at 23–26.

48   *See, e.g., Microsoft,* 253 F.3d 34 (D.C. Cir. 2001) (holding that evidence of intent is permissible to prove anticompetitive effects); *Aspen Skiing,* 472 U.S. 585 (holding that unexplained changes in course of dealing can give rise to inference of anticompetitive effects); Brooke Group Ltd. v. Brown & Williamson Tobacco Corp., 509 U.S. 209, 222–24 (1993) (holding that to prevail under a predatory pricing claim, the plaintiff must show, first, that the defendant priced its products below an appropriate measure of its costs, and, second, that there was a dangerous probability that the defendant would recoup its investment in below-cost prices, but not addressing the appropriate measure of cost because the parties agreed that the relevant measure of cost was average variable cost).

49   *Supra* note 43, *Guidance* at 12-13 (discussing use of evidence of efficiencies as a defense to a claim of exclusionary conduct).

50   *Id.* at 12.

51   Philip Lowe, *The European Commission Formulates its Priorities as Regards Exclusionary Conduct by Dominant Undertakings,* GLOBAL COMPETITION REVIEW (February 2009).

52   United States v. Baker Hughes, Inc., 908 F.2d 981 (D.C. Cir. 1990) (Thomas, J.).

The Legend of Price Fixing by U.S. Trade Associations

Theodore Voorhees, Jr.

tvoorhees@cov.com

Partner, Covington Burling LLP

Abstract

There has long been a widespread preconception in the United States that membership in trade associations and participation in association activities indicate a propensity to engage in anticompetitive activity. This viewpoint seems to be the long tail residuum of many antitrust enforcement proceedings against trade associations, including criminal prosecutions, that occurred during the early and middle decades of the 20th century, and of the stigmatizing impact of a quaint and often-recited aphorism by the 18th Century political economist Adam Smith. Given the plethora of international cartel activities and criminal prosecutions by the U.S. Department of Justice in recent years, one might have expected to see widespread involvement by U.S. trade associations. This review of the last three decades of Department of Justice and Federal Trade Commission enforcement actions and private antitrust litigation reveals, however, that the days of rampant antitrust abuses by U.S. trade associations are long over, most likely the result of improved internal association governance measures and increased self-policing to deter and avoid anti-competitive activity by and among trade association members.

There was a time, long ago, when U.S. trade associations were generally held in suspicion for their presumed role as prime incubators for criminal antitrust price-fixing conspiracies. For many years growing numbers of federal antitrust indictments issued against associations seemed to confirm this common view. But times have changed. A fresh examination of this subject is long overdue. The modern U.S. record, reviewed in this article, will surprise those who may still cling to the old way of thinking.

The reputation for fomenting antitrust mischief has long bedeviled the trade association sector, and may have originated two centuries ago with the casual but often-quoted reflections of the Scottish moral philosopher and "father of modern economics,"[1] Adam Smith, who wrote in 1776 that: "People of the same trade seldom meet together, even for merriment and diversion, but the conversation ends in a conspiracy against the public, or in some contrivance to raise prices."[2]

Smith made this assertedly intuitive observation[3] long before the rise and rapid proliferation of national trade associations in the United States. Nevertheless, U.S. trade association experience during the early decades of the 20th century seemed to bear out the Scottish sage's insights, as the Antitrust Division of the United States Department of Justice (hereafter "Antitrust Division") repeatedly launched successful enforcement actions against industry boycotts, price-fixing, and related anti-competitive schemes carried out by or in connivance with industry associations. The Division secured a drum-beat of landmark U.S. Supreme Court rulings—*Eastern States Retail Lumber Dealers' Ass'n, American Column & Lumber, American Linseed Oil, Trenton Potteries, Sugar Institute*—that would long stigmatize the modern American trade association as a sinister threat to competition.[4]

I. The Early Years of Criminal Prosecutions

These early Antitrust Division victories cast a long shadow of subsequent criminal enforcement proceedings against many U.S. trade associations in mid-century. The darkest days were the two decades between 1955 and 1975, when 88 associations were indicted for Sherman Act violations, including 18 in 1959 alone.[5] The rate of indictments began gradually tapering off during the late 1960s and early 1970s and then sharply declined to three in each year from 1976-78, one in 1979 and none in 1980. Only six associations were criminally prosecuted after 1980; none since 1995.[6]

Based on a scan of the names of the six trade associations that were prosecuted between 1980 and 1995, what is most noteworthy is the relatively narrow focus of all six organizations when compared to many of the targets of earlier prosecutions:

> National Turtle Farmers & Shippers Association (1995)
>
> Lake Country Optometric Society (1995)
>
> Northwest Chapter of the Arkansas Society of Professional Surveyors (1992)
>
> Midwest Steel Drum Manufacturer's Association (1991)
>
> Wholesale Produce Dealers Association of Hawaii (1986)
>
> Association of Ship Brokers and Agents (1983)

It appears that one must go very far back in time to find the last two instances of a criminal antitrust proceeding against a U.S. trade association of real national stature. Thus, it has been more than 30 years since the Antitrust Division's successful 1979 prosecution of the Society of Independent Gasoline Marketers, and more than forty years ago since the Division won a guilty verdict against the Plumbing Fixtures Manufacturers Association in 1970.[7]

1. Transition to Civil Proceedings

The disappearance of criminal proceedings does not mean U.S. trade associations have fallen outside the legal spotlight. To the contrary, associations continue to be the subject of numerous government and private enforcement actions. But the key difference is that all of these are *civil* rather than *criminal* proceedings. Somewhat surprisingly, however, academic commentators do not appear to have taken notice of this marked shift from criminal to civil enforcement, or sought to offer an explanation for the change.

Government Civil Actions and Speeches—Trade associations continue to engage in a wide variety of antitrust-sensitive activities on behalf of their members. These include establishment of membership rules and standard-setting, both of which have the potential to result in exclusionary effects, and formulation of business practice standards and rules that could have direct or indirect effects on price.[8] There is no doubt that federal enforcement agencies maintain vigilance in this sphere, as evidenced by the steady stream of civil actions the Antitrust Division and the FTC have filed against trade associations in all of these areas, most recently concentrating on the real estate brokerage and health care sectors.[9]

The key distinction, however, is that in each of these recent enforcement actions the government used its *civil* rather than *criminal* authority, essentially acknowledging that the association practices in question were generally subject to application of the antitrust rule of reason. Even when they have involved trade practices that had a fairly clear and direct impact on price—such as the Antitrust Division's 1980s cases challenging brokerage commissions in the oil tanker chartering business[10] and the broadcast industry's rules restricting television advertising,[11] the Division's more recent actions against "traditional" real estate broker practices disfavoring limited-service, lower-cost internet brokers,[12] and the FTC's recent actions against health care professional associations[13]—the federal enforcement agencies have recognized that the trade association practices in question did not warrant criminal enforcement.[14] Unlike naked price-fixing and bid-rigging, which have no pro-competitive justification and are typically conducted covertly, the trade association practices that have come under enforcement agency scrutiny in the modern era are conducted in the open and tend to have arguable economic and pro-competitive justifications.[15]

Private Antitrust Plaintiffs—Although criminal prosecutions of U.S. trade associations have essentially vanished, associations are nevertheless regularly named as defendants in private treble damage actions charging participation in or facilitation of industry price-fixing conspiracies.[16] A number of such efforts by private plaintiffs to characterize conventional trade association conduct as price fixing have foundered on defense motions to dismiss or for summary judgment,[17] but numerous others have survived such motions,[18] even after the U.S. Supreme Court in its *Twombly* decision raised the bar for plaintiffs attempting to plead antitrust conspiracy.[19] It remains rare, however, to find a prevailing plaintiff at the conclusion of one of these cases.[20] Nevertheless, traces of anti-association stigma remain in some court rulings. In 1988 and then again in 2002 the United States Court of Appeals for the Fifth Circuit found it necessary to observe that "a trade association is not by its nature a 'walking conspiracy.'"[21] The Fifth and Eleventh Circuits repeated this "damned by faint praise" refrain in 2008 and 2010, respectively.[22]

Academic Commentary—Contemporary antitrust scholars still treat trade associations harshly, almost reflexively labeling them either willing facilitators of cartelization, or providers of ready "cover" for conspiratorial meetings. A closer look at the academic literature, however, reveals that the examples of association misconduct to which they point involve either foreign trade organizations, or U.S. association activities that pre-date the 1980s, or "cover" situations surrounding trade *conferences or conventions,* not trade *associations.* As will be seen below, the difference in the latter case is substantive, not semantic.

The surge of trade association criminal prosecutions in the U.S. during the 1950s and 1960s produced a cluster of papers in academic journals during the 1970s and early 1980s that focused on the facilitating role trade associations often played in price-fixing conspiracies.[23] These articles in turn inspired more recent commentators who have echoed the same message. Thus, Christopher Leslie, one of the more prolific of these contemporary authors, observed in a lengthy 2004 article that:

> For most of the past century, the history of cartels in America parallels the history of trade associations. Many trade associations were created as a cover for cartel schemes.[24]

Four years later, Professor Leslie was still advancing the notion that trade associations work hand-in-glove with cartelists:

> In sum, while some trade associations came to facilitate illegal price fixing, some cartelists created trade associations for the purpose of concealing an illegal conspiracy. Importantly, when trade associations are employed as cover for cartels, it is harder for member firms' own internal antitrust compliance programs to spot price fixing. In any case, the relationship between trade associations and price fixing suggests that any efforts to thwart cartelization must pay special attention to trade associations.[25]

Purdue University Professor John M. Connor, another leading cartel scholar and the author of *Global Price Fixing*,[26] cited the infamous lysine and citric acid cartels uncovered during the 1990s as examples of continuing trade association misconduct:

> "Cartels frequently utilized industry trade associations as covers for their illegal meetings, prepared false agendas and false minutes, and took many other steps to hide their conspiracies."[27]

Most recently, a 2011 article by Professor Leslie and co-author Herbert Hovenkamp featured an extensive survey of the 20th century history and dynamics of cartelization, which the authors summarized as follows:

> In sum, the trade association provides the structure for cartel decisionmaking, the cover for why competitors are gathering, and 'may also foster a social climate conducive to collusion.' All of this facilitates a relatively democratic decisionmaking process for the cartel."[28]

Though numerous cartel-trade-association combinations are surveyed in the Leslie-Hovenkamp paper, none involved conduct of a U.S. trade association after the 1970s.

II. Prevalence of International Cartels — But Where Are the U.S. Trade Associations?

There can be no doubt that international cartels remain a very significant problem both in the United States and abroad, as demonstrated by the lengthy and seemingly ever-replenishing list of indictments and plea agreements covering a wide array of industries in recent years. The aggregate annual levels of criminal fines that have been paid by the wrongdoers in price-fixing cases have reached breathtaking levels. The Antitrust Division alone reported collecting $4.661 billion in cartel fines from 2000 through 2010, including $1 billion for fiscal year 2009 alone.[29]

What seems to have gone largely unnoticed, however, is the absence of indictments against any U.S. trade associations in the affected industries. This is especially noteworthy given that a very high percentage of these cartel prosecutions benefited from cooperating companies that either sought leniency or entered into plea agreements under the Justice Department's highly successful leniency/amnesty program.[30] Cooperating firms are required to provide full disclosure to prosecutors regarding everything they know about the cartel activity in question, which often produces leads to other price-fixing schemes of which the cooperating firm may also be aware. If U.S. trade associations had been involved in any of these uncovered cartels, or even if domestic associations were only being taken advantage of as "cover" for the underlying criminal activity, one would expect to see related indictments and prominent press release mentions of the trade association connection, as has increasingly been the case overseas.[31] But whereas the torrent of recent prosecutions has uncovered a host of miscreants in many countries, the wrongdoers appear to have conspired almost everywhere *except* within U.S. trade associations.

The U.S. Antitrust Division lists its largest fines assessed in cartel prosecutions in a chart entitled "*Sherman Act Violations Yielding a Corporate Fine of $10 Million or More.*"[32] The chart includes international and domestic cartels in 32 industry sectors prosecuted since 1995. Tellingly, no U.S. trade association was indicted in connection with any of these criminal price-fixing conspiracies. The notable *absence* of U.S. trade association involvement is all the more remarkable given the hundreds or even thousands of separate conspiratorial meetings and conversations[33] that occurred among companies and corporate officials in diverse locations including:

- within or near the corporate headquarters of the conspirators themselves,[34]

- in connection with tours of one of the conspirators' plants,[35]

- in hotels,[36]

- at famous restaurants,[37]

- in executives' homes,[38]

- even in a horse barn.[39]

One would think that if U.S. trade associations are as conducive to cartel conduct as some persist in arguing, at least a few of these diverse meetings and contacts would have taken place under the auspices of a U.S. association. One is left with the impression that, although many business executives the world over still exhibit an unhealthy appetite for price fixing, the bad actors seem to be *avoiding* rather than infiltrating or involving trade associations located in the United States.

III. Possible Explanation for Disappearance of U.S. Trade Associations from the Division's Criminal Enforcement Docket

Certainly the absence of a criminal prosecution against any major U.S. trade association since 1979 (or against even a small or regional U.S. association since 1995) is not explained either by diminution of prosecutorial effort against cartels or by loss of enforcement community interest in trade association activities. Rather, it would appear the most likely explanation for this important development is a combination of enhanced self-policing by U.S. trade associations and successful deterrence of international cartelists from conducting conspiratorial meetings on U.S. soil.

Self-Policing—Although there appears to be no official or comprehensive survey of the matter, it is evident that most, if not all, national trade associations in the United States have established detailed antitrust compliance programs and procedures to avoid falling into antitrust danger. In many cases U.S. associations require attendance by counsel whenever members meet or hold conference calls under association auspices. This positive development reflects a desire for verifiable compliance emanating both from the associations themselves and from their members, as noted at a recent American Bar Association symposium on U.S. cartel enforcement:

> Question: I understand that many companies these days are actually vetting trade associations, before they actually allow their members to participate, to see whether trade associations have these types of requirements in place.
>
> Diane Bieri (Pharma): I am sure that's true, and in our case we frequently interact with the antitrust counsel of the member companies to reassure them that we are taking measures to ensure compliance.[40]

The Antitrust Division recognizes that compliance efforts have proliferated among U.S. trade associations and has even complimented associations for affirmatively providing useful information in aid of Justice Department enforcement actions. In a 1995 address before the Trade Association and Antitrust Law Committee of the Bar Association of the District of Columbia, Willard K. Tom, counselor to the Assistant Attorney General of the Antitrust Division stated:

> We often tell members of the private bar that they are the first line of defense for preserving competition in our economy, because the advice they give their clients to keep them in compliance with the antitrust laws amounts to far more effective and efficient law enforcement than trying to prosecute violators after the fact. That goes equally well for trade associations, whose antitrust compliance activities can help keep both the associations themselves and their members out of trouble.[41]

Antitrust compliance by U.S. trade associations has produced a growing literature, as illustrated by two recent publications of the ABA Antitrust Section.[42]

Deterrence—Antitrust Division officials have frequently observed that foreign cartelists take pains to avoid dealings with one another on American soil lest they fall within the grasp of U.S. antitrust enforcers. As Hammond and colleagues stated most recently in a paper delivered at the Georgetown Global Antitrust Enforcement Symposium in Washington, DC on September 22, 2011:

> On numerous occasions, the Antitrust Division has interviewed members of international cartels who provided first-hand accounts of their participation in cartels that spanned the globe but stopped at the US border because the participants feared going to jail. This eyewitness testimony is compelling evidence that enforcement in the United States is deterring cartel activity.[43]

IV. Trade Associations Distinguished from Trade Conferences and Conventions

In two of the thirty-two Justice Department cartel prosecutions listed on the Antitrust Division's chart of largest criminal fines[44]—the Choline Chloride (Vitamins) cartel and the Marine Hose cartel—secret meetings of the conspirators occurred in the United States under "cover" of a trade event but these two instances did not involve a U.S. trade association but rather a US *trade conference* or *convention*.[45] Thus, the Marine Hose conspirators apparently chose to hold one of their meetings in a Houston Texas hotel under cover of the 2007 Offshore Technology Conference,[46] and the Choline Chloride (Vitamins) conspirators met in January 1998 "over dinner on the fringes of the Southeast Poultry Convention in Atlanta."[47] Notably, there are several important differences between a trade conference or convention, which are essentially *events* that provide an opportunity to gather and collude on the periphery, and a trade association, which is a formal business membership enterprise that typically features a governance structure that provides mechanisms to avert unauthorized activities and promote active vigilance, in particular to prevent cartel behavior.

First, a trade conference or convention is typically a discrete *event* rather than a broad-scale enterprise, a venue rather than a membership organization. The conference or convention normally takes place during a limited time period, and though it is often repeated, most typically on an annual or biannual cycle, it does not usually have the full organizational infrastructure, including in-house counsel and antitrust safeguards, needed for conducting the ongoing business of a trade association. Thus the trade conference is not only an "opportunity" for holding illicit meetings, it can be a relatively un-policed occasion since the absence of direct trade association involvement will often mean no antitrust compliance program oversight has been activated.

Second, trade associations are full-service membership bodies with broad policy and action agendas to foster their members' business interests in the public and governmental spheres. Trade conferences and conventions, on the other hand, are events that attract diverse audiences of incidental attendees, not year-round members. Thus, one would not expect mere incidental attendance of this kind to provide sufficient incentive for any individual or group of corporate attendees to insist that the organizers provide antitrust guidance, oversight, or self-policing for their diverse collection of visitors. And lacking such due diligence pressure from attendees, no trade conference or convention is likely to feel any particularized need to provide elaborate legal structures and governance disciplines for protection against what will surely seem to be only theoretical and highly tenuous legal liability risks facing unspecified individuals within their broad audience.

Third, trade conferences and conventions are often massive public events drawing thousands or more attendees, including many organizations and individuals that have few or no connections or business dealings with one another. In these circumstances, any attempt to develop internal governance rules and due diligence safeguards to police all possible interactions among the diverse participants would be a very tall order, yet attract no core group of interested stakeholders having a direct and vital self-interest in assuring that the governance structure is in place and works. This is fundamentally different from the case of a trade association, whose members can readily appreciate the direct legal hazard they will be exposed to if the organization does not take adequate measures to avoid antitrust risk.

For these reasons, one would not expect the organizers of a trade conference or convention to be as strongly motivated as most major U.S. trade associations, or as adequately resourced, to create systematic antitrust safeguards.

V. The Cartelists' Search for Protective "Cover"

While it cannot be denied that conspirators might use their planned joint presence at a large public event such as a trade conference or convention as "cover" for an unlawful meeting, that does not distinguish a trade conference from any other mass function, such as a sporting event or a political convention. By its very nature, "cover" can be afforded by any event—without it being necessary for there to be a connection between the event's "host" and the conspirators. Indeed, an argument could be made that the farther removed the conspirators' business focus is from the "covering" venue, the better the cover story. Being in the same city where a political convention or Olympic or World Cup sporting event is taking place would arguably arouse less suspicion than assembling at a trade association's offices. When considered in combination with the fact that many U.S. associations monitor member behavior to prevent wrongdoing, it might be said that for business rivals to seek supposed "cover" within their own industry's trade association would appear logically to be their worst option—the choice most easily discovered by their association's internal policing mechanism, and the occasion that prosecutors can most readily link back contextually to the very wrongdoing they are trying to conceal.

Several conclusions can be drawn from the relative ease with which cartels can find "cover" options in the modern business world. First, no organization, whether trade association or otherwise, that hosts an event which draws business executives for legitimate reasons can absolutely prevent those individuals from arranging to meet "offsite" for illegal purposes. Second, trade associations are nevertheless singularly motivated to institute due diligence mechanisms designed to reduce that risk from happening exactly because their core business of bringing their competitor-members together will inevitably draw enhanced scrutiny by antitrust enforcers and others. Third, the need to safeguard trade associations from even the appearance of antitrust wrongdoing and consequent liability risks has become keenly appreciated by the associations themselves as well as their members, especially in the United States where a century of highly publicized prosecutions have made the severity of punishment readily apparent. And finally, it logically follows that the apparent disinclination of international cartels in the modern era to select a U.S. trade association as the host for their unlawful gatherings—whether as a direct venue or as an occasion providing "cover"—is most likely explained as much by their fear of detection *by the trade association* as by their healthy respect for vigilant U.S. enforcement authorities.

VI. Conclusion

U.S. trade association indictments have become nearly extinct. Of course, this does not mean that trade association gatherings are immune to infection. Antitrust compliance programs, careful monitoring of association proceedings by counsel, and close vigilance have had salutary effects and obviously need to continue. Nevertheless, the record over the last several decades provides a compelling case for recalibrating the rhetoric about U.S. trade association vulnerabilities, if only to recognize the demonstrable progress that has been made since *Plumbing Fixtures*. One can fairly conclude from the record that U.S. trade associations have probably become the *least* rather than the *most* hospitable venue for price fixing over the last 30 years. And as to Adam Smith's off-hand remark, the United States Court of Appeals for the District of Columbia Circuit may have said it best in a 1984 antitrust ruling involving Sherman Act Section 1 charges against trade associations of dentists and periodontists:

> No matter how true [Smith's observation] may have been in the eighteenth century, after nearly a century of American business operating under the Sherman Act we can no longer subscribe to such a near-sighted view of the business world . . . .[48]

Figure 1

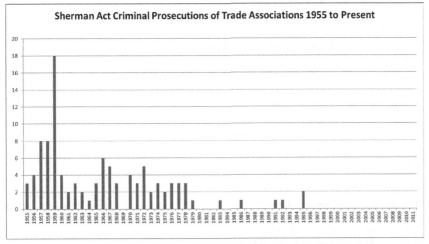

Sherman Act Criminal Prosecutions of Trade Associations 1955 to Present

SOURCE: JAMES M. CLABAULT & MICHAEL K. BLOCK, SHERMAN ACT INDICTMENTS: 1955-1980 (Federal Legal Publications 1980); Trade Regulation Reporter (CCH) Transfer Binder, U.S. Antitrust Cases—Summaries Complaints, Indictments, Developments, ¶¶ 45,070-45,088 1980-1988; Trade Regulation Reporter (CCH) Transfer Binder, U.S. Antitrust Cases—Summaries, ¶¶ 45,080-45,096 1988-1996; DOJ Antitrust Case Filings—Dec. 1994-present, available at http://www.usdoj.gov/atr/cases.html.

Appendix A

Sherman Act Criminal Prosecutions of Trade Associations 1955-Present[49]

Index 1 "Chronological Index By Calendar Year" (pp. 917-932)

1955 (3)

Fish Smokers Trade Council
MD and VA Milk Producers Ass'n
National Rifle Ass'n of America

1956 (4)

International Boxing Guild
Erie County Malt Beverage Distributors Ass'n
Shoulder Pads Mfrs. Ass'n of California
Philadelphia Radio & Television Broadcasters Ass'n

1957 (8)

Concrete Form Ass'n of Central New England
Toy Guidance Council

Nassau & Suffolk County Retail Hardware Ass'n
Chicago Boiler Mfrs. Ass'n
Tri-County Beer Distributors Ass'n
Automatic Merchandisers Ass'n of Western Pa.
Maine Lobstermen's Ass'n
Venetian Blind Mfrs. Credit Ass'n

1958 (8)
New York Pickle & Condiment Dealers Ass'n
Greater New York Food Processors Ass'n
Frozen Food Distributors Ass'n of Greater New York
Greater Washington Chevrolet Dealers Ass'n
Ford Dealers Advertising Ass'n
Oakland Zone Chevrolet Dealers Ass'n
Plymouth Dealers Ass'n of Northern California
Fur Shearers Guild

1959 (18)
Detroit Chevrolet Dealers Ass'n
Seam Binding Mfrs. Ass'n
Rubber Mfrs. Ass'n
Greater Blouse Skirt & Neckwear Contractors Ass'n
National Ass'n of Blouse Mfrs.
Greater New York Chrysler Corp. Automobile Dealers
Metropolitan Buick Dealers Ass'n
Automobile Merchants Ass'n of New York
Nassau-Suffolk DeSoto Dealers Group
Brooklyn & Queens Dodge Dealers Group
Nassau-Suffolk Dodge Dealers Group
Nassau-Suffolk Chrysler Dealers Ass'n
Arizona Consolidated Masonry and Plastering Contractors Ass'n
San Diego Grocers Ass'n
Auto Glass Dealers Ass'n
Philadelphia Ass'n of Linen Suppliers
Gasoline Retailers Ass'n
Bituminous Concrete Ass'n

1960 (4)
Southeast Texas Chapter, Nat'l Electric Contractors
Carbonated Beverage Manufacturers Ass'n of Washington, DC
Durable Building Materials Council
Northern California Pharmaceutical Ass'n

1961 (2)
Milk Distributors Ass'n
The Greater New York Tailor's Expressmen Ass'n

1962 (3)
Conn. Package Stores Ass'n
Greater New York Roll Bakers Ass'n
Interborough Delicatessen Dealers Ass'n

1963 (2)
Duluth Clearing House Ass'n
Pennsylvania Refuse Removal Ass'n

1964 (1)

New Oleans Chapter, Associated General Contractors of America

1965 (3)

Association of North American Directory Publishers
National Hose Assemblies Manufacturers Ass'n
Northern Virginia Beer Wholesalers

1966 (6)

Associated Cement Contractors of Michigan
Chicago Linen Supply Ass'n
Bowling Proprietors Ass'n of Northern Ohio
Plumbing Fixture Manufacturers Ass'n
Montana State Food Distributors Ass'n
Ohio Honda Dealers' Sales Ass'n

1967 (5)

Fuel Oil Dealers Div. of the Central Montgomery Cnty Chamber of Commerce
California Shell Dealers Ass'n
Marin Independent Service Station Ass'n
Automotive Service Dealers Ass'n
United Oil Dealers Ass'n

1968 (3)

Independent Body Shop Ass'n of Reno and Sparks
Oregon Restaurant and Beverage Ass'n
Columbus Bowling Proprietors Ass'n

1969 (0)

1970 (4)

Federacion de Transporte de Puerto Rico
Kansas City Music Operators Ass'n
Metro Denver Concrete Ass'n
Manufacturers Ass'n of the Relocatable Building Industry

1971 (3)

Independent Garage Owners of Athens
Athens Automobile Dealers Ass'n
National Association for Air Freight

1972 (5)

Overhead Door Distributors Ass'n of Greater Delaware Valley
Garage Door Manufacturers Ass'n
Central Michigan Gasoline Dealers Ass'n
Professional Petroleum Merchants Ass'n
St. Petersburg Automobile Dealers Ass'n

1973 (2)

Jackson Hole Service Station Ass'n
Georgia Automatic Merchandising Council

1974 (3)

Clovis Retail Liquor Dealers Trade Ass'n
National Board of Fur Farm Organizations
Custom Brokers and Forwarders Ass'n of Miami

1975 (2)

Korean Hair Goods Ass'n of America
Hawaii Conference of Tour Operators

1976 (3)
Society of Independent Gasoline Marketers of America
Lubbock County Beverage Ass'n
Metal Insulation Jacketing Manufacturers Ass'n

1977 (3)
Wholesale Tobacco Distributors of New York
Florida Portable Sanitation Ass'n
Greater Syracuse Board of Realtors

1978 (3)
Electric Fuse Manufacturers Guild
Detroit Lumbermen's Ass'n
Midlands Chapter of Registered Land Surveyors

1979 (1)
Tobacco Distributors Association of New Jersey
1980 (0)
1981 (0)
1982 (0)

1983 (1)
Association of Ship Brokers and Agents (USA)
1984 (0)
1985 (0)

1986 (1)
Wholesale Produce Dealers Association of Hawaii

1987 (0)
1988 (0)
1989 (0)
1990 (0)

1991 (1)
Midwest Steel Drum Manufacturer's Association

1992 (1)
Northwest Chapter of the Arkansas Society of Professional Surveyors

1993 (0)
1994 (0)

1995 (2)
Lake Country Optometric Society
National Turtle Farmers & Shippers Association

1996 (0)

Theodore Voorhees, Jr.

1997 (0)
1998 (0)
1999 (0)
2000 (0)
2001 (0)
2002 (0)
2003 (0)
2004 (0)
2005 (0)
2006 (0)
2007 (0)
2008 (0)
2009 (0)
2010 (0)
2011 (0)

NOTES

1 *See* PAUL A. SAMUELSON & WILLIAM D. NORDHAUS, ECONOMICS 376 (McGraw-Hill Companies 14th ed. 1992).

2 Adam Smith, *An Inquiry Into The Nature and Causes of the Wealth of Nations*, in 39 GREAT BOOKS OF THE WESTERN WORLD 55 (R. Hutchins & M. Adler eds., 1952).

3 In *Bell Atlantic v. Twombly*, 550 U.S. 544 (2007), Justice Souter, writing for the majority, called Smith's comment a "tongue-in-cheek remark", 550 U.S. at 567 n.12, and even Justice Stevens, who invoked Smith's observation in dissent, acknowledged that "I am not so cynical as to accept that sentiment at face value . . . ." 550 U.S. at 501 (Stevens, J., dissenting).

4 *See, e.g., E. States Retail Lumber Dealers' Ass'n v. United States*, 234 U.S. 600, 608-09 (1914) (group boycott orchestrated by trade association of retail lumber dealers); Am. Column & Lumber Co. v. United States, 257 U.S. 377, 410-11 (1921) (price fixing pursuant to "Open Competition Plan" of American Hardwood Manufacturers' Association); United States v. Am. Linseed Oil Co., 262 U.S. 371, 389-90 (1923) (broad suppression of competitive conditions in the industry implemented by a trade association called "Armstrong Bureau of Related Industries"); United States v. Trenton Potteries Co., 273 U.S. 392 (1927) (price fixing orchestrated by Sanitary Potters' Association); Sugar Inst., Inc. v. United States, 297 U.S. 553, 601 (1936) (price fixing by national trade association of U.S. sugar industry). Of course, the 1920s Supreme Court also recognized that trade association activities can be wholly innocent and even pro-competitive. *See* Maple Flooring Ass'n v. United States, 268 U.S. 563, 584 (1925) ("We do not conceive that the members of trade associations become such conspirators merely because they gather and disseminate information . . . bearing on the business in which they are engaged and make use of it in the management and control of their individual businesses . . . ."); Cement Mfr's Protective Ass'n v. United States, 268 U.S. 588, 604 (1925) ("we cannot regard the procuring and dissemination of information which tends to prevent the procuring of fraudulent contracts... as an unlawful restraint of trade even though such information be gathered and disseminated by those who are engaged in the trade or business principally concerned.").

5 Charts listing Antitrust Division criminal proceedings against trade associations, year-by-year from 1955-2011, are provided in Attachment A and Figure 1.

6 *Id.* Given this sharp downward trend, it is noteworthy that in the federal government's mid-1970s criminal prosecution of the gypsum wallboard industry for price-fixing, the Gypsum Association was not indicted but rather was named in the complaint as an unindicted co-conspirator. United States v. U.S. Gypsum Co., 438 U.S. 422, 427 n.2 (1978). All of the gypsum defendants were found guilty but their convictions were reversed by the United States Court of Appeals for the Third Circuit, whose opinion was affirmed by the U.S. Supreme Court. *Id.*, 438 U.S. at 433-34.

7 *See* United States v. Am. Radiator & Standard Sanitary Corp., 433 F.2d 174, 180 (3d Cir. 1970); United States v. Soc'y of Indep. Gasoline Marketers, 624 F.2d 461 (4th Cir. 1980).

8 *See* ABA SECTION OF ANTITRUST LAW, ANTITRUST AND TRADE ASSOCIATIONS HANDBOOK (2009).

9 *See, e.g.*, Sw. Health Alliances, Inc., FTC Docket No. C-4327, July 8, 2011 (consent order resolving claims against association of physicians charged with fixing prices physicians charge insurers), *available at* http://www.ftc.gov/os/caselist/0910013/110715southwestdo.pdf; United States v. Nat'l Ass'n of Realtors, No. 05 C 5140, 2006 U.S. Dist. LEXIS 86963, at *2-3 (N.D. Ill. Nov. 27, 2006); *see also* Press Release, Dep't of Justice, Justice Department Announces Settlement With the National Association of Realtors (May 27, 2008), http://www.usdoj.gov/atr/public/

press_releases/2008/233605.htm; N. Tex. Specialty Physicians v. FTC, 528 F.3d 346 (5th Cir. 2008); Conn. Chiropractic Ass'n (2008) (FTC Consent); Press Release, Dep't of Justice, Justice Department Reaches Settlement With the Arizona Hospital and Healthcare Association and its Subsidiary (May 22, 2007), http://www.usdoj.gov/atr/public/press_releases/2007/223470.htm; Carlsbad Physician Ass'n, 135 F.T.C. 804, 807 (2003) (consent order); United States v. Scuba Retailers Ass'n, No. 96-6112, (S.D. Fla. complaint filed Jan. 30, 1996), *complaint available at* http://www.usdoj.gov/atr/cases/f3700/3720.htm; United States v. Nat'l Council on Problem Gambling, Inc. (D.D.C. *complaint filed* June 6, 2003), *complaint available at* http://www.usdoj.gov/atr/cases/f201000/201082.htm; United States v. Nat'l Ass'n of Police Equip. Distribs., Inc., No. 02-80703, (S.D. Fla. *complaint filed* July 25, 2002) *complaint available at* http://www.usdoj.gov/atr/cases/f11600/11655.htm; Press Release, Dep't of Justice, Justice Department Moves to stop Anticompetitive Actions of National Medical Residency Trade Association, (May 28, 1996), http://www.usdoj.gov/atr/public/press_releases/1996/0669.htm; Press Release, Dep't of Justice, Travel Agent Trade Association Agrees to End Anticompetitive Practices, (Oct. 25, 1994), http://www.usdoj.gov/atr/public/press_releases/1994/211931.htm.

10   United States v. Ass'n of Ship Brokers & Agents (U.S.A.), Inc., Trade Reg. Rptr. (CCH) Transfer Binder, U.S. Antitrust Cases Summaries, ¶ 45,080 (Case 2805).

11   United States v. Nat'l Ass'n of Broadcasters, 536 F. Supp. 149, 156 (D.D.C. 1982):

> The per se rule is thus inappropriate in a supply limitation case if the industry which is the subject of the litigation possesses attributes which in a fundamental way contradict the assumed link between supply and price that underlies the per se treatment of supply restrictions . . . . An examination of television broadcasting reveals that it possesses unusual characteristics which may be disruptive of that linkage.

12   *See* Press Release, Dep't of Justice, Justice Department Announces Settlement With The National Association of Realtors (May 27, 2008), http://www.usdoj.gov/atr/public/press_releases/2008/233605.htm.

13   *See, e.g.,* Sw. Health Alliances, Inc., FTC Docket No. C-4327, (July 8, 2011) (consent order resolving claims against association of physicians charged with fixing prices physicians charge insurers), *available at* http://www.ftc.gov/os/caselist/0910013/110715southwestdo.pdf.

14   *See, e.g.,* Joel I. Klein, Acting Ass't Att'y Gen., Antitrust Div., U.S. Dep't of Justice, Criminal Enforcement in a Globalized Economy, Address Before the Advanced Criminal Antitrust Workshop (Feb. 20, 1997), *available at* http://www.usdoj.gov/atr/public/speeches/1054.htm:

> Although this practice did involve a horizontal agreement, with dimensions of a traditional price fix, in our view it clearly didn't merit criminal consideration. The principal reason for this conclusion was that the convention, while satisfying the traditional requirements for ripening into a section 1 agreement, nevertheless was different from the kind of agreement that we charge criminally. It was really an industry practice—a way of life—that traders followed as a matter of custom; and when it was violated, the reactions were varied: sometimes there was retaliation; sometimes there was annoyance; and sometimes nothing appeared to happen. All in all, we concluded that the agreement was "thin" and therefore we weren't prepared to proceed criminally.

15   In a recent enforcement action by the FTC involving alleged price fixing in the U.S. pipe fitting supply industry, the Commission filed suit against three companies, alleging that they conspired to set and maintain prices and exchanged information about their monthly sales through a trade association. Notably, the trade association wasn't charged with wrongdoing. http://www.ftc.gov/os/caselist/1010080/120104sigmado.pdf.

16   *See, e.g.,* Kleen Prods. LLC v. Packaging Corp. of Am., No. 1:10-cv-05711 (N.D. Ill., *complaint filed* Sept. 9, 2010) (alleging price fixing under auspices of two trade associations); Minn-Chem Inc. v. Agrium Inc. et al., Civ. No. 08-cv-05162 (D. Minn. *complaint filed* Sept. 11, 2008) (complaint includes claims of conspiracy to fix prices for potash products at meetings of International Fertilizer Industry Association and Fertilizer Institute). *But see In re* Pressure Sensitive Labelstock Antitrust Litig., 2008-2 Trade Cas. (CCH) ¶ 76,253 (M.D. Pa. 2008) (complaint includes allegations regarding price-fixing discussions at meetings of Tag & Label Manufacturers Institute (TLMI), but TLMI was not named as a defendant); *In re* Rail Freight Fuel Surcharge Antitrust Litig., 2008-2 Trade Cas. (CCH) ¶ 76,366 (D.D.C. 2008) (complaint includes allegations that defendant railroads used Association of American Railroads (AAR) to facilitate price fixing, but AAR apparently was not named as a defendant).

17   *See, e.g., In re* Processed Egg Prods. Antitrust Litig., (CCH) 2011-2 Trade Cas. ¶ 77,659 (E.D. Pa. 2011) (granting motion to dismiss filed by United Egg Association); Am. Dental Ass'n v. Cigna Corp., 605 F.3d 1283 (11th Cir. 2010) (affirming district court's dismissal of complaint under *Twombly*); Reifert v. S. Cent. Wis. MLS Corp., 450 F.3d 312, 314 (7th Cir. 2006) (grant of summary judgment affirmed); *Gregory v. Fort Bridger Rendezvous Ass'n*, 448 F.3d 1195, 1205 (10th Cir. 2006) (*grant of summary judgment affirmed*); Jack Russell Terrier Network of N. Cal. v. Am. Kennel Club, Inc., 407 F.3d 1027, 1034-36 (9th Cir. 2005) (*grant of summary judgment affirmed* on finding that defendant association and affiliates were single entity incapable of conspiring); Corner Pocket of Sioux Falls, Inc. v. Video Lottery Techs., Inc., 123 F.3d 1107, 1109 (8th Cir. 1997) (upholding grant of summary judgment, finding that trade association and members did not conspire to fix prices or allocate territories); Ad/SAT v. Associated Press, 181 F.3d 216, 234 (2d Cir. 1999) (per curiam) (upholding grant of summary judgment because plaintiff failed to show that association members "consciously committed themselves to a common [unlawful] scheme"); Wilk v. Am. Med. Ass'n, 895 F.2d 352, 374-78 (7th Cir. 1990) (trade association found to be uninvolved in alleged conspiracy); Consol. Metal Prods. v. Am. Petroleum Inst., 846 F.2d 284, 293-94, 297 (5th Cir. 1988) (summary judgment in favor of trade association affirmed); *In re* Late Fee & Over-Limit Litig., 528 F. Supp. 2d 953, 963-65, 967 (N.D. Cal. 2007) (granting motion to dismiss); JES Props., Inc. v. USA Equestrian, Inc., No. 802CV1585T24, 2005 WL 1126665 (M.D. Fla. May 9, 2005) (association and individual promoters did not conspire), *aff'd*, 458 F.3d 1224 (11th Cir. 2006).

18 *In re* Text Messaging Antitrust Litig., 630 F.3d 622, 628 (7th Cir. 2010) (*cert. denied*, 131 S. Ct. 2011) (participation in a trade association is "a practice, not illegal in itself, that facilitates price fixing that would be difficult for the authorities to detect"); *In re* Plasma-Derivative Protein Therapies Antitrust Litig., 764 F. Supp. 2d 991 (N.D. Ill. 2011) (motion to dismiss denied, citing *In re* Text Messaging Antitrust Litig., based on allegation that trade association assisted association members in concealing their unlawful activities); Starr v. Sony BMG Music Entm't, 592 F.3d 314 (2d Cir. 2010), *cert denied*, 131 S. Ct. 901 (2011) (motion to dismiss denied after *Twombly* based on alleged trade association involvement in price fixing); *In re* Packaged Ice Antitrust Litig., 723 F. Supp. 2d 987 (E.D. Mich., 2010) (membership in trade association along with other allegations sufficient to withstand motion to dismiss). *See also* Tunica Web Adver. v. Tunica Casino Operators Ass'n, 496 F.3d 403, 411 (5th Cir. 2007) (reversing grant of summary judgment because issue of fact existed on whether association members engaged in concerted action; but note that the trade association in question had earlier been dismissed from the lawsuit evidently on a voluntary basis, *see* Tunica Web Adver., Inc. v. Barden Miss. Gaming, *LLC*, 2008-2 Trade Cas. (CCH) ¶ 76,369 (N.D. Miss. 2008)); Denny's Marina, Inc. v. Renfro Prods., Inc., 8 F.3d 1217, 1219 (7th Cir. 1993) (reversing grant of summary judgment because genuine issue of fact existed on whether trade association and members engaged in horizontal price fixing scheme); Fears v. Wilhelmina Model Agency, No. 02 Civ. 4911, 2004 WL 594396 (S.D.N.Y. Mar. 23, 2004) (summary judgment granted in part and denied in part because genuine issue of fact existed on whether members of association colluded to fix commissions).

19 *See Twombly, supra* note 3, 550 U.S. at 570 (requiring that an antitrust complaint plead "enough facts to state a claim to relief that is plausible on its face.").

20 *See, e.g.*, Freeman v. San Diego Ass'n of Realtors, 322 F.3d 1133, 1154 (9th Cir. 2003) (summary judgment granted to plaintiffs on price fixing claim); Vandervelde v. Put & Call Brokers & Dealers Ass'n, 344 F. Supp. 118 (S.D.N.Y. 1972) (combination of association's rule requiring discount in certain commodity sales, and defendant's suspension for violating rule held unlawful).

21 *See* Consol. Metal Prods., Inc. v. Am. Petroleum Inst., 846 F.2d 284, 293-94 (5th Cir. 1988); Viazis v. Am. Ass'n of Orthodontists, 314 F.3d 758, 764 (5th Cir. 2002); *see also* Five Smiths Inc. v. Nat'l Football League Players Ass'n, 788 F. Supp. 1049, 1040 n.5 (D. Minn. 1992) ("A trade association is not a 'walking conspiracy' of its members.").

22 N. Tex. Specialty Physicians v. FTC, 528 F.3d 346, 356, 358 (5th Cir. 2008); *Am. Dental Ass'n, supra* note 17, 605 F.3d at 1296.

23 *See, e.g.*, George A. Hay and Daniel Kelley, *An Empirical Survey of Price Fixing Conspiracies* 17 J.L. & Econ. 13, 21 (1974) ("In seven out of eight cases with more than fifteen firms in the conspiracy, a formal industry trade association was involved"); Arthur Fraas and Douglas Greer, *Market Structure and Price Collusion: An Empirical Analysis* 26 J. Indus. Econ. 21 (1977) (noting that trade associations were involved in almost one-third of U.S. price fixing conspiracies); R. Bruce Rich, *The Conduct of Trade Association Meetings* 46 Brook. L. Rev. 205, 206 n.7 (1980) ("A review of government antitrust litigation, both civil and criminal commenced during the past two decades, reveals the extent to which price-fixing and other illegal activities have been undertaken under the aegis of trade associations. From 1965 to 1969, for example, 23 of the 50 price-fixing suits instituted by the Antitrust Division of the Department of Justice named trade associations as defendants").

24 Christopher R. Leslie, *Trust, Distrust, and Antitrust*, 82 Texas L. Rev. 515, 599 (2004) (footnote omitted).

25 Christopher R. Leslie, *Cartels, Agency Costs, and Finding Virtue in Faithless Agents*, 49 Wm. & Mary L. Rev. 1621, 1688-89 (2008) (footnote omitted).

26 (2d Updated and Revised Edition 2007) [hereinafter Global Price Fixing].

27 *Id.* at 11.

28 Herbert Hovenkamp & Christopher R. Leslie, *The Firm as Cartel Manager*, 64 Vand. L. Rev. 813, 839 (2011) (citing Arthur G. Fraas & Douglas F. Greer, *Market Structure and Price Collusion: An Empirical Analysis*, 26 J. Indus. Econ. 21, 39 (1977)). The authors were quick to add that "[o]f course, not all trade associations are fronts for illegal activity." and that "the great majority of trade associations' activities are procompetitive." 64 Vand. L. Rev., *supra* at 839 and n.136 (citation and internal quotation marks omitted).

29 *See* Dep't of Justice, Antitrust Div., Criminal Enforcement, Fine and Jail Charts 2000-2010, *available at* http://www.usdoj.gov/atr/public/criminal/264101.html.

30 Such cooperation arrangements have become pervasive in recent years. As stated by Ann O'Brien, Senior Counsel to the Deputy Assistant Attorney General for Criminal Enforcement in a June 2008 speech in Europe:

> The Antitrust Division of the U.S. Department of Justice . . . has a long history of settling cartel cases with plea agreements. Over 90 percent of the hundreds of defendants charged with criminal cartel offenses during the last 20 years have admitted to the conduct and entered into plea agreements with the Division.

See Message from the AAG, Criminal Antitrust Fines (2000-2007) (Spring 2008), *available at* http://usdoj.gov/atr/public/231424.htm; Ann O'Brien, Senior Counsel to the Deputy Ass't Att'y Gen. for Criminal Enforcement, Antitrust Div., U.S. Dep't of Justice, Cartel Settlements in the U.S. and E.U.: Similarities, Differences & Remaining Questions, Presented at 13th Annual EU Competition Law and Policy Workshop, Florence, Italy, at 1 (June 6, 2008), *available at* http://www.usdoj.gov/atr/public/speeches/235598.htm. Antitrust Division officials have confirmed that amnesty agreements were reached with cooperating companies and executives in at least the following cartels: DRAM, Rubber Chemicals, Vitamins, Graphite Electrodes, Fine Arts Auctions, and USAID Construction cartels. Scott D. Hammond, Deputy Ass't Att'y Gen. for Criminal Enforcement, Antitrust Div., U.S. Dep't of Justice, An Update of the Antitrust Division's Criminal Enforcement Program, Remarks Before the ABA Section of Antitrust Law Cartel Enforcement Roundtable, 2005 Fall Forum (Nov. 16, 2005), *available at* http://www.usdoj.gov/atr/public/speeches/213247.htm.

31 Trade associations have recently been subject to fines or government enforcement action for alleged price fixing in Spain (National Perfumery and Cosmetics Association, Feb. 23, 2011, *see Spain Fines Cosmetics Cartel €51 Million*, Global Competition Rev. (Mar. 7, 2011), http://www.globalcompetitionreview.com/news/article/29829/spain-fines-cosmetics-cartel-51-million/); China (Zhejiang Fuyang Paper Making Industry Association, Jan. 4, 2011, *see The Asia-Pacific Antitrust Review 2011*, Global Competition Rev., http://www.globalcompetitionreview.com/reviews/33/sections/117/chapters/1208/); and Norway (chartered bus association, July 6, 2009, *see generally Trade Associations as Cartels*, Fin. Express (Oct. 13, 2011), http://www.financialexpress.com/news/trade-associations-as-cartels/859262/0); France (*Géfil Syndicat National de l'Ingénierie des Loisirs, de la Culture et du Tourisme*), Jan. 12, 2011, *French Agency Metes Out Fines for Collusion on Prices*, Bloomberg BNA Antitrust & Trade Reg. Rpt., Jan 20, 2012.

32 *Available at* http://www.justice.gov/atr/public/criminal/sherman10.html.

33 In the case of the lysine cartel, for example, there were hundreds of conspiratorial contacts:

> The lysine cartel held ten formal meetings to fix prices . . . . In addition, at least 22 other significant face-to-face meetings were held . . . . Finally, there were hundreds of telephone calls made during the conspiracy to coordinate list price changes and to report monthly sales information to the secretary of the lysine association.

Global Price Fixing 193.

34 Citric Acid cartel, Global Price Fixing 138; Choline Chloride (Vitamins) cartel, Global Price Fixing 311-12.

35 Lysine cartel, Global Price Fixing 193.

36 Lysine cartel, Global Price Fixing 194; Vitamins cartel, Global Price Fixing 281, 285, 310.

37 Lysine cartel, Global Price Fixing 214.

38 Vitamins cartel, Global Price Fixing 286.

39 Ready Mix Concrete cartel. *See* United States v. Beaver, 515 F.3d 730 (7th Cir. 2008).

40 Remarks on Mergers, Cartels and Single Firm Conduct, George Mason Law Review Antitrust Symposium, *Cartels: Public and Private Enforcement*, 14 Geo. Mason L. Rev. 879, 909 (2007).

41 *See* Willard K. Tom, Counselor to the Ass't Att'y Gen., Antitrust Div., U.S. Dep't of Justice, Antitrust and Trade Associations, Address Before the Trade Association and Antitrust law Committee of the Bar Association of the District of Columbia (Feb. 22, 1995), *available at* http://www.usdoj.gov/atr/public/speeches/0106.htm.

42 *See* ABA Section of Antitrust Law, Antitrust Compliance: Perspectives and Resources for Corporate Counselors (2d Ed. 2010) (Ch. 17: An Antitrust Primer for Attending Trade Association Meetings and Assessing Antitrust Compliance); ABA Section of Antitrust Law, Antitrust and Associations Handbook (2009) (*see* Ch. XI: "Antitrust Compliance for Associations").

43 Scott D. Hammond, Deputy Ass't Att'y Gen., Antitrust Div. U.S. Dep't of Justice, Gregory J. Werden, Senior Econ. Counsel, Antitrust Div. U.S. Dep't of Justice, and Belinda A. Barnett, Deputy Gen. Counsel, Antitrust Div. U.S. Dep't of Justice, *Recidivism Eliminated: Cartel Enforcement In The United States Since 1999*, Paper presented before the Georgetown Global Antitrust Enforcement Symposium (Sept. 22, 2011) *available at* http://www.usdoj.gov/atr/public/speeches/275388.pdf.

44 *See supra* note 32.

45 *See* Global Price Fixing 310.

46 *See* Complaint and Affidavit in Support of Criminal Complaint and Arrest Warranty at ¶ 26, United States v. Peter Whittle No.: 07-2553 (S.D. Fla. Apr. 24, 2007), *available at* http://www.usdoj.gov/atr/cases/f223000/223056.htm.

47 Global Price Fixing 310.

48 Kreuzer v. Am. Academy of Periodontology, 735 F.2d 1479, 1489 (D.C. Cir. 1984). *See also* United States v. Taubman, 297 F.3d 161, 166 (2d Cir. 2002):

> If, as the Government told the District Court, it 'frequently use[s]' the [Smith] quotation in antitrust cases . . . , then it should reevaluate the practice, and district courts should carefully consider the tendency of any such quotation to taint the jury's understanding of the law. Indeed, were this a case where the Government asked the jury to infer the existence of or a defendant's participation in a price-fixing conspiracy, we might well have vacated the conviction and remanded for a new trial. We now consider the Government to be on notice that future uses of a quotation such as the one used in this case might well prove fatal to the case.

49 James M. Clabault & Michael K.,Block, Sherman Act Indictments: 1955-1980 (Federal Legal Publications 1980); Trade Regulation Reporter (CCH) Transfer Binder, U.S. Antitrust Cases—Summaries Complaints, Indictments, Developments, ¶¶ 45,070-45,088 1980-1988; Trade Regulation Reporter (CCH) Transfer Binder, U.S. Antitrust Cases—Summaries, ¶¶ 45,080-45,096 1988-1996; DOJ Antitrust Case Filings—Dec. 1994-present, *available at* http://www.usdoj.gov/atr/cases.html.

The Normative Limits of Comparative Competition Law

Andre Fiebig

Andre.Fiebig@bakermckenzie.com
Partner, Baker & McKenzie, LLP
Adjunct Professor of Law, Northwestern University School of Law

Abstract

Professor Kovacic has played an influential role in the development of the relatively young field of comparative competition law. At the core of many of his articles is a search for a better way of achieving the underlying objectives of competition law. His writings provide advice not only to the mature antitrust jurisdictions such as the U.S. and the EU, but also countries which have recently adopted competition law regimes. At the same time, however, Kovacic recognizes that competition law is interpreted and applied around the world in different social, political and economic contexts. As the number of competition law regimes continues to grow, so will the importance of the field of comparative competition law. This article addresses the limits encountered by comparative competition law when it moves from a purely analytical exercise to a normative application.

I. Introduction

The myriad of Professor Kovacic's articles and speeches reveals a search for—or at least the recognition of the possibility of—objective standards for judging the conduct of competition regulators worldwide. Given his breath of knowledge and experience, this has, in my view, been one of Kovacic's most valuable contributions to antitrust law and policy not only in the United States, but also in jurisdictions with relatively young competition law regimes. Kovacic has made important contributions to the field of comparative competition law scholarship, which are both descriptive as well as normative. For example, his idea of a "superior effectiveness report card"[1] assumes the ability to identify objective normative criteria for judging the performance of antitrust and competition law agencies. At other points, his writing reveals a belief in the existence of "superior norms"[2] and "superior practices"[3] for antitrust enforcement. It is this normative aspect of Kovacic's advice and scholarship that makes them particularly valuable.

Yet, it is apparent that Kovacic, similar to many other comparativists, is sensitive to the limits of the application of a normative analysis in the international context due to differences in the political, economic, social, and cultural influences on competition law and its application and enforcement. Kovacic observes, for example, that: "Decisions about the appropriate design of antitrust systems in emerging economies must acknowledge the distinctive features of the transition environment . . . . Approaches that have proven effective in Western countries are hardly assured of success when transplanted into a transition economy setting."[4] As characterized by Professor Waller in his contribution to this *Festschrift/Mélanges*, the "humility" present in Kovacic's writing is an expression of the recognition of the normative limits of a comparative approach to competition law.[5] This article uses the occasion of Kovacic's *Festschrift/Mélanges* to explore the normative limits of comparative law in the field of antitrust.

II. Comparative Law

Comparative competition law grew out of and can be considered a branch of comparative law in general. The longstanding debate in the comparative law literature over the normative value of comparative law provides insights into the limits of comparative competition law. Comparative law is not a specific set of autonomous legal norms. Rather, the field of comparative law refers to the study and comparison of legal norms or institutions in two or more jurisdictions. Admittedly, this is a very broad definition. The absence of a specific definition has made it difficult for comparative law to establish itself as an independent discipline. Further adding to the identity crisis is the absence of an agreed comparative method. The one comparative method which has achieved a level of recognition above the others is functionality.[6] According to two leading comparative law scholars: "From this basic principle stem all the other rules which determine the choice of laws to compare, the scope of the undertaking, the creation of a system of comparative law, and so on."[7]

The functional method of comparative law starts by identifying the particular social issue or problem, which the law in a particular jurisdiction is designed to address. "Law is the concrete 'social problem' or 'legal need'. The objects of comparison are the solutions to such problems in different legal systems."[8] In other words, the functional method asks: What is the function of the specific legal norm? This is a deceptively difficult task as a legal norm may serve several diverse functions in a particular society. In addition, there are often direct and indirect functions of a legal norm. For example, one direct function of a law prohibiting the abuse of a dominant position may be to prevent companies with market power from engaging in particular practices that the legislator considers anti-competitive. However, that same law might have indirect functions. For example, a law prohibiting the commercial abuse of market power may legitimately serve to protect consumers, protect competitors or insure the efficient allocation of resources. The functional method of comparative law does not question the legitimacy of the purpose of the legal norm.

Assuming that one gains an understanding of the function (or functions) of the particular legal norm being examined, the second step in the functional approach is to determine whether the society in the particular foreign jurisdiction being examined encounters those same issues. If so, one is able to examine how that foreign society addresses those issues. In some instances, the foreign jurisdiction may not even rely on legal norms to resolve the particular issues. For example, one could imagine a foreign society that deals with the issue of abuse of market power through social norms rather formal legal norms. This creates what the comparativists refer to as the comparability problem.[9] If, however, legal norms have been adopted in the foreign jurisdiction to address the same issues, the comparativist is able to compare those legal norms to the legal norms in her home jurisdiction. One might, for example, compare the legal norms codified in the Treaty on the Formation of the European Union prohibiting the abuse of a dominant position with similar legal norms in the United States codified in Section 2 of the Sherman Act.

III. Purpose of Comparative Law

The question then becomes: Why do comparativists engage in this exercise? Comparative law is used for many purposes, and its goals have been adequately delineated and elaborated on by prominent jurists.[10] The uses for comparative law range from the practical to the theoretical and from the descriptive to the normative.[11] For example, a German court may engage in a comparative exercise when confronted with the issue whether to recognize a U.S. civil judgment for punitive damages. In that circumstance, the German court may need to determine whether the concept of punitive damages in civil proceedings is contrary to German notions of *ordre public*. The primary function of punitive damages in civil cases in the United States is deterrence of particular conduct. Applying a comparative approach, the German court may then conclude that the recognition of awards for punitive damages in civil cases is contrary to German notions of *ordre public* because the same function is achieved by the state in Germany in administrative or criminal proceedings rather than through civil courts.[12]

Comparative law encounters greater challenges when it is applied normatively, i.e., what Michaels refers to "a yardstick to determine the 'better law'."[13] Comparativists recognize the potential normative use of comparative law. According to Rheinstein, "The question for comparative law is not only which function a law serves in contemporary society, but also whether this function is adequately fulfilled and whether another norm would serve that function better."[14] As recognized by Rheinstein, the normative use of comparative law builds on and goes one step further than the descriptive or analytical use of comparative law. Once an understanding is gained of a foreign law, the normative approach to comparative law may be used to determine strengths and weaknesses in the foreign or even the domestic law. According to the comparativists, every legal norm has to justify its existence by asking whether there is another rule which is superior.[15]

The notion of superiority of a legal norm discussed here refers to the comparison of legal norms between or among separate legal systems rather than to the relationship between or among legal norms within a legal system. Every advanced legal system requires rules to determine which legal norm applies in the event of the simultaneous, potential application of those norms to the particular facts of the case. Legal systems therefore need to establish what Hans Kelsen referred to as a hierarchy of norms.[16] Within this hierarchy there are superior legal norms and inferior legal norms. This intra-system relationship needs to be distinguished from the relationship of legal norms between systems. Whereas the superiority of legal norms in Kelsen's *Stufenlehre* refers to the vertical relationship of legal norms within a system, the concept of superiority of legal norms in the context of comparative law refers to the relationship between legal norms of different jurisdictions designed to achieve the same purpose. The concept of superior or better legal norms often appears in the comparative literature surrounding harmonization of law efforts.[17]

Comparative law is often used normatively for practical purposes. The legislative process in most democracies often relies on comparative law to examine a foreign legal system to determine whether it contains laws appropriate for adoption into one's own legal system.[18] According to Zweigert and Kötz, "Legislators all over the world have found that on many matters good laws cannot be produced without the assistance of comparative law, whether in the form of general studies or of reports specially prepared on the topic in question."[19] One need not look any further than Brussels for an example. The current discussion over the introduction of private remedies in European competition law is largely a comparative law exercise with normative elements. One of the fundamental issues is whether and how far is the U.S. system of private enforcement is better than the enforcement system currently prevalent in Europe and how much of it can be imported into Europe.[20]

IV. Law as Sozialwissenschaft

The normative use of comparative law is not without its critics. Many comparativists have traditionally questioned the use of comparative law to determine whether a particular legal norm is superior to others.[21] According to Reitz: "Comparison is a relatively weak basis for normative argument . . . . The argument for domestic law reform has to be made in terms of normative claims acceptable within the domestic legal system."[22] At the core of the debate over the normative use of comparative law lies the recognition of the relative nature of a particular legal norm. Law belongs to the realm of social sciences and not the physical sciences. Even Montesquieu, in his *The Spirit of the Laws*, recognized that law was embedded in and particular to the society in which it exists.[23] As a consequence, according to Schmitthoff, "We are today accustomed to consider law as a sociological phenomenon which cannot be separated from the other components of the structure of modern society. In consequence, every comparative study of law which claims to deserve the name has to consider its subject-matter both as a product and as a cause of those general sociological tendencies."[24]

The recognition of the relative nature of legal norms presents a challenge for comparative law. If a law is unique to a society, how is it useful as a subject of comparative exercise? Even more questionable is the usefulness of comparing laws in different jurisdictions to derive normative conclusions. To a certain extent, comparative law tries to address these challenges by employing the functional method discussed above. The threshold requirement for the application of the function method is comparability: the social issues, which legal norms in different jurisdictions are trying to address, must be comparable.[25] This is, admittedly, not a perfect approach to solving the problem of the relativity of law because there are often an unlimited number of functions a law serves within a society. For this reason, the relative nature of law continues to be a thorn in the side of comparative law and serves as a limit on its normative application.[26] It is pervasive in the debate over the "transplantability" of laws[27] as well as in the unification or harmonization of laws.[28]

Further complicating matters for the normative use of comparative law is the existence of superiority biases.[29] Sociologists and psychologists recognize that there is a natural tendency to assume that one's own practices and understandings are superior to those of others.[30] This is particularly prevalent in the legal community—probably because of the commitment and discipline required to become a lawyer in most jurisdictions, the personality types the discipline seems to attract and the parochial training that seems to pervade contemporary legal training in many countries.[31] As most jurists are trained in one legal system and then later engage in comparative exercises, there is a tendency to examine the foreign law through the lens of one's own legal system. "Even experienced comparatives sometimes look for the rule that they want only in the particular place in the foreign system where their experience of their own system leads them to expect it: they are unconsciously looking at the problem with the eyes of their own system."[32] It is the challenge of the comparative lawyer applying comparative law normatively to "disentangle" themselves from their preferences for their "own" law.[33] The results of the normative application of comparative law are therefore often vulnerable to the criticism of superiority bias in the comparative literature.[34]

V. Comparative Competition Law

The discipline of comparative law developed over the last century largely independent of competition law. The focus of comparative law was traditionally on private law and not public law such as competition law. Even as late as 50 years ago, only a handful of jurisdictions had adopted competition laws, and even fewer actively enforced them.[35] There are now over 100 countries around the world that have adopted some form of laws that may be called competition laws. The rise of the field of comparative competition law parallels this increase in the adoption of legal norms regulating competition around the world. Professor Kovacic has played a prominent and influential role in this development over the last 20+ years both as a scholar and a regulator.

Although the term is used frequently in the literature,[36] there is no uniform definition of "comparative competition law." Many competition law scholars use the term without committing to or attempting to adopt a precise definition.[37] The term "comparative competition law" generally refers to the application of comparative law methodology to the field of competition law.[38] As with comparative law in general, comparative competition law attempts to understand and compare the content, purposes and application of different competition law regimes. The rapid increase in the number of jurisdictions that have adopted competition laws in the last 20 years has created a unique opportunity for comparative competition law. Compliance costs and inconsistent outcomes across jurisdictions have been cited as reasons for harmonization, unification, or an international antitrust code.[39] In recognition of the political difficulties in these methods to address the multiplicity of competition laws around the globe, the focus has shifted to softer approaches such as education (technical assistance), peer review, best practices or efforts to rate regimes or enforcement agencies.[40]

All of these efforts have a normative component. Any attempt at harmonizing, unifying, reviewing or identifying best practices requires a normative evaluation of appropriate laws, procedures or enforcement practices. The issue which all of these efforts is addressing is: "Are the principles we now regard as essential for a soundly based antitrust law universal?"[41] For example, when the International Competition Network adopts "best practices," it engages in a normative exercise.[42] One of its stated original objectives was to "formulate proposals for procedural and substantive convergence through results-oriented agenda and structure."[43] It has sought to achieve this objective by preparing and issuing "best practices" for countries to emulate.[44] This is commensurate with its current mission of the ICN of advocating "the adoption of superior standards and procedures in competition enforcement and policy around the world, formulate proposals for procedural and substantive convergence, and seek to facilitate effective international cooperation."[45]

If comparative competition law is the application of comparative methods to competition law, one needs to first ask the functional question: what is the issue which competition law is designed to address? It is as this stage where we begin to recognize the significant challenges inherent in comparative competition law. As Professor Kovacic's scholarship appropriately discusses, even within legal systems there is a lack of consensus over the goals of competition law.[46] A survey of U.S. antitrust law, for example, reveals a lack of a uniform objective.[47] The task becomes even more challenging when this question is posed in the international context. If, for example, the purpose of competition law in one jurisdiction is to promote economic efficiency, but in another jurisdiction it is to promote market integration, can we meaningfully compare (not to even mention rate) the competition laws of the two jurisdictions?

The answer to this question depends on the objective of such comparative exercise. If the purpose of the exercise is to gain a greater understanding of the foreign competition law — for academic or practical purposes — comparative competition law may still be useful even if confronted with different functions across jurisdictions. If used normatively, however, comparative competition law experiences the same limitations comparative scholars have been struggling with for over a century. As the writings of Kovacic correctly identify, competition law is interpreted, enforced and applied in a social, political, economic and cultural context.[48] The validity of normative conclusions about a foreign competition law regime based upon reference to another competition law regime are therefore inherently difficult as it is necessary to accommodate all of the relevant contextual differences influencing the respective competition laws. As Waller correctly observes, "Antitrust law, like all law, is not universal, but specific to a time, place, and culture."[49] A particular rule, procedure or institutional component appropriate for one particular competition law regime may not be the best rule, procedure or institutional structure for another jurisdiction. Professor Gal refers to "the ecology of competition law."[50] What she means is that competition law exists and is applied in the context of a particular socio-economic ideology (soil) under institutional and organizational constraints (sun and water) in the realities of political economy conditions (pesticides). If not all jurisdictions share the same soil, sun, water and use of pesticides, can we expect them to yield similar crops?

This limitation applies not only when deriving normative conclusions about a foreign competition law regime, but also when making conclusion about one's own competition law regime based upon a comparison with another jurisdiction. In the past 20 years, for example, many countries that have introduced competition laws have employed comparative methods in the drafting, structuring and enforcing their national rules.[51] Kovacic's scholarship and leadership have been enormously influential in this assimilation process. This introspective use of comparative law is by no means limited to the jurisdictions that have recently adopted competition laws. As suggested by Judge Wood, even the United States can improve its antitrust laws through a comparative approach: "[W]e need to understand both why our own antitrust laws work well for us; to consider whether different rules might be working equally well for others; and to ask whether there is anything we might learn from the experience of others in this burgeoning field. This effort should repay us richly, as we strive to improve our laws, create greater coherence between the federal and state antitrust systems, and reap the benefits of competition in the future."[52]

Competition law — perhaps more so than other fields of law — is particularly constrained in its normative uses because of its dependency on assumptions about rational human behavior in the commercial context. In the United States, for example, certain business decisions are often considered exclusionary because of the absence of a rational business reason for the decision.[53] "Generally, a finding of exclusionary conduct requires some sign that the mono-

polist engaged in behavior that—examined without reference to its effects on competitors—is economically irrational."[54] Rationality, in the commercial context, is equated by
U.S. courts with a constant search for short-term financial gain.[55] These assumptions about
human behavior are not always applicable across borders. Comparative law, when used
normatively in the field of competition law, runs into what Lescano and Teubner call "rationality conflicts in a polycentric global society."[56]

The normative limits of comparative competition law are nothing new to comparative
competition lawyers including Professor Kovacic. Comparative competition law scholars
recognize that there is not one correct standard for competition law or its institutions.[57]
Kovacic, as both an academic and a regulator, has illustrated his sensitivity to the normative
limits of comparative competition law.[58] For example, in suggesting that other jurisdictions
should consider adopting legal norms rewarding individuals for informing the government
of certain competition law violations—similar to *qui tam* informers under the U.S. False
Claims Act [59]—Kovacic recognizes that "the acceptability in any jurisdiction of such an
approach depends heavily on its consistency with existing social and political norms."[60]

The normative use of comparative competition law often manifests itself as criticism by a
jurist trained in a particular jurisdiction of the laws, institutions or policies of a foreign
jurisdiction. Professor Gerber has been particularly poignant in his criticism of the U.S.
antitrust community in this respect: "Pervasive within the U.S. antitrust community is the
view that the U.S. has the right answers to basic antitrust questions, specifically, that it has
the best methods of analysis and generally the best institutional framework (primarily
because it accords a dominant role to courts and private enforcement mechanisms). In this
view, others should emulate U.S. Antitrust law because it is the best system."[61] This same
concern is expressed by Kovacic and other scholars in other jurisdictional contexts (albeit
in less direct terms).[62] Regarding the relatively recent efforts of China to adopt a competition law regime, the normative use of comparative competition law has been criticized as
"antitrust functionalism"—i.e., "an unstated and unwarranted assumption about the background similarities between China and elsewhere."[63]

The tendency to use comparative competition law normatively is particularly acute because
of the apparent similarity of the function of competition law in economic systems sharing
the same reliance on the market for the allocation of scarce resources. Fundamental differences between economic systems have been identified as a major impediment to the usefulness of a comparative law approach between such systems.[64] The collapse of the planned
economy of the Soviet Union and the adoption of a more market-based system was interpreted by many as the "end of economic history," i.e., the global recognition of the superiority of a market economy. The naive assumption is, therefore, that all competition issues
should be resolved similarly. This applies, for example, to a functional comparative analysis of the U.S. and EU competition laws. Observers often express their dismay with the
divergence between the United States and EU competition laws: "Since both the United
States and the EU explicitly identify the protection of consumer welfare as the main objective of competition law, the very existence of such significant transatlantic divergence
seems fundamental, remarkable, and unsettling."[65] This deductive reasoning ignores the
relative nature of competition law and the differences that exist even between market
economies. Even if there is a consensus on the superiority of the market over the state as
the appropriate allocator of scarce resources, there remain significant differences among
market economies and the role of competition law in those economies.

Exacerbating this tendency to ignore the relative nature of competition law is the perceived
"universalist posture"[66] of economics. Competition law regulates the economic behavior
of firms. For this reason, its interpretation and application is guided—and in some jurisdictions one could say dictated—by prevailing economic theories. Of all the fields of law
subject to comparative analysis, competition law is perhaps the most strongly influenced

by economics. This characteristic of competition law makes it particularly attractive for normative uses because of the treatment of economics as a science.[67] The assumption is that competition law, if guided by the "science" of economics, should be consistent in all market economies.[68] "Universality is at the core of the scientific enterprise, and thus as a social science, economics seeks universally valid principles. The language of economics is, therefore, necessarily abstract, and its methods are intended to be applicable everywhere. In general, economists assume that economics is the same here, there and everywhere, regardless of cultural or other contexts."[69] Because the application of competition law is currently dependent on economics, this same universalist posture is often taken in the field of comparative competition law.

Some comparative competition law scholars, aware of the normative constraints of their trade, have proposed ways to continue to use a comparative approach in the field of competition law. Gerber, for example, proposes "the development of an analytical framework — and, eventually, a language — that can effectively detect, express and convey both commonalities and differences in the operations of legal systems."[70] Waller in this *Festschrift Mélanges* as well as elsewhere[71] suggests an empirical approach to comparative competition law based on the increased wealth of data available on foreign competition laws and institutions. Although these valuable proposals address the traditional weakness of comparative law, they do not remedy it entirely. They would not explain, for example, the need for a competition law system to use specific, codified market share thresholds for identifying market dominance because of the need of that particular legal system and culture for legal certainty.

The influence of behavioral economics will likely lead to a greater sensitivity to the normative limits of comparative competition law. The core recognition of behavioral economics is that behavior of individuals is not always consistent with the model of a utility maximizer posited by neo-classical economics.[72] Decisions, even economic ones, are influenced by the cultural, political and social context in which the decision maker exists. By introducing a differentiated approach to human conduct, behavioral economics is challenging the general model of economic behavior on which competition law has been based for at least the last half century.[73] As this differentiated approach is increasingly accepted, it is likely to lead to a greater awareness of the limits to the normative use of comparative competition law.

VI. Conclusion

Although it still lacks precise contours, comparative competition law continues to develop into its own discipline. Similar to comparative law in general, comparative competition law has value at many levels. The limits on its normative application should not be interpreted to preclude the normative use of comparative competition law entirely. Most comparativists will recognize at least a potential for normative uses of comparative law — and some would even argue that: "The quest for the 'better solution'. . . is the essential purpose of Comparative Law in many of its practical application."[74] As Kovacic has aptly illustrated, comparative competition law can be used effectively, provided that one is sensitive to the relative nature of competition law. Certain characteristics of competition law make it particularly vulnerable to misuse. One admirable aspect of Kovacic's scholarship and teaching has been his awareness of this limit and the willingness to be critical of those who ignore them: "Operating without adequate knowledge of local conditions, foreign advisors have a tendency to provide ill-fitting, off-the-track solutions imported from cities such as Brussels, Canberra, London, Ottawa, Paris or Washington, DC."[75] His involvement with and influence on the work of the International Competition Network has helped that organization from becoming a lectern from which the Europeans and the Americans teach the rest of the world how to do competition law.[76] If comparative competition law is to develop into its own discipline as a normative method of analysis, we are well advised to follow the humility that Professor Kovacic has exhibited in his career and writings.

NOTES

1   William E. Kovacic, *Rating the Competition Agencies: What Constitutes Good Performance?*, 16 GEO. MASON L. REV. 903, 923 (2008-2009).

2   William E. Kovacic, *Competition policy in the European Union and the United States: convergence or divergence in the future treatment of dominant firms?*, 4 COMPETITION L. INT'L 8, 10 (2008).

3   William E. Kovacic & Hugh M. Hollman, *The International Competition Network: Its Past, Current and Future Role*, 20 MINN. J. INT'L L. 274 (2011).

4   William E. Kovacic, *Institutional Foundations for Economic Legal Reform in Transition Economies: The Case of Competition Policy and Antitrust Enforcement*, 77 CHI.-KENT L. REV. 265, 301-302 (2001-2002). *See also* William E. Kovacic, *Lucky Trip? Perspectives from a Foreign Advisor on Competition Policy, Development and Technical Assistance*, 3 EUR. COMPETITION J. 319, 322 (2007).

5   Spencer W. Waller, *The Next Generation of Competition Law*, in WILLIAM E. KOVACIC: AN ANTITRUST TRIBUTE - VOL. 1 (Nicolas Charbit et al. eds., Institute of Competition Law 2012).

6   Ralf Michaels, *The Functional Method of Comparative Law*, in THE OXFORD HANDBOOK OF COMPARATIVE LAW (M. Reimann & R. Zimmermann eds. 2006) 339, 364 – 366; David J. Gerber, *Comparative Antitrust Law*, id. 1194, 1201.

7   KONRAD ZWEIGERT & HEIN KÖTZ, AN INTRODUCTION TO COMPARATIVE LAW (2nd ed. 1987) 31.

8   Catherine Valcke, *Comparative Law as Comparative Jurisprudence – The Comparability of Legal Systems*, 52 AM. J. COMP. L. 713 (2004); Konrad Zweigert & Hans-Jürgen Puttfarken, *Critical Evaluation in Comparative Law*, 5 ADEL. L. REV. 343, 345 (1973).

9   Konrad Zweigert & Hans-Jürgen Puttfarken, *Critical Evaluation in Comparative Law*, 5 ADEL. L. REV. 343, 355 (1973).

10 David J. Gerber, *System Dynamics: Toward a Language of Comparative Law?*, 46 AM. J. COMP. LAW 719, 720-21 (1998); MAX RHEINSTEIN, EINFÜHRUNG IN DIE RECHTSVERGLEICHUNG (1974); P. Pierre Lepaulle, *The Function of Comparative Law*, 35 HARV. L. REV. 838 (1922); Ralf Michaels, *The Functional Method of Comparative Law*, in THE OXFORD HANDBOOK OF COMPARATIVE LAW (M. Reimann & R. Zimmermann eds. 2006) 339, 364–366.

11 Certain comparativists such as Rheinstein and Gerber distinguish between a descriptive use and a comparative use. MAX RHEINSTEIN, EINFÜHRUNG IN DIE RECHTSVERGLEICHUNG (1974) 22 (distinguishing between *Auslandrechtskunde* and *Rechtsvergleichung*); David J. Gerber, *Comparative Antitrust Law*, in THE OXFORD HANDBOOK OF COMPARATIVE LAW (M. Reimann & R. Zimmermann eds. 2006) 1194, 1201.

12 *See* German Bundesgerichtshof, [BGH] [Federal Court of Justice] IX ZR 149/91 June 4, 1992 [reported in NJW 3096 (1992) (Ger.)].

13 Ralf Michaels, *The Functional Method of Comparative Law*, in THE OXFORD HANDBOOK OF COMPARATIVE LAW (M. Reimann & R. Zimmermann eds.) 339, 373.

14 MAX RHEINSTEIN, EINFÜHRUNG IN DIE RECHTSVERGLEICHUNG (1974) 26.

15 Max Rheinstein, *Teaching Comparative Law*, 5 U. CHI. L. REV. 615, 617 (1937-38).

16 HANS KELSEN, GENERAL THEORY OF LAW AND STATE (2006) 123.

17 ALAN WATSON, LEGAL TRANSPLANTS. AN APPROACH TO COMPARATIVE LAW (1993); Del Duca et al, *Impact of Legal Culture and Legal Transplants on the Evolution of the U.S. Legal System*, 58 AM. J. COMP. L. 1 (Supp. 2010); Leone Niglia, *Of Harmonization and Fragmentation: The Problem of the Legal Transplants in the Europeanization of Private Law*, 17(2) MAASTRICHT J. EUR. & COMP. L. 116 (2010); Julie Paquin, *Cross-Cultural Business Law Transplants: The Neglected Issue of the Fit*, 17 TRANSNAT'L L. & CONTEMP. PROBS. 331 (2008).

18 *See* Constantine E. McGuire, *Legislator's Interest in Comparative Legal Studies*, 8 TUL. L. REV. 171 (1933-1934).

19 ZWEIGERT & KÖTZ, AN INTRODUCTION TO COMPARATIVE LAW (2nd ed. 1987) at 15.

20 *See* Robert H. Lande and Joshua P. Davis, *Comparative Deterrence from Private Enforcement and Criminal Enforcement in the U.S. Antitrust Laws*, 2011 (2) BYU L. REV. 315 (2011); Monique Hazelhorst, *Private Enforcement of EU Competition Laws: Why Punitive Damages are a Step Too Far*, 18 EUR. REV. PRIVATE L. 757 (2010); Wouter P.J. Wils, *The Relationship between Public Antitrust Enforcement and Private Actions for Damages*, 32 WORLD COMPETITION 3 (2009).

21 GUSTAV RADBRUCH, ÜBER DIE METHODE DER RECHTSVERGLEICHUNG, 1906 (2) Monatsschrift für Kriminalpsychologie und Strafrechtsreform 422; BERNARD GROSSFELD, MACHT UND OHNMACHT DER RECHTSVERGLEICHUNG (1984); FELIX HOLLDACK, GRENZEN DER ERKENNTNIS AUSLÄNDISCHEN RECHTS (1919); William P. Alford, *On the Limits of "Grand Theory" in Comparative Law*, 61 WASH. L. REV. 945 (1986); JULIUS OFNER, DIE JURISPRUDENZ ALS SOZIALE TECHNIK (1894); Max Rheinstein, *Legal Systems: Comparative Law and Legal Systems*, INT'L ENCYCL. OF THE SOCIAL SCIENCES IX (1968) 210; MAX RHEINSTEIN, EINFÜHRUNG IN DIE RECHTSVERGLEICHUNG (1974) 28.

22 John C. Reitz, *How to Do Comparative Law*, 46 AM. J. COMP. L. 617, 624-25 (1998).

23 CHARLES DE SECONDAT, BARON DE MONTESQUIEU, THE SPIRIT OF THE LAWS (4th ed. T. Nigent trans. 1766) Book I, Chapter 3, p.7.

24 Clive M. Schmitthoff, *The Science of Comparative Law*, 7 CAMBRIDGE L.J. 94, 97 (1939-1941).

25 BERNHARD GROSSFELD, THE STRENGTH AND WEAKNESS OF COMPARATIVE LAW (1990) 71-74; Ralf Michaels, *The Functional Method of Comparative Law*, in THE OXFORD HANDBOOK OF COMPARATIVE LAW (M. Reimann & R. Zimmermann eds.) 339, 345; ZWEIGERT & KÖTZ, AN INTRODUCTION TO COMPARATIVE LAW (2nd ed. 1987) at 31; Rodolfo Sacco, *Legal Formants: A Dynamic Approach to Comparative Law*, 39 AM. J. COMP. L. 1, 6 (1991); Catherine Valcke, *Comparative Law as Comparative Jurisprudence*, 52 AM. J. COMP. L. 713, 720-21 (2004).

26 John C. Reitz, *How to Do Comparative Law*, 46 AM. J. COMP. L. 617, 624-25 (1998); MAX RHEINSTEIN, EINFÜHRUNG IN DIE RECHTSVERGLEICHUNG (1974) 20-21; Konrad Zweigert, Die kritische Wertung in der Rechtsvergleichung, in: FESTSCHRIFT FÜR SCHMITTHOFF (1973) 403; OTTO SANDROCK, ÜBER SINN UND METHODE ZIVILISTISCHER RECHTSVERGLEICHUNG (1966).

27 Pierre Legrand, *The Impossibility of Legal Transplants*, 4 MAASTRICHT J. EUR. & COMP. L. 111 (1997); Michele Graziadei, *Comparative Law as the Study of Transplants and Receptions*, in THE OXFORD HANDBOOK OF COMPARATIVE LAW (M. Reimann & R. Zimmermann eds. 2007) 441, 466.

28 MAX RHEINSTEIN, EINFÜHRUNG IN DIE RECHTSVERGLEICHUNG (1974) 13; Harry First, *Theories of Harmonization: A Cautionary Tale*, in COMPARATIVE COMPETITION LAW: APPROACHING AN INTERNATIONAL SYSTEM OF ANTITRUST LAW 17 (Hanns Ullrich, ed., 1998) 17-18.

29 Ralf Michaels, *The Functional Method of Comparative Law*, in THE OXFORD HANDBOOK OF COMPARATIVE LAW (M. Reimann & R. Zimmermann eds. 2007) 339, 378.

30 Vera Hoorens, *Self-enhancement and Superiority Biases in Social Comparison*, 4(1) EUROPEAN REVIEW OF SOCIAL PSYCHOLOGY 113 (1993); J. R. Eiser, S. Pahl, and Y. R. A. Prins, *Optimism, Pessimism, and the Direction of Self-other Comparisons*, 37 JOURNAL OF EXPERIMENTAL SOCIAL PSYCHOLOGY 77 (2001); J. D. Brown, *Evaluations of Self and Others: Self-enhancement Biases in Social Judgments*, 4 SOCIAL COGNITION 353 (1986).

31 *See* Adelle Blackett, *Globalization and Its Ambiguities: Implications for Law School Curricular Reform*, 37 COLUM. J. TRANSNAT'L L. 57 (1998-1999).

32 ZWEIGERT & KÖTZ, AN INTRODUCTION TO COMPARATIVE LAW (2nd ed. 1987) at 31.

33 *Id.*

34 Konrad Zweigert, *Die kritische Wertung in der Rechtsvergleichung*, in LAW AND INTERNATIONAL TRADE: FESTSCHRIFT FÜR CLIVE M. SCHMITTHOFF ZUM 70. GEBURTSTAG (1973) 403; Franz von Liszt, Das *"Richtige Recht" in der Strafgesetzgebung*, 26 ZEITSCHRIFT FÜR DIE GESAMTE STRAFRECHTSWISSENSCHAFT 553 (1906); G.-R. de Groot & H. Schneider, *Das Werturteil in der Rechtsvergleichung. Die Suche nach dem besseren Recht*, in COMPARABILITY AND EVALUATION (K. Boele-Woelki, F. W. Grosheide, E. H. Hondius & G. J. W. Steenhoff, eds. 1994) 53.

35 For a discussion of this historical development *see* DAVID J. GERBER, GLOBAL COMPETITION: LAW, MARKETS, AND GLOBALIZATION (2010).

36 The term started to become frequently used in the 1990's primarily because of the apparent superiority of a market economy over a planned economy and the consequent need for laws regulating competition. HANNS ULLRICH (ed.), COMPARATIVE COMPETITION LAW: APPROACHING AN INTERNATIONAL SYSTEM OF ANTITRUST LAW (1997); David J. Gerber, *Comparative Antitrust Law*, in OXFORD HANDBOOK OF COMPARATIVE LAW 1193 (M. Reimann & R. Zimmermann, eds. 2007).

37 *See, e.g.*, HANNS ULLRICH (ed.), COMPARATIVE COMPETITION LAW: APPROACHING AN INTERNATIONAL SYSTEM OF ANTITRUST LAW (1997); Spencer W. Waller, *Comparative Competition Law as a Form of Empiricism*, 23 BROOK. J. INT'L L. 455, 455 (1997); David J. Gerber, *Comparative Antitrust Law*, in OXFORD HANDBOOK OF COMPARATIVE LAW 1193 (M. Reimann & R. Zimmermann, eds. 2007).

38 In the comparative literature, competition law is generally used synonymously with antitrust law to the exclusion of legal norms applicable to unfair trade practices. David J. Gerber, *Comparative Antitrust Law*, in OXFORD HANDBOOK OF COMPARATIVE LAW 1193 (M. Reimann & R. Zimmermann, eds. 2007). *But see* Ivo E. Schwartz & Jürgen Basedow, *Restrictions on Competition*, in III INTERNATIONAL ENCYCLOPEDIA OF COMPARATIVE LAW (1995) 3.

39 Douglas H. Ginsburg & Scott H. Angstreich, *Multinational Merger Review: Lessons from Our Federalism*, 68 ANTITRUST L.J. 219, 220 (2000); Spencer W. Waller, *The Internationalization of Antitrust Enforcement*, 77 B. U. L. REV. 343, 385-86 (1997); Kenneth J. Hamner, *The Globalization of Law: International Merger Control and Competition Law in the United States, the European Union, Latin America and China*, 11 J. TRANSNAT'L L. & POLICY 385, 403 (2002).

40 Daniel Sokol, *Designing Antitrust Agencies for More Effective Outcomes: What Antitrust Can Learn from Restaurant Guides*, 41 LOY. U. CHI. L.J. 573 (2010).

41 Diane P. Wood, *The U.S. Antitrust Laws in a Global Context*, 2004 COL. BUS. L. REV. 265, 281 (2004).

42 For a discussion of the work of the ICN, *see generally* Merit E. Janow & James F. Rill, *The Origins of the ICN*, in: THE INTERNATIONAL COMPETITION NETWORK AT TEN: ORIGINS, ACCOMPLISHMENTS AND ASPIRATIONS (P. Lugard ed. 2011). For a discussion of the work of the ICN in developing "best practices" *see* Maria Coppola, *One Network's Effect: The Rise and Future of the ICN*, CONCURRENCES N 3-2011, 222 (2011); William E. Kovacic & Hugh M. Hollman, *The International Competition Network: Its Past, Current and Future Role*, 20 MINN. J. INT'L L. 274 (2011).

43 MEMORANDUM ON THE ESTABLISHMENT AND OPERATION OF THE INTERNATIONAL COMPETITION NETWORK, *available at* www. internationalcompetitionnetwork.org/uploads/library/docs579.pdf.

44 *Id.*

45 ICN, THE ICN's VISION FOR ITS SECOND DECADE, *available at* www.internationalcompetitionnetowrk.org/uploads/library/doc755.pdf.

46 William E. Kovacic, *Comments and Observations on the Sherman Act: The First Century*, 59 ANTITRUST L.J. 119 (1990); William E. Kovacic, *The Changing Equilibrium of Antitrust Policy*, in II THE ANTITRUST IMPULSE: AN ECONOMIC, HISTORICAL AND LEGAL ANALYSIS 575 (Theodore P. Kovaleff ed. 1994).

47 RUDOLPH J. R. PERITZ, COMPETITION POLICY IN AMERICA 1888-1992 (1996); Joseph F. Brodley, *The Economic Goals of Antitrust: Efficiency, Consumer Welfare, and Technological Progress*, 62 N. Y. U. L. REV. 1020 (1987); Kenneth G. Elzinga, *Goals of Antitrust: Other Than Competition and Efficiency, What Else Counts*, 125 U. PA. L. REV. 1191 (1976-1977); Louis B. Schwartz, *Justice and Other Non-Economic Goals of Antitrust*, 127 U. PA. L. REV. 1076 (1978-1979).

48 *See, e.g.*, William E. Kovacic, *Institutional Foundations for Economic Legal Reform in Transition Economies: The Case of Competition Policy and Antitrust Enforcement*, 77 CHICAGO-KENT L. REV. 265 (2002); William E. Kovacic, *Designing and Implementing Competition and Consumer Protection Reforms in Transitional Economies: Perspectives from Mongolia, Nepal, Ukraine, and Zimbabwe*, 44 DEPAUL L. REV. 1197 (1995); William E. Kovacic, *Getting Started: Creating New Competition Policy Institutions in Transition Economics*, 23 BROOK. J. INT'L L. 403 (1997).

49 Spencer W. Waller, *Comparative Competition Law as a Form of Empiricism*, 23 BROOK. J. INT'L L. 455, 463 (1997).

50 Michal S. Gal, T*he Ecology of Antitrust Preconditions for Competition Law Enforcement in Developing Countries*, in UNCTAD, COMPETITION, COMPETITIVENESS AND DEVELOPMENT (June 2004) 20.

51 William E. Kovacic, *Designing and Implementing Competition and Consumer Protection Reforms in Transitional Economies: Perspectives from Mongolia, Nepal, Ukraine, and Zimbabwe*, 44 DEPAUL L. REV. 1197 (1995); William E. Kovacic, *Getting Started: Creating New Competition Policy Institutions in Transition Economies*, 23 BROOK. J. INT'L L. 403 (1997).

52 Diane P. Wood, *The U.S. Antitrust Laws in a Global Context*, 2004 COL. BUS. L. REV. 265, 280-81 (2004). *See also* Spencer W. Waller, *Comparative Competition Law as a Form of Empiricism*, 23 BROOK. J. INT'L L. 455, 459 (1997) ("Throughout the world, comparative competition law is in full flourish, not for the purpose of imitating U.S. or EU law, but to understand and apply whatever may be relevant to the unique foreign national problem being studies. Through contacts with both the U.S. and EU systems, foreign lawmakers and competition enforcers have learned to pick and choose what they need for their own economies, unless the dictates of regional integration or preferential trade access requires them to sign up wholesale to one of these two dominant models.").

53 *See, e.g.*, Taylor Publishing Company v. Jostens, Inc., 216 F.3d 465, 475 (5th Cir. 2000) ("To determine whether the conduct if exclusionary, we look to the proffered business justification for the act. Where the conduct has no rational business purpose other than its adverse effects on competitors, an inference that it is exclusionary is supported.").

54 Stearns Airport Equipment Company v. FMC Corporation, 170 F.3d 518, 522 (5th Cir. 1999).

55 *See, e.g.*, ID Security Systems Canada, Inc. v. Checkpoint Systems, Inc., 198 F. Supp. 2d 598, 611 (E.D. Penn. 2002).

56 Andrea Fischer-Lescano & Gunther Teubner, *Regime-Collisions: The Vain Search for Legal Unity in the Fragmentation of Global Law*, 25 MICH. J. INT'L L. 999, 1005 (2004).

57 Diane P. Wood, *The U.S. Antitrust Laws in a Global Context*, 2004 COL. BUS. L. REV. 265, 280-81 (2004); Spencer W. Waller, *Neo-Realism and the Institutional Harmonization of Law: Lessons from Antitrust*, 42 U. KAN. L. REV. 557 (1994); Spencer W. Waller, *Comparative Competition Law as a Form of Empiricism*, 23 BROOK. J. INT'L L. 455, 455 (1997); David J. Gerber, *Competition Law*, in OXFORD HANDBOOK OF COMPARATIVE LAW (2005).

58 Spencer W. Waller, *The Next Generation of Competition Law*, WILLIAM E. KOVACIC: AN ANTITRUST TRIBUTE - VOL. 1 (Nicolas Charbit et al. eds., Institute of Competition Law 2012).

59 31 U.S.C. § 3729 et seq.

60 William E. Kovacic, *Private Participation in the Enforcement of Public Competition Law, Third Annual Conference on International and Comparative Competition Law: The Transatlantic Dialogue* (May 15, 2003) *available at* http:// www.ftc.gov/speeches/other/030514biicl.shtm.

61 David J. Gerber, *Comparative Antitrust Law*, in OXFORD HANDBOOK OF COMPARATIVE LAW 1193 (M. Reimann & R. Zimmermann, eds. 2007). *See also* DAVID J. GERBER, GLOBAL COMPETITION: LAW, MARKETS, AND GLOBALIZATION (2010), 156 ("It is common for members of this community to assume that the U.S. antitrust system is generally superior to others and that others should follow it, perhaps shorn of some of its inconsistencies and weaknesses.").

62   William E. Kovacic, *Designing and Implementing Competition and Consumer Protection Reforms in Transitional Economies: Perspectives from Mongolia, Nepal, Ukraine, and Zimbabwe*, 44 DEPAUL L. REV. 1197 (1995); William E. Kovacic, *Getting Started: Creating New Competition Policy Institutions in Transition Economies*, 23 BROOK. J. INT'L L. 403 (1997); Eleanor M. Fox, *India: The Long Road to a Full-Function Competition Law*, 21 ANTITRUST 72 (2007); John O. Haley, *Competition Policy for East Asia*, 3 WASH. U. GLOBAL STUD. L. REV. 277 (2004); Tobor Varady, *The Emergence of Competition Law in (Former) Socialist Countries*, 47 AM. J. COMP. L. 229 (1999).

63   Salil Mehra & Meng Yanbei, *Against Antitrust Functionalism: Reconsidering China's Antimonopoly Law*, 49 VA. J. INT'L L. 379, 385-86 (2009); *see also* Xiaoye Wang, *Highlights of China's New Anti-Monopoly Law*, 75 ANTITRUST L. J. 133 (2008).

64   Ulrich Drobnig, *Möglichkeiten und Grenzen intersystemarer Rechtsvergleichung auf dem Gebiete des Zivilrechts*, in PROBLEME SYSTEMVERGLEICHENDER BETRACHTUNG (Gernot Gutmann & Siegfried Mampel eds. 1986) 195; Konrad Zweigert & Hans-Jürgen Puttfarken, *Critical Evaluation in Comparative Law*, 5 ADEL. L. REV. 343, 353 (1973); Dietrich A. Loeber, *Rechtsvergleichung zwischen Ländern mit verschiedener Wirtschaftsordnung*, 26 RABELS ZEITSCHRIFT FÜR RECHTSVERGLEICHUNG 201 (1961); Ulrich Drobnig, *The Comparability of Socialist and Non-Socialist Systems of Law*, 3 TEL AVIV U. STUD. L. 45 (1977).

65   Alan Devlin & Michael Jacobs, *Antitrust Divergence and the Limits of Economics*, 104 N.W.L. REV. 253, 280 (2010).

66   David J. Gerber, *Competition Law and the Institutional Embeddedness of Economics*, in ECONOMIC THEORY AND COMPETITION LAW (Josef Drexl, Laurence Idot & Joël Monéger eds. 2009) 20, 23.

67   The tendency to treat economics as a science can be traced back to at least Lionel Robbins, An Essay on the Nature and Scientific Significance of Economic Science (1932) 121 ("Economic laws describe inevitable implications. If the data they postulate are given, then the consequences they predict necessarily follow. In this sense they are on the same footing as other scientific laws.").

68   Comparativists often reference economic theory in an effort to substantiate their claim that their particular understanding of competition law is superior. *See e.g.*, William J. Kolasky, *What is competition? A comparison of U.S. and European perspectives*, 2004 ANTITRUST BULL. 29, 31-36 (2004).

69   David J. Gerber, *Competition Law and the Institutional Embeddedness of Economics*, in ECONOMIC THEORY AND COMPETITION LAW (Josef Drexl, Laurence Idot, and Joël Monéger eds. 2009) 20, 23.

70   David J. Gerber, *System Dynamics: Toward a Language of Comparative Law?*, 46 AM. COMP. L. REV. 719, 726-27 (1998).

71   Spencer W. Waller, *Comparative Competition Law as a Form of Empiricism*, 23 BROOK. J. INT'L L. 455 (1997).

72   *See generally* Amitai Etzioni, *Behavioral Economics: Toward a New Paradigm*, 55 AM. BEHAVIORAL SCIENTIST 1099 (2011).

73   Maurice E. Stucke, *Behavioral Economics at the Gate: Antitrust in the Twenty-First Century*, 38 LOY. U. CHI. L.J. 513 (2007).

74   Konrad Zweigert & Hans-Jürgen Puttfarken, *Critical Evaluation in Comparative Law*, 5 ADEL. L. REV. 343, 343 (1973).

75   William E. Kovacic, *Lucky Trip? Perspectives from a Foreign Advisor on Competition Policy, Development and Technical Assistance*, 3 EUR. COMPETITION J. 319, 322 (2007).

76   *See, e.g.*, William E. Kovacic & Hugh M. Hollman, *The International Competition Network: Its Past, Current and Future Role*, 20 MINN. J. INT'L L. 274 (2011).

Article 102 TFEU: The Case for a Remedial Enforcement Model along the Lines of Section 5 of the Federal Trade Commission Act

Jean-Francois Bellis

jfbellis@vbb.com

Partner, Van Bael & Bellis
Professor, Institute of European studies, University of Brussels (ULB)

Abstract

In his writings, Bill Kovacic has made the case for applying more widely Section 5 of the FTC Act in U.S. antitrust enforcement, and in particular vis-à-vis dominant firms. Among other things, Bill advocates that Section 5 should be enforced independently of Section 2 of the Sherman Act and applied to new types of anti-competitive conduct going beyond the Sherman Act as well as to "frontier" cases. Section 5 of the FTC Act presents many substantive similarities with Article 102 TFEU but, unlike Article 102 TFEU, is not enforced by fines but rather by cease-and-desist orders. This article argues that Article 102 TFEU calls for a different enforcement model patterned after that of Section 5 of the FTC Act in view of the increasing uncertainty introduced by the use of a more economic "effects-based" approach and the constraints imposed by the European Convention for the protection of Human Rights and Fundamental Freedoms ("ECHR").

I. Introduction

This article draws its inspiration from the contribution by Bill Kovacic to the recent debate about the role of Section 5 of the Federal Trade Commission Act ("FTC Act") in U.S. antitrust enforcement. In his article entitled "Competition policy and the application of section 5 of the Federal Trade Commission Act,"[1] Bill Kovacic makes the case for applying more widely Section 5 of the FTC Act in U.S. antitrust enforcement, and in particular *vis-à-vis* dominant firms. Among other things, Bill advocates that Section 5 should be enforced independently of Section 2 of the Sherman Act and applied to new types of anti-competitive conduct going beyond the Sherman Act as well as to *frontier* cases. As it will be discussed in this article, the debate about the role of Section 5 of the FTC Act in the United States may be of direct relevance to the enforcement of EU competition rules.

In the U.S. antitrust system, the FTC is the authority that most closely resembles the European Commission. The FTC is an administrative body created by the FTC Act 1914 with the aim of complementing the U.S. antitrust enforcement system. Section 5 of the FTC Act entrusts the FTC with expert administrative enforcement powers in relation to "unfair methods of competition" or "unfair or deceptive practices" which go beyond the Sherman Act.[2] Concretely, the FTC investigates alleged antitrust infringements and, where necessary, issues decisions enjoining the relevant firms, through cease-and-desist orders, from engaging in or continuing the relevant conduct. FTC's powers are therefore purely remedial as the agency cannot impose fines or criminal sanctions on businesses, although it does have the power to seek civil penalties and court injunctions in case of non-compliance.[3] FTC decisions can then be reviewed by the U.S. Federal Courts of Appeal.

The principal motivations behind the adoption of FTC Act were: (i) to counter the rigidity of U.S. courts in addressing competition concerns, (ii) to introduce a flexible administrative mechanism capable of adapting itself to new business realities, (iii) to create an expert authority simultaneously capable of conducting investigations, preparing studies and bringing well-informed administrative cases, (iv) to create an independent and responsive body, and (v) to have a broad authority to impose remedies lighter than under the Sherman Act.[4] Even though in practice the significance of Section 5 has been limited,[5] Bill Kovacic takes the view that there is a potentially important role for the FTC in the development of U.S. competition policy. He specifically recommends that the FTC devise a strategy involving the use of policy statements or guidelines to establish clear principles and analytical concepts as to what constitutes unfair methods of competition. Under this approach, unfair methods of competition should continue to be analysed under an economic, effects-based, *rule of reason* rather than under a *per se* illegal basis. This, in turn, would support the gradual development of a stand-alone Section 5 regime.

As this article will discuss, the scope of Section 5 FTC Act is probably closer to that of Article 102 Treaty on the Functioning of the European Union ("TFEU") than any other provision of U.S. antitrust law, including Section 2 of the Sherman Act. Yet, Article 102 TFEU is enforced by the European Commission essentially through the adoption of infringement decisions accompanied by increasingly harsh fines which are criminal in all but name, even though there is a recent tendency to deal with abuses of dominance in commitment decisions without fines.[6] This article will explore the reasons why the European Commission should develop an enforcement model in which fines are imposed only in exceptionally clear cases of abuse and, for the rest, Article 102 TFEU is enforced through cease-and-desist orders like Section 5 of the FTC Act.

II. Article 102 TFEU — A Constantly Evolving Provision

1. Section 5 of the FTC Act and Article 102 TFEU

Section 5 of the FTC Act presents interesting similarities with Article 102 TFEU.

To begin with, Section 5 refers to *unfairness*, a concept also present in Article 102. Indeed, the first example of abuse in Article 102 TFEU is the imposition of "unfair purchase or selling prices or other unfair trading conditions." While many older Article 102 cases have been centred on the concept of unfair prices or trading conditions,[7] even one of the most recent judgments, *Deutsche Telekom*, describes margin squeezes, a new form of abuse recently identified by the Commission, as "unfair pricing practices."[8]

Equally importantly, as already noted, the enforcement of Section 5 of the FTC Act is entrusted to an administrative authority, the FTC. That enforcement model corresponds exactly to that embraced by the European Union ("EU") in which the European Commission was granted far-reaching enforcement powers by Regulation 17/62 and its successor, Regulation 1/2003 on the implementation of the rules on competition laid down in Articles 81 and 82 of the Treaty.[9]

There is, however, one important difference between the FTC and the Commission: while the Commission has the power to impose substantial fines on undertakings found to have infringed Article 102 TFEU, the FTC is only entitled to issue civil cease-and-desist orders. The reason why the FTC was not allowed to impose penalties was that it was granted broad substantive authority to enjoin anti-competitive practices that might not be caught by the Sherman Act. As previously mentioned, the FTC was also expected to serve as an advisor to the business community on the legality of business practices. As a result, the FTC's powers were essentially designed to be "persuasive and corrective rather than punitive."[10]

As will be discussed below, the concerns reflected in the FTC's limited remedial powers are also applicable to the enforcement of Article 102 TFEU, which has frequently been applied to novel forms of anti-competitive practices.

2. Article 102 TFEU

Article 102 TFEU (formerly Article 86 and then 82 EC) provides that "[a]ny abuse by one or more undertakings of a dominant position within the internal market or in a substantial part of it shall be prohibited as incompatible with the internal market in so far as it may affect trade between Member States."

Like Section 5 of the FTC Act, Article 102 TFEU is a broad and open-ended provision, which prohibits abusive conduct by dominant undertakings without defining what is meant by either *dominant position* or *abuse*.

Early commentators of Article 102 had assumed that the concept of "*dominant position*" corresponded to that of monopoly or quasi-monopoly.[11] But the Commission, with the support of the Court of Justice, has transformed Article 102 into a provision which imposes duties on undertakings which merely hold a pre-eminent market position.[12] In *AKZO Chemie BV v. Commission*, the European Court of Justice found that a market share above 50% was evidence of a dominant position[13] but, in some instances, undertakings with market shares even below 40% have been held to be dominant.[14] In practice, any company, which holds a leading market position may find itself subject to the rigours of Article 102.

The concept of abuse has been subjected to a similarly expansive interpretation. As discussed more in detail below, the concept of abuse in Article 102 TFEU has already undergone two *mutations* through administrative and judicial interpretation. The first *mutation* took place in the early years of EU competition law enforcement when the concept of abuse, initially designed to cover only exploitative conduct, was expanded to also cover exclusionary practices. The second *mutation* is more recent and is still ongoing: it involves the substitution of an effects-based approach for a form-based approach hitherto applied to the identification of abusive conduct. This considerable transformation of the scope of Article 102 over the years has effectively turned it into something very much like what Section 5 of the FTC Act was meant to be, namely a provision aimed at covering a broad range of anti-competitive conduct, including novel situations, which had not been previously envisaged.

3. The First Mutation: From Exploitative to Exclusionary Abuses

One of the early commentators of Article 102 TFEU (which was then Article 86 of the Rome Treaty), René Joliet, observed that, unlike Section 2 of the Sherman Act, which was concerned with monopolisation practices, Article 102 only targeted direct exploitation of market power.[15] As René Joliet stressed, all the examples of abusive practices listed in Article 102 referred to instances where market power is exploited, used, or exercised to the detriment of suppliers or purchasers.[16] None of the examples refers to practices by which a dominant position is acquired or maintained. The purpose of Article 102 was thus to establish a supervision system of the dominant firms' use of their market power, in other words, *exploitative* abuses.

It did not take long for the Commission to put forward a radical rewriting of Article 102 under which the concept of abuse was expanded to also cover exclusionary abuses. In its 1966 Memorandum on concentration,[17] the Commission took the view that Article 102 could also reach practices of dominant undertakings that result in a lessening of competition such as mergers and acquisitions or predatory pricing. In other words, abuses could not only be exploitative but also exclusionary.

On this issue, as on many other jurisdictional issues, the Commission's expansive interpretation of Article 102 was backed by the European Court of Justice. In its 1973 *Continental Can* judgment, the Court of Justice held that Article 102 was:

> . . . not only aimed at practices which may cause damage to consumers directly but also at those which are detrimental to them through their impact on an effective competition structure, such as is mentioned in article 3 (f) of the treaty. Abuse may therefore occur if an undertaking in a dominant position strengthens such position in such a way that the degree of dominance reached substantially fetters competition, i.e. that only undertakings remain in the market whose behaviour depends on the dominant one.[18]

Ironically, the definition of the concept of abuse, which is currently most often cited from the *Hoffmann-La Roche*19 judgment, almost completely overlooks that exploitative abuses, which historically were the main subject of Article 102, are also covered by Article 102:

> The concept of abuse is an objective concept relating to the behaviour of an undertaking in a dominant position which is such as to influence the structure of a market where, as result of the very presence of the undertaking in question, the degree of competition is weakened and through recourse to methods which, different from those which condition normal competition in products or services on the basis of the transactions of commercial operators, has the effect of hindering the maintenance of the degree of competition existing in the market or the growth of that competition.[20]

As a matter of fact, the Commission has rarely, if at all, dealt with exploitative abuses since the eighties. In its 2008 Guidance Paper on its enforcement priorities in applying Article 82 (now 102 TFEU) of the Treaty,[21] the Commission stressed that exclusionary abuses were a matter of higher priority than exploitative abuses because it considered safeguarding the competitive process in the internal market of paramount importance. The Commission did not exclude the possibility of intervening in relation to exploitative conducts, such as charging of excessively high prices, where the protection of consumers could not be otherwise adequately ensured, but did not consider this to be a priority.[22]

In addition to this mutation from exploitative to exclusionary abuses, Article 102 has undergone (and is still undergoing) another equally important mutation with the gradual introduction of an *effects-based* approach to replace the *form-based* approach traditionally applied by the Commission.

4. The Second *Mutation:* From *Form-based* to *Effects-based*

Following the modernisation of the enforcement of Article 101 TFEU reflected in Regulation 1/2003, Commissioner Kroes announced in 2004 that the Commission had started reviewing its enforcement policy under Article 102 TFEU.[23] In July 2005, at the Commission's request, the Economic Advisory Group on Competition Policy issued a report entitled "An economic approach to Article 82" advocating for a more economics-based approach to Article 102, in line with the reform of Article 101 and merger control.[24] The Group stated that it supported an effects-based rather than a form-based approach to competition policy that focuses on the presence of anti-competitive effects that harm consumers and examination of each specific case, based on sound economics and grounded in facts. In December 2005, DG Competition published a discussion paper on the application of Article 82 to exclusionary abuses and invited all interested parties to provide comments.[25]

After intensive internal debates, the Commission adopted in 2008 a Guidance Communication on enforcement priorities in applying Article 102 TFEU.[26] This communication was intended to provide greater clarity and predictability regarding the general framework of analysis, which the Commission intends to use in determining whether it should pursue a case against exclusionary conduct by a dominant undertaking.[27] The Commission made it clear, however, that the Communication was not intended to be a statement of the law and was without prejudice to the interpretation of Article 102 TFEU by the EU Courts.[28] The central concept on which the Communication is based is that of *anti-competitive foreclosure*. According to the Guidance Communication, *anti-competitive foreclosure* describes a situation where effective access of actual or potential competitors to supplies or markets is hampered or eliminated as a result of the conduct of the dominant undertaking whereby the dominant undertaking is likely to be in a position to profitably increase prices to the detriment of consumers.[29] The Commission stated that it will *normally* intervene where, on the basis of *cogent and convincing evidence*, the allegedly abusive conduct is likely to lead to anti-competitive foreclosure.[30]

Even though it was only in 2008 that the Commission formally embraced the effects-based approach by issuing its Guidance Communication, such approach had already been applied with respect to the tying allegations in the 2004 *Microsoft* decision.[31] In that decision, the Commission recognised that the bundling of Windows Media Player (WMP) with the Windows operating system did not directly foreclose competition since users remained free to install any third party media player of their choice and OEMs were not prevented from pre-installing as many third party media players as they wished to install. The Commission accepted that the conduct at issue was not a *classical* tying case of the type found to be abusive through the form-based analysis in *Hilti*[32] and *Tetra Pak I*[33] and that further analysis was required before its compatibility with Article 102 could be assessed. To that effect, the Commission developed a theory of indirect foreclosure summarised as follows in the decision: "[i]n a nutshell, tying WMP with the dominant Windows makes WMP the platform of choice for complementary content and applications which in turn risks foreclosing competition in the market for media players."[34]

In other words, the Commission took the view that the integration of WMP in the Windows operating system would lead to WMP eventually dominating the market because of the incentives for content suppliers to encode their content in the WMP format, thereby causing other media players to exit the market. In its application to the Court of First Instance, Microsoft presented evidence showing that many of the assumptions on which the Commission's reasoning was based were unfounded.[35] That evidence, however, was ignored by the Court on the grounds that the Commission did not need to establish the existence of foreclosure. According to the Court, the Commission could correctly conclude that the bundling of WMP with the ubiquitous Windows platform provided WMP with a distributional advantage over competing media players and this was all the Commission had to establish to find Microsoft's conduct abusive.[36] The Microsoft judgment shows the difficulty of trying to inject an effects-based approach into a system that has traditionally had a form-based architecture.

Whether or not dominant undertakings may safely rely on the Guidance Communication to assess their exposure to Article 102 TFEU liability is far from clear. The ambivalence of the Commission on this point is particularly manifest in the *Intel* decision in which the Commission devotes not less than 156 pages (out of a total of 538) to the "as efficient competitor" ("AEC") analysis of Intel's rebates of the type discussed in the Guidance Communication.[37] Surprisingly, however, the Commission stresses that such analysis is "not indispensable for finding an infringement under Article 82 of the Treaty according to the case-law."[38] As a matter of fact, the finding of abuse in the *Intel* decision essentially rests on the traditional form-based case law, going back to the 1979 *Hoffmann-La Roche* case.[39]

This raises a serious question. The Commission cannot provide an analytical framework "to help undertakings better assess whether certain behaviour is likely to result in intervention by the Commission under Article 82" and at the same time, proceed to fine dominant undertakings for abusive conduct that is defined on the basis of pre-Guidance standards. Such attitude seems to be in direct contradiction with the principles of equal treatment and legitimate expectations applied by the Court in *Dansk Rorindustri* in relation to fining guidelines issued by the Commission.[40] It is not because the Communication was labelled as "guidance" rather than "guidelines," a choice of word which was apparently the subject of lengthy discussions within DG Competition, that it is immune to the *Dansk Rorindustri* case law.

The approach set out in the Guidance Communication has been applied by the Commission in new abuse cases such as *Deutsche Telekom* in which a finding of abuse in relation to the practice of margin squeeze was based on an AEC analysis, which was upheld by both the Court of First Instance and the Court of Justice.[41] It remains to be seen whether this approach will also be extended in the future to more traditional abusive practices subject of an abundant form-based case law. The objection that such a shift is inconsistent with the interpretations of Article 102 laid down in the past by the EU Courts is not a valid one. There is very little original thinking by the EU Courts reflected in that old case law which essentially consists in judgments upholding interpretations of the then Article 82 EC (or former 86) which the Commission put forward. In effect, these old judgments are nothing but a mirror in which the Commission can contemplate the reflection of its own past practice. They should not be perceived as an obstacle to a change in the Commission policy better attuned to modern economic thinking.

If, as expected, a more economic effects-based approach is increasingly used in the enforcement of Article 102 TFEU in the future, one important characteristic of that approach, namely the greater uncertainty that it introduces in the identification of abusive conduct, will need to be given due weight. As the EAGCP has noted, "an economics-based approach will naturally lend itself to a 'rule of reason' approach to competition policy, since careful consideration of the specifics of each case is needed."[42] This raises the question of whether the Commission can legitimately continue to sanction abuses of dominance with fines. The novel use of an effects-based, somewhat speculative, foreclosure theory in the *Microsoft* case did not prevent the Commission from imposing what was then the highest antitrust fine ever. Subjecting to fines conduct which is identified as illegal further to a *rule of reason* analysis creates a growing tension with another recent development in the EU, namely, the realisation that competition law fines are of a criminal nature, which in turn raises significant fundamental rights issues.

III. The Impact of Fundamental Rights

Recent developments in the area of fundamental rights may be signalling a shift in how the EU competition order views itself. Two 2011 judgments, one from the European Court of Human Rights and the other from the European Court of Justice, have addressed the question of whether the administrative enforcement model of competition law adopted by the EU and a number of Member States is compatible with fundamental rights.

In *Menarini*,[43] the European Court of Human Rights in Strasburg recognised the criminal nature of competition law fines[44] but accepted that such fines could be imposed by decisions adopted by administrative non-judicial competition authorities, provided that they were subject to a full judicial review on points of law and fact by independent courts having full jurisdiction. In its subsequent *KME* and *Chalkor* judgments,[45] which appear to echo *Menarini*, the Court of Justice elaborated on the scope and extent of the judicial review which the General Court must perform when ruling on appeals against Commission decisions imposing pecuniary sanctions for competition law infringements. According to the Court of Justice, the General Court cannot "refrain from reviewing the Commission's interpretation of information of an economic nature. Not only must [the Court] establish, among other things, whether the evidence relied on is factually accurate, reliable and consistent but also whether that evidence contains all the information which must be taken into account in order to assess a complex situation and whether it is capable of substantiating the conclusions drawn from it."[46]

These developments must be seen against the background of the Lisbon Treaty, which provides for the accession of the EU to the European Convention for the protection of Human Rights and Fundamental Freedoms (ECHR). This development will give even higher prominence to the question of compatibility of competition proceedings with the rights protected under this Convention such as, in particular, the principle of legality of criminal offences and penalties.[47]

This is where the Commission's practice of imposing heavy fines to sanction infringements of Article 102, defined for the first time in the very decision that imposes the fine, will increasingly come under fire. Imposing criminal sanctions for the violation of a provision merely prohibiting abusive conduct without defining it cannot be consistent with the fundamental principle *nulla poena sine lege*.[48] The Commission should stop imposing fines in Article 102 cases, except perhaps for the most manifest and well-established violations.[49] Like the FTC in Section 5 cases, the Commission should in most cases limit itself to ordering the discontinuance of abusive practices without imposing pecuniary sanctions. Such decisions, which would no longer present a criminal character, could then be appealed to the General Court under a standard of limited judicial review consistent with their essentially regulatory nature under which there could be more room for a margin of discretion for the Commission.[50]

At this point, however, it is necessary to take stock of a recent development in the Commission's practice, namely, the increasing reliance on commitment decisions in abuse of dominance cases, and examine whether commitments, rather than cease-and-desist decisions, could be the alternative to infringement decisions with fines.

IV. Commitment Decisions — The Alternative to Infringement Decisions with Fines?

It is interesting to note that, since the introduction of a commitment procedure under Article 9 of Regulation 1/2003, the Commission has extensively used this new provision, particularly in abuses of dominance cases.[51] Since the entry into force of Regulation 1/2003 on 1 May 2004, twenty-one commitment decisions have been adopted, the majority of which involving infringements of Article 102 TFEU.

It is not surprising that so many recent Article 102 cases have ended in commitment decisions. One of the main attractions of the commitment procedure for undertakings resides in the fact that Article 9 does not allow the Commission to impose fines. In view of the high level of fines,[52] and the fact that EU Courts have upheld practically all Commission decisions in dominance cases in the last thirty years,[53] understandably, undertakings may prefer to offer commitments rather than take the risk of defending their case before the Courts.

Interestingly, the sector in which commitment decisions have been most prevalent is the energy sector, where the Commission has maintained the pressure on undertakings to support the ongoing liberalization process in these markets. No less than eight commitment decisions were issued between 2007 and 2011 in relation to Article 102 cases in the energy sector alone.[54]

In *Distrigaz*,[55] for instance, the Commission had expressed concerns that Distrigaz' long-term gas supply agreements in the Belgian market breached Article 102 by limiting the ability of other gas suppliers to conclude agreements with Distrigaz' customers, thereby foreclosing the market. In response to these concerns, Distrigaz agreed to reduce the gas volumes tied up in long-term agreements and to limit contract durations to five years in order to open up the Belgian gas market to greater competition.

In another somewhat politically-charged case, *E.ON*,[56] Germany's largest electricity and gas undertaking agreed to break itself up by proposing to sell its electricity transmission system network to an operator with no interests in electricity generation and/or supply businesses and to commit to divest a sizeable generation capacity to competitors. In this case, the Commission effectively managed to secure from E.ON voluntary but legally binding structural commitments through competition enforcement at a time when its parallel negotiations with Member States on the regulatory unbundling of their energy companies were struggling. Again, it was the threat of heavy fines that incited E.ON to propose voluntary commitments.

A number of commitment decisions have also been adopted in the high tech sector. Thus, in *Microsoft (Tying)*,[57] the Commission sent to Microsoft a Statement of Objections in which it took the view that the integration of Internet Explorer with the Windows operating system violated Article 102 and indicated that it was considering adopting a decision ordering Microsoft to take the necessary measures to terminate the abuse and impose a fine. Since this practice had started in 1996, the fine, which the Commission could have imposed on Microsoft, might have been very substantial.[58] Following discussions with the Commission, Microsoft agreed to make available a mechanism enabling OEMs and users in the European Economic Area ("EEA") to turn Internet Explorer off and on. Under the commitments proposed by Microsoft, OEMs will be free to pre-install any web browsers of their choice on PCs and set as default any web browser. Finally, Microsoft offered to distribute a choice screen software update to users of Windows PCs within the EEA offering them a choice of web browsers, and presenting them with links where they could find more information about the web browsers presented on the screen.

The Commission also accepted commitments offered by Rambus that put a cap on its royalty rates for certain patents for DRAMs.[59] These commitments were offered after the Commission had expressed the preliminary view in a Statement of Objections that Rambus had engaged in a *patent ambush*, intentionally concealing that it had patents and patent applications relevant to the technology used in the JEDEC standard, and subsequently, claiming royalties for those patents.

More recently, following the issuance of a Preliminary Assessment (rather than a formal Statement of Objections), the Commission accepted commitments by IBM in the mainframe maintenance market.[60] The Commission was concerned that IBM might be in breach of Article 102 for imposing unreasonable conditions on independent *mainframe maintainers* which needed access to spare parts and technical information in order to compete effectively in this market. To address these concerns, IBM committed to make spare parts and technical information readily available, under commercially reasonable and non-discriminatory terms, to its independent competitors.

Of all the commitment decisions adopted thus far, the one that attracted the most attention is the famous *Alrosa case*,[61] in which the Commission had accepted commitments by De Beers, the world's largest producer of rough diamonds, in relation to a supply agreement it had concluded with Alrosa, the world's second largest producer.

The initial agreement between the two undertakings had provided that De Beers would purchase annually from Alrosa, for a period of five years, U.S. $800 million of rough diamonds, which represented roughly half of the latter's annual production. The Commission expressed concerns that such an agreement would appreciably restrict competition on the worldwide rough diamonds market by eliminating competition from Alrosa, De Beers' largest competitor, and therefore constituted an abuse of dominant position by De Beers. To address these concerns, De Beers finally offered commitments to the Commission agreeing to progressively phase out its purchases of rough diamonds from Alrosa by 2009. On 22 February 2006, the Commission issued a decision making these commitments binding and Alrosa subsequently challenged this decision in an appeal before the General Court.

In its 2007 judgment, the General Court annulled the Commission's commitment decision on the grounds that the Commission had breached the principle of proportionality by imposing on De Beers an obligation to end its supply agreement with Alrosa, which the Court found to be manifestly disproportionate.[62]

That judgment, however, was quashed by the European Court of Justice which made it clear that commitment decisions are not subject to the same degree of judicial scrutiny as infringement decisions due to the voluntary nature of commitments.[63] The Court of Justice stated that undertakings which offer commitments consciously accept that these may go beyond what the Commission could itself impose on them in an infringement decision following a thorough examination. The commitments procedure is effectively intended to provide a quicker and more flexible solution to competition concerns identified by the Commission in comparison to fully-fledged investigations resulting in infringement decisions.[64] As a result, the principle of proportionality does not apply to the same extent to commitment decisions, and must not be assessed on the same basis as infringement decisions.[65]

In addition, the Court of Justice considered that the General Court had unlawfully interfered with the Commission's discretion with regard to the acceptance of the commitments. According to the Court of Justice, the General Court wrongly "put forward its own assessment of complex economic circumstances and thus substituted its own assessment for that of the Commission, thereby encroaching on the discretion enjoyed by the Commission instead of reviewing the lawfulness of its assessment."[66] The Court of Justice made it clear that the Commission was not obliged to seek out less onerous and more moderate solutions than the proposed commitments and could limit itself to ascertaining whether the latter were sufficient to address its competition concerns.[67]

In light of the above, therefore, it is manifest that commitment decisions cannot be the sole alternative to infringement decisions with fines. Commitment decisions are adopted further to summary investigations and are nothing but the product of a bargaining process. The Court of Justice itself has recognised that they may go beyond what could be ordered by the Commission in a decision adopted under Article 7 of Regulation 1/2003. For this reason, they are not a suitable vehicle for providing guidance on how Article 102 TFEU should be applied in novel situations.

V. Conclusion

In the last ten years, increasingly harsh penalties have been imposed on dominant undertakings for engaging in conduct found to be illegal under the vague standard of *abuse* set in Article 102 TFEU. While the inherent lack of clarity and predictability of Article 102 makes it unsuitable for enforcement by means of pecuniary sanctions, the introduction of a more economic, effects-based, and thus more speculative, approach in the interpretation of that provision compounds the problem. For the reasons discussed above, commitment decisions cannot be the sole alternative to fines. Article 102 calls for a different enforcement model, in which abusive exclusionary practices of dominant undertakings are the subject of cease-and-desist decisions without fines, along the lines of the FTC Section 5 model. In this respect at least, Brussels might perhaps benefit from being a little more like Washington.

NOTES

1   William E. Kovacic & Marc Winerman, *Competition policy and the application of section 5 of the Federal Trade Commission Act*, 76 Antitrust L.J. 929 (2010) *available at* http://www.ftc.gov/speeches/kovacic/2010kovacicwin ermanpolicyapp.pdf.

2   The FTC Act is codified at 15 U.S.C. § 41 et seq. 15 U.S.C. § 45.

3   5 U.S.C. § 45 (l) – (m) (on civil penalties and injunctions).

4   *See supra*, note 1, at p. 931.

5   The last time the U.S. Supreme Court had to review exclusionary practices by a dominant firm under Section 5 was in 1927 where it ruled against the FTC in Federal Trade Commission v. Eastman Kodak Co., 274 U.S. 619 (1927).

6   *See infra*, note 54.

7   This provision was applied, for instance, in Case 127/73, BRT v. SABAM, 1974 E.C.R 313, where an obligation on members of a copyright society to assign all present and future copyrights to the society and to allow it to exercise these rights for five years after withdrawal was found in violation of Article 102 (a). Similarly, in Case 7/82, GVL v. Comm'n, 1983 E.C.R. 483, Article 102 was relied upon by the Commission to prohibit discriminatory treatment on grounds of nationality.

8   Case T-271/03, Deutsche Telekom v. Commission, 2008 E.C.R. II-47, ¶ 167.

9   Council Regulation (EC) No 1/2003 of 16 December 2002 on the implementation of the rules on competition laid down in Articles 81 and 82 of the Treaty, 2003 OJ (L 1) 1-25. Following the entry into force of the Lisbon Treaty, Articles 81 and 82 are now Articles 101 and 102 TFEU.

10   Amy Marshak, *The Federal Trade Commission on the frontier: Suggestions for the use of section 5*, (2011) 86 N.Y.U.L. REV.1128.

11   RENÉ JOLIET, MONOPOLIZATION AND ABUSE OF DOMINANT POSITION: A COMPARATIVE STUDY OF AMERICAN APPROACHES TO THE CONTROL OF ECONOMIC POWER (1967, Martinus Nijhoff, The Hague).

12   Case 27/76, United Brands v. Comm'n, 1978 E.C.R. 207 ¶¶ 65-129.

13   Case 62/86, 1991 E.C.R. I-3359 ¶ 50.

14   *See* Case T-219/99, British Airways v. Comm'n, 2003 E.C.R. II-05917 ¶¶ 211, 225 (finding BA to be dominant under Article 102 for a market share which had fallen from 46% to 40% during the period of the abuse); *see also* Commission Decision Wanadoo Interactive, Case COMP/38.233 in which the Commission found that Wanadoo was dominant with a 39% market share when its main competitors had market shares of 6.5% and 16% respectively.

15   *See supra*, note 11.

16   *Id.* 247.

17   EUROPEAN COMMISSION, MEMORANDUM ON THE PROBLEMS OF CONCENTRATION IN THE COMMON MARKET (1966).

18   Case 6/72, Europemballage & Continental Can v. Comm'n, 1973 E.C.R. 215, at 245 ¶ 26.

19   Case 85/76, Hoffmann La Roche v. Comm'n, 1979 E.C.R. 461.

20   *Id.* 541, ¶ 91.

21   Guidance on Commission enforcement priorities in applying Article 82 to exclusionary conduct by dominant firms, *available at* http://eur-lex.europa.eu/LexUriServ/LexUriServ.do?uri=OJ:C:2009:045:0007:0020:EN:PDF.

22   *Id.* ¶¶ 6-7.

23   *See* SPEECH (04)477, 28 October 2004.

24   EAGCP REPORT, AN ECONOMIC APPROACH TO ARTICLE 82 (2005) *available at* http://ec.europa.eu/dgs/competition/economist/eagcp_july_21_05.pdf.

25   PUBLIC CONSULTATION, DG COMPETITION DISCUSSION PAPER ON THE APPLICATION OF ARTICLE 82 OF THE TREATY TO EXCLUSIONARY ABUSES, December 2005, *available at* http://ec.europa.eu/competition/antitrust/art82/discpaper2005.pdf.

26   *See supra*, note 21.

27   *Id.* ¶ 2.

28   *Id.* ¶ 3.

29   *Id.* ¶19.

30   *Id.* ¶ 20.

31   Case COMP/C-3/37.792, Microsoft (2004).

32   Case IV/30.787, Eurofix-Bauco/Hilti, 1998 OJ (L 65/19).

33   Case IV/31.043, OJ [1992] L 72/1, Tetra Pak II; *See also* Jean-Francois Bellis & Tim Kasten, *The Microsoft Windows Media Player tying case*, in LUCA RUBINI, MICROSOFT ON TRIAL: LEGAL AND ECONOMIC ANALYSIS OF A TRANSATLANTIC ANTITRUST CASE (2010, Edward Elgar) Chapter 4, pp. 144-145 and 154-155.

34   *See supra*, note 31, Microsoft, ¶ 842.

35   *See supra*, note 33, Jean-Francois Bellis & Tim Kasten.

36   Case T-201/04, Microsoft v. Commission, 2007 E.C.R. II-03601, ¶ 1058.

37   Case COMP/C-3/37.990, Intel (2009).

38   *Id.* ¶ 925.

39   *See supra*, note 19.

40   Joined cases C-189/02 P, C-202/02 P, C-205/02 P to C-208/02 P and C-213/02 P, Dansk Rorindustri and Others v. Commission, 2005 E.C.R. I-05425, ¶¶ 2112011.

41   Case T-271/03, Deutsche Telekom v. Commission, 2008 E.C.R. II-00477; C-280/08 P Deutsche Telekom v. Commission, 2010 E.C.R.___(not yet reported).

42   *See supra*, note 24.

43   A. Menarini Diagnostics S.R.L. v. Italy (application number 43509/08), 27 September 2011.

44 Even though Article 23(5) of Regulation 1/2003 expressly describes fines as not being of criminal nature, Advocate General Sharpston stated in her Opinion in Case C-272/09 P, KME, 10 February 2011, ¶ 64, that she had "little difficulty in concluding that the procedure whereby a fine is imposed for breach of the prohibition on price-fixing and market-sharing agreements in Article 81(1) EC falls under the 'criminal head' of Article 6 ECHR as progressively defined by the European Court of Human Rights."

45 Case C-389/10 P, KME v. Commission, 2011 E.C.R. – not yet reported, C-386/10 P - Chalkor v. Commission, 2011 E.C.R. ___(not yet reported).

46 *Id*. KME ¶ 121.

47 *See* Donald Slater, Denis Waelbroeck, & Sébastien Thomas, *Competition law proceedings before the European Commission and the right to a fair trial: no need for reform?*, GCLC Working Paper 04/08 *available at* http://www.coleurop.be/content/gclc/documents/GCLC%20WP%2004-08.pdf; *See also* Wouter Wils, *The Increased Level of EU Antitrust Fines, Judicial Review, and the European Convention on Human Rights*, 33 WORLD COMPETITION: LAW AND ECONOMICS REVIEW 1, March 2010, *available at* http://papers.ssrn.com/sol3/papers.cfm?abstract_id=1492736.

48 *See* Bo Vesterdorf, *Article 102 TFEU and sanctions: appropriate when*, 2011, ECLR 573.

49 As a matter of fact, the Commission has refrained in the past from imposing fines in abuse of dominance cases raising novel issues. *See e.g.*, joined Cases C-241/91P and C-242/91P, Radio Telefis Eireann v. Comm'n, 1995 E.C.R. 1995 I-00743 ["*Magill*" case]; *See also* Case C-418/01, IMS Health, 2004 E.C.R. I-05039 ¶ 12, in which the Commission adopted an interim decision which limited itself to ordering IMS to immediately grant a licence to its competitor.

50 *Supra*, note 48.

51 Article 9(1) of Regulation 1/2003 provides that:

> Where the Commission intends to adopt a decision requiring that an infringement be brought to an end and the undertakings concerned offer commitments to meet the concerns expressed to them by the Commission in its preliminary assessment, the Commission may by decision make those commitments binding on the undertakings. Such a decision may be adopted for a specified period and shall conclude that there are no longer grounds for action by the Commission.

At the end of 2011, the Commission had accepted so far some twenty-one commitments decisions. Eight concerned Article 101, twelve related to Article 102, and one related to both Articles 101 and 102.

52 *See in particular Microsoft* and *Intel* where fines of respectively €497million and €1.06 billion were imposed.

53 *See* Damien J. Neven, *Competition Economics and Antitrust in Europe*, 2006, 21 ECONOMIC POLICY 48, 741 791 (research demonstrating that between 1990 and 2006, the Commission had won 75% of Article 101 TFEU cases, 58% of merger cases, but as much as 98% of Article 102 TFEU cases on appeals before the General Court), *available at* http://ec.europa.eu/dgs/competition/economist/economic_policy.pdf.

54 *See* Case COMP/B-1/37966, Distrigaz (2007); Case COMP/39.388, E.ON German Electricity Wholesale Market (2008); Case COMP/39.402, RWE Gas Foreclosure (2009); Case COMP/39.316, GDF Suez (2009); Case COMP/39.386, EDF (2010); Case 39351, Swedish Interconnectors (2010); Case COMP/39.317, E.ON Gas Foreclosure (2010); Case COMP/39.315, *ENI* (2010).

55 *Id*. *Distrigaz* (2007).

56 *Id*. *E.ON* (2008).

57 Case COMP/C-3/39.530, Microsoft (tying) (2009).

58 Under ¶¶ 19-24 of the Commission's 2006 Fining Guidelines, fines may be based on a proportion of up to 30% of the undertaking's annual sales to which the infringement relates, multiplied by the number of years of participation in the infringement.

59 Case COMP/38.636, Rambus (2009).

60 Case COMP/C-3/39.692, IBM (Maintenance Services) (2011).

61 Case COMP/B-2/38.381, De Beers (2006).

62 Case T-170/06, Alrosa v. Comm'n 2007, E.C.R. II-02601.

63 Case C-441/07 P, Comm'n v. Alrosa, 2010 E.C.R. I-05945 ¶¶ 47-48. *See also*, the General Court judgment in the same case, ¶ 106, in which the General Court noted that commitments may be seen as a form of assent given to the undertakings concerned in a decision which the Commission was empowered to adopt unilaterally. Indeed, commitments are voluntary only in appearance whenever the alternative to not offering them is the imposition of a substantial fine.

64 Id. ¶ 37.

65 Id. ¶ 50.

66 Id. ¶ 67.

67 Id. ¶ 61.

Has the European Commission Become More Severe in Punishing Cartels? Effects of the 2006 Guidelines: Revision*

John M. Connor

jconnor@purdue.edu
Professor, Purdue University

Abstract

This paper analyzes the first 22 cartel decisions of the European Commission under its 2006 revised fining Guidelines. I find that the severity of the cartel fines relative to affected sales is about double the fines decided under the previous 1998 Guidelines. EC fines now regularly disgorge the monopoly profits accumulated by cartelists. Yet, the new fine guidelines are no more severe than U.S. DOJ criminal fines. Nearly all recent cartel decisions reward one or more participants with full or partial leniency. There is no evidence that leniency discounts have led to larger percentage reductions in cartel-wide fines. Moreover, despite more severe fines, the share of defendants requiring reductions under the Commission's 10% cap or ability-to-pay considerations has not risen. Contrary to expectations, the size of the percentage discounts for recidivism has gone down under the new guidelines. There is evidence that the Commission has been inconsistent in applying recidivism penalties in the manner promised it its 2006 Guidelines. In particular, it has been overly lenient by failing to account for numerous previous hard-core cartel violations in the EU.

"... European fines have become astronomical. Certain folks are very concerned that the fines have gotten to the level where they are threatening the competitive viability of the companies." — Comment of Roxanne E. Henry, Howrey LLP at the Roundtable Conference with Enforcement Officials, American Bar Association Section of Antitrust Law Spring Meeting, Washington, D.C. (April 23, 2010).

"As regards the fines and the level of our fines, it is true that the level has increased quite substantially since we introduced new fining guidelines a couple of years ago. We recognized that the level of our fines was clearly not deterrent beforehand, so we had to increase it in order to increase the deterrence. I would say that the absolute level of the fines may sound astronomical, but it is not so important per se because we are very often looking at quite a large group of offenders with very large turnovers. So I think that has to be related to the turnovers of the companies." — Reply of Alexander Italianer, Director General for Competition, European Commission (same meeting).

I. Introduction

When the European Commission ("EC") introduced its second set of cartel-fining guidelines in late 2006, the Commission's intention was to treat hard-core cartel infringements more severely. Commentators were universally of the opinion that fines for comparable cartels would increase considerably compared to the earlier 1998 guidelines — perhaps too severely in the minds of antitrust defense counsel. EC officials defended the higher fines as necessary for deterrence and suggested that — when corrected for affected sales — were not as large as they seemed.

At the same time that absolute fines were rising, the EC's 2002 Leniency Program became highly successful in attracting more applicants than earlier years; discounts on fines mandated for leniency will countervail the trends in increasing corporate and cartel-wide severity under the new guidelines. Moreover, the "10%-of-sales cap" rule has remained unchanged since the 1960s; with higher fines and the world financial crisis that began in 2008, more cartelists may qualify for reductions in their fines. Thus, leniency decisions and the 10% upper limit may dampen the intended increases in severity. The outcome of these three policy changes is an empirical question. Now that the EC has implemented the new guidelines for about four years, an assessment of these expectations is feasible.

The objective of this chapter is to examine the size and severity of the EC cartel-fining decisions through the end of 2011, assess changes in severity, and discuss the main factors affecting severity. Severity is measured in two ways: by the ratio of the fine to the undertaking's global annual sales and the ratio of the fine to affected commerce during the entire collusive period.

European Commission's decisions frequently suppress information on the affected sales that were used to derive fines for each addressee (defendant) that is judged to have violated EU competition rules. Sales data are suppressed in some final redacted decisions and in nearly all summaries of the decisions. This chapter is an exercise in "reverse engineering." The EC's formula for computing fines is reformulated to solve for a defendant's affected sales when the final fine is published together with some of the following: the starting-point multiplier for gravity, duration of the offense, aggravating or mitigating adjustments, deterrence premium, reductions due to ability to pay or to the 10% global sales cap, or leniency or "settlement" discounts. Indeed, four alternative formulas are applied, and these serve as cross-checks on the derivations of affected sales employed as the bases of the fines. Once a company's affected sales is known, the severity of the EC's fine can be calculated exactly.

The trend in EC severity is also compared to comparable cartel fines imposed by the Antitrust Division of the U.S. Department of Justice (DOJ).[1] Calculating severity in this manner is difficult, but alternative indicators that rely on more convenient numbers can be misleading.[2] By including decisions through the end of 2011, the severity of cartel fines may be used as an indicator of the commitment of EC Competition Commissioner Almunia relative to his predecessors.

Trends in severity reveal that cartel fines imposed by the EC under its 2006 Guidelines have been higher than those under its 1998 Guidelines. Fine reductions for successful leniency applicants have been substantial, but no higher than under the 1998 Guidelines. However, the size and severity of EC cartel fines since 2007 are still lower than those of the DOJ. Commissioner Almunia has approved less severe cartel fines than his predecessors. One reason for less-than-expected severity is a lenient application of the aggravating penalty enhancements for recidivism.

II. The 2006 EC Fining Guidelines

The EC sanctions cartels solely with fines. The EC first adopted detailed *Penalty Guidelines* in 1998 for calculating firm-by-firm cartel fines, though they may be regarded as a written notice of unwritten practices of the early 1990s (Wils 1998). A detailed explanation of how the 1998 Guidelines were applied can be found in Harding and Joshua (2003: 240-252) and Joshua and Camesasca (2004).

Corporate leniency programs are intended to increase the proportion of clandestine cartels that are discovered by antitrust authorities. Before leniency programs were implemented, the probability of discovery was estimated to be only about 15% (Bryant and Eckard 1991). The EC's first Leniency Notice was in effect from July 1996 to February 2002, but during that time only 16 final decisions were rendered as a result of immunity applications.[3] This modest record led to the proclamation of a second Leniency Notice, which took effect in February 2002. The new program offered nearly automatic immunity for qualified applicants, which had the effect of attracting much larger numbers of applicants.[4]

In September 2006, revised European Union ("EU") fining guidelines were adopted (EC 2006). The Commission wished to increase the size and severity of cartel fines. The new Guidelines were predicted to double average fines for comparable cartels (Veljanovski 2009). Generally, the revised guidelines have been praised by scholars as more transparent, predictable, and a step forward toward optimally deterring fines (Camilli 2006, Wils 2007, Motta 2008). In a departure from previous practice, the new EC starting point is a percentage of the violator's affected European Economic Area ("EEA") sales for the entire duration of the cartel, net of taxes (EC 2006: §13-§17).[5] In the case of global cartels, the EC asserts a bold concept of extraterritoriality: a company's basic fine will be calculated as a percentage of the addressee's annual global sales[6] in the cartelized market, not merely EU sales (EC 2006: §18). For hard-core cartels the starting-point range is 15% to 30% of affected sales (EC 2006: §19-§26). The percentage chosen within this range is affected by the nature of the violation, the cartel's market share, and the geographic scope of the cartel. The starting percentage is then multiplied by the number of years the cartel endured. In addition, an amount of from 15% to 25% of affected sales will be applied to hard-core cartel fines. Thus, for a typical hard-core cartel of five years' duration, the "basic amount" of the fine will range from 90% to 175% of affected sales.[7]

The basic amount is adjusted for a defendant's culpability. It can be increased up to 100% for *each* previous infringement of the EU's competition laws, a doubling of the previous percentage (EC 2006: §28-§29).[8] Obstruction of an investigation, cartel leadership, and cartel instigation are examples of additional aggravating factors. Mitigating circumstances include negligence, substantial cheating,[9] and conduct approved by governments. Other than recidivism, no specific percentages are suggested for culpability adjustments to the basic amount. A special additional "deterrence" penalty may be added for large, diversified members of cartels or those for which the gain from collusion is known to be larger than the fine (EC 2006: §30-§31). After culpability adjustments are made, there are three possible downward adjustments: the 10% sales cap, total or partial leniency discounts[10] for cooperation with prosecutors, and inability to pay.

III. Data Sample and Method

The first cartel decision made under the EC's 2006 Notice was *Professional Videotapes*. This case began with unannounced inspections on May 28-29, 2002 and ended with a decision of the Commission on November 20, 2007 (EC 11/20/2007).[11] Information of the decision was released in four stages: first, a terse press release posted on November 20, 2007; second, a three-page Summary of the decision published in the *Official Journal* on March 1, 2008; third, the redacted, non-official 59-page Web version of the decision in one or two languages later in 2008; and, fourth, the redacted official decision in about 11 languages in the *Official Journal*. The time lag in *Professional Videotape* of 5.5 years from raid to the first detailed non-official decision was longer than most for the EC. The most recent decision is for the *Glass for Cathode Ray Tubes* cartel in October 2011.

The data needed for analyzing the 2006 Guidelines decisions are extracted from the Summary or non-official, redacted final versions of the decisions post on the EC's Website. There are 22 EC decisions regarding 128 cartel participants (Table 1).[12] The type of redacted data varies across decisions, and this can be problematic. Some of the cartel decisions suppressed so much information that it was impossible to calculate firm-level affected sales for every participant (and, hence, severity). For example, at one extreme, the *Flat Glass* decision suppressed seven items: the starting-point percentage, duration, basic amount, deterrence premium, adjusted basic amount, and reductions, if any, due to the 10% cap or ability to pay. For four cartel decisions severity cannot be calculated for the amnesty recipient because a pre-leniency fine is not revealed.

The sample of 22 cartels appears to be roughly representative of the types of cartels convicted in the past in terms of numbers of participants, industry distribution, and other characteristics (*see Connor* 2009). This chapter compares decisions under the 2006 Guidelines with previous EC decisions and contemporary U.S. decisions. Information about these other cartels also comes from the EC's published decisions, from guilty pleas posted on the DOJ's Website, or from academic and industry trade publications.[13]

The method employed to calculate severity is quite straightforward. The numerator of the fine/sales ratio is the violator's fine reported in the EC decision, converted to U.S. dollars on the day of the decision; if a leniency reduction was awarded, then a pre-leniency fine is easily computed.[14] The affected EEA sales of a cartel participant is seldom reported, so an algorithm was deduced algebraically from the underlying formula that is employed by the Commission to set cartel fines under the 2006 Guidelines (*European Commission* 2006). Essentially, the fine amount is a linear function of affected sales, and a combination of the starting-point, aggravating-factors, mitigating factors, deterrence-premium, leniency-discount, and final adjustment percentages.[15] This equation is solved for affected sales. Several internal consistency checks are performed.[16]

IV. Analysis and Results

1. Absolute Levels of Cartel Fines

The final fines imposed by the EC under its 2006 Guidelines total $8.433 billion (€6.187 billion) (Table 2). The mean average final fine imposed on the 22 cartels in the sample was $383 million. However, because the fines are highly skewed, the *median* average[17] cartel fine is much lower $178 million (Table 2). The mean average cartel fine under the 2006 Guidelines was 99% higher than the average fine per cartel (€141.6 million) imposed during 1999-2009 under the EC's 1998 Guidelines (Veljanovski 2009: 5). This large increase in EC fines is due in part to an increase in affected sales and in part to the tougher provisions of the new fining guidelines (Connor and Miller 2010).

Final fines are available for 128 companies ("undertakings" in EC jargon).[18] The mean average corporate fine is $65.9 million (€48.3 million) and the median is $15.6 million (€10.5 million). Under the 1998 EC Guidelines, the mean final fine was €38.7 million (Veljanovski 2010: 4). Thus, the mean per firm fine increased by only 25% under the new 2006 Guidelines, and much of this increase can be ascribed to general inflation.

2. Choice of the Starting Point

Under the previous Guidelines, it was virtually impossible to ascertain the starting point for cartel fines, something for which the Commission was roundly criticized (Joshua and Camesasca 2004). Under the new Guidelines, all hard-core cartels have mandated starting points of 15% to 30% of affected sales. The Commission has a good deal of discretion within that range, but it is apparent that it has been cautious in choosing the starting-point percentages. All but three starting points hovered near the bottom of the range. *Marine Hose* had a starting point of 25%, *PCP rubber* 21%, and *Tin Heat Stabilizers* 20%. The remaining 19 cartels had average starting points of 17%. What made the gravity of *Marine Hose* so special is difficult to discern from the decisions. True, the marine-hose market was dominated by the cartel, but so were other cartels with lower starting points. One lesson is that the EC has plenty of leeway to increase average fines by about 80% should it use 30% starting points in place of the typical 16-17% points in the sample.

3. How Severe?

Recall that for the purposes of this chapter, fine severity is relative to the addressee's global annual sales *or* to its total affected sales. The first measure of severity takes into account the defendant's ability to pay from earnings in the EU and elsewhere from the relevant line of business. The second measure incorporates a somewhat societal standard: the customers' point of view. These ratios can be calculated for the entire cartel or for an individual cartelist.

The severity of final EC fines imposed under the 2006 Guidelines on the 22 cartels is shown in Table 2. There is a wide variation in global-sales variation across cartels.[19] Whole-cartel severity ranges from 6.7% of global company sales for *Bananas 2* to 412% for *Marine Hose* (Table 2). The simple arithmetic mean average severity is 90%, the mean sales-weighted average[20] is 59%, and the median severity is 68%.[21] These are high averages, but because most cartels endure for several years, the alternative measure of severity is lower.

The more conventional measure of severity is to divide by the company's sales during its involvement in the cartel. The severity of *final* EC fines imposed under the 2006 Guidelines on the 22 cartels is shown in Table 3. Again, this measure of severity is highly variable.[22]

Whole-cartel severity ranges from 1.2% of global company sales for *Glass for CRTs* to 76% for *MEGAL Gas Pipeline* (Table 3).[23] The simple arithmetic mean average severity is 19.4%, the mean sales-weighted average[24] is 5.4% and the median severity is 21.3%. Measured this way, average severity is much more modest.

Here are some severity benchmarks. The maximum criminal cartel fine under the U.S. Sentencing Guidelines is 80% of affected sales in the jurisdiction; in Brazil the upper limit is 30%; and in Japan and Korea maximal fines are close to 10% (Connor 2008: 585). Another yardstick is the overcharges generated by cartels operating in Western Europe. Connor (2010: 112) reports that the mean average overcharge for cartels active across most of the EU is 60% of affected sales, and the median is 40%. Restricting the sample to cartels condemned by the EC, the mean is 55% and the median 33%. The majority of the cartel fines under the 2006 Guidelines are about half of the likely damages caused in the EU.[25]

Another standard of comparison is the severity of fines imposed on international cartels by the DOJ. Information is available for 1999-2011 U.S. criminal fines and affected U.S. sales for 30 cartels (Table 4). During 1999-2011, the median average degree of severity for the 87 cartels fined by the EC is 7.7%; by comparison, the DOJ fines had a median severity of 15.8%. For the whole period, U.S. fines were twice as severe as EC fines. However, during 2007-2011 under the 2006 Guidelines, median EC fines rose to become almost equally severe as U.S. cartel fines.

There are at least two reasons for less severe fines. Reductions in fines because of full leniency (immunity) have significant effects on fine severities. For the 124 companies for which pre-leniency fines were published, fines totaled €9.192 million, whereas after the 12 immunized defendants' fines were made zero, the total dropped to €6.187 million—a 33% reduction.[26] Another reason for relatively lenient fines is that the affected sales of recent cartels are larger than the earlier cartels, and the Commission through its discretion over the starting-point percentage and other discretionary choices imposes less severe fines on the biggest cartels.[27] In its Guidelines, there are no provisions for issuing less severe fines for larger cartels.

4. Changes in Severity

To gauge trends in the severity of EC fines fined under the 2006 Guidelines, two standards of comparison are developed: previous EC decisions and comparable U.S. DOJ decisions. For the comparative cartel decisions affected sales estimates are often derived from official documents, but trade and academic sources are also used where reasonably precise.[28]

The median affected-sales severity of EC final fines on the 22 cartels under the 2006 Guidelines was 14.3% (Table 2). Within the EC decisions under both Guidelines, median severity was virtually unchanged from the base period 1999-2006 (7.7%) to the years 2007-2011 (7.5%) (Table 4). However, if one compares severity of the 22 cartel fines under the 2006 Guidelines with the 16 cartel fines under the old guidelines, the new guidelines produce much more severe fines. For the 16 cartels sanctioned under the 1998 Guidelines during 2007-2011, the median severity was 4.68% of EU affected sales. *Thus, the new 2006 Guidelines produced hard-core cartel fines that were more than three times as severe as comparable fines imposed under the 1998 Guidelines.*[29]

How do trends in EC severity compare to those imposed by U.S. courts? From the base period 1999-2006, median affected-sales severity rose by 32% (Table 4). By contrast, the trend in EC fine severity is basically flat. The increase in severity brought about by adopting new guidelines kept the 2007-2011 severity from falling.

A final benchmark for EC changes in cartel-fines severity is the policy regime instilled by the Competition Commissioner. Previous research shows that, after accounting for variation in market characteristics and cartel conducts, cartel fines during the Kroes commissio-nership were significantly higher than those of previous commissioners (Connor and Miller 2010). An examination of the six decisions made under the 2006 guidelines under the leadership of Commissioner Almunia shows that severity has declined by more than 50% compared to the 16 decisions under Commissioner Kroes. While the first 18 months of his leadership may not be indicative of the entire five-year appointment, Almunia does seem to be off to a cautious start.[30]

5. Firm-Level Severity of Fines

So far I have examined severity of fines of the 22 cartels as observations, but severity varies considerably across the corporate participants of a cartel. In this section I analyze severity of 124 individual violators' fines. The great majority of the EC's published decisions main-tain corporate secrecy by suppressing defendants' affected sales or precise market shares.[31] However, computing the affected sales of convicted corporations was made feasible by the transparent formula applied by the Commission in most cases decided under the 2006 Guidelines.[32]

The 45 defendants (36% of the sample) with the most severe cartel fines—100% of annual global sales or more—are shown in Table 5.[33] Or these top 45 firms, median severity is 190% of annual sales. Three infringers—all in *Marine Hose*—display an unprecedented 500% to 650% this measure of severity. Of the remaining 79 companies, median fine/annual sales ratios are 44%. If one assumes that competitive profits are generally less than 25% of sales, the great majority of these defendants face full disgorgement, i.e., they are being required to pay fines from more than one year's future profits in the relevant line of business (or sell assets to pay the fines).[34]

The severity of fines is far lower when measured by total affected sales. For all 128 firms, the more conventional indicator of severity is two-thirds lower than the one based on annual global sales (Table 5). From this multi-year perspective, the burden of cartel fines seems more bearable. The median average duration of collusion was 5.5 years and defendants are frequently allowed to repay in five-year installments. Thus, a competitive profit rate of 20% of sales would be sufficient to generate repayment of a median fine.

6. Aggravating Factors: Recidivism Penalties

The 2006 Guidelines were remarkable for what promised to be more severe fines for repeat price-fixing offenders under EU competition law or the competition laws of the Member States. Wils (2007), in his discussion of "repeated infringements"[35] identified them as a "particularly important" indicator of gravity in setting fines (pp. 21-28). The 2006 Guide-lines specified a maximum 100% boost in the basic amount for *each* prior infringement.[36] Indeed, of all the possible aggravating factors, recidivism is in practice almost the only one with large upward adjustments.[37]

However, the Guidelines offer only a few specifics on how to count repeated previous in-fringements. Under the 2006 guidelines, any previous decision for a "similar infringement" under Articles 101 and 102 of the Treaty on the Functioning of the European Union (TFEU) by either the EC or by the EU NCAs counts as a repeated infringement (ibid. pp. 23-27).[38] All previous price-fixing infringements are similar to a price-fixing infringement under current consideration. Affiliates under common ownership and control of a single group have their infringements summed. Beyond these two rules, counting instances of recidivism is discretionary.

There are some ambiguities in EC rules for counting previous EU infringements. One would expect that all price-fixing infringements from EC decisions that resulted in fines in the past decade or two would be penalized, but this rule is not specified. There is no absolute time limit (other than 1966, the year of the first adverse EC decision on price fixing[39]), but the EC has discretion to ignore old decisions.[40] Contemporaneous infringements, i.e., those that began before a previous decision date and overlapped with a second violation, apparently do not count (Wils 2007: 26). Decisions of the EU's National Competition Authorities (NCAs) ought to be added to the count, but here too the Commission has discretion.[41] It is not clear whether previous violations that resulted in amnesty ought to be counted, nor whether two subsidiaries of an addressee convicted for the same cartel violation are counted twice. Transparency demands that these details be known to the business and legal communities.

In its first five years of applying the 2006 Guidelines, the EC has been cautious and perhaps inconsistent in applying extra penalties for recidivism. Out of 124 firms in the sample, 14 (1%) were identified and penalized as recidivists (Table 7). Penalty uplifts ranged from 50% to 100% and averaged 61%. Under the 1998 Guidelines the recidivism penalty was almost always 50% (Wils 2007: 23), so the average recidivism penalty has increased only 11 percentage points under the 2006 fining guidelines. A member of the Competition Commissioner's Cabinet agrees:

> ". . . the Commission has not made full use of the possibilities offered by its 2006 Fining Guidelines, increasing in practice fines by 50 % in case of one prior infringement, 60 % in case of two prior infringements, 90 % in case of three prior infringements, and 100 % in case of four prior infringements. The Commission has thus stayed relatively close to its practice preceding the 2006 Fining Guidelines . . ." (Wils 2012: 16).

Additional evidence of caution by the Commission in applying the recidivism penalty is contained in Table 7. The 14 recidivists (11 unique firms) were penalized a total of 885 percentage points for their involvement in 26 previous infringements cited in the EC decisions. Imposing an average of 34 points per previous infringement is less severe than the Commission's previous practice of adding 50 points per violation. In addition, for these 14 violations I have found from 58 to 62 previous EC violations by these 14 companies that met EU definitions and should have been counted as instances of recidivism. That is, the EC could have added a maximum of 58,000 to 62,000 percentage points added to the basic amounts of the recidivists' fines. Finally, the Commission has ignored all hard-core cartel decisions against these 14 recidivists by the EU NCAs. By my reckoning, fine enhancements of up to 43,000 more percentage points could have been added by counting qualifying cartel decisions by EU NCAs. Unless the Commission was unaware of 75 or more previous convictions in the EU, these data show an inexplicable reticence in applying the Guidelines.[42] One wonders whether such a severe undercounting is an unannounced policy or simply the result of poor record-keeping by the Commission.

To be more concrete, let us examine two examples. The first violator to receive an extra recidivism penalty was ENI in the *Chloroprene Rubber* decision of December 5, 2007. The EC decision cites *Polypropylene* and *PVC II* as the two previous violations that were decided on April 23, 1986 and July 27, 1994, respectively. For the two previous infringements, ENI had its fine raised by 60% (30 percentage points per violation). The Commission ignored its *Butyl Rubber* decision of November 29, 2006, which clearly qualifies under EC practice. In addition, ENI was previously convicted of price fixing in four EU NCA decisions: *Gasoline* (Italy 1999), *Gasoline* (Czech Republic 2002), *Diesel Fuel* (Italy 2003), and *Aviation Fuel* (Italy 2004). Thus, ENI was guilty of three to seven previous EU violations, not just two. A second example is the 90% penalty enhancement imposed on both Akzo in the *Plastic Tin Heat Stabilizers* cartel decision of November 11, 2011. The EC decision cites three former EC infringements, but I have located an additional seven or eight EC convictions plus one Italian conviction of Akzo and its subsidiaries.

A proportional application of the guidelines might be expected to result in roughly equal percentage penalties for each prior EU price-fixing violation, as was the EC's practice under the 1998 Guidelines. To do otherwise is to require the Commission to discriminate across prior violations for hard-core price fixing and assign them to different classes of gravity. Using the number of prior violations listed in the decisions, the Commission has so far applied from 25% to 50% extra for each *cited* additional infringement, which may be low but is at least an acceptably narrow, predictable range (Table 7). However, when one adds other appropriate but uncited violations, the mean average recidivism penalty is six to ten percentage points per violation.

7. Mitigating Factors

The Commission more often grants mitigating reductions than it does aggravating increases. Of the 128 violators in the sample, only 16 (13%) received fine reductions for attenuating circumstances, including settlement incentives. Under the 1998 Guidelines, 20% of all cartelists had their fines attenuated (Veljanovski 2010: 10). The reductions ranged from 5% to 70% per firm, but counting cartelists with no reductions, the mean average was 2.7% of affected sales. By far the most important mitigation factor was the (erroneous) belief by cartelists in the *Banana 1 and 2* cases that they had government approval for price fixing conduct. The rest of the reductions were almost evenly spread across three factors: non-cooperation for the full duration of the cartel, agreeing to settlement, and extraordinary cooperation with the Commission's prosecution.

8. Impact of the Leniency Program

A general issue in setting appropriate fines for cartels is the impact of leniency awards on deterrence. The presence of an effective leniency program in a given jurisdiction destabilizes existing cartels by raising discovery rates, but also has an effect on the beginning of the violation. Legal-economic theory of deterrence of crimes holds that the decision of a firm to form an illegal cartel or to join an existing cartel requires the firm to form a conjecture about the size of monetary penalties that it will be required to pay should the cartel be discovered in the future. Little is known about how this expectation is formed, but presumably rational would-be criminals look at existing penalties being paid by those criminals that were caught and punished for comparable crimes.[43] *Ceteris paribus*, the higher is the expected future penalty, the lower is the number of newly established cartels.[44] Deterrence is improved. Conversely, the lower the expected penalties if caught, the greater the number of cartel formations. Deterrence worsens. Thus, overly generous leniency rewards (discounts on the fine that otherwise would be paid) can undermine the benefits of leniency programs.

The operation of the 2006 EC Guidelines offer a uniquely detailed insight into the impact of leniency on cartel fines, because the formulas employed to calculate fines reveal the affected sales of individual infringers. Prior to the application of the new guidelines, most published decisions did not reveal either total cartel affected sales or the market shares of the cartel participants. Without both types of data, precise calculations of individual participants' affected sales are not possible from the decisions themselves. To derive estimates would require external sales or share data of dubious precision.

First, leniency is offered to one or more cartelists in almost all EC decisions. In *MEGAL Gas Pipeline* no leniency was offered, but in the remaining 21 cartels (95%) there was at least one recipient, which is higher than the rate than previously (id. 14). A total of 53 cartelists (41%) were leniency-discount recipients (of which 16 were for 100%), which is a slightly lower proportion than previously (id.) Second, leniency concessions reduce fines considerably. On average post-leniency cartel fines were 33% to 35% lower than the pre-leniency fines (those that would have been imposed, absent the rewards due to the Leniency Program).[45] By comparison, a careful analysis of 56 cartel decisions made under the EC's 1998 Guidelines finds that leniency discounts caused pre-leniency fines to decline by 36.3% (Veljanovski 2009: 8). Therefore, so far, Commission leniency discounts under the 2006 Guidelines have been similar to those under the 1998 Guidelines. Third, the range in leniency discounts is quite wide. The most extreme cases are: *Washing Powder* (69% fine reduction) and *Sodium Chlorate* (61%) on the high side and *Marine Hose* (11%) on the low side.

The EC is on the record that the purpose of the 2006 Guidelines is to serve general deterrence. An optimal degree of leniency is difficult to determine. Outsiders are in no position to second-guess the appropriateness of particular leniency decisions, because assessing the "value added" of various proffers of inculpatory information by leniency applicants would require access to all the files on the case.

9. The 10%-of-Sales Upper Limit

The Commission is not permitted to impose fines that exceed 10% of an infringer's global sales[46] in the year prior to the decision. This rule has been in effect and unchanged since 1960. So, one issue is whether the EC's more severe fines are causing the 10% cap to be reached more frequently. If that is the case, it could imply that this half-century-old rule ought to be revisited.

Commission final decisions frequently withhold the identity and size of ability-to-pay discounts.[47] However, our "reverse-engineering" method yields reliable inferences for the missing data. For the 128 cartelists fined under the 2006 Guidelines in 2007-2011, only 8% had their fines reduced by the cap. The average reduction was 53%. The ratio was slightly above 9% for the cartel participants fined under the 1998 Guidelines. Therefore, so far the new guidelines and world financial crisis have not required the use of the 10% cap with any greater frequency than formerly.

V. Conclusions

Looking at absolute fines alone reveals nothing about severity. Severity of fines in this paper is measured by dividing by two values: by the annual global sales in the relevant market and by total affected cartel sales in the EU. Both measures show high variation across cartels and cartel participants. Applying a formula to the 128 defendants that have been fined under the new guidelines, I find that the medial severity is 80%, but 45 (36%) of them displayed annual-sales severities above 100%. Three firms in *Marine Hose* ranged as high as 500% to 650% of affected sales—possible (but rare) examples of supra-deterrence. EC fines regularly disgorge the monopoly profits accumulated by most cartelists. However, the more conventional index of severity shows that median fines were only 26% of affected sales.

The average affected-sales severity of EC cartel fines rose considerably under the 2006 Guidelines. The new fines were about two times higher than those issued under the 1998 Guidelines. Yet, EC severity and they were slightly less severe than those imposed by the U.S. DOJ during 2007-2011. Looking at the trend in severity between the Kroes and Almunia regimes, fine severity under the 2006 Guidelines fell by more than 50%.

Increases in severity under the new Guidelines have been held back by low starting-point percentages and generous applications leniency discounts. Nearly all 2007-2011 cartel decisions have rewarded one or more participant with full or partial leniency. However, there is no evidence that leniency discounts have led to larger percentage reductions in EC cartel fines than under the 1998 Guidelines. Indeed, the average leniency discount per cartelist has declined. Moreover, the share of defendants requiring reductions under the Commission's 10% cap or ability-to-pay considerations has not risen.

The EC needs to revisit its policy with regard to recidivism uplifts. The frequency and size of recidivism discounts has declined markedly under the new Guidelines—the opposite of what was intended. There is ample evidence that the Commission has been overly cautious and inconsistent in applying recidivism penalties under the 2006 Guidelines. Not only has the EC been more lenient in its choice of percentage discounts, but it has ignored many numerous previous EU violations, including all appropriate decisions of the EU National Competition Authorities. The result has been millions of euros lower fines from missing recidivism enhancements and possible adverse effects on cartel deterrence.

REFERENCES

Almunia, Joaquín. *Antitrust Anforcement: Challenges Old and New*. Speech at the 19th International Competition Law Forum, St. Gallen (June 8, 2012).

Bryant, Peter J., and E. Woodward Eckard, Jr. "The Probability of Price Fixing: Evidence From Stock Market Reaction to Federal Indictments." *The Review of Economics and Statistics* 73 (May 1991): 309-317.

Camilli, Enrico Leonardo. "Optimal and Actual Fines in Cartel Cases: The European Challenge." Paper presented at the Amsterdam Center for Law and Economics Conference *Remedies and Sanctions in Competition Policy*. Amsterdam (17-18 February 2005). [Available at http://www.kernbureau.uva.nl/acle/object.cfm/objectid=F07DE744-C1D1-4F2E-876EEB31F7FA5B9F]

_____. "Optimal Fines in Cartel Cases and the Actual EC Fining Policy." *World Competition* 29 (2006): 575- 605.

Connor, John M. "Price-Fixing Overcharges: Legal and Economic Evidence." Chapter 4, pp. 59-153 in John B. Kirkwood (editor), Volume 22 of *Research in Law and Economics*. Oxford, Amsterdam and San Diego: Elsevier (January 2007).

_____. "Global Antitrust Prosecutions of International Cartels: Focus on Asia." *World Competition* 31 (December 2008): 575-605.

_____. *Cartels & Antitrust Portrayed: Private International Cartels from 1990 to 2008: AAI Working Paper #09-06*. (August 31, 2009). [Available at http://ssrn.com/abstract=1467310]

_____. *Price Fixing Overcharges: Revised 2nd Edition: SSRN Working Paper* (April 27, 2010). [Available at SSRN: http://ssrn.com/abstract=1610262]

_____. *Private International Cartels Spreadsheet*, prepared by the author (August 2012).

Connor, John M., and Douglas Miller. Determinants of EC Antitrust Fines of Corporate Participants of Global Cartels. (manuscript under journal review available from author).

European Commission. *Guidelines on the method of setting fines imposed pursuant to Article 23(2)(a) of Regulation No 1/2003* [2006] Official Journal C210/2.

_____. *Commission Decision of 20 November 2007 relating to a proceeding under Article 81 of the EC Treaty and Article 53 of the EEA Agreement: Case COMP/38.432 – Professional Videotape* (C(2007)5469 final). Brussels: European Commission (11/20/2007). [Available at http://ec.europa.eu/competition/antitrust/cases/decisions/38432/en.pdf]

Harding, Christopher, and Julian Joshua. *Regulating Cartels in Europe: A Study of Legal Control of Corporate Delinquency*. New York: Oxford University Press (2003).

Joshua, Julian M., and Peter D Camesasca. "EC fining policy against cartels after the *Lysine* rulings: the subtle secrets of x." *Global Competition Review* (2004). [Available at http://howrey.info/docs/ECfiningCartel.pdf]

Motta, Massimo. "On Cartel Deterrence and Fines in the European Union." *European Competition Law Review* 29 (2008): 209-220.

Spagnolo, Giancarlo. "Leniency and Whistleblowers in Antitrust." Prepared for P. Buccirossi (Ed.), *Handbook of Antitrust Economics*. Cambridge, Mass.: MIT Press (2008). [Available at http://www.cepr.org/meets/wkcn/6/6641/papers/spagnolo.pdf]

Veljanovski, Cento. *European Commission Cartel Prosecutions and Fines, 1998-2009 – An Updated Statistical Analysis of Fines under the 1998 Penalty Guidelines*. (March 3, 2009, revised version November 21, 2010). [Available at http://ssrn.com/abstract=1016014]

_____. *European Cartel Fines under the 2006 Penalty Guidelines: A Statistical Analysis*. (December 10, 2010a). [Available http://ssrn.com/ abstract=1723843]

Has the European Commission Become More Severe in Punishing Cartels?
Effects of the 2006 Guidelines: Revision

Gregory J. Werden, Gregory J., Scott D. Hammond, and Belinda A. Barnett. *Recidivism Eliminated: Cartel Enforcement in the United States Since 1999*. Speech at the Georgetown Global Antitrust Enforcement Symposium, Washington, D.C. (September 22, 2011). [Available at http://www.justice.gov/atr/public/speeches/275388.pdf]

Wils, Wouter P. J. "The Commission's New Method for Calculating Fines in Antitrust Cases." *European Law Review* 23 (1998): 252-263.

_____. "Is Criminalization of EU Competition Law the Answer?" *World Competition* 28 (June 2005): 117-159.

_____. "Optimal Antitrust Fines: Theory and Practice." *World Competition* 29 (2006): 183-208.

_____. "The European Commission's 2006 Guidelines on Antitrust Fines: A Legal and Economic Analysis." *World Competition: Law and Economics Review* 30 (June 2007). [Available at SSRN: http://ssrn.com/abstract=962654]

_____. "Recidivism in EU Antitrust Enforcement: A Legal and Economic Analysis." *World Competition* 35 (March 2012).

Table 1. Sample of EC Cartel Decisions, by Date of Decision, 2007-2011.

Cartel Name	Number of Companies [a]	Date of Investigation [b]	Date of Decision	Decision Time
				Years
Professional Videotape	3	5/28/2002	11/20/2007	5.48
Flat Glass	4	2/22/2005	11/28/2007	2.77
Chloroprene Synthetic Rubber	6	3/27/2003	12/5/2007	4.69
Nitrile Butadiene Synthetic Rubber	2	3/27/2003	1/23/2008	4.82
International Removal Services	11	9/16/2003	3/11/2008	4.49
Sodium Chlorate	4	9/10/2004	6/11/2008	3.75
Aluminum Flouride	4	3/2005	6/25/2008	3.32
Paraffin Wax	10	5/2/2005	10/1/2008	3.41
Bananas 1 (No. EU)	3	6/2/2005	10/15/2008	3.37
Car Glass	4	2/22/2005	11/12/2008	3.72
Marine Hose	6	5/2/2007	1/28/2009	1.74
MEGAL Gas Pipeline	2	5/16/2006	7/8/2009	3.14
Calcium Carbide	8	1/16/2007	7/22/2009	2.52
Power Transformers	7	2/7/2007	10/7/2009	2.67
Plastic Additives: Tin Heat Stabilizers	8	2/12/2003	11/11/2009	6.75
Plastic Additives: Epoxidized Soy Oil Stabilizers	8	2/12/2003	11/11/2009	6.75
Steel, pre-stressed	17	9/2002	6/30/2010	7.83
Animal Feed Phosphates	5	11/28/2003	7/20/2010	6.64
LCDs TFT Type	6	NA	12/8/2010	NA
Detergent («Washing Powder»)	3	6/2008	4/13/2011	2.87
Bananas 2 (So. EU)	2	11/28/2007	10/12/2011	3.87
Glass for Cathode ray Tubes	4	3/2009	10/19/2011	2.64
Total: 22 cartels	128			
Average				4.15

NA = Not available
a) Number of ultimate parents; the number of addressees may be larger.
b) The date on which the first amnesty application received or a request for information was sent.

Table 4. Median Severity of EC and U.S. DOJ Cartel Fines Compared, Affected Sales Basis, 1999-2011.

Decision Date [a]	Number of Cartels in the Decisions [b]		Median Severity of Fines		Relative Severity of EC to DOJ Fines
	EC, All Guidelines	U.S. DOJ [c]	EC	U.S. DOJ [c]	
			Percent		Ratio
2011	4	6	2.0	0.46	23.0
2010	6	3	2.8	16.1	0.17
2009	7	5	8.7	22.7	0.38
2008	9	6	13.4	23.5	0.57
2007	12	6	8.0	43.4	0.18
2006	6	4	6.7	15.5	0.43
2005	6	3	9.7	9.1	1.07
2004	8	5	17.5	13.5	1.30
2003	6	6	1.7	5.7	0.30
2002	9	5	4.1	5.7	0.72
2001	15	2	9.0 [d]	NA	--

2000	2	5	9.1	43.7	0.21
1999	3	13	0.26	15.8 d	0.02
1999-2006	65	43	7.7	12.7	0.61
2007-2011	32	26	7.5	16.7	0.45
2007-2011 New 2006 Guidelines	22	--	14.3 e	--	--

Source: Private International Cartels spreadsheet (Connor 2012).
a) All members of cartels are fined simultaneously by the EC. However, as the DOJ fines cartel participants sequentially, the date is the year that the first company in the cartel pleads guilty.
b) The number of cartels fined may exceed the number of observations used to calculate the medians because of availability of affected sales data. Non-monetary-penalty decisions are omitted. Some decisions (e.g., *Vitamins* in 2001) refer to multiple cartels.
c) International cartels only; year is date first member of cartel is sanctioned. The number of U.S. severity ratios computed from affected sales data from plea agreements is small (30). There are 58 observations that use industry trade sources for the sales data; these have a mean severity of 12.4% and a median severity of 4.4%.
d) Dominated by Vitamins cartels.
e) Median whole-cartel fine under the 2006 Guidelines seen in 3rd column of Table 3.

Table 5. Highest Known EC Corporate Cartels' Severities, Two Sales Bases Compared, 2006 Guidelines.

Cartel	Subsidiary/ Ultimate Parent	Final Fine	Global Annual Sales Severity	Affected Sales Severity
		€ million	*Percent*	*Percent*
Marine hose	Bridgestone Corp.	58.500	650.00	75.58
Marine hose	Parker ITR Srl	25.610	650.00	75.58
Phosphates, animal feed	FMC	14.400	612.00	55.74
Plastic additives: tin heat stabilizers for PVC	Ackros Chemicals/Akzo Nobel NV	21.800	585.20	74.29
Phosphates, animal feed	Timab Industries	59.850	581.40	52.96
Phosphates, animal feed	Ercros Industrial SA	14.850	550.80	50.17
Marine hose	Trelleborg Industrie	24.500	500.00	58.14
Polychloroprene syn. Rubber (PCP)	Syndial Spa/Enichem SpA/ENI	132.160	468.16	77.34
Phosphates, animal feed	Jose de Mello/Quimitecnica	1.751	459.00	41.81
Paraffin wax (a/k/a Candle Wax)	Total SA	128.163	416.50	56.39
Paraffin wax (a/k/a Candle Wax)	Exxon Mobil BVBA	83.588	406.88	58.57
Plastic additives: epoxidized soy oil stabilizers for PVC	Ackros Chemicals/Akzo Nobel NV	18.800	377.25	63.83
Moving and storage, Belgium-Intl., EU	Ziegler	9.200	340.00	39.53
Sodium chlorate	Atochem and Elf Aquitaine/Total SA	59.020	296.40	72.38
Paraffin wax (a/k/a Candle Wax)	MOL	23.700	252.00	34.12
Phosphates, animal feed	Tessanderlo Chemie	83.752	244.80	22.30
Paraffin wax (a/k/a Candle Wax)	RWE	37.440	231.00	35.87
Marine hose	Dunlop Oil & Marine Limited	18.000	225.00	39.71
Plastic additives: tin heat stabilizers for PVC	Elementis UK (f/k/a Harcros Chemical)	16.834	220.00	31.47
Polychloroprene syn. Rubber (PCP)	Denka Seiken	47.000	209.00	34.53
Moving and storage, Belgium-Intl., EU	Gosselin	4.500	204.00	30.05
Plastic additives: tin heat stabilizers for PVC	Ciba Geigy	61.320	204.00	27.79
Plastic additives: epoxidized soy oil stabilizers for PVC	Chemson/Metallgesellschaft AG/ GEA Group	3.802	190.00	28.77
Paraffin wax (a/k/a Candle Wax)	Repsol	19.800	186.30	28.24
Paraffin wax (a/k/a Candle Wax)	Sasol Wax GmbH/Sasol	318.200	183.75	24.88
Paraffin wax (a/k/a Candle Wax)	ENI	29.120	181.44	59.01
Moving and storage, Belgium-Intl., EU	Coppens	0.104	176.81	26.04
Paraffin wax (a/k/a Candle Wax)	Tudapetrol	12.000	171.00	29.18

Marine hose	Manuli Rubber industry	4.900	157.50	27.80
Polychloroprene syn. Rubber (PCP)	Du Pont Dow Elastomers/E I Du Pont	37.125	156.75	25.90
Glass, auto (Carglass)	Saint-Gobain	896.000	153.60	37.51
Plastic additives: epoxidized soy oil stabilizers for PVC	Elementis UK (f/k/a Harcros Chemical)	15.741	152.00	29.14
Plastic additives: epoxidized soy oil stabilizers for PVC	AC Treuhand	0.174	152.00	29.14
Moving and storage, Belgium-Intl., EU	Exel	8.900	144.50	26.50
Plastic additives: tin heat stabilizers for PVC	AC Treuhand	0.174	140.00	29.88
Moving and storage, Belgium-Intl., EU	Team Relocations	3.490	136.00	26.22
Polychloroprene syn. Rubber (PCP)	Du Pont Dow Elastomers/Dow Chemical	26.550	129.11	26.39
Steel, prestressed	Austria Draht/Voestalpine Stahl	22.000	120.83	27.86
Transformers, power	ABB Asea Brown Boveri	33.750	120.00	34.89
Plastic additives: epoxidized soy oil stabilizers for PVC	Ciba Geigy	7.104	114.00	21.85
MEGAL gas pipeline, DE + FR	E.ON AG	553.000	112.50	23.00
MEGAL gas pipeline, DE + FR	GDF Suez SA	553.000	112.50	23.00
Polychloroprene syn. Rubber (PCP)	Tosoh	4.800	104.50	17.26
Video tape, professional for TV	Sony Corp.	47.190	101.53	37.46
Steel, prestressed	Siderurgica Latina Martin (SLM)/ Ori Martin Group	15.956	100.58	22.64
MEDIAN	45 Highest Companies		190.00	31.47
MEDIAN	79 Lower Companies		44.0*	20.2*
MEDIAN	124 Companies		79.79*	25.74*
*= There are ten immunity recipients for which pre-leniency fines are used.				

Table 6. Severity of EC Cartel Fines, Almunia versus Predecessor, 2006 Fining Guidelines, 2007-2011.

Cartel Name	Date of Decision	Affected Cartel Sales	Fine/ Global Annual Sales	Fine/ Total Affected Sales
		$ million a	Percent	
Earlier Decisions:				
Professional Videotape	11/2007	537.0	20.4	23.8
Flat Glass	11/2007	3116.0	22.5	24.0
Chloroprene Synthetic Rubber	12/2007	2912.0	17.5	33.4
Nitrile Butadiene Synthetic Rubber	1/2008	307.3	16.1	23.0
International Removal Services	3/2008	568.0	22.2	12.3
Sodium Chlorate	6/2008	311.0	7.4	19.2
Aluminum Flouride	6/2008	27.3	16.8	20.3
Paraffin Wax	10/2008	7009.0	13.8	22.5
Bananas 1	10/2008	5987.0	1.0	3.3
Car Glass	11/2008	8501.0	20.7	22.4
Marine Hose	1/2009	659.0	22.7	30.7
MEGAL Gas Pipeline	7/2009	2023.0	76.0	76.0
Calcium Carbide	7/2009	533.0	16.2	22.2
Power Transformers	10/2009	686.0	14.7	22.3
Plastic Additives: Tin Heat Stabilizers	11/2009	1071.0	17.1	22.2
Plastic Additives: Epoxidized Soy Oil Stabilizers	11/2009	752.0	14.0	19.2
Almunia Decisions:				

Steel, pre-stressed	6/2010	21662.0	1.7b	1.4 b
Animal Feed Phosphates	7/2010	8165.0	3.5b	5.2 b
LCDs TFT Type	12/2010	13998.0	6.1	17.0
Detergent («Washing Powder»)*	2/2011	74100.0	0.6	1.9
Bananas 2 (So. EU)*	10/2011	503.0	2.4	3.2 b
Glass for Cathode ray Tubes*	10/2011	2029.0	0.9	1.2
Mean average of 16 earlier cartels			101.4	21.1
Median average of 16 earlier cartels			70.2	16.6
Mean average, 6 Almunia cartels			57.7	3.7
Median average, 6 Almunia cartels			31.9	2.6

*Summary decision is source, so not as accurate as other calculations.
a) Translated from euros on the day of the decision. No inflation adjustment. Ignores court appeals.
b) Projected EEA (or smaller appropriate region) affected sales with an adjustment for either the unrevealed sales or pre-leniency fine of an amnesty recipient. Future publication of the final decision may eliminate the need for estimation.

Table 7. Recidivism Penalties under the 2006 EC Fining Guidelines, 2007-2011, by Date of EC Decision and by Ending Date of Previous Collusion

Major Subsidiaries/ Parent Group	Cartel	Decision, Infringement Dates	Previous EC, EU NCA, or Other Infringements: Cartel and Decision Date b (M/D/Y)	Collusive Period for Likely or Possible Previous Infringements c	Added Penalty	Comment
					Pct.	
ENI	Chloroprene (PCP) Rubber	12/5/07 5/13/93-5/13/02	Polypropylene (EC)—4/23/86 PVC Plastic (EC)—7/27/94 Diesel fuel (Italy)—3/6/03 Gasoline (Italy)—10/14/99 Aviation fuel (Italy)—12/17/04 Gasoline (Czech)—7/10/02 EPDM (US)—4/18/05 Butyl Rubber (EC)—11/29/06 Nigeria LNG (US)—7/19/10 Paraffin wax (EC)—10/1/08 Gasoline (Romania)—1/10/12	6/1977-11/1983 8/1980-7/1984 1991-1998 1/1994-6/2000 1990-2000 1/2001-12/2001 1/1996-10/2002 5/20/1996-11/28/2002 1995-2004 2/21/2002-4/28/2005 ?/2006-?/2006	60	Two previous EC violations by ENI mentioned in Decision: *Polypropylene* and *PVC II*; I find three violations in EC decided before 12/5/07 and four in NCAs. Two US cartels overlapped.
Bayer	Chloroprene (PCP) Rubber	12/5/07 3/13/93-5/13/02	Insecticides (CA)—6/3/93 BT insecticide (CA)—6/3/93 X-Ray film (US)—8/7/98 Radiological media (IT)—11/00 Citric Acid (EC+)—12/5/01 Diabetes tests (Italy)—4/30/03 Polyols polyester (US)—9/30/04 Diabetes tests (Portugal)—1/1/05 EPDM (US)—4/18/05 Diabetes tests 2 (PT)—10/13/05 Rubber Chem. (EC)—12/21/05 Polyols polyether (US)—8/06 Urethane (US)—11/17/06 Nitrile rubber (EC+)—12/5/07 Butyl Rubber (EC+)—11/29/06 NBR rubber (EC)—1/23/08 Pyrethroid (IBRD)—3/17/08 Pharmaceticals (RO)—3/19/12	1/1982-12/1988 10/1991-10/1992 1989-1993 1995-1999 2/1991-5/1995 1990-1/2001 1998-2002 1990-1/2001 1/1996-10/2002 7/2001-12/2004 1/1996-12/2001 1998-2002 1/1998-12/2004 10/2000-10-2002 5/20/1996-11/28/2002 10/9/2000- 10/30/2002 1999-2004 12/2008-3/2012	50	One previous EC violation mentioned in Decision: *Citric Acid*; I find three EC violations decided before 12/5/07 and one decided on same day in EC and five in NCAs

Bayer	Nitrile Rubber (NBR)	1/23/08 10/9/00-9/30/02	Insecticides (CA)—6/3/93 BT insecticide (CA)—6/3/93 X-Ray film (US)—8/7/98 Radiological media (IT)—11/00 Citric Acid (EC+)—12/5/01 Diabetes tests (Italy)—4/30/03 Polyols polyester (US)—9/30/04 Diabetes tests (Portugal)—1/1/05 EPDM (US)—4/18/05 Diabetes tests 2 (PT)—10/13/05 Rubber Chem. (EC)—12/21/05 Polyols polyether (US)—8/06 Urethane (US)—11/17/06 Butyl Rubber (EC+)—1/29/06 PCP Rubber (EC+)—1/23/08 Pyrethroid (IBRD)—3/17/08 Pharmaceticals (RO)—3/19/12	1/1982-12/1988 10/1991-10/1992 1989-1993 1995-1999 2/1991-5/1995 1990-1/2001 1998-2002 1990-1/2001 1/1996-10/2002 7/2001-12/2004 1/1996-12/2001 1998-2002 1/1998-12/2004 5/20/1996-11/28/2002 5/13/1993-5/13/2002 1999-2004 12/2008-3/2012	50	One previous EC violation mentioned in Decision: *Citric Acid*; I find three previous violations in EC and one same-day violation in EC and four in NCAs
Atochem or Arkema/ Total SA a	Sodium Chlorate	6/11/08 5/17/95- 2/9/00	Polypropylene (EC)—4/23/86 (1st subsidiary) Polypropylene (EC)—4/23/86 (2nd subsid.) Peroxygen products—2/7/85 PVC Plastic (EC)—7/27/94 Lease Oil (US)—5/10/99 Gasoline (Italy)—6/8/00 Gasoline (Spain)—6/5/01 Diesel (Italy)—3/6/03 Gasoline (France)—4/1/03 Organic Perox (EC)—12/10/03 Bitumen (Sweden)—12/15/04 Hydrogen Perox (EC)—5/3/06 Acrylic Glass (EC+)—5/31/06 Aviation fuel (IT)—6/20/06 Bitumen in NL (EC)—9/13/06 MCAA (EC)—1/19/06 Polypropylene (KR)—2/20/07 LPG (France)—3/2/07 Gasoline 2 (IT)—12/20/07 Polyethylene (KR)—12/26/07 Paraffin wax (EC)—10/1/08 Soda ash (ZA)—11/5/08 Aviation fuel (FR)—12/4/08 Gasoline 2 (ES)—7/31/09 Plastic additive (EC+)—11/11/09 Bitumen (ZA)—3/4/10 Petrol products (ZA)—10/12/11	6/1977-11/1983 6/1977-11/1983 1958-12/13/1980 1/1983-5/1984 1/1986-12/1993 1/1994-6/2000 10/1998-8/2001 1991-1998 1/1999-6/2002 1/1971-12/1997 1999-6/2003 1994-2001 1/23/1997-9/2002 2002-2003 4/1994-10/2002 1/1984-8/1999 4/1994-4/2005 5/2001-12/2005 2002-2008 4/1994-4/2005 9/3/1992-4/28/2005 1983-11/5/2008 2002-2003 2002-2008 1987-2000 2000-12/2009 2003-8/2008	90	Three previous EC violations mentioned in Decision: *Peroxygen Products*, *Polypropylene*, and *PVC*; I find eight or nine relevant prior decisions in EC and eight in NCAs
Shell International Petroleum/ Royal Dutch Shell	Candle Wax c	10/1/08 9/3/92-5/17/05	Polypropylene (EC)—4/23/86 Polyethylene (EC)—12/21/88 PVC plastic (EC)—7/27/94 Lease oil (US)—5/10/99 Gasoline (IT)—6/8/00 Gasoline (SE)—6/29/00 Gasoline (Czech)—9/16/02 Gasoline (FR)—4/1/03 Petroleum (IS)—1/29/05 LPG (BR)—9/27/05 Aviation fuel (IT)—6/20/06 Bitumen in NL (EC)—9/13/06 Butyl rubber (EC)—11/29/06 LPG gas (FR)—3/2/07 Petroleum (EL)—10/3/07 Gasoline 2 (IT)—12/20/07 Tobacco retail (UK)—7/11/08 Petroleum (GR)—11/29/08 Aviation fuel (FR)—12/4/08 Bitumen (ZA)—3/4/10 Petroleum (ZA)—10/12/11	6/1977-11/1983 9/1976-11/1984 10/1980-7/1984 1/1986-12/1993 1991-1998 1999-6/2003 1/2001-12/2001 1/1999-6/2002 1993-2003 2000-9/2002 1990-2000 4/1994-10-2002 1996-2002 2000-9/2002 ????-2007 12/2004-1/2007 3/1/2001-8/15/2003 2006-11/2008 2002-2003 2002-12/2009 2003-8/2008	60	Two previous EC violations mentioned in Decision: *Polypropylene* and "*PVC II*" *(LdPE Polyethylene)* ; I find five previous violations in EC and ten in NCAs

ENI	Candle Wax c	10/1/08 2/21/02-4/28/05	Polypropylene (EC)—4/23/86 PVC Plastic (EC)—7/24/94 Diesel fuel (Italy)—3/6/03 Gasoline (Italy)—10/14/99 Aviation fuel (Italy)—12/17/04 Gasoline (Czech)—7/10/02 EPDM (US)—4/18/05 Butyl Rubber (EC)—11/29/06 PCP rubber (EC+)—12/5/07 Nigeria LNG (US)—7/19/10 Gasoline (Romania)—1/10/12	6/1977-11/1983 10/1980-7/1984 1991-1998 1/1994-6/2000 1990-2000 1/2001-12/2001 1/1996-10/2002 5/20/1996-11/28/2002 3/13/1993-5/13/2002 1995-2004 ?/2006-?/2006	60	Two previous EC violations mentioned in Decision: *Polypropylene* and *PVC II*; I find four previous violations in EC and four in NCAs
Saint-Gobain	Car Glass	11/12/ 2008 3/10/98-3/11/03	Flat glass-Benelux (EC)—7/23/84 Flat glass-Italy (EC)—12/7/88 Abrasive grains (US)—5/8/97 Flat Glass 1 (EC+)—11/28/07 Glass, insulated (NL)—1/6/11	9/1/1978-10/9/1981 6/1/1983-4/10/1986 1/1985-12/1994 1/9/2004-2/22/2005 5/18/2004-9/15/2005	60	Two previous EC violations mentioned in Decision: *Flat Glass (Benelux)* and *Flat Glass (Italy)*; I find three previous violations in EC and none in NCAs
Degussa/ Evonik Industries AG/SKW AG (penalty on Degussa)	Calcium carbide	7/22/09 4/22/04-10/13/ 2006	Polypropylene (EC)—10/13/84 PVC Plastic (EC)—7/27/94 Vitamin B3 (US+)—3/1/99 Methionine (EC+)—7/2/02 Organic Perox (EC)—12/10/03 Organic Perox (EC)—12/10/03 (2nd subsidiary) Carbon Black (US)—1/07 Hydrogen Perox (EC+)—5/3/06* Acrylic Glass (EC)—5/31/06*	1979-11/1983 1/1983-5/1984 1/1992-3/1998 2/1986-2/1999 1/1/1971-12/31/1997 1/1/1971-12/31/1997 1/1999-11/2002 1994-2001 1/23/1997-9/2002	50	Decision mentions one previous violation (*Methionine*), but I find six or seven violations in EC and none in NCAs
Casco Carbide/ Akzo Nobel (penalty on Akzo)	Calcium carbide	7/22/09 11/3/04-10/13/ 2006	Choline Chloride No. Am. (US+)—3/29/99 Organic Perox (EC)—12/10/03* Sodium Gluconate (EC)—9/29/04 Choline Chloride Europe (EC+)—12/9/04 MCAA (EC+)—1/19/05 MCAA (US+) (2nd subsid.)—1/19/05 Pharmaceuticals (BR)—10/14/05 Rubber Chem. (EC+)—12/21/05* Hydrogen Perox (EC)—5/3/06 Auto paints (US)—1/8/07 Marine paints (IT)—2/9/07 Sodium Chlorate (EC)—6/11/08* Plastic stabilizer tin (EC+)—11/11/09 Plastic stabilizer soy (EC+)—11/11/09	1/1988-10/1998 1/1/1971-12/31/1997 2/1987-6/1995 11/1992-9/29/99 1/1984-8/1999 1/1984-8/1999 2002-2009 1/1996-12/2001 12/1994-2001 1/1993-12/2000 1/1999-12/2003 12/1994-1/2000 1987-2000 1/1990-2/12/2003	100	Decision mentions four previous violations (*Sodium Gluconate, Organic Peroxide, Choline Chloride (Europe)*, and *MCCA*); I find seven or eight violations in EC and one in an NCA.
ABB	Transfor-mers, electric power	10/7/ 2009 6/9/99-5/15/03	Hydro-electric power equipment (Norway)—5/99 Pre-Insulated Pipe (EC)—10/21/98 USAID contracts in Egypt (US) —8/18/00 Heating equip (Sweden)—7/7/03 Switchgear GIS (EC+)—1/24/07* Switchgear GIS-type (Czech)—2/12/07* Switchgear GIS-type (Hungary)—1/24/07* Switchgear GIS-type (Slovakia)—1/21/08* Switchgear, air insulated (Brazil)— pending Undersea cable (EC+)—amnesty pending	1990-1997 - 11/1990-6/1996 6/1998-9/1996 9/1996-9/2001 4/15/1988-3/2/2004 1/1988-3/2004 1/1998-5/2004 1/1988-5/2004 1985-3/2006 ?-2009	50	One previous EC violation mentioned in Decision: *Pre-Insulated Pipe*; I find seven or eight violations in EC and Y in NCAs; I find X continuing violations in EC and five in NCAs

Ackros Chemicals / Akzo Nobel NV	Plastic additives: tin heat stabilizers	11/11/2009 2/24/87-3/21/00	Polypropylene (EC)—10/13/84 PVC plastic (EC)—7/27/94 Choline Chloride No. Am. (US+)—3/29/99 Organic Perox. (EC)—12/10/03* Sodium Gluconate (EC)—9/29/04 Choline Chloride Europe (EC+)—12/9/04 MCAA (EC+)—1/19/05 MCAA (US+) (2nd subsid.)—1/19/05 Pharmaceuticals (BR)—10/14/05 Rubber Chem. (EC+)—12/21/05* Hydrogen Perox. (EC)—5/3/06 Auto paints (US)—1/8/07 Marine paints (IT)—2/9/07 Sodium Chlorate (EC)—6/11/08* Calcium carbide (EC)—7/22/09 Plastic additive soy (EC+)—1/11/09	1979-11/1983 10/1980-7/1984 1/1/1971-12/31/1997 2/1987-6/1995 11/1992-9/29/99 1/1984-8/1999 1/1984-8/1999 2002-2009 1/1996-12/2001 12/1994-2001 1/1993-12/2000 1/1999-12/2003 12/1994-1/2000 4/7/2004-1/16/2007 1/1990-2/12/2003	90	Three previous EC violations mentioned in Decision, *Peroxygen products*, *Polypropylene*, and *PVC*; I find ten or eleven violations in EC and one in NCAs
Trefil-union + Trefil-europe + Fontain-union + Unimetal + Emesa + Galycas + Usinor +Trefil-arbed + Arbed / Arcelor-Mittal SA	Steel, pre-stressing	6/30/10 1/1/84-9/19/2002 d	Stainless Steel (EC)—1/21/98 Steel Mesh (EC)—2/8/89 Steel Mesh (EC) (2nd subsidiary) 2/8/89 Steel Beams (EC)—11/8/06 Steel Beams (EC)—11/8/06 (re-adoption, 2nd subsidiary) Metal scrap (ZA)—4/7/08 Steel Distrib. (FR)—12/16/08 Steel (Turkey)—6/19/09 Steel rebars (ZA)—9/1/09 Steel tinplate (ZA)—pending	12/1993-11/1996 1981-11/1955 1981-11/1955 7/1/1988-12/1990 7/1/1988-12/1990 1998-7/23/2007 6/1999-6/2004 ????-2007 ????-2008 4/2009-10-20/2009	60	Previous EC violations of three current subsidiaries of ArcelorMittal mentioned in Decision: for Trefilunion in *Welded Steel Mesh*, for Fontainunion in *Welded Steel Mesh*, and for Unimetal in *Steel Beams*; I find four or five violations in EC and one in NCAs
DWK Drahtwerk Koeln/ Saarstahl	Steel, pre-stressing	6/30/10 2/9/94-11/6/01	Steel Beams (EC)—11/8/06	1/1984-12/1990	50	One previous EC violation mentioned in Decision: for Saarstahl AG in *Steel Beams*; I find one violation in EC and none in an NCA
14 Penalties on 11 Unique Violators	9 Cartels				885 percentage points	26 previous EC and zero NCA violations noted in EC decisions, but I find a total of 58 to 62 previous EC violations and 43 NCA violations

▨ = EC's decision.
▨ = NCA's decision.
= Possibly simultaneous cartel violation.
* = Guilty but received full amnesty.
a) Complex ownership and name changes before, during and after the cartel period.
b) EC decisions unless EU NCA or other antitrust authority listed in parentheses; EC+ means that other non-EU authorities also punished the global cartel. To save space, the jurisdiction is identified through its Internet address abbreviation.
c) Generally longest date proven in any jurisdiction, but EC date for EC infringements. Where there is uncertainty about the precise starting date, the author has used external information to hazard a date.
d) Duration is very difficult to determine because of multiple changes in ownership; ArcelorMittal's three major French subsidiaries (owned from 7/1/99) began colluding at various dates (1/1/84, 12/20/84, and 4/3/95) but all ended on 9/19/2002; its three major Spanish subsidiaries (owned from 2/18/2002) began on various dates (11/30/92, 15/15/92, and 4/2/95) but ended on 9/19/2002; and its two major Italian subsidiaries (owned from 12/15/92) began on 1/7/99 and ended on 9/19/2002. *See* Decision Recitals 701 to 733.

APPENDIX: DISCUSSION OF REVISIONS

Several adjustments were made to the data and the sample employed for this chapter. First, The present sample drops a couple of cartel decisions later found to have been based on the 1998 fining Notice (*Air Cargo, DRAMs and Rambus DRAMs*). Second, this chapter draws data from mostly final redacted EC cartel decisions. Three that were published during 2010-2011 were used to expand the sample (*Calcium Carbide, Flat Glass, and Paraffin Wax*). Some newly released final decisions permitted revisions of estimates formerly based on only brief summaries of decisions (*Aluminum Flouride, Animal Feed Phosphates, Detergents, LCD Panels, Tin Heat Stabilizers for PVC*, and *Epoxidized Soy Oil Stabilizers for PVC*). Third, three new decisions are added on the basis of preliminary information contained in summaries (*Glass CRT Tubes, Bananas 2, and Detergents*). In summary, I added six cartels to the data set (a net addition of four cartels). The additional years included permit an assessment of the Almunia commissionership relative to its predecessors. I also double-checked some data entries that readers thought were incorrect and expanded the number of internal consistency checks.

Second, this revision also extends and clarifies the concept of affected sales. There are two valid measures of severity of EC fines. In the 2010 law review, severity was calculated using *global annual* sales of the undertaking in the year before the EC decision was taken. In this chapter, I also calculate severity relative to the company's *total affected sales* for the duration of the cartelist's participation in the cartel.

Finally, preliminary responses are offered to criticisms of the original article. Many of the comments received concerned the previous findings on recidivism. Therefore, I expanded the discussion of recidivism discounts.

NOTES

*   This revision adds new information on EC cartel decisions posted by the European Commission from mid 2010 to the end of 2011. In addition, it addresses certain comments received from readers of my December 2010 SSRN Working Paper "Has the European Commission Become More Severe in Punishing Cartels? Effects of the 2006 Guidelines" and an article that appeared in the European Competition Law Review 1/2011: 27-36. Details of the changes made may be found in the Appendix.

1   The DOJ posts most of the sentencing memoranda of cartelists that have pleaded guilty to criminal price fixing. These memoranda almost always show how the defendant's fine range was calculated in accordance with federal Sentencing Guidelines, which start with the company's affected sales.

2   A previous analysis of the 2006 EC penalty guidelines does not examine severity of fines (*Veljanovski 2010a*). In an earlier analysis of the 1998 EC guidelines, *Veljanovski* (2010: 13-14) does calculate the ratio of fines relative to the global sales of infringers in a single year prior to the EC decision. He finds that the mean ratio is 2.7%. This information is relevant for assessing the average constraint of the EC's 10%-cap rule, but it is not fine severity in the usual sense. Veljanovski's approach understates severity of EC fines by dividing fines (that refer to periods averaging nine years) by firms' global sales for *one* year. Moreover, *Veljanovski* (2009: Figure 3) shows that a second crude measure of severity, the mean average EC final fine per firm, declined by 35% from 2007 to 2010. Our more appropriate measure of severity shows the opposite trend.

3   A few more decisions that were made later resulted from the 1996 Leniency Program, but still less than half of the immunity applications produced convictions.

4   In December 2006 the third Leniency Program came into force, but it was little changed from the Second Notice.

5   More precisely, the violator's last full year of collusive sales will be multiplied by the number of years, where the years are rounded up to the nearest half year. As noted by *Wils* (2006: 15), the EC before 2006 had imposed cartel fines in the range of 2% to 9% of the violator's global sales for one year only, the last year of the cartel's life. Under the 2006 revisions, a fine for a single-line firm *starts at* 15% of its affected sales in the last year of collusion multiplied by the years of duration of the cartel; for a typical five-year duration, the basic fine could be from 45% to 150% of affected sales in the final year of collusion, which is an enormous increase for a specialized firm. For diversified firms, the new sales method could be lower than the previous method.

6   The year is normally the last previous fiscal year's company's sales everywhere in the world of the relevant product. Thus, multinational firms will owe larger fines than otherwise comparable national firms.

7   Let affected sales be AS. Then, for a relatively "benign" five-year cartel the basic amount would be (0.15x5) AS+0.15AS = 0.90AS. For an especially injurious cartel, the basic amount can be (0.3x5)AS+0.25AS = 1.75AS.

8   The period of look-back for recidivism now extends to all adverse EC decisions; moreover, decisions of the Member States are now counted. The maximum 100% increase is to be multiplied for each occurrence of recidivism.

9   Note that cheating creates more profits for a firm than rigidly adhering to the cartel agreement.

10 Technically, both full immunity and partial leniency are handled under the 1998 or 2001 *Leniency Notices*, not the Guidelines themselves, but published decisions typically treat leniency simply as a penultimate step in the fine calculation.

11 There were two press releases prior to the decision, one confirming the raids and another dated March 20, 2007 announcing that a Statement of Objections was sent to alleged defendants in the cartel. Not all raids are confirmed by the EC. The mean average decision time in the sample of 22 cartels is 4.15 years.

12 The first 16 cartel decisions were made in the latter half of the Kroes Commissionership. Six cartels, beginning with *Prestressing Steel* in June 2010, have been sanctioned under the present Competition Commissioner Almunia. Three recent decisions (*Washing Powder, Exotic Fruits* (*"Bananas 2"*), and *Glass for CRTs*) should be regarded as preliminary because they are analyzed using incomplete data from summaries of the decisions.

13 These data have been collected in the Private International Cartels spreadsheet built and maintained by the author.

14 Pre-leniency fines are usually reported in the EC's press releases. However, for eight firms that received full immunity, no pre-leniency fine was reported and cannot be calculated.

15 The share of EU commerce controlled by the cartel requires judgment is six cases. My interpretation of this datum is 60% for *Aluminum Flouride*, 95% for *Transformers*, 90% for *Detergents*, 75% for *International Removal*, 80% for *Phosphates*, 95% for *CRT Glass*, and 50% for *Bananas 2*.

16 Affected sales can be computed from either the basic amount, adjusted basic amount, or final fine plus a few of the percentages mentioned above. There is no indication that the Commission adjusts reported nominal sales for inflation. Sales in euros are converted to dollars on the day of the decision, which means that they may be slightly overstated and severity understated.

17 When a data sample is skewed, the median is considered a more representative average figure than the mean. *Veljanovski* (2010) does not report medians, so 1998-2006 comparisons are not possible.

18 Undertakings may include consultancies and trade associations.

19 The standard variation of this severity index is 93.4 percentage points. Seven of the 22 cartel fines had severity exceeding 100% of global annual company sales.

20 That is, total fines divided by total affected sales.

21 Not shown in Table 2, the mean and median average individual cartelists' severities are 121.3% and 67.6% of sales, respectively.

22 The standard variation is 16.3 percentage points.

23 The second highest is *Sodium Chlorate* (40%), and there are four above 20%.

24 That is, total fines divided by total affected sales.

25 For comparisons with other authorities, *see* Connor (2009).

26 Pre-leniency fines were customarily published in the Commission's press releases, a practice that would seem to aid in cartel deterrence. However, in all four of the cartel decisions during the Almunia commissionership that immunized a defendant, beginning with *Steel Prestressing* in June 2009, the press releases no longer reveal the "but-for fine." Moreover, the three summary decisions and the one final decision posted by September 2012 also suppress the but-for fine. Only final fines are revealed. This new policy reduces transparency.

27 The correlation between fine severity and annual global company sales is -0.29; between severity and total affected sales the correlation is -0.31. Further research may discover whether the inverse relationship between severity and size is accounted for by some hidden factor other than size per se.

28 The source of these data is Connor (2012). In general, sales data derived from industry sources is larger than affected sales employed by the EC and DOJ for fining purposes. Industry sources include both affected sales and sales of fringe (non-participating) firms. Sales employed by antitrust authorities must survive possible appeals to higher courts, so curtailed product, geographic, and temporal definitions are applied. Thus, severity calculations using industry trade data generally understate severity.

29 If one compares the 22 cartel fines under the new 2006 Guidelines with the earlier 1999-2006 fines, the former are twice as severe as the latter (Table 4).

30 The median fine severity using the global-annual-sales basis fell from 70% under Kroes to 32% under Almunia. The median total-affected-sales measure fell from 16.6% to 2.6%. Six decisions is a rather small sample that could contain an unusually large number of low-impact cartels. Almunia has spoken little about cartel enforcement during his administration. In one speech, he noted the small number of cartel decisions and lower fines in decisions from mid-2010 to 2011 (Almunia 2012: 4).

31 Out of 21 cartel decisions, only three revealed exact firm-level affected sales.

32 I was able to compute precisely affected sales for 126 of the 134 firms. The missing firms were full amnesty recipients.

33 The 11 cartelists at the bottom of Table 5 received very generous leniency discounts from the EC; four were immunized. Without leniency, each would have paid fines greater than 100% of their affected sales.

34 Only 12 of the 112 (8%) defendants that were not immunized had an annual-sales ratio below 25%.

35 "The use by the Commission of the term "repeated infringement" rather than "recidivism" may have reflected a desire to distinguish EU antitrust enforcement from (hard-core) criminal law" (Wils 2011: note 14).

36 Out of 74 cartel decisions under the 1998 Guidelines up to 2006, 17 (23%) imposed recidivism penalties 28 participants; the penalty was almost always 50% (*Wils* 2007: 23).

37 Of the 94 cartelists in the sample with information about aggravating factors, 16 (17%) received extra penalties; 13 of the 16 were for recidivism. More firms (31 out of 94 or 33%) qualified for mitigating discount.

38 This formula excludes counting contemporaneous infringements or indeed any infringement that post-dates the adoption date of a previous infringement decision.

39 Harding and Joshua (2003:113-121) seem to identify a January 1966 EC decision against the *Noordwijks Cement Accoord* as the first well documented adverse cartel decision. The *Quinine* and *Dyestuffs* decisions of July 1969 were the first cartel decisions with fines imposed.

40 Wils (2012: 15) notes that some NCAs have imposed 10- or 15-year limits.

41 Indeed, *Connor and Miller* (2010) found statistical evidence that instances of recidivism *outside* the EU's jurisdiction raised EC fines on global cartels.

42 Table 7 also shows that these 14 recidivists are in many cases extending their cartel conduct to jurisdictions outside the EU.

43 That is, corporate price fixers in Europe would estimate their likely future EC fines by gathering information about recently fined cartelists, adjusting their own estimate according to the size of the cartel to be formed or joined. In addition, *ex ante*, the firm might take into account any long-term trends in the size of contemporaneous fines.

44 The actual relationship of leniency discounts to overall deterrence is more complicated. *See Spagnolo* (2008).

45 The leniency reduction is not yet available for eight amnestied cartelists. I suspect that when these are published, the average reduction will rise to 23% or 24%.

46 "Global sales" is the company's after-tax net revenues in all lines of business and all geographic regions.

47 In the 22-cartel sample, five were suppressed.

Enforcement under China's Anti-Monopoly Law: So Far, So Good?*

XIAOYE WANG

wangxiaoye88@yahoo.com.cn
Professor of Law, Hunan University

ADRIAN EMCH

adrian.emch@hoganlovells.com
Counsel, Hogan Lovells
Lecturer, IP School Peking University

Abstract

With the launch of the Opening-Up and Reform Policy in the late 1970's, China has undertaken the difficult transition from a planned economy to a market economy. In parallel with the significant economic reforms, China's legal system has been remodelled. The Anti-Monopoly Law is a key law in China's effort to lay out the legal framework for an effective market economy. Each of the three antitrust enforcement agencies in China has achieved progress, and private litigation in courts is evolving quickly. Nonetheless, as China's transition has not been completed, it is natural that antitrust enforcement encounters considerable challenges. The lawsuit against the General Administration of Quality Supervision, Inspection and Quarantine, the questions raised in relation to the *China Unicom/ China Netcom* merger and the issue in the *TravelSky* case illustrate some of these challenges. China should continue its efforts to increase the effectiveness of antitrust enforcement. In particular, it is necessary to raise the awareness in society about the concept of competition and the importance of competition policies, and to improve the authorities' antitrust enforcement capabilities.

In parallel with China's significant economic reforms, its legal system has developed at rapid pace in the recent past, particularly from the perspective of laying out the legal framework for an effective market economy. The Chinese government has enacted groundbreaking laws and regulations in the field of civil, business and economic law, and has put forward rules to safeguard freedom of contract, enforcement of rights and interests, and free competition—all of which are core principles of a market economy. To this end, laws such as the Company Law,[1] the Contract Law,[2] the Property Rights Law,[3] and, in 2007, the Anti-Monopoly Law ("AML")[4] have been enacted. But, unlike the Contract Law or the Property Rights Law, the AML does not rely on "individual autonomy" or "freedom of contract" as absolute principles, as present in general business and commercial law. Rather, the AML confers the government a right to intervene in the economy to oppose monopolies, protect competition, and safeguard the market economy. The AML stands for the idea that the marketplace is the best decision-maker for allocating resources. Hence, in China, the promulgation and implementation of the AML is a milestone in the process of China's economic reform.[5] Nonetheless, as China's current economic system is still in a transitional phase, it is natural that, in these early stages, antitrust enforcement encounters considerable challenges. As Kovacic and Winerman argued, there is an identifiable life cycle that characterizes the development of competition policy-making or that of an antitrust agency.[6]

I. Track Record by China's Antitrust Agencies So Far

Since the AML took effect in August 2008, the enforcement of the law has received much attention around the world. This is particularly true for the merger control arena. Many multinational companies have a considerable presence in China and, given that the merger filing thresholds in China are *inter alia* based on sales revenues generated within China, their mergers and acquisitions frequently trigger filings not only in Europe, the United States and elsewhere but also with the authorities in China. In addition, the parties to a merger often put approval by the Chinese authorities as a "condition precedent" to completion of the transaction. Against this background, it is not surprising that, apart from the antitrust regimes of the United States and the European Union, the AML is becoming one of the most influential antitrust laws in the world.

The pages that follow will give an overview of the progress achieved by each of the three antitrust enforcement agencies in China, as well as the situation of private litigation in courts.

1. The Ministry of Commerce

The Ministry of Commerce ("MOFCOM") has jurisdiction over the control of "concentrations between business operators" (as "mergers" in the antitrust sense are called in China). In September 2008, MOFCOM established its Anti-Monopoly Bureau, granting it power to receive notifications and review mergers. After the AML came into effect, the State Council enacted the Regulation on the Notification Thresholds for Concentrations between Business Operators,[7] and the Anti-Monopoly Commission under the State Council issued the Guidelines on the Definition of the Relevant Market.[8]

The remaining supporting legislation on merger control aspects was essentially drafted by MOFCOM's Anti-Monopoly Bureau. As such, the bureau released the Measures on the Calculation of Sales Revenues for the Notification of Concentrations between Business

Operators in the Financial Sector (together with other governmental bodies),[9] the Measures on the Notification of Concentrations between Business Operators,[10] the Measures on the Review of Concentrations between Business Operators,[11] the Provisional Regulation on the Divestiture of Assets or Businesses in Concentrations between Business Operators,[12] the Provisional Regulation on Assessing the Impact of Concentrations between Business Operators on Competition,[13] and so on.

From the AML's entry into force until early 2012, MOFCOM's Anti-Monopoly Bureau examined and completed the review of close to 400 merger filings, among which one transaction was prohibited, 11 transactions were approved conditionally, and the remaining transactions were approved unconditionally (and a few of filings were withdrawn by the parties). The percentage of unconditional clearances thus represents over 95% of the total filings reviewed and completed. By way of example, the mergers approved conditionally by MOFCOM in the latter half of 2011 include the acquisition of Savio Macchine Tessili by private equity fund Alpha V,[14] the establishment of the joint venture between General Electric and Shenhua,[15] Seagate's acquisition of the Samsung hard disk drive business[16] and, in February 2012, MOFCOM cleared the joint venture between Henkel and Tiande Chemical subject to conditions.[17] These cases demonstrate that even where MOFCOM believes a merger has significant negative effects on competition in the market, it may still be willing to grant approval so long as the parties can come up with a way to remove those effects. Naturally, there is room for improvement of when and how MOFCOM decides to impose remedies.[18]

Perhaps the MOFCOM decision, which aroused the most intense and widespread reaction, was the decision in 2009 to prohibit the acquisition of Huiyuan by Coca-Cola. The opinions on this case diverged and continue to diverge.[19] Some people think that this decision was made from the industrial policy perspective rather than to protect competition. In their view, the motive behind such a decision would be to protect national brands and domestic small and medium-sized enterprises.[20] Other people had a different opinion, arguing that this decision was made to protect competition in the market (even admitting that, as one of the first antitrust enforcement cases in China, the MOFCOM announcement was not transparent enough).[21] Those taking the view that the *Coca-Cola/Huiyuan* decision was exclusively based on antitrust grounds often point to the decision by the Australian Competition & Consumer Commission ("ACCC") in 2003. In that case, the ACCC prohibited the acquisition of Berri by Coca-Cola, and this case was based on facts similar to Coca-Cola's proposed acquisition of Huiyuan.[22]

A. The National Development and Reform Commission

The National Development and Reform Commission ("NDRC") is responsible for handling price-related antitrust offences, including monopoly agreements, abuses of dominance and administrative monopoly conduct related to pricing. NDRC's Price Supervision and Anti-Monopoly Bureau has jurisdiction for enforcing not only the AML, but also the Price Law.[23] In 2011, around 20 additional officials joined the Price Supervision and Anti-Monopoly Bureau to work on antitrust matters. This indicates the importance NDRC now attaches to antitrust enforcement.

NDRC has also been active on the normative front. In January 2011, it promulgated the Anti-Price Monopoly Regulation24 and the Regulation on the Administrative Law Enforcement Procedure for Anti-Price Monopoly.[25] These regulations are important tools for NDRC's enforcement of the AML.

In addition, in coordination with NDRC's local offices, the Price Supervision and Anti-Monopoly Bureau has handled more than ten cases including the tying by the salt companies in Hubei and Jiangsu, and sanctioned the cartel between rice noodle producers in

Nanning and Liuzhou and the price-fixing implemented through a paper industry association in Zhejiang.[26] Due to the limited experience at these early stages of antitrust enforcement under the AML, the basis for most of the above-mentioned investigations was the Price Law, promulgated in 1997.

In November 2011, however, the Price Supervision and Anti-Monopoly Bureau relied on the AML to impose heavy penalties on two pharmaceutical enterprises located in Weifang, Shangdong Province, confiscating the illegal gains and imposing fines in the amount of RMB 6,877,000 (around USD 1.1 million) and RMB 152,600 (around USD 24,000), respectively.[27] The agency held that the two enterprises had significantly raised the price of the raw materials necessary to produce compound reserpine tablets by way of entering into restrictive agreements with the only two domestic producers of those raw materials. The effect of the price rise led many pharmaceutical enterprises to suspend production of reserpine tablets, thereby inflicting significant harm upon consumers.

In a different development, on November 9, 2011, the nightly news program News30Minutes reported that NDRC was investigating potential abuses by China Telecom and China Unicom in the broadband sector. According to the statements made by an NDRC official, if the investigation were to bring to light clear evidence confirming the abuses, then a penalty in the range of hundreds of millions could be imposed upon the companies, in line with Article 47 of the AML.

Without a doubt, NDRC's investigations in the two above-mentioned cases (the *Reserpine* case and the *China Telecom/China Unicom* matter) have significantly raised the agency's profile as an antitrust enforcer. This is especially true for the investigation against the two state-owned telecommunications incumbents China Telecom and China Unicom, given the significant impact the case could have both in China and abroad. Whatever the conclusion of this case, NDRC's investigation conveys the message that the AML is not a "toothless tiger" when it comes to tackling state-owned enterprises with significant market power. If these enterprises were found to exclude or restrict competition by means of abusing their dominant position and thereby harming consumers, NDRC has indicated its willingness to sanction the companies according to the provisions of the AML.[28]

B. The State Administration for Industry and Commerce

In line with the State Council's directives, the State Administration for Industry and Commerce ("SAIC") is in charge of those antitrust cases that do not fall under the remit of MOFCOM and NDRC. In particular, SAIC's competence encompasses cases involving restrictive agreements, abuses of dominance and administrative monopoly conduct that are not related to pricing.

As it is generally hard to draw a clear line between pricing conduct and non-pricing conduct, there exists widespread concern among academics and practitioners about potential jurisdictional conflict between NDRC's and SAIC's antitrust enforcement. By way of example, in a cartel organized by the paper industry association in Fuyang, Zhejiang Province, investigated and sanctioned by NDRC, the anti-competitive conduct consisted both of price-fixing (i.e., "pricing conduct") and restriction of output (i.e., "conduct not related to pricing").[29] As far as we are aware, NDRC and SAIC have reached an agreement to coordinate their enforcement essentially on the basis of the "first come, first serve" principle: if one authority accepts a complaint, the other one will refuse to accept a complaint in the same case. In our view, in the longer run, this general and relatively simple principle may need to be replaced by a more detailed working arrangement between the two agencies that, ideally, should be made public to guide the conduct of market players.

Following the entry into force of the AML, SAIC has made substantial efforts to enact rules implementing the law in its field of jurisdiction. As such, it has promulgated the Regulation on the Procedure for the Handling of Cases Involving Monopoly Agreements and Abuses of a Dominant Market Position,[30] the Regulation on the Procedure for the Prevention of Conduct Abusing Administrative Power to Eliminate or Restrict Competition,[31] the Regulation on the Prohibition of Monopoly Agreement Conduct,[32] the Regulation on the Prohibition of Conducting Abusing a Dominant Market Position,[33] and the Regulation on the Prevention of Conduct Abusing Administrative Power to Eliminate or Restrict Competition.[34]

local office in Jiangsu—the Jiangsu Administration for Industry and Commerce ("AIC")—investigated a case involving a restrictive agreement executed by the construction material and machinery association in the city of Lianyungang. This was the first published case accepted and concluded by a local AIC. SAIC and the Jiangsu AIC confiscated illegal earnings of RMB 140,000 (approximately USD 22,000) and imposed a fine of RMB 730,000 (approximately USD 116,000) upon the association and five of its members.[35]

C. The Courts

Article 50 of the AML provides that "if a business operator implements monopolistic conduct and causes loss to others, it shall be responsible for civil liabilities in accordance with the law." Since the AML took effect, the courts have accepted more than 40 antitrust actions filed on the basis of this provision,[36] including *Zhou Ze v. China Mobile*,[37] *Tangshan Renren v. Baidu*,[38] *Sursen v. Shanda*,[39] *Li Fangping v. China Netcom*,[40] *Huzhou Yiting Termite Control Services v. Huzhou City Termite Control Research Institute*,[41] *Liu Dahua v. Hunan Huayuan Industrial*[42] and so on. The vast majority of court actions were abuse of dominance cases.[43] To the best of our knowledge, all abuse of dominance actions so far have been dismissed or settled.

As an example of a settlement, in the *China Mobile* case, plaintiff Zhou Ze—a lawyer—alleged that the imposition of a mobile "monthly rental fee" by China Mobile constituted an abuse of a dominant market position in violation of the AML. Following intermediation by the court, the case was settled. Defendant China Mobile agreed to pay Mr. Zhou an amount of RMB 1,000 (approximately USD 160) in the concept of "expressing gratitude" (rather than indemnification for any wrongdoing).[44]

In addition, there is a string of cases where the courts dismissed the allegations of abuse of dominance essentially on the grounds that the plaintiffs had not provided sufficient evidence: the *Tangshan Renren v. Baidu*, *Sursen v. Shanda*. *Li Fangping v. China Netcom*, *Huzhou Yiting Termite Control Services v. Huzhou City Termite Control Research Institute*, *Liu Dahua v. Hunan Huayuan Industrial* all had relatively similar lines of reasoning by the courts.[45]

From these cases it can be seen that plaintiffs in private litigation have experienced difficulties in meeting the burden of proof. In reaction to this perceived weakness of existing rules, the Intellectual Property Bench of the Supreme People's Court circulated for comment the Provisions of the Supreme People's Court on Several Issues concerning the Application of the Law in Adjudication of Monopoly-Related Civil Disputes (Draft for Comments)[46] in April 2011. If these provisions were enacted in unchanged form, the burden of proof for plaintiffs, in particular in abuse of dominance actions, would be considerably lowered.[47]

On a more general level, it should be highlighted that the courts have accepted several dozens of private actions filed under the AML since its entry into effect over three years ago. In a certain way, this demonstrates the relative importance of private antitrust litigation in China.

II. Challenges During the Initial Phase of Antitrust Enforcement

As noted above, there has been quite notable progress at these early stages of enforcement of the AML. However, as the examples below show, various problems persist.

• **The AQSIQ administrative monopoly case.** On August 1, 2008, the day that the AML came into force, four Beijing-based companies offering systems to combat counterfeits were reported to have brought a lawsuit before the Intermediate People's Court in Beijing against the alleged administrative monopoly conduct by the General Administration of Quality Supervision, Inspection and Quarantine ("AQSIQ").

> The plaintiffs alleged that AQSIQ had misused its administrative powers by making a specific electronic supervision code owned by a single enterprise — CITIC National Inspection Information Technology Co., Ltd. — compulsory for all companies selling a range of products on the market. The plaintiffs contended that AQSIQ's conduct would restrict competition (between them and CITIC National Inspection Information Technology) and hence violate the AML. AQSIQ appears to have imposed this requirement to use the electronic supervision code of CITIC National Inspection Information Technology first in 2005, but significantly expanded the list of products subject to it in 2007.[48] (Reports also indicate that, for some period, AQSIQ had actually held a shareholding in CITIC National Inspection Information Technology.)[49]
>
> A month after the action was filed, the court dismissed the case on the grounds that the statute of limitation had expired.[50] Under the rules governing the litigation procedure, the action would be time-barred after two years.[51] Hence, the court appears to have taken the initial moment of the obligation to use the supervision code, in 2005, as the starting point to calculate the time period.[52] Nonetheless, other interpretations would also have been possible, namely that the extension of the requirement in 2007 to cover other products would be the relevant benchmark (in which case less than two years would have passed), or that the time period for the statute of limitation had not started to run at all, as the infringement would be "ongoing." In a way, this case is a signal that court litigation under the AML still faces challenges.

• **The merger between China Unicom and China Netcom.** According to the State Council Regulation on the Notification Thresholds for Concentrations between Business Operators, companies are under an obligation to file for merger approval if their combined annual sales revenues exceeded RMB 10 billion (approximately USD 1.6 billion) worldwide or RMB 2 billion (approximately USD 317 million) in China and at least two of the parties to the transaction individually generated annual sales revenues in China over RMB 400 million (approximately USD 63 million).

> In 2008, the acquisition by China Unicom of competing telecommunications operator China Netcom was announced. Reportedly, the sales revenues in 2007 (i.e., the year prior to the merger) of China Unicom exceeded RMB 100 billion (around USD 16 billion) and those of China Netcom were around RMB 87 billion (around USD 14 billion), meaning that the notification thresholds prescribed by the State Council were exceeded. Nonetheless, China Unicom and China Netcom appear to have implemented their merger without filing a merger notification.[53]

Beyond this merger in the telecommunications sector, there is a strong sentiment of suspicion on the ground in Beijing that many other restructuring transactions involving state-owned enterprises, especially those between companies on the national level, were carried out without filing a notification before implementation as required by the AML.[54] This situation shows that there is still resistance for compliance with the AML by large state-owned enterprises.

• **The TravelSky case**. On April 20, 2009, Air China, China Eastern, China Southern and several other companies established a joint venture, TravelSky Technology Limited ("TravelSky"), to sell air tickets. They also announced the adoption of a new airfare pricing system.[55] The new pricing system both raised the price of tickets and set a maximum level for ticket discounts. As such, even if an airline granted the maximum discount, it would in reality be around three times the price of the tickets before the introduction of the new airfare pricing system.

> Not surprisingly, there was a public outcry upon this announcement, and many observers denounced the system as anti-competitive. Indeed, it is difficult to understand how the airlines would be able to simultaneously resort to such a complex pricing system without there being any agreement between them.[56] Reportedly, NDRC initiated an investigation and publicly stated that they adopted a "zero tolerance" approach toward price-fixing cartels.[57] However, until today, consumers are still waiting to see any final decision by NDRC in this matter.

As mentioned above, in the *China Unicom/China Netcom* merger, the companies appear to have failed to notify MOFCOM as required under the AML, and the investigation against TravelSky has not been completed. Against this background, there are grounds for people to question whether the AML applies to large state-owned enterprises at all. Of course, in our view, the AML should treat all enterprises in the marketplace equally, regardless of whether they are state-owned or private enterprises, or domestic or multinational companies. In a way, the AML works like the rules of a sports game: if the referee applies different rules to Liu Xiang and Li Xiang, then the game is inherently unfair.

III. How to Reform China's Antitrust Enforcement Regime

In the three plus years since the AML's implementation first began, the three enforcement agencies have obtained achievements in their respective fields of jurisdiction, to a certain extent, such as the show of strength displayed by NDRC in the China Telecom and China Unicom investigation indicates. In a sense, people have realized that the AML is not a "toothless tiger" when confronted with large companies.

That said, many people still lack confidence in effective antitrust enforcement. This may be due to the fact that the ultimate success of the AML as an effective enforcement tool to protect competition depends on a variety of factors such as the economic and political regime, the capabilities and skills of the enforcement agencies, the culture of competition throughout the country, etc. At present, China should continue its efforts, both at the macro- and micro-levels, to increase the effectiveness of antitrust enforcement.

1. Raising Awareness of Society

It is necessary to raise the awareness in society about the concept of competition, in order to transmit the message that competition policies matter. Beyond legislation and enforcement activities, competition policies also need to include the reform of governmental rules that unreasonably restrict competition and state monopolies that are unreasonable. As Kovacic pointed out, "[g]overnment regulations that restrict entry, pricing, and trade often curb new business development and distort the competitive process."[58]

The need to raise awareness of the benefits of competition as a factor driving economic progress and prosperity should not only target private companies and individuals, but also state-owned enterprises and governmental officials. In particular, law- and policy-makers should be aware of the significant impact that competition policies can have on the development of the national economy and the transition to a market-oriented economic regime. Kovacic correctly found that "[o]ne important role for a competition agency is to educate business officials, consumers, and government policymakers about the merits of market processes."[59]

We believe that the State should re-consider the relationship between government and market, and should re-define the role played by the government in the economy. In other words, the State should defer to competition and market mechanisms as the best way to achieve an optimal allocation of resources rather than reinforce the government's direct control over the economy. If the government plays a double role as referee and player in the marketplace, there will be an inherent conflict of interest.[60]

The question of whether China's economic reforms can continue the path towards a free market economy is, of course, of prime importance for the reform process of its entire economic and political system. At the same time, the answer to this question will crucially shape the implementation of the AML in the years to come. As Bork said, "it is not far-fetched to view antitrust as a microcosm in which larger movements of our society are reflected and perhaps, in some small but significant way, reinforced or generated."[61]

At present, in the current environment, government restrictions to competition are pervasive, and state-owned enterprises face few obstacles to seek "protection" from government or engage in "rent seeking" behavior.[62] China's White Paper on the rule of law, for example, acknowledged that "local protectionism, departmental protectionism and difficulties in law enforcement occur from time to time."[63] Hence, effective implementation of the AML remains difficult at this point in time. That is why NDRC's investigation into the conduct of China Telecom and China Unicom has drawn widespread attention, as it is targeted at two powerful companies from a state-owned sector that in many ways is closed to private investment.

Clearly, if state-owned enterprises do not (need to) abide by the AML's provisions—i.e., if they fail to file notifications for their mergers, or their cartels or abuses of dominance are "exempted" in practice—then it is basically no longer possible to view the AML as the safeguard for market competition.

2. Improving the Capabilities for Antitrust Enforcement

There are at least three aspects to be considered for improving antitrust enforcement capabilities: (i) increasing law enforcement resources, (ii) increasing the independence and authority of the enforcement agencies, and (iii) refining the normative regime set up by the AML.

i. Increasing the resources available for antitrust law enforcement

No law enforces itself. No matter how perfect a law is, if it does not have people enforcing it, it will remain a piece of paper.

In addition, to a large extent, the impact of a law enforcement agency depends upon its human and financial resources. Consequently, in order to improve antitrust enforcement capabilities, the State should deploy a sufficient number of personnel and provide adequate financial resources for the enforcement work. In particular, sufficient resources for antitrust enforcement in China must be set aside for the following reasons. First, the scope of the AML is broad and covers basically all sectors and companies. Second, China has a vast and booming economy. Hence, the resources available for antitrust enforcement in China should not trail behind those of other jurisdictions.

At present, the resources available for antitrust enforcement in China seem insufficient for a country its size. To illustrate the inadequacy of the antitrust enforcement resources in China, the personnel and financial budgets for the past few years assigned to antitrust enforcement agencies across a number of countries can be compared. In 2010, the Antitrust Division of the United States Department of Justice had a budget of around USD 163 million and counted 809 staff members (among which 591 lawyers, economists and other professionals) in its ranks.[64] The Federal Trade Commission, in turn, had a budget of USD 211 million and 1,100 staff members in 2010.[65] At the same time, there were 791 staff working at the Japan Fair Trade Commission, which had a budget of JPY 8,962 million (around USD 113million) in 2010.[66]

In comparison, the resources available for antitrust enforcement in China are much smaller than those of the above-mentioned enforcement agencies. Currently, with its six departments and approximately 30 staff members, MOFCOM's Anti-Monopoly Bureau can draw from the largest pool of resources in China. The institution with the least resources is SAIC's Anti-Monopoly and Anti-Unfair Competition Enforcement Bureau which has only two departments and a headcount of less than 10 officials at the national level. As mentioned, in 2011, close to 20 staff members joined NDRC's Price Supervision and Anti-Monopoly Bureau in Beijing representing a considerable improvement over the previous situation.

However, the problem of the inadequacy in the number of antitrust enforcement staff remains. Of course, in practice, increases of antitrust enforcement resources can only be achieved step by step, rather than at one go. However, the low number of antitrust officials should draw the attention of the leadership at various levels in China.

ii. Improving the independence and authority of the antitrust enforcement agencies

Independent antitrust enforcement means that the antitrust procedure should be free from interference by other governmental bodies. Such independence is a specific requirement of the AML. As is well known, the AML prohibits agreements significantly restricting competition, unjustified abuses of dominance and anti-competitive mergers. In practice, an investigation by an antitrust enforcement agency generally has a large impact, potentially affecting an entire market or sector. For example, more often than not, an abuse of dominance can involve large state-owned enterprises or multinational companies. In that scenario, if the enforcement agency does not enjoy sufficient independence or authority, it might be prone to influence by other government bodies or institutions with an interest in the outcome of the case.

Considering that antitrust agencies should enjoy full independence, the World Bank proposed in a 2002 report that the agencies' chairmen be appointed by Parliament and that the agencies have their own budget. According to the survey on 50 developed countries contained in this report, 63% of these countries were found to have an independent antitrust agency—i.e., an agency with no subordination to other governmental bodies.[67]

In China, it seems currently impossible to set up antitrust enforcement agencies with no subordination at all towards other governmental bodies.[68] However, it would not be correct to state that nothing can be done to increase the independence and authority of the antitrust agencies. In particular, we believe that the most suitable remedy is to consolidate the three antitrust enforcement agencies into a single authority.[69]

When submitting a draft version of the AML to the Standing Committee of the National People's Congress in 2006, Cao Kangtai—the Director of the Legal Affairs Office of the State Council—pointed out that, on the one hand, the AML provisions on the setup of the antitrust agencies should focus on what is feasible in practice and, at the same time, maintain the existing structure of law enforcement through the various competent agencies to ensure implementation after the AML's publication. On the other hand, he noted that room should be left open for making institutional reforms and functional adjustments in the future.[70] This indicates that, in the long run, it is perfectly possible that antitrust enforcement in China can be integrated into a single, unified agency.

Unlike single-agency enforcement foreseen by other laws, antitrust law enforcement by multiple institutions is an unsatisfactory arrangement that leads to high costs and low efficiency in enforcement.[71] In addition, such an arrangement will inevitably cause jurisdictional conflict, in particular between NDRC and SAIC.[72]

A key weakness with this three-head law enforcement structure is that all three agencies are part of larger ministries or commissions under the State Council, and are therefore at a relatively low level within the administrative hierarchy, equipped with relatively little authority. Furthermore, NDRC for instance is a key government institution in China that formulates and implements the State's macro-economic policies, and MOFCOM and SAIC play similarly important roles. Not surprisingly, it may be difficult for the antitrust agencies, which are just a small part of these larger institutions, to be independent in their antitrust enforcement work.[73] Hence, in our view, the State Council should take the decision to merge the three antitrust agencies into a single authority in order to optimize the benefits that AML enforcement can bring about.

iii. Refining the normative regime of the AML

As a law that has only been in force for three plus years, the normative regime set up by the AML lends itself to further refinement. Many provisions of the AML are framed as relatively high-level principles, rather than detailed rules ready to be implemented. For example, Article 55 provides that "this law shall apply to the conduct of a business operator which eliminates or restricts competition by abusing intellectual property rights." However, the law does not provide guidance on how to define the types of conduct that amount to an anti-competitive abuse of intellectual property rights.

Likewise, at the current stage of antitrust law enforcement, many issues relating to restrictive agreements, abuses of dominance and the merger control procedure still require further guidance through implementing rules. Clearly, China's normative process to improve its antitrust regime has still a long way to go.

IV. Conclusions

In the three plus years of the AML's existence, Chinese antitrust law has made considerable progress. Nonetheless, anti-competitive conduct by companies and restrictions created by government actors are still widespread, and enforcement is still lagging behind its potential. Law- and policy-makers should keep up their efforts to create a level-playing field for all market players.

Free competition in the marketplace can be achieved through a variety of legal and policy measures. As Kovacic indicated, "competition policy encompasses a large collection of policy instruments by which a country can promote business rivalry."[74]

In the long-term, the market will allocate resources optimally only when the government takes a "neutral" stance in the marketplace or limits itself to providing only those essential public services that cannot be satisfactorily provided by the market. In particular, the government should not be "judge and party" at the same time—i.e., simultaneously act as regulator and market player.

To effectively protect competition in the market and deter illegal conduct, an antitrust regime must be equipped with sufficient authority and status. China needs to back up antitrust enforcement efforts with the necessary human and financial resources.

Clearly, only when antitrust laws apply equally to all businesses, without regard to ownership or nationality, can China truly complete its transition from a state-planned to a market economy. Conversely, as Kovacic pointedly remarked, "a competition policy system can facilitate the transition from planning to markets by demonstrating the government's commitment to address serious market failures."[75]

NOTES

*   The authors would like to thank Reed Anderson for his helpful research.

1   Company Law of the People's Republic of China (promulgated by Presidential Order No. 42, October 27, 2005 as amended, effective Jan. 1, 2006) (China).

2   Contract Law of the People's Republic of China (promulgated by Presidential Order No. 15, March 15, 1999 as amended, effective Oct. 1, 1999) (China).

3   Property Rights Law of the People's Republic of China (promulgated by Presidential Order No. 63, March 16, 2007, effective Oct. 1, 2007) (China).

4   Anti-Monopoly Law of the People's Republic of China (promulgated by Presidential Order No. 68, August 30, 2007).

5   *See* Xiaoye Wang, *Highlights of China's New Anti-Monopoly Law*, ANTITRUST LAW JOURNAL 133, 134 (2008).

6   *See*, for example, Marc Winerman & William E. Kovacic, *Outpost Years for a Start-Up Agency: The FTC from 1921-1925*, ANTITRUST L.J. 146 (2010).

7   Regulation on the Notification Thresholds for Concentrations Between Business Operators (promulgated by State Council Order No. 529, August 3, 2008).

8   Guidelines on the Definition of the Relevant Market (adopted on May 24, 2009 and promulgated on July 7, 2009 by the Anti-Monopoly Commission of the State Council and the Anti-Monopoly Bureau of the Ministry of Commerce).

9   Measures on the Calculation of Sales Revenues for the Notification of Concentrations between Business Operators in the Financial Sector (promulgated with Order No. 10 by the People's Bank of China, China Banking Regulatory Commission, China Securities Regulatory Commission and China Insurance Regulatory Commission, July 15, 2009).

10   Measures on the Notification of Concentrations between Business Operators, Notice of the Ministry of Commerce of the People's Republic of China (promulgated by Order No. 11, November 21, 2009).

11   Measures on the Review of Concentrations between Business Operators, Notice of the Ministry of Commerce of the People's Republic of China (promulgated by Order No. 12, November 24, 2009).

12   Provisional Regulation on the Divestiture of Assets or Businesses in Concentrations between Business Operators, Notice of the Ministry of Commerce of the People's Republic of China (promulgated by Order No. 41, July 5, 2010).

13   Provisional Regulation on Assessing the Impact of Concentrations between Business Operators on Competition, Notice of the Ministry of Commerce of the People's Republic of China (promulgated by Order No. 55, August 29, 2011).

14   Notice of the Ministry of Commerce of the People's Republic of China [2011] Order No. 73, *Penelope/Savio Macchine Tessili*, October 31, 2011.

15   Notice of the Ministry of Commerce of the People's Republic of China [2011] Order No. 74, *General Electric China/Shenhua Coal to Liquid and Chemical*, November 10, 2011.

16   Notice of the Ministry of Commerce of the People's Republic of China [2011] Order No. 90, *Seagate/Samsung Hard Disk Drive*, December 12, 2011.

17   Notice of the Ministry of Commerce of the People's Republic of China [2012] Order No. 6, *Henkel Hong Kong/ Tiande Chemical*, February 9, 2012.

18   *See*, for example, Francois Renard, *A Practitioner's Look at Merger Control Remedies*, CPI ANTITRUST CHRONICLE (JANUARY 2012).

19   Notice of the Ministry of Commerce of the People's Republic of China [2009] Order No. 22, *Coca-Cola/Huiyuan*, March 18, 2009.

20   *See*, for example, Terry Calvani & Karen Alderman, *BRIC in the International Merger Review Edifice*, 43 CORN. INT. L.J. 131 (2010).

21   *See* Wang Xiaoye, *The Anti-Monopoly Law Should Apply to Domestic Enterprises Equally*, 21st Century Business Insight, March 24, 2009 (in Chinese).

22   The ACCC believed that, post-transaction, Coca-Cola could leverage its market power to bundle the Berri product with its own beverages and that retailers would be willing to accept the bundled sales for their own economic benefits. Consequently, consumers would have fewer options and the product prices would ultimately be higher. *See* ACCC Opposes Coca Cola's Proposed Fruit Juice Acquisition (2003), *available at* http://www.accc.gov.au/content/index.phtml/itemId/407482/fromItemId/378016 (last visited on February 19, 2012).

23   Price Law of the People's Republic of China (promulgated by Presidential Order No. 92, December 29, 1997, effective).

24   Anti-Price Monopoly Regulation, (promulgated by Order No. 7 of the National Development and Reform Commission, December 29, 2010).

25   Regulation on the Administrative Law Enforcement Procedure for Anti-Price Monopoly (promulgated by Order No. 8 of the National Development and Reform Commission, December 29, 2010).

26   *See* JRJ.com website, *NDRC's Price Supervision Bureau holds an anti-monopoly seminar*, 2010, *available at* http://finance.jrj.com.cn/2010/12/0714358728278.shtml (last visited on February 28, 2012).

27   *See* NDRC website, *Two pharmaceutical companies receive significant sanctions for monopolizing compound reserpine BPC*, November 14, 2011, *available at* http://www.sdpc.gov.cn/xwfb/t20111114_444330.htm (last visited on February 28, 2012).

28   *See* Xiaoye Wang, *China Telecom and China Unicom: Main Legal Questions*, ed. 2, December 7, 2011, *available at* http://www.iolaw.org.cn/showArticle.asp?id=3168 (last visited on February 9, 2012).

29   NDRC press release, Significant sanctions imposed on paper manufacturing industry association in Fuyang, Zhejiang Province for organizing business operators to conclude a price monopoly agreement, *available at* http://jjs.ndrc.gov.cn/gzdt/t20110104_389453.htm (last visited on February 22, 2012).

30   Regulation on the Procedure for the Handling of Cases Involving Monopoly Agreements and Abuses of a Dominant Market Position (promulgated by Order No. 42 of the State Administration for Industry and Commerce, June 10, 2009).

31   Regulation on the Procedure for the Prevention of Conduct Abusing Administrative Power to Eliminate or Restrict Competition (promulgated by Order No. 41 of the State Administration for Industry and Commerce, June 10, 2009,).

32   Regulation on the Prohibition of Monopoly Agreement Conduct, Regulation on the Prohibition of Conducting Abusing a Dominant Market Position, (promulgated by Order No. 53 of the State Administration for Industry and Commerce, December 31, 2010).

33   Regulation on the Prohibition of Conducting Abusing a Dominant Market Position (promulgated by Order No. 54 of the State Administration for Industry and Commerce, December 31, 2010, effective…) (China).

34   Regulation on the Prevention of Conduct Abusing Administrative Power to Eliminate or Restrict Competition (promulgated by Order No. 55 of the State Administration for Industry and Commerce, December 31, 2010) (China).

35   *See* SAIC press release, The first monopoly case to imposed administrative penalty by the Industry and Commerce Administration has been closed, January 26, 2011, *available at* http://www.saic.gov.cn/ywdt/gsyw/dfdt/xxb/201101/t20110126_103772.html (last visited on February 28, 2012).

36 *See* Kong Xiangjun, Several issues on Chinese Anti-Monopoly civil litigation, 7th International Seminar for Competitive Law and Policy of the Law Institute of the Chinese Academy of Social Sciences, June 3-4, 2011 (in Chinese).

37 *See* Zhou Ze's Sina Blog, *The plaintiff and defendant reached a settlement in the case of China Mobile being sued for monopolistic conduct*, October 25, 2009, *available at* http://blog.sina.com.cn/s/blog_4bdb1fa00100g27j.html (last visited on February 28, 2012).

38 Beijing Intermediate People's Court No. 1, *Tangshan Renren v Baidu*, [2009] Yi Zhong Min Chu Zi No. 845, December 18, 2009. Upheld on appeal by Beijing High People's Court, *Renren v Baidu*, [2010] Gao Min Zhong Zi No. 489, July 9, 2010.

39 Shanghai Intermediate People's Court No. 1, *Sursen v Shanda*, October 20, 2009, [2009] Hu Yi Zhong Min Wu (Zhi) Chu Zi No. 113. Upheld on appeal by Shanghai High People's Court, *Sursen v. Shanda*, December 15, 2009, [2009] Hu Gao Min San (Zhi) Zhong Zi No. 135.

40 Beijing Intermediate People's Court No. 2, *Li Fangping v China Netcom (Group) Co. Ltd. Beijing Branch*, December 18, 2009, [2008] Er Zhong Min Chu Zi No. 17385. Upheld on appeal by Beijing High People's Court, *Li Fangping v China Netcom (Group) Co. Ltd. Beijing Branch*, June 9, 2010, [2010] Gao Min Zhong Zi No. 481.

41 Huzhou Intermediate People's Court, *Huzhou Yiting Termite Control Services Co., Ltd. v. Huzhou City Termite Control Research Institute Co., Ltd.*, [2009] Zhe Hang Zhu Chu Zi No. 553, June 7, 2010. Upheld on appeal by Zhejiang High People´s Court, *Huzhou Yiting Termite Control Services Co., Ltd. v. Huzhou City Termite Control Research Institute Co., Ltd.*, [2010] Zhe Zhi Zhong Zi No. 125, August 27, 2010.

42 Changsha Intermediate People's Court, *Liu Dahua v. Hunan Huayuan Industrial*, December 12, 2011, [2011] Chang Zhong Min Wu Chu Zi N0. 158.

43 Zhu Li, *New Developments in Civil Antitrust Litigation in China*, CPI ANTITRUST CHRONICLE, JANUARY 2012, AT 3.

44 *See* Zhou Ze's Sina Blog, *supra* note 37.

45 Adrian Emch, *Abuse of a Dominant Market Position in China—The First Cases*, in CAPACITY BUILDING FOR THE ENFORCEMENT OF COMPETITION LAW (XIAOYE WANG ED., SOCIAL SCIENCES ACADEMIC PRESS, FORTHCOMING IN 2012) (IN CHINESE).

46 Provisions of the Supreme People's Court on Several Issues concerning the Application of the Law in Adjudication of Monopoly-Related Civil Disputes (Draft for Comments), April 25, 2011, *available at* http://www.court.gov.cn/gzhd/zqyj/201104/t20110425_19850.htm (last visited on February 29, 2012).

47 Emch, *Abuse of a Dominant Market Position in China – The First Cases*, *supra* note 45.

48 Circular on Implementing Special Provisions of the State Council on Strengthening the Safety Supervision and Administration of Food and Other Products and Carrying Out Electronic Supervision on Product Quality, [2007] AQSIQ Order No. 582, November 29, 2007.

49 *See* Luneng Information Port, *Four security companies brough antitrust lawsuit against General Administration of Quality Supervision, Inspection and Quarantine*, August 2, 2008, *available at* http://www.luneng.com/html/2008-08-02/947415055.htm (last visited on February 28, 2012).

50 *See* Xinhua, *The Court dismissed the case by four security companies against the General Administration of Quality Supervision, Inspection and Quarantine*, September 5, 2008, *available at* http://news.xinhuanet.com/legal/2008-09/05/content_9773194.htm (last visited on February 28, 2012).

51 Supreme People's Court Interpretation of Several Issues regarding the Implementation of the Administrative Litigation Law of People's Republic of China, [2000] Judicial Interpretation No. 8 of the Supreme People's Court, March 10, 200, art. 41.

52 *See* Adrian Emch, *Das chinesische Antimonopolgesetz in der Praxis*, Zeitschrift für Immaterialgüter, Informations- und Wettbewerbsrecht 905, 911 (2009) (in German).

53 *See* Ifeng, *MOFCOM officials confirmed that it suspected the China Unicom/CNC merger was illegal*, April 30, 2009, *available at* http://finance.ifeng.com/news/industry/20090430/609480.shtml (last visited on February 28, 2012).

54 *Id.*

55 The new tickets system are mainly about: (1) the discount rate is based on 0.4 as its lowest floating rate; (2) the discount part is subject to RMB 0.75 per person and per kilometre provided by the country as a benchmark, with no more than 25% benchmark price allowed that does not apply to the discount rate; and (3) the air ticket will not show the discount rate.

56 *See* Sun Jibin, *TravelSky Technology Limited: New round of price hikes for airplane tickets—who is to blame?*, Legal Daily Weekend, April 23, 2009 (in Chinese).

57 *See* Wang Biqiang & Liu Weixun, *Suspected of manipulating the rise of flight ticket prices—NDRC investigates TraveSsky*, May 17, 2009, *available at* http://www.eeo.com.cn/finance/other/2009/05/16/137823_1.shtml (last visited on February 28, 2012).

58 William E. Kovacic, *Institutional Foundations for Economic Legal Reform in Transition Economies: The Case of Competition Policy and Antitrust Enforcement*, CHICAGO-KENT LAW REVIEW 265, 282 (2001).

59 *Id.*

60 *See*, for example, Paul Conway, Richard Herd, Thomas Chalaux, Ping He & Jianxun Yu, *Product Market Regulation and Competition in China*, (OECD Economics Department Working Papers N. 823, December 16, 2010, at 25) ("Chinese policymakers need to increasingly focus on setting framework conditions for private sector activity and maintaining an arm's length relationship between the state and the market.").

61 ROBERT H. BORK, THE ANTITRUST PARADOX – A POLICY AT WAR WITH ITSELF (1978), AT 10.

62 *See* Wang, *Highlights of China's New Anti-Monopoly Law, supra* note 5, at 147.

63 State Council Information Office, *White Paper: China's Efforts and Achievements in Promoting the Rule of Law*, February 2008.

64 *See* GLOBAL COMPETITION REVIEW, THE 2010 HANDBOOK OF COMPETITION ENFORCEMENT AGENCIES, AT 311.

65 *See* FEDERAL TRADE COMMISSION, PERFORMANCE AND ACCOUNTABILITY REPORT FISCAL YEAR 2011, AT 132.

66 *See* GLOBAL COMPETITION REVIEW, THE 2011 HANDBOOK OF COMPETITION ENFORCEMENT AGENCIES, AT 165.

67 *See* World Bank World Development Report 2002, *Building Institutions for Markets*, at 142.

68 OECD, *The Challenges of Transition for Competition Law in China*, January 27, 2009, DAF/COMP/GF(2008)2/REV1, paragraph 91.

69 Wang, *Highlights of China's New Anti-Monopoly Law, supra* note 5, at 144-145; Adrian Emch & Qian Hao, *The New Chinese Anti-Monopoly Law - An Overview*, eSapience Center for Competition Policy (November 2007), at 21; and Adrian Emch, *The Antimonopoly Law and its Structural Shortcomings*, Global Competition Policy Magazine, (August 2008), at 3-6.

70 Cao Kangtai, *Interpretation of the Draft of the Anti-Monopoly Law of the People's Republic of China*, June 24, 2006, *available at* http://www.npc.gov.cn/npc/zt/2006-06/24/content_1382613.htm (last visited on February 28, 2012).

71 William E. Kovacic, *Downsizing Antitrust: Is it Time to End Dual Enforcement?*, 41 ANTITRUST BULLETIN 505-540 (1996); and OECD, *The Challenges of Transition for Competition Law in China, supra* note 68, paragraph 90.

72 Emch, *The Antimonopoly Law and its Structural Shortcomings, supra* note 69, at 5.

73 *Id.*

74 Kovacic, *Institutional Foundations for Economic Legal Reform in Transition Economies: The Case of Competition Policy and Antitrust Enforcement, supra* note 58, at 281.

75 Id. at 298.

Antitrust Enforcement in a Network Culture: Opportunities and Challenges in the 21st Century

RACHEL BRANDENBURGER

Special Advisor, International, Antitrust Division, U.S. Department of Justice

Abstract

This article addresses, from an antitrust enforcer's perspective, the vital question of what competition agencies need to do to participate effectively in today's globalized economy, in which nearly 130 competition agencies enforce the laws of their respective jurisdictions. The myriad economic connections of the global economy mean that the mergers and conduct that these competition agencies investigate will often impact competition enforcement in many other jurisdictions, and this will require greater cooperation between and among agencies than ever before. Professor Anne-Marie Slaughter has characterized international networks of government agencies as a "key feature of world order in the 21st century." While competition agencies will need to focus constantly and carefully on making cooperation effective, they will not need to attempt a fundamental redesign of the manner in which they cooperate, precisely because competition agencies—including the U.S. antitrust agencies—have discovered the value of participating in one, two, or several complementary multilateral competition networks. These include, to cite two examples, the Organization for Economic Cooperation and Development and the International Cooperation Network, whose memberships overlap to a significant degree. As the article describes in detail, each of these networks has developed its own ways of organizing work, but all share the goal of improving both substantive competition law and policy and the effectiveness of competition law enforcement. The article then describes the evolving cooperation relationships between the U.S. antitrust agencies and their traditional cooperation partners as well as new agencies, particularly those of the BRICS countries. The article also explains that no aspect of antitrust enforcement work will be more important than creating an environment where effective case cooperation among multiple jurisdictions occurs as a matter of course, and suggests seven guiding principles to which agencies should have regard in carrying out their enforcement activities. The article concludes by identifying four factors that will likely shape the global competition community in the future: 1) the collaborative approach to policy-making and enforcement will intensify; 2) future competition and cooperation approaches will reflect the impact of new competition agencies, particularly those of the BRICS countries; 3) government austerity plans will make cooperation and collaboration with other agencies more attractive; and 4) globalization will enhance the importance of the first three factors and the recognition of mutual advantage.

It is an honor to contribute to this volume of articles in praise of the work of Bill Kovacic in the international antitrust community.[1]

I. The Globalization of Antitrust

This article addresses, from an antitrust enforcer's perspective, the vital question of what competition agencies need to do to participate effectively in today's globalized economy. The number of competition enforcement agencies has increased exponentially in the past 20 years: from a handful in 1990 to roughly 130 today.[2] These agencies include the BRICS—Brazil, the Russian Federation, India, China, and South Africa—all of which possess, or are rapidly developing, significant competition enforcement regimes. Competition agency officials, global firms, and their advisers all must now pay serious attention to the rules in many different jurisdictions around the world in order to be effective in our globalized environment.

The relatively recent proliferation of competition regimes and multijurisdictional enforcement matters often is attributed, at least in part, to "globalization." The past decade, of course, has been marked by significant global economic changes. Total U.S. international trade, for example, more than doubled between 2000 and 2011.[3] (There was some decline in 2009 in the wake of the global economic downturn.) China is now the United States' second largest trading partner (after Canada) and has become the world's leading exporter.[4] Similarly, between 2000 and 2011, U.S. trade in goods with Brazil has increased by nearly 150 per cent, and U.S. trade in goods with India has more than tripled.[5]

Globalization is, of course, about more than just trade flow statistics. Globalization also includes technological innovations that enable there to be many more connections among our various economies. For example, even if a product is made largely for U.S. consumption, it may have been assembled in another jurisdiction and its key components may have been made in yet other jurisdictions. The supply chain disruptions following the devastating earthquake and tsunami in Japan last year were a grave reminder of just how closely the pieces of the global economy fit together.

From a competition enforcement perspective, the myriad economic connections of the global economy mean that the mergers and conduct that agencies investigate will increasingly impact competition enforcement in multiple jurisdictions. These developments have profound implications for the future of international competition policy and practice. The new reality is that it is increasingly insufficient for competition agencies to cooperate on investigations with only one or two other jurisdictions. The challenge for us all is how to adapt today's cooperation protocols to a world that increasingly involves multiple enforcers investigating the same matter.

Significant as these changes are, we will not need a fundamental redesign of the way that international cooperation occurs. Indeed, we already have in place many of the basic building blocks we need to take international cooperation into the future on a broad scale. There are numerous ways in which competition enforcement agencies can effectively participate in the current global environment. First, many agencies derive great information-gathering, analytical, networking, and other benefits from participating actively in multilateral organizations. Second, many agencies establish strong bilateral and plurilateral[6] relationships with other agencies, which lead (sometimes very quickly) to a mutually improved understanding of competition policy issues and to improved quality in all aspects of competition agency organization and work. Finally—and this is especially important—agencies are increasingly working together effectively on competition enforcement matters, in both bilateral and plurilateral contexts.

II. Participation in Multilateral Organizations

Nowhere is the globalization of antitrust so obvious as in the several networks of competition agencies, including the Organisation for Economic Cooperation and Development ("OECD") , the International Competition Network ("ICN") , the United Nations Conference on Trade and Development ("UNCTAD") and the Asia Pacific Economic Cooperation ("APEC") . Professor Anne-Marie Slaughter of Princeton University has written incisively on the role of international networks of government agencies as a "key feature of world order in the 21st century."[7] As she explains in general, and I will discuss in particular, these international networks "build trust and establish relationships among their participants that then create incentives to establish a good reputation and avoid a bad one. These are the conditions essential for long-term cooperation."[8]

OECD, ICN, UNCTAD, and APEC each provide differentiated venues for competition agencies around the world to participate in meaningful discussions of policy and practical experience, and to the extent possible, substantive and procedural convergence on a broad scale. In today's world of limited resources, all competition agencies must calibrate their participation in these various venues in a way that best suits their interests and resources. But taken as a whole, the consensus work produced though multilateral dialogue promotes consistency of basic objectives and common approaches among competition enforcers. Multilateral dialogue also provides a point of comparison for agencies' own approaches via the exchange of innovative ideas and best practices.

1. OECD

OECD—described by Professor Slaughter as "the quintessential host of trans-governmental regulatory networks"[9]—is an organization of 34 developed countries that discuss and formulate consensus views on a wide range of public policy issues, ranging from micro— and macro—economic policy to telecommunications, corporate governance, education and environmental protection. Delegates from member governments attend meetings of many different committees in Paris, where the OECD headquarters and Secretariat are located.[10]

The competition interests of the U.S. antitrust agencies (the Antitrust Division of the Department of Justice and the Federal Trade Commission) in OECD are centered in the Competition Committee ("CC") , whose predecessor, the Committee on Restrictive Business Practices, was one of the first OECD committees to be established in December 1961. Then-Assistant Attorney General Lee Loevinger of the Antitrust Division attended the Committee's first meetings, with the encouragement of then-Attorney General Robert Kennedy, and the Division has traditionally played a leading role in the CC.

The CC has three primary goals: to identify best practices in competition policy and antitrust enforcement, to foster convergence among national competition policies, and to promote increased cooperation among competition agencies. The CC has produced numerous non-binding OECD Council recommendations (e.g., on enforcement cooperation, hard core cartel enforcement, and the merger review process).[11] Over the years, the CC has also produced many useful reports (e.g., impact of hard core cartels, leniency), held roundtables on nearly every conceivable antitrust subject, and encouraged many members in a generally market-oriented and deregulatory direction. Most recently, the CC has adopted two "strategic themes," on enforcement cooperation and agency performance evaluation, respectively, which will occupy much of the CC's agenda over the next two years.

The CC consistently attracts a high level of participation by senior competition officials, and is widely regarded as one of the most successful OECD committees. Accordingly, many non-members seek to be observers; at this point, the CC has 15 observers,[12] which fully participate in roundtable discussions, while China and others often participate on an *ad hoc* basis.

The CC has effectively promoted competition law enforcement based on consumer welfare and sound antitrust principles. For example, the 1998 Council recommendation on hard-core cartels, a U.S. initiative, successfully focused the community of antitrust agencies on the need to combat cartels and to cooperate in doing so. Because OECD Council recommendations are adopted by member governments, they are powerful tools for advancing competitive principles at government-wide levels. In the same way, the CC, by interacting closely with the many other OECD policy committees, highlights the importance of pro-competitive approaches in other policy areas.

The practice of holding roundtables where each delegation can, and normally does, present its experience and views on particular issues has been a valuable one for promoting sound convergent approaches to competition issues.[13] Members choose the topics for these round-tables based on current competition interests, ranging from theoretical (e.g., the meaning of "competition on the merits") to very practical (techniques for detecting bid-rigging or training antitrust officials). The Secretariat often provides a comprehensive background paper, and outside experts often participate as speakers and produce valuable papers. The CC also benefits from private sector input through the OECD's Business and Industry Advisory Committee. Roundtable proceedings are published on the OECD website, and provide a valuable resource on a wide range of topics.

The CC's in-depth peer reviews of members' competition regimes have provided valuable insights into areas for improvement; the United States was the first jurisdiction to undergo an "examination" of its antitrust laws and policies, and all OECD members have been peer reviewed at least once, as have many CC observers (on a voluntary basis). These peer reviews result in comprehensive public reports, and the OECD's great prestige in many member and non-member countries strengthens the impact of its recommendations in members' domestic policy-making.

The CC's Working Party No. 3 ("WP3") covers enforcement and international cooperation and has often been chaired by the Assistant Attorney General ("AAG") in charge of the Antitrust Division. Under the leadership of former AAG Christine Varney, the OECD initiated a global dialogue on procedural fairness and transparency issues, holding two roundtables on those topics in 2010, covering transparency, agency decision-making, and confidentiality, while a third roundtable focusing on the role of courts in antitrust procee-dings was held in October 2011. Working Party 3 concluded its exercise in March 2012 by publishing a 112-page booklet containing a summary of the three roundtables, with an introduction by then-Acting AAG Sharis Pozen.[14] In addition, WP3 has recently held round-tables on state-owned enterprises, arbitration, and economic tools in merger analysis.

Working Party No. 2 ("WP2") covers the interface between competition and regulatory matters, and holds two or three roundtables every year at which OECD members and obser-vers compare their approaches to addressing competition issues in particular regulated sectors. Over the past several years, WP2 has developed a "competition assessment toolkit"[15] intended to provide government regulators and legislators with background ma-terials for considering the competitive effects of existing and proposed laws and regula-tions. In the next two years, much of WP2's work will be devoted to the "strategic theme" of agency evaluation.

Responding directly to the challenges of globalization, OECD has created the Global Forum on Competition ("GFC") , an outreach program that enables OECD members to share their experience with a large number of developing countries, to promote best practices, and to hear non-member views about technical assistance and problems faced by transition and developing economies. The GFC meets once a year in Paris; its most recent meeting, in February 2012, attracted more than 90 delegations, including 18 international organizations. Finally, the OECD Secretariat organizes its own technical assistance programs, often with the participation of staff from the Division, the Federal Trade Commission ("FTC") , and other OECD member competition agencies, and operates regional centers for technical assistance in Seoul and Budapest.

2. ICN

The ICN is a working collaboration—a virtual network—of competition enforcement officials from around the world. Its current membership represents 127 national and multinational competition agencies from 111 jurisdictions. It is the only international body devoted exclusively to competition law policy and enforcement, providing its member agencies with ready access to a specialized, informal venue for maintaining regular contacts and addressing practical competition concerns.

The ICN concept originated in recommendations made by the International Competition Policy Advisory Committee ("ICPAC") , an advisory group formed in 1997 by then-Attorney General Janet Reno and then-AAG Joel Klein to address competition issues in the context of globalization.[16] In its 2000 report, ICPAC recommended the creation of a new venue—a "global competition initiative"—for government officials, private firms and non-governmental organizations to consult on competition issues.[17] ICPAC recommended that such an initiative "foster dialogue directed toward greater convergence of competition law and analysis, common understanding, and common culture."[18]

In October 2001, the Antitrust Division, the FTC, and competition agencies from Australia, Canada, the European Union, France, Germany, Israel, Italy, Japan, Korea, Mexico, South Africa, the United Kingdom, and Zambia launched the ICN in New York.[19] The ICN celebrated its 11th annual conference in April 2012 in Rio de Janeiro, which attracted roughly 450competition enforcers and non-governmental advisors from more than 80 jurisdictions.[20]

From the start, the Division and FTC have played central roles in the ICN and have been closely involved with all aspects of the ICN's work. At the launch of the ICN, the Division expressed the hope that ICN will provide an environment in which antitrust officials from dozens of countries can work together to achieve consensus on ways to make international antitrust enforcement more efficient and effective, to the benefit of consumers and companies around the world."[21] The Division and FTC are members of the ICN Steering Group and participate in the full range of ICN substantive projects. After co-chairing the Merger Working Group for many years, the Division now co-chairs the Cartel Working Group, together with the German and Japanese competition agencies, and co-chairs a subgroup of the Cartel Working Group with the Japan Fair Trade Commission.[22]

The ICN has no permanent secretariat, although the Canadian Competition Bureau provides administrative support. The ICN is guided by a Steering Group of 18 members selected every two years.[23] Senior agency officials represent their agencies on the Steering Group, which provides oversight to the ICN's work and sets its strategic direction. Its Chair is also selected every two years.

From its inception, the ICN has been inclusive. All competition agencies that enforce competition laws are welcomed as members and encouraged to add their perspectives and expertise to the ICN's work. By embracing a global scope, the ICN seeks to broaden the competition culture beyond the established players and deepen competition policy discourse. The ICN work products are intended to be inclusive, reflecting the diversity of its membership, including the different sizes and stages of development of the economies that member agencies represent. From the beginning, the ICN also has welcomed the participation of "non-governmental advisers," who include individuals from the legal, economic, business, academic and consumer communities with interest and expertise in competition law.

The ICN is a project-based network. Projects are advanced in a virtual structure of 'working groups' and other *ad hoc* formats. There are five substantive working groups, addressing mergers, cartels, unilateral conduct, advocacy, and agency effectiveness. The ICN does not exercise any binding rule-making function. Rather, where the ICN approves recommendations arising from its projects, individual competition agencies decide whether and how to implement the recommendations. In practice, the broad agency participation that underlies the consensus ICN recommendations has contributed to the wide implementation of those recommendations around the world.

The ICN's best-known and influential achievements have come in the form of "Recommended Practices" built on practical guidance informed by member experiences. Notably, the ICN has produced Recommended Practices for Merger Notification and Review Procedures, Recommended Practices for Merger Analysis, and Recommended Practices on the Assessment of Dominance/Substantial Market Power.[24]

In addition, ICN members have developed practical case-handling and enforcement manuals promoting "good practices," tips and techniques, and examples of successful member experience on topics such as anti-cartel enforcement, market studies, and merger and unilateral conduct investigative techniques. ICN work products have inspired improvements to the practices of many of the ICN's member agencies, and have influenced legal and policy reforms in many jurisdictions.

The ICN's impact goes beyond its written outputs. An important achievement of the ICN (and of OECD) is the way in which it fosters personal relationships between agency heads and agency staff—relationships that engender familiarity and trust which makes effective case cooperation more likely. The ICN and OECD thus provide vehicles for competition agency officials to work together, increase understanding, and build trust with their counterparts around the world. As Professor Eleanor Fox of New York University School of Law has written in her excellent article assessing the ICN's work, "These networks of relationships deepen understanding, respect, and trust, build community, and provide ready-made avenues for mutual assistance and cooperation."[25]

3. UNCTAD

UNCTAD, based in Geneva, has been involved in competition issues for more than 30 years. In the 1970s, UNCTAD was the forum for lengthy negotiations (in which the Antitrust Division played a leading role), that led to the United Nations General Assembly's adoption of the Set, a non-binding multilateral code of conduct for the prevention of private anticompetitive behavior.[26] UNCTAD has 194 members and a relatively small competition-dedicated Secretariat, which is responsible for preparing the annual meetings and providing developing countries with technical assistance on competition issues.

UNCTAD conducts a review conference on the Set every five years, the last in 2010, and holds annual meetings in Geneva of its Intergovernmental Group of Experts ("IGE"), which was established by the Set. UNCTAD's competition focus is on issues of particular interest to developing countries, and many developing countries attend review conferences and IGE meetings; more than 90 UN members attended the 2012

IGE meeting. The UNCTAD format is similar to that of OECD: two or three roundtables on previously agreed topics (in 2012, e.g., competition policy and public procurement) and a peer review of a developing or transition country (in 2012, Tanzania, Zambia, and Zimbabwe).

4. APEC

APEC is a relative newcomer to multilateral competition work. APEC is an organization of 21 member economies in the Asia-Pacific region, including the United States. It was established in 1989 to facilitate economic growth, cooperation, trade, and investment in the region, and its Competition Policy and Law Group ("CPLG") was created in 1996; both U.S. antitrust agencies are very involved in the CPLG's work. Each year, the CPLG holds one meeting that discusses one or two competition-related topics; at its last meeting—in Moscow in February 2012, the CPLG held discussions/roundtables on information-sharing and competition assessment. The CPLG also holds a competition policy training session for member economies each year.

* * *

This review of the participation of competition agencies in multilateral competition organizations shows that the identity of participants and the nature of their participation varies significantly among the organizations: all OECD members are also members of ICN, but not vice-versa; nearly all ICN members are members of UNCTAD, but not vice-versa. Taken together, these fora offer many meaningful opportunities for competition agencies to engage with their counterparts in other jurisdictions on important competition policy and enforcement issues in a collegial setting.

These multilateral efforts address differences in national and regional approaches to competition that have international consequences. The existing multilateral competition-related fora have proven to be effective tools for promoting inter-agency cooperation and convergence. The depth and regularity of interaction among so many agencies within the OECD, ICN, UNCTAD, and APEC have improved mutual knowledge, trust, and respect, and increased understanding of each agency's laws, policies, and practices. This, in turn, has strengthened inter-agency cooperation, and will continue to do so in the future.

III. Agency-to-Agency Relations

1. Cooperation Generally

As illustrated by the text of the U.S. antitrust agencies' 2011 Memorandum of Understanding ("MOU") with China's competition agencies,[27] "cooperation" is a broad concept in the competition law context. It ranges from capacity-building in the form of seminars and international exchanges of visits by competition experts to and from relatively new agencies—something that the U.S. agencies have done over the past 20 years with many other agencies around the world, to our mutual advantage—to very close working relationships between and among enforcement agencies in analyzing particular competition enforcement cases.

Competition agencies repeatedly find it useful for their experts to talk to one another generally about competitive issues in particular sectors or particular investigations. Valuable cooperation of this sort often can be accomplished solely with a discussion of public information, particularly where one agency has accumulated a great deal of experience in a sector while the other agency is dealing with an issue in that sector for the first time. This sort of cooperation enables the latter agency's experts to move up the learning curve on a particular subject in a short time. It can also be appropriate and useful for two agencies to cooperate closely in a particular law enforcement investigation, including exchanging views about evidence, competitive concerns, and possible remedies.

2. Cooperation Agreements

In addition to the multilateral networks and generalized bilateral cooperation, another broad avenue for agency participation in the global competition community is the establishment of bilateral relationships between competition agencies. While informal relationships are common, there are many formal relationships as well. One instrument used to establish a basic framework for closer agency-to-agency cooperation is the cooperation agreement, of which there are now a great many around the world.[28] Such cooperation agreements between governments or agencies set out practical parameters for cooperation and coordination between the agencies, but do not confer any additional legal powers on them. The United States concluded its first antitrust cooperation agreement in 1976 with Germany, before cooperation between competition agencies was widely accepted—indeed, even before the value of competition laws was widely accepted.

Today's era of constructive, comprehensive and routine international cooperation began in earnest in the early 1990s, and advanced significantly when the United States and the European Commission ("EC") signed their first cooperation agreement in 1991.[29] Spurred by the adoption of the European Merger Regulation,[30] the U.S. agencies and the EC recognized that they would need to work together more often and more closely than previously, because large, multinational mergers would more commonly come under review by both jurisdictions. The U.S.-EC agreement establishes general notification requirements when an enforcement action by an agency in one jurisdiction may affect the interests of the other country. It sets out a general duty to cooperate and render assistance in enforcement activities, subject to respective domestic laws, and it lists factors that go into a decision of whether to coordinate with the other jurisdiction.

Antitrust cooperation between the U.S. antitrust agencies and the EC has been a success story. The U.S. agencies and the EC have largely consistent enforcement policies, directed at the common goal of promoting consumer welfare, and both sides are deeply committed to cooperating closely on enforcement matters and exchanging views on policy matters. Over 20 years after the initial cooperation agreement, today's relationship is an organic process of frequent enforcement and policy collaboration on many competition issues at all levels.[31]

From the late 1990s through the present, as bilateral relationships have strengthened and case cooperation has became more commonplace, the United States has concluded a total of 12 government to government or agency-to-agency cooperation agreements, with counterparts in Australia, Brazil, Canada, Chile, China, the EC, Germany, Israel, Japan, Mexico, Russia, and most recently with India.[32]

3. New Competition Regimes: The BRICS

At this point, I would like to illustrate my discussion of how a broad range of competition agencies can participate effectively in the global competition community with some examples of how some relatively new agencies are successfully doing so, as illustrated by the U.S. antitrust agencies' recent MOUs with the Russian and Chinese agencies. The recent creation and development of competition regimes in the BRICS nations illustrates the near universal globalization of competition enforcement and the growing need for all enforcers to work effectively with a wide variety of colleagues all over the world. Given the size and importance of the BRICS' economies, their entry into competition enforcement is a significant development for global firms and competition enforcers. Their actions, and their participation in the global competition community, will certainly influence future international competition policy dialogue and cooperation.

4. China

China enacted a comprehensive Antimonopoly Law ("AML") in 2007, and has allocated AML enforcement jurisdiction among three established agencies: the Ministry of Commerce ("MOFCOM") for mergers; the National Development and Reform Commission ("NDRC") for price-related anticompetitive conduct; and the State Administration for Industry and Commerce ("SAIC") for non-price-related conducted. A fourth key institution is the Supreme People's Court, which is preparing rules for the conduct of private lawsuits seeking damages or other relief for alleged violations of the AML. China has been an *ad hoc* observer in OECD.

Building a solid relationship with China's AML institutions is a key international priority for the U.S. agencies, and our signing last year of an MOU with MOFCOM, NDRC, and SAIC is an important step in solidifying that relationship;[33] this MOU was supplemented in November 2011 by a guidance document on cooperation between MOFCOM and the U.S. agencies in merger cases.[34] The U.S. agencies have been actively engaging the three Chinese competition agencies on a frequent basis, with the aim of building a cooperative relationship and encouraging China to implement its AML in a procompetitive, transparent, and non-discriminatory manner. The U.S. agencies' engagement has consisted of frequent meetings and training workshops, both in China and the United States, to discuss substantive antitrust analysis and effective investigative techniques, submission of written comments on draft implementing rules and guidelines, and less formal exchanges that deepen our cooperative relationships. The U.S. agencies will continue to build our cooperative relationships with China's competition enforcement agencies.

5. India

In India, the national legislature enacted a comprehensive competition law in 2002 and created a new agency, the Competition Commission of India ("CC I"), to enforce it. It has taken time for the CCI to hire staff and begin to enforce the entirety of its mandate, but in 2011, the premerger filing regulations came into force, so that the CCI is now a "full-service" competition agency. India has recently become an observer on OECD, and is an ICN member. The U.S. agencies have engaged with the CCI for several years—hosting CCI officials in Washington and sending experts to India to share our enforcement and administrative experience. We have begun to build a good cooperative relationship with the CCI, and signed an MOU in September 2012 with the Indian Ministry of Corporate Affairs and CCI.

6. Brazil

The Brazil competition regime was reorganized in 2011; it includes two agencies: the Administrative Council for Economic Defense ("CADE") and the Secretariat for Economic Monitoring ("SEAE").[35] The Brazilian agencies are important participants in the global competition community; they have long been observers at OECD and leaders in ICN. CADE sits on the ICN Steering Group and the Brazilian agencies hosted the 2012 ICN conference. The United States signed a cooperation agreement with Brazil in 1999, and that agreement, together with the U.S./Brazil MLAT, has led to increased enforcement cooperation between the U.S. and Brazilian agencies in merger and cartel cases.

7. Russian Federation

The Russian Federal Antimonopoly Service ("FAS") is, like the Brazilian agencies, a well-established participant in the global competition community. The Russian Federation is an active observer in the OECD Competition Committee and a leading participant in ICN. Among other things, FAS sits on the ICN Steering Group, is a co-chair of the ICN Advocacy Working Group and hosted the 2006 ICN Conference. Over the years, FAS has entered into many bilateral cooperation agreements with other competition agencies, including a 2009 MOU with the U.S. agencies to promote enhanced communication and cooperation on competition law enforcement and policy developments.

8. South Africa

Since the enactment of the Competition Act in 1998, the two South African competition agencies—the Competition Commission and the Competition Tribunal—have played an important role in the global competition community. South Africa is a longtime observer at OECD, and the South African agencies—like the Brazilian agencies and FAS—have long made important contributions to ICN. To take three examples: senior South African competition officials have been members of the ICN Steering Group; David Lewis, the former Chairperson of the Tribunal, was ICN Chair in 2009; and the South African agencies hosted the ICN conference in 2005. The U.S. agencies have worked closely with the South African agencies on policy matters since the enactment of the Competition Act, and that cooperative relationship has grown to include working together on enforcement matters.

IV. Cooperation: Working Together in a Globalized World

No aspect of antitrust enforcement work will be more important in the future than creating and sustaining a legal and policy environment where effective and efficient case cooperation among multiple jurisdictions occurs as a matter of course. Getting cases right is the most important task that competition enforcement agencies have, and in the era of globalization, getting them right will increasingly mean getting them right *together*, with agencies from all over the world. Ultimately, this will be the true test of how competition agencies can participate meaningfully in the global environment.[36]

1. Guiding Principles for Agency-to-Agency Relations

Competition law enforcers around the globe, whether long established or much more recently established, should have regard to several guiding principles in carrying out their competition enforcement activities.[37] These guiding principles include: transparency; mindfulness of other jurisdictions' interests; respect for other jurisdictions' legal, political and economic cultures; trust among agencies; ongoing dialogue on all aspects of international competition enforcement; convergence, where possible, in policy and enforcement results; and cooperation between and among agencies. The principles of transparency, convergence and cooperation were first articulated in this context some 12 years ago, in the Department of Justice's ICPAC report. To these principles, the Division has recently added the four other principles, based on our international experience since 2000. While none of these principles is completely new to international competition enforcement, we believe that it will be increasingly important to place a high priority on each of them in the future.

As to transparency, if competition agencies are to communicate, cooperate and respect each other, or converge effectively with one another, they must be able to understand each others' approaches. Likewise, it is crucial for businesses to be able to develop an understanding of the competition rules that apply to them generally, and—equally importantly—how these rules are likely to be applied to them in particular cases.

Competition officials should strive to ensure openness and transparency between a competition agency and the party or parties under investigation about the conduct at issue, the nature of the potential violation at issue, and the procedures that will apply, as well as a willingness by the agency to discuss with the parties the core issues and analysis throughout the investigative process. Agencies should also strive for openness and transparency with other competition agencies about our agency's policies, practices and decisions, and be willing to exchange views throughout the investigative process with other competition agencies investigating the same transaction or conduct. (Of course, transparency must operate consistently with legal, statutory and prudential obligations to respect confidential information and the rights of the parties to make their case to each agency.)

Once competition agencies understand the ways in which colleagues in other jurisdictions operate, they can constantly be mindful of the impact their actions and approaches outside of their jurisdictions, and the effects that other agencies' actions and approaches may have within their respective jurisdictions. Mindfulness of other competition authorities' jurisdictions, practices and traditions allows agencies to work together to minimize inconsistent or conflicting approaches. Divergent enforcement outcomes should occur, if at all, only for well-founded reasons, and not arbitrarily or unexpectedly. Mindfulness helps prevent arbitrary or unexpected differences.

Respect involves two critical components: openness to the ideas of others, and respect for our differences. No one has a monopoly on good ideas. In terms of openness to one another's ideas, greater cooperation and convergence will not be possible if any of us comes to the table with the notion that our agency has all the right answers and that other jurisdictions should therefore adopt our own agency's standards or processes wholesale. The fact is that all competition agencies are, or should be, interested in protecting their consumers, and though agencies may not always agree on the best course, we all should listen to, learn from, and respect the various voices in the global enforcement community. It is only in this way that effective antitrust enforcement across the globe can truly become a reality.

Building trust among enforcement agencies is also essential. Trust can be born of working productively together, whether in negotiating documents like our cooperation agreements and MOUs; having detailed discussions on particular substantive or procedural issues on a sustained basis; working closely together on individual investigations; or through capacity building activities. The more familiar we become with one another, the more we appreciate that we share a common purpose and the more we realize just how similar our approaches and challenges often are.

Competition law enforcers must build trust, not just between enforcement authorities, but also with the business community. Competition agencies' ability to work together effectively is often not solely in their hands. In merger cases, for example, U.S. law appropriately provides strong protections to confidential business information that merging parties and third parties provide to the federal antitrust agencies during the merger review process. For the U.S. agencies, for example, to share such information with other competition agencies with which they cooperate in a merger review, the merging parties must agree to provide written waivers of their confidentiality rights with respect to the protected information that is to be shared. Accordingly, businesses need to have confidence that confidentiality waivers designed to allow cooperation between enforcement agencies will not result in compromised corporate information. By the same token, in order to achieve cooperation around the globe, competition agencies need to have confidence that parties are not seeking to play one agency off against another.

Ensuring an ongoing dialogue is similarly essential for effective competition policy and practice in today's world. This dialogue should occur not just among competition agencies, but also with the business community, consumers, practitioners, academics and the general public. Each can provide important insights and different perspectives on what is, and what is not, working well in the international world of competition law enforcement.

Sustained, meaningful dialogue within the world's competition community, based on the principles just mentioned, has led to a significant degree of convergence around the world on a wide range of competition issues. Not surprisingly, attaining convergence among 130 jurisdictions around the world, each with its unique legal culture, enforcement regime, political structure and economic situation, is not always easy, and it may be unrealistic to expect convergence on everything.[38] Of course, convergence does not necessarily guarantee that competition enforcement agencies will arrive at precisely the same results in the context of a particular case.[39] Importantly, the convergence that the global competition community has already achieved and will achieve in the future is closely intertwined with cooperation among competition agencies, the last of the guiding principles.

Cooperation is a broad word in the competition context. It includes capacity building, discussing substantive legal and economic concepts and procedural issues, sharing general knowledge about a given industry, and working together on individual cases. Cooperation reduces uncertainty and unnecessary burdens on competition agencies and firms involved in competition enforcement matters. In addition, cooperation helps to manage differences. Even in the presence of legal or procedural differences, the U.S. antitrust agencies have generally tended to reach the same conclusions with other competition agencies when we are fully engaged with one another in analyzing the same matter. While this type of cooperation among competition agencies on individual enforcement matters is becoming increasingly commonplace, experience suggests that each matter raises its own combination of issues, some familiar and others unusual or unprecedented.

The Antitrust Division is committed to intensifying our strong focus on the ways that we cooperate with our counterparts around the globe in our day-to-day work on individual matters.[40] In Fiscal Years 2010 through 2012, for example, the Antitrust Division worked on scores of investigations with an international dimension, most of which involved cooperation with competition agencies in other jurisdictions. During 2011, for example, we cooperated on merger reviews—often with waivers from parties and third parties—with competition agencies including those in Australia, Brazil, Canada, Columbia, the European Union, Germany, Japan, Mexico, South Africa and the United Kingdom. The Division also cooperates with many competition agencies on civil non-merger and criminal matters.[41]

V. The Future of International Competition Policy and Enforcement

1. Sources for New Ideas

Just as the current state of accelerated agency-to-agency cooperation has developed as a result of the need to address global market realities, the lessons agencies learn and global economic developments are likely to lead to new ways of interaction in the future. Some agencies are pursuing closer ties with their neighbors, creating regional groupings of agencies from jurisdictions with close economic ties, similar enforcement cultures, and significant overlaps in the matters they investigate. Examples can be found in Europe, Latin America, Africa and Asia.

2. European Competition Network

Over the past 55 years, the European Union has crafted a very successful approach that combines both supranational enforcement by the EC, for conduct that affects trade between and among the 27 EU member states, and enforcement by the individual member states, which often cooperate among themselves and with the EC on particular enforcement matters, through the European Competition Network ("ECN").

The EC is the primary enforcer of EU competition rules, but the member states are also empowered to enforce these rules in national administrative proceedings or courts, and to notify the EC when they do so, if conduct affecting intra-EU trade is involved. Each of the EU member states has its own competition law and enforcement agency (or agencies), and has concurrent jurisdiction with the EU to enforce Articles 101 and 102 of the European Treaty[42] when cross-border trade is affected. Member states apply their national competition laws to cases with purely domestic effects involving anticompetitive agreements, mergers and abuse of dominance. In order to ensure uniformity of application, the EC monitors member state enforcement of the EU rules, and has the right to displace the national enforcers in cases of sufficient EU-wide interest.

To facilitate cooperation and ensure the consistent application of European competition rules, the EC and member states established the ECN as a forum for discussion and cooperation among competition authorities.[43] Through the ECN, the EC and member state agencies inform each other of new cases and contemplated enforcement decisions, coordinate investigations, exchange evidence and discuss issues of common interest, including in sector or topic specific working groups. The ECN framework allows the member agencies to share work on specific cases, exchange experiences and build a common enforcement culture, for example, via policy efforts such as the ECN model leniency program.[44]

3. Africa

African regional organizations that aim for regional economic cooperation and more integrated markets, such as the 19-member Common Market for Eastern and Southern Africa ("COMESA") and the eight-member West African Economic and Monetary Union ("WAEMU"), have included competition policy and strengthening competitive markets as key elements of their agendas. Both organizations also participate in the broader international competition dialogue. Last year, representatives of 23 national and regional competition agencies from across Africa launched the African Competition Forum ("ACF"). The ACF aims to help build the capacities of member competition agencies and to promote the awareness and adoption of competition principles in national economic policies.[45]

4. Latin America and the Caribbean

The Caribbean Community ("CARICOM") is another illustration of a regional approach to competition policy among smaller jurisdictions. CARICOM is an organization of 15 jurisdictions in the Caribbean and Central and South America, whose member are seeking, over time, to create a single market and economy. The CARICOM Revised Treaty contains competition provisions, and a CARICOM Competition Commission was created in 2008.

The Competition Commission's underlying functions are to work with the member states to apply competition rules to cross-border anticompetitive conduct, to promote and protect competition in the Community, and to coordinate the implementation of CARICOM competition policy. While the Competition Commission is not yet fully operational and has not yet initiated any enforcement proceedings, it is fully engaged in capacity-building in the region and has joined the ICN.[46]

5. Asia–Pacific

Yet another example of regional experimentation with cooperation and coordination in competition matters comes from Australasia. In recent years, the governments of Australia and New Zealand have entered into a series of agreements on a wide range of legal and economic subjects, including competition, that are intended to integrate their economies more effectively and efficiently. In addition to the usual series of enforcement cooperation agreements,[47] the two agencies have agreed on a comprehensive staff exchange program that has recently led to a Commissioner of the Australian Competition & Consumer Commission becoming an Associate Commissioner of the New Zealand Commerce Commission as well. This is an idea certainly worth considering in other jurisdictions.[48]

6. Work Sharing

There are other interesting ideas for international competition enforcement that have yet to be tried in a meaningful way. For instance, the 2000 ICPAC report discussed above recommended the consideration of the concept of "work sharing" for multi-jurisdictional merger investigations.[49] As the ICPAC report explained, "work sharing" could "be accomplished in incremental steps with each step reflecting a different degree of cooperation and each step built upon successful approaches to cooperation and coordination that enforcement authorities have already implemented. An important objective is to reduce duplication, while preserving the freedom for jurisdictions to take their own measures under their own laws, as necessary and appropriate. In ICPAC's view, such work sharing could include agencies working together to reduce duplication, for example, by jointly negotiating merger remedies, limiting the number of jurisdictions conducting second-stage reviews, or identifying one jurisdiction to coordinate particular merger investigations. While we have seen progress on the joint negotiation of remedies in individual transactions,[50] other possible forms of work sharing have not yet been deeply explored. While certain aspects of work sharing can raise sensitive issues, perhaps it is the type of idea that could be developed in the proposed work of OECD and ICN on enforcement cooperation, and prove valuable to agencies in this time of fiscal constraint.

V. Conclusion: A Future Working Environment for Global Competition Policy

It is probably impossible to anticipate all of the variables affecting the future of competition enforcement, based on the current state of play, but there are some factors that will likely shape the global competition community of the future.

First, the current collaborative approach to international competition policy and enforcement through multilateral networks and strong agency-to-agency cooperation will very likely intensify. The global competition community's enthusiastic embrace of collaborative effort as a model for policy and enforcement work thoroughly validates Professor Slaughter's observations about the value of networks of agencies from different jurisdictions.[51]

One of the salient aspects of this development in our context is the manner in which competition agencies have calibrated their participation in the various networks and other collaborative efforts: OECD, ICN, regional competition networks, and a wide variety of bilateral cooperation on enforcement matters. Some agencies focus their resources on one or two of these options—which may vary over time—while other, often larger, agencies participate in many networks. The goal for each agency, however situated, is to derive value from these options, whether in substantive competition theory, best practices for enforcement, or individual law enforcement matters. What that means for the future is that our various networks and relationships, including our ways of cooperation, will evolve in order to continue offering significant value to a wide range of competition agencies, while minimizing possible redundancy.

Second, future competition and enforcement approaches will reflect the impact of new enforcement agencies, which has yet to be fully realized. To take an obvious example, the competition agencies of the BRICS jurisdictions—which themselves constitute a type of network—already participate to varying degrees in a wide range of competition networks (e.g., OECD and ICN) and their voices will be heard more often on competition issues in the years to come, while their participation will be sought (and needed) more in enforcement cooperation.

There are also many scores of small agencies in the world whose policy and enforcement issues and needs may in some ways be quite different from the ones that large, established agencies are accustomed to addressing. In some cases, particularly in matters of broad competition analysis and process issues, the large multilateral networks (OECD, ICN, and UNCTAD) will offer experiences and guidance that newer and small agencies will find useful, while regional networks (e.g., ECN, COMESA, and CARICOM) will offer experiences that may sometimes be better tailored to smaller agencies' practical needs.

Third, in the current economic environment, competition agencies will necessarily be impacted by general government austerity plans, and thus will need to do more international work with fewer resources. Accordingly, cooperation, collaboration and efficiency will be even more highly valued than they have been in the past. Competition networks obviously can help with this, but they must be careful to work in ways that complement the activities of other networks, and not duplicate them. Making this happen, of course, will be the responsibility of the network members themselves.

Finally, globalization has brought about broader and more frequent participation of many competition agencies through networks and closer agency-to-agency relationships forged via case-specific cooperation. The unprecedented depth and regularity of interaction among so many agencies has improved mutual understanding of other jurisdictions' laws, policies, and practices. This, in turn, has advanced the beginnings of a next stage of inter-agency cooperation, driven by the recognition of mutual advantage.

There is much unrealized potential within the current system of multilateral dialogue, and increasingly frequent case-specific interaction. The depth of agencies' knowledge about each other and how they operate and decide matters continues to grow through multilateral initiatives and cooperation on individual cases. The agency-driven process of frequent enforcement and policy collaboration at all levels has led to the growing recognition of core enforcement principles and common objectives, which in turn, reinforces such collaboration.

In today's global competition community, much of what we do will be increasingly international. The U.S. antitrust agencies and many of our counterparts are working to bring about improved inter-agency cooperation and greater dialogue and convergence in thinking about competition agency practices and policies. Continued participation by many agencies will help develop common practices, expectations and approaches across all competition agencies—established and new, from jurisdictions large and small, developed and developing. In short, the global competition community must take advantage of its diversity to meet the challenges of globalization with sustainably effective, efficient and complementary networks, both formal and informal, of competition enforcement agencies on a worldwide scale.

NOTES

1 I am very grateful to my colleagues, Ed Hand and Paul O'Brien, for their help with the preparation of this article.

2 The International Competition Network's membership, for example, currently includes 127 members in 111 jurisdictions around the world.

3 U.S. Trade in Goods and Services, http://www.bea.gov/newsreleases/international/trade/trad_time_series.xls.

4 U.S. Trade Balance, by Partner Country 2010, http://dataweb.usitc.gov/scripts/cy_m3_run.asp; Country Comparison: Exports, https://www.cia.gov/library/publications/the-world-factbook/rankorder/2078rank.html; *compare*, World Trade in 2001—Overview, http://wto.org/english/res_e/statis_e/its2002_e/chp_1_e.pdf

5 Trade in Goods with Brazil, http://www.census.gov/foreign-trade/balance/c3510.html#2000; Trade in Goods with Africa, http://www.census.gov/foreign-trade/balance/c0013.html#2000; Trade in Goods with India, http://www.census.gov/foreign-trade/balance/c5330.html#2000.

6 In this article, I use the term "plurilateral" to mean several jurisdictions or competition agencies—more than two, which would be "bilateral," but not many, which would be "multilateral."

7 SLAUGHTER, A NEW WORLD ORDER 1 (2004).

8 *Id.* at 3.

9 *Id.* at 46.

10 OECD members are Australia, Austria, Belgium, Canada, Chile, Czech Republic, Denmark, Estonia, Finland, France, Germany, Greece, Hungary, Iceland, Ireland, Israel, Italy, Japan, Korea, Luxembourg, Mexico, Netherlands, New Zealand, Norway, Poland, Portugal, Slovakia, Slovenia, Spain, Sweden, Switzerland, Turkey, the United Kingdom, and the United States. The European Commission also participates.

11 OECD Council Recommendations and Best Practices on Competition Law and Policy, *available at* http://www.oecd.org/document/59/0,3746,en_2649_34685_4599739_1_1_1_1,00.html.

12 Brazil, Bulgaria, Chinese Taipei, Colombia, Egypt, India, Indonesia, Latvia, Lithuania, Malta, Peru, Romania, Russia, South Africa, and Ukraine.

13 It is not unusual for 25 or 30 OECD members and observers to submit papers for roundtables held by the CC and its Working Parties.

14 The booklet is *available at* http://www.oecd.org/daf/competition/abuseofdominanceandmonopolisation/rpoceduralfairnessandtransparency-2012.htm. ("A key theme emerging from the discussions was a broad consensus on the need for, and importance of, transparency and procedural fairness in competition enforcement . . ." *Id.*)

15 OECD Competition Assessment Toolkit, *available at* http://www.oecd.org/document/48/0,3746, en_2649_34753_42454576_1_1_1_1,00.html.

16 International Competition Network, History, *available at* http://www.internationalcompetitionnetwork.org/about/history.aspx.

17 INTERNATIONAL COMPETITION POLICY ADVISORY COMMITTEE, FINAL REPORT TO THE ATTORNEY GENERAL AND ASSISTANT ATTORNEY GENERAL FOR ANTITRUST (Feb. 28, 2000) [hereinafter ICPAC REPORT], *available at* http://www.justice.gov/atr/icpac/finalreport.html.

18 ICPAC REPORT, Executive Summary at 29, *available at* http://www.justice.gov/atr/icpac/execsummary.pdf.

19 Press Release, U.S. DOJ, *U.S. and Foreign Antitrust Officials Launch International Competition Network* (Oct. 25, 2001), *available at* http://www.justice.gov/atr/public/press_releases/2001/9400.htm.

20 Press Release, U.S. DOJ, *International Competition Network Launches New Initiatives on Enforcement Cooperation, Investigative Process and Working with the Courts* (April 20, 2012), *available at* http://www.justice.gov/atr/public/press_releases/2012/282485.htm.

21 Oct. 25, 2001 Press Release, *supra* note 19.

22 FTC co-chairs the Agency Effectiveness Working Group, together with the Mexican and Norwegian competition agencies.

23 International Competition Network, Operational Framework, *available at* http://www.internationalcompetitionnetwork.org/about/operational-framework.aspx.

24 *See* International Competition Network, Recommended Practices for Merger Notification and Review Procedures, *available at* http://www.internationalcompetitionnetwork.org/uploads/library/doc588.pdf; International Competition Network, Recommended Practices for Merger Analysis, *available at* http://www.internationalcompetitionnetwork. org/uploads/library/doc316.pdf; International Competition Network, Recommended Practices for Dominance/ Substantial Market Power Analysis Pursuant to Unilateral Conduct Laws, *available at* http://www.international-competitionnetwork.org/uploads/library/doc317.pdf.

25 Eleanor M. Fox, *Linked-In: Antitrust and the Virtues of a Virtual Network*, 43 Int'l Lawyer 51 (2009). In preparation for the ICN's 10th anniversary, then-ICN Steering Group Chair John Fingleton led a network-wide consultation to evaluate the ICN's strengths and identify possible improvements. The resulting report identifies four high-level goals for the future of the ICN: to promote experience sharing among the ICN's diverse membership, pressure appropriate convergence efforts, promote competition advocacy, and facilitate effective international cooperation. As part of the Second Decade project, the ICN Steering Group embarked on three projects: cooperation, investigative process, and agency relationships with courts, respectively. The ICN's Vision for its Second Decade is *available at* http://www.internationalcompetitionnetwork.org/uploads/library/doc755.pdf.

26 The Set of Multilaterally Agreed Principles and Rules for the Control of Restrictive Business Practices, *available at* www.unctad.org/Templates/StartPage.asp?intItemID=4106&lang=1.

27 The U.S.-China MOU and a subsequent Guidance document on merger cooperation are *available at* http://www.justice.gov/atr/public/international/docs/273310a.pdf.

28 To take just three examples, the United States has antitrust cooperation agreements or memoranda of understanding involving 12 jurisdictions. Canada has 11 such agreements, and the European Union has "dedicated" bilateral cooperation agreements with seven jurisdictions, plus broader agreements with roughly 30 jurisdictions that contain some competition provisions.

29 At roughly the same time, the U.S. antitrust agencies' relationship with Canada also became mutually reinforcing and cooperative. This was prompted in part by Canada's adoption in 1986 of a new Competition Act and the U.S.-Canada Mutual Legal Assistance Agreement, which came into effect in 1990. Mutual Legal Assistance Agreements—(MLATs)—are agreements that provide generally for assistance in criminal law enforcement, including the obtaining of evidence and sharing of information.

30 Council Regulation (EEC) No. 4064/89 (Dec. 21, 1989), [1989] O.J. L395/1, on the control of concentrations between undertakings.

31 *See* Rachel Brandenburger, *Twenty Years of Transatlantic Antitrust Cooperation: the Past and the Future*, *available at* http://justice.gov/atr/public/articles/279068.pdf; Press Release, U.S. DOJ, *United States and European Union Antitrust Agencies Issue Revised Best Practices for Coordinating Merger Reviews*, *available at* http://www.justice. gov/atr/public/press_releases/2011/2763078.htm.

32 The U.S. antitrust cooperation agreements are *available at* http://www.justice.gov/atr/public/international/int-arrangements.html.

33 *See* Christine Varney, Remarks on the Signing of the Memorandum of Understanding on Antitrust Cooperation (July 27, 2011), *available at* http://www.justice.gov/atr/public/speeches/273347pdf.

34 Guidance for Case Cooperation between the Ministry of Commerce and the Department of Justice and Federal Trade Commission on Concentration of Undertakings (Merger) Cases (Nov. 29, 2011), *available at* http://www.justice.gov/atr/public/international/docs/277772.pdf.

35 The organization of the BCPS is outlined at http://www.cade.gov.br.

36 On international antitrust cooperation generally, *see, e.g.*, Rachel Brandenburger, *The Many Facets of International Cooperation at the Antitrust Division* (June 15, 2012), *available at* http://www.justice.gov/atr/public/ speeches/284239.pdf.; Interview with Rachel Brandenburger & Randy Tritell, *Global antitrust policies: How wide is the gap?*, Concurrences Competition L.J., No. 1-2012, 3-11 (2012).

37 *See, e.g.*, Christine A. Varney, Asst. Attorney General, *International Cooperation: Preparing for the Future* (Sept. 21, 2010), *available at* http://www.justice.gov/atr/public/speeches/262606.htm; Rachel Brandenburger, *International Competition Policy and Practice: New Perspectives?* (Oct. 29, 2010), *available at* http://www.justice.gov/atr/public/speeches/270980.pdf.

38 Former Assistant Attorney General Christine A. Varney has explained in some detail why this is so. *See International Cooperation: Preparing for the Future*, *supra* note 37, and Professor Slaughter has emphasized the utility of "informed divergence." Slaughter, *supra* note 7, at 181. *See also* John Fingleton, *The International Competition Network: Planning for the Second Decade* (April 27, 2010), *available at* http://www.oft.gov.uk/shared_oft/ speeches/689752/0410.pdf. (The ICN "should aim for convergence where it can be achieved, and 'informed divergence' – acknowledging the need for, and reasoning behind, potential differences in standards between jurisdictions – where appropriate.")

39 As former Assistant Attorney General Varney has explained, merger analysis in a particular case may vary among jurisdictions, not because there is disagreement about theory, but because "the market and industry structures and dynamics may differ by country of origin." Varney, *supra* note 37.

40 *See* Joseph Wayland, *International Cooperation at the Antitrust Division* (Sept. 14, 2012), *available at* http://www.justice.gov/atr/public/speeches/286979.pdf.

41 *See* Wayland, *supra*, at pages 4-9; *see generally* Rachel Brandenburger, *Intensification of International Cooperation: the Antitrust Division's Recent Efforts* (Feb. 17, 2012), *available at* http://www.justice.gov/atr/public/speeches/281609.pdf.

42 Consolidated Version of the Treaty on the Functioning of the European Union art. 15 (Sept. 5, 2008), 2008 O.J. (C 115) 47.

43 For an overview of the ECN, *see* http://ec.europa.eu/competition/ecn/index_en.html.

44 The ECN Model Leniency Program is *available at* http://ec.europa.eu/competition/ecn/model_leniency_en.pdf.

45 Press Release, *African Competition Forum launched in Nairobi* (Mar. 8, 2011) *available at* http://www.compcom.co.za/assets/Uploads/AttachedFiles/MyDocuments/ACF-Launch-Conference-press-release-final.pdf.

46 *See generally* K.L. Menns & DeCoursey Eversley, *The Appropriate Design of the CARICOM Competition Commission* (May 20, 2011), *available at* http://vi.unctad.org/files/studytour/stuwi11/Presentations/Tuesday%2024/Eversley.Menns.Appropriate%20Design%20of%20the%20CCC.ACLE.pdf.

47 *See, e.g.*, ACCC Press Release, Trans-Tasman merger protocol agreed (2006), *available at* http://www.accc.gov.au/content/index/phtml/ItemId/757850/fromItemId/720536.

48 In March 2012, a senior Vietnamese competition official suggested that the Association of Southeast Asian Nations (ASEAN), of which Vietnam is a member, should consider, as a medium-term project, the creation of a regional competition authority along the lines of the EC's Directorate-General for Competition. This is yet another interesting idea from the Asia-Pacific region. *See* http://www.globalcompetitionreview.com/news/article/31483.

49 *See* ICPAC Report at 4, 7-9.

50 *See* Press Release, U.S. DOJ, Justice Department Requires Divestitures in Order for United Technologies Corporation to Proceed with Its Acquisition of Goodrich Corporation (July 26, 2012), *available at* http://www.justice.gov/opa/pr/2012/July/12-at-925.html, *e.g.*, *CPTN/Novell*, Press Release, U.S. DOJ, *CPTN* Holdings LLC and Novell Inc. Change Deal in Order to Address Department of Justice's Open Source Concerns (Apr. 20, 2011), *available at* http://www.justice.gov/atr/public/press_releases/2011/270086.htm; Press Release, German Bundeskartellamt, http://www.bundeskartellamt.de/wEnglisch/News/Archiv/ArchivNews2011/2011_04_20.php (Apr. 20, 2011), *available at* http://www.bundeskartellamt.de/wEnglish/News/press/2011_04_20.php; for *Ticket Master/Live Nation*, *see* Press Release, U.S. DOJ, *Department Requires Ticketmaster Entertainment Inc. to Make Significant Changes to Its Merger with Live Nation Inc.* (Jan. 25, 2010), *available at*; Press Release, Canadian Competition Bureau, *Competition Bureau Requires Divestitures by Ticketmaster-Live Nation to Promote Competition* (Aug. 25, 2010), *available at* http://www.competitionbureau.gc.ca/eic/site/cb-bc.nsf/eng/03191.html.

51 As Prof. Slaughter says, in imagining the future of international governmental networks:

> Governments would not only produce convergence and informed divergence, improve compliance with international rules, and enhance international cooperation through regulation by information. They would also regulate themselves in ways that would deliberately improve the governing performance of both actual and potential members; create forums for multilateral discussion and argument by all their members, and create opportunities to harness the positive rather than the negative power of conflict.

SLAUGHTER, *supra* note 7, at 195.

Rachel Brandenburger

The Institute of Competition Law

The Institute of Competition Law is a think tank, founded in 2004 by Dr. Nicolas Charbit, based in Paris and New-York. The Institute cultivates scholarship and discussion about antitrust issues though publications and conferences. Each publication and event is supervised by editorial boards and scientific or steering committees to ensure independence, objectivity, and academic rigor. Thanks to this management, the Institute has become one of the few think tanks in Europe to have significant influence on antitrust policies.

AIM

The Institute focuses government, business and academic attention on a broad range of subjects which concern competition laws, regulations and related economics.

BOARDS

To maintain its unique focus, the Institute relies upon highly distinguished editors, all leading experts in national or international antitrust: Bill Kovacic, Mario Monti, Eleanor Fox, Barry Hawk, Laurence Idot, Fred Jenny, etc.

AUTHORS

2,500 authors, from 55 jurisdictions.

PARTNERS

- Universities: University College London, King's College London, Queen Mary University, Paris Sorbonne Panthéon-Assas, etc.

- Law firms: Allen & Overy, Cleary Gottlieb Steen & Hamilton, Hogan Lovells, Jones Day, White & Case, Kinstellar, Vogel & Vogel, etc.

EVENTS

More than 130 events since 2004 in Brussels, London, New York, Paris and Washington DC.

ONLINE VERSION

Concurrences website provides all articles published since its inception, and around 1,000 articles published online only, in the electronic supplement.

PUBLICATION

The Institute publishes Concurrences Journal, a print and online quarterly peer-reviewed journal dedicated to EU and national competitions laws. Launched in 2004 as the flagship of the Institute of Competition Law, the journal provides a forum for both practitioners and academics to shape competition policies.

Concurrences Journal

Concurrences is a print and online quarterly peer reviewed journal dedicated to EU and national competitions laws. It has been launched in 2004 as the flagship of the Institute of Competition Law in order to provide a forum for academics, practitioners and enforcers. The
Institute's influence and expertise has garnered interviews with such figures as Christine
Lagarde, Doug Melamed, Bill Kovacic, François Hollande and Nicolas Sarkozy.

CONTENTS

More than 7400 articles, print and/or online.
Quarterly issues provide current coverage with
contributions from the EU or national or foreign
countries thanks to more than 800 authors in
Europe and abroad. Approximately 25 % of the
contributions are published in English, 75 % in
French, as the official language of the General
Court of justice of the EU; all contributions
have English abstracts.

FORMAT

In order to balance academic contributions with
opinions or legal practice notes, Concurrences
provides

its insight and analysis in a number of formats:

- Forewords: Opinions by leading academics
  or enforcers
- Interviews: Interviews of antitrust experts
- Trends: 4 to 6 short papers on hot issues
- Law & Economics: Short papers written
  by economists for a legal audience
- Doctrines: Long academic papers
- Case Summaries: Case commentary
  on EU and French case law
- Legal Practice Short papers for in-house
  counsels
- International: Medium size papers
  on international policies
- Books Review: Summaries of recent
  antitrust books
- Articles Review: Summaries of leading
  articles published in 45 antitrust journals

BOARDS

The Scientific Committee is headed by Laurence Idot, Professor at Panthéon Assas University. The International Committee is headed by
Frederic Jenny, OECD Competition Comitteee
Chairman. Boards members include Bruno Las-
serre, Mario Monti, Richard Whish, Wouter
Wils, etc.

ONLINE VERSION

Concurrences website provides all articles
published since its inception, in addition to selected articles published online only in the electronic
supplement.

- Interviews: Interviews of antitrust experts
- Trends: 4 to 6 short papers on hot issues
- Law & Economics: Short papers written
  by economists for a legal audience
- Doctrines: Long academic papers
- Case Summaries: Case commentary
  on EU and French case law
- Legal Practice Short papers for in-house
  counsels
- International: Medium size papers
  on international policies
- Books Review: Summaries of recent
  antitrust books
- Articles Review: Summaries of leading
  articles published in 45 antitrust journals

e-COMPETITIONS

e-Competitions Bulletin

CASE LAW DATABASE

e-Competitions is the only online resource that provides consistent coverage of antitrust cases from 55 jurisdictions, organized into a searchable database structure. e-Competitions concentrates on cases summaries taking into account that in the context of a continuing growing number of sources there is a need for factual information, i.e., case law.

- 8,000 case summaries
- 1,850 authors
- 55 countries covered
- 24,000 subscribers

SOPHISTICATED EDITORIAL AND IT ENRICHMENT

e-Competitions is structured as a database. The editors make a highly sophisticated technical and legal work on all articles by tagging these with key words, drafting abstracts and writing html code to increase Google ranking. There is a team of antitrust lawyers – PhD and judges clerks - and a team of IT experts. e-Competitions makes comparative law possible. Thanks to this expert editorial work, it is possible to search and compare cases.

PRESTIGIOUS BOARDS

e-Competitions draws upon highly distinguished editors, all leading experts in national or international antitrust. Advisory Board Members include: Sir Christopher Bellamy, Ioanis Lianos (UCL), Eleanor Fox (NYU), Damien Géradin (Tilburg University), Barry Hawk (Fordham University) Fred Jenny (OECD), Jacqueline Riffault-Silk (Cour de cassation), Wouter Wils (DG COMP), etc.

LEADING PARTNERS

- Association of European Competition Law Judges: The AECLJ is a forum for judges of national Courts specializing in antitrust case law. Members timely feed e-Competitions with just released cases.

- Academics partners: Antitrust research centres from leading universities write regularly in e-Competitions: University College London, King's College London, Queen Mary University, etc.

- Law firms: Global law firms and antitrust niche firms write detailed cases summaries specifically for e-Competitions: Allen & Overy, Hogan Lovells, Jones Day, White & Case, etc.

CPSIA information can be obtained at www.ICGtesting.com
Printed in the USA
LVOW010415280113

3338LVUK00001B/1/P